Controversies in Constitutional Law

Collections of Documents and Articles on Major Questions of American Law

General Editor

Paul Finkelman
University of Tulsa School of Law

A ROUTLEDGE SERIES

Contents of the Collection

Volume 1
The State as Child Protector

Volume 2
The State and the Schooling of Children

Volume 3
Child vs. State

Children and the Law

Volume 1

The State as Child Protector

Edited with introductions by

Janet W. Steverson

Northwestern School of Law
of Lewis and Clark College

ROUTLEDGE
New York/London

Published in 2002 by
Routledge
29 West 35th Street
New York, NY 10001

Published in Great Britain by
Routledge
11 New Fetter Lane
London EC4P 4EE

Routledge is an imprint of the Taylor & Francis Group.

10 9 8 7 6 5 4 3 2 1

Library of Congress Cataloging-in-Publication Data

Children and the law / edited with introductions by Janet W. Steverson.
p. cm. — (Controversies in constitutional law)
Includes bibliographical references.
Contents: v. 1. The State as Child Protector — v. 2. The State and the Schooling of Children — v. 3. Child vs. State.
ISBN 0-415-93803-1 (set : alk paper) — ISBN 0-415-93804-X (vol. 1 : alk. paper) — ISBN 0-415-93805-8 (vol. 2 : alk. paper) — ISBN 0-415-93806-6 (vol. 3 : alk. paper)
1. Children—Legal status, laws, etc.—United States. 2. Parent and child (Law)—United States. 3. Juvenile justice, Administration of—United States. I. Steverson, Janet W. II. Series.
KF479.A75 C478 2002
346.7301'35—dc21 2002020626

Contents

vii Series Introduction
ix Volume Introduction

I. Overview

2 Why Parental Rights Laws are Necessary
Christopher J. Klicka and Douglas W. Phillips
7 Child Abuse, The Constitution, and the Legacy of *Pierce* v. *Society of Sisters*
Barbara Bennett Woodhouse

II. Who is a Parent?

18 The Tie that Binds: The Constitutional Right of Children to Maintain Relationships with Parent-Like Individuals
Gilbert A. Holmes
73 Contested Adoption and the Liberty Interest of the Child
Marcus T. Boccaccini and *Eleanor Willemsen*
91 The Changing American Family: A Reevaluation of the Rights of Foster Parents When Biological Rights Have Been Terminated
Cassandra S. Haury

III. Custody and Adoption of Children

123 *Palmore* v. *Sidoti*
129 *Santosky* v. *Kramer*
177 An Analysis of Realistic Due Process Rights of Children Versus Parents
Raymond C. O'Brien

IV. Corporal Punishment of Children by Parents or Guardians

229 The Child's Right to Humane Discipline under the U.N. Convention on the Rights of the Child: The Mandate Against All Corporal Punishment of Children
Susan H. Bitensky

237 Spanking and Other Corporal Punishment of Children by Parents: Overvaluing Pain, Undervaluing Children
David Orentlicher

V. Parent's Refusal of Medical Treatment for Children

277 Medical Decision Making for and by Children: Tensions Between Parent, State, and Child
Walter Wadlington
303 Spiritual Treatment Exemptions to Child Medical Neglect Laws: What We Outsiders Should Think
James G. Dwyer

VI. State's *Obligation* to Protect Children from Harm

334 Affirmative Duties, Systemic Harms, and the Due Process Clause
Barbara E. Armacost

VII. Third-Party Visitation with Children

393 Protecting Children's Relationships with Extended Family: The Impact of *Troxel* v. *Granville*
Barbara Bennett Woodhouse
397 Nonparent Visitation Rights v. Family Autonomy: An Abridgement of Parents' Constitutional Rights?
Elizabeth Weiss
445 Grandparent Visitation: The Best Interests of the Grandparent, Child, and Society
Erica L. Strawman

463 Acknowledgments

Series Introduction

This ongoing series, *Controversies in Constitutional Law,* provides teachers, scholars, and students convenient access to the debates and scholarly literature surrounding major questions of constitutional law. Each set of books—from two to four volumes—consists of four elements: an extended introduction to the issue by the editor; reprints of the significant cases and briefs on the subject; congressional testimony, and other primary documents on the issue; and a selection of the best scholarly articles on the subject. By conveniently gathering all this material in one place, each set of volumes allows users to become familiar quite quickly with the arguments and positions surrounding a particular constitutional controversy.

Scholars and students interested in constitutional law and public policy are often overwhelmed by the sheer amount of material published on controversial subjects. The topics in *Controversies in Constitutional Law* are timely, politically significant, and intellectually compelling. They are the issues that bring the legal academy, courts, politicians, and general public together—although not always in harmony.

Many scholars are barely able to keep up with the material in their own fields. Yet there is a need to learn about issues beyond our own specialties. A new course may require an introduction to a problem; our own research may lead us to a new issue. The series *Controversies in Constitutional Law* is designed to meet these needs, enabling scholars and teachers to come up to speed quickly on the topics in each volume.

This series also serves students at all levels of higher education. Students often encounter controversial topics without the background in how the problem developed. These volumes provide such a background. The important cases are reprinted in full; the introductions provide students with a map of the issues; the briefs, congressional testimony, and scholarly articles give convenient access to the arguments and debates.

The volumes bring together in one place a wide variety of sources and materials that are unlikely to be found in any one library. The primary documents include cases, briefs, testimony from legislative committee hearings, and, on occasion, executive branch publications. Few law libraries, university libraries, or public libraries will have all these materials. The secondary literature comes from the scholarly literature of law, history, political science, economics, criminology, and other relevant fields. Some of the articles also may be from serious nonacademic journals.

The related government publications, briefs, and congressional testimony are particularly important. Too often scholars overlook them. There is a tendency to focus on court opinions—what the Supreme Court said. Obviously this is important for understanding doctrine, but briefs, especially amicus briefs, are also an important source of information about the larger constitutional controversy the case represents. The politics of a case are often more apparent in these briefs than in either the oral arguments or the Court's opinion. Similarly, congressional hearings illustrate the social, philosophical, and political dimensions of these questions.

The goal of limiting each collection—two to four focused volumes—and the occasional inability to secure a reasonable copyright permission fee for some important articles often forces hard and judicious choices. Important articles that are not reprinted here are listed in the further reading sections at the end of the introductions.

The ongoing series *Controversies in Constitutional Law* provides in one single place comprehensive introductions to topics that will satisfy most lawyers, scholars, and students. By combining cases, briefs, legislative debates, and testimony from committee hearings with secondary articles, it is hoped to facilitate access to the issue presented in each set of volumes.

Paul Finkelman

Volume Introduction

As its title suggests, I initiated this three-volume series on children and the law in an effort to provide some insight into how children are treated under the United States Constitution. As is true with any collection, however, there are page limits that must be adhered to lest the reader be overwhelmed. Therefore, by necessity, the scope of this collection is not nearly as broad as its title might suggest. Thus, although one might think that such a series should explore the treatment of children in the criminal arena, the constitutional issues that arise under criminal law and procedure are so vast that those issues must be explored separately, if one does not want to give short shrift to both the civil and the criminal issues. Further, even in the civil arena, a overview collection such as this cannot adequately examine all of the constitutional issues affecting children. Such a collection can, however, give the reader a general sense of how the United States Supreme Court has chosen to apply the Constitution to children as a class and such is the purpose of this collection. The collection will achieve this purpose by taking an in-depth look at some of the major Supreme Court cases in this area, as well as by exploring some of the pressing constitutional issues that have not yet made their way to the Supreme Court. In general, the format of the collection will be to provide background information concerning a particular issue followed by opposing viewpoints concerning the proper resolution of the issue.

The focus of this first volume is on the parent, the state, and the child because children's destinies are controlled in large part by their parents and by the state. Thus, no collection on children would be complete if it did not focus, in part, upon the rights of parents vis-a-vis their children and the interests of the state in its children. Towards that end, the materials in this volume explore the question of what is the proper balance between the parents' rights to raise their children as they see fit, free from state intervention, and the state's interest in intervening in the family to protect the child and to promote her/his interests. Part one of this volume contains two articles that explore the above issue in a general way, while parts two though seven grapple with some specific contexts in which this parent versus state issue arises.

Part two explores the question of who is a parent in the eyes of the Constitution, because one must first resolve this issue before one can discuss the protections that the Constitution affords to parents. More specifically, part two deals with the constitutional issues pertaining to unwed parents, foster parents, and other parent-like third parties.

The next three sections then wrestle with the question of when *may* the state interfere with the parent-child relationship without violating a parent's constitutional rights, while the final two sections deal with the issue of when *must* the state act to protect children from harm. In general, the law presumes that the parent or parents of a child are best situated and equipped to raise, nurture and protect that child. Based in part upon this belief, but also based upon our Country's emphasis upon individual rights, the traditional stance has been that parents can best perform their functions if the interference of the state in this process is minimal. Thus, it has generally become recognized that, under the Constitution, parents have a fundamental right to the care, custody and management of their children and to raise their children as they fit. As a result, the state may infringe upon this right only if it has a sufficient reason. The protection of children from abuse and/or neglect at the hands of their parents or others is one such reason. As a result, it is generally recognized that the state, in its *parens patriae* role, can interfere in the parent-child relationship and even end that relationship in order to protect a child from harm. Parts three through five specifically cover the question of the type of harm that justifies intervention and the process that the state must afford the parents prior to and/or after such intervention.

Part three focuses on the custody and adoption of children. When the custody of a child is at stake, the nature of the constitutional issues that are involved in a given case will depend upon the state's role in that case. If the state seeks to remove a child from her/his parents due to alleged harm, the issues revolve around whether the child is being harmed so as to justify the state's intervention, the way in which the state may intervene if harm is involved, and the type of process the state must afford to the parents prior to and/or after such intervention. The *Santosky v. Kramer* case holds that because parents have a fundamental liberty interest in the care, custody, and management of their children the state has a very high burden to overcome before it may terminate a parent's right to a relationship with her/his child. The Raymond O'Brien article takes issue with this holding and contends that the court cannot place such a high burden upon the state because to do so violates the child's constitutional rights.

If, however, instead of seeking to sever the parent-child relationship, the state is merely deciding which parent will receive custody of a child upon divorce, then the Constitution is involved only if one or more of the factors used in determining custody infringes upon the constitutional rights of one of the parents. In such a case the focus will often be upon whether the consideration of the factor by the state is designed to, and will, protect the child from harm. The *Palmore v. Sidoti* case is provided as an example of such a case where the trial judge inappropriately used the factor of race to remove a child from the custody of its mother.

The second area of potential harm to a child is corporal punishment. In this area we again see the tension between the state's interest in protecting children from harm, or at least promoting their best interests and the parents' rights to raise their children as they see fit, which for some includes the use of corporal punishment. One of the key issues in this area is whether the child's interest in not receiving corporal punishment is strong enough to justify state intervention. The subject covered in part five is the parent's refusal of medical treatment for children. Two articles in this section present differing views as to the relative strengths of the interests of the parents, the child and the state.

Part six moves away from the question of when may the state act to protect its children, to the question of when must the state act to protect its children. While it is accepted that the state *may* act to protect children if it so chooses, it is also accepted that, in general, the state has no affirmative duty to protect its children. In fact, in general, the government has no duty under the Constitution to protect any individual from harm caused to him by other private individuals.[1] The materials debate the correctness of this constitutional stance.

Finally, part seven delves into the question of when the state may grant visitation to a third-party over the objections of a parent. In *Troxel v. Granville*, decided by the Supreme Court in the year 2000, the Supreme Court struck down a Washington state third-party visitation statute as it was applied to the custodial mother in the case. Due to the very specific nature of the Court's ruling, and the extremely broad nature of the statute, the *Troxel* case still leaves room for the states to adopt less broad visitation statutes. The three articles in this part explore the question of whether the interests of the children and the third-parties are strong enough to justify the state intervention in this area.

Janet W. Steverson

Note

[1] Nowak, Rotunda, Constitutional Law (4th Ed.) §12.4 p. 477.

Children and the Law

Volume 1

The State as Child Protector

Christopher J. Klicka and Douglas W. Phillips

Why Parental Rights Laws Are Necessary

The steady erosion of parental rights requires a legislative solution to protect the parent-child relationship against unwarranted interference and to reinstate this bedrock principle of a free society.

Last year, news hit the press concerning 59 6th graders in Pennsylvania's East Stroudsburg Area School District who were forced against their will by school officials to strip to their underwear and submit to a full genital examination. According to some of the parents, this exam included digital penetration. Many of the 11-year-olds objected, wept, and sought permission to call their parents. School officials ridiculed the students, blocked the door, called them "babies," and refused their request.

One of the more astonishing aspects of this episode was the incredulity expressed by East Stroudsburg officials that their authority could be questioned by parents. One pediatrician summed up the school's position, stating, "Even a parent doesn't have a right to say what's appropriate for a physician to do when they are doing an exam." As news of the incident spread across the country, thousands of parents expressed outrage, echoing the cry: "Not with my child, you don't!"

When the Massachusetts Court of Appeals upheld the right of a school to require children to sit through a 90-minute presentation by "Hot, Sexy and Safer Productions, Inc." in which children were told to participate in a "group sexual experience," parents were incensed. Although male and female children were told to engage in lewd play with condoms as part of the exercise, the court held that the right of parents to direct the upbringing of their children does not encompass a broad-based right to restrict this form of information from their children in public schools. When news of the court's decision circulated, outraged parents proclaimed: "Not with my child, you don't!"

Earlier this year one of the authors received a phone call from a member family of The Home School Legal Defense Association. The panicked mother reported that a social worker was at her door demanding entry and an immediate private interview of her four young children. It seems that a member of the extended family who had been diagnosed with mental problems had used the anonymous tip hot line to report to the Department of Social Services that various members of his family were abusing their children.

The social worker knew there was no evidence of

For more than a thousand years, the doctrine of parental rights had been a bedrock principle of the Western legal tradition, expressed throughout the common law.

© John Boal

abuse and that the anonymous tipster was a mentally unstable family member with a reputation for making false charges. Nevertheless, she verbally abused the family for their reluctance to cooperate and, when refused entry, threatened to make things worse for the family if she had to get a court order.

Under duress, the family allowed her to enter and interview the children. During the interview, the social worker asked the children numerous sexually explicit questions. The distraught mother stated that her previously innocent children had been defiled by the questioning and were having horrible nightmares as a result. Her tearful message: "Never again with my children, they won't!"

All of this would be minimally significant in the grand scheme of American law and jurisprudence if the above examples represented isolated instances of abuse—mere glitches in the system and not symptomatic problems. However, such abuses of parental rights have become all too commonplace.

It is fair to say that somewhere today a parent will be threatened with child abuse charges for using reasonable corporal discipline on a child because an "expert" thinks the practice is inherently abusive; that somewhere today a social worker will challenge a parent's right to educate a child at home; and that somewhere today a public school official will rebuff a parent who objects to the curriculum being taught to her child.

The Origins of the Parental Rights Movement

The Home School Legal Defense Association has been fighting since 1983 to protect the right of parents to direct the education and training of their children. Based on thousands of experiences with social workers, truant officers, and school superintendents, it is our observation that the system is out of balance. This imbalance has precipitated the national movement to reestablish parental rights protections.

During the 1990s a grassroots movement emerged to seek statutory and judicial protections over the parent-child relationship. The timing is significant. For more than three decades Americans have witnessed the widescale erosion of parental rights. A hodgepodge of judicial decisions has called into question the common-law presumption of parental competence that undergirds our Constitution, leaving one to wonder whether parental rights are still considered fundamental.

Widespread "family abuse" by the child protective services industry, as well as a growing feeling that parents have been disenfranchised from the education of their children by "experts" and heavy-handed bureaucrats, has led many to call for legislation that will protect the right of parents to make independent decisions about the education and discipline of their offspring. The threat of the United States ratifying the United Nations Convention on the Rights of the Child, which would give children fundamental rights enforceable against their parents, has also sparked action. Still others simply want the freedom to reject what they perceive as a politically correct, assembly-line, one-size-fits-all approach to their children's education.

To rectify these problems, attempts at parental rights legislation often focus on one or more of the following points: (1) formal legislative recognition that parental rights are fundamental and, consequently, deserve the highest level of protection against government interference; (2) enforcement of due process restrictions on child protective services workers, so that intact families will not be subject to abusive treatment by state officials who disagree with the family's religious beliefs or child training practices; and (3) the rights of parents to have greater control over their children's public education, including the ability to opt out of morally offensive programs.

Roots in Common Law

The United States Constitution does not explicitly mention parental rights. Like other legal principles at the time of the nation's founding, the right of parents to direct the education and upbringing of their children was an implicit and necessary assumption of society. That parents had a God-given duty as well as right to make all decisions with respect to the future of their unemancipated children was part of the higher law that the Declaration of Independence termed "the laws of nature and of nature's God." For more than a thousand years, the doctrine of parental rights had been a bedrock principle of the Western legal tradition, expressed throughout the "common law." This common law was eventually incorporated by reference.

Modern proponents of parental rights look not only to common law but also to several key provisions of the Bill of Rights that safeguard the family. These include the religious liberty and free speech provisions of the First Amendment; the due process and liberty provisions of the Fourth, Fifth, and Fourteenth Amendments; and the limitation on federal interference in the family that would be the necessary result of a government bound by the strictures of the Tenth Amendment.

Yet it is precisely because confusion reigns regarding the proper interpretation and application of these very constitutional provisions, and interpretive discrepancies exist among the various lower courts, that organizations such as the Home School Legal Defense Association believe the time has come for a legislative remedy.

Parents should be applauded, not penalized, for investing time in the discipline and nurturing of their children.

Opponents of parental rights argue that such rights are not expressly enumerated in the Constitution. They fail to recognize that when drafting the Bill of Rights, the Framers specifically addressed those rights that had been challenged by the Crown during colonial days. Amendments such as the Third, which prohibits the quartering of troops in private residences, may appear to be mostly of historical significance, yet even within this provision, one finds the simple principle that agents of the state should hold the sanctity of the home inviolable.

Thus, the fact that the Constitution does not explicitly mention parental rights does not mean that the framers considered them of little consequence. In fact, the opposite was true. Parental rights were the functional equivalent of the right to breathe—a right so obvious and fundamental as to be unnecessary of mention. But just in case future generations might have any doubts, the Framers ratified the Ninth Amendment, which states: "The enumeration in the Constitution of certain rights shall not be construed to deny or disparage others retained by the people." In sum, parental rights have long been recognized as implicit in the concept of ordered liberty.

Although lower courts have repeatedly denied parental rights, the United States Supreme Court has consistently recognized the fundamental rights of parents to direct their children, as the following decisions indicate:

> This case involves the fundamental interest of parents, as contrasted with that of the state, to guide the religious future and education of their children. The history and culture of Western civilization reflect a strong tradition of parental concern for the nurture and upbringing of their children. This primary role of the parents in the upbringing of their children is now established beyond debate as an enduring tradition. *Wisconsin v. Yoder*, 406 U.S. 233 (1972).

> The fundamental liberty interest of natural parents in the care and management of their child does not evaporate simply because they have not been model parents or have lost temporary custody of their child to the state. *Santosky v. Kramer*, 455 U.S. 745, 753 (1982).

Finally, in *Meyer v. Nebraska*, the Court held that the right of parents to instruct their children was within the liberty of the 14th Amendment.

It is important to note that the Supreme Court employs two basic levels of protection in its analysis of constitutional rights. It uses a higher level of protection in cases involving "fundamental rights" (speech, press, religion, parental rights). It provides a significantly lower level of protection to rights it has labeled "nonfundamental." The standards of review for such fundamental rights is called the "compelling interest test." When government regulations conflict with a fundamental right, the government has the burden to prove the regulations are "essential" and "the least restrictive means" to fulfill a compelling interest. When nonfundamental rights conflict with government regulation, the government need only prove its regulations are "reasonable."

For example, homeschool parents were thrilled by the 1993 decision of the Supreme Court of Michigan, in a case handled by the Home School Legal Defense Association, which declared that teacher certification was unconstitutional as applied to religiously motivated homeschooling parents *(People v. DeJonge*, 501 N.W. 2d 127 1993). However, in a companion case decided the same day, the Michigan Supreme Court held that secular homeschooling parents suffered no constitutional violation when forced to comply with the certification requirement *(People v. Bennett*, 501 N.W. 2d 88 1993).

The difference between these two decisions was simple, but profound. The Michigan Supreme Court, on one hand, held that the right to freely exercise religions was a fundamental right, whereas "parents' rights" were "nonfundamental" in nature. The result was that Christian parents were allowed to homeschool but secular parents were not. Within a few years, the Michigan Legislature restored the proper balance by enacting the following language:

> It is the natural, fundamental right of parents and legal guardians to determine and direct the care, teaching, and education of their children. *M.C.L.A. 380.10.*

Due to a grassroots outcry for explicit recognition of parental rights, two other states—Kansas and Texas—have enacted similar parental rights laws.

A Response to Critics

Critics of parental rights legislation have raised concerns that such limitations would inhibit the state's ability to protect genuinely abused children. Our response is that well-drafted legislation would protect only those rights that should lawfully belong to parents. For example, no parent would ever have a right to disable, starve, or abuse (as the term has been historically understood) a child. In such cases the state has an absolute obligation to criminally prosecute the parent. Ideally, parents' rights legislation would make it difficult for the state to harass parents for their religious beliefs, choice of education, or decision to use corporal discipline, without undermining the ability of law enforcement to prosecute genuine abusers.

In the final analysis, stronger families mean a stronger nation. Families must feel secure in their liberty to raise their children according to the dictates of their conscience. Parents should be applauded, not penalized, for investing time in the discipline and nurturing of their children. Parents, not social workers or teachers, are in the best position to make decisions for their children. Other than in cases of genuine child abuse, which should be treated as a crime, the fundamental right of parents to direct the education and upbringing of their children should in every case trump the policy objectives of bureaucrats and social workers.

We want to return to an America where 11-year-old girls will not be stripped against their will by school officials, where parents can say no to public school programs that expose children to sexually explicit material, and where the Fourth Amendment still prevents warrantless officials from entering homes to harass parents. Well-crafted parental rights legislation will help to reestablish the sanctity of the home as a fundamental principle of liberty for our free society. ■

Christopher J. Klicka is Executive Director and **Douglas W. Phillips** is Attorney at The National Center for Home Education, a division of The Home School Legal Defense Association. They can be reached at P.O. Box 3000, Purcellville, VA 20134 (e-mail: hslda@hslda.org; Web site: http://www.hslda.org).

Editor's note: In an "Information Release," the East Stroudsburg Area School District affirmed that it had complied with the legal requirements of the Pennsylvania Public School Code regarding health examinations. The district sent parents several notifications of the scheduled examination, advised them to have the exam performed by their family physician, and advised them of the opportunity to be present at the examination, the report said. A female physician, assisted by a female school nurse, performed the examinations on those students whose parents had not submitted reports from their family physician. Investigations by independent legal counsel and the Pennsylvania state police "concluded that there were no improprieties on the part of the physician or district employees."

Child Abuse, the Constitution, and the Legacy of *Pierce v. Society of Sisters*

BARBARA BENNETT WOODHOUSE*

My fascination with *Pierce v. Society of Sisters* began almost twenty years ago when I was a law student at Columbia, participating in one of the earliest child advocacy clinics. The case that made *Pierce* come alive for me had nothing to do with education. It involved two boys (my first live clients) caught in the coils of the child welfare system. The term "child welfare system" refers to the network of state and federal laws, civil courts, and social programs intended to protect children from abuse and neglect by their caretakers. In 1982, it was still a fairly novel idea to assign lawyers to represent children, even in criminal and juvenile delinquency proceedings where the children's "liberty" was clearly at issue. However, New York State, aware of the high stakes such proceedings raised for the families involved, was experimenting with appointing counsel for children as well as parents in cases that involved involuntary removal of children from their homes and termination of parental rights.[1]

Many readers may not realize that the child welfare system as we know it is barely twenty-five years old.[2] Children without proper parental care and control have always been dealt with at the local level. In colonial times, local poor law authorities had the power to seize vagrant and unruly children and indenture them to work for their keep. During the nineteenth century, private charities such as the Society Against Cruelty to Children and the Children's Aid Society intervened to remove poor, largely immigrant children from homes they considered unsafe or unsavory. The first federal involvement in the child welfare system dates to the New Deal and the Social Security Act of 1935, which provided states with funds for foster care for homeless children. Only with the "discovery" of child abuse by physicians in the 1960s, did violence against children become a federal issue. The 1974 Child Abuse Prevention and

---

* Ms. Woodhouse is a Professor of Law and Co-Director of the Center for Children's Policy Practice and Research at University of Pennsylvania.

1. See Santosky v. Kramer, 455 U.S. 745 (1982) and Smith v. Organization of Foster Families for Equality and Reform, 431 U.S. 816 (1977) for discussion of statutory reforms and processes in the state of New York in the late seventies and early eighties.

2. For a history of child welfare law in the United States, see *Child Abuse and Neglect*, *in* FUTURE OF FAMILIES FROM THE PACKARD FOUNDATION.

Treatment Act opened the modern era of federal involvement, by tying eligibility for federal funding to the states' adoption of model legislation for reporting and investigating charges of child maltreatment.

During the past twenty-five years, federal child welfare policy has vacillated between concern about over-intervention endangering family autonomy, and concern about "under-intervention" endangering children. Today, every state has an elaborate system of laws and courts governing state intervention in the family. Reports of abuse have grown exponentially, straining the system beyond its limits. Between 1976 and 1993, the number of children officially reported as abused or neglected grew by more than 374%. Currently, over 3,000,000 reports of abuse are filed annually. Despite difficulties of proof, approximately 1,000,000 of these reports are substantiated upon investigation. In 1995, half a million children were living in foster care and hundreds of thousands of other children were under in-home supervision of local departments of human services or child welfare.[3]

If this description conjures up images of a smoothly functioning system that precisely calibrates its interventions to match the level of risk, you have not been reading your newspapers or law reporters or listening to NPR or Oprah. Approximately half of the state child welfare agencies and many more local systems - including Philadelphia, New York, Arkansas, and Washington D.C.—are being sued or have been placed under federal court supervision because of their gross failures of care.[4] Too many children, especially children of color, are being removed from their homes because of poverty and its associated ills.[5] At the same time, the system is failing those who need it most. Half of the 1,000 children who die each year at the hands of caregivers are already known to child welfare authorities.[6]

But what, you may ask, does all of this have to do with *Pierce v. Society of Sisters*? Isn't *Pierce* all about parents' right to send their children to private schools? In the past 75 years, *Pierce*, and its sister case, *Meyer v. Nebraska,* have come to stand for much more than the proposition that government may not standardize our children by

---

3. Richard J. Gelles and Ira Schwartz, Article: *Children and the Child Welfare System,* 2 U. PA. J. CONST. L. 95 (1999).

4. *See* Baby Neal v. Casey, 43 F.3d 48 (3d Cir. 1994) and In re Marisol, 520 U.S. 1211 (1997).

5. Dorothy Roberts, Article: *Is There Justice in Children's Rights? The Critique of Federal Family Preservation Policy,* 2 U. PA. J. CONST. L. 112 (1999); and Martin Guggenheim, Commentary: *The Foster Care Dilemma and What To Do About It: Is the Problem That Too Many Children Are Not Being Adopted Out of Foster Care or That Too Many Children Are Entering Foster Care?,* 2 U. PA. CONST. L. 141 (1999).

6. *See supra* note 3.

forcing all into a single educational mold. These cases have taken on a life of their own, giving birth to a branch of constitutional doctrine that has extended into every area where state and family intersect. In cases about abortion, contraception, and sterilization, *Pierce* is cited for the principle that individuals have a privacy right to make decisions about child-bearing free of state intervention.[7] In cases about unmarried father's rights, *Pierce* is cited for the principle that a man has a liberty interest in raising his biological children.[8] In cases about religious training, *Pierce* is cited for the principle that parents have a right to inculcate their children with moral values.[9] Like most students of law in the latter quarter of the twentieth century, I had been taught as a 1L student that *Pierce* was the good substantive due process left when the evil dross of *Lochner* and economic due process had been burned away. I accepted it as the liberal icon celebrated by forward-thinking scholars, such as Laurence H. Tribe, for protecting the rights of individuals and groups to "heed the music of different drummers."[10] In the child welfare system, I was confronted with the dark side of *Meyer* and *Pierce.*

The Columbia child advocacy clinic was my first exposure to child welfare law. In the chaos of New York family court, I picked up my first clinic case. My clients were siblings, age 12 and 14, whose biological father was seeking their return from foster care.[11] When I met with my youthful clients, their position was clear. The two boys, raised by kinship foster parents (a great-aunt and step-grandfather), loved their father, who had maintained contact with them throughout their childhood. However, they did not want to leave the safety and stability of the home and neighborhood where they had lived since infancy. They feared, quite rationally, that their charismatic but unstable father was ill equipped to guide them through the dangers facing African American teens growing up in New York City. They wanted me to ask for more contact with their father, but they wanted to remain in the custody of their foster grandfather, from whom they drew enormous security and strength.

On researching the law, I quickly learned that arguments about the children's wishes, their best interests, or the foster family's twelve

---

7. Planned Parenthood v. Casey, 510 U.S. 1309 (1994); Roe v. Wade, 410 U.S. 113 (1973); Griswold v. Connecticut, 361 U.S. 479 (1965); LAURENCE H. TRIBE, AMERICAN CONSTITUTIONAL LAW 11-3 (2d ed. 1988) (reviewing how *Pierce* and its progeny paved the way for subsequent reproductive rights cases such as *Griswold*).

8. Lehr v. Robertson, 463 U.S. 248 (1983).

9. Wisconsin v. Yoder, 406 U.S. 205 (1972).

10. Tribe, *supra* note 7, at § 15-6.

11. Barbara Bennett Woodhouse, *"It All Depends on What You Mean by Home:" Towards a Communitarian Theory of the Nontraditional Family,* 1996 Utah L. Rev. 569 (1996).

year investment in these children, were beside the point. Since their father had never technically "abandoned" the children, prevailing law said he had a constitutional "right" to repossess them on demand, unless we could show clear and convincing evidence that he was "unfit."[12] Without a showing that the father posed an imminent danger to his children, the children's wishes and the evidence I had gathered on their best interests would not even be admissible. To me, it seemed that the law treated these very thoughtful and expressive adolescents not as persons, but as insentient articles of parental property. Foster care functioned, in their case, as a baggage check where children could be left and reclaimed at the owner's convenience. Where, I asked myself, had this principle of constitutional law originated? The trail of citations lead back to dicta in *Meyer* and *Pierce*. In passing, Justice McReynolds had listed control and custody of one's children as among those fundamental liberties guaranteed by the due process clause of the Fourteenth Amendment.[13]

I will not rehash here the story I told in "'Who Owns the Child?': *Meyer* and *Pierce* and the Child as Property,"[14] To make a very long article short, I looked at the cases in social and historical context, relating them to populist and progressive movements for child labor laws, mandatory public schooling and children's rights. I found another story hidden between the lines. The cases were about family autonomy and freedom from state tyranny, but they were also about ownership of children. The cases reflected deeply rooted divisions in American politics and conflicts about the culture of family and state. One camp conceptualized children primarily as private property belonging to their parents and viewed any limits on parental authority as an assault on parents' "God-given" rights. The other camp conceptualized children primarily as future citizens, belonging to their communities and their nation, and viewed state regulation of education, labor and maltreatment as justified by the State's interest in children's welfare and in their growth to autonomous citizenship.

While *Pierce* reached what I and most would agree were the "right" results, rejecting a law that would force all children into a state-dictated mold, it also perpetuated an adult-centric concept of parents' ownership and control that still pervades the constitutional law of the family. The Court's dicta in *Meyer* and *Pierce* gave constitutional status to a vision of the family already becoming outdated in 1925.

---

12. *See Santosky*, *supra* note 1.

13. *Meyer*, 262 U.S. at 400 (constitutionalizing the power of parents to control the education of their own).

14. 33 WM. & MARY L. REV. 995 (1992).

What a strange form of "liberty" that endows one person with control of another? Viewed in historical context, however, *Pierce* was not so hard to fathom. It was a relic of a time when substantive due process theory provided a bulwark against all forms of state intervention in so-called private enterprises. The family figured as one of many private arenas in which a man should be free from state intermeddling. The same Supreme Court that decided *Pierce* had taken a highly expansive view of Fourteenth Amendment liberty and property. Laws regulating hours and conditions of work, protecting women from exploitive labor practices, and imposing limits on child labor had been challenged as infringing the individual's constitutionally protected liberty to enter into contracts, to pursue a calling, and generally to deploy one's labor and assets as one wished. Just as the common law protected a man's rights to hire and fire at will and to use his property as he wished, so common law also protected his right to govern his family as he wished.

These Supreme Court decisions shared at least one basic fallacy. They treated commerce and labor, the family and the market, as even playing fields, ignoring the imbalances of power and the deeply embedded structural barriers to liberty that made state intervention necessary as a tool for achieving real justice. Substantive due process theory does a poor job of discriminating between rights and wrongs. In assessing whether a right is fundamental, substantive due process doctrine asks whether it is deeply rooted in tradition and necessary to ordered liberty. Unlike equal protection clause analysis, it does not force the lawmaker to justify legislative policies with empirical evidence. In substantive due process analysis, the entrenched inequality of nineteenth century family life, where men ruled, women obeyed, and children were seen but not heard, were accepted as natural phenomena, like the laws of gravity.[15] As timeless as they may have seemed to McReynolds and his brethren, we now understand that these laws were merely man-made arrangements. Common law rights, although firmly rooted in tradition and necessary to maintenance of the traditional order, often reinforced inequalities of power and justified the oppression of the weaker by the stronger. As historian Reva Siegel has demonstrated, conduct we now criminalize as wife battering was sanctioned and sheltered from scrutiny by the husband's common law privilege to administer appropriate correction.

Women may have escaped the separate spheres of *Bradwell v. Illinois,* but children remain trapped in the time warp of *Pierce.*

15. By 1969, we find Justice Black, in *Tinker v. Des Moines Independent Community School District,* 393 U.S. 503 (1969), mourning the fact that children are no longer "seen but not heard" and predicting the deterioration of civil society.

Parents' rights proponents, in state and federal bills such as the Parental Rights and Responsibilities Act and the Religious Liberty Protection Act, cite *Meyer* and *Pierce* to argue that the common law privilege excusing corporal punishment of children is a fundamental right that cannot be tampered with by those who would reform the common law.[16] Knowing the potential of the common law to make abuse and exploitation seem ordinary and natural, we ought to treat "rights" rooted in the common law with heightened suspicion rather than with heightened respect.

Many have argued that the parental rights we trace to *Meyer* and *Pierce* are necessary to establish "family autonomy" and "family privacy."[17] In order to protect the family unit from undue intervention we must erect a barrier between the family unit and the overbearing state. There is nothing wrong with this analysis as long as we remember that there is no such thing as "the family unit." The family is a group of persons, often with shared values and interests, but individuals nonetheless. When the interests of parents and children coincide, as in the original education cases, endowing the family patriarch or matriarch with autonomy from state intervention empowers all family members. Most of us would agree that children need powerful parents who can advocate for them and protect them from harm. However, when family members' interests clash, the notions of family autonomy and family privacy simply place intra-family disputes outside the law, to be decided in a state of nature where raw power rules. When children are abused or not protected by their parents, the fiction of family unity becomes a dangerous illusion.

One case can often be worth a thousand words. Let me use the landmark child welfare case of *Santosky v. Kramer*[18], decided in 1982, to illustrate what I see as the problematic legacy of *Pierce*. This case involved a challenge to the standard of proof for the termination of parental rights (or TPR). New York's child welfare law, enacted in response to CAPTA and AACWA, the federal laws described earlier, created an elaborate scheme for dealing with cases of abuse and neglect. The Court's opinion provides a primer, useful even today, on

---

16. Barbara Bennett Woodhouse, Symposium: *Meeting the Basic Needs of Children: Defining Public and Private Responsibilities: A Public Role in the Private Family: The Parental Rights and Responsibilities Act and the Politics of Child Protection and Education*, 57 OHIO ST. L.J. 393 (1996).

17. Martha Fineman, Symposium: *Privacy and the Family: Panel III, What Place for Family Privacy?*, 67 GEO. WASH. L. REV. 1207 (1999); Naomi R. Cahn, Symposium: *Privacy and the Family: Panel III, Models of Family Privacy*, 67 GEO. WASH. L. REV. 1225 (1999); Barbara Bennett Woodhouse, Symposium: *Privacy and the Family: Panel III, The Dark Side of Family Privacy*, 67 GEO. WASH. L. REV. 1247 (1999).

18. 455 U.S. 745 (1982).

child welfare laws. The Santosky's three children had been removed after the three-year-old suffered a broken femur and multiple bruises and the one-year-old was hospitalized with malnutrition, bruises, blisters and multiple pin pricks apparently inflicted intentionally. After six years of foster care, including an unsuccessful attempt at reunification and many court hearings, the family court found the children "permanently neglected" and granted the state agency's petition to terminate parental rights so the children could be freed for adoption. The statute specified that the state must prove the grounds for a TPR by a preponderance of the evidence. The Supreme Court, in a five to four decision, held that only a requirement of clear and convincing evidence could adequately protect the parent against erroneous deprivation of so fundamental a liberty. To reach its conclusion, the majority had to apply the *Mathews v. Eldridge* test for determining what process is due. *Mathews* balances the private interests at stake against the State's interests, and assesses whether the risk of error can be diminished by adding procedural protections. The majority took the position that the Santosky children's interests in family preservation were coextensive with those of their parents. Only after a finding of parental unfitness could their interests diverge. Employing a clear and convincing evidence standard would assure that the fact finder erred on the side of parents' (and children's) interest in family unity. Even if the child's interests could be seen as divergent, the risk of error should not be distributed evenly.

> For the child, the likely consequences of an erroneous failure to terminate is preservation of an uneasy status quo. For the natural parents, however, the consequence of an erroneous termination is the unnecessary destruction of their natural family. A standard that allocates the risk of error evenly between these two outcomes does not reflect properly their relative severity.

The dissenters first challenged the myth of family unity.

> The child has an interest in the outcome of the fact finding hearing independent of that of the parent. To be sure, 'the child and his parents share a vital interest in preventing erroneous termination of their natural relationship.' But the child's interest in a continuation of the family unit exists only to the extent that such a continuation will not be harmful to him. An error in the fact-finding hearing that results in a failure to terminate a parent-child relationship which rightfully should be terminated may well detrimentally affect the child.

The dissenters also challenged the majority's balancing of the harms. If the family court makes an erroneous factual determination resulting in a wrongful denial of the TPR, "the child involved must return either to an abusive home or to the often unstable world of foster care." As the dissenters noted, before a TPR could be brought, the child would have been adjudicated neglected or abused by a court of law or voluntarily surrendered by his parents. He would have spent at least a year and usually far longer in foster care. By this point, the myth of family unity could be painfully out of tune with the child's reality.

By constitutionalizing the rights of parents, *Pierce* set the framework for opinions such as *Santosky*, that leave little room for a theory of children's rights and ignore the reality of children's lives. Other avenues exist for honoring family ties and protecting families from wrongful intervention without treating children like chattels or imprisoning them in abusive or dysfunctional families. One promising approach is to adopt a "functional" as opposed to a "formal" definition of family. The child who has spent six years in foster care may actually have formed family attachments that now supercede his biological ties. For this child, the "natural family" of Supreme Court doctrine is a mere abstraction. Another avenue is to conceptualize family rights as relational rights of association, rather than individual rights of possession. Such a model would encourage courts to look for reciprocal attachments, shared by parent and child. Such an approach would force courts to focus not only on the loss to a parent deprived of his child, but on the value to children of the parent-child relationship. It would also force us to recognize the price paid by children like the infamous Gregory K., living in foster care limbo. The media made a joke out of Gregory, calling him the child who wanted to "divorce" his parents. His real story was the story of a child who had grown up in foster care while his mother went from one abusive relationship to the next. Gregory was not seeking a no fault divorce – his mother had left him so many times, and broken so many promises, he had stopped counting. Children should not be deprived of real and sustaining family relationships out of deference to an absentee parents' abstract rights.

Another case that illustrates the power of the common law is *DeShaney v. Winnebago County*,[19] decided in 1989. The *DeShaney* Court never cites *Pierce* or *Meyer*, but parents' common law and constitutional rights are the engine that drive this case to its tragic conclusion. The question presented was whether the Winnebago County Department of Social Services could be held responsible under Section 1983 of the Civil Rights Act for failing to protect

19. 489 U.S. 189 (1989).

Joshua after he was released to his father's custody. Although DSS continued to monitor his case, it left him in his home despite evidence of danger. The majority accepts at face value that the father's battering of his child is a private matter, and does not implicate state action. As the dissenters point out, the Court ignores the network of laws that empower the parent and disempower the child and his neighbors. Once Joshua's case had been reported to the state, and he had been released to his father's custody, only DSS could effectively come to his aid. The law, not God or nature, placed Joshua at the mercy of his father. As Akhil Amar and Daniel Widawsky wrote in Child Abuse as Slavery: A Thirteenth Amendment response to DeShaney,[20] "Like the antebellum slave, the abused child is subject to near domination and degradation by another person, and is treated more like a possession than as a person." This is the tradition of parental rights we need to re-examine and reject.

Perhaps the Court is learning to approach the constitutionalization of parents' common law rights with greater caution. One of the traditional rights of custody has been the right to exclude others from contact with the child. In *Troxel v. Granville,* decided just last term, the Court was invited to announce that a "fit" parent possess a *constitutional* right to exclude other family members - in this case, paternal grandparents - from contact with a child and that the state has no power to intervene in such cases. The grandparents had invoked a Washington state law that granted standing to "any person at any time" to petition the family court for visitation. The family court was authorized to grant visitation if in "the best interest" of the child. The Washington statute was, as Justice O'Connor noted in her plurality opinion, "breathtakingly broad." But some form of third party visitation statute had been passed in every state. These laws represented a trend away from a rigid hierarchy of exclusionary rights in children, and towards a child-centered perspective that recognizes the importance to children of key attachment relationships. These laws limited parents' absolute freedom to make and unmake their children's families, in circumstances where parental liberty clashed with children's needs for continuity and stability.

At oral argument, counsel for the mother, Tommie Granville, argued that virtually all of these statutes were unconstitutional. In her view, *Pierce* and its progeny established an absolute wall of separation. Unless the biological parent had been proven unfit, the state had no business overriding her child-rearing decisions, no matter how arbitrary and selfish. Justice Stevens, attempting to test the limits of her position, posed the following hypothetical: imagine

20. 105 HARV. L. REV. 1359 (1992).

an unmarried mother who has lived with her own parents since her child's birth, relying on them for child care and support. After an argument with her parents, she takes her six-year-old child and leaves home in a snit. The mother refused to let the child visit the grandparents who raised her from infancy. The attorney held firm. It was the mother's right to make bad decisions as well as good ones, and the state must not intervene. Fortunately, the Court stopped short of endorsing this absolutist view.

Writing for a fractured court, Justice O'Connor recites the litany of cases, beginning with *Meyer* and *Pierce,* as establishing perhaps the oldest of fundamental liberties, the parent's liberty interest in custody, care and control of his child. However, she carefully did NOT affirm the extreme position that a fit parent's rights may always trump the child's best interest. She states that some material weight must be given to the parent's judgment. O'Connor notes that Tommie Granville had never terminated or even threatened to terminate all contact between the little girls and their grandparents. The disagreement before the court was over where and how often contact should take place. Adopting a narrow fact-specific approach, O'Connor concluded that the Washington court, on the facts of this case, failed to give sufficient deference to Tommie Granville's decision. The judge simply presumed that seeing grandparents was in every child's best interests, and engaged in inappropriate second-guessing of the mother's reasonable choices.

The most striking aspect of the opinion in *Troxel* was the justices' inability to reach consensus. While Thomas approached *Troxel* as a classic substantive due process analysis calling for strict scrutiny, Scalia rejected entirely the notion that the Constitution has anything to say about parents' rights to deny access to a child. Stevens, as one might predict from his question at oral argument, would not allow a parent's right of control to trump the child's countervailing rights and interests. By my count, at least seven justices acknowledge some room for state regulation, refusing to hew blindly to the common law tradition giving parents virtually absolute powers.[21] After wading through the welter of opinions – a plurality, two concurrences and three dissents – only one thing is perfectly clear. Evaluating the scope of parents' constitutional rights in light of the emerging rights of children will not be an easy task. I predict that it will occupy the Court for many years to come.

Meanwhile, let us recognize, on this 75th birthday, that *Pierce,* like the Roman God Janus, has two faces. This complex case has left

21. David Meyer, in a forthcoming article skillfully dissects the *Troxel* opinion and predicts that the court is shifting away from strict scrutiny towards a more complex model of the interests at stake in cases involving family autonomy.

behind a complex legacy. On its smiling side, we see those principles of individual liberty and of family privacy and pluralism that allow children to grow into unique individuals, secure in the protective power of caring parents. On its weeping side, we see the stories of children like Joshua DeShaney, Tina Santosky, and Gregory K., trapped in dangerous homes or held hostage in the child welfare system by a distorted vision of the family and of the Constitution.

THE TIE THAT BINDS: THE CONSTITUTIONAL RIGHT OF CHILDREN TO MAINTAIN RELATIONSHIPS WITH PARENT-LIKE INDIVIDUALS

GILBERT A. HOLMES*

TABLE OF CONTENTS

INTRODUCTION 359
I. CURRENT LAW AND JURISPRUDENCE 363
A. *Constitutional Protection of the Child-Parent Relationship* . 363
B. *Deficiencies in the Jurisprudence* 370
1. *Case Law* 370
a. *Controversy Between a Birth Parent and an Unrelated Adult with a Significant Parental Relationship* 370
b. *Controversy Between Natural Parents and Adoptive Parents* 376
c. *Controversy Between Birth Mother, Foster Parents, and Child* 377
2. *Common Threads and Fallacies* 380
II. LEGAL SUPPORT FOR CHILDREN'S LIBERTY INTERESTS IN CHILD-PARENT RELATIONSHIPS 385
A. *Children's Constitutional Rights* 385
B. *Expanding Legal Protection to Other Adult-Child Relationships* 387
III. EMPIRICAL SUPPORT FOR CHILDREN'S LIBERTY INTERESTS IN CHILD-PARENT RELATIONSHIPS 388
IV. SPECIFICS OF CHILDREN'S LIBERTY INTERESTS IN CHILD-PARENT RELATIONSHIPS 390
A. *Definition of "Parent"* 391
1. *A Test for Identifying Parent-Like Individuals* 393
2. *Standing* 396

---

* Associate Professor of Law, Seton Hall University School of Law; B.A., 1969, Bucknell University; J.D., 1972, New York University School of Law. I am grateful to Twila Perry, Kathleen Boozang, Marc Poirier, Charles Sullivan, and Michael Zimmer for their helpful comments on earlier drafts and to Holly Robinson, James Boskey, Carol Goldforth, and Catherine McCauliff for their valuable insight and support in the preparation of this Article. I also wish to thank John Sellers (Class of 1995), Henry Greenberg and Eric Probst (Class of 1994), and John Johnson (Class of 1993) for their invaluable assistance.

B. *Establishing a Right of Companionship* 398
1. *The Substantive Right of Companionship in the Family Dissolution Context* 399
2. *The Substantive Right of Companionship in the 42 U.S.C. § 1983 Context* 399
C. *The Effect of Recognizing Children's Liberty Interests in Child-Parent Relationships* 404
1. *A Constitutional Basis for Visitation* 404
2. *Custodial Parent Status for Parent-Like Individuals* . 409
CONCLUSION 410

WE ARE GUILTY
OF MANY ERRORS AND MANY FAULTS
BUT OUR WORST CRIME
IS ABANDONING THE CHILDREN,
NEGLECTING THE FOUNTAIN OF LIFE.
MANY OF THE THINGS WE NEED
CAN WAIT. THE CHILD CANNOT.
RIGHT NOW IS THE TIME
HIS BONES ARE BEING FORMED, HIS
BLOOD IS BEING MADE, AND
HIS SENSES ARE BEING DEVELOPED.
TO HIM WE CANNOT ANSWER
"TOMORROW."
HIS NAME IS "TODAY."[1]

INTRODUCTION

Children are the most important foundation of every society. As the sole source of tomorrow's leaders and participants, children are the link between the past, the present, and the future. They are the tools by which each culture perpetuates its way of life. Children preserve a society's legacy—its heritage, culture, history, and folklore.[2] Because children play this vital role, their transition to adulthood is an essential component of a society's preservation. To ensure that its culture and values will endure from generation to generation, a society should adopt policies that positively affect the

1. *In re* S.L.H., 342 N.W.2d 672, 681 (S.D. 1984) (Henderson, J., concurring in part and dissenting in part) (quoting Gabriela Mistral, Nobel Laureate of Chile).

2. For an insightful discussion of children and families as the agents for the transmission of heritage, culture, traditions, beliefs, and folklore, see HERBERT G. GUTMAN, THE BLACK FAMILY IN SLAVERY AND FREEDOM, 1750-1925, at 3-44 (1976).

raising, nurturing, and education[3] of children.

In the past four years, courts have confronted an increasing number of disputes involving children and their familial relationships that raise perplexing legal, social, and psychological questions. For example, in 1989, the United States Supreme Court decided that the biological father of a child born into an adulterous relationship with a married woman did not have a right to maintain a relationship with the child.[4] In 1991, the New York Court of Appeals held that a member of a dissolved same-sex family lacked standing to seek visitation with a child that her partner conceived via artificial insemination during the relationship.[5] In the same year, the Wisconsin Supreme Court refused to enforce a coparenting agreement executed by the members of a dissolved same-sex family and denied standing to one member of the family to pursue visitation of the child despite a statute authorizing standing.[6] In 1992, a Florida court decided that a minor could commence a proceeding to terminate his birth mother's parental rights so that his foster parents could legally adopt him.[7] In 1993, the Michigan Supreme Court ruled that Michigan did not have jurisdiction to issue a custody order contrary to an Iowa order issued two years earlier awarding custody of a child in a preadoptive placement to the birth father, who never consented

---

3. The term "education" encompasses more than formal schooling. Education includes the transformation of "uninitiated and seemingly alien beings [children] into robust trustees of [society's] own resources and ideals." JOHN DEWEY, DEMOCRACY AND EDUCATION: AN INTRODUCTION TO THE PHILOSOPHY OF EDUCATION 12 (1916).

4. Michael H. v. Gerald D., 491 U.S. 110 (1989). For further discussion of the competing issues in and the importance of *Michael H.*, see Mary Kay Kisthardt, *Of Fatherhood, Families and Fantasy: The Legacy of* Michael H. v. Gerald D., 65 TUL. L. REV. 585 (1991).

5. Alison D. v. Virginia M., 572 N.E.2d 27 (N.Y. 1991). For further discussion of *Alison D.*, see Kimberly P. Carr, Alison D. v. Virginia M.: *Neglecting the Best Interests of the Child in a Nontraditional Family*, 58 BROOK. L. REV. 1021 (1992); Note, *New York Court of Appeals Refuses to Adopt a Functional Analysis in Defining Family Relationships*—Alison D. v. Virginia M., 105 HARV. L. REV. 941 (1992) [hereinafter Note, *Defining Family Relationships*].

6. *In re* Z.J.H., 471 N.W.2d 202, 209 & n.12 (Wis. 1991). The statute provided in pertinent part:

> Upon petition by a grandparent, great-grandparent, stepparent or person who has maintained a relationship similar to a parent-child relationship with the child, the court may grant reasonable visitation rights to that person if the parents have notice of the hearing and if the court determines that visitation is in the best interest of the child.

WIS. STAT. ANN. § 767.245 (West 1987).

7. *In re* Kingsley, No. JU 90-5245, 1992 WL 551484 (Fla. Cir. Ct. Oct. 21, 1992), *aff'd in part & rev'd in part sub nom* Kingsley v. Kingsley, 623 So. 2d 780 (Fla. Dist. Ct. App. 1993).

to the adoption.[8]

All of these cases involved delicate, complex, and troubling questions of social policy, legal doctrine, and psychological data on child-rearing, and all of them scrutinized the significance of the child's biological, actual, and perceived relationships. Their respective resolutions have stirred public debate about the definition of "family" and the effect of current public policy in family-relationship-dispute resolution.[9]

A common deficiency in all of these cases, however, is the courts' utilization of an adult-centered approach to resolve disputes that affect primarily the lives and development of children. By refusing to permit an "adulterous" unwed father to visit his child,[10] recognizing another unwed father's right to challenge his child's adoption,[11] refusing to allow visitation between a child and an unrelated adult who has functioned as the child's parent,[12] and requiring the termination of all parental rights to free a child for adoption,[13] courts perpetuate the exclusivity accorded the relationship between the child and the legal parent. Child-rearing is an important community effort—parents, teachers, religious leaders, legislators, judges, social workers, and children themselves have a significant impact on a child's transition to adulthood.[14] Traditional jurisprudence, however, grants exclusive child-rearing authority to the legal

---

8. DeBoer v. Schmidt, 502 N.W.2d 649, 659 (Mich. 1993).

9. *See, e.g.*, Tony Bizjak, *Family Images Focusing in on New Definitions*, SACRAMENTO BEE, June 28, 1992, at A1; Susan Canfield, *Defining Family Becomes More Flexible*, SEATTLE TIMES, June 14, 1993, at E3; *Gay Families Deserve Equality*, PHOENIX GAZETTE, July 28, 1989, at A13; Peggy O'Crowley, *New Ties That Bind in the Home, Tradition Gives Way to Diversity*, NORTHERN N.J. REC., Mar. 25, 1990, at 101; Clarence Page, *Partnership is what Marriage is About*, OREGONIAN, Oct. 10, 1989, at B06; Kathleen Parker, *Women are at the Core of Family Values Debate*, ORLANDO SENTINEL, Aug. 28, 1992, at E1; Leslie Phillips, *Family Ties: New Meanings; Cities Recognizing Non-Traditional Living Arrangements*, USA TODAY, July 12, 1989, at 03A; Tom Schaefer, *Readers Divided on Family Values and What Makes a Family*, WICHITA EAGLE, Sept. 5, 1992, at 8C; Linell Smith, *'Family Values': What Are They? The Meanings Are Varied*, BALT. SUN, Aug. 26, 1992, at 1G; *YWCA Redefines the Family*, ATLANTA CONST., June 3, 1992, at B3; *What Is Family?*, WASH. POST, July 13, 1989, at A22.

10. Michael H. v. Gerald D., 491 U.S. 110 (1989).

11. *See* DeBoer v. Schmidt, 502 N.W.2d 649 (Mich. 1993).

12. *See* Alison D. v. Virginia M., 572 N.E.2d 27 (N.Y. 1991); *In re* Z.J.H., 471 N.W.2d 202 (Wis. 1991).

13. *See In re* Kingsley, No. JU 90-5245, 1992 WL 551484 (Fla. Cir. Ct. Oct. 21, 1992), *aff'd in part & rev'd in part sub nom.* Kingsley v. Kingsley, 623 So. 2d 780 (Fla. Dist. Ct. App. 1993).

14. There is an African proverb that teaches that it takes an entire village to raise a child.

parents,[15] particularly with respect to governing the child's relationships with other adults.[16] This approach creates an all-or-nothing resolution of familial conflicts, one that is particularly inadequate when the dispute is between an adult who has both a legal and an actual relationship with the child and an adult who has only an actual relationship with the child. As a general rule, the former will prevail and the latter will lose all access to the child.[17] In applying the current approach, courts focus on the adult's status and legal relationship with the child, but ignore the importance of the personal relationship to the child.[18]

This Article uses recent cases to illustrate the inadequacy of the adult-centered approach to reconciling the rights of children with those of adults.[19] It argues that the law should accord children an independent liberty interest in their relationships with both "legal parents"[20] and "nonlegal parents"[21] irrespective of biological ties. The Article analyzes (a) the development of children's constitutional

---

15. In *Meyer v. Nebraska*, 262 U.S. 390 (1923), the Court attempted to define the rights protected by the liberty provision of the Fourteenth Amendment, noting:

> Without doubt, it denotes not merely freedom from bodily restraint but also the right of the individual to contract, to engage in any of the common occupations of life, to acquire useful knowledge, to marry, establish a home and bring up children, to worship God according to the dictates of his own conscience, and generally to enjoy those privileges long recognized at common law as essential to the orderly pursuit of happiness by free men.

Id. at 399. In acknowledging the parents' child-rearing role, the Court also has observed that "the child is not the mere creature of the State; those who nurture him and direct his destiny have the right, coupled with the high duty, to recognize and prepare him for additional obligations." Pierce v. Society of Sisters, 268 U.S. 510, 535 (1925).

16. *Alison D.*, 572 N.E.2d 27; *Z.J.H.*, 471 N.W.2d 202; Katharine T. Bartlett, *Rethinking Parenthood as an Exclusive Status: The Need for Legal Alternatives When the Premise of the Nuclear Family has Failed*, 70 VA. L. REV. 879 (1984).

17. *See, e.g.*, *Alison D.*, 572 N.E.2d at 29 ("Petitioner concedes that she is not the child's 'parent'. . . . Rather she claims to have acted as a 'de facto parent'. . . . Therefore, she claims to have standing to seek visitation rights. These claims, however, are insufficient . . . .").

18. *See infra* Part III (discussing the psychological studies indicating the relative importance of noncustodial parental relationships to children).

19. The rights of *legal* parents to the custody and care of their children are protected under the liberty clause of the Fourteenth Amendment.

20. As used in this Article, "legal parent" means an adult who is related to a child by conception, birth, or adoption. A legally related adult includes both a legal parent and any other person whose relationship with the child is recognized by a statute according that individual a right to maintain the relationship. *See, e.g.*, N.Y. DOM. REL. LAW § 72 (McKinney 1988) (grandparents); WIS. STAT. ANN. § 767.245 (West 1993) (stepparents).

21. A nonlegal parent is an individual who does not have a legal relationship with the child, but who has served as a parent to the child. *See infra* Part IV.A.1 (describing the criteria for identifying individuals with whom a child would have a liberty interest in maintaining relationships).

rights; (b) recent statutory changes expanding the categories of individuals who have standing to pursue visitation; (c) empirical studies recognizing a child's need to maintain relationships with parent-like figures; and (d) the impact that a child-centered approach would have on the parents' constitutional right to control and care for their children. This Article advocates the recognition of children's liberty interest in familial relationships and suggests a model for conducting a child-centered analysis. Finally, it proposes a test for identifying nonlegal parents with whom children could maintain protected relationships.

I. CURRENT LAW AND JURISPRUDENCE

A. *Constitutional Protection of the Child-Parent Relationship*

Courts have repeatedly invoked the United States Constitution to protect the parent-child relationship. Although this protection has been extended to the full range of familial relationships, the jurisprudence generally does not address a variety of "nontraditional"[22] relationships that exist in today's society. Thus, the case law provides guidance with respect to the "traditional" parent-child relationship, but leaves many questions unanswered in the nontraditional realm. More important, the jurisprudence is silent with respect to the children's interest in maintaining certain relationships.

The Supreme Court initiated the constitutional protection of family relationships in *Meyer v. Nebraska*[23] and *Pierce v. Society of Sisters*,[24] placing the parent-child relationship within the private autonomy paradigm of the Constitution.[25] In both cases, the Court

22. The term "traditional family" is extremely misleading. Generally, it has been applied to a family consisting of married parents with children born from the marriage. This definition assumes that families come in one dominant style and designates all other types "nontraditional." Recent census data refutes this assumption. In 1988, so-called "traditional families" represented only 27% of households with minor children. *See* Note, *Looking for a Family Resemblance: The Limits of the Functional Approach to the Legal Definition of Family*, 104 HARV. L. REV. 1640 n.1 (1991) [hereinafter Note, *Family Resemblance*]. By 1991, "traditional families" comprised only 22% of the households with children. *See* Jennifer L. Heeb, Note, *Homosexual Marriage, the Changing American Family, and the Heterosexual Right to Privacy*, 24 SETON HALL L. REV. 347, 349 n.11 (1993). Given that households consisting of a husband, wife, and their children constitute the minority of families with children, it is difficult, if not ludicrous, to assume that the traditional family predominates or should continue to receive preferential treatment.

23. 262 U.S. 390 (1923).

24. 268 U.S. 510 (1925).

25. *See Meyer*, 262 U.S. at 400; *Pierce*, 268 U.S. 534-35 (both cases involved the exercise of parental control over their children's education). Although the Constitution does not expressly delineate parental rights, these rights comprise a portion of the "liberty"

acknowledged that the liberty provision of the Fourteenth Amendment[26] limits a state's ability to interfere with parents' child-rearing and education decisions.[27] In these initial discussions, the Court did not clearly indicate that parents' right to control family decision-making was a fundamental liberty interest.[28] Subsequently, however, the Court clarified that the liberty interest in family relationships was

---

guaranteed to "persons" throughout the document. As Professor Tribe summarized:

> [R]ights have been located in the "liberty" protected by the due process clauses of the fifth and fourteenth amendments. They have been cut from the cloth of the ninth amendment—conceived as a rule against cramped construction—or from the privileges and immunities clauses of article IV and of the fourteenth amendment. Encompassing rights to shape one's inner life and rights to control the face one presents to the world, they have materialized from the "emanations" and "penumbras"—most recently dubbed simply the "shadows"—of the first, third, fourth, and fifth amendments. They elaborate the "blessings of liberty" promised in the Preamble, and have been held implicit in the eighth amendment's prohibition against cruel and unusual punishments.

LAURENCE H. TRIBE, AMERICAN CONSTITUTIONAL LAW § 15-3 (2d ed. 1988) (footnotes omitted). For an insightful discussion of family privacy and autonomy, see Judith G. McMullen, *Privacy, Family Autonomy, and the Maltreated Child*, 75 MARQ. L. REV. 569 (1992). For a discussion of the history and development of parents' constitutional rights, see Francis Barry McCarthy, *The Confused Constitutional Status and Meaning of Parental Rights*, 22 GA. L. REV. 975 (1988).

26. U.S. CONST. amend. XIV, § 1. In pertinent part, the Fourteenth Amendment provides:

> All persons born or naturalized in the United States, and subject to the jurisdiction thereof, are citizens of the United States and of the State wherein they reside. No State shall make or enforce any law which shall abridge the privileges or immunities of citizens of the United States; nor shall any State deprive any person of life, liberty, or property, without due process of law; nor deny to any person within its jurisdiction the equal protection of the laws.

Id.

27. In *Meyer*, the Court proclaimed that "without doubt, [liberty] denotes not merely freedom from bodily restraint but also the right of the individual to . . . establish a home and bring up children . . . ." *Meyer*, 262 U.S. at 399. In *Pierce*, the Court announced that compulsory public schooling "unreasonably interferes with the liberty of parents and guardians to direct the upbringing and education of children under their control." *Pierce*, 268 U.S. at 534-35. For an in depth discussion of the role of *Meyer* and *Pierce* in the birth of constitutional theory applicable to the relationships between the child, parent, and state, see Barbara B. Woodhouse, *"Who Owns the Child?":* Meyer *and* Pierce *and the Child as Property*, 33 WM. & MARY L. REV. 995 (1992).

28. The Court had not yet developed its tripartite constitutional analysis involving strict scrutiny, rational basis, and the middle tier tests when it decided *Meyer* and *Pierce*. Therefore, the Court did not need to resolve the issue of whether or not the parents' liberty interest was fundamental. *See* Griswold v. Connecticut, 381 U.S. 479, 504 (1965) (citing Skinner v. Oklahoma, 316 U.S. 535 (1942) as authority for the proposition that strict scrutiny analysis is required when fundamental rights are in danger). For a discussion of the standards of review that apply when a statute or policy is challenged on constitutional grounds, see JOHN E. NOWAK & RONALD D. ROTUNDA, CONSTITUTIONAL LAW § 11.4 & 14.3 (4th ed. 1991).

indeed fundamental and granted the highest constitutional protection to the family decision-making process.[29]

The Court affirmed the protection of the parent-child relationship in subsequent related cases. In *West Virginia State Board of Education v. Barnette*,[30] the Court held that the state could not require school children to recite the Pledge of Allegiance against parental objection.[31] Because the state could not demonstrate a compelling interest in such a requirement,[32] the Court upheld the parents' freedom to refuse—and to permit their children to refuse—to endorse official dogma under the Establishment Clause of the First Amendment.[33]

In *Prince v. Massachusetts*,[34] however, the Court permitted the state to prohibit a parent from allowing her ward to proselytize their

---

29. *See* Santosky v. Kramer, 455 U.S. 745, 753 (1982) (declaring parents' liberty interest in the "care, custody and management" of their children to be fundamental and requiring states to prove parental unfitness sufficient to terminate those rights by clear and convincing evidence); Wisconsin v. Yoder, 406 U.S. 205 (1972) (holding that the state's interest in compulsory education was not sufficiently compelling to overcome parents' fundamental right to raise their children).

30. 319 U.S. 624 (1943).

31. *Id.* at 642.

32. The State asserted that it had the right to "condition access to public education on making a prescribed sign and profession and at the same time to coerce attendance by punishing both parent and child." *Id.* at 630-31. The Court answered the State's assertion of this power by proclaiming that

> [i]f there is any fixed star in our constitutional constellation, it is that no official, high or petty, can prescribe what shall be orthodox in politics, nationalism, religion, or other matters of opinion or force citizens to confess by word or act their faith therein. If there are any circumstances which permit an exception, they do not now occur to us.

Id. at 642.

33. *Id.* Although the majority opinion did not expressly analyze the parents' liberty interest in child-rearing, the Court in Prince v. Massachusetts, 321 U.S. 158 (1944), characterized *Barnette* as a decision that "respected the private realm of family life which the state cannot enter." *Id.* at 166. In *Prince*, the Court explained:

> The rights of children to exercise their religion, and of parents to give them religious training and to encourage them in the practice of religious belief, as against preponderant sentiment and assertion of state power voicing it, have had recognition here, most recently in *West Virginia State Board of Education v. Barnette*. Previously in *Pierce v. Society of Sisters*, this Court had sustained the parent's authority to provide religious with secular schooling, and the child's right to receive it, as against the state's requirement of attendance at public schools. And in *Meyer v. Nebraska*, children's right to receive teaching in languages other than the nation's common tongue were guarded against the state's encroachment. It is cardinal with us that the custody, care, and nurture of the child reside first in the parents, whose primary function and freedom include preparation for obligations the state can neither supply nor hinder.

Id. at 165-66 (citations omitted).

34. 321 U.S. 158 (1944).

religion on the grounds that those activities violated the state child labor laws.[35] Despite its prior holdings protecting parental discretion over a child's secular and religious training in *Meyer*, *Pierce*, and *Barnette*, the Court in *Prince* found that the state's compelling interest in the child's health outweighed Ms. Prince's constitutionally supported right to direct the upbringing of the child.[36] Notwithstanding this conclusion, the majority recognized that the parents have a constitutionally based right to raise their children.[37]

In *Wisconsin v. Yoder*,[38] the Court again acknowledged the existence of the parents' child-rearing authority and underscored the importance of protecting familial relationships against governmental intrusion.[39] The Court declared a state policy requiring children to attend school until they were sixteen years old unconstitutional as applied to Amish children, because it violated both the parents' rights under the Free Exercise Clause of the First Amendment and their liberty interest under the Fourteenth Amendment.[40]

In the preceding cases, the parents' liberty interest in child-rearing served as a shield against governmental intrusion when there was no compelling state interest in the intrusive policy or action. The jurisprudence safeguarding family autonomy springs from the constitutional protection of individual decisions regarding intrafamily relationships.[41] Interestingly, although it is often a factor in the Court's analysis, the Court has never required marriage as a prerequisite to the Constitutional protection of the parent-child relationship.

---

35. *Id.* at 168-69. Massachusetts's Child Labor Law section 69 provided: "No boy under twelve and no girl under eighteen shall sell, expose or offer for sale any newspapers, magazines, periodicals or any other articles of merchandise of any description, or exercise the trade of bootblack or scavenger, or any other trade, in any street or public place." *Id.* at 160-61 (quoting MASS. GEN. L. ch. 149, § 69 (1939)).

36. *See id.* at 166, 170. The Court stated:

> [T]he family itself is not beyond regulation in the public interest, as against a claim of religious liberty. And neither rights of religion nor rights of parenthood are beyond limitation. Acting to guard the general interest in youth's well being, the state as *parens patriae* may restrict the parent's control by requiring school attendance, regulating or prohibiting the child's labor, and in many other ways.

Id. at 166 (citations omitted).

37. *See id.* at 171. It is interesting to note that the Court used the parental autonomy analysis even though Ms. Prince was not the biological mother of the child. In fact, she was the child's aunt and custodian. *Id.* at 159.

38. 406 U.S. 205 (1972).

39. *Id.* at 213-14.

40. *Id.* at 233-34.

41. *See* McMullen, *supra* note 25, at 575 ("As social reforms began to protect children and other workers, the American idealized image of the independent individual continued to develop. Courts adjusted their reasoning to gradually create a rhetoric of family autonomy and 'parental rights' which could be limited only by significant state interests.").

The clearest examples of the minimal impact of the existence or absence of a marital relationship appear in cases that recognize unwed fathers' liberty interests in maintaining relationships with their children.[42] Although the Court has limited the class of unwed fathers who can assert their constitutional rights[43] and has distinguished unwed fathers' rights from those of mothers,[44] it has accorded unwed fathers who establish actual relationships with their children constitutional protection of the parent-child relationship. The unwed father cases demonstrate that the liberty interest in family relationships is personal and is dependent not only upon a biological tie, but also upon the manifestation of an actual parent-child relationship.[45]

---

42. *Compare* Caban v. Mohammed, 441 U.S. 380 (1978) *and* Stanley v. Illinois, 405 U.S. 645 (1972) (recognizing an unwed father's liberty interest in his relationship with his children) *with* Lehr v. Robertson, 463 U.S. 248 (1983) *and* Quilloin v. Walcott, 434 U.S. 246 (1978) (denying constitutional protection to unwed fathers' relationships with their children because they had not established an actual relationship with the children). In *Lehr*, the Court explained that

> [w]hen an unwed father demonstrates a full commitment to the responsibilities of parenthood by "com[ing] forward to participate in the rearing of his child," his interest in personal contact with his child acquires substantial protection under the Due Process Clause. At that point it may be said that he "act[s] as a father toward his children." But the mere existence of a biological link does not merit equivalent constitutional protection. The actions of judges neither create nor sever genetic bonds.

Lehr, 463 U.S. at 261 (quoting Caban v. Mohammed, 441 U.S. 380, 389 n.7, 392 (1979)). For a discussion of the development of unwed fathers' liberty interests, see Elizabeth Buchanan, *The Constitutional Rights of Unwed Fathers Before and After* Lehr v. Robertson, 45 OHIO ST. L.J. 313 (1984).

43. An unwed father's constitutional right to maintain a relationship with his child is dependent upon both a biological connection and the maintenance of a relationship. *See Lehr*, 463 U.S. at 261 (stating that constitutional protection of a parental relationship stems not just from a biological link but also from a continuing interaction with the child); *Quilloin*, 434 U.S. at 255 (determining that a biological father who never established a relationship with his child cannot prevent the child's adoption); *Caban*, 434 U.S. at 393 (stating that an unwed father should not be treated differently than an unwed mother when he has established a relationship with his children and admitted paternity).

Although Justice Stevens believed that the Court had not denied unwed fathers a liberty interest in their children, *see Lehr*, 463 U.S. at 261, others viewed the Court's limitation of unwed fathers' procedural rights as a denial of constitutional protection. *Id.* at 276 (White, J., dissenting) (characterizing the failure to provide an unwed father notice and a hearing before his child's adoption as a violation of the Due Process Clause). *See generally* Buchanan, *supra* note 42.

44. *See Lehr*, 463 U.S. at 263-64 & n.20; *Caban*, 441 U.S. at 404-07 (Stevens, J., dissenting).

45. Justice Stevens has promoted the concept that a parent's liberty interest requires both a biological and an actual relationship with the child. The mother's actual relationship arises during the pregnancy and childbirth, but the father's actual relationship requires additional effort. Thus, in *Caban v. Mohammad*, he explained:

The Court also has refused to adopt a rigid definition of "family" that would obstruct constitutional protection of other important interpersonal relationships. For example, in *Moore v. City of East Cleveland*,[46] the Court prohibited the state from applying its single family zoning statute to exclude Ms. Moore's family—which consisted of her son, his child, and another grandchild—from an area zoned for single family occupancy.[47] The Court applied the constitutional protection of family relationships articulated in *Meyer v. Nebraska*[48] and *Pierce v. Society of Sisters*[49] to Ms. Moore's family even though it did not consist of the traditional parent-child relationship.[50] The Court recognized that the historical and traditional foundations of the Constitution required a flexible definition of family.[51]

Likewise, in *Smith v. Organization of Foster Families for Equality and Reform*,[52] the Court acknowledged that constitutional protection of family relationships is not limited to relationships based on blood,

---

> Both parents are equally responsible for the conception of the child out of wedlock. But from that point on through pregnancy and infancy, the differences between the male and the female have important impact on the child's destiny. Only the mother carries the child; it is she who has the constitutional right to decide whether to bear it or not. In many cases, only the mother knows who sired the child, and it will often be within her power to withhold that fact, and even the fact of her pregnancy, from that person. If during pregnancy the mother should marry a different partner, the child will be legitimate when born, and the natural father may never even know that his 'rights' have been affected.

Caban, 441 U.S. at 404-05 (Stevens, J., dissenting) (citations omitted). Writing for the majority in *Lehr*, Justice Stevens continued his biological tie-actual relationship requirement:

> The significance of the biological connection is that it offers the natural father an opportunity that no other male possesses to develop a relationship with his offspring. If he grasps that opportunity and accepts some measure of responsibility for the child's future, he may enjoy the blessings of the parent-child relationship and make uniquely valuable contributions to the child's development. If he fails to do so, the Federal Constitution will not automatically compel a State to listen to his opinion of where the child's best interests lie.

Lehr, 463 U.S. at 262.

46. 431 U.S. 494 (1977). For further discussion of the definition of family in the application of constitutional doctrine, see Note, *Family Resemblance*, *supra* note 22.

47. *Moore*, 431 U.S. at 496.

48. 262 U.S. 390 (1923).

49. 268 U.S. 510 (1925).

50. *Moore*, 431 U.S. at 503-06.

51. *Id.* Justice Powell explained that "our decisions establish that the Constitution protects the sanctity of the family precisely because the institution of the family is deeply rooted in this Nation's history and tradition. . . . Ours is by no means a tradition limited to respect for the bonds uniting the members of the nuclear family." *Id.* at 503-04 (citations omitted).

52. 431 U.S. 816 (1977).

marriage, or adoption.[53] Specifically, the Court reasoned that

> the importance of the familial relationship, to the individuals involved and to the society, stems from the emotional attachments that derive from the intimacy of daily association, and from the role it plays in "promot[ing] a way of life" through the instruction of children . . . as well as from the fact of blood relationship. No one would seriously dispute that a deeply loving and interdependent relationship between an adult and a child in his or her care may exist even in the absence of a blood relationship.[54]

Despite its permissive definition of a family, the Court refused to extend constitutional protection to the Smiths' foster family because a foster family is a creation of the state. The Court reasoned that the foster parents' interest "derives from a knowingly assumed contractual relation with the State, [and] it [thus] is appropriate to ascertain from state law the expectations and entitlements of the parties."[55] Consequently, foster families are bound "by the limited recognition accorded to [them] by the [state] statutes."[56] Furthermore, the Court was aware that extending constitutional protection to foster families would transgress the legal parents' liberty interest in their children.[57]

The jurisprudence protecting family relationships presents substantial difficulties. It leaves open the question of whether a birth mother can deny an unwed father his substantive due process rights by refusing him access to the child[58] or by failing to advise him of

53. *Id.* at 843-44.

54. *Id.* at 844 (quoting Wisconsin v. Yoder, 406 U.S. 205, 231-33 (1972)). For a discussion of the need to recognize a different definition of "family," see Mary P. Treuthart, *Adopting a More Realistic Definition of "Family,"* 26 GONZ. L. REV. 91 (1990-91).

55. *Smith*, 431 U.S. at 845-46.

56. *Id.* at 846.

57. *See id.* The state can provide constitutional protection to the foster family relationship only by terminating the legal parents' parental rights and authorizing the adoption of the children by the foster parents. Because this process transforms the foster family into a "legal family," it requires according the legal parents due process. *See* Santosky v. Kramer, 455 U.S. 745, 747-48 (1982) ("Before a State may sever completely and irrevocably the rights of parents in their natural child, due process requires that the State support its allegations by at least clear and convincing evidence.").

58. *See* Lehr v. Robertson, 463 U.S. 248, 268 (1983) (White, J., dissenting) (framing the issue in terms of whether denying a putative father notice and an opportunity to be heard in an adoption proceeding when his whereabouts are known is consistent with due process); *In re* Adoption of Kelsey S., 823 P.2d 1216 (Cal. 1992) (declaring unconstitutional a statutory provision that permitted an unwed mother to consent to her child's adoption shortly after the child's birth and before the father had an opportunity to establish an actual relationship with the child). *See generally* Buchanan, *supra* note 42.

her pregnancy or the birth of the child. It also leaves unanswered the question of whether substantive due process rights are implicated when adults, rather than the state, consensually create family relationships without the benefit of marriage. Moreover, the Court sends conflicting messages by failing to define "family" adequately and failing to identify specifically the class of adults who are entitled to maintain a relationship with the child.[59] Most importantly, however, the courts have remained silent regarding the question of whether children have an independent liberty interest in their own familial relationships. As will be discussed below, this silence presents a major deficiency in the jurisprudence.

B. *Deficiencies in the Jurisprudence*

1. Case Law.—In the cases that have examined constitutional rights in family relationships—involving traditional families, unwed fathers, or other family-type relationships—the courts have not addressed the *children's* interest in maintaining the relationships. Several recent cases, discussed below, demonstrate this troubling oversight.

a. Controversy Between a Birth Parent and an Unrelated Adult with a Significant Parental Relationship.—In *Michael H. v. Gerald D.*,[60] Michael, the birth father, sought to continue his relationship with Victoria, his biological child, whose birth mother was Gerald's wife, Carole.[61] Victoria also sought to maintain her relationship with Michael, relying on the Fourteenth Amendment to the United States Constitution.[62] Gerald, who was married to Carole at the time of Victoria's conception and birth, acknowledged Victoria as his daughter, but did not dispute that Michael was her biological father.[63]

---

59. In Stanley v. Illinois, 405 U.S. 645 (1972), the Court held that a state cannot terminate constitutional parental rights absent evidence of unfitness. *Id.* at 658. In Quilloin v. Walcott, 434 U.S. 246 (1978), however, the Court found that biology alone was insufficient to create a liberty interest in familial relationships and did not address the notion of unfitness. *See id.* at 255. Justice Marshall hinted, however, that states could not terminate parental rights absent a showing of unfitness. *See id.* at 251. Finally, in Smith v. Organization of Foster Families for Equality and Reform, 431 U.S. 816 (1977), Justice Brennan indicated that a parental liberty interest can exist even absent a biological relationship. *Id.* at 842-43.

60. 491 U.S. 110 (1989).

61. *Id.* at 113-14.

62. *Id.* at 130.

63. *Id.*

Michael also acknowledged Victoria as his child, lived with her, supported her, held her out to the world as his daughter, and sought to be her custodial parent.[64] These factors satisfied the Supreme Court's previously articulated prerequisites for permitting an unwed father to maintain a relationship with his child.[65] In opposing Michael's custody claim, Gerald and Carole relied on the fact that California recognized Gerald as Victoria's legal father under an evidentiary presumption of legitimacy[66] and argued that California permitted only the legal mother or father to challenge that presumption.[67]

---

64. *Id.* at 114.

65. *See supra* notes 42-45 and accompanying text (explaining that an unwed father must have both a biological and an actual relationship with a child in order to maintain the relationship).

66. Under California evidentiary rules, the California courts declared Gerald to be Victoria's father because of his marriage to Carole at the time of Victoria's birth. *Michael H.*, 491 U.S. at 115. The Court relied on a California statute that stated, in pertinent part:

> (a) Except as provided in subdivision (b), the issue of a wife cohabiting with her husband, who is not impotent or sterile, is conclusively presumed to be a child of the marriage.
>
> (b) Notwithstanding subdivision (a), if the court finds that the conclusions of all the experts, as disclosed by the evidence based upon blood tests performed pursuant to Chapter 2 (commencing with Section 890) of Division 7, are that the husband is not the father of the child, the question of paternity of the husband shall be resolved accordingly.
>
> (c) The notice of motion for blood tests under subdivision (b) may be filed . . . not later than two years from the child's date of birth by the husband. . . .
>
> (d) The notice of motion for blood tests under subdivision (b) may be raised by the mother of the child not later than two years from the child's date of birth if the child's biological father has filed an affidavit with the court acknowledging paternity of the child.
>
> (e) Subdivision (b) shall not apply to any case coming within Section 7005 of the Civil Code, or to any case in which the wife, with the consent of the husband, conceived by means of a surgical procedure.
>
> (f) The notice of motion for the blood tests pursuant to subdivision (b) shall be supported by a declaration under oath submitted by the moving party stating the factual basis for placing the issue of paternity before the court. This requirement shall not apply to any case pending before the court on September 30, 1980.
>
> (g) Subdivision (b) shall not apply to any case which has reached final judgment of paternity on September 30, 1980.

CAL. EVID. CODE § 621 (West Supp. 1989), *repealed by* Act effective Jan. 1, 1994, ch. 162, § 8, 1992 Cal. Legis. Serv. 412 (West). This section was moved and recodified at CAL. FAM. LAW CODE § 7540-41 (West 1994) (codifying former Evidence Code § 621(a) at Family Law § 7540 and codifying former § 621(b)-(g), with modifications, at Family Law § 7541).

67. *Michael H.*, 491 U.S. at 120; *see* CAL. EVID. CODE § 621(c), (d), (West Supp. 1989) (permitting the husband or the mother of the child to request blood tests), *repealed by* Act effective Jan. 1, 1994, ch. 162, § 8, 1992 Cal. Legis. Serv. 412 (West); *supra* note 66 (quoting the pertinent portion of the statute).

The Supreme Court dismissed Michael's claim, reasoning that California was entitled to adopt a public policy that gave a priority to one potential father over another.[68] The Court distinguished Michael's claim from those of the unwed fathers in other cases[69] on the grounds that Michael was an "adulterous father."[70] According to the Court, Michael's claim did not seek to protect a relationship "deeply rooted in this Nation's history and tradition"[71] and, therefore, did not warrant constitutional protection.[72]

Victoria also sought to have *both* relationships protected under the Due Process Clause, with Michael as her biological father and Gerald as her legal father.[73] Her claim was separate and distinct from Michael's claim and did not seek to create a priority for either father.[74] Although the Court did not rule out the possibility of a claim by a child like Victoria, it rejected her claim without addressing or analyzing its legal basis.[75] The Court did not even discuss whether Victoria had a constitutional right to maintain her relationship with either Michael or Gerald.[76] Furthermore, assuming,

---

68. *Michael H.*, 491 U.S. at 129-30. Carole and Gerald argued, and the Court agreed, that Michael's paternity was immaterial. Implicit in the Court's reasoning is the view that a biological relationship was insufficient to preserve Michael's constitutional right, and therefore, that it did not provide the essential component of a parent-child relationship that could be protected by the Due Process Clause. *Id.* at 125-27.

69. *See supra* notes 43-45 (describing other unwed father cases).

70. *Michael H.*, 491 U.S. at 130.

71. *Id.* at 124 (quoting Moore v. City of E. Cleveland, 431 U.S. 494, 503 (1977)).

72. *Id.* at 129-30.

73. *Id.*

74. *Id.*

75. *Id.* at 130-31. The Court stated:

> We have never had occasion to decide whether a child has a liberty interest, symmetrical with that of her parent, in maintaining her filial relationship. We need not do so here because, even assuming that such a right exists, Victoria's claim must fail. Victoria's due process challenge is, if anything, weaker than Michael's. Her basic claim is not that California has erred in preventing her from establishing that Michael, not Gerald, should stand as her legal father. Rather, she claims a due process right to maintain filial relationships with both Michael and Gerald. This assertion merits little discussion, for, whatever the merits of the guardian ad litem's belief that such an arrangement can be of great psychological benefit to a child, the claim that a State must recognize multiple fatherhood has no support in the history or traditions of this country. Moreover, even if we were to construe Victoria's argument as forwarding the lesser proposition that, whatever her status vis-a-vis Gerald, she has a liberty interest in maintaining a filial relationship with her natural father, Michael, we find that, at best, her claim is the obverse of Michael's and fails for the same reasons.

Id.

76. *Id.* Victoria's constitutional right to maintain relationships with family members would emanate from her status as a person under the Constitution and from her liberty interest, protected by Fourteenth Amendment substantive due process.

arguendo, that Victoria had a constitutional right, the Court identified no state interests sufficiently compelling to overcome that right. The Court did not even address whether Victoria's status as a minor justified limiting her share of the constitutional rights traditionally afforded adults in their family relationships.[77] As a result of the Court's decision, neither Michael nor Victoria could maintain a legally recognized relationship with each other.

Several state courts also have confronted claims involving nontraditional families where disputes arose between a birth parent and an adult with a significant parental relationship. In *Alison D. v. Virginia M.*,[78] the New York Court of Appeals decided that Alison, a member of a dissolved lesbian partnership, was not entitled to maintain a relationship with A.D.M., a child born to her partner during the partnership.[79] Although Alison was not A.D.M.'s biological mother, she claimed that she was a psychological parent,[80] a de facto parent,[81] and an equitable parent[82] to A.D.M.[83] She maintained that she and her partner, Virginia, mutually decided to bring A.D.M. into the world, and that she (Alison) had provided financial and emotional support to A.D.M. during the two and one-half years in which the parties lived together and after they separated.[84] The essence of Alison's claim was that she, Virginia, and A.D.M. constituted a "family" under New York law.[85]

---

77. *See supra* text accompanying notes 23-59 (discussing the development of jurisprudence acknowledging individuals' liberty interest in their family relationships); *infra* note 171 (discussing cases limiting the constitutional protection accorded children because of their special status as minors, or because of the need to balance their rights against their parents' and society's interests).

78. 572 N.E.2d 27 (N.Y. 1991).

79. *Id.* at 29. Alison and Virginia had all the appearances of a traditional family, except that the adults were of the same sex and were unmarried. After living together for three years, they decided to add children to the family. *Id.* at 28. Virginia underwent artificial insemination and gave birth to A.D.M. *Id.*

80. *See* Bartlett, *supra* note 16, at 946 ("Psychological parents are adults who provide for the physical, emotional, and social needs of the child . . . .").

81. Most jurisdictions have defined a de facto parent as an individual who fulfills the child's physical and psychological needs on a daily basis. *E.g.*, *In re* Hirenia C., 22 Cal. Rptr. 2d 443 (Cal. Ct. App. 1993); *In re* Baby Girl B., 618 A.2d 1 (Conn. 1992); *In re* L.W., 613 A.2d 350 (D.C. App. 1992); *In re* Dependency of J.H., 815 P.2d 1380 (Wash. 1991); *In re* B.G., 523 P.2d 244 (Cal. 1974).

82. *See* Nancy D. Polikoff, *This Child Does Have Two Mothers: Redefining Parenthood to Meet the Needs of Children in Lesbian-Mother and Other Nontraditional Families*, 78 GEO. L.J. 459, 483-86 (1990) (discussing equitable parenthood).

83. *Alison D.*, 572 N.E.2d at 29.

84. *Id.* at 28.

85. *Id.* at 28-29. *See* Braschi v. Stahl Assocs., 543 N.E.2d 49 (N.Y. 1989) (adopting a functional definition of "family" under state rent control law). *See also* CARMEL, N.Y., CODE

In rejecting Alison's claim, the court stated that although she may have an "understandable concern for and interest in the child," Alison was not a "parent" within the meaning of the statute governing visitation.[86] Because she was not a parent under the statute and because the court declined to extend the definition of parent to include "functional" or "psychological" parents, the court concluded that Alison lacked standing to seek visitation rights.[87] Like the Supreme Court in *Michael H.*, the New York Court of Appeals used the state policy embodied in a statute to exclude an adult with a significant parental relationship from access to the child. The fact that Michael was a birth parent while Virginia was not was irrelevant in each court's emphasis on the legal rather than the actual relationship. The New York Court of Appeals did not address whether A.D.M. had a right to maintain his relationship with Alison.[88] Unlike the Court in *Michael H.*, however, the New York court was not directly presented with any claims on behalf of the child.

In *In re Z.J.H.*,[89] the Wisconsin Supreme Court also was confronted with custody and visitation issues arising from a dissolved

---

§ 63-7 (1983) (defining family as "[t]wo (2) or more persons related by blood, marriage or legal adoption, or five (5) unrelated adults living together as a single housekeeping unit"). Alison and Virginia lived in Carmel, New York.

86. *Alison D.*, 572 N.E.2d at 29. Specifically, New York law provides that:

> (a) Where a minor child is residing within this state, either *parent* may apply to the supreme court for a writ of habeas corpus to have such minor child brought before such court; and on the return thereof, the court, on due consideration, may award the natural guardianship, charge and custody of such child to either *parent* for such time, under such regulations and restrictions, and with such provisions and directions, as the case may require, and may at any time thereafter vacate or modify such order. . . .

N.Y. DOM. REL. LAW § 70 (McKinney 1994) (emphasis added); *see also* Ronald FF v. Cindy GG, 511 N.E.2d 75 (N.Y. 1987) (denying visitation rights to a heterosexual male partner in an unmarried family unit who was legally unrelated to the child).

87. *Alison D.*, 572 N.E.2d at 29. The court acknowledged the undisputed facts that Alison participated in the decision to conceive A.D.M., that she treated A.D.M. in all respects as her child, and that Virginia consented to Alison's sharing in A.D.M.'s upbringing. *Id.* Alison's and Virginia's behavior comports with the definitions of psychological parent, de facto parent, and equitable parent, and the doctrine of *in loco parentis*. *In loco parentis* applies when a person undertakes the care and control of another in the absence of such supervision by that person's natural parents and in the absence of formal legal approval; it is a temporary relationship that is not to be likened to an adoption, which is permanent. BLACK'S LAW DICTIONARY 787 (6th ed. 1990). *Cf.* Ray v. Ray, 1989 WL 150825 (Ohio Ct. App. Dec. 14, 1989) (granting custody to a stepfather over the birth mother pursuant to the doctrine of *in loco parentis*).

88. Some commentators have asserted that the New York court missed an opportunity to declare that children's rights stand on the same footing as parents' rights. *See, e.g.*, Carr, *supra* note 5, at 1024; Note, *Defining Family Relationships*, *supra* note 5, at 942, 943.

89. 471 N.W.2d 202 (Wis. 1991).

lesbian relationship. Wendy Sporleder and Janice Hermes lived together in a committed relationship for eight years.[90] After an unsuccessful attempt to add a child to the relationship through the artificial insemination of Sporleder, they agreed that Hermes would adopt a child.[91] In March 1988, the child, Z.J.H., was placed in the couple's home for a six-month preadoptive placement.[92] During this time, Sporleder provided the primary care for the child and Hermes worked.[93] Sporleder and Hermes executed a coparenting agreement, which provided, *inter alia*, for mediation to determine the physical placement of Z.J.H. and for liberal visitation for the non-placement party, in the event the parties separated.[94] Shortly thereafter the parties did separate.[95] Subsequently, Hermes formally adopted Z.J.H. and refused Sporleder access to the child.[96]

In affirming the dismissal of Sporleder's petition to obtain custody or visitation rights and to enforce the coparenting agreement, the Wisconsin Supreme Court determined that Sporleder had no standing to acquire custody, that she was not entitled to visitation rights, and that the coparenting agreement was unenforceable.[97] The court reached this result even though the Wisconsin legislature had recently enacted a liberal visitation statute providing individuals like Sporleder standing to seek visitation rights.[98] The court's interpretation of the statute was consistent with Wisconsin case law that denied standing to individuals such as Sporleder.[99] This case law, however, predated the liberal revision of the statute.[100] The

---

90. *Id.* at 204.
91. *Id.*
92. *Id.*
93. *Id.*
94. *Id.*
95. *Id.*
96. *Id.*
97. *Id.*
98. *Id.* at 208-10. The applicable statute provided:

> *Visitation Rights of Certain Persons:* 1) Upon petition by a grandparent, great-grandparent, step parent, or *person who has maintained a relationship similar to a parent-child relationship with the child*, the court may grant reasonable visitation rights to that person if the parents have notice of the hearing and if the court determines that visitation is in the best interest of the child.

WIS. STAT. § 767.245(1) (West 1993) (emphasis added).

99. *In re* Z.J.H., 471 N.W.2d at 210; *see In re* Soergel, 453 N.W.2d 624, 627 (Wis. 1990) (predicating the applicability of the visitation rights statute on the existence of an underlying proceeding affecting the family unit). The *Z.J.H.* court determined that because Sporleder was not legally related to Z.J.H. and did not have standing to seek custody, she could not commence a proceeding affecting the family unit or take advantage of the liberal language of the statute. *In re* Z.J.H., 471 N.W.2d at 205.

100. *See In re* Z.J.H., 471 N.W.2d at 209-10.

Wisconsin Supreme Court, therefore, employed a restrictive construction of the old version of the statute to circumvent the clear mandate of the liberal revision.[101]

b. Controversy Between Natural Parents and Adoptive Parents.—In *In re B.G.C.*,[102] Cara Clausen gave birth to a child without informing the child's natural father, Daniel Schmidt.[103] Immediately after birth, Cara, an Iowa resident, surrendered the child for adoption to Jan and Roberta DeBoer, a Michigan couple.[104] Cara signed a release of custody, as did Scott Seefeldt, whom Cara had falsely identified as the child's father.[105] The DeBoers named the child Jessica[106] and prepared to adopt her at the end of the six month waiting period mandated by Iowa law.[107]

Shortly after she executed the adoption consent, Cara revealed the fact of Daniel Schmidts's paternity and sought to vacate her consent.[108] Simultaneously, Daniel petitioned the court to intervene in the adoption proceeding.[109] The trial court ordered a blood test,

---

101. In essence, the *Z.J.H.* court's interpretation of the new statute would bestow standing upon a "person who has maintained a relationship similar to a parent-child relationship," WIS. STAT. § 767.245(1) (West 1993), only when there also is litigation that affects the adult relationships in the family unit, such as a divorce proceeding between the child's parent and a stepparent.

102. 496 N.W.2d 239 (Iowa 1992) ("B.G.C." stands for Baby Girl Clausen).

103. *Id.* at 241.

104. *Id.* at 240-41.

105. *Id.* at 241. It is unclear whether Scott Seefeldt knew that he was not the child's father. Because Cara was dating Scott when she learned that she was pregnant, he may have believed that he was the father. *Id.* at 246. Certainly, Cara represented to Scott and to the court that he was the father. *Id.* at 241.

106. Lucinda Franks, *The War for Baby Clausen*, THE NEW YORKER, Mar. 22, 1993, at 57. The Schmidts subsequently named the child Anna. *Id.* at 62. This Article will refer to the child as Jessica/Anna.

107. *Id.*; *see* IOWA CODE ANN. § 600.10 (West 1993) ("The adoption of a minor person shall not be decreed until that person has lived with the adoption petitioner for a minimum residence period of one hundred eighty days.").

108. *In re* B.G.C., 496 N.W.2d at 241.

109. *Id.* at 241. Daniel challenged the adoption under an Iowa statute that provides:

> An adoption petition shall not be filed until a termination of parental rights has been accomplished except in the following cases: (a) No termination of parental rights is required if the person to be adopted is an adult. (b) If the stepparent of the child to be adopted is the adoption petitioner, the parent-child relationship between the child and the parent who is not the spouse of the petitioner may be terminated as part of the adoption proceeding by the filing of that parent's consent to the adoption.

IOWA CODE ANN. § 600.3(2) (West 1993). Daniel claimed that the adoption petition was invalid because his parental rights had not been terminated and because he had not abandoned the child. *In re* B.G.C., 496 N.W.2d at 241.

which confirmed that Daniel was the birth father.[110] Thereafter, the trial court denied Cara's petition to vacate her consent to the adoption, but granted Daniel's petition to dismiss the adoption proceeding.[111] The court reasoned that because paternity was established in Daniel's favor, there was no factual or statutory basis upon which to terminate his paternal rights.[112] On appeal, the Supreme Court of Iowa affirmed the award of custody to Daniel and remanded the denial of Cara's petition.[113]

Undaunted, the DeBoers refused to return the child to Daniel and Cara and commenced a proceeding in Michigan to modify the Iowa courts' determinations.[114] The trial court granted the DeBoers's petition and awarded them custody.[115] The Michigan Court of Appeals, however, reversed and reinstated the custody decision of the Iowa courts.[116] The Michigan Supreme Court affirmed the Court of Appeals in a lengthy opinion.[117] The United States Supreme Court declined to stay the enforcement of the Michigan Supreme Court decision,[118] and in an emotionally charged climax to the litigation, the DeBoers returned Jessica to Daniel and Cara, who subsequently named her Anna.[119]

c. Controversy Between Birth Mother, Foster Parents, and Child.—In *Kingsley v. Kingsley*,[120] Rachel Kingsley placed her son, Gregory, with the Orange County, Florida, Department of Health and Rehabilitative Services in an attempt to ensure that he would receive adequate

---

110. *See In re* B.G.C., 496 N.W.2d at 246 (discussing the trial court's analysis of the attempt to terminate Daniel's parental rights). The trial court opinion is sealed and unavailable.

111. *See id.* at 241.

112. *See id.* at 246.

113. *Id.* at 241. On remand, the district court restored Cara's parental rights. While the appeal had been pending, Daniel and Cara were married. Franks, *supra* note 106, at 67. The court reasoned that, because Daniel had been awarded custody, "[i]t would be ludicrous not to [award custody] to the mother." *Id.* at 72.

114. *See In re* Clausen, 501 N.W.2d 193, 194 (Mich. Ct. App. 1993).

115. *See id.* at 195-96.

116. *Id.* at 198.

117. *In re* Clausen, 502 N.W.2d 649, 651-52 (Mich. 1993). The court found that the Michigan courts did not have jurisdiction to entertain the DeBoers's petition and were obligated to enforce the Iowa Supreme Court's decision. *Id.* at 652.

118. DeBoer v. Schmidt, 114 S. Ct. 1 (1993).

119. *See* Maryanne George, *DeBoers, Supporters Share Pain, Anger*, DETROIT FREE PRESS, Aug. 5, 1993, at 1B; *Sobbing Toddler Returned to Her Biological Parents*, LOS ANGELES TIMES, Aug. 3, 1993, at A10.

120. 623 So. 2d 780 (Fla. Dist. Ct. App. 1993).

care.[121] While Gregory was in foster care, Rachel did not maintain significant contact with him,[122] and he quickly became dissatisfied with his life as a foster child.[123] When his last foster family, the Russes, appeared to provide a happy and safe environment, Gregory expressed a desire to join the foster family legally.[124]

On June 25, 1992, Gregory filed a petition to terminate his mother's parental rights along with a complaint for declaration of rights and adoption by his foster parents.[125] The trial court granted

---

121. *In re* Kingsley, No. JU 90-5245, 1992 WL 551484, at *2 (Fla. Cir. Ct. Oct. 21, 1992), *aff'd in part & rev'd in part sub nom.* Kingsley v. Kingsley, 623 So. 2d 780 (Fla. Dist. Ct. App. 1993). *See also* Sarah Tippit, *I've Got the Family I Always Wanted*, LADIES HOME J., Apr. 1993, at 150. "[Rachel] placed her two older sons in foster care twice; Gregory lived first with foster families, then in the Lake County Boys Ranch, a group home for abused and neglected boys." *Id.* at 204.

122. *In re* Kingsley, 1992 WL 551484, at *2.

> Gregory Kingsley . . . [was] placed in foster case in September, 1989. [He] remained in foster care until the following August. [He] remained with the natural mother only two months before she again placed [him] in foster care. Many services were provided to her during this period and she failed to take advantage of these services in order to keep [Gregory] in her home.

Id. *See also* Phil Long & Susan Bloodworth, *Family Ties Are Put to Test as Boy's 'Divorce' Case Opens*, MIAMI HERALD, Sept. 24, 1992, at 1A, 11A ("Gregory has lived with his mother only seven months out of the past nine years.").

123. *See* Tippit, *supra* note 121, at 204.

124. *Id.*

125. Kingsley v. Kingsley, 623 So. 2d 780, 782 (Fla. Dist. Ct. App. 1993). He filed the petition in the juvenile division of the circuit court and the complaint for adoption in the civil division of the circuit court. *Id.* The adoption complaint subsequently was transferred to the juvenile division by court order. *Id.*

Unless parental rights have been terminated, parental consent is required for an adoption under Florida law. *See* FLA. STAT. ANN. § 63.062(1) (West 1993). Although Gregory's father consented to the adoption, Rachel refused to consent; thus, Gregory sought to terminate her parental rights under Florida law. *See* FLA. STAT. ANN. § 39.464 (West 1993). Section 39.464 provides, in pertinent part:

> The department, the guardian ad litem, or a licensed child-placing agency may petition for the termination of parental rights under any of the following circumstances:
>
> . . . .
>
> (3) Severe or continuing abuse or neglect.—The parent or parents have engaged in conduct towards the child or towards other children that demonstrates that the continuing involvement of the parent or parents in the parent-child relationship threatens the life or well-being of the child regardless of the provision of services. Provision of services is evidenced by having had services provided through a previous performance agreement, permanent placement plan, or offer of services in the nature of a case plan from a child welfare agency. A current performance agreement or permanent placement plan need not be offered to the parent or parents, and the petition may be filed at any time before a performance agreement or permanent placement plan has been accepted by the court.

Id.

Gregory the right to commence the termination proceeding, but did not rule on his standing to file an adoption petition.[126] Subsequently, both Gregory's *guardian ad litem* (the County Department of Health and Rehabilitative Services) and the Russes filed petitions to terminate Rachel's parental rights.[127] The Russes also filed an adoption petition.[128] After hearing from the various parties, the trial court granted the petitions to terminate Rachel's parental rights and the Russes's petition for adoption over Rachel's objection.[129] The Florida District Court of Appeal reversed the trial court's determination that Gregory had standing to terminate Rachel's parental rights, but upheld the termination sought by the other two petitions on the grounds that abandonment had been established.[130]

Although the media touted Gregory as a child seeking to "divorce" his parents,[131] the case simply was a termination of parental rights proceeding based on parental unfitness.[132] The trial court employed the same legal analysis and the same statute that it would apply in an ordinary termination of parental rights proceeding.[133] The only difference between *Kingsley* and other termination proceedings was that Gregory—instead of the state foster care system or his foster parents—initiated the proceeding.[134] This difference was

---

126. *In re* Kingsley, 1992 WL 551484, at *5. *See also Kingsley*, 623 So. 2d at 782; Ike Flores, *Boy, 11, Can File Suit to "Divorce" Parents; Judge OKs Action in Adoption Case*, S.F. EXAMINER, July 10, 1992, at A10.

127. *Kingsley*, 623 So. 2d at 783.

128. *Id.* at 782-83.

129. *Id.* at 783.

130. *Id.* at 790; *see also A Boy's "Divorce" Is Upheld in Court*, N.Y. TIMES, Aug. 20, 1993, at A21; *Court Voids Boy's "Divorce" from Mom; Adoption Out*, CHI. TRIB., Aug. 19, 1993, at 18; *Court Reverses Boy's "Divorce" from Mother*, L.A. TIMES, Aug. 19, 1993, at A16.

131. *See supra* notes 121-122, 126, 130 (citing articles discussing Gregory's case).

132. *See Kingsley*, 623 So. 2d at 790 (Harris, C.J., concurring in part and dissenting in part) ("This rather ordinary termination of rights case was transformed into a *cause celebre* by artful representation and the glare of klieg lights.").

133. *In re* Kingsley, No. JU 90-5245, 1992 WL 551484, at *1-*5 (Fla. Cir. Ct. Oct. 21, 1992), *aff'd in part & rev'd in part sub nom.* Kingsley v. Kingsley, 623 So. 2d 780 (Fla. Dist. Ct. App. 1993).

134. Most states charge public and private agencies with responsibility for reuniting foster children with their families or seeking termination of the legal parents' rights so that the children can be adopted. *See, e.g.*, CAL. WELF. & INST. CODE § 361.5 (West 1994), FLA. STAT. ANN. § 409.145 (West 1993), N.Y. FAM. CT. ACT § 1055 (McKinney 1994). Florida, like many states, also permits foster parents to file a petition to terminate the legal parents' rights when the foster care agencies are unable or unwilling to do so. *See* FLA. STAT. ANN. § 39.454 (1987); *see also* 42 U.S.C. §§ 620-628, 670-687a (1988 & Supp. III 1991) (requiring states to implement a plan making reasonable efforts to reunite families).

neither unique[135] nor a factor in the court's decision.[136]

2. *Common Threads and Fallacies.*—Although the above cases arose from dissimilar controversies, they uniformly failed to recognize that children have an independent right to maintain or sever family relationships. The courts in each of these cases achieved results arguably consistent with the "best interests of the child" doctrine,[137] but the individual decisions, in reality, were inconsistent with that doctrine because each focused on the adults'—rather than the child's—status and rights in the relationship. As a result, the courts in these cases in many respects victimized, rather than protected, the children by denying them a voice in resolving questions of and access to relationships with important parent figures.[138]

These cases demonstrate the courts' attitude toward the issue of whether children have a constitutional right to maintain family relationships. First, the courts viewed the "families" in these cases as falling outside the constitutional protection of the liberty interest because they were comprised of individuals who were not legally

135. *In re* Appeal in Pima County Juvenile Severance Action No. S-113432, No. 2 CA-JV 93-0003, 1993 WL 339248 (Ariz. Ct. App. Sept. 9, 1993); *see also* Joe Salkowski, *Ariz. Court Upholds Children's Right to "Divorce" Parents*, ARIZONA DAILY STAR, Sept. 14, 1993, at 1 ("'[J]udges preside over one or two cases each year in which children ask that custodial rights of one or both of their parents be severed.'") (quoting the Presiding Judge of the Pima County Juvenile Court).

136. Even though the trial court determined that Gregory had standing to commence the proceeding, it decided the case based on its determination of Rachel's unfitness as defined in the statute, and not on Gregory's "rights" in the relationship. *See Kingsley*, 623 So. 2d at 790.

137. The "best interests of the child" doctrine refers to the standard utilized in determining child custody. *See, e.g.*, Marcia O'Kelly, *Blessing the Tie that Binds: Preference for the Primary Caretaker as Custodian*, 63 N.D. L. REV. 481, 488-89 (1987). In applying the doctrine, "the primary goal of courts is to secure the best interests of the child." Gary Crippen, *Stumbling Beyond Best Interests of the Child: Reexamining Child Custody Standard-Setting in the Wake of Minnesota's Four Year Experiment with the Primary Caretaker Preference*, 75 MINN. L. REV. 427, 433 (1990); *see also* UNIF. MARRIAGE AND DIVORCE ACT § 402, 9A U.L.A. 561 (1987) (listing factors that courts must consider). The doctrine, which "emerged as a reform aimed at mitigating the possessive, patriarchal model of children as property," Barbara B. Woodhouse, *Hatching the Egg: A Child-Centered Perspective on Parents' Rights*, 14 CARDOZO L. REV. 1747, 1756 (1993), has had various definitions over time. For a discussion of the various definitions, see Crippen, *supra*, at 432-35; O'Kelly, *supra*, at 495-532; Harvey R. Sorkow, *Best Interests of the Child: By Whose Definition?*, 18 PEPP. L. REV. 383 (1991).

138. *See* Michael H. v. Gerald D., 491 U.S. 110, 136 (1989) (Brennan, J., dissenting); Alison D. v. Virginia M., 572 N.E.2d 27, 30 (N.Y. 1991) (Kaye, J., dissenting); *In re* Z.J.H., 471 N.W.2d 202, 214 (Wis. 1991) (Bablitch, J., dissenting); *In re* Clausen, 502 N.W.2d 649, 668 (Mich. 1993) (Levin, J., dissenting). Arguably, in *In re Kingsley*, Gregory's mother was not an "important" figure, and the court could have denied the continued relationship on that basis.

related.[139] In other words, the courts refused to extend constitutional protection to nontraditional families, implicitly advancing a very narrow view of the personal liberty interest attendant to family relationships. A majority of the Supreme Court has rejected this narrow view of the liberty interest.[140]

Second, to the extent that these decisions acknowledged the child's claim, they linked it to an adult's claim.[141] This approach subordinates the child's rights to the adult's rights and is inconsistent with current jurisprudence in other areas of the law that recognize children's constitutional rights.[142] Moreover, this approach improperly limits the constitutional examination of family relationships to a parent-centered model, despite the Supreme Court's expansion of this model in prior cases.[143]

Finally, these decisions reduce the child to an object instead of treating the child as a person.[144] The child becomes a nonentity and is not accorded any rights, consideration, or value. As the dissent in *Z.J.H.* aptly concluded:

---

139. In *Michael H.* and *In re* Z.J.H., the courts specifically invoked this view. *See Michael H.*, 491 U.S. at 130-31; *In re* Z.J.H., 471 N.W.2d at 211-12. In *Alison D.* and *In re B.G.C.*, the courts arguably adopted this view by default, by failing to consider the liberty interests of anyone other than the birth parents. In *In re Kingsley*, the court similarly incorporated this view by failing to consider Gregory's liberty interest in his relationship with his mother, although this failure is understandable because Gregory himself sought to end the relationship.

140. Writing for the plurality in Planned Parenthood v. Casey, 112 S. Ct. 2791 (1992), Justice O'Connor, along with Justices Kennedy and Souter, specifically rejected the restrictive definition of the personal liberty interest in family relationships adopted by Justice Scalia in *Michael H.*, stating that "such a view would be inconsistent with our law. It is a promise of the Constitution that there is a realm of personal liberty which the government may not enter." *Id.* at 2805. In *Michael H.*, Justices O'Connor and Kennedy, Stevens, Brennan, Marshall, and Blackmun, and White all rejected Justice Scalia's view. *See Michael H.*, 491 U.S. at 133 (O'Connor, J., concurring); *id.* (Stevens, J., concurring); *id.* at 137 (Brennan, J., dissenting); *id.* at 157 (White, J., dissenting).

141. *See, e.g., Michael H.*, 491 U.S. at 131 ("[W]e find that, at best, [Victoria's] claim is the obverse of Michael's and fails for the same reasons."); *In re* Clausen, 502 N.W.2d at 665 ("It is true that children, as well as their parents, have a due process liberty interest in their family life. However, in our view those interests are not independent of the child's parents.").

142. *See infra* Part II.A. (discussing jurisprudence recognizing children's constitutional rights).

143. *See* Moore v. City of E. Cleveland, 431 U.S. 494, 506 (1977) (applying the constitutional protection of family relationships to a family unit consisting of a grandmother, her son, and her two grandsons); Smith v. Organization of Foster Families for Equality and Reform, 431 U.S. 816, 843 (1977) (acknowledging that constitutional protection of family relationships can apply to members of family units who are not related by blood).

144. *See In re* Z.J.H., 471 N.W.2d 202, 215 (Wis. 1991) (Bablitch, J., dissenting).

> [T]he majority opinion[] focus[es] solely on the rights of the adults in this non-traditional relationship that is dissolving. Lost in . . . the majority opinion [is] the interests of at least [an] equal if not paramount concern: the interests of the child . . . .
>
> The majority denies him any legal significance. He is a nonentity in this battle between two parents. Because this is a non-traditional parental relationship, the result of the majority's decision is that the child's interests will not even be considered. It is as if he does not even exist.[145]

This attitude toward the children is painfully obvious when one observes that courts rarely refer to a child by name[146] and that statutes often refer to the child as "it."[147] This treatment of the child is reminiscent of the time when constitutional rights were afforded only to a privileged few.[148]

The real tragedy of these cases, however, is that the rationale used for denying the claim of the "nonlegal" parent, whether based

---

145. *Id.*

146. *See, e.g.*, Klipstein v. Zalewski, 533 A.2d 1384 (N.J. Super. 1988):

> He has not shown why a residential relationship with *the child* for a period of only one year, during which *the child* maintained a good relationship with her natural father, is of such great importance to *this child* that we should compel visitation over the objections of not only both natural parents but, equally important, of *the child* herself.

Id. at 1388 (emphasis added). In *Alison D.*, the court found it unnecessary to refer to any of the parties by name, noting that:

> *Petitioner* and *respondent* agreed to a visitation schedule whereby *petitioner* continued to see *the child* a few times a week. . . . By this time, *the child* had referred to both *respondent* and *petitioner* as "mommy". *Petitioner's* visitation with *the child* continued until 1986, at which time *respondent* bought out *petitioner's* interest in the house and then began to restrict *petitioner's* visitation with *the child.* In 1987 *petitioner* moved to Ireland to pursue career opportunities, but continued her attempts to communicate with *the child.* Thereafter, *respondent* terminated all contact between *petitioner* and *the child,* returning all of *petitioner's* gifts and letters.

Alison D. v. Virginia M., 572 N.E.2d 27, 28 (N.Y. 1991) (emphasis added).

147. *See, e.g.*, N.Y. DOM. REL. LAW § 70 (McKinney 1994) ("In all cases there shall be no prima facie right to the custody of the child in either parent, but the court shall determine solely what is for the best interest of the child, and what will best promote *its* welfare and happiness, and make award accordingly." (emphasis added)).

148. In Scott v. Sanford, 60 U.S. 393 (1856) (the Dred Scott case), the Supreme Court remarked:

> Undoubtedly, a person may be a citizen, that is, a member of the community who form the sovereignty, although he exercises no share of the political power, and is incapacitated from holding particular offices. Women and minors, who form a part of the political family, cannot vote; . . . yet they are citizens.

Id. at 422. Although minors still cannot vote, the Supreme Court now accords them more rights than those recognized, or more specifically, ignored, in 1856. *See infra* Part II.A. (discussing children's constitutional rights).

on legal presumptions,[149] a lack of biological ties, or the adults' legal status,[150] usually is irrelevant to a child's interest in protecting important family relationships. A child takes no part in creating the "legal" barriers that prevent a parent-like adult[151] from maintaining the relationship. Victoria did not commit the adultery that ultimately precluded her relationship with her biological father.[152] Neither A.D.M. nor Z.J.H. had any say in determining whether the parties who decided to bring them into their respective families were heterosexual, married, or otherwise possessed a biological or legal tie to them. Jessica/Anna did not cause Daniel and Cara to be unmarried at the time of her conception and birth, nor did she cause Cara to place her for adoption and then seek her return or cause the DeBoers to resist her return.[153] Gregory did not participate in Rachel's decision to place him in foster care. Yet these children were profoundly, and arguably detrimentally, affected by these factors because the courts focused on them in analyzing the cases.

There are two sides to a child-parent[154] relationship—the parent's and the child's. Yet courts have applied the Constitution to protect only the parent's interest in the relationship. Because the courts' analysis of the traditional liberty interest in child-parent relationships is parent-centered, it overlooks any liberty interest the child may have in preserving the relationship.[155] A child-centered

149. *See supra* text accompanying notes 66-72 (discussing how the *Michael H.* Court applied the presumption of legitimacy to reject a biological father's liberty interest in his relationship with his daughter).

150. *See supra* text accompanying notes 78-101 (discussing how lack of biological ties and appropriate legal status foreclosed standing in *Alison D.* and *Z.J.H.*).

151. For a definition of "parent-like adult," see *infra* Part IV.A.1.

152. In *Michael H.*, Justice Scalia distinguished Michael's claim from the unwed father's claims in Stanley v. Illinois, 405 U.S. 645 (1982), Caban v. Mohammed, 441 U.S. 380 (1979), and Lehr v. Robertson, 463 U.S. 248 (1983), because Michael was an "adulterous father." Michael H. v. Gerald D., 491 U.S. 110, 123-24, 128-29 (1989).

153. *In re* Clausen, 502 N.W.2d 649, 653 (Mich. 1993).

154. The traditional nomenclature for this relationship is "parent-child." This term denotes absolute dominance by the parent and the subservience of the child. In many respects this dominance is appropriate: the parent provides the child with food, clothing, shelter, nurturing, and education. But the focus on the absolute dominance of the parent obscures the fact that the child's view of the world is relevant to his or her best interests. *See generally* Woodhouse, *supra* note 137. By describing the relation herein as "child-parent," I am attempting to use the child to focus and define the relationship for liberty interest analysis—something the law has rarely done.

155. An analysis of the child's liberty interest must extend to children the privileges and immunities accorded "persons" under the Constitution or must provide an acceptable rationale for excluding children from this constitutional protection. As one commentator has noted:

approach[156] to constitutional analysis of child-parent relationships, on the other hand, assumes that the child is the focal point of the relationship and defines the scope of constitutional protection according to a child-centered view.[157]

By concentrating on the flaws in the adult's claims, the courts have neglected to examine the possibility and reality of a loving and caring relationship between a child and a legally unrelated adult and to preserve that relationship by employing a child-centered approach. Instead, the courts have terminated important relationships in a child's life, denied the child a chance to enhance his or her psychological and sociological development, and missed an opportunity to further the child's dignity judicially.[158] This result is detrimental to the child and certainly does not advance his or her best interest.

> Under traditional constitutional analysis, a statute that infringes fundamental rights can survive judicial scrutiny only if the government can show that the statute is both necessary and narrowly drawn to serve a compelling state interest. Given that children are persons under the Constitution, logic would seem to demand such strict scrutiny for infringements not only of adult's rights, but of children's rights as well.

Note, *Assessing the Scope of Minors' Fundamental Rights: Juvenile Curfews and the Constitution*, 97 HARV. L. REV. 1163, 1169 (1984) (citations omitted) (discussing the development of a compelling state interest in statutes or policies infringing on children's constitutional rights under the strict scrutiny test).

156. The analysis offered in this Article places the liberty interest of children in family relationships on par with the parents' liberty interest in their companionship with their children. *See infra* text accompanying notes 216-269 (discussing children's liberty interest as a right of companionship). Therefore, I could have easily termed this approach "child right equalization" rather than "child-centered." I chose to use the term "child-centered" because it promotes a greater recognition of the child's view of the world as a basis for analysis. For an interesting general discussion of the child's perspective as a basis of analysis, see Woodhouse, *supra* note 137.

157. The recognition of children's liberty interest embodies a jurisprudence and social policy that identifies children as persons who need protection. The liberty interest of children rests philosophically on the need to facilitate the transition of developing citizens from childhood to adulthood and doctrinally on the recognition of children as persons under the Constitution. For an insightful discussion of the jurisprudence and social policy that identifies children as individuals needing protection, see Michael S. Wald, *Children's Rights: A Framework for Analysis*, 12 U.C. DAVIS L. REV. 255 (1979).

158. For an intriguing discussion of the child's dignity and constitutional doctrine, see Charles R. Tremper, *Respect for the Human Dignity of Minors: What the Constitution Requires*, 139 SYRACUSE L. REV. 1293 (1988).

II. LEGAL SUPPORT FOR CHILDREN'S LIBERTY INTERESTS IN CHILD-PARENT RELATIONSHIPS

A. *Children's Constitutional Rights*

The recognition of children's liberty interests in familial relationships logically follows from existing jurisprudence protecting children's constitutional rights. The Supreme Court has recognized children's constitutional rights in several contexts and has announced that children are entitled to both procedural and substantive due process.[159] Additionally, a number of Supreme Court cases have been interpreted as supporting children's liberty interests in areas other than family dispute litigation.[160]

In *In re Gault*,[161] the Supreme Court held for the first time that children are "persons" under the Constitution.[162] As a result, the *Gault* Court recognized that children have a right to due process in juvenile proceedings.[163] Subsequent cases have expanded procedural due process rights to apply in other proceedings involving juveniles.[164] The Court also has found that children have constitutional rights to obtain abortions[165] and contraceptives[166] and to the free-

---

159. *See infra* notes 161-174 and accompanying text (discussing the cases identifying children's procedural and substantive due process rights).

160. *See infra* notes 216-269 and accompanying text (discussing cases recognizing children's constitutional rights to companionship).

161. 387 U.S. 1 (1967).

162. *Id.* at 30-31.

163. *Id.* at 21. In *Gault*, an Arizona juvenile court adjudicated 15-year-old Gregory Gault a juvenile delinquent and ordered him confined to a detention facility until he reached age eighteen. Because the Arizona legislature had characterized juvenile proceedings as civil in nature, rather than criminal, the proceedings did not include any procedural due process protection. *Id.* at 4-6. Specifically, the complainant did not appear at the proceeding, the juvenile's parents did not receive notice of the proceeding, the juvenile was not represented by counsel, the juvenile was permitted to make damaging admissions, and a transcript of the proceeding was not maintained. *Id.* The absence of these constitutional guarantees was critical to the Court's analysis and application of the Fourteenth Amendment. *See id.* at 18 ("Juvenile Court history has again demonstrated that unbridled discretion, however benevolently motivated, is frequently a poor substitute for principle and procedure.").

164. *See* New Jersey v. T.L.O., 469 U.S. 325, 341 (1985) (concluding that school officials' search and seizure of a student's purse had satisfied the applicable due process requirements); Parham v. J.R., 442 U.S. 584, 616 (1979) (stating that civil commitment procedures met due process requirements); Goss v. Lopez, 419 U.S. 565, 582 (1975) (holding that school suspensions without a hearing violated procedural due process).

165. Planned Parenthood v. Casey, 112 S. Ct. 2791, 2832 (1992) (recognizing a minor's right to obtain an abortion subject to parental consent or court authorization); Belotti v. Baird, 443 U.S. 622, 647 (1979) ("every minor must have the opportunity . . . to go directly to a court without first consulting or notifying her parents"); Planned Parenthood v.

dom of expression.[167]

In applying the Constitution to children, courts have sought primarily to protect them from arbitrary state action,[168] insensitive government policies,[169] and their own folly.[170] While courts have afforded children's constitutional rights only limited protection in comparison to adults, they usually restricted children's rights to preserve the corresponding rights of the adults who take care of them or to promote the children's best interests.[171] Courts have analyzed children's constitutional rights in institutional settings analogous to the familial setting.[172] While children spend much of their child-

---

Danforth, 428 U.S. 52, 74 (1976) (ruling that a minor's liberty interest in the abortion decision precludes a parental veto).

166. Carey v. Population Servs. Int'l, 431 U.S. 678, 694 (1977) (holding that restrictions on distribution of contraceptives to minors violated their substantive due process rights).

167. *See* Board of Educ. v. Mergens, 496 U.S. 226, 247 (1990) (holding that public school officials cannot restrict extra-curricular activities based on content); Hazelwood Sch. Dist. v. Kuhlmeier, 484 U.S. 260, 273 (1988) (allowing public schools to limit school-sponsored speech, but only on legitimate pedagogical grounds); Island Trees Union Free Sch. Dist. No. 26 v. Pico, 457 U.S. 853, 872 (1982) (holding that public schools cannot arbitrarily remove books from the school library); Tinker v. Des Moines Indep. Community Sch. Dist., 393 U.S. 503, 513 (1969) (holding that public schools cannot restrict private speech unless it disrupts school activities); Hedges v. Wauconda Community Unit Sch. Dist. No. 118, 807 F. Supp. 444, 465 (N.D. Ill. 1992) (holding that school officials cannot restrict students' distribution of religious material before and after school, nor can officials establish a particular location for such distribution during school hours without violating the students' First Amendment rights), *aff'd in part and vacated in part*, 9 F.3d 1295 (7th Cir. 1993) (upholding the prohibition of restrictions on free speech, but permitting certain limitations on the place and manner of the speech).

168. *See Island Trees*, 457 U.S. at 873; *Tinker*, 393 U.S. at 513.

169. *Casey*, 112 S. Ct. at 2832; *Bellotti*, 443 U.S. at 647; *Carey*, 431 U.S. at 694; *Hedges*, 807 F. Supp. at 465.

170. *See, e.g.*, *Carey*, 431 U.S. at 695-96 (taking judicial notice of the high incidence of sexual activity among minors and the "frequently devastating" consequences).

171. *See, e.g.*, New Jersey v. T.L.O., 469 U.S. 325, 339 (1985) (weighing students' Fourth Amendment rights against school officials' interests); *Tinker*, 393 U.S. at 511 (limiting students' right to freedom of expression in the school context). *See also* Christopher L. Blakesley, *Child Custody—Jurisdiction and Procedure*, 35 EMORY L.J. 291, 377 (1986) (observing that "each time a child's rights have been considered less expansive than those of an adult, it has been based on a view that the restriction was in the best interest of the child"); Wendy D. Bowie, *Multiplication and Division—New Math for the Courts: New Reproductive Technologies Create Potential Legal Time Bombs*, 95 DICK. L. REV. 155, 172 (1990) (commenting that because "a child's rights are often less extensive than an adult's, a frozen embryo's rights may be less extensive than a child's"); Peter L. Scherr, *The Juvenile Curfew Ordinance: In Search of a New Standard of Review*, 41 WASH. U.J. URB. & CONTEMP. L. 163, 191 (1992) (proposing that the Supreme Court apply the intermediate scrutiny test to infringements of minor's fundamental rights).

172. *See, e.g.*, *Tinker*, 393 U.S. 503 (symbolic speech in school); Hazelwood Sch. Dist. v. Kuhlmeier, 484 U.S. 260 (1988) (printed speech in school); Board of Educ. v. Mergens, 496 U.S. 226 (1990) (religious content of speech in school); Parham v. J.R., 442 U.S. 584 (1979) (due process in mental hospital admissions); *In re* Gault, 387 U.S. 1 (1967) (due

hood in various institutions, such as schools, hospitals, psychiatric centers, and the juvenile justice system, they spend their entire childhood in families.[173] Like families, these institutions seek to promote children's best interests. Extending the children's constitutional rights to the familial setting, as in other institutional settings, will limit the courts' ability to deny children constitutional rights merely because they are in the protective institution of the family. As with schools and other institutions, the protective nature of the family should not insulate the child from receiving the guarantees of the Constitution.[174]

B. Expanding Legal Protection to Other Adult-Child Relationships

With a few minor exceptions, the common law of the United States limited the scope of legal protection that is accorded adult-child relationships to legal parents, guardians, and their children and wards.[175] In 1966, New York initiated a movement to expand the category of individuals who were entitled to pursue the continuation of familial relationships by enacting the first grandparent visitation statute.[176] Many states followed suit by expanding and codifying the legal protection accorded to nonlegal parents' visitation claims.[177]

---

process in juvenile justice system); *T.L.O.*, 469 U.S. 325 (search and seizure in school).

173. *See* William S. Geimer, *Juvenileness: A Single-Edged Constitutional Sword*, 22 GA. L. REV. 949, 951 (1988) (arguing that because juveniles "live, work, and learn in places owned by others," their constitutional rights necessarily conflict with adult views and orthodoxy).

174. *See, e.g., Gault*, 387 U.S. 1; *Tinker*, 393 U.S. 503; *Belotti*, 444 U.S. 669.

175. For example, only the child's legal parents and guardians had standing to pursue the continuation of the child-parent relationship when the government or an individual threatened to interrupt it. *See supra* notes 23-59 and accompanying text (discussing cases in which parents and guardians have sought constitutional protection of the child-parent relationship).

176. The statute provides: "Where either or both of the parents of a minor child . . . is or are deceased, or where circumstances show that conditions exist [in] which equity would see fit to intervene, a grandparent or the grandparents of such child may apply for a writ of habeas corpus to have such child brought before such court . . . ." N.Y. DOM. REL. LAW § 72 (McKinney 1992).

177. Forty-nine of the fifty states have statutes that permit relatives at least as close as grandparents to seek visitation. Many of these permit others to petition as well.

The thirty-four jurisdictions that permit grandparents to petition for visitation include: Alabama, ALA. CODE § 30-3-4 (1989); California, CAL. CIV. CODE § 197.5 (1982); Colorado, COLO. REV. STAT. ANN. § 19-1-117 (West 1988 & Supp. 1993); Delaware, DEL. CODE ANN. tit. 10, § 950 (1975 & Supp. 1992); Florida, FLA. STAT. ANN. § 752.01 (West 1993); Georgia, GA. CODE ANN. § 19-7-3 (1993); Idaho, IDAHO CODE § 32-1008 (1983); Indiana, IND. CODE ANN. § 31-1-11.7-2 (Burns 1993); Iowa, IOWA CODE ANN. § 598.35 (1993); Kansas, KAN. STAT. ANN. § 38-129 (1993); Kentucky, KY. REV. STAT. § 405.021 (Baldwin 1993); Maine, ME. REV. STAT. ANN. tit. 19, § 1003 (West 1993); Maryland, MD. CODE ANN., FAM. LAW § 9-102 (1993); Massachusetts, MASS. GEN. LAWS ANN. ch. 119, § 39D (West

By the end of the 1980s, only Washington and the District of Columbia had not enacted expansive visitation statutes. By expanding their visitation statutes to include grandparents, great-grandparents, stepparents, siblings, and others, state legislatures announced a new policy that promotes the best interests of children by encouraging the continuation of meaningful familial relationships. This policy arguably elevates children's constitutional rights in familial relationships to the same level as parents' constitutional rights.

III. EMPIRICAL SUPPORT FOR CHILDREN'S LIBERTY INTERESTS IN CHILD-PARENT RELATIONSHIPS

Child-parent relationships have been the subject of significant social science research and legal discourse.[178] Social scientists have closely examined the effect of the dissolution of the family unit on a minor's well-being.[179] For example, studies have shown that high

---

1993); Michigan, MICH. COMP. LAWS ANN. § 722.27b (West 1993); Mississippi, MISS. CODE ANN. § 93-16-3 (1993); Missouri, MO. ANN. STAT. § 452.402 (Vernon 1993); Montana, MONT. CODE ANN. § 40-4-217 (1993); Nebraska, NEB. REV. STAT. ANN. § 43-1802 (1988); Nevada, NEV. REV. STAT. ANN. § 125A.330 (1993); New Hampshire, N.H. REV. STAT. ANN. § 458:17-d (1992); New Mexico, N.M. STAT. ANN. § 40-9-2 (Michie 1993); New York, N.Y. DOM. REL. LAW § 72 (McKinney 1993); North Carolina, N.C. GEN. STAT. § 50-13.2 (1987); Oklahoma, OKLA. STAT. ANN. tit. 10, § 5 (West 1994); Oregon, OR. REV. STAT. § 109.121 (1994); Rhode Island, R.I. GEN. LAWS § 15-5-24.3 (1993); South Carolina, S.C. CODE ANN. § 20-7-420 (Law. Co-op. 1993); South Dakota, S.D. CODIFIED LAWS ANN. § 25-4-52 (1992); Tennessee, TENN. CODE ANN. § 36-6-301 (1991); Texas, TEX. FAM. CODE ANN. § 14.03 (West 1986 & Supp. 1994); Vermont, VT. STAT. ANN. tit. 15, § 1013 (1989); West Virginia, W. VA. CODE § 48-2B-2-6 (1993); and Wyoming, WYO. STAT. § 20-7-101 (1993).

The six jurisdictions that permit both grandparents and great-grandparents to petition for visitation include: Arizona, ARIZ. REV. STAT. ANN. § 25-337.01 (1993); Arkansas, ARK. CODE ANN. § 9-13-103 (Michie 1991); Minnesota, MINN. STAT. ANN. § 257.022 (West 1992 & Supp. 1994); North Dakota, N.D. CENT. CODE § 14-09-05.1 (1993); Pennsylvania, PA. CONST. STAT. § 5311-13 (1993); and Wisconsin, WIS. STAT. ANN. § 767.245 (West 1993).

Two jurisdictions permit grandparents and siblings to petition for visitation, including: Louisiana, LA. REV. STAT. ANN. § 9:344 (West 1994); and New Jersey, N.J. STAT. ANN. § 9:2-7.1 (West 1993).

Illinois allows grandparents, great-grandparents, and siblings to petition for visitation. ILL. REV. STAT. ch. 750, para. 5/607 (Smith-Hurd 1993).

Utah allows "grandparents and other immediate family members" to petition for visitation. UTAH CODE ANN. § 30-5-2 (1993).

Alaska and Ohio permit a grandparent or other person to seek visitation. ALASKA STAT. § 25.24.150 (1993); OHIO REV. CODE ANN. § 3109.05.01 (Anderson 1992).

Connecticut, Hawaii, and Virginia permit any person to seek visitation. CONN. GEN. STAT. ANN. § 46b-59 (West 1986); HAW. REV. STAT. § 571-46 (West 1993); VA. CODE ANN. § 16.1-278.15 (1993).

178. For an in-depth review of the psychological studies of divorce on children, see Joan B. Kelly, *Current Research on Children's Post Divorce Adjustment: No Simple Answers*, 31 FAM. & CONCILIATION CTS. REV. 29 (1993).

179. *Id.* at 36-42.

self-esteem and respect for authority are instrumental to child development[180] and that both parents' participation in the child-parent relationship fosters the child's ability to acquire these traits.[181] One of the earliest long-term studies demonstrated that during the first five years of a child's separation from his or her parent, "the relationship between the child and *both* original parents did not diminish in emotional importance to the child . . . ."[182] Other longitudinal studies make similar observations and offer varying explanations.[183] Subsequent studies also have identified other factors affecting children's development.

Recent studies, however, have found that continued contact with the noncustodial parent is less relevant to child development than previously believed,[184] making classifying the factors that influence the development of post-divorce children more complex and unpredictable.[185] Notwithstanding this disagreement over the extent of the impact of the child-noncustodial parent relationship on the child's development,[186] the current consensus remains that children

---

180. *See, e.g.*, Joseph M. Healy, Jr. et al., *Children and Their Fathers After Parental Separation*, 60 AM. J. ORTHOPSYCHIATRY 531 (1990) (recognizing the correlation between the frequency of father-child visitation and the child's self-esteem).

181. *See id.; see also* JUDITH S. WALLERSTEIN & JOAN B. KELLY, SURVIVING THE BREAKUP: HOW CHILDREN AND PARENTS COPE WITH DIVORCE 307 (1980) (finding that the self-image of children from divorced families was "firmly tied to their relationship with both parents and [the children] thought of themselves as children with two parents who had elected to go their separate ways.").

182. WALLERSTEIN & KELLY, *supra* note 181, at 307 (emphasis added).

183. *See, e.g.*, Lise M. C. Bisnaire et. al., *Factors Associated with Academic Achievement in Children Following Parental Separation* 60 AM. J. ORTHOPSYCHIATRY 67, 92 (1990) (recognizing that maintaining a relationship with the noncustodial parent improves the child's academic performance, but identifying other factors, such as the noncustodial parent's income and ability to work less, that also may affect the child's academic performance).

184. *See, e.g.*, James L. Peterson & Nicholas Zill, *Marital Disruption, Parent-Child Relationships, and Behavior Problems in Children*, 48 J. MARRIAGE & FAM. 295, 306-07 (1986) (identifying parental conflict and the custodial parent's sex and remarriage as factors influencing children's post-divorce behavior).

185. *See* Thomas E. Smith, *Parental Separation and Academic Self-Concepts of Adolescents: An Effort to Solve the Puzzle of Separation Effects*, 52 J. MARRIAGE & FAM. 107, 113-14 (1990) (noting that the child's age, race, and gender and the parents' pre- and post-divorce marital conflict all complicate the effect of divorce on children).

186. *See* Janet R. Johnston et. al., *Ongoing Post Divorce Conflict: Effects on Children of Joint Custody and Frequent Access*, 59 AM. J. ORTHOPSYCHIATRY 576, 588 (1989) (concluding that a continued child-noncustodial parent relationship does not enhance the child's well-being); JOSEPH GOLDSTEIN ET AL., BEYOND THE BEST INTERESTS OF THE CHILD 116-18 (1979) (explaining that strengthening the custodial parent's role and minimizing, if not eliminating, the noncustodial's parent's role enhances the child's well being). *But see* Frank F. Furstenberg, Jr. & Christine W. Nord, *Parenting Apart: Patterns of Childrearing After Marital Disruption*, 47 J. MARRIAGE & FAM. 893, 899 (1985); WALLERSTEIN & KELLY, *supra* note 181, at 142-44 (concluding that a child's relationship with a noncustodial parent is

benefit from continued contact with noncustodial parents.[187]

Based on this consensus, the law must recognize the importance of child-parent relationships in the resolution of familial disputes. By taking these relationships into account, the law will enrich children's lives and soften the harmful effects of familial dissolution. Although the empirical and psychological studies do not prove that all children will benefit from maintaining all of their child-parent relationships, the studies support the view that it is better to inquire into the nature of the relationship to determine whether it is beneficial than it is to prohibit the relationship altogether.

Using psychological studies to support children's liberty interest in maintaining relationships with nonlegal parents has its drawbacks. One criticism of the argument is that the psychologists studied children who had lived in legally recognized marriages prior to the divorce.[188] Notwithstanding this limitation, the studies provide observations relevant to this Article in that they have found generally that marital blood relationships do not appear to be key factors in the importance of the parental relationship to the child. Rather, the key factor in the child-parent relationship is the emotional bond forged by the child's continuous cohabitation with the parents before divorce.[189] In short, these studies support the proposition that parental influence is not limited to or defined by biology.[190] Therefore, a functional definition of parent is more appropriate to an analysis of policies addressing the impact of family dissolution on children.

IV. SPECIFICS OF CHILDREN'S LIBERTY INTERESTS IN CHILD-PARENT RELATIONSHIPS

Adopting a child-centered analytic structure presents two basic issues: first, who qualifies as the "parent" in the relationship?; and second, what is the nature and extent of the right being protected? Each issue will be addressed below.

---

important and meaningful to the child).

187. Kelly, *supra*, note 178, at 39; FURSTENBERG & NORD, *supra* note 186, at 899; WALLERSTEIN & KELLY, *supra* note 181, at 142-44.

188. Divorce proceedings records are a social scientist's primary source of dissolving families. Because only traditional marriages are entitled to divorce as a means of dissolution, dissolving nontraditional families are absent from the records.

189. *See* WALLERSTEIN & KELLY, *supra* note 181; *see also* Woodhouse, *supra* note 137.

190. Courts also have adopted this observation. *See, e.g.*, Smith v. Organization of Foster Families for Equality and Reform, 431 U.S. 816, 844 (1977) ("No one would seriously dispute that a deeply loving and interdependent relationship between an adult and a child in his or her care may exist even in the absence of a blood relationship.").

A. *Definition of "Parent"*

Current jurisprudence limits constitutional protection of adult-child relationships to cases in which the adult is statutorily defined as a legal parent.[191] The recognition of a legal child-parent relationship is wholly dependent on the actions of the adults. If the adults biologically conceive the child, marry before or after the birth of the child, or adopt the child, then the resultant adult-child relationship will receive constitutional protection.[192] When the adult has not established a relationship with the child in the legally correct manner, however, the relationship generally is not entitled to constitutional protection.[193] Therefore, in order to assure that the child's liberty interest in his or her relationship with a nontraditional or legally unrelated parent figure will be protected, it is necessary to expand the definition of "parent."

Because children do not participate in the formation of their biological or legal child-parent relationships, they are wholly blameless for the shortcomings of their relatives—legal, biological, or otherwise. This innocence absolves them of responsibility for any moral objection attached to the nontraditional child-parent relationship. For example, it is easy, although not necessarily appropriate, to limit or deny constitutional protection to adults whose behavior does not

---

191. *See supra* text accompanying notes 23-59 (discussing the constitutional protection of child-parent relationships).

192. Current jurisprudence protects the traditional child-parent relationship. *See id.* This, however, does not mean that the deficiencies created by the adult-centered analysis are inapplicable to these relationships, however. For example, in adoption proceedings, the Constitution bestows procedural and substantive due process rights upon legal parents in order to protect their rights. *See* GOLDSTEIN ET AL., *supra* note 186, at 22 ("Legal adoption cancels out the legal rights of the biological parents. To safeguard their interests, even in cases where these run counter to the child's interests, either parental consent or abandonment is generally an essential preliminary to adoption in present-day law.") (citations omitted). But the constitutional analysis of adoption proceedings has never considered the child's liberty interest in the terminated child-parent relationship. A fair application of such an analysis would lend constitutional support for "open" adoptions, which allow the child to continue his or her relationship with the biological parent even though the legal tie has been severed. For a detailed discussion of open adoptions, see Carol Amadio & Stuart L. Deutsch, *Open Adoption: Allowing Adopted Children to 'Stay in Touch' with Blood*, 22 J. FAM. L. 59 (1983); Laurie A. Ames, *Open Adoptions: Truth and Consequences*, 16 LAW & PSYCHIATRY R. 137 (1992); Joseph R. Carrieri, *The Open Adoption: Parental Visitation After Adoption*, *in* THE FOSTER CHILD 1989: FROM ABANDONMENT TO ADOPTION, at 313 (PLI Litig. & Admin. Practice Course Handbook Series No. 151, 1989); Michael Spry, *Open Adoption*, 1 KY. CHILDREN'S RTS. J. 13 (1991).

193. *See supra* Part I.B. (discussing the deficiencies of the current jurisprudence constitutionally protecting child-parent relationships).

meet prevailing social norms.[194] Unmarried individuals and same-sex partners in nontraditional families represent easy targets for policies that seek to promote a "standard" way of life.[195] Yet children play no part in the creation of their families; they merely participate in, and are the beneficiaries of, the relationships that arise out of the families.

Therefore, a child-centered approach necessarily must recognize both the children's innocence and participation in child-parent relationships and not deprive them of these important relationships solely because of the adult's behavior or status. Accordingly, an expanded definition of "parent" should include not only individuals who are legally related to the child under the appropriate state statutes,[196] but also individuals who are not legally related to the child but have voluntarily assumed parenting responsibilities,[197] and

---

194. Social norms are constantly changing, pressuring the courts to address the changes. When the law responds to changing social values, caution generally is advisable to avoid repression in the name of progress. As one commentator stated:

> Society alters, some say evolves. Values change. Majorities grow more complacent; factions rigidify. Locked into frozen configurations, legislators may either ignore sound opportunities for progress, or opt for novelty without adequate thought of consequences. An unchecked spiral of change ultimately entails the same danger threatened by the most stubborn opposition to change. Either possibility can impart a teleology to positivist lawgiving which may equal legislated perpetual conformity.

TRIBE, *supra* note 25, at 1308. Using social acceptability to limit the application of constitutional doctrine, therefore, threatens our pluralistic society.

195. Occasionally, courts expressly promote the standard way of life. *See, e.g.*, Michael H. v. Gerald D., 491 U.S. 110, 113 (1989) (stating that "the facts of this case are, *we must hope*, extraordinary") (emphasis added). More often, courts implicitly adopt a standard way of life by denying nontraditional families the same privileges and immunities they accord traditional families. *Compare Michael H.*, 491 U.S. 110 (denying constitutional protection to an unwed father who established an actual relationship with his daughter because the mother was married and living with her husband) *and In re* Z.J.H., 471 N.W.2d 202 (Wis. 1991) (refusing to permit visitation by an unrelated lesbian family member) *with* Moore v. City of E. Cleveland, 431 U.S. 494 (1977) (extending constitutional protection to a family consisting of a grandmother, her son, and her two grandsons) *and In re* D.M.M., 404 N.W.2d 530 (Wis. 1987) (extending visitation statute, which prescribed grandparent and great-grandparent visitation, to a great-aunt).

196. *See e.g.*, ILL. ANN. STAT. ch. 705 para. 405/1-3(11) (Smith-Hurd 1993) (defining a "parent" under the Juvenile Court Act of 1987 as "the father or mother of a child [including] any adoptive parent").

197. Parenting responsibilities are the daily responsibilities of caring for a child. Although general in nature, parenting responsibilities are child-specific and, therefore, elude precise definition. One of the major qualities of a parent-like individual is the voluntary assumption of parenting responsibilities. The relationship, however, need not be created in a voluntary manner. Individuals can become parents involuntarily, whether through unintended conception or through the illness, death, or irresponsibility of the birth parents. The important criterion is that they assume the responsibilities that have

who either have resided with the child or were barred from residing with the child by the child's custodian. The list of parent-like individuals should include foster parents, stepparents, second-parents,[198] other relatives of the child, or other adults who have lived with the child and acted as parents for a significant period of time. The requirement that a parent-like individual voluntarily assume parenting responsibilities precludes a person who has contracted to care for the child for payment from asserting the claim of a parent-like individual.[199]

1. A Test for Identifying Parent-Like Individuals.—The parent-like individual can be identified through a two-part test: (1) an individual who has (a) participated in the act or decision to create a family unit that included the child;[200] or (b) executed written acknowledgement of the child or had his or her name placed on the birth certificate of the child; or (c) executed an irrevocable written provision for the child's future *and,* (2) who has (a) lived with the child while assuming daily child-rearing responsibilities for a significant period of time; or (b) provided significant, regular support for and attempted to maintain consistent contact with the child when continued cohabitation with the child was prevented by the legal custodian. Individuals satisfying both parts of this test would be considered "parents" in a child-parent relationship. And children could protect their relationship with these "parents" by claiming liberty interests in the relation-

---

been thrust upon them. Whether the parenting responsibilities are undertaken voluntarily or involuntarily, it is the *continued* assumption of responsibilities that must be voluntary for the individual to qualify as "parent-like."

198. A second-parent is someone who has lived with the child and his or her legal parent, but unlike a stepparent, is not married to the child's legal parent. A second-parent who adopts the child becomes the child's "legal parent." *See* Carrie Bashaw, Comment, *Protecting Children in Nontraditional Families: Second Parent Adoptions in Washington*, 13 U. PUGET SOUND L. REV. 321 (1990).

199. At first glance, it might appear that foster parents are paid to assume parenting responsibilities. The foster parent stipend, however, covers only the child's expenses and often is insufficient to meet those expenses. *See* Smith v. Organization of Foster Families for Equality and Reform, 431 U.S. 816, 824-28 (1977) (describing the role of foster parents). Clearly, the stipend does not compensate foster parents for their child-care. Regardless of whether the stipend is reimbursement or compensation, the full-time nature of the foster parents' commitment distinguishes them from the *au pair*, nanny, or other child care provider whose commitment is supplemental to that of the individual who actually and legally exercises parental responsibilities.

200. Creation of the family unit includes the marriage or cohabitation of individuals, one of whom has a child from a different relationship, the addition of a child to an existing family unit *via* the adoption or by artificial insemination of one of the adults, or any similar voluntary consensual act of the adults in forming a family that includes children.

ships. In contrast, such individuals would not meet the traditional definition of "parent" unless they were related to the child as a result of conception, birth, or adoption.[201]

This definition of parent-like individuals addresses several important issues in the analysis of the child's liberty interest in preserving a child-parent relationship. First, the definition limits the group of individuals with whom the child may have a constitutionally protected relationship. One major objection to the creation of new categories of individuals who can exert control over or affect the lives of children is that there must be a limit on who might have standing to seek to preserve a relationship. The concern is that opening the door to a new category of persons who are not related to the child in a manner presently recognized will undermine the family and place the legal parents at the mercy of anyone wishing to claim a relationship with the child.[202] This concern raises legitimate issues because neither judges, lawyers, child development experts, nor parents wish to see an increase in family-relationship litigation, nor do they want to undermine the legal parents' liberty interest by opening the door to frivolous claims.[203]

---

201. Parent-like individuals who are not legally related to the child would not qualify to preserve the child-parent relationship through their own liberty interest claim. This limitation, while supporting the current jurisprudence and avoiding the difficulties of increasing the number of individuals who can assert conflicting constitutional claims, requires further examination. *See supra* text accompanying notes 23-59 (discussing the current jurisprudence providing constitutional protection to relationships between legal parents and their children); *infra* text accompanying notes 202-205 (discussing the concern of unnecessarily increasing the number of individuals who can claim a liberty interest in their relationship with a child); *see also* Bartlett, *supra* note 16, at 944-51 (discussing a policy according parent-like individuals legal parental status).

202. The archetypal objection to a new policy according a liberty interest to an unrelated or third party adult is that it would prompt visitation claims by discharged babysitters, nannies or *au pairs*, concerned teachers, neighbors, relatives, or friends. The general argument against such visitation claims is that they compromise the parents' liberty interest to determine with whom the child will associate.

The importance of child-adult relationships, however, already has led to statutes and decisions that expand the categories of individuals who can litigate claims to maintain adult-child relationships. *See supra* Part II.B. Legislative initiatives and lawsuits by grandparents for visitation exemplify this expansion. Only three states and the District of Columbia have not enacted a statute granting grandparents standing to seek visitation. *See infra* notes 176-177 and accompanying text (setting forth and discussing the grandparent visitation statutes). Some states have permitted grandparents to seek and obtain visitation rights even when both parents are living with the child and object to the visitation. *See, e.g.*, Tufano v. Tufano, 556 A.2d 1036 (Conn. App. 1989); King v. King, 828 S.W.2d 630 (Ky. 1992).

203. This concern may be overstated. At least two states presently permit "any person" to seek visitation and permit courts to grant visitation if the applicant demonstrates that it would be in the child's best interests. *See* CONN. GEN. STAT. ANN. § 46b-59 (1986); HAW.

These concerns, however, should not prevent children from asserting their right to maintain important relationships. The child's liberty interest in family relationships should be paramount, not concerns about the parents' liberty interest or an increase in meritless claims.[204] Moreover, recognizing a *child's* liberty interest in a child-parent relationship would not expand the category of *adults* who could assert a liberty interest in that relationship[205] because only children or individuals acting on their behalf could seek protection of the child-parent relationship.

Second, the definition of a parent-like individual also would assist judges in determining who could initiate litigation on behalf of the child. The petitioner in custody and visitation litigation is often someone other than the child. Furthermore, children are often, if not always, represented by others when they assert their constitutional rights.[206] In cases where a child asserts a liberty interest in a child-parent relationship, the parent-like individual could serve as the child's *guardian ad litem* and present the claim to the court. Any individual whom the court deems to have the interests of the child at heart and who is capable of representing and protecting the child's interests can assert the child's claim.[207] In determining whether an

---

REV. STAT. ANN. § 571-46 (1993) (limiting "any person" to those who have had "de facto custody of the child"). The research for this Article has not uncovered any dismissals of cases in these jurisdictions because of the frivolous nature of the claim.

204. This approach also fails to distinguish between a person's standing to bring a claim and subsequent review of the merits of the claim. Although the best interests of the child are important, if not paramount, to a determination of the merits of any claim for custody or visitation, that standard is not a sound basis for rejecting standing to a party seeking to assert a claim for the right to visitation.

205. *See generally* Bartlett, *supra* note 16; Polikoff, *supra* note 82.

206. In all of the major children's constitutional rights cases, the child's claim was presented by a guardian acting on the child's behalf. *See, e.g.*, Board of Educ. Westside Comm. Sch. v. Mergens, 496 U.S. 226 (1990) (parents asserted that a public school violated children's First Amendment rights by refusing students permission to form a Christian club on campus); Bethel Sch. Dist. v. Fraser, 478 U.S. 675 (1986) (father asserted that public school violated his son's First Amendment rights by suspending him because of the content of a nominating speech he made in a student government election); Tinker v. Des Moines Indep. Community Sch. Dist., 393 U.S. 503 (1969) (fathers asserted that public school violated students' First Amendment rights in suspending them for wearing a black arm band in protest of the Vietnam war); Brown v. Board of Educ., 347 U.S. 483 (1954) (parents asserted that board of education violated students' Fourteenth Amendments rights by maintaining a segregated school system); Hedges v. Wauconda Community Unit Sch. Dist., 807 F. Supp. 444 (N.D. Ill. 1992) (parents asserted that principal and public school board violated their daughter's First Amendment rights by prohibiting distribution of religious material written by nonstudents), *aff'd in part and vacated in part*, 9 F.3d 1295 (7th Cir. 1993).

207. *See* HARRY D. KRAUSE, FAMILY LAW 1034 (1976) (defining *guardian ad litem* and his or her responsibilities).

individual meets the criteria, a court could apply the parent-like individual test to distinguish a total stranger from a legal stranger.[208]

On the other hand, a court may appoint an independent law guardian or a *guardian ad litem* to represent the child's interest precisely because it might be inappropriate for the nonrelated adult who is the subject of the proceeding to assert the child's interest. The appointment of an independent guardian, however, presents one difficulty. The guardian may decide to withdraw the proceeding based on the guardian's subjective determination that the asserted child-parent relationship is unsuitable. One safeguard against this problem could be a requirement that the guardian seek judicial approval of a decision to withdraw the proceeding and provide notice to the parent-like individual.

The guardian's decision to cut off the proceeding should receive judicial approval only upon a showing that continuation of the relationship with the parent-like individual would actually harm the child, a standard similar to the one employed to limit or terminate visitation in a case involving a child and a legal parent.[209] Absent such a showing, the court should not permit the guardian's value judgment to substitute for a determination on the merits of the claim asserted based on the liberty interest of the child.

2. *Standing.*—Recognizing the child's liberty interest in child-parent relationships and expanding the definition of "parent" mandates an examination of the role of standing in family-relationship litigation and the correlation between standing and substantive due process. The Supreme Court has held unconstitutional state statutory schemes that do not accord standing to individuals who have substantive due process rights in family relationships.[210] Thus, if the

---

208. Courts generally prefer to select a family member over a total stranger when appointing a *guardian ad litem* because of the concern that family members generally have for their relatives. *See, e.g., In re* Klein, 538 N.Y.S.2d 274 (1989) (denying the petition of a total stranger seeking appointment as the *guardian ad litem* for a comatose adult when her husband was also seeking appointment as the *guardian ad litem*), *appeal denied*, 539 N.Y.S.2d 298 (1989). Although a parent-like individual is technically a legal stranger rather than a "family" member, by definition he or she would have a greater relationship and a stronger concern for the child's interest than a total stranger.

209. *See* Zummo v. Zummo, 574 A.2d 1130 (Pa. 1990) (holding that restrictions on visitation require a showing of a "substantial threat" of present or future "physical or mental" harm).

210. *E.g.*, Stanley v. Illinois, 405 U.S. 645, 658 (1972) (stating that an unwed father has a liberty interest in his relationship with his children and declaring a statute prohibiting his assertion of that interest unconstitutional); Caban v. Mohammed, 441 U.S. 380, 393-94 (1979) (stating that Mr. Caban, an unwed father, had established a liberty interest in his

Supreme Court recognized a child's liberty interest in a child-parent relationship, it also would be forced to recognize the child's substantive due process right in the relationship. As a result, other courts would have to grant children standing in family-relationship disputes and correspondingly strike down as violative of substantive due process any state statute that failed to accord children standing to assert their claims. In response to any recognition of a child's liberty interest, states would be compelled to amend their statutes to accord children standing to assert their claims.[211]

As the unwed father cases demonstrate, states are empowered to limit the class of people who may raise a visitation claim, but these limits may not interfere with family members' substantive due process rights absent a compelling state interest.[212] Although the unwed father cases permit states to prescribe the conduct that is required before a person can assert a liberty interest, states may not prevent entirely an individual from raising a liberty interest claim.[213] The test for a parent-like individual enumerated above[214] provides a method by which states can evaluate the conduct of individuals who are the subject of the child's liberty interest claim, without eliminating the child's ability to raise the claim. Therefore, an expanded definition of "parent" that includes parent-like individuals places limits on the child's liberty interest in a child-parent relationship and creates a constitutionally-based test for standing to initiate claims based on the child's liberty interest. Finally, an expanded definition of "parent" allows the courts to address the most important question—the best interests of the child—without the artificial restrictions found in the current jurisprudence.[215]

---

relationship with his children and declaring a statute that did not afford him an opportunity to protest his children's adoption unconstitutional).

211. The history of the New York statute regarding parental consent for adoption serves as an excellent example of the impact that recognizing a liberty interest in family relationships has had on legislative enactments. In 1980, in response to Caban v. Mohammed, 441 U.S. 380 (1978), the New York Legislature amended § 111(1) of the New York Domestic Relations Law to add sub paragraphs (d)-(f), which require the consent of unwed fathers who maintain substantial and continuous or repeated contact, or live with, the child, before an adoption can take place. *See* N.Y. DOM. REL. LAW § 111(1)(d)-(f) (McKinney 1988 & Supp. 1994).

212. *See supra* notes 42-45 and accompanying text.

213. *See id.*

214. *See supra* text accompanying notes 200-201.

215. *See* Alison D. v. Virginia M., 572 N.E.2d 27, 30 (N.Y. 1991) (Kaye, J., dissenting) (noting that the majority proclaimed that it was powerless to consider the child's interests); *In re* Z.J.H., 471 N.W.2d 202, 214-15 (Wis. 1991) (Bablitch, J., dissenting) (explaining that the result of the majority's opinion "is that the child's interest will not even be considered").

B. Establishing a Right of Companionship

Although the Supreme Court has constitutionally protected the right of companionship,[216] the Court has yet to decide whether children have a liberty interest in the companionship of their parents. There are indications, however, that the Court would recognize such an interest.

In *Stanley v. Illinois*,[217] the Court acknowledged parents' liberty interest in the "companionship, care, custody, and management of their children,"[218] and in *Roberts v. United States Jaycees*,[219] the Court noted that the right to maintain a family relationship through "cohabitation with one's relatives" is entitled to constitutional protection.[220] The substantive right of companionship in familial relationships has been recognized in two contexts. The first context is the family dissolution cases involving marital and nonmarital children and their parents.[221] The second context is the cases brought under 42 U.S.C § 1983[222] for deprivation of substantive due

216. *See* Santosky v. Kramer, 455 U.S. 745, 758-59 (1982); Stanley v. Illinois, 405 U.S. 645, 651 (1972).

217. 405 U.S. 645 (1972).

218. *Id.* at 651.

219. 468 U.S. 609 (1984).

220. *Id.* at 619. *Roberts* is generally regarded as supporting the proposition that the right of freedom of association under the First Amendment cannot justify discrimination based on gender. *See, e.g.*, Gerald L. Edgar, Note, Roberts v. United States Jaycees*: Does the Right of Free Association Imply an Absolute Right of Private Discrimination?*, 1986 UTAH L. REV. 373; Ann H. Jameson, Note, Roberts v. United States Jaycees*: Discriminatory Membership Policy of a National Organization Held Not Protected by First Amendment Freedom of Association*, 34 CATH. U. L. REV. 1055 (1985). The *Roberts* Court did identify a freedom of "intimate association" attributable to families and similar groups that are small and selective, however, and acknowledged that this aspect of freedom of association protects family relationships. *See Roberts*, 486 U.S. at 620. *See also* William P. Marshall, *Discrimination and the Right of Association*, 81 NW. U. L. REV. 68, 80-83 (1986) (criticizing the Court's suggestion that some private organizations may enjoy the freedom of "intimate association"); William Buss, *Discrimination by Private Clubs*, 67 WASH. U. L.Q. 815, 839-41 (1989) (discussing the Court's analysis of the freedom of "intimate associations").

221. *E.g.*, Stanley v. Illinois, 405 U.S. 645, 658-59 (1972) (holding that unwed fathers have a constitutional right to a hearing to determine their fitness before they are denied custody of their children); May v. Anderson, 345 U.S. 528, 535 (1953) (establishing that a mother's right to custody is personal and that, accordingly, the courts must possess proper jurisdiction over her before adjudicating that right).

222. 42 U.S.C § 1983 (1988) provides in pertinent part:

> Every person who, under color of any statute, ordinance, regulation, custom, or usage, of any State . . . subjects, or causes to be subjected, any citizen of the United States . . . to the deprivation of any rights, privileges, or immunities secured by the Constitution and laws, shall be liable to the party injured in an action at law, suit in equity, or other proper proceeding for redress.

process rights in family relationships.[223]

1. *The Substantive Right of Companionship in the Family Dissolution Context.*—The right of companionship was an essential part of the family dissolution cases discussed earlier in this Article. In *Michael H.*, Victoria and Michael sought but did not receive constitutional protection of their companionship relationship with each other.[224] Similarly, in *Alison D.*, Alison sought protection of a companionship relationship with A.D.M., but the New York State Court of Appeals denied her application.[225] Likewise, in *Z.J.H.*, the Wisconsin Supreme Court refused to protect Wendy Sporleder's companionship relationship with Z.J.H.[226] And in *B.G.C.*, although the DeBoers sought custody of Jessica/Anna, they were generally interested in maintaining contact and involvement with her.[227] Finally, in *Kingsley*, Rachel fought to maintain a relationship with her son Gregory even though he was living with his foster parents.[228] All of these cases could have had different outcomes if the courts had taken into account the children's liberty interest rather than focusing on the adults' liberty interest. The courts could have constitutionally protected only the child's companionship right and not the adult's custodial right. In this way, the courts would have afforded the child the right to maintain a visiting relationship with the parent-like adult with minimal impact on the liberty interest of the legal parent. Thus, these courts could have recognized at least the visitation rights of Victoria with Michael, A.D.M. with Alison, Z.J.H. with Wendy, Gregory with Rachel, and Jessica/Anna with the DeBoers even though the adults ultimately may have desired a stronger legal relationship than one protecting only visitation rights.

2. *The Substantive Right of Companionship in the 42 U.S.C. § 1983 Context.*—Both parents and children have asserted a similar substantive right of companionship in familial relationships in cases arising under 42 U.S.C. § 1983.[229] In these cases, almost all federal courts have

---

Id.

223. *See infra* note 230 (citing cases protecting family relationships).

224. Michael H. v. Gerald D., 491 U.S. 110, 124 (1989).

225. Alison D. v. Virginia M., 572 N.E.2d 27, 29 (N.Y. 1991).

226. *In re* Z.J.H., 471 N.W.2d 202, 204 (Wis. 1991).

227. *See* Franks, *supra* note 106, at 72.

228. *In re* Kingsley, No. JU 90-5245, 1992 WL 551484 (Fla. Cir. Ct. Oct. 21, 1992), *aff'd in part & rev'd in part sub nom.* Kingsley v. Kingsley, 623 So. 2d 780 (Fla. Dist. Ct. App. 1993).

229. *See supra* note 222 (setting forth the pertinent language of § 1983).

recognized the *parents'* right to assert a liberty interest in the continued association and companionship of their children in certain circumstances.[230] Additionally, in *Smith v. City of Fontana*,[231] the United States Court of Appeals for the Ninth Circuit held that the parents' constitutional interest in their familial companionship "logically extends to protect *children* from unwarranted state interference with their relationships with their parents."[232] In so holding, the court concluded that a child whose father was killed by police officers has an interest that "is sufficiently weighty by itself to constitute a cognizable liberty interest."[233] Indeed, the court reasoned that a child's loss of the support, society, and companionship of a parent presents a *stronger* case for recovery than that of a parent who seeks to recover for the loss of a child.[234] The court emphasized that even in the context of claims made by parents, such claims are not based on any custodial interest, but rather arise solely from the familial relationship.[235] As support for this proposition, the *Fontana* court noted that in *Strandberg v. City of Helena*,[236] parents were allowed to assert a companionship claim under § 1983 after their twenty-two-year-old son committed suicide while incarcerated.[237]

Some federal courts have also implicitly recognized children's substantive due process rights to the companionship of their parents

230. *E.g.*, Trujillo v. Board of County Comm'rs, 768 F.2d 1186, 1189 (10th Cir. 1985) (recognizing a mother's and a sister's interest in their relationship with their son and brother who had died in jail); Bohn v. City of Dakota, 772 F.2d 1433, 1434 (8th Cir. 1985) ("The privacy and autonomy of familial relationships . . . are unarguably among the protectible interests which due process protects."), *cert. denied*, 475 U.S. 1014 (1986); Bell v. City of Milwaukee, 746 F.2d 1205, 1245-46 (7th Cir. 1984) (finding that the father of a man killed by a police officer possessed a liberty interest in the companionship of his son); Morrison v. Jones, 607 F.2d 1269, 1275 (9th Cir. 1979) (holding that a mother whose child was transported to Germany by county officials had a constitutionally protected interest in her relationship with her son), *cert. denied*, 445 U.S. 962 (1980); Duchesne v. Sugarman, 566 F.2d 817, 825 (2d Cir. 1977) (stating that a mother whose children were taken from her by city welfare officials had a liberty interest in the care and companionship of her children); *see also* Logan v. Hollier, 711 F.2d 690, 691 (5th Cir. 1983) (acknowledging that courts have upheld the constitutional protection of familial relationships), *cert. denied*, 466 U.S. 936 (1984).

231. 818 F.2d 1411 (9th Cir.), *cert. denied*, 484 U.S. 935 (1987).

232. *Id.* at 1418 (emphasis added).

233. *Id.* at 1419.

234. *Id.*

235. *Id.*

236. 791 F.2d 744 (9th Cir. 1986).

237. *Fontana*, 818 F.2d at 1419 (citing *Strandberg*, 791 F.2d at 748). The *Strandberg* trial court had reasoned that the parent's right of companionship was separate from the right of custody and that parental control did not terminate when the child was emancipated. *Strandberg*, 791 F.2d at 748 n.1.

in contexts other than the parents' death. In *Duchesne v. Sugarman*,[238] for example, the plaintiffs asserted a deprivation of liberty interest in the unlawful removal of children from their mother by local welfare officials.[239] In remanding the case for trial, the United States Court of Appeals for the Second Circuit noted that the right "to the preservation of family integrity encompasses the reciprocal rights of both parent[s] and children."[240] The court emphasized that, with respect to children, the right is in "not being dislocated from the 'emotional attachments that derive from the intimacy of daily association' with the parent."[241]

In *Franz v. United States*,[242] a birth father brought a claim to enforce his visitation rights with his child who had been placed in a witness protection program without the father's consent.[243] In determining that the trial court had jurisdiction to hear the claim, the United States Court of Appeals for the District of Columbia noted that "[a] child's corresponding right to protection from interference in the relationship derives from the psychic importance to him of being raised by a loving, responsive, reliable adult."[244]

Even when children have brought unsuccessful § 1983 claims, the courts have recognized that the Constitution protects children's companionship relationships with family members. These courts, however, generally dismissed the cases because the plaintiffs were unable to establish that the state action intentionally caused the deprivation of the companionship relationship. For example, in *Ortiz v. Burgos*,[245] the United States Court of Appeals for the First Circuit held that a plaintiff may assert a violation of a Fourteenth Amendment liberty interest only if the state action was aimed directly at the child-parent relationship.[246] The court determined that prior Supreme Court cases invoking substantive due process protection for the family relationship fit into two categories.[247] First, the court noted that some cases prevent government interference in "particular-

238. 566 F.2d 817 (2d Cir. 1977).
239. *Id.* at 821.
240. *Id.* at 825.
241. *Id.* (quoting Smith v. Organization of Foster Families for Equality and Reform, 431 U.S. 816, 844 (1977)).
242. 707 F.2d 582 (D.C. Cir. 1983).
243. *Id.* at 585.
244. *Id.* at 599.
245. 807 F.2d 6 (1st Cir. 1986).
246. *Id.* at 8.
247. *Id.* at 7-8.

ly private family decisions."[248] Second, the court identified other cases holding that due process requires strict scrutiny[249] of procedural protections whenever the state, "in furtherance of a legitimate state interest," seeks to interfere with the child-parent relationship.[250] Thus, when presented with a claim by a stepfather and siblings of an adult inmate killed by prison guards, the court affirmed the dismissal of the claim on the grounds that the deprivation was only incidental to the relationship.[251] Significantly, the court's dismissal of the claim was not based on the absence of a protected relationship.

Similarly, in *Manarite v. City of Springfield*,[252] the court rejected a claim brought by the daughter of a detainee who committed suicide while in protective custody.[253] Citing *Ortiz*, the court reasoned that in failing to prevent the suicide, the city was not directly interfering with a child-parent relationship and thus "'*only the person toward whom the state action was directed, and not those incidentally affected*, may maintain a § 1983 claim [for a violation of the familial association right].'"[254]

These cases establish that courts have recognized children's liberty interest in the companionship of their family members. They are distinguishable from *DeShaney v. Winnebago County Department of Social Services*,[255] wherein the Supreme Court found that the state officials' failure to intervene in the family life of a child, Joshua, did not constitute a denial of his substantive due process rights.[256] In that case, social services officials received information that Joshua's father may have physically abused him.[257] The officials conducted several investigations and even removed Joshua from the home for a period of time.[258] They also directed Joshua's father to take parent-

---

248. *Id.* at 8 (citing Moore v. City of E. Cleveland, 431 U.S. 494 (1977); Griswold v. Connecticut, 381 U.S. 479 (1965); Pierce v. Society of Sisters, 268 U.S. 510 (1925)).

249. *See supra* note 28 (referring to the standards of review utilized when a statute or policy is challenged on constitutional grounds).

250. *Ortiz*, 807 F.2d at 8 (citing Santosky v. Kramer, 455 U.S. 745 (1982); Little v. Streater, 452 U.S. 17 (1981); Stanley v. Illinois, 405 U.S. 645 (1972)).

251. *Id.* at 10.

252. 957 F.2d 953 (1st Cir.), *cert. denied*, 113 S. Ct. 113 (1992).

253. *Id.* at 960.

254. *Id.* (quoting Pittsley v. Warish, 927 F.2d 3, 8 (1st Cir. 1991) (emphasis and alteration in *Manarite*).

255. 489 U.S. 189 (1989). For an in depth discussion of *Deshaney*, see Laura Oren, *The State's Failure to Protect Children and Substantive Due Process:* Deshaney *in Context*, 68 N.C. L. REV. 659 (1990).

256. *DeShaney*, 489 U.S. at 201.

257. *Id.* at 192-93. The officials obtained the information from the mandatory reports of the doctors and hospitals that had treated Joshua. *Id.*

258. *Id.*

ing classes and to remove his paramour from the home, and assigned a caseworker to monitor Joshua's condition.[259] The caseworker made several visits to Joshua's home and reported that several times she was denied access to Joshua because he was "ill," that the girlfriend was still living in the home, and that Joshua's father had not taken the parenting classes.[260] Subsequently, Joshua was admitted to the hospital suffering from massive and permanent brain damage resulting from physical blows to his head.[261] Joshua's father was tried and convicted of child abuse.[262] Joshua's mother commenced an action against the county under § 1983, seeking damages for the county's deprivation of Joshua's constitutional rights, including his right of companionship with her.[263] The Supreme Court affirmed the dismissal of this claim on the grounds that the state's failure to intervene did not constitute a state action affecting Joshua's constitutional rights.[264] His father had caused the injuries, not state action.[265]

In the cases that have recognized the substantive right of companionship, the specific acts creating the harm were committed by state officials.[266] Thus, the only question in these cases was whether or not the acts directly impaired any substantive due process rights. In *Smith* and *Franz*, the courts found a deprivation and, accordingly, granted relief.[267] Conversely, in *Ortiz* and *Manarite*, the courts found no direct deprivation and dismissed the proceedings.[268] Combined with prior Supreme Court pronouncements protecting family relationships arising out of intimate associations, or

---

259. *Id.* at 192.
260. *Id.* at 193.
261. *Id.*
262. *Id.*
263. *Id.*
264. *Id.* at 203.
265. *Id.*
266. Manarite v. City of Springfield, 957 F.2d 953 (1st Cir.) (adjudicating a claim against the city and its police chief for failing to prevent the suicide of a man detained in jail), *cert. denied*, 113 S. Ct. 113 (1992); Smith v. City of Fontana, 818 F.2d 1411 (9th Cir.) (involving the use of excessive force by police officers), *cert. denied*, 484 U.S. 935 (1987); Strandberg v. City of Helena, 791 F.2d 744 (9th Cir. 1986) (adjudicating an action against the city and its police officers by the parents of a son who committed suicide in jail); Ortiz v. Burgos, 807 F.2d 6 (1st Cir. 1986) (deciding a suit brought against prison guards for beating an inmate to death); Franz v. United States, 707 F.2d 582 (D.C. Cir. 1983) (involving a claim against the United States for separating a child from his father as part of a witness protection program); Duchesne v. Sugarman, 566 F.2d 817 (2d Cir. 1977) (adjudicating a mother's claim against a city child welfare bureau).
267. *Smith*, 818 F.2d at 1420, 1424; *see Franz*, 707 F.2d at 610.
268. *See Ortiz*, 807 F.2d at 10; *Manarite*, 957 F.2d at 959-60.

arising by blood or marriage,[269] these cases support, if not compel, the recognition of children's liberty interest in companionship relationships with parent-like adults.

C. *The Effect of Recognizing Children's Liberty Interests in Child-Parent Relationships*

1. *A Constitutional Basis for Visitation.*—Recognizing a child's liberty interest in a companionship relationship would affect litigation in nontraditional family-relationship disputes in two significant ways. First, as already discussed, it would eliminate the court's ability to use the status of the unrelated adult as a barrier to seeking judicial intervention.[270] Second, it would establish a constitutional basis for visitation rights between the child and the parent-like individual. This would require courts to grant applications to maintain child-parent relationships unless there was a narrowly tailored, compelling state interest that supported the denial of visitation.[271] Recognizing the child's liberty interest would require the court to balance the liberty interest of the child, the liberty interest of the legal parent, and the state's interest in the welfare of the child. Thus, in order to deny visitation between the child and the parent-like adult, it would be necessary to show a compelling state interest identical to the state interest that would sustain a denial of visitation between the child and the legal parent.

The manner in which the recognition of the child's liberty interest could affect family dispute resolution in nontraditional family settings can be illustrated by applying this approach to the cases discussed at the beginning of this Article. In *Michael H. v. Gerald D.*,[272] the Supreme Court declined to recognize that the Constitu-

---

269. *See, e.g.*, Moore v. City of E. Cleveland, 431 U.S. 494, 503-55 (1977) (explaining that the Constitution implicitly recognizes the tradition of family, which extends beyond the nuclear family); Smith v. Organization of Foster Families for Equality and Reform, 431 U.S. 816, 844 (1977) (holding that constitutional protection of the family encompasses relationships that "ste[m] from the emotional attachments that derive from the intimacy of daily association . . . as well as from the fact of a blood relationship").

270. *See supra* text accompanying notes 210-215 (discussing the relationship between substantive due process rights and standing).

271. The jurisprudence governing granting, reviewing, modifying, and denying visitation rights is well established. *See* HOMER H. CLARK, JR., THE LAW OF DOMESTIC RELATIONS IN THE UNITED STATES § 19.4(g) (2d ed. 1988). This jurisprudence supports a liberal view of visitation and favors awarding visitation unless it would seriously harm the child. *Id.* § 19.4(h); *see also* Zummo v. Zummo, 574 A.2d 1130, 1141 (Pa. Super. Ct. 1990) (holding that restrictions on visitation rights require a showing of a "substantial threat" of present or future "physical or mental" harm).

272. 491 U.S. 110 (1989).

tion afforded protection to Michael's relationship with his daughter Victoria.[273] Although the Supreme Court's analysis of Michael's liberty interest raises serious questions,[274] the Court's decision concerning his liberty interest should not have affected its recognition of Victoria's liberty interest in her relationship with her father.[275] In fact, the recognition and protection of Victoria's liberty interest would have provided a better mechanism by which the trial court could consider Victoria's petition and declare unconstitutional any California statute or policy that prohibited her from presenting her claim.[276] The trial court would apply the best interests of the child standard to consider the propriety of Victoria's petition and would appraise the benefit and harm to Victoria associated with continuing the relationship. Absent a demonstration of harm to Victoria, the court would grant Victoria visitation rights with Michael.[277]

The recognition of Victoria's liberty interest would not require the state to recognize the multiple fatherhood concept rejected by Justice Scalia.[278] Rather, it would compel the court to protect Victoria's significant child-parent relationship not only with Gerald and Carole, her legal parents, but also with Michael, a parent-like individual.[279] Because Victoria's child-parent relationship with Michael would entitle her to a visitation right only and would not interfere with her legal parents' custody right, the current policy of granting certain priorities to legal parents would be preserved.

Similarly, in *Alison D. v. Virginia M.*[280] and *In re Z.J.H.*,[281] recognition of A.D.M.'s and Z.J.H.'s liberty interests would not have influenced the denial of Alison's or Wendy's petition, nor mandated the acceptance of a functional definition of parent for the purpose of granting parental rights to legally unrelated adults. Recognizing the

---

273. *Id.* at 127-30.

274. *See supra* note 140 and accompanying text (discussing the Court's subsequent rejection of the liberty interest analysis proffered by Justice Scalia in *Michael H.*).

275. *See supra* text accompanying note 205, 224-229 (discussing the possible effects of limiting the child's liberty interest to the child's claim and not applying it to an adult claim).

276. *See supra* text accompanying notes 210-215 (explaining that statutes denying standing to parties with a substantive due process claim are unconstitutional).

277. *See* CLARK, *supra* note 271, § 19.4(h).

278. *See* Michael H. v. Gerald D., 491 U.S. 110, 130-31 (1989).

279. Michael qualifies as a parent-like individual because he participated in the act of begetting Victoria, lived with Victoria, and assumed daily child-rearing responsibilities for Victoria. See *Michael H.*, 491 U.S. at 113-14; *supra* Part IV.A.1. (describing the criteria for identifying a parent-like individual).

280. 572 N.E.2d 27 (N.Y. 1991).

281. 471 N.W.2d 202 (Wis. 1991).

children's liberty interests, however, would have required the trial courts to permit either Alison and Wendy or a *guardian ad litem* to present a claim on behalf of the children. Moreover, the courts would be obliged to declare unconstitutional any state statute or policy that prohibited the children from presenting their claims.[282] In both *Alison D.* and *Z.J.H.*, the courts would apply the best interests of the child standard to consider the merits of the children's petitions and to assess the potential harm in continuing the relationships. Absent a showing of harm to the children, the court would grant the children visitation rights with the parent-like individuals.[283]

At the same time, a court that recognized a child's liberty interest in maintaining a relationship with a parent-like individual would not be forced to treat the parent-like individual as the child's legal parent. Rather, the courts would apply the criteria for ascertaining parent-like individuals[284] in determining the qualifications of the unrelated adults. This result would provide constitutional protection for nontraditional consensual relationships and would promote the constitutional policy of honoring individual autonomy in family decision-making.[285]

If the *B.G.C.* court[286] had recognized Jessica/Anna's liberty interest, the outcome also may have been different. If the court had applied the approach advanced in this Article, it would have been obliged to consider the DeBoers's petition for custody as an application on behalf of Jessica/Anna for visitation.[287] If the court then found such visitation to be in the best interests of the child, the court could have protected Jessica/Anna's relationship with both the Schmidts, her legal parents, and the DeBoers, her nonlegal parents. Had the Iowa courts utilized this approach, rather than the traditional

282. *See supra* text accompanying notes 210-215 (explaining that statutes denying standing to parties with a substantive due process claim are unconstitutional).

283. *See* CLARK, *supra* note 271, § 19.4(h).

284. *See supra* Part IV.A.1. (describing the criteria for identifying a parent-like individual). In their respective child-parent relationships, Alison was a parent to A.D.M. and Wendy was a parent to Z.J.H. under the parent-like individual test. Alison participated in the decision to beget A.D.M. through the artificial insemination of Virginia and supported him for several years. *Alison D.*, 572 N.E.2d at 28. Similarly, Wendy participated in the decision to add Z.J.H. to the family *via* adoption and lived with and supported him during the preadoption placement. *In re* Z.J.H., 471 N.W.2d at 204.

285. *See supra* note 25 and accompanying text (discussing the protection of child-parent relationships as a part of the private autonomy paradigm of the Constitution).

286. 496 N.W.2d 239 (Iowa 1992).

287. The court would not be obliged to grant the Deboers's petition for custody, however, because the child's liberty interest only supports the child's claim for visitation, not custody.

approach, the protracted litigation arising from this case may have been avoided.[288]

In re Kingsley[289] illustrates the dilemma of applying the child's liberty interest when the child clearly expresses a desire to sever the child-parent relationship.[290] In considering this issue, it is important to remember that *Kingsley* is different from the other cases discussed in this Article because it involved a termination of parental rights rather than the granting of custody or visitation. This difference is significant because a proceeding to terminate parental rights examines the fitness of a parent to continue in that status and, with a finding of unfitness, transforms a legal parent into a legally unrelated individual. A termination proceeding also permits the creation of a legal relationship—protected even from interference by the former legal parent—between the child and previously legally unrelated adults. In the custody and visitation cases, however, the parent-like individual's fitness was not at issue and the determination does not substitute one legal relationship with another.[291]

In *Kingsley*, Gregory, who was represented by counsel, had articulated his desire to terminate his relationship with Rachel, his biological mother.[292] Gregory's claim challenges a fundamental assumption underlying the thesis of this Article—that protecting the child's liberty interest mandates the continuation of the child-parent relationships through visitation, unless visitation would harm the child. That challenge materializes, however, if the analysis of the child's liberty interest only applies when there is an expressed preference by the child.

---

288. Such a decision may have facilitated the early transfer of the child back to the Schmidts, averted the two years of bonding between Jessica/Anna and the DeBoers, and prevented the child's painful removal from a home she had known for two years. *See* Sandra G. Boodman, *Uprooting Jessica: Psychiatrists Say Childhood Loss Can Have a Lifelong Impact*, WASH. POST, Aug. 10, 1993, at Z07 (discussing the harm children may suffer from early separation from their parents); *Jessica: Legal Struggle Offers Lessons on Love and Law*, DETROIT FREE PRESS, July 28, 1993, at 10A (noting the increasing harm to Jessica from the protracted litigation).

289. No. 90-5245, 1992 WL 551484 (Fla. Cir. Ct. Oct. 21, 1992, *aff'd in part & rev'd in part sub nom.* Kinglsey v. Kingsley, 623 So. 2d 780 (Fla. Dist. Ct. App. 1993).

290. Gregory Kingsley sought to sever his relationship with his birth mother. *Id.* The parental figure, however, could just as easily have been a parent-like individual in a nontraditional family.

291. *See, e.g., In re* B.G.C., 496 N.W.2d 239 (Iowa 1992). Although the DeBoers alleged that Daniel Schmidt should not receive custody of Jessica/Anna because he was an unfit parent, *id.* at 246, the Schmidts did not contest the DeBoers's fitness. In fact, the courts did not need to reach that question because the case turned on the determination that the Schmidts's parental rights had never been terminated in the first place.

292. *See generally Kingsley*, 1992 WL 551484.

Such a limitation is unjustified because it unduly restricts the assertion of the liberty interest to cases in which the child is capable of expressing his or her wishes. Although there is profound value in acknowledging children's familial desires,[293] at most ages between birth and majority, children's statements regarding familial relationships tend to be incomprehensible or unreliable.[294] Thus, if courts allowed only children who are mature enough to make complicated choices about familial relationships and articulate these choices clearly to assert their liberty interests, the liberty interest of most children in child-parent relationships would remain unprotected. In short, courts would continue to disregard the liberty interests of most children because most children would not be able to articulate an opinion about their interest in their child-parent relationships. On the other hand, categorically ignoring the statements of children unable to make independent decisions would minimize the court's ability to recognize dangerous situations and perhaps would allow unfit parent-like individuals to assert a child's "liberty interest" as a ploy for achieving something denied them. Striking a balance between these legitimate but opposing concerns will require the same sensitive inquiry that so often is a part of family law.

Striking this balance in *Kingsley* would not have prevented the trial court from terminating Rachel's parental rights. Rachel, or a *guardian ad litem*, could request a visitation arrangement based on Gregory's liberty interest in the child-parent relationship despite his expressed desire to terminate the legal parent-child relationship. Rather, striking the balance would have allowed the court to implement a visitation relationship between Gregory and Rachel, provided that such a relationship would not cause Gregory harm and even though the court may have been powerless to force Gregory to see Rachel.[295]

---

293. *See generally* Woodhouse, *supra* note 137, at 829-41.

294. *See* Albert J. Solnit, Truth Telling: The Child as Witness (June 11, 1993) (unpublished paper presented at North American Conference of the International Society of Family Law).

295. Once a child reaches a certain age, neither courts nor custodial parents can force the child to visit a noncustodial parent. Some courts have even acknowledged that, in some cases, forced visitations may not be in a child's best interests. *See, e.g.*, Stringfellow v. Stringfellow, 553 So. 2d 1161, 1162 (Ala. Civ. App. 1989) (acknowledging that visitation rights may be discontinued "where adverse psychological damage would result and no good would result from forced visitation"); Hagler v. Hagler, 460 So. 2d 187, 189 (Ala. Civ. App. 1984) (explaining that in rare cases, if it is in the best interest of the child, a court may discontinue visitation rights if the child refuses to visit the parent).

2. *Custodial Parent Status for Parent-Like Individuals.*—The lack of a constitutional basis for a custody or visitation claim by a parent-like individual does not completely preclude the parent-like individual from raising such a claim. Although the legal parent's liberty interest is paramount to that of the parent-like individual,[296] in the event the legal parent were to lose the superior custody claim,[297] the parent-like individual's claim would become viable.[298]

In the absence of a legal parent's superior claim, awarding custody to a parent-like individual also would be consistent with the current trend in custody jurisprudence toward continuity of care and permanency planning.[299] Awarding custody to a parent-like individ-

---

296. *See* Bartlett, *supra* note 16; Polikoff, *supra* note 82 (discussing the jurisprudence granting a priority to legal parents' liberty interest claims).

297. The principal reason legal parents lose their custody claims is their abuse, neglect, or abandonment of the child. *See, e.g.*, N.Y. FAM. CT. ACT § 1022(a)(ii) (McKinney 1994) (specifying that parents may be temporarily deprived of custody upon a finding of neglect and abuse); N.Y. SOC. SERV. LAW § 384-b(4)(b), (c) (McKinney 1992) (specifying that parental rights may be terminated upon a finding of neglect and abuse); ILL. ANN. STAT. ch. 705, para. 405/2-23 (Smith-Hurd 1992) (specifying that children may be removed from their parents' custody upon a finding of neglect and abuse); *see also* Bennett v. Jeffreys, 356 N.E.2d 277, 280 (N.Y. 1976) (holding that "[t]he State may not deprive a parent of his child's custody absent surrender, abandonment, persisting neglect, unfitness or other like extraordinary circumstances").

A third party's claim may also gain viability when the legal parent is unavailable due to illness or death. *See, e.g., In re* Carey, 544 N.E.2d 1293, 1300 (Ill. App. Ct. 1989) (stepmother granted custody of child over noncustodial natural mother upon natural father's death), *appeal denied*, 550 N.E.2d 554 (1990); Nabstedt v. Barger, 121 N.E.2d 781 (Ill. 1954) (relying on a statute listing the parents' mental illness as a ground for their child's adoption by a third party); *see also* N.Y. SOC. SERV. LAW § 384-b(4)(b) (McKinney 1992) (authorizing termination of parental rights due to parent's mental illness).

298. *See Bennett*, 356 N.E.2d 277 (establishing parental abandonment, neglect, or abuse of the child as a prerequisite for applying the best interests of the child doctrine in granting custody to a third party over a birth parent); *In re* J.C., 608 A.2d 1312 (N.J. 1992) (requiring parental unfitness or the lack of a child-parent relationship before terminating parental rights based on the bond between the child and the foster parent); *In re* K.L.F., 608 A.2d 1327, 1333-34 (N.J. 1992) (refusing to award custody of children in foster care to the Commissioner of Social Services without proof of neglect, abuse, or abandonment of the children).

299. Both continuity of care and permanency are emerging concepts in the jurisprudence. Continuity of care has been applied in custody determinations as an important factor for promoting stability in a child's life. *See* Smith v. Smith, 615 So. 2d 926, 930-31, 935 (La. Ct. App.) (explaining that continuity of care is a polestar consideration in child custody cases), *cert. denied*, 617 So. 2d 916 (La. 1993); Delzer v. Winn, 491 N.W.2d 741, 743 (N.D. 1992) (holding that maintaining stability and continuity in the child's life is a compelling consideration in child custody cases); *In re* L.W., 613 A.2d 350, 357 (D.C. 1992) (explaining that continuity of care must be considered in determining the best interest of the child). In the foster care context, courts strive toward achieving permanency and stability in a foster care placement. *See generally* THE NEW YORK TASK FORCE ON

ual when the legal parents are unqualified is also consistent with the best interests of the child and with the continuity of care doctrine. In short, if courts were to recognize the child's liberty interest in a child-parent relationship, they would be promoting stability and fostering the continuation of relationships that are beneficial to the child.

CONCLUSION

The recognition of a child's independent liberty interest in continuing a child-parent relationship through visitation would protect the relationship from both the parent's and the child's perspective. Granting the child a right to visitation, however, also raises complicated questions concerning the applicability of other legal obligations attendant to the relationship.[300]

Although this Article favors granting parent-like individuals greater consideration than the current jurisprudence affords,[301] it does not seek to secure for them a full liberty interest in the child-parent relationship. When parent-like individuals have lived with a child for a significant period of time, however, they probably should have the opportunity to seek custody of the child in the event of a dissolution of the family. Recognizing the liberty interest of such parent-like individuals should follow as a proper consequence of recognizing and protecting their children's liberty interest[302] and would further legally solidify the relationships. Such a limited recognition of the parent-like individuals' liberty interest would not necessarily open the door to frivolous claims because the definition of parent-like individuals could be sufficiently narrow to minimize the number of claims.[303]

PERMANENCY PLANNING FOR CHILDREN IN FOSTER CARE, STATE OF NEW YORK UNIFIED COURT SYSTEM, PERMANENCY PLANNING: A SHARED RESPONSIBILITY (1986).

300. For example, questions arise concerning whether the parent-like individual would have an obligation to support the child while enjoying the benefits of visitation of the child and whether a child could inherit from a parent-like individual and vice versa.

301. *See supra* Part I.B. (discussing the deficiencies of the current jurisprudence affecting child-parent relationships).

302. Just as children's liberty interest arose as a reciprocal right of the parents' liberty interest, courts could recognize parent-like individuals' liberty interest as a reciprocal right of the children's liberty interest. *See supra* text accompanying notes 216-269 (discussing children's substantive due process right to the companionship of their parents).

303. *See supra* text accompanying notes 196-201 (setting forth a test for identifying parent-like individuals). And, if that test is not sufficiently narrow, limiting custody claims to parent-like individuals who lived with the child for a significant period of time would further minimize claims for custody.

The approach adopted in this Article would allow individuals to choose freely the family type appropriate for them and would protect all families regardless of their social acceptance. It would protect both traditional and nontraditional families and would permit courts to fashion equitable remedies in complex family disputes. Finally, according children a right to maintain important family relationships would legitimize the efforts of a growing number of nontraditional families to provide for the development of our most valuable future resource—our children. To ignore these efforts or to sanction the manipulation of children's lives based solely on the adult's status serves neither our children's, nor our future's, best interests.

CONTESTED ADOPTION AND THE LIBERTY INTEREST OF THE CHILD

MARCUS T. BOCCACCINI*

ELEANOR WILLEMSEN, PH.D.**

I. INTRODUCTION

Children have protected constitutional rights in their family relationships. These rights are conventionally known as "liberty interests"[1]—an idea based on the connection between empirical psychological research about young children's relationships and the concept of a person's protected constitutional right to retain family relationships.[2] Yet, the Supreme Court of the United States has refused to decide whether a child has a liberty interest consistent with that of the parent in maintaining a filial relationship.[3]

A number of recent court cases,[4] involving attempts by an unwed biological father to prevent the adoption of his biological child by prospective

---

* Marcus T. Boccaccini is a doctoral candidate in Clinical Psychology/Psychology-Law at the University of Alabama. Department of Psychology, Box 870348, Tuscaloosa, AL 35487-0348.

** Eleanor Willemsen received her Ph.D., M.A., and B.A. from Stanford University. She is a Professor of Psychology at Santa Clara University. Department of Psychology, 500 El Camino Real, Santa Clara, CA 95053. E-mail Ewillemsen@mailer.scu.edu.

1. *See* Michael H. v. Gerald D., 491 U.S. 110, 130 (1988).

2. In *Tinker v. Des Moines Independent Community School District*, 393 U.S. 503, 511 (1969), the Court recognized that children are "persons" under the Constitution and that they possess "fundamental rights which the State must respect, just as they themselves must respect their obligations to the state." *See also* Kirsten Korn, *The Struggle for the Child: Preserving the Family in Adoption Disputes Between Biological Parents and Third Parties*, 72 N.C. L. REV. 1279, 1289 (1994).

3. *See Michael H.*, 491 U.S. at 130.

4. *See, e.g.*, *id.* at 126 (holding that the family unit was a traditionally protected liberty interest, but that a father's right to a relationship with his child born from an adulterous relationship is not a traditional liberty interest); Lehr v. Robertson, 463 U.S. 248, 262 (1983) (stating that although the mere biological link does not merit constitutional protection, an unwed father who takes advantage of that opportunity and accepts some measure of responsibility for the child's future may enjoy the constitutional protections of that relationship); Caban v. Mohammed, 441 U.S. 380, 393-94 (1979) (requiring an established relationship between the unwed father and his child in order to warrant constitutional protection); Quilloin v. Walcott, 434 U.S. 246, 256 (1978) (holding that constitutional protection would not be afforded to a putative father on the mere existence of a biological link unless there exists some affirmative action by him to acknowledge and accept his responsibilities); Stanley v. Illinois, 405 U.S. 645, 658 (1972) (recognizing that putative fathers have parental rights in their children which deserve due process protection where an established family relationship existed).

adoptive parents with whom the child has already been placed, have evolved into legal contests pitting the rights and interests of children against those of their biological parents.[5] Attempts have been made to standardize the process by which these contested adoption cases are decided, and catch phrases such as "in the best interests of the child" further imply that consistency is the foundation of the system.[6] However, variability in decisions from court to court and in laws from state to state served to create a myriad of confusing precedents that lack useful consistency.[7] Even though there is no doubt that the protracted legal battles that these cases involve are emotionally trying on each of the participants, the harm done to an innocent child by a delayed change of custody indisputably exceeds the combined suffering of the other participants.[8]

The Supreme Court of the United States has gone to significant lengths to outline an unwed father's rights in adoption cases,[9] but has yet to address the child's rights in similar cases.[10] It is these constitutionally protected rights, which are usually referred to as "liberty interests," that will be discussed in this Article. Unfortunately, the current trend in the majority of contested adoption decisions is to view the issue of what is in the child's best interests as answered largely by the determination of the father's parental fitness.[11] Due to a myriad of complex deciding elements in the custody equation, the problem in many of these cases is that the child has resided with prospective adoptive parents for a period of years.[12] Although children's interests are often addressed, in contested adoption cases, they remain dormant until a finding is made that the father's rights have not been vio-

---

5. *See generally* Lynn Kirsch, Note, *Unwed Fathers and Their Newborn Children Placed for Adoption: Protecting the Rights of Both in Custody Disputes*, 36 ARIZ. L. REV. 1011 (1994).

6. Courts applying a best interest of the child standard generally consider the claims of competing parents on "equal footing" and require that each party present evidence demonstrating that awarding custody in his favor would serve the best interests of the child. *See* Suzette M. Haynie, *Biological Parents v. Third Parties: Whose Right to Child Custody is Constitutionally Protected?*, 20 GA. L. REV. 705, 721-22 (1986).

7. *See* Kirsch, *supra* note 5, at 1019.

8. *See id.* at 1031.

9. *See* Karen C. Wehner, *Daddy Wants Rights Too: A Perspective on Adoption Statutes*, 31 HOUS. L. REV. 691, 692 (1994).

10. *See* Michael H. v. Gerald D., 491 U.S. 110, 130 (1988).

11. *See* Haynie, *supra* note 6.

12. *See* Robert S. Rausch, Note, *Unwed Fathers and the Adoption Process*, 22 WM. & MARY L. REV. 85, 113-14 (1980). "Time is most critical to the child. By the time the court enters the final order of adoption, a child already has begun to develop substantial ties to his new parents and siblings." *Id.* However, "[m]any states have specific requirements relating to giving notice of the adoption and locating and terminating the rights of absent biological parents, particularly unwed fathers. These procedures are by far the worst offenders of expediency." *Id.* at 116-17.

lated.[13]

Children have protected constitutional rights to their established intimate family relationships, conventionally known in constitutional law as "liberty interests." In contested adoption cases, these liberty interests should have priority over the rights and interests of their biological parents. This proposal is founded upon the large body of psychological research which shows that a disruption of the close, significant, emotional bond between a psychological parent, or parents, and a child can be extremely harmful to that child's long-term well-being.[14] Moreover, because children have protected interests and are too young to assist in the making of any custody decisions, we must take into account the implications of psychological research in order to advocate for the child's best interests and their rights to have these interests considered in contested adoption cases.

II. LIBERTY INTERESTS AND CHILDREN'S NEEDS

A. LIBERTY INTEREST

The term "liberty" is a cornerstone of the Constitution of the United States[15] and, therefore, of the judiciary system. Perhaps the best definition of liberty was proffered by the Supreme Court in *Meyer v. Nebraska*:[16]

> [Liberty] denotes not merely freedom from bodily restraint but also the right of the individual to contract, to engage in any of the common occupations of life, to acquire useful knowledge, to marry, establish a home and bring up children, to worship God according to the dictates of his own conscience, and generally to enjoy those privileges long recognized . . . as essential to the orderly pursuit of happiness.[17]

Therefore, liberty denotes freedom of the mind as well as freedom of action, and liberty interest denotes the limitation on the states to abuse an individ-

13. *See id.* at 132, noting that,

> [T]he determination of an unwed father's rights involves several factors. All unwed fathers are at least entitled to notice and a chance to be heard before their parental rights can be terminated. Any additional substantive rights to which they may be entitled depends on the quality of their relationship with their children.

Id.

14. *See* William H. Berman & Michael B. Sperling, *The Structure and Function of Adult Attachment*, *in* ATTACHMENT IN ADULTS 5, 7-8 (Michael B. Sperling & William H. Berman eds., 1994).

15. *See* U.S. CONST. amend. XIV, § 1 ("No state shall . . . deprive any person of life, liberty, or property, without due process of law; nor deny to any person within its jurisdiction the equal protection of the laws.").

16. 262 U.S. 390 (1923).

17. *Id.* at 399.

ual's said freedom.[18]

The Due Process Clause of the Fourteenth Amendment maintains that no state shall "deprive any person of life, liberty, or property, without due process of law."[19] Therefore, it is a Fourteenth Amendment violation to deprive a person of a liberty interest without due process of law.[20] Similar to the concept of liberty interest, the concept of due process has not been reduced to a concise formula or definition.[21] Generally, due process incorporates notions of fair notice, fair warning, and especially the opportunity to be heard in a meaningful time and manner.[22]

Due process rights are generally separated into two categories: substantive and procedural.[23] Substantive due process rights are rights such as those listed in the Bill of Rights and those rights considered to be so fundamental that a state may not take them away unless a "compelling state interest" requires it.[24] Rights such as abortion,[25] privacy,[26] marriage,[27] and physical safety[28] have been found to constitute such fundamental rights.[29] Procedural due process rights involve expectations created by state law and may be taken away if the state affords a proper hearing before or after deprivation of such a right.[30] Therefore, because procedural due process rights can be legally violated through due process, while substantive due process rights cannot unless a compelling state interest is shown, substantive due process rights are afforded more legal protection than are procedural due process rights.[31]

Certain liberty interests have been identified in case law which directly pertain to family relationships.[32] Of specific relevance to our discussion of

---

18. *See* JOHN E. NOWAK & RONALD D. ROTUNDA, CONSTITUTIONAL LAW 518 (1995).
19. U.S. CONST. amend. XIV, § 1.
20. *See id.*
21. *See* Moore v. City of East Cleveland, 431 U.S. 494, 501-02 (1977).
22. *See* Thadd Llaurado, Comment, *The Actionability Under Section 1983 of a Negligent Deprivation of a Liberty Interest in Light of* Daniels *and* Davidson, 69 MARQ. L. REV. 599, 626 (1986).
23. *See* NOWAK & ROTUNDA, *supra* note 18, at 346.
24. *See id.* at 518.
25. *See* Roe v. Wade, 410 U.S. 113, 154 (1972).
26. *See* Griswold v. Connecticut, 381 U.S. 479, 485 (1964).
27. *See* Loving v. Virginia, 388 U.S. 1, 12 (1966).
28. *See* Mapp v. Ohio, 367 U.S. 643, 656-57 (1960).
29. *See generally* JOAN BISKUPIC & ELDER WITT, THE SUPREME COURT AND INDIVIDUAL RIGHTS 295-99 (1997).
30. *See* NOWAK & ROTUNDA, *supra* note 18, at 510.
31. *Compare* Mathews v. Eldridge, 424 U.S. 319, 334-35 (1976), *with* Roe v. Wade 410 U.S. 113, 154-55.
32. *See, e.g.*, Michael H. v. Gerald D., 491 U.S. 110 (1988); Lehr v. Robertson, 463 U.S. 248 (1983); Caban v. Mohammed, 441 U.S. 380 (1979); Quilloin v. Walcott, 434 U.S. 246 (1978);

contested adoption is the Supreme Court's identification and specification of circumstances under which a biological father's liberty interest in forming a relationship with his child is constitutionally protected.[33]

B. THE SUPREME COURT OF THE UNITED STATES

Before 1972, an unwed father had neither a right to notice of an adoption nor a right to prevent mothers from placing their children for adoption.[34] Regardless of the circumstances surrounding the biological parents' relationship, most states only required the mother's consent in order to place a child for adoption.[35] In 1972, the Supreme Court heard the first of four cases that drastically changed the law affecting an unwed father's parental rights.[36] These cases reflect an increasingly explicit finding that an unwed father has a liberty interest in forming and maintaining a parent-child relationship with his child.[37]

The first of these cases was *Stanley v. Illinois*.[38] In *Stanley*, the Court ruled that parental fitness could not be determined solely on the basis of marital status, and that unwed fathers have a protected liberty interest in their "established" relationship with their children.[39] The Court used *Quilloin v. Wallcott*[40] to clarify the tacit assumption in *Stanley* that a biological father has to act like a nurturing father in order to "establish" a constitutionally protected interest in the father-child relationship.[41] *Caban v. Mo-*

Stanley v. Illinois, 405 U.S. 645 (1972).

33. *See* Daniel C. Zinman, Note, *Father Knows Best: The Unwed Father's Right to Raise His Infant Surrendered for Adoption*, 60 FORDHAM L. REV. 971, 1000 (1992).

34. *See* Wehner, *supra* note 9, at 693.

35. *See* Norman E. Allen, Adoption of Kelsey S.: *When Does an Unwed Father Know Best?*, 24 PAC. L.J. 1633, 1637 (1993).

36. *See id.*

37. *See* Elizabeth A. Hadad, *Tradition and the Liberty Interest: Circumscribing the Rights of the Natural Father*, 56 BROOK. L. REV. 291, 313 (1990).

38. 405 U.S. 645 (1972). Joan and Peter Stanley lived together for eighteen years without getting married. *See id.* at 646. When Joan died, their three children were taken away from Peter in accordance with an Illinois law, which required that children of unwed mothers become wards of the state and be placed with court-appointed guardians upon the mother's death. *See id.* Stanley asserted that his Fourteenth Amendment rights to due process and equal protection were violated because he was never shown to be an unfit parent. *See id.* The Supreme Court held that the sta-tute certainly deprived Stanley of his Fourteenth Amendment right to due process because parental unfitness had to be established on a case-by-case basis instead of the overall assumption that all unmarried fathers are unfit to care for their children. *See id.* at 649-57. Furthermore, denying Stanley a fitness hearing because of his marital status violated the Equal Protection Clause. *See id.* at 658.

39. *Id.* at 645.

40. 434 U.S. 246 (1977).

41. *Id.* at 248, 256.

hammed[42] reiterated the Court's position in *Stanley* and *Quilloin* that a father needed more than a biological tie in order for his paternal rights to be protected, and specified that a state may not treat an unwed father differently than the mother when he has admitted paternity and has established a substantial relationship with the child.[43] In *Lehr v. Robertson*,[44] the Court held that a potential relationship based on a biological connection provides the father with a unique opportunity to develop an actual relationship with his child, but that he must promptly "grasp" this opportunity in order for his rights to be protected by the Constitution.[45] Thus, the current standard for deciding if an unwed father has a constitutionally protected right to a relationship with his child is to determine whether or not he acted promptly in his assertion and maintenance of his parental rights.[46]

In summary, the Supreme Court has maintained that in order for an unwed father to have a constitutionally protected relationship with his child, he must act like a father and shoulder responsibility for the child.[47] As the Court has expressed, he must grasp the opportunity he is given as a result of the biological connection.[48] Only then will he be allowed to be heard regarding his child's circumstances.[49] Interestingly, children's interests in their family relationships are usually encompassed in determining what "is in the best interests of the child" and are frequently discussed in court decisions

42. 441 U.S. 380 (1978). In *Caban*, the biological father, Caban, and mother, Mohammed, lived together out of wedlock for several years. *See id.* at 382. After the mother moved out, both parents developed relationships that ended up in marriage. *See id.* at 382. Mohammed petitioned for her husband to adopt the children but Caban and his wife cross-petitioned to adopt the children themselves. *See id.* at 383. Caban was not allowed to block the petition for adoption unless he could show that the adoption was not in the "child's best interest." *Id.* at 386-87. Mohammed was allowed to adopt the children. *See id.* at 383. The Court found the New York statute unconstitutional and recognized that the distinction drawn between unwed fathers and mothers discriminates against fathers by excluding them from participating in the adoption process on the basis of gender. *See id.* at 394.

43. *See id.* at 394. *See also* Kirsch *supra* note 5, at 1015.

44. 463 U.S. 248 (1982). Lehr had not lived or established a relationship with his child. *See id.* at 249-50. When the child was over two years old, the mother and her husband filed a petition for adoption. *See id.* at 250. The Court granted the adoption without giving notice to the biological father. *See id.* Lehr claimed that his due process and equal protection rights were violated since he was not given advance notice of the adoption proceeding. *See id.* at 250. The Court distinguished between the cases where the father developed a relationship with the child and cases where there was an opportunity to develop the relationship. *See id.* at 261. Since Lehr never established such a relationship, his rights were not violated. *See id.* at 267-68.

45. *Id.* at 262.

46. *See* Zinman, *supra* note 33, at 980.

47. *See id.*

48. *See Lehr*, 463 U.S. at 262.

49. *See id.*

but have never been explicitly outlined.[50] The current assumption is that by examining the biological father's parental fitness and the timeliness of his declaration of intent to care for the child, the child's relationship interests will be vicariously served.[51] The following Section uses empirical evidence from years of psychological research in order to show that this current trend of viewing the child's interests as largely dependent upon the biological father's parental fitness is not only inadequate, but can inadvertently result in irreparable harm to the child. We must identify children's interests in their intimate family relationships as "liberty interests" requiring due process protection in order to protect children from this preventable harm.

C. THE IMPORTANCE OF ATTACHMENT IN INFANCY

"Attachment" is the term used by psychologists to describe the sense of special connection that babies who are psychologically well cared for feel towards their caregivers.[52] We believe that psychological evidence about the role of attachment in development supports the idea of the centrality of attachment in any infant's normal development and, therefore, to that infant's orderly pursuit of happiness. Children's attachment bonds with their caregivers develop out of the experience of having their caregiver respond to their signals about what they need and want.[53] This early experience of attachment is represented in the mind of the child and it is this mental model of attachment that comes to have a powerful life-long influence.[54]

There are several reasons why the child's experience of attachment is so crucial to child development. First, the experience of secure attachment teaches the child that he or she is lovable and loving.[55] Through this significant lesson, the child forms the willingness and the ability to connect to other people, such as new caregivers at daycare, school, or in the extended family, and peers in those same settings.[56]

Second, the attachment relationship forms the "secure base" from which the toddler can "go out" to the world of other people, things, and

---

50. Zinman, *supra* note 33, at 987.

51. *See id.* at 1000-01.

52. *See* Berman & Sperling, *supra* note 14, at 5; *see also* Mary D. Salter Ainsworth, *Attachments Beyond Infancy*, 44 AM. PSYCHOLOGIST 709, 709 (1989).

53. *See* Elizabeth Anisfeld et al., *Does Infant Carrying Promote Attachment? An Experimental Study of the Effects of Increased Contact on the Development of Attachment*, 61 CHILD DEV. 1617 (1990).

54. *See* Berman & Sperling, *supra* note 14, at 7.

55. *See* Douglas M. Teti & Karen E. Ablard, *Security of Attachment and Infant Sibling Relationships: A Laboratory Study*, 60 CHILD DEV. 1519 (1989).

56. *See id.* at 1519-20.

events and explore them and learn from them.[57] Paradoxically, this close connection provides the basis for independence and learning on one's own. Research shows that insecurely attached babies have, with greater frequency than securely attached babies, less advanced development of their understanding of objects, connections involved in what happens around them, and the use of tools, along with less advanced communication skills.[58] Finally, the mental representation of this early attachment experience is the centerpiece of a child's self awareness and awareness of the "other" as a separate person with whom one can nevertheless connect.[59]

Attachment relationships develop gradually over the course of the first year of life.[60] The extent to which caregivers understand and respond to the baby's signals throughout the first year are predictors of attachment security at year one and beyond.[61] Early in the first year, the attachment bond develops as a result of a caregiver's "getting the message" when the baby is hungry, tired, over or under-stimulated, etc.[62] Later, in mid-year, the bond develops as the caregiver helps the baby interact with the environment through such activities as proffering a toy that has attracted interest, noticing a wary reaction to a newly arrived stranger, or recognizing that the baby wants to crawl away and do her own thing.[63] By the year's end, there will develop a complex interplay of communication, both nonverbal and, soon, verbal.[64] The sensitivity of care has been measured at all these points in various studies, and it reliably relates to security of attachment at year one and beyond.[65]

Secure attachment has been shown in research to predict more complex and better language skills and higher levels of intellectual development.[66] These facts are seen by child development researchers to demonstrate the positive results of the rich exploratory play, including that with other people, engaged in by the securely attached toddler with a secure base.[67] These

---

57. Adriana G. Bus & Marunus H. Van Ijzendoorn, *Attachment and Early Reading: A Longitudinal Study*, 149 J. GENETIC PSYCHOL. 199, 199-200 (1989).

58. *See* ATTACHMENT IN THE PRESCHOOL YEARS: THEORY, RESEARCH, AND INTERVENTION 200-01 (Mark T. Greenberg et al. eds., 1990) [hereinafter PRESCHOOL]; *see also* JEREMY HOLMES, JOHN BOWLBY AND ATTACHMENT THEORY 109-10 (1993).

59. *See* JEROME KAGAN, THE SECOND YEAR: THE EMERGENCE OF SELF AWARENESS 118-19 (1981).

60. *See* Berman & Sperling, *supra* note 14, at 7.

61. *See* Anisfeld, *supra* note 53.

62. *See* Salter Ainsworth, *supra* note 52, at 710.

63. *See* PRESCHOOL, *supra* note 58, at 202-03.

64. *See* HOLMES, *supra* note 58, at 75.

65. *See id.* at 111.

66. *See id.*

67. *See* PRESCHOOL, *supra* note 58, at 202-03.

positive effects of secure attachment persist into the later grade school years.[68] Indeed, it seems probable that all important aspects of development are related to the quality of this early experience.

Attachment issues do not only affect children; they carry over to adulthood.[69] Adults have mental representations of their remembered and continuously experienced relationships of attachment with their important caregivers.[70] These representations strongly influence the intimate relationships of romance and parenting and have been studied by researchers.[71] The scientific literature demonstrates a consistent relationship between the quality of attachment history in individuals' mental representations and the success and satisfaction they have in their romantic relationships.[72] Those with insecure attachment are less trusting, less satisfied, and less optimistic about the future of the relationship than those with secure attachment.[73] Insecure attachment can thus be seen to lead to more frequent problems in maintaining stable relationships and long-term marriages than those with secure histories would have.[74] Similarly, the sensitivity of mothers' behavior with these infants is predictable from their mental representations of attachment.[75]

In sum, a young child's experiences with attachment, its disruption or its secure continuity, can influence the capacity to form important close relationships and to sustain them over time during adult life. Disruptions to early relationships resulting in insecure attachment experiences and representations make it difficult for these individuals to relate well to other people for the rest of their lives. Thus, disrupted early attachment is a risk factor for the development of problems with relationships throughout the life span.

D. ATTACHMENT AND THE IDEA OF LIBERTY INTEREST IN ONE'S RELATIONSHIPS

If a child is removed from the only secure home she has known, she is at risk for difficulties in human interaction and relationships, underachieve-

68. *See* ATTACHMENT IN ADULTS 41 (Michael B. Sperling & William H. Berman eds., 1994).

69. *See* Berman & Sperling, *supra* note 14, at 8.

70. *See* Judith Crowell & S. Shirley Feldman, *Mothers' Working Models of Attachment Relationships and Mother and Child Behavior During Separation and Reunion*, 27 DEV. PSYCHOL. 597 (1991).

71. *See* Cindy Hazan & Phillip Saver, *Romantic Love Conceptualized as an Attachment Process*, 52 J. PERSONALITY & SOC. PSYCHOL. 511, 521 (1987).

72. *See id.* at 511.

73. *See generally id.* at 514-15.

74. *See id.*

75. *See* Crowell & Feldman, *supra* note 70, at 604.

ment, and failure to successfully parent the next generation.[76] Disruption of an existing safe, secure, and loving relationship can prevent a child from exercising a liberty interest in pursuing the ordinary activities of life known as normal development.[77] Although a child's liberty interest in the early family relationship has been identified,[78] it has not yet been used as the primary deciding factor in a contested adoption case.

In fact, when discussing the confounding nature of biological fathers' and children's rights in contested adoption cases, one disconcerted commentator has appropriately noted that "there is no definitive test which serves the dual purpose of protecting a father's fundamental rights and considering the interests of the child."[79] As illustrated above, the trend in Supreme Court decisions has been to view the child's liberty interests as largely dependent upon a determination of the biological father's parental fitness and a show of timely responsibility.[80]

It does seem that because of the harm that would result to the child from a severance of the familial relationships and emotional ties that are formed when a child has resided with prospective adoptive parents for a significant amount of time, that children in contested adoption cases have a substantive due process right in remaining with the only parents that they have ever known. Conversely, because a biological father may be legally deprived through due process of his right in forming a relationship with his child, he has only a procedural due process right to forming a relationship with his child. Therefore, it appears that constitutionally, children's rights in these cases are and should be considered paramount to those of the father. Unfortunately, as the next section illustrates, they usually are not.

III. RECENT CASES: INCONSISTENCIES IN THE LAW

In contested adoption cases, the Supreme Court has outlined certain guidelines to be followed under specific circumstances.[81] Problems arise when novel circumstances render the Supreme Court's guidance inadequate.

76. *See generally* Zinman, *supra* note 33, at 986-87.

77. *See id.* at 987.

78. *See In re* Jasmon O., 878 P.2d 1297, 1308 (Cal. 1994); *In re* Bridget R., 49 Cal. Rptr. 2d 507, 524 (Cal. Ct. App. 1996).

79. Je'Nell Blocher Gustafson, *The Natural Father, I Presume: The Natural Father's Rights Versus the Best Interests of the Child*, 1 SAN DIEGO JUST. J. 489, 497 (1993).

80. *See* Kirsch, *supra* note 5, at 1018.

81. Courts usually follow either a "best interest of the child" standard, *see* Haynie *supra* note 6, or a "biological-parental fitness" standard which assumes that by placing a child in the custody of the natural parent, absent a showing that the natural parent is unfit, the child's best interests will be served. *See* Gregory S. Hilderbran, Comment, *In re* Baby Girl Eason: *Balancing Three Competing Interests in Third Party Adoptions*, 22 GA. L. REV. 1217, 1234 (1988).

Under these circumstances, decisions become idiosyncratic and lack the underlying consistency that is needed to protect all children in contested adoption cases.[82] The five cases below are provided to illustrate this point.

A. *IN RE BABY GIRL CLAUSSEN*

In re Claussen,[83] publicly known as the "Baby Jessica" case,[84] is perhaps the best known case involving what has become known as "the thwarted father."[85] A thwarted father is a father who genuinely wants to take responsibility for his child but has been thwarted of the opportunity to do so.[86] In this Iowa case, the biological mother knowingly named the wrong man as the father of the child and subsequently placed the child for adoption.[87] When the biological father found out about his child, he immediately pursued legal recourse in order to obtain custody of Jessica.[88] He argued that he never abandoned his child.[89] In the end, two-and-a-half-year-old Baby Jessica was returned under court order to her biological father and mother, who had subsequently married, rather than to the only parents that she had ever known, without primary regard to what was in her best interests.[90] As a result of the focus on the biological father's rights, Jessica has been inauspiciously placed at an elevated risk for future difficulties with human interaction, relationships, and achievement.

B. *MICHAEL H. V. GERALD D.*

In *Michael H. v. Gerald D.*,[91] a biological father was denied paternity and visitation rights by the Supreme Court because the mother was, and remained, married to someone else throughout the affair and the birth of their child.[92] The biological father had established a significant relationship with the child while she and the mother had resided with him for a significant period of time after the birth.[93] The Court was again willing to forsake the lib-

82. *See* Kirsch, *supra* note 5, at 1011-12.
83. 502 N.W.2d 649 (Mich. 1993).
84. *See id.* at 652.
85. *See* Tonya M. Zdon, *Putative Fathers' Rights: Striking the Right Balance in Adoption Laws*, 20 WM. MITCHELL L. REV. 929, 940 (1994).
86. *See id.*
87. *See Clausen*, 502 N.W.2d at 652.
88. *See id.* at 652.
89. *See id.*
90. *See id.* at 668.
91. 491 U.S. 110 (1989).
92. *See id.* at 113-16.
93. *See id.* at 113-14.

erty interests of the child in preserving developed bonds of attachment, in this case with her biological father, and gave prominence to the rights of an adult party.[94] Here, it is proper for the biological father to receive paternity and visitation rights. Thus, giving priority to all developed healthy attachment bonds regardless of the person to whom the child may be attached.

C. *ADOPTION OF MICHAEL H.*

In *Adoption of Michael H.*,[95] the Supreme Court of California found that a biological father who expressed interest in raising his child, but did not make his intentions formally known until after the child had been placed, had failed to grasp his opportunity interest.[96] The Court noted that the father had only announced his intentions to prevent adoption two weeks after the placement had taken place, and that "[i]t would seem inequitable to give preference to an unwed father who failed to fully grasp his parental obligations in a timely fashion."[97] Because the father did not promptly come forward during the prenatal period and demonstrate a full commitment to his parental responsibilities, his interest in his child was not constitutionally protected. Superficially, the decision in *Michael H.* appears to be in agreement with our position. However, the rationale in *Michael H.* is inapposite because consideration of the child's interests was limited to evaluating whether the biological father was a fit and responsible father. Following this reasoning, the court would have similarly accounted for the father's failure to "grasp his opportunity interest," but only after it had considered the child's protected liberty interests in the continuity and stability of his home and protection from physical and emotional negligence. The ultimate custody placement in *Michael H.* would not change if the children's substantive due process rights had rightfully been used as the deciding criteria, but the reasoning behind the custody placement would.

D. *IN RE BRIDGET R.*

In the case of *In re Bridget R.*,[98] the Second District Court of Appeal in California found that the Indian Child Welfare Act (ICWA)[99] did not automatically allow a biological father to revoke his consent to the adoption

94. *See id.* at 113-15.
95. 898 P.2d 891 (Cal. 1995).
96. *See id.* at 901.
97. *Id.* at 899.
98. 49 Cal. Rptr. 2d 507 (Cal. Ct. App. 1996).
99. 25 U.S.C. §§ 1901-1923 (1994).

of his twin girls.[100] The ICWA imposes requirements for the voluntary termination of parental rights of children who are members of an Indian tribe or eligible to be a member and the biological child of a member.[101] The ICWA gives jurisdiction and special privileges in such custody cases to the tribal court in order to facilitate the placement of eligible adoptees into an existing tribal community.[102] In its decision, the appellate court invoked the "existing Indian family" doctrine, which holds that the ICWA does not apply "without first determining that the biological parents had a significant social, cultural, or political relationship with the tribal community,"[103] and remanded the case to the trial court for a decision on that issue.[104] It was doubtful that Richard, who lived hundreds of miles from the reservation, ever "participated in tribal life or maintained any significant social, cultural or political relationship with the Tribe."[105] The adopting parents argued that the ICWA creates an impermissible racial classification unless it is limited by the doctrine.[106] Without the ICWA, the court could have rendered a decision similar to *Michael H.*, declaring the father unfit and deciding in favor of the adoptive placement based on the biological father's failure to "grasp his opportunity interest." Thus, the decision in *Bridget* would not have required a basis in the child's liberty interest.

Nonetheless, it is most promising that in *Bridget* the applicability of the ICWA was questioned primarily because of the children's rights. The court's opinion that "the interests of the tribe and the biological family may be in direct conflict with the children's strong needs, which we find to be constitutionally protected, to remain through their developing years in one stable and loving home,"[107] reflects a meaningful acknowledgment of the centrality of children's developmental needs and indeed identifies them as "liberty interests." This is a truly important opinion denoting the importance of the child's best interests.

IV. ISSUES, PROBLEMS, AND ANSWERS

The liberty interests of the child in contested adoption cases are of greater legal concern than are those of the biological father. Psychological studies suggest that in contested adoption cases, children are entitled to sub-

100. *See Bridget R.*, 49 Cal. Rptr. 2d at 536.
101. *See* 25 U.S.C. § 1913.
102. *See id.* § 1911.
103. *Bridget R.*, 49 Cal. Rptr. 2d at 536.
104. *See id.* at 530.
105. *Id.* at 515-16.
106. *See id.* at 519.
107. *Bridget R.*, 49 Cal. Rptr. 2d at 522-23.

stantive due process rights or liberty interests in the continuity and stability of their homes, and in protection from physical and emotional negligence, while biological fathers in the aforementioned cases have only a procedural due process right or liberty interest in establishing a relationship with their child. The Supreme Court has ruled on the rights of the father in these cases, but has yet to directly address the child's rights in a similar manner.[108] As a result, in lower courts, the determining factor in these cases reduces to a combination of the biological father's parental fitness and his coming forward to accept responsibility in a timely manner. This trend in decisions not only ignores the empirical evidence, but is judicially contradictory because it holds the child's substantive due process rights as subordinate to the procedural due process rights of the biological father.

This Article by no means implies that the biological father's fitness and timely acceptance of responsibility are not important criteria for determining whether or not a father should be able to receive custody of his child, but rather that the attachment issues surrounding the child's needs must be addressed before the father is allowed to be heard concerning his fitness. A child does have an important interest in having a psychologically fit father, but that is not his or her only need. Ideally, if an unwed mother wants to place her child with someone else but the father desires to raise the child himself, it might well be in the best interests of the child to be placed with the father. As can be seen in the cases previously discussed, the situation is rarely, if ever, this ideal. A myriad of complicating factors intervene and slow the placement process. Meanwhile, the child's life continues in the family presently nurturing him, and there the vital attachment process proceeds without regard either for the biological connection or identity of the parent(s).

A. WHAT CAN BE DONE?

There is universal agreement among legal commentators that most of the problematic issues which arise in contested adoption cases are the result of delays in the legal system.[109] Attachment issues are directly related to time.[110] Therefore, the longer a contested adoption case stays in the legal system, the greater the potential harm that can be done to the child.[111] Effi-

108. *See* Michael H. v. Gerald D., 491 U.S. 110, 130 (1988).

109. *See* Rausch, *supra* note 12, at 116-17, 127; *see also* Allen, *supra* note 35, at 1677-79; Kirsch, *supra* note 5, at 1031; Wehner, *supra* note 9, at 12-13, 716, 719; Zdon, *supra* note 85, at 949.

110. *See* Salter Ainsworth, *supra* note 52.

111. *See* Rausch, *supra* note 12.

cient resolution of custody disputes raised by unwed fathers will serve the child's interests by reducing uncertainty and preventing him or her from being uprooted after emotional ties with pre-adoptive parents have been established.[112]

Statutory reform is needed to speed up the process by which biological fathers are notified and heard on issues of fitness and responsibility, and final custody decisions reached.[113] More emphasis needs to be placed on getting unwed fathers to act earlier than has previously been required. Acknowledgment of the father's intentions earlier in the adoption process will help to prevent the lengthy court battles that create the dilemma between the rights of the thwarted father and the right of the child to stay in an environment which is secure and stable.[114] It is in the best interest of the child to be placed permanently with either the biological father or the adoptive parents, as soon as possible.[115] The sooner that it can be determined whether the biological father is either fit or unfit, the sooner the child can be permanently placed. However, caution must be taken in reforming the adoption process so as not to further treat the child's interests as if subsumed in the biological father's or presumptively lying with him.[116]

Reform must do more than simply speed up the process by which a biological father's rights are identified. There are general steps that could be implemented in order to speed up decisions about permanent placement of the children in these cases. First, universal implementation of a state run registry, such as the existing one in New York, that would promptly notify registered unwed fathers of any pending adoption of their child, would allow fathers sufficient time to grasp their opportunity interest and effectively prevent most thwarted father scenarios.[117] Any man who even suspects that he may be a father could register with the state. Second, legal hearings on the issues of the father's right to be heard, his parental fitness, and the best interests of the child could be condensed into one hearing. Third, this one

---

112. *See Recent Developments—Family Law—Unwed Fathers' Rights—New York Court of Appeals Mandates Veto Power Over Newborn's Adoption for Unwed Father Who Demonstrates Parental Responsibility—In re* Raquel Marie X., 559 N.E.2d 418, (1990), *cert. denied*, 59 U.S.L.W. 3386 (U.S. Nov. 27, 1990) (No. 90-597), 104 HARV. L. REV. 800, 807 (1991) [hereinafter *Recent Developments*].

113. *See* Kirsch, *supra* note 5, at 1011-12. *See also* Wehner, *supra* note 9, at 719; Zdon, *supra* note 85, at 956.

114. *See* Rausch, *supra* note 12, at 113.

115. *See id.* at 114.

116. *See* Kirsch, *supra* note 5, at 1026. *See also* Barbara Bennett Woodhouse, *Hatching the Egg: A Child Centered Perspective on Parents' Rights*, 14 CARDOZO L. REV. 1747, 1785 (1993).

117. *See* Wehner, *supra* note 9, at 717-18. *See also* Zdon, *supra* note 85, at 940-41, 950, 956.

hearing could be "fast tracked" so that a calendar date for it takes priority over other civil cases.

B. PROBLEMS WITH THE CENTRALITY OF THE CHILD'S RIGHTS

A persuasive argument exists in opposition to a reformation of the adoption process reflecting the centrality of the child's rights. In contested adoption cases, the father is in a no-win situation because the child is developing attachment bonds with the adoptive parents, while he has not been allowed the same opportunity to form attachment bonds.[118] This suggests that all prospective adoptive parents have to do to be awarded custody is to physically secure the child and drag the case out in court. This is obviously unfair to a fit and responsible father who genuinely wants to raise his own child, but this situation would rarely, if ever, occur if the reforms proposed above are implemented by the states.

Although the discussion up to this point has dealt with determining the proper balance between the father's and the child's rights in contested adoption cases, the rights of the mother should not be overlooked.[119] In some circumstances, the mother may have excellent reasons for not naming a father. Based on the constitutional right to privacy, it has been suggested that a mother's right to remain silent outweighs a father's right to notice.[120] Currently, a woman has a right to make child bearing decisions regardless of the father's objections.[121] However, a mother cannot unilaterally preclude the biological father from asserting his right to establish a relationship with the child.[122] In order to facilitate the best interests of the child, the mother's rights may have to be balanced against those of the father in these cases. The actions of both parents, the mother's relinquishment of legal custody and the father's show of desire to take the child into his home, must be evaluated against the criterion of which prospect provides the best chance for a safe, secure, and stable home.

One final concern that arises from this discussion is this: If we take a child-centered approach to contested adoption cases, what are the implica-

118. *See* Kirsch, *supra* note 5, at 1026 n.161, 1029 & n.178, 1030. *See also Recent Developments*, *supra* note 112.

119. *See* Rausch, *supra* note 12, at 127.

120. *See id.* at 124, 127. *See also* Zdon, *supra* note 85, at 960 n.235. *But see* Rausch, *supra* note 12, at 128 (stating that the Supreme Court has declared that unwed fathers require notification of any legal proceedings that have an effect on their parental rights and that procedural due process demands, at a minimum, notice and a chance to be heard).

121. *See* Planned Parenthood v. Danforth, 428 U.S. 52, 92-93 (1976). *See also* Rausch, *supra* note 12, at 124.

122. *See* Rausch, *supra* note 12, at 124, 126, 128.

tions for custody decisions involving older children and/or other parenting situations? The Supreme Court adequately touched on many issues concerning rights in custody cases involving unwed fathers of older children.[123] Indeed, there might be a "compelling state interest" in limiting the substantive due process right of the child for one context, say, custody following divorce, and not another, such as contested adoption. Based on the variability of scenarios and issues involved in custody cases, such as the age of the children, the marital status of the parents, and each parent's fitness, even a succinct discussion of these issues is beyond the scope of this paper. However, we acknowledge that identifying a child's placement interest as a constitutional right raises issues for placement disputes that go beyond those of adoption.

V. CONCLUSION

The current tacit standard of viewing children's rights in contested adoption cases are largely determined by the biological father's parental fitness and the timeliness of his proclamation to take responsibility for the child is simply inadequate. Empirical evidence establishes that children ought to have constitutionally protected substantive due process rights, or liberty interests, in the continuity and stability of their homes, and in protection from physical and emotional negligence. Furthermore, inadequacies and delays in the current contested adoption process add to the already deficient standard of subjugating the rights of the child. Unless the current process in which contested adoption cases are resolved is reformed, children will continue to be needlessly harmed.

123. *See generally* Caban v. Mohammed, 441 U.S. 380 (1979); Quilloin v. Walcott, 434 U.S. 246 (1978); Stanley v. Illinois, 405 U.S. 645 (1972).

NOTES

THE CHANGING AMERICAN FAMILY: A REEVALUATION OF THE RIGHTS OF FOSTER PARENTS WHEN BIOLOGICAL PARENTAL RIGHTS HAVE BEEN TERMINATED

> *When biological parenting does not work . . . there is a noble alternative, a human grace that has stood the test of time. It is based on something more profound than blood. It is based on love.*[1]

I. INTRODUCTION

In the late 1990s, the Massachusetts courts ruled that a small boy the court called "Hugo" should be removed from the custody of his foster mother, with whom he had lived for approximately one year, and placed in the permanent custody of his biological aunt.[2] Hugo was taken from his biological mother by the Department of Social Services for the state of Massachusetts three days after his birth in 1994 and has never lived with either of his biological parents.[3] Due to his mother's use of cocaine during her pregnancy,[4] Hugo has special physical, mental, and developmental challenges.[5] After spending the first part of his life in another foster home, Hugo

---

[1] Jean Bethke Elshtain, *The Chosen Family*, THE NEW REPUBLIC, Sept. 14, 1998, at 45, 54.

[2] Adoption of Hugo, 700 N.E.2d 516, 518 (Mass. 1998).

[3] *Id.* at 518.

[4] *Id.* at 519 n.5.

[5] *Id.* at 519.

was placed in the home of foster mother Ms. L.[6] In Ms. L.'s care, Hugo began to receive services including speech therapy as well as physical and occupational therapy to address his special needs.[7] During his one-year placement with Ms. L., Hugo steadily adapted to his new home and his new foster mother, bonding with her and calling her "Mommy."[8] Additionally, Hugo's older sister, Gloria, was also in the care of Ms. L. at that time and was subsequently adopted by her in 1996.[9] Hugo developed a close relationship with his sister, to whom he turned for support and reassurance in his activities and help with interpreting his speech.[10]

Shortly after Hugo's foster mother filed papers to adopt him, the child's biological aunt decided that she also wanted to seek custody of Hugo.[11] In the end, the Massachusetts Supreme Court ruled for the biological aunt in the custody battle.[12] After the Massachusetts Court of Appeals ruled that the decision of the Juvenile Court of Suffolk County to give custody to Hugo's paternal aunt was "risk-laden,"[13] the Supreme Judicial Court of Massachusetts overruled,[14] stating that although separating Hugo from his foster family would have negative consequences for Hugo, his aunt could provide better services to address Hugo's developmental problems.[15]

In the end, the battle over custody of Hugo "highlights a fundamental flaw in our nation's child custody system: the law recognizes biological ties, not emotional ones."[16] In fact, to date, the United States Supreme Court has refused to recognize any fundamental right based on a child-parent relationship where biological ties were

---

[6] *Id.* at 518.

[7] *Id.* at 519.

[8] *Id.*

[9] *Id.* at 518.

[10] *Id.* at 524 n.20.

[11] *Id.* at 518.

[12] *Id.* at 516.

[13] Adoption of Hugo, 694 N.E.2d 377, 380 (Mass. App. Ct. 1998).

[14] Adoption of Hugo, 700 N.E.2d at 516.

[15] *See id.* at 519 (stating that "Hugo's aunt planned to spend 'a lot of quality time with him and working in areas where he needs help.'"). The court also took into consideration the fact that Hugo's aunt had been "heavily, consistently, and directly" involved with the treatment of her son, who was also born with special needs and developmental disabilities. *Id.* Her son, however, did not have behavioral problems. *Id.*

[16] Mary Ann Mason, *Fostering Family: When Love is Thicker than Blood*, THE NEW REPUBLIC, Aug. 30, 1999, at 14, 15.

not involved. The courts need to reevaluate this denial of due process rights in light of the changing dynamics of our society and the state of our evolving system of family connections.

At the end of the twentieth century, the dominance of the traditional nuclear family formed by a heterosexual couple and their children, and the values associated with nuclear families, have faded.[17] Many children no longer grow up in a stable home surrounded by two loving parents dedicated to the upbringing of their children.[18] In fact, divorce and remarriage have increasingly become the reality for a large percentage of American parents and their children.[19]

With the disappearance of the traditional nuclear family, a number of unconventional families have begun to develop.[20] For example, lesbian and gay parents are increasingly asserting their rights to raise their own children; sometimes turning to the practice of surrogacy or sperm and egg donation in order to have children.[21] Additionally, single parents, both mothers and fathers, have formed successful family environments for their children.[22] Finally, other adult caregivers, such as grandparents, blood relatives, and

---

[17] *See* Janet L. Dolgin, *The Fate of Childhood: Legal Models of Children and the Parent-Child Relationship*, 61 ALB. L. REV. 345, 347-50 (1997) (discussing transformation of childhood in light of changing family dynamics and values and legal system's response to those changes); *see also* Barbara Shapiro, *"Non-Traditional" Families in the Courts: The New Extended Family*, 11 J. AM. ACAD. MATRIM. L. 117, 125 (1993) (remarking that, according to 1990 census, only 26% of U.S. households now consist of two married parents of opposite sex living together with children).

[18] *See* Barbara Bennett Woodhouse, *"It All Depends on What You Mean by Home": Toward a Communitarian Theory of the "Nontraditional" Family*, 1996 UTAH L. REV. 569, 570 ("The majority of Americans now live in households that do not mirror the nuclear family model of a wage-earner husband, homemaker wife, and their biological children, all sharing one domicile.").

[19] *See* Ann Laquer Estin, *Family Governance in the Age of Divorce*, 1998 UTAH L. REV. 211, 211 n.8 (reporting disturbing divorce statistics). In 1990, there were 1,182,000 divorces in the United States, involving 1,075,000 children. *Id.*

[20] *See generally*, Alison Harvison Young, *Reconceiving the Family: Challenging the Paradigm of the Exclusive Family*, 6 AM. U. J. GENDER & L. 505 (1998) (describing development of new family systems including single parent families, stepparent families, adoptive families, and lesbian or gay parent families).

[21] *Id.* at 539-49.

[22] *Cf.* Estin, *supra* note 19, at 211 (suggesting that single parenthood often results from either divorce or birth of children to unmarried parents). The 116th edition of the Bureau of Census report found that of 4,000,240 total births, 1,240,000 were to unmarried mothers. *Id.* at 211 n.7.

stepparents have sought recognition from society and from the legal system as members of a child's family.[23]

Foster parents, however, have been and continue to be outsiders in this growing group of unconventional family systems.[24] In general, courts consistently deny foster parents any legal rights to the children they raise, and society has frequently failed to recognize the vital role that foster parents play in the lives of their foster children.[25]

Due to the development of these new family systems, and because of the breakdown in the traditional family system, family life has become much more public.[26] As a result, "[c]ourts are required to referee the relationships of parents and stepparents, or parents and grandparents, or biological and adoptive parents. As the once-stigmatized status of illegitimacy has been normalized . . . complex issues of parental rights" arise.[27] Courts frequently make difficult decisions regarding the rights of respective parties and the rights of children in cases involving child custody.[28] As the legal approach to custody has evolved, the courts have become more liberal in allowing parties other than married parents to assert legally protected rights to their children. For example, the United States Supreme Court, in *Stanley v. Illinois*,[29] recognized the rights of unwed fathers to their children.[30] The Court, however, has failed to rule on the rights

---

[23] *See, e.g.*, Lockhart v. Lockhart, 603 N.E.2d 864, 866-67 (Ind. Ct. App. 1992) (holding that Grandparent Visitation Rights Act does not violate equal protection but denying standing to grandparents to seek visitation under particular circumstances of case).

[24] *See infra* Part II.A. (discussing nature and purpose of foster care system).

[25] *See infra* Part II.B. (tracing evolution of judicial approach to existence of substantive and procedural due process rights).

[26] *See* Estin, *supra* note 19, at 212 (discussing significant relocation of public authority over families during last twenty-five years).

[27] *Id.*

[28] *See, e.g.*, DeBoer v. DeBoer, 509 U.S. 1301 (1993) (denying petition by foster parents to stay order giving custody to child's biological father); Twigg v. Mays, No. 88-4489-CA-01, 1993 WL 330624 (Fla. Cir. Ct. Aug. 18, 1993) (denying visitation rights to biological parents after child was raised from birth by unrelated man child thought was her biological father); Kingsley v. Kingsley, 623 So. 2d 780 (Fla. Dist. Ct. App. 1993) (holding that minor child could not unilaterally terminate rights of his biological parents).

[29] 405 U.S. 645 (1972).

[30] *Id.* at 649.

> [A]s a matter of due process of law, Stanley was entitled to a hearing on his fitness as a parent before his children were taken from him and that, by denying him a hearing and extending it to all other parents whose

of non-biological parents to custody of children in their care.[31] The United States Supreme Court discusses the rights of foster parents in only one case, *Smith v. Organization of Foster Families for Equality and Reform* ("*OFFER*").[32] In the *OFFER* case, the Court avoided a ruling on the constitutional rights of foster parents by basing its decision on state law provisions.[33]

Part II.A. explores the nature and purpose of the foster care system and its functioning in modern society.[34] Part II.B. addresses the evolution of the courts' approach to custody issues, including the standards applied in custody determinations.[35] Further, Part III.A. proposes that the legal system should recognize the fundamental due process rights of foster parents to retain custody of their foster children, particularly when biological parents have relinquished custody of their children.[36] Finally, in Part III.B., this Note recommends the adoption of an objective standard upon which to base custody decisions when biological parents, whose parental rights have been terminated, and third parties, including blood relatives, are battling with foster parents to obtain custody of the children.[37]

II. BACKGROUND

A. THE NATURE AND PURPOSE OF THE FOSTER CARE SYSTEM

The early development of the notion of foster care began with the practice of the church boarding abandoned children with worthy widows.[38] Additionally, another early counterpart to the modern foster care system was the historical practice of indenturing

---

> custody of their children is challenged, the State denied Stanley the equal protection of the laws guaranteed by the Fourteenth Amendment.

Id. But see, Lehr v. Robertson, 463 U.S. 248, 263-65 (1983) (denying unwed father right to block stepparent adoption); Quilloin v. Walcott, 434 U.S. 246, 255-56 (1978) (same).

[31] Mason, *supra* note 16, at 15.

[32] 431 U.S. 816 (1977) [hereinafter *Smith v. OFFER*].

[33] *Id.* at 847.

[34] *See infra* notes 38-59 and accompanying text.

[35] *See infra* notes 60-150 and accompanying text.

[36] *See infra* notes 151-178 and accompanying text.

[37] *See infra* notes 179-195 and accompanying text.

[38] ALFRED KADUSHIN, CHILD WELFARE SERVICES 346 (4th ed. 1988).

children as apprentices.[39] Under Elizabethan Poor Laws, children whose parents could no longer afford to keep them could agree to enter apprenticeships with a master lasting until the child turned twenty-one years of age.[40] The parents of indentured children lost all custody rights to their children,[41] but the children received room and board in exchange for their work.[42]

The modern foster care system, founded by Charles Loring Brace in the mid-nineteenth century,[43] developed as a temporary welfare service to provide emotional and economic support for children whose parents were unable to provide such care.[44] Foster care evolved from the notion that children receive better, more nurturing care and independent attention living in a family environment than in an institution like an orphanage.[45] Thus, "[t]he purpose of the foster care system is to provide a child with a stable, non-institutionalized environment when that child's biological parents cannot properly minister to her physical, emotional, and financial needs."[46]

Under the modern approach, states accept children into the foster care system using one of two methods of placement. First, parents who are unable to care for their children may voluntarily place their children in the temporary custody of the state, which agrees to take responsibility for the day-to-day care of the children.[47] The parents normally retain the right to revoke the foster care agreement and, thereby, have their children returned to their custody within a

---

[39] *Id.*; Kristin J. Brandon, Comment, *The Liberty Interests of Foster Parents and the Future of Foster Care*, 63 U. CIN. L. REV. 403, 406 n.13 (1994).

[40] Brandon, *supra* note 39, at 406 n. 13; *see also*, Marsha Garrison, *Parents' Rights vs. Children's Interests: The Case of the Foster Child*, 22 N.Y.U. REV. L. & SOC. CHANGE 371, 374 (1996) (noting that first historical basis for termination of parental rights was poverty).

[41] Garrison, *supra* note 40, at 374.

[42] KADUSHIN, *supra* note 38, at 346.

[43] KADUSHIN, *supra* note 38, at 347-49. Brace developed a system that placed vagrant children living in New York City with families in rural homes. *Id.*

[44] Brandon, *supra* note 39, at 406; *see also* Cristina Chi-Young Chou, *Renewing the Good Intentions of Foster Care: Enforcement of the Adoption Assistance and Child Welfare Act of 1980 and the Substantive Due Process Right to Safety*, 46 VAND. L. REV. 683, 683 (1993) (discussing development of foster care system and purposes of its structure).

[45] Brandon, *supra* note 39, at 407.

[46] Vincent S. Nadile, Note, *Promoting the Integrity of Foster Family Relationships: Needed Statutory Protections for Foster Parents*, 62 NOTRE DAME L. REV. 221, 221 (1987).

[47] Brandon, *supra* note 39, at 406.

designated period of time.[48] Second, involuntary placement occurs when a court removes the child from the custody of his parents after a showing of neglect or abuse.[49] Although parents are not entitled to the return of their child on demand when custody is awarded to the state in a court proceeding,[50] the court does not terminate the rights of parents upon involuntary placement. Only after engaging in further analysis can the court order permanent termination of the rights of natural parents.[51] Overall, most placements in the foster care system originate as voluntary placements.[52]

Foster care is typically viewed as a temporary placement with the goal of achieving parent-child reunification.[53] Although the system contemplates short-term care, with the goal of returning children to the custody of their biological parents, children often spend several years in the care of foster families.[54]

A foster parent is generally recognized "as an adult who is not a relative of the natural parents, and who is granted physical custody of a child, either by the child's natural parents or by a child welfare agency."[55] The foster parent plays only one role, that of primary

---

[48] *See id.* at 407 (stating that although in most situations state must automatically return child to biological parents, courts may grant custody to state through use of state's juvenile laws).

[49] *Id.*

[50] *OFFER*, 431 U.S. 816, 828 (1977) (noting that, following involuntary placement, "termination of foster care must then be consented to by the court").

[51] Brandon, *supra* note 39, at 407.

[52] *OFFER*, 431 U.S. at 824; *see also* Marian F. Dobbs, *Foster Care and Family Law: A Look at* Smith v. OFFER *and the Constitutional Rights of Foster Children and Their Families*, 17 J. FAM. L. 1, 2 n.3 (1979).

[53] Garrison, *supra* note 40, at 375.

[54] *See* Karen P. Wackerman, *The Due Process Rights of Foster Parents*, 50 BROOK. L. REV. 483, 503-04 (1984) (stating that most children in foster care can expect to stay in system for at least two-and-a-half years and that up to 20% of foster children remain in care system for more than ten years); *see also* Nadile, *supra* note 46, at 222 (noting that most foster children remain in system for at least two-and-a-half years). This contradiction between the expressed goals of the foster care system and the realities inherent in the system is another reason to reevaluate judicial treatment of foster parents.

Increasingly, the foster care system is spinning out of control due to factors such as the AIDS epidemic and rising rates of drug abuse and homelessness. *See* Brandon, *supra* note 39, at 408-10 (describing effects of epidemics on foster care and foster parents). Children are left for extended periods of time in foster homes and often find themselves lost in the system of foster care with little chance of returning to their natural parents and little hope of being freed for adoption. *Id.*

[55] Claudio DeBellis & Marta B. Soja, *Gregory K.: Child Standing in Parental Termination Proceedings and the Implications of the Foster Parent - Foster Child Relationship*

caregiver, in the structure of the system, which is primarily based in contract law.[56] Parental functions are divided among social service agencies, foster parents, and natural parents.[57] Foster parents are required to sign a contract detailing their agreement to provide specified services for the child while that child is in their care.[58] The state maintains the right to temporary custody of the child, thereby reserving the right to remove the child at any time.[59]

B. EVOLUTION OF THE JUDICIAL APPROACH TO CHILD CUSTODY MATTERS

In order to understand the modern judicial approach to matters of child custody, it is helpful to briefly trace the development of two forms of constitutional rights: substantive rights and procedural due process rights.[60]

1. The Development of Substantive Due Process Rights of Parents and Children. As the American family began to redefine itself in the nineteenth and twentieth centuries, the Supreme Court responded with increasing recognition of family relationships within the fundamental constitutional protections provided by the Four-

---

on the Best Interests Standard, 8 ST. JOHN'S J. LEGAL COMMENT. 501, 520 (1993).

[56] *See* Matthew R. Asman, Note, *The Rights of a Foster Parent Versus the Biological Parent Who Abandoned the Child: Where Do the Best Interests of the Child Lie?*, 8 CONN. PROB. L.J. 93, 113 (1993) (noting that some courts have found that since foster relationship originates in state law, it is contractual arrangement); *see also OFFER*, 431 U.S. at 826 (stating that, under New York law, foster parents provide care to foster children under contractual arrangement with social service agency).

[57] *See* KADUSHIN, *supra* note 38, at 380 (suggesting that social service agency is responsible for balancing needs of children, foster parents, and natural parents).

[58] *See id.* at 402-03 (stating that foster parents "do not assume parenting responsibility; they *share* it" and suggesting that most foster parents are responsible for child for only limited segment of child's life) (citation omitted).

[59] *Id.*; *see also OFFER*, 431 U.S. at 826 (noting that "typical contract expressly reserves the right of the agency to remove the child on request"). However, under many state statutes the social service agency must provide some form of notice to foster parents before removal can take place.

[60] *See* U.S. CONST. amend. XIV, § 1 (guaranteeing due process rights). The Fourteenth Amendment states, in part, that

> [n]o State shall make or enforce any law which shall abridge the privileges or immunities of citizens of the United States; nor shall any State deprive any person of life, liberty, or property, without due process of law; nor deny to any person within its jurisdiction the equal protection of the laws.

Id.

teenth Amendment.[61] The Court first recognized a substantive due process interest for families in *Meyer v. Nebraska*.[62] In striking down a statute that prohibited the teaching of foreign languages to children who had not passed the eighth grade,[63] the Court held that the right of teachers to instruct their students, as well as the rights of parents to encourage this instruction, fell within the protection of a liberty interest under the Fourteenth Amendment.[64] Although the Supreme Court's decision striking down the statute dealt primarily with the right of a teacher to teach foreign languages to a student, the Court also noted the unreasonable intrusion into the parent-child relationship created by the statute.[65] Thus, in later judicial determinations, the Court has interpreted *Meyer* as protecting the substantive due process right of parents to raise their children as they see fit.[66]

A few years later, in *Pierce v. Society of Sisters*,[67] the United States Supreme Court held that a parent's right to due process was violated where a state law required parents to send their children to public schools.[68] According to the Court, the statute interfered

---

[61] *See, e.g.*, Zablocki v. Redhail, 434 U.S. 374 (1978) (acknowledging constitutionally protected right to marry); Wisconsin v. Yoder, 406 U.S. 205 (1972) (acknowledging fundamental right of parents to control upbringing of their children); Loving v. Virginia, 388 U.S. 1 (1967) (acknowledging right to establish home and raise children); Griswold v. Connecticut, 381 U.S. 479 (1965) (acknowledging right to use contraception); Skinner v. Oklahoma, 316 U.S. 535 (1942) (acknowledging right to procreate).

[62] 262 U.S. 390 (1923).

[63] *See id.* at 396-97. The text of the statute reads as follows:

> Section 1. No person, individually or as a teacher, shall, in any private, denominational, parochial or public school, teach any subject to any person in any language other than the English language.
> Section 2. Languages, other than the English language, may be taught as languages only after a pupil shall have attained and successfully passed the eighth grade as evidenced by a certificate of graduation issued by the county superintendent of the county in which the child resides.

Id.

[64] *Id.* at 400.

[65] *Id.* at 400-03.

[66] *See, e.g.*, Pierce v. Society of Sisters, 268 U.S. 510, 534-35 (1925) (suggesting that doctrine of *Meyer* is that government may not unreasonably interfere with "the liberty of parents and guardians to direct the upbringing and education of children under their control").

[67] *Id.* at 510.

[68] *Id.* at 533-35.

with the right of parents to guide the development of their children.[69]

In cases following *Meyer* and *Pierce*, the Court further defined the scope of the substantive due process rights of families.[70] Although the Supreme Court seems to be moving toward recognizing a liberty interest in the "family," the scope of Constitutional protection has not been extended to nontraditional families.[71] The Supreme Court has held, however, that the Due Process Clause not only protects nuclear families, but also protects a family consisting of a grandmother, her son, and two of her grandchildren who were cousins.[72] In *Moore v. City of East Cleveland*, the Supreme Court invalidated a New York zoning ordinance that would have forced a grandmother to obtain separate housing arrangements for her grandsons.[73] The case was significant because it directly recognized a substantive interest in an extended family relationship.[74]

Children have also been afforded increasing constitutional protection.[75] The United States Supreme Court first extended constitutional rights to children in *In re Gault*.[76] In that case, the Court held that minors, as well as adults, are entitled to due process and fair judicial treatment as provided by the Fourteenth Amend-

---

[69] *Id.* at 535 ("The child is not the mere creature of the State; those who nurture him and direct his destiny have the right, coupled with the high duty, to recognize and prepare him for additional obligations.").

[70] *See infra* notes 71-74 and accompanying text (discussing cases in which Supreme Court further defined due process rights of families).

[71] *See, e.g.*, Michael H. v. Gerald D., 491 U.S. 110 (1989) (holding that because of statutory presumption that any child born into marriage was natural child of those parents there was no fundamental liberty interest between unwed father and his biological daughter when child was born during mother's marriage to another man).

[72] Moore v. City of E. Cleveland, 431 U.S. 494, 504 (1977). This case dealt with the constitutionality of a zoning ordinance that allowed only specific kinds of relatives to live together. *Id.* at 495-96. The ordinance essentially limited the kind of individuals who could live in a household to those in a traditional nuclear family relationship. *Id.* at 502.

[73] *Id.* at 499-500.

[74] Brandon, *supra* note 39, at 412.

[75] *See* Suzette M. Haynie, Note, *Biological Parents v. Third Parties: Whose Right to Child Custody is Constitutionally Protected?*, 20 GA. L. REV. 705 (1986) (arguing that any custody standard giving preference to biological parents is unconstitutional). Haynie observes that "[h]istorically, the law viewed children as property." *Id.* at 706. It was only in the twentieth century that the "courts began to recognize the basic right of children to be free from gross neglect or abuse by their parents." *Id.* at 706-07.

[76] 387 U.S. 1 (1967).

ment and the Bill of Rights.[77] Although the Court did not hold that the due process rights of minors accused of criminal wrongs are coextensive with those of adults, the Court did hold that some constitutional protections should be afforded to minors in the juvenile justice system because due process is a primary foundation for individual freedom.[78] The Supreme Court also recognized a minor's right to privacy in *Bellotti v. Baird*[79] by holding unconstitutional a Massachusetts statute that required minors to obtain parental consent for an abortion but that did not provide for adequate bypass procedures to avoid parental participation in the abortion decision.[80]

2. Judicial Recognition of Procedural Due Process Rights. The Supreme Court has not only recognized substantive due process rights of parents and children, but has also recognized procedural due process rights in familial relationships.[81] For example, in *Stanley v. Illinois*,[82] the United States Supreme Court recognized the due process right of an unwed father to a hearing on his fitness as a parent before the State could take custody of his children in a dependency proceeding.[83] In *Stanley*, after the death of the natural mother of the children, the State of Illinois declared the children

---

[77] *Id.* The *Gault* case involved the rights of a minor who was charged with making obscene phone calls. *Id.* at 4. Adequate notice of the charges was not given to the minor's parents. *Id.* at 31-34. Nor were the parents or minor informed of a right to counsel. *Id.* at 34.

[78] *See id.* at 31-57 (specifically recognizing right of minors and their parents to constitutionally adequate notice of charges against minor, notice of minor's right to counsel, and confrontation of accused minor through sworn testimony by witnesses available for cross-examination in court proceedings).

[79] 443 U.S. 622, 647-48 (1979). The Supreme Court held that state laws requiring pregnant minors to obtain parental consent for abortion must include alternative procedures whereby pregnant minors can obtain authorization for abortion without parental consent through judicial bypass procedures. *Id.* at 643-44.

[80] *Id.* at 643-44. The Supreme Court had already held that states could not lawfully authorize an absolute parental veto over the decision of a minor to obtain an abortion. Planned Parenthood of Cent. Missouri v. Danforth, 428 U.S. 52, 74-75 (1976).

[81] Brandon, *supra* note 39, at 414. The concept of substantive and procedural due process comes from the recognition of a liberty interest protected by the Constitution. "A liberty interest may be defined as the constitutionally protected right of an individual to enjoy those privileges that are essential to proper functioning of a liberal democratic society." Nadile, *supra* note 46, at 232 n.76.

[82] 405 U.S. 645 (1972).

[83] *Id.* at 649.

wards of the state and placed them with court-appointed guardians.[84] At the time, Illinois had in effect a dependency statute that allowed state officials to "circumvent neglect proceedings on the theory that an unwed father is not a 'parent' whose existing relationship with his children must be considered."[85] While recognizing that due process of law does not require a hearing in every case where there is governmental impairment of a private interest, the Court held that the private interest of the father to retain custody of his children was "cognizable and substantial."[86] Additionally, the Court held that the Illinois statute was "inescapably contrary to the Equal Protection Clause"[87] because while the statute provided a hearing on the fitness of married parents, divorced parents, and unmarried mothers before removal of their children from their custody, it denied unwed fathers the same opportunity.[88]

Several years later, a case came before the United States Supreme Court which presented the Court with the opportunity to rule on the question of whether New York statutory and regulatory procedures for removal of foster children from foster homes violated the Due Process and Equal Protection Clauses of the Fourteenth Amendment.[89] Instead of addressing the Due Process arguments, however, the Court ruled that the New York procedures were adequate to protect "whatever liberty interests appellees may have."[90] The Court did recognize that "[f]oster care of children is a sensitive and emotion-laden subject"[91] and that, because many children in foster care often remain in the care of the system for much longer than contemplated, children thereby develop great

---

[84] *Id.* at 646.

[85] *Id.* at 649-50.

[86] *Id.* at 652.

[87] *Id.* at 658.

[88] *Id.*

[89] *Smith v. OFFER*, 431 U.S. 816 (1974). *OFFER* represents the first and only case decided by the Supreme Court regarding the issue of the constitutional rights of foster families. With all of the changes in societal impressions of family relationships that have taken place since *OFFER* was decided, *see supra* notes 17-25 and accompanying text, it would be interesting to discover whether the Supreme Court would now take those changes into account when addressing the rights of foster parents.

[90] *Id.* at 856.

[91] *Id.* at 833.

emotional ties to their foster parents.[92] In recognizing the similarities between foster parents and biological parents, the Court also cautioned that there are several important distinctions between the two sets of parents.[93] First, the relationship between foster family and child has its origins in state law and contract.[94] Second, the Court suggested that tension between the rights of foster parents and natural parents was unavoidable since it was not possible to offer one group procedural protection without derogating the rights of the other group.[95] Although the ruling in *OFFER* did not foreclose the possibility of constitutional rights arising, it is unclear under what circumstances, if any, a due process liberty interest would exist in a foster parent-foster child relationship.[96]

The United States Supreme Court has not granted certiorari on any other case where it would have had the occasion to address the existence of due process rights of foster parents. Despite the continued reluctance of the Supreme Court to rule on the question of liberty interests of foster parents, many lower courts have ruled on the issue.[97] The results of such cases have been mixed. For

---

[92] *Id.* at 835-36. Justice Brennan, writing for the majority, stated:

> No one would seriously dispute that a deeply loving and interdependent relationship between an adult and a child in his or her care may exist even in the absence of blood relationship. At least where a child has been placed in foster care as an infant, has never known his natural parents, and has remained continuously for several years in the care of the same foster parents, it is natural that the foster family should hold the same place in the emotional life of the foster child, and fulfill the same socializing functions, as a natural family. For this reason, we cannot dismiss the foster family as a mere collection of unrelated individuals.

Id. at 844-45.

[93] *Id.* at 845.

[94] *Id.* Justice Brennan stated that "[w]hile the Court has recognized that liberty interests may in some cases arise from positive-law sources . . . particularly where, as here, the claimed interest derives from a knowingly assumed contractual relation with the State, it is appropriate to ascertain from state law the expectations and entitlements of the parties." *Id.* at 845-46.

[95] *Id.* at 846; *see also*, Brandon, *supra* note 39, at 416 ("A liberty interest in the foster family, founded on the principle of a permanent foster family relationship, would inevitably conflict with this absolute right of the natural parents.").

[96] *See OFFER*, 431 U.S. at 847 (stating that "[i]t is unnecessary for us to resolve those questions definitively in this case, however, for like the District Court, we conclude that 'narrower grounds exist to support' our reversal").

[97] *See infra* notes 98-134 and accompanying text (exploring lower court cases discussing liberty interests of foster parents).

example, the United States Court of Appeals for the Fifth Circuit, in *Drummond v. Fulton County Department of Family & Children's Services*,[98] held that a liberty interest did not exist in foster family relationships.[99] *Drummond* involved an attempt by white foster parents to adopt a mixed-race foster child.[100] The agency decision to remove the child from his foster family was based almost entirely on considerations of race.[101] In fact, the court agreed that the agency's consideration of race was proper in that it would "prevent the problems faced by parents unequipped to rear a child of a different race and would encourage adoptions based partially on the child's physical resemblance to the adoptive parents."[102] Additionally, the court emphasized both the contractual nature of foster care and its temporary aims and goals in ruling that no deprivation of Fourteenth Amendment due process rights took place when the foster child was removed from the home of his potential adoptive parents.[103]

The Seventh Circuit agreed with the holding in *Drummond* when the case *Procopio v. Johnson*[104] came before the court. *Procopio* involved a child named Ashley whom the court involuntarily placed in foster care after ruling that Ashley was a neglected and dependent minor.[105] Ashley's foster parents, the Procopios, had taken Ashley into their home because the social service agencies repeatedly assured them that Ashley would almost surely be available for adoption.[106] However, the Department of Children and Family Services developed a plan that included a goal of returning Ashley to her biological parents.[107] Five years later, the juvenile court

---

[98] 563 F.2d 1200 (5th Cir. 1977).
[99] *Id.* at 1206-08.
[100] *Id.* at 1203.
[101] Wackerman, *supra* note 54, at 488 n.27.
[102] *Id.*; *see also Drummond*, 563 F.2d at 1204-07 (recognizing that race was given substantial weight in decision of social service agency to remove foster child and holding that consideration of race was not unconstitutional).
[103] *Drummond*, 563 F.2d at 1207.
[104] 994 F.2d 325 (7th Cir. 1993).
[105] *Id.* at 326-27. Ashley's mother was addicted to heroin and cocaine and had prostituted herself during pregnancy. *Id.*
[106] *Id.* at 327.
[107] *Id.*

returned Ashley to the custody of her biological parents.[108] This suit arose out of the Procopio's allegations of a constitutional violation of their liberty interest in their foster family.[109] The Court of Appeals for the Seventh Circuit affirmed the decision of the District Court holding that the Procopios failed to demonstrate that their long-term foster relationship with Ashley or assurances of adoption by social service agencies created a liberty interest.[110] The Court of Appeals emphasized that since the state expressed a mandate that foster care would serve a temporary purpose, with the goal of returning the child to the custody of his biological parents, the foster parents could not claim that they expected a permanent relationship.[111]

In contrast, several other courts have disagreed with the reasoning in *Drummond* and *Procopio*. In *Brown v. County of San Joaquin*,[112] a California district court recognized a liberty interest of foster parents where biological parental rights had been terminated.[113] The court reasoned that since provision of a stable and permanent home is the primary goal of foster care, once reunification with the child's biological parents is no longer possible, the law should recognize the emotional ties between foster parents and foster children and that the best interests of the foster child may be served by protecting those ties.[114] According to the court, after termination of biological parental rights, foster parents and foster children are permitted by California law to expect an enduring relationship.[115] Further, in recognizing that foster parents are entitled to procedural due process, the court found it artificial to treat a foster parent relationship differently from a biological parent relationship since "the emotional sustenance and enrichment, the very sense of self, derived from an intimate relationship with one's

---

[108] *Id.*
[109] *Id.* at 328.
[110] *Id.* at 333.
[111] *Id.* at 328-30.
[112] 601 F. Supp. 653 (E.D. Cal. 1985).
[113] *Id.* at 664.
[114] *Id.* at 661.
[115] *Id.*

parent or one's child cannot be discounted by the niceties of the relationship's creation."[116]

Additionally, the United States Court of Appeals for the Second Circuit, in *Rivera v. Marcus*,[117] affirmed a Connecticut district court decision that held that a foster mother, the half-sister of two foster children, was deprived of due process when her foster children were removed from her home without proper procedural protections.[118] The Connecticut District Court, however, based its decision on limited grounds.[119] The district court did not hold that foster relationships in general require recognition of due process rights, but that the blood relationship between the foster mother and her foster children brought the foster mother "within the status of a 'parent' under federal constitutional law."[120] The Court of Appeals for the Second Circuit agreed with the district court decision and explained that there was essentially no legal distinction between the claim of Rivera and that of the grandmother in *Moore v. City of East Cleveland*.[121] The court of appeals analogized the two cases, stating that since both cases involved extended family relationships, Rivera and her related foster children likewise had a liberty interest requiring due process protection.[122] The Second Circuit Court of Appeals also recognized that "children surely possess a liberty interest in maintaining, free from arbitrary state interference, the

---

[116] *Id.* at 664. In addition, the court states:

> [T]he foster family relationship is sufficiently similar to other familial relationships held by the Supreme Court to be entitled to constitutional protection. The court reaches this conclusion because the foster parent-foster child relationship has precisely the same form and content as a healthy biological parent-child relationship, and in the face of that reality, the circumstances of its creation are immaterial.

Id. at 665.

[117] 696 F.2d 1016 (2d Cir. 1982).

[118] Rivera v. Marcus, 533 F. Supp. 203, 207 (D. Conn. 1982).

[119] *Id.*

[120] *Id.*; *see also* Wackerman, *supra* note 54, at 490 (stating that blood relationship brought foster mother within status of parent under federal constitutional law).

[121] *Rivera*, 696 F.2d at 1025; *see also* Wackerman, *supra* note 54, at 492 (noting that Second Circuit held that Mrs. Rivera and her stepbrother and stepsister, like Mrs. Moore and her family, have liberty interest requiring due process protection).

[122] *See Rivera*, 696 F.2d at 1024-25 ("[W]e find that Mrs. Rivera possesses an important liberty interest in preserving the integrity and stability of her family. We believe that custodial relatives like Mrs. Rivera are entitled to due process protections when the state decides to remove a dependent relative from the family environment.").

family environment that they have known since birth."[123] Thus, the court acknowledged not only the due process rights of the foster mother under the particular circumstances of the case but also the rights of children to maintain ties to members of their family, including foster parents.

Finally, and most recently, Judge Kimba Wood of the United States District Court for the Southern District of New York took an additional step towards recognizing inherent rights of foster parents when she held that a foster mother, who had cared for her child continuously for four years and had subsequently initiated adoption proceedings, had a constitutionally protected liberty interest in the stability and integrity of the relationship between herself and her foster child.[124] In *Rodriguez*, the foster mother asserted a procedural due process claim that she was deprived of liberty protected by the Due Process Clause when her foster children were removed without notice from her home.[125] The court stated that although "[p]rocedural due process protection embraces the parent-child relationship, whether biological or formalized through adoption," there is still a question "whether due process protection extends to a parent-child relationship that has its origin in state law and contract, but in which emotional and psychological ties hoped for in biological families, as well as an expectation of permanency, have developed."[126] Judge Wood suggests in her opinion that the Supreme Court's discussion of foster family relationships in *Smith v. OFFER*[127] provides some guidance as to what factors should be considered in deciding whether a due process liberty interest exists.[128] The court focused on the discussion in *OFFER* of the

---

[123] *Id.* at 1026.

[124] Rodriguez v. McLoughlin, 49 F. Supp. 2d 186 (S.D.N.Y. 1999).

[125] *Id.* at 194. The foster children, Andrew and Thomas, were removed under "emergency" removal procedures after a child welfare official found the two young boys in the care of Ms. Rodriguez's grandson Edwin, a twelve-year-old special education student. *Id.* at 190-91. The child welfare official determined that Edwin was having a difficult time managing the children and the official wondered about the propriety of the decision to leave the children in Edwin's care. *Id.* at 191. Thus, the official removed the children from the Rodriguez home without any official notice and without providing their foster mother any reason for the removal. *Id.* at 191.

[126] *Id.* at 194.

[127] 431 U.S. 816 (1977).

[128] *Rodriguez*, 49 F. Supp. 2d at 195.

differences between the relationship between foster parents and their foster children and the relationship between biological families and their children.[129] The New York District Court interpreted *OFFER* as recognizing three major distinctions in these relationships:

> First, there is generally no biological relationship between foster parents and foster children . . . . Second, there is a 'virtually unavoidable' tension between the rights of biological parents and those of foster parents . . . . Third, 'whatever emotional ties may develop between foster parent and foster child,' the relationship has its origins, 'in state law and contractual arrangements.'[130]

The district court proceeded to explain why the distinctions between foster parents and natural parents did not come into play in the *Rodriguez* case. For example, the court differentiated the relationship of the foster mother to her foster child Andrew from the type of relationship addressed in *OFFER*, finding two principle distinctions. First, the *Rodriguez* case was distinguishable from the *OFFER* case based on the fact that the rights of Andrew's biological parents were terminated, avoiding any possible conflict with the rights of his foster mother.[131] Secondly, the court differentiated the case through its factual findings that Andrew's foster mother had an expectation of permanency in her relationship with her foster child, evidenced by her pending petition for his adoption.[132] The fact that Andrew's foster mother had entered into an Adoptive Placement Agreement showed, according to the court, that although the foster mother may not have had expectations of permanency at the outset of her relationship with Andrew, she had subsequently developed the intention to make the relationship permanent.[133] Finally, the court also found it significant that Andrew had lived with his foster

---

[129] *Id.*
[130] *Id.* (citations omitted).
[131] *Id.* at 195-96.
[132] *Id.*
[133] *Id.*

mother for the first four years of his life.[134] Thus, the New York District Court recognized a liberty interest where biological parental rights have been terminated, when foster parents have cared continuously for the foster child for more than twelve months since infancy, and when the foster parents have entered into an adoptive placement agreement for their foster child.[135]

C. STANDARDS USED BY THE COURTS IN DECISIONS CONCERNING CHILD CUSTODY

In addition to societal development of goals and expectations for foster care,[136] the judiciary has developed a number of standards upon which to base decisions in custody proceedings. The legal system has reacted to the changing definitions of family by recognizing a variety of interests in decisions concerning the custody and care of children. There are three basic interests that the courts seek to protect through legal standards: (1) the child's interest in being in the care of an adult who will provide the best possible upbringing; (2) the adult's interest in the custody and companionship of the child; and (3) society's interest in the form and function of the family.[137]

The first standard, which reflects all three of these interests, is the parental fitness standard.[138] When courts apply this standard to decide whether parental rights should be terminated, it requires that the child endure serious actual or threatened harm before the state will intervene.[139] The second standard is often called the "best interests of the child" standard.[140] This standard allows courts to give attention solely to the needs and interests of the child when

---

134 *Id.*

135 *Id.* at 199 (noting that "[t]his holding recognizes such a liberty interest in only a discretely identifiable set of foster parents.").

136 *See infra* Parts II.A., B. (discussing nature and purpose of foster care system and evolution of judicial approach to custody by foster parents).

137 Eric G. Anderson, *Children, Parents, and Nonparents: Protected Interests and Legal Standards*, 1998 BYU L. REV. 935, 939.

138 *Id.* at 949-50.

139 *Id.*

140 *Id.* at 950-51. For a detailed summary of criticisms of the best interests standard see Carl E. Schneider, *Discretion, Rules, and Law: Child Custody and the UMDA's Best-Interest Standard*, 89 MICH. L. REV. 2215, 2219-25 (1991).

deciding with whom the child should reside.[141] Finally, some courts recognize an intermediate standard, under which a non-parent must show not only that their relationship with the child is in the child's best interests, but also that "actual detriment" to the child may occur if the non-parent's relationship with the child is not protected.[142] Thus, the intermediate standard is essentially a hybrid of the best interests of the child standard and the parental fitness standard that results from consideration of three basic interests: those of children, adults, and society.[143]

Other commentators have recommended a "psychological parent" standard.[144] A psychological parent is one who fulfills the physical and emotional needs of the child through constant contact and nurturing.[145] Psychological parent-child relationships can occur when a child is temporarily placed in foster care or in the home of a relative or a close friend by a biological parent or while a child is living with potential adoptive parents.[146] One can determine who is a psychological parent by looking at three factors: (1) the continuity of the relationship between the child and adult in terms of proximity and duration; (2) the love of the adult toward the child; and (3) the affection and trust of the child toward the adult.[147] The concept of the psychological parent is based on the idea that children need stable relationships with adults and that disruptions of those relationships can be traumatic to the child, possibly resulting in

---

141 Anderson, *supra* note 137, at 950-51.

142 *Id.* at 952.

143 *Id.* at 952-53.

144 *See, e.g.*, JOSEPH GOLDSTEIN ET AL., BEYOND THE BEST INTERESTS OF THE CHILD 27 (1973) (advocating use of psychological parent standard in child custody cases). For judicial discussion of the psychological parent standard, see *In re* B.G.C., 496 N.W.2d 239, 240-41 (Iowa 1993) (involving dispute between biological parents and potential adoptive parents); Snyder v. Scheerer, 436 S.E.2d 299, 301 (W. Va. 1993) (recognizing that nonparent with whom child resides for long time becomes psychological parent); Doe v. Mitchell, 244 N.W.2d 827, 843 (Mich. 1976) (recognizing that psychological parent-child relationship may be more important than biological parent-child relationship), *overruled by* Bowie v. Arder, 490 N.W.2d 568 (Mich. 1992); *In re* Stell, 783 P.2d 615, 622 (Wash. Ct. App. 1989) (declining to reject psychological parent theory).

145 GOLDSTEIN, *supra* note 144, at 98.

146 *Id.*; Vanessa L. Warzynski, *Termination of Parental Rights: The "Psychological Parent" Standard*, 39 VILL. L. REV. 737, 748 (1994).

147 Warzynski, *supra* note 146, at 767. 767.

permanent psychological harm.[148] Parental rights would thus be terminated only where the biological parent has deprived the child of a loving and caring relationship.[149]

In recent years, courts have increasingly turned to the best interests of the child standard. Courts generally determine a child's "best interests" by evaluating such factors as the preference of the child for a particular custodian; the identity of the current custodian of the child; the opportunity to keep siblings together; the age, sex and health of the child; the child's emotional relationship with the non-custodial third party; the duration of the relationship with the third party seeking custody; the moral fitness of the competing parties; and the comparative environments offered by the parties.[150] Although the best interests standard does not have specifically defined factors and is, thus, naturally vague, courts continue to use the term "best interests" of the child and to apply the standard in the way each individual court or judge sees fit.

---

148 *Id.* at 765-66. Warzynski states:

> A stable, continuous and caring relationship is critical to a child's development. A child separated from his of her psychological parent may suffer separation anxiety, trauma, distress, a profound sense of loss and setbacks in the quality of his or her future emotional attachments . . . . Separations profoundly impact children because they have not yet developed the adult ability to cope with threats to their emotional security. Thus, it is not the biological tie that bonds a child to an adult, but the psychological relationship. The law, therefore, should protect this relationship, regardless of whether or not the psychological parent is also the biological parent.

Id.

149 At least one commentator suggests that using the psychological parent standard in proceedings to terminate biological parental rights would help resolve confusion in the law regarding the applicable standard and would, therefore, avoid the emotional damage that uncertainty causes the child. *See, e.g., id.* at 770-71 (arguing for use of psychological parent standard).

150 Haynie, *supra* note 75, at 707-08 n.9. For an example of a specific state's "best interests" test, see Sharon J. Fleming, *Custody Standards in New Mexico: Between Third Parties and Biological Parents, What is the Trend?*, 27 N.M. L. REV. 547, 557 (1997) (describing statutorily mandated standard in New Mexico).

III. ANALYSIS

A. RECOGNITION OF PROCEDURAL DUE PROCESS RIGHTS OF FOSTER PARENTS WHEN THE STATE HAS TERMINATED THE RIGHTS OF BIOLOGICAL PARENTS

Foster parents who care for children whose biological parents have had their parental rights terminated for reasons such as abandonment, abuse, neglect, or permanent mental illness, should have a recognized liberty interest in maintaining their family structure.[151] Although foster families are not traditional in the historical sense, our society increasingly recognizes families of many different origins and types.[152] Consequently, our legal system should recognize that foster parents who have provided continuous care, love, and financial and emotional support are parents just as biological parents are parents.[153]

The liberty interest of foster parents in maintaining a relationship with their foster children should be interpreted as requiring procedural due process when the state seeks to remove foster children from the homes of their foster parents.[154] First, the

---

[151] *See* Moore v. City of E. Cleveland, 431 U.S. 494, 501 (1977) ("[U]nless we close our eyes to the basic reasons why certain rights associated with the family have been accorded shelter under the Fourteenth Amendment's Due Process Clause, we cannot avoid applying the force and rationale of these precedents to [other areas of] family choice. . . .").

[152] *See supra* text accompanying notes 17-31 (describing decline of traditional nuclear family and subsequent increase in societal and legal recognition of unconventional families).

[153] Smith v. OFFER, 431 U.S. 816, 843 (1977) (recognizing that biological relationships are not exclusive determination of existence of family). In fact, one justice has noted that a biological relationship alone may not be sufficient to create a constitutionally protected family. *Moore*, 431 U.S. at 536-40 (Stewart, J., dissenting).

[154] It is highly unlikely that the Supreme Court will ever recognize a fundamental substantive right of foster parents to their foster children. The identification of substantive rights of foster parents would naturally interfere with the substantive rights of biological parents since such fundamental rights do not disappear based upon the circumstances. Thus, foster parents can not have fundamental substantive rights to their foster children when biological parental rights are terminated but not possess those same substantive rights when biological parents retain parental rights. *But see*, Mendel Shapiro, *Constitutional Protection of Long-Term Foster Families*, 79 COLUM. L. REV. 1191, 1206-1208 (1979) (describing showing necessary for recognition of substantive rights of long-term foster families and concluding that where rights of natural parents are not implicated, long-term foster families are functional equivalent of natural family and should be accorded same substantive constitutional protection).

problems inherent in the recognition of procedural due process rights would not apply when biological parental rights no longer exist.[155] Second, because of the failure of the modern foster care system to achieve temporary care for children followed by reunification with biological parents, it is necessary that courts and legislatures create a more effective system.[156] Reform will help guard both the interests of foster parents and the interests of foster children.[157]

1. Problems Inherent in the Recognition of Due Process Rights of Foster Families to Custody of Their Foster Children Would Not Apply When the State has Terminated the Child's Biological Parents' Rights. One of the most convincing arguments against the recognition of a liberty interest for foster families in maintaining their relationship with their foster children is that such a recognition would inevitably cause a conflict of interest with the rights of biological parents.[158] The argument is that if the court recognized a liberty interest for foster parents, foster parents could potentially use that liberty interest to prevent or delay removal of their foster child from their care, thus interfering with the recognized substantive due process rights of a child's biological parents.[159] This concern, however, is eliminated when the court orders permanent termination of all biological parental rights.[160] Because the

---

[155] *See infra* Part III.A.1. (arguing that conflict between liberty interests of biological parents and liberty interests of foster parents would not occur when state has terminated biological parents' rights).

[156] *See infra* Part III.A.2. (suggesting that failure of modern foster care system dictates judicial recognition of interests of foster parents).

[157] For a discussion of a constitutionally protected interest already acquired by prospective adoptive parents when there is a reasonable expectation of a permanent parent-child relationship, see Thelen v. Catholic Social Servs., 691 F. Supp. 1179, 1185 (E.D. Wis. 1988) (holding that prospective adoptive parents have "a limited, but not wholly insignificant constitutionally protected liberty interest in their family unit during the initial six month period that a child is placed in their home").

[158] *See OFFER*, 431 U.S. at 846 (suggesting that procedural protection for foster parents would derogate from substantive liberty interests of biological parents).

[159] Nadile, *supra* note 46, at 233.

[160] *See supra* notes 89-96 and accompanying text (discussing distinctions between foster parents and biological parents that justify different rights for two groups). Recall that one of the central concerns in recognizing due process rights of foster parents, as expressed by the United States Supreme Court in *OFFER*, was the "inevitable" conflict of those rights with the substantive rights of biological parents. *OFFER*, 431 U.S. at 846. When the conflict between the rights of foster families and biological families was eliminated through termination of biological parental rights, several courts held that foster parents were entitled to procedural

biological parents no longer have any judicially recognized right to raise, or even to maintain custody of their children, there is no longer a conflict with any recognized right of the foster family.[161]

Although some commentators argue that the judiciary is unsuited for the job of creating adequate protections for foster families,[162] they do not deny that foster families are in need of constitutionally protected rights in order to assure that their children are not arbitrarily removed from their custody.[163] A ruling by the United States Supreme Court recognizing the existence of procedural due process rights of foster parents would assure foster families that the state would not remove foster children from their homes without proper protections. Foster families who have sustained relationships with their foster children, when there is no possibility that the children will return to the custody of their biological parents, deserve this assurance. Although state law governs the foster care system,[164] such a ruling by the Supreme Court would provide significant motivation for legislative reform regarding removal procedures for foster children since states would be required to provide the constitutionally necessary protections to foster parents. Further, the Supreme Court could provide guidelines for removal procedures that would meet minimum constitutional standards.[165]

---

due process. *See Brown v. County of San Joaquin*, 601 F. Supp. 663, 664 (1985) (holding that since reunification with biological parents was impossible, foster parents should be granted liberty interest); *Rodriguez v. McLoughlin*, 49 F. Supp. 2d 186, 195 (1999) (ruling that foster families should be accorded due process protection when court has terminated biological parental rights, when foster parents have cared for foster child for extended period of time, and when foster parents have entered into adoptive placement agreement).

[161] *See* Jehnna Irene Hanan, Comment, *The Best Interest of the Child: Eliminating Discrimination in the Screening of Adoptive Parents*, 27 GOLDEN GATE U.L. REV. 167, 182 ("If the biological parents' rights have been terminated, there is no longer a competing interest to protect.").

[162] *See, e.g.*, Nadile, *supra* note 46, at 233 (stating that despite recent focus on judicial solutions, judiciary is unsuited to fashion adequate protections on which foster parents may rely).

[163] *Id.* at 234-35. Nadile suggests that the legislature should be responsible for creating procedures necessary to protect foster parents from "capricious state-imposed removals" of their foster children. *Id.*

[164] *See* Megan M. O'Laughlin, Note, *A Theory of Relativity: Kinship Foster Care May be the Key to the Pendulum of Termination vs. Reunification*, 51 VAND. L. REV. 1427, 1430 (1996) (noting that foster care system is implemented by individual states).

[165] For one example of Supreme Court approval of a constitutionally adequate removal procedure, see Smith v. OFFER, 431 U.S. 816, 820 n.30 (1977) (holding that New York

Several commentators have suggested that New York State statutory procedures could serve as an adequate basic model for removal of children from foster homes.[166]

2. Concern Over the Tension Between Liberty Interests of Foster Parents and the Nature of Foster Care. Although upon cursory examination it seems that recognition of procedural due process rights of foster parents conflicts with the goals of the foster care system, that conflict has not materialized due to the changing nature of the foster care system.[167] Each year, a greater number of children remain in foster care for an extended or indefinite period of time.[168] Thus, instead of arguing that the purpose of foster care is only to provide temporary care,[169] society and the judicial system should recognize that foster care actually serves as more than a resource for temporary care. In particular, courts should recognize that foster care may be the only avenue that some children have to find a permanent and stable home.[170] Additionally, when dealing with a situation in which the return of a foster child to the home of his or her biological parents is impossible because the biological parents no longer possess parental rights, another solution is needed to find the child a stable, loving home.[171] If ultimate

---

removal procedure is constitutionally adequate to protect whatever liberty interest foster parents possess). The New York Social Service Laws provide that (1) foster families will receive written notice of removal; (2) the agency will conduct a conference, if requested, between foster parents and the agency, to which foster parents may bring counsel; (3) the agency will make a decision about removal within five days of the conference; (4) the agency will stay removal of the child until a decision is rendered; and (5) the agency will conduct a full adversarial hearing for the foster parents if the agency recommends removal. Nadile, *supra* note 46, at 235; *see also* N.Y. SOC. SERV. LAW §§ 383(2), 400 (McKinney 1983) (reciting text of statute).

166 Nadile, *supra* note 46, at 235. *See also* Wackerman, *supra* note 54, at 514 (stating that New York's statutory framework should serve as constitutionally acceptable model).

167 *See* discussion *supra* Part II.A. (describing failure of modern foster care system to meet its goal of temporary care and reunification with biological parents).

168 *See* O'Laughlin, *supra* note 164, at 1432-33 (suggesting that of more than half-a-million children currently in foster care system, most spend an average of three years in system while one in ten children spend more than seven years in foster care).

169 *See OFFER*, 431 U.S. at 846 (arguing that purpose of foster care is to provide temporary care).

170 *Cf.* O'Laughlin, *supra* note 164, at 1433 (finding that children often wait from three-and-a-half to five-and-a-half years to find a placement for adoption).

171 *See, e.g.*, Hanan, *supra* note 161, at 182 ("When foster parents seek to adopt a child who has been in their care for a long time, the foster care arrangement, while intended to be temporary, has, in reality, become indefinite.").

permanence of home life is a goal of the foster care system,[172] it would actually be in furtherance of that goal to afford due process rights to foster parents when biological parental rights would not interfere.[173] Foster parents would then be able to assert rights to foster children, giving those parents the opportunity to present evidence that their home is a stable and loving environment for the foster child.[174]

Although the foster family is created pursuant to state contractual laws, the strong bonds that form between foster parents and their foster children should not be ignored simply because of the origin of those bonds.[175] When biological parental rights are terminated, the original contractual arrangement among the social service agency, the foster parents, and the biological parents is discontinued.[176] Only a relationship between the state and the foster parents remains, with neither party holding constitutionally protected rights to the foster child. Thus, it is impractical to deny foster parents a liberty interest because their right to provide care for their foster children began as a contract right. When the child is freed from the domain of parental decisionmaking, the interests of the child and of the foster parents are furthered by recognizing

---

[172] *See* Susan L. Brooks, *A Family Systems Paradigm for Legal Decision Making Affecting Child Custody*, 6 CORNELL J.L. & PUB. POL'Y 1, 17 (1996) (describing notion of permanency, widely supported by policy makers, as concept of placing every child in permanent home whether that be with biological or adoptive parents); *see also* ANTHONY N. MALUCCIO ET AL., PERMANENCY PLANNING FOR CHILDREN: CONCEPTS AND METHODS 3-90 (1986) (exploring theoretical and practice framework of permanency planning).

[173] For one criticism of the current focus of the courts when making custody determinations, see Nicole L. Sault, *Many Mothers, Many Fathers: The Meaning of Parenting Around the World*, 36 SANTA CLARA L. REV. 395, 406 (1996), *quoted in* Young, *supra* note 20, at 555 n.316 (" '[M]any of the problems that people face in the United States today are the consequences of cultural definitions of family that ignore the traditional kinship functions of sharing, cooperation, nurturing and mutual support, while asserting the values of biology, independence and control.' ").

[174] *See id.* at 555 ("[T]he 'channeling function' of law could be deployed to encourage and support the creation and maintenance of more connections with those who may have special interests. . . . [S]ocial policy should be contemplating ways of encouraging more people to feel greater levels of responsibility for more children.").

[175] Asman, *supra* note 56, at 113.

[176] *See* discussion *supra* Part II.A. (describing interplay between biological parental rights, foster parent contractual rights, and state custodial powers). There is no longer a balance of interests and responsibilities among the three groups of participants in the foster care system.

that a new agreement concerning the rights and responsibilities of the parties is necessary.

In addition, there is another concern expressed by the courts about recognizing a liberty interest in foster parents. Some commentators have expressed a fear that there will be a drop in the number of voluntary placements of children in the foster care system if there is judicial recognition of a liberty interest in foster parents.[177] Although parental reluctance to use foster care is an important issue to consider, recognition of procedural due process rights of foster parents *after* court-ordered termination of biological parental rights should not affect the frequency of voluntary placements. Additionally, the state could make clear to biological parents who are concerned about the possibility of foster-parent intervention that biological parental rights are normally extinguished only after a showing of parental unfitness or in cases where a child's safety is jeopardized by a parent. Because of the strong desire of the state to avoid arbitrary interference in the private lives of families,[178] the termination of parental rights does not usually occur when a parent is forced to resort to the use of the foster care system because of financial problems or a temporary inability to properly provide for the physical needs of their children. Thus, biological parents will not be deterred from voluntarily placing their children in foster care if they know that the foster parents will be able to assert a limited liberty interest in their children only after their rights are terminated.

B. THE APPROPRIATE STANDARD FOR MAKING CUSTODY DECISIONS

The primary difference among the standards used by courts to decide in whose custody to place a child is the weight given to the competing interests of parents, children, and society.[179] Although the legal system should recognize the right of foster parents to a liberty interest in their children following the termination of the

---

[177] *See* Brandon, *supra* note 39, at 425-26 (noting that recognition of liberty interest may discourage use of foster care system by biological parents who might otherwise take advantage of the service).

[178] U.S. CONST. amend. XIV, § 1 (guaranteeing right to privacy in family life).

[179] *See* discussion *supra* Part II.B. (tracing judicial approach to child custody matters).

parental rights of the child's biological family, any subsequent battle over the custody of the child should be decided by a revised "best interests" standard.[180] By attempting to provide only for a child's welfare, courts can better maintain stability in a child's life and simultaneously provide an environment in which the child can thrive. The courts should strongly consider evidence of a long-term relationship between foster parents and their children when making custody determinations. Additionally, judges should consider evidence of a child's adjustment to the environment of the foster home as well as evidence of the child's current ability to thrive in that environment based on a psychological assessment.

There are a number of reasons that the "best interests" standard needs to be reevaluated or revised. First, most state statutes now "employ generic language merely directing courts to consider the best interests of the child," and thereby leave "courts and parties with little direction."[181] The vagueness of the standard means that no two courts actually apply exactly the same factors in deciding child custody issues, causing inconsistency and uncertainty in the law.[182] In fact, although statutory provisions may provide for a best interests standard, many courts actually employ a balancing test between parental rights and a child's best interests.[183] Secondly, because the standard for custody determination is so undefined, judges often apply their personal and intuitive feelings to determine the best interests of the child.[184] This can result in unexpected rulings tainted with the personal biases of a judge.[185]

---

[180] For one example of a typical "best interests" test, see N.M. STAT. ANN. § 40-4-9(A) (Michie 1994) (mandating that courts consider (1) wishes of child's parent or parents as to his custody; (2) wishes of child; (3) interaction and interrelationship of child with his parents, siblings, and any other person who may significantly affect child's best interest; (4) child's adjustment to his home, school, and community; (5) mental and physical health of all individuals involved; and (6) potential negative effect that custody change may have on child).

[181] Elizabeth P. Miller, Note, DeBoer v. Schmidt *and* Twigg v. Mays*: Does the "Best Interests of the Child" Standard Protect the Best Interests of Children?*, 20 J. CONTEMP. L. 497, 509 (1994).

[182] Warzynski, *supra* note 146, at 752.

[183] *Id.*

[184] Miller, *supra* note 181, at 509.

[185] *See* John Dewitt Gregory, *Blood Ties: A Rationale for Child Visitation by Legal Strangers*, 55 WASH. & LEE L. REV. 351, 387 (1998). Gregory states:

> [The] best interests standard is both vague and indeterminate and gives precious little guidance to judicial decision makers. It provides to judges

Because of the problems inherent in the current state standards, states should adopt a uniform "best interests" standard applicable in custody decisions between foster parents and third parties after biological parents are removed from consideration for custody.[186] In particular, in applying the uniform best interests standard, courts should place significant weight on the importance of the psychological parent and the theory of attachment that supports that idea.[187] Because the focus of the best interests standard is on the child, psychology should play a key role in custody determinations.[188] The theory of attachment can play a crucial role in anticipating the psychological results of removing a child from his current environment or changing his custodial environment. Attachment theory focuses on a behavioral and emotional bond that results from the proximity of the child to one certain individual, normally the child's primary caregiver.[189] An attachment in a child's infancy allows a child to find a "secure base" in her caregiver from which she

---

> the invitation, which they frequently accept with alacrity, to engage in virtually untrammeled exercises of discretion in deciding issues of child custody and visitation. It serves poorly the interests of children in custody or visitation cases, speaking rather to the interests of contending adults. The standard lacks any settled meaning and is more a rubric than an analytical tool for deciding child custody and visitation cases. It has meant different things at different points in time.

Id.; *see also* Janet W. Weinstein, *And Never the Twain Shall Meet: The Best Interests of Children and the Adversary System*, 52 U. MIAMI L. REV. 79, 109 (1997) (noting that personal biases of judge may be deciding factor in best interests determinations).

[186] *See* Miller, *supra* note 181, at 514 (suggesting that uniform standard will also help resolve child custody issues in more expeditious manner). A faster determination may help to avoid the emotional trauma inflicted upon children such as "Baby Jessica" whose ordeal lasted for two-and-a-half-years. *Id.* at 515-16.

[187] For a discussion of attachment theory, see MARY D. SALTER AINSWORTH ET AL., PATTERNS OF ATTACHMENT: A PSYCHOLOGICAL STUDY OF THE STRANGE SITUATION 3-28, 302-04 (1978) (providing theoretical background of attachment theory and distinguishing attachment as an affectional band or tie between infant and mother figure from attachment behaviors through which such bond first forms and is maintained, mediated, and further developed).

[188] Some commentators have even suggested that judges should be trained specifically to preside over custody matters, thereby allowing judges with knowledge and experience in matters of child custody to review information provided by the child, the foster family, the third party, and psychologists or social workers. *See, e.g.*, John J. Musewicz, *The Failure of Foster Care: Federal Statutory Reform and the Child's Right to Permanence*, 54 S. CAL. L. REV. 633, 649-650 (arguing that judges' lack of training and expertise in child placement decisions, where jurisprudence, philosophy, psychology and culture merge, is intolerable given judges' power to alter family relationships).

[189] AINSWORTH, *supra* note 187, at 302.

explores the world around her.[190] A child develops social skills and investigates her surroundings, returning to the attachment figure in times of fear.[191] Thus, the existence of an attachment provides a basis for self-reliance, competence, and a capacity to form relationships.[192]

In the context of child custody cases, attachment theory illustrates the importance of maintaining a familiar and consistent environment for children, particularly for very young children. Attachment theory also illustrates the scope of psychological damage that can occur if there is a disruption in the attachment relationship.[193]

Attachment theory provides the basis for the psychological parent standard, which suggests that the law should protect the psychological relationship that has formed between a parent and a child, regardless of biology.[194] That standard advocates the evaluation of three factors: (1) the continuity of the relationship between the child and the adult caregiver in terms of duration and proximity; (2) the love of the adult towards the child; and (3) the affection and trust of the child towards the adult.[195] Based on the psychological parent standard, no other inquiry is necessary. If a psychological parent exists, custody is automatically awarded to that parent under this standard. Because the psychological parent standard is fairly speculative and subjective, it should not be the sole measure to evaluate options for custody. Instead, courts can use the psychological parent standard to create a rebuttable presumption that the foster family should receive custody over third parties, whether those parties are adoptive families or blood relatives of the child. If a member of the foster family is determined to be the

---

190 *See generally*, JOHN BOWLBY, A SECURE BASE: PARENT-CHILD ATTACHMENT AND HEALTHY HUMAN DEVELOPMENT 1-38, 119-36 (1988) (discussing origins and meaning of attachment theory and exploring role of attachment in personality development).

191 *Id.*

192 James G. O'Keefe, Note, *The Need to Consider Children's Rights in Biological Parent v. Third Party Custody Disputes*, 67 CHI. KENT L. REV. 1077, 1101 (1991).

193 *See id.* at 1102 (suggesting that separation or loss in early childhood of attached caregiver can result in conduct problems, cognitive disturbances, depression, suicide risk, and increased risk of psychiatric disturbance).

194 Warzynski, *supra* note 146, at 766.

195 *Id.*

psychological parent to the foster child, the court must then determine whether the presumption for custody of the child could be rebutted by considering factors typically examined in a best interests of the child analysis. If those factors are established to be at least equal to those of the third party seeking custody, the foster parents should be awarded custody. As the standard is currently applied, judges sometimes prefer biological relatives of the child, even though they may be strangers, over foster parents who have provided extended care for the child. Although biology is an important consideration, the more important question is where the child will thrive. Judges should not be allowed to speculate that children are better off living with blood relatives. The new standard would allow judges to avoid preferences of biological relatives in child custody determinations and would provide additional protection for foster families without requiring judicial recognition of substantive due process rights.

IV. CONCLUSION

In light of the evolution of the American family in the twentieth century, the judiciary should respond by broadening its recognition of non-traditional families. In particular, foster families are in desperate need of fundamental constitutional protections that could save those families from arbitrary governmental interference in their private lives. The failure of the modern foster care system to serve its original goals of reunification with biological parents, as well as the plight of foster children trapped in that system, require that society and the judicial system take steps to remedy the condition of parentless children by allowing loving foster parents the ability to keep those children in their homes. Recognizing foster parents' fundamental liberty interest in their foster children after the child's biological parents no longer have rights to the child would increase the possibility that foster children could find permanent homes. Additionally, the use of a revised best interests standard, in which the existence of a psychological parent in the foster family creates a rebuttable presumption favoring custody by the foster family, helps to protect the interests of foster families while allowing analysis to remain focused on a child's best interests.

It is the duty of the judiciary to respond to a changing society. If courts do not reevaluate both the rights of foster parents in light of modern society and the standards used in custody determinations, the foster care system will, year after year, continue to fail more foster children and foster parents.

CASSANDRA S. HAURY

PALMORE v. SIDOTI

CERTIORARI TO THE DISTRICT COURT OF APPEAL OF FLORIDA, SECOND DISTRICT

No. 82–1734. Argued February 22, 1984—Decided April 25, 1984

When petitioner and respondent, both Caucasians, were divorced in Florida, petitioner, the mother, was awarded custody of their 3-year-old daughter. The following year respondent sought custody of the child by filing a petition to modify the prior judgment because of changed conditions, namely, that petitioner was then cohabiting with a Negro, whom she later married. The Florida trial court awarded custody to respondent, concluding that the child's best interests would be served thereby. Without focusing directly on the parental qualifications of petitioner, her present husband, or respondent, the court reasoned that although respondent's resentment at petitioner's choice of a black partner was insufficient to deprive petitioner of custody, there would be a damaging impact on the child if she remained in a racially mixed household. The Florida District Court of Appeal affirmed.

Held: The effects of racial prejudice, however real, cannot justify a racial classification removing an infant child from the custody of its natural mother. The Constitution cannot control such prejudice, but neither can it tolerate it. Private biases may be outside the reach of the law, but the law cannot, directly or indirectly, give them effect. Pp. 431–434.

426 So. 2d 34, reversed.

BURGER, C. J., delivered the opinion for a unanimous Court.

Robert J. Shapiro argued the cause and filed a brief for petitioner.

John E. Hawtrey argued the cause and filed a brief for respondent.*

---

*Briefs of *amici curiae* urging reversal were filed for the United States by *Solicitor General Lee, Assistant Attorney General Reynolds, Deputy Solicitor General Wallace, Deputy Assistant Attorney General Cooper, Kathryn A. Oberly*, and *Brian K. Landsberg;* for the American Civil Liberties Union Foundation et al. by *Burt Neuborne, William D. Zabel, Marcia Robinson Lowry, Thomas I. Atkins, Ira G. Greenberg*, and *Samuel Rabinove;* for Leigh Earls et al. by *Jay L. Carlson, James P. Tuite, Roderic V. O. Boggs, James D. Weill, Justin J. Finger, Jeffrey*

CHIEF JUSTICE BURGER delivered the opinion of the Court.

We granted certiorari to review a judgment of a state court divesting a natural mother of the custody of her infant child because of her remarriage to a person of a different race.

I

When petitioner Linda Sidoti Palmore and respondent Anthony J. Sidoti, both Caucasians, were divorced in May 1980 in Florida, the mother was awarded custody of their 3-year-old daughter.

In September 1981 the father sought custody of the child by filing a petition to modify the prior judgment because of changed conditions. The change was that the child's mother was then cohabiting with a Negro, Clarence Palmore, Jr., whom she married two months later. Additionally, the father made several allegations of instances in which the mother had not properly cared for the child.

After hearing testimony from both parties and considering a court counselor's investigative report, the court noted that the father had made allegations about the child's care, but the court made no findings with respect to these allegations. On the contrary, the court made a finding that "there is no issue as to either party's devotion to the child, adequacy of housing facilities, or respectability of the new spouse of either parent." App. to Pet. for Cert. 24.

The court then addressed the recommendations of the court counselor, who had made an earlier report "in [another] case coming out of this circuit also involving the social consequences of an interracial marriage. *Niles v. Niles*, 299 So. 2d 162." *Id.*, at 25. From this vague reference to that earlier case, the court turned to the present case and noted the counselor's recommendation for a change in custody because

---

P. Sinensky, *Leslie K. Shedlin*, and *Marc D. Stern;* and for the Women's Legal Defense Fund et al. by *Sally Katzen*, *Lynn Bregman*, and *Nancy Polikoff*.

"[t]he wife [petitioner] has chosen for herself and for her child, a life-style unacceptable to the father *and to society*. . . . The child . . . is, or at school age will be, subject to environmental pressures not of choice." Record 84 (emphasis added).

The court then concluded that the best interests of the child would be served by awarding custody to the father. The court's rationale is contained in the following:

> "The father's evident resentment of the mother's choice of a black partner is not sufficient to wrest custody from the mother. It is of some significance, however, that the mother did see fit to bring a man into her home and carry on a sexual relationship with him without being married to him. Such action tended to place gratification of her own desires ahead of her concern for the child's future welfare. *This Court feels that despite the strides that have been made in bettering relations between the races in this country, it is inevitable that Melanie will, if allowed to remain in her present situation and attains school age and thus more vulnerable to peer pressures, suffer from the social stigmatization that is sure to come.*" App. to Pet. for Cert. 26–27 (emphasis added).

The Second District Court of Appeal affirmed without opinion, 426 So. 2d 34 (1982), thus denying the Florida Supreme Court jurisdiction to review the case. See Fla. Const., Art. V, § 3(b)(3); *Jenkins* v. *State*, 385 So. 2d 1356 (Fla. 1980). We granted certiorari, 464 U. S. 913 (1983), and we reverse.

II

The judgment of a state court determining or reviewing a child custody decision is not ordinarily a likely candidate for review by this Court. However, the court's opinion, after stating that the "father's evident resentment of the mother's choice of a black partner is not sufficient" to deprive her of custody, then turns to what it regarded as the damaging impact on the child from remaining in a racially mixed household. App. to Pet. for Cert. 26. This raises important federal concerns arising from the Constitution's commitment to eradicating discrimination based on race.

The Florida court did not focus directly on the parental qualifications of the natural mother or her present husband, or indeed on the father's qualifications to have custody of the child. The court found that "there is no issue as to either party's devotion to the child, adequacy of housing facilities, or respectability of the new spouse of either parent." *Id.*, at 24. This, taken with the absence of any negative finding as to the quality of the care provided by the mother, constitutes a rejection of any claim of petitioner's unfitness to continue the custody of her child.

The court correctly stated that the child's welfare was the controlling factor. But that court was entirely candid and made no effort to place its holding on any ground other than race. Taking the court's findings and rationale at face value, it is clear that the outcome would have been different had petitioner married a Caucasian male of similar respectability.

A core purpose of the Fourteenth Amendment was to do away with all governmentally imposed[1] discrimination based on race. See *Strauder* v. *West Virginia*, 100 U. S. 303, 307–308, 310 (1880). Classifying persons according to their race is more likely to reflect racial prejudice than legitimate public concerns; the race, not the person, dictates the category. See *Personnel Administrator of Mass.* v. *Feeney*, 442 U. S. 256, 272 (1979). Such classifications are subject to the most exacting scrutiny; to pass constitutional muster, they must be justified by a compelling governmental interest and must be "necessary . . . to the accomplishment" of their

[1] The actions of state courts and judicial officers in their official capacity have long been held to be state action governed by the Fourteenth Amendment. *Shelley* v. *Kraemer*, 334 U. S. 1 (1948); *Ex parte Virginia*, 100 U. S. 339, 346–347 (1880).

legitimate purpose, *McLaughlin* v. *Florida*, 379 U. S. 184, 196 (1964). See *Loving* v. *Virginia*, 388 U. S. 1, 11 (1967).

The State, of course, has a duty of the highest order to protect the interests of minor children, particularly those of tender years. In common with most states, Florida law mandates that custody determinations be made in the best interests of the children involved. Fla. Stat. § 61.13(2)(b)(1) (1983). The goal of granting custody based on the best interests of the child is indisputably a substantial governmental interest for purposes of the Equal Protection Clause.

It would ignore reality to suggest that racial and ethnic prejudices do not exist or that all manifestations of those prejudices have been eliminated. There is a risk that a child living with a stepparent of a different race may be subject to a variety of pressures and stresses not present if the child were living with parents of the same racial or ethnic origin.

The question, however, is whether the reality of private biases and the possible injury they might inflict are permissible considerations for removal of an infant child from the custody of its natural mother. We have little difficulty concluding that they are not.[2] The Constitution cannot control such prejudices but neither can it tolerate them. Private biases may be outside the reach of the law, but the law cannot, directly or indirectly, give them effect. "Public officials sworn to uphold the Constitution may not avoid a constitutional duty by bowing to the hypothetical effects of private racial prejudice that they assume to be both widely and deeply held." *Palmer* v. *Thompson*, 403 U. S. 217, 260–261 (1971) (WHITE, J., dissenting).

This is by no means the first time that acknowledged racial prejudice has been invoked to justify racial classifications. In *Buchanan* v. *Warley*, 245 U. S. 60 (1917), for example,

[2] In light of our holding based on the Equal Protection Clause, we need not reach or resolve petitioner's claim based on the Fourteenth Amendment's Due Process Clause.

this Court invalidated a Kentucky law forbidding Negroes to buy homes in white neighborhoods.

> "It is urged that this proposed segregation will promote the public peace by preventing race conflicts. Desirable as this is, and important as is the preservation of the public peace, this aim cannot be accomplished by laws or ordinances which deny rights created or protected by the Federal Constitution." *Id.*, at 81.

Whatever problems racially mixed households may pose for children in 1984 can no more support a denial of constitutional rights than could the stresses that residential integration was thought to entail in 1917. The effects of racial prejudice, however real, cannot justify a racial classification removing an infant child from the custody of its natural mother found to be an appropriate person to have such custody.[3]

The judgment of the District Court of Appeal is reversed.

It is so ordered.

---

[3] This conclusion finds support in other cases as well. For instance, in *Watson* v. *Memphis*, 373 U. S. 526 (1963), city officials claimed that desegregation of city parks had to proceed slowly to "prevent interracial disturbances, violence, riots, and community confusion and turmoil." *Id.*, at 535. The Court found such predictions no more than "personal speculations or vague disquietudes," *id.*, at 536, and held that "constitutional rights may not be denied simply because of hostility to their assertion or exercise," *id.*, at 535. In *Wright* v. *Georgia*, 373 U. S. 284 (1963), the Court reversed a Negro defendant's breach-of-peace conviction, holding that "the possibility of disorder by others cannot justify exclusion of persons from a place if they otherwise have a constitutional right (founded upon the Equal Protection Clause) to be present." *Id.*, at 293.

SANTOSKY ET AL. *v.* KRAMER, COMMISSIONER, ULSTER COUNTY DEPARTMENT OF SOCIAL SERVICES, ET AL.

CERTIORARI TO THE APPELLATE DIVISION, SUPREME COURT OF NEW YORK, THIRD JUDICIAL DEPARTMENT

No. 80-5889. Argued November 10, 1981—Decided March 24, 1982

Under New York law, the State may terminate, over parental objection, the rights of parents in their natural child upon a finding that the child is "permanently neglected." The New York Family Court Act (§ 622) requires that only a "fair preponderance of the evidence" support that finding. Neglect proceedings were brought in Family Court to terminate petitioners' rights as natural parents in their three children. Rejecting petitioners' challenge to the constitutionality of § 622's "fair preponderance of the evidence" standard, the Family Court weighed the evidence under that standard and found permanent neglect. After a subsequent dispositional hearing, the Family Court ruled that the best interests of the children required permanent termination of petitioners' custody. The Appellate Division of the New York Supreme Court affirmed, and the New York Court of Appeals dismissed petitioners' appeal to that court.

Held:

1. Process is constitutionally due a natural parent at a state-initiated parental rights termination proceeding. Pp. 752–757.

(a) The fundamental liberty interest of natural parents in the care, custody, and management of their child is protected by the Fourteenth Amendment, and does not evaporate simply because they have not been model parents or have lost temporary custody of their child to the State. A parental rights termination proceeding interferes with that fundamental liberty interest. When the State moves to destroy weakened familial bonds, it must provide the parents with fundamentally fair procedures. Pp. 752–754.

(b) The nature of the process due in parental rights termination proceedings turns on a balancing of three factors: the private interests affected by the proceedings; the risk of error created by the State's chosen procedure; and the countervailing governmental interest supporting use of the challenged procedure. *Mathews* v. *Eldridge*, 424 U. S. 319, 335. In any given proceeding, the minimum standard of proof tolerated by the due process requirement reflects not only the weight of the public and private interests affected, but also a societal judgment about how the risk of error should be distributed between the litigants. The minimum standard is a question of federal law which this Court may resolve. Retrospective case-by-case review cannot preserve fundamental fairness when a class of proceedings is governed by a constitutionally defective evidentiary standard. Pp. 754–757.

2. The "fair preponderance of the evidence" standard prescribed by § 622 violates the Due Process Clause of the Fourteenth Amendment. Pp. 758–768.

(a) The balance of private interests affected weighs heavily against use of such a standard in parental rights termination proceedings, since the private interest affected is commanding and the threatened loss is permanent. Once affirmed on appeal, a New York decision terminating parental rights is *final* and irrevocable. Pp. 758–761.

(b) A preponderance standard does not fairly allocate the risk of an erroneous factfinding between the State and the natural parents. In parental rights termination proceedings, which bear many of the indicia of a criminal trial, numerous factors combine to magnify the risk of erroneous factfinding. Coupled with the preponderance standard, these factors create a significant prospect of erroneous termination of parental rights. A standard of proof that allocates the risk of error nearly equally between an erroneous failure to terminate, which leaves the child in an uneasy status quo, and an erroneous termination, which unnecessarily destroys the natural family, does not reflect properly the relative severity of these two outcomes. Pp. 761–766.

(c) A standard of proof more strict than preponderance of the evidence is consistent with the two state interests at stake in parental rights termination proceedings—a *parens patriae* interest in preserving and promoting the child's welfare and a fiscal and administrative interest in reducing the cost and burden of such proceedings. Pp. 766–768.

3. Before a State may sever completely and irrevocably the rights of parents in their natural child, due process requires that the State support its allegations by at least clear and convincing evidence. A "clear and convincing evidence" standard adequately conveys to the factfinder the level of subjective certainty about his factual conclusions necessary to satisfy due process. Determination of the precise burden equal to or greater than that standard is a matter of state law properly left to state legislatures and state courts. Pp. 768–770.

75 App. Div. 2d 910, 427 N. Y. S. 2d 319, vacated and remanded.

BLACKMUN, J., delivered the opinion of the Court, in which BRENNAN, MARSHALL, POWELL, and STEVENS, JJ., joined. REHNQUIST, J., filed a dissenting opinion, in which BURGER, C. J., and WHITE and O'CONNOR, JJ., joined, *post*, p. 770.

Martin Guggenheim argued the cause for petitioners. With him on the briefs was *Alan N. Sussman*.

Steven Domenic Scavuzzo argued the cause *pro hac vice* for respondents. With him on the brief was *H. Randall Bixler*. *Wilfrid E. Marrin* and *Frederick J. Magovern* filed a brief for respondents Balogh et al.*

JUSTICE BLACKMUN delivered the opinion of the Court.

Under New York law, the State may terminate, over parental objection, the rights of parents in their natural child upon a finding that the child is "permanently neglected." N.Y. Soc. Serv. Law §§ 384–b.4.(d), 384–b.7.(a) (McKinney Supp. 1981–1982) (Soc. Serv. Law). The New York Family Court Act § 622 (McKinney 1975 and Supp. 1981–1982) (Fam. Ct. Act) requires that only a "fair preponderance of the evidence" support that finding. Thus, in New York, the factual certainty required to extinguish the parent-child relationship is no greater than that necessary to award money damages in an ordinary civil action.

Today we hold that the Due Process Clause of the Fourteenth Amendment demands more than this. Before a State may sever completely and irrevocably the rights of parents in

---

*Briefs of *amici curiae* urging reversal were filed by *Marcia Robinson Lowry*, *Steven R. Shapiro*, and *Margaret Hayman* for the American Civil Liberties Union Children's Rights Project et al.; and by *Louise Gruner Gans*, *Catherine P. Mitchell*, *Norman Siegel*, *Gary Connor*, and *Daniel Greenberg* for Community Action for Legal Services, Inc., et al.

Briefs of *amici curiae* urging affirmance were filed by *Robert Abrams*, Attorney General, *Shirley Adelson Siegel*, Solicitor General, and *Lawrence J. Logan* and *Robert J. Schack*, Assistant Attorneys General, for the State of New York; and by *Dave Frohnmayer*, Attorney General, *William F. Gary*, Solicitor General, and *Jan Peter Londahl*, Assistant Attorney General, for the State of Oregon.

their natural child, due process requires that the State support its allegations by at least clear and convincing evidence.

I

A

New York authorizes its officials to remove a child temporarily from his or her home if the child appears "neglected," within the meaning of Art. 10 of the Family Court Act. See §§ 1012(f), 1021–1029. Once removed, a child under the age of 18 customarily is placed "in the care of an authorized agency," Soc. Serv. Law § 384–b.7.(a), usually a state institution or a foster home. At that point, "the state's first obligation is to help the family with services to . . . reunite it . . . ." § 384–b.1.(a)(iii). But if convinced that "positive, nurturing parent-child relationships no longer exist," § 384–b.1.(b), the State may initiate "permanent neglect" proceedings to free the child for adoption.

The State bifurcates its permanent neglect proceeding into "fact-finding" and "dispositional" hearings. Fam. Ct. Act §§ 622, 623. At the factfinding stage, the State must prove that the child has been "permanently neglected," as defined by Fam. Ct. Act §§ 614.1.(a)–(d) and Soc. Serv. Law § 384–b.7.(a). See Fam. Ct. Act § 622. The Family Court judge then determines at a subsequent dispositional hearing what placement would serve the child's best interests. §§ 623, 631.

At the factfinding hearing, the State must establish, among other things, that for more than a year after the child entered state custody, the agency "made diligent efforts to encourage and strengthen the parental relationship." Fam. Ct. Act §§ 614.1.(c), 611. The State must further prove that during that same period, the child's natural parents failed "substantially and continuously or repeatedly to maintain contact with or plan for the future of the child although physically and financially able to do so." § 614.1.(d). Should the State support its allegations by "a fair preponderance of the evidence," § 622, the child may be declared permanently neglected. § 611. That declaration empowers the Family Court judge to terminate permanently the natural parents' rights in the child. §§ 631(c), 634. Termination denies the natural parents physical custody, as well as the rights ever to visit, communicate with, or regain custody of the child.[1]

New York's permanent neglect statute provides natural parents with certain procedural protections.[2] But New York permits its officials to establish "permanent neglect" with less proof than most States require. Thirty-five States, the District of Columbia, and the Virgin Islands currently specify a higher standard of proof, in parental rights termination proceedings, than a "fair preponderance of the evidence."[3] The only analogous federal statute of which we are aware

---

[1] At oral argument, counsel for petitioners asserted that, in New York, natural parents have no means of restoring terminated parental rights. Tr. of Oral Arg. 9. Counsel for respondents, citing Fam. Ct. Act § 1061, answered that parents may petition the Family Court to vacate or set aside an earlier order on narrow grounds, such as newly discovered evidence or fraud. Tr. of Oral Arg. 26. Counsel for respondents conceded, however, that this statutory provision has never been invoked to set aside a permanent neglect finding. *Id.*, at 27.

[2] Most notably, natural parents have a statutory right to the assistance of counsel and of court-appointed counsel if they are indigent. Fam. Ct. Act § 262.(a)(iii).

[3] Fifteen States, by statute, have required "clear and convincing evidence" or its equivalent. See Alaska Stat. Ann. § 47.10.080(c)(3) (1980); Cal. Civ. Code Ann. § 232(a)(7) (West Supp. 1982); Ga. Code §§ 24A-2201(c), 24A-3201 (1979); Iowa Code § 600A.8 (1981) ("clear and convincing proof"); Me. Rev. Stat. Ann., Tit. 22, § 4055.1.B.(2) (Supp. 1981-1982); Mich. Comp. Laws § 722.25 (Supp. 1981-1982); Mo. Rev. Stat. § 211.447.2(2) (Supp. 1981) ("clear, cogent and convincing evidence"); N. M. Stat. Ann. § 40-7-4.J. (Supp. 1981); N. C. Gen. Stat. § 7A-289.30(e) (1981) ("clear, cogent, and convincing evidence"); Ohio Rev. Code Ann. §§ 2151.35, 2151.414(B) (Page Supp. 1982); R. I. Gen. Laws § 15-7-7(d) (Supp. 1980); Tenn. Code Ann. § 37-246(d) (Supp. 1981); Va. Code § 16.1-283.B (Supp. 1981); W. Va. Code § 49-6-2(c) (1980) ("clear and convincing proof"); Wis. Stat. § 48.31(1) (Supp. 1981-1982).

Fifteen States, the District of Columbia, and the Virgin Islands, by court decision, have required "clear and convincing evidence" or its equivalent. See *Dale County Dept. of Pensions & Security* v. *Robles*, 368 So. 2d 39, 42

permits termination of parental rights solely upon "evidence beyond a reasonable doubt." Indian Child Welfare Act of 1978, Pub. L. 95–608, § 102(f), 92 Stat. 3072, 25 U. S. C. § 1912(f) (1976 ed., Supp. IV). The question here is whether

---

(Ala. Civ. App. 1979); *Harper* v. *Caskin*, 265 Ark. 558, 560–561, 580 S. W. 2d 176, 178 (1979); *In re J. S. R.*, 374 A. 2d 860, 864 (D. C. 1977); *Torres* v. *Van Eepoel*, 98 So. 2d 735, 737 (Fla. 1957); *In re Kerns*, 225 Kan. 746, 753, 594 P. 2d 187, 193 (1979); *In re Rosenbloom*, 266 N. W. 2d 888, 889 (Minn. 1978) ("clear and convincing proof"); *In re J. L. B.*, 182 Mont. 100, 116–117, 594 P. 2d 1127, 1136 (1979); *In re Souza*, 204 Neb. 503, 510, 283 N. W. 2d 48, 52 (1979); *J.* v. *M.*, 157 N. J. Super. 478, 489, 385 A. 2d 240, 246 (App. Div. 1978); *In re J. A.*, 283 N. W. 2d 83, 92 (N. D. 1979); *In re Darren Todd H.*, 615 P. 2d 287, 289 (Okla. 1980); *In re William L.*, 477 Pa. 322, 332, 383 A. 2d 1228, 1233, cert. denied *sub nom. Lehman* v. *Lycoming County Children's Services*, 439 U. S. 880 (1978); *In re G. M.*, 596 S. W. 2d 846, 847 (Tex. 1980); *In re Pitts*, 535 P. 2d 1244, 1248 (Utah 1975); *In re Maria*, 15 V. I. 368, 384 (1978); *In re Sego*, 82 Wash. 2d 736, 739, 513 P. 2d 831, 833 (1973) ("clear, cogent, and convincing evidence"); *In re X.*, 607 P. 2d 911, 919 (Wyo. 1980) ("clear and unequivocal").

South Dakota's Supreme Court has required a "clear preponderance" of the evidence in a dependency proceeding. See *In re B. E.*, 287 N. W. 2d 91, 96 (1979). Two States, New Hampshire and Louisiana, have barred parental rights terminations unless the key allegations have been proved beyond a reasonable doubt. See *State* v. *Robert H.*, 118 N. H. 713, 716, 393 A. 2d 1387, 1389 (1978); La. Rev. Stat. Ann. § 13:1603.A (West Supp. 1982). Two States, Illinois and New York, have required clear and convincing evidence, but only in certain types of parental rights termination proceedings. See Ill. Rev. Stat., ch. 37, ¶¶ 705–9(2), (3) (1979), amended by Act of Sept. 11, 1981, 1982 Ill. Laws, P. A. 82–437 (generally requiring a preponderance of the evidence, but requiring clear and convincing evidence to terminate the rights of minor parents and mentally ill or mentally deficient parents); N. Y. Soc. Serv. Law §§ 384–b.3(g), 384–b.4(c), and 384–b.4(e) (Supp. 1981–1982) (requiring "clear and convincing proof" before parental rights may be terminated for reasons of mental illness and mental retardation or severe and repeated child abuse).

So far as we are aware, only two federal courts have addressed the issue. Each has held that allegations supporting parental rights termination must be proved by clear and convincing evidence. *Sims* v. *State Dept. of Public Welfare*, 438 F. Supp. 1179, 1194 (SD Tex. 1977), rev'd on other grounds *sub nom. Moore* v. *Sims*, 442 U. S. 415 (1979); *Alsager* v. *District Court of*

New York's "fair preponderance of the evidence" standard is constitutionally sufficient.

B

Petitioners John Santosky II and Annie Santosky are the natural parents of Tina and John III. In November 1973, after incidents reflecting parental neglect, respondent Kramer, Commissioner of the Ulster County Department of Social Services, initiated a neglect proceeding under Fam. Ct. Act § 1022 and removed Tina from her natural home. About 10 months later, he removed John III and placed him with foster parents. On the day John was taken, Annie Santosky gave birth to a third child, Jed. When Jed was only three days old, respondent transferred him to a foster home on the ground that immediate removal was necessary to avoid imminent danger to his life or health.

In October 1978, respondent petitioned the Ulster County Family Court to terminate petitioners' parental rights in the three children.[4] Petitioners challenged the constitutionality of the "fair preponderance of the evidence" standard specified in Fam. Ct. Act § 622. The Family Court Judge rejected this constitutional challenge, App. 29–30, and weighed the evidence under the statutory standard. While acknowledging that the Santoskys had maintained contact with their children, the judge found those visits "at best superficial and devoid of any real emotional content." *Id.*, at 21. After

---

Polk County, 406 F. Supp. 10, 25 (SD Iowa 1975), aff'd on other grounds, 545 F. 2d 1137 (CA8 1976).

[4] Respondent had made an earlier and unsuccessful termination effort in September 1976. After a factfinding hearing, the Family Court Judge dismissed respondent's petition for failure to prove an essential element of Fam. Ct. Act § 614.1.(d). See *In re Santosky*, 89 Misc. 2d 730, 393 N. Y. S. 2d 486 (1977). The New York Supreme Court, Appellate Division, affirmed, finding that "the record as a whole" revealed that petitioners had "substantially planned for the future of the children." *In re John W.*, 63 App. Div. 2d 750, 751, 404 N. Y. S. 2d 717, 719 (1978).

deciding that the agency had made "'diligent efforts' to encourage and strengthen the parental relationship," *id.*, at 30, he concluded that the Santoskys were incapable, even with public assistance, of planning for the future of their children. *Id.*, at 33–37. The judge later held a dispositional hearing and ruled that the best interests of the three children required permanent termination of the Santoskys' custody.[5] *Id.*, at 39.

Petitioners appealed, again contesting the constitutionality of § 622's standard of proof.[6] The New York Supreme Court, Appellate Division, affirmed, holding application of the preponderance-of-the-evidence standard "proper and constitutional." *In re John AA*, 75 App. Div. 2d 910, 427 N. Y. S. 2d 319, 320 (1980). That standard, the court reasoned, "recognizes and seeks to balance rights possessed by the child . . . with those of the natural parents . . . ." *Ibid.*

The New York Court of Appeals then dismissed petitioners' appeal to that court "upon the ground that no substantial constitutional question is directly involved." App. 55. We granted certiorari to consider petitioners' constitutional claim. 450 U. S. 993 (1981).

II

Last Term, in *Lassiter* v. *Department of Social Services*, 452 U. S. 18 (1981), this Court, by a 5–4 vote, held that the

[5] Since respondent Kramer took custody of Tina, John III, and Jed, the Santoskys have had two other children, James and Jeremy. The State has taken no action to remove these younger children. At oral argument, counsel for respondents replied affirmatively when asked whether he was asserting that petitioners were "unfit to handle the three older ones but not unfit to handle the two younger ones." Tr. of Oral Arg. 24.

[6] Petitioners initially had sought review in the New York Court of Appeals. That court *sua sponte* transferred the appeal to the Appellate Division, Third Department, stating that a direct appeal did not lie because "questions other than the constitutional validity of a statutory provision are involved." App. 50.

Fourteenth Amendment's Due Process Clause does not require the appointment of counsel for indigent parents in every parental status termination proceeding. The case casts light, however, on the two central questions here—whether process is constitutionally due a natural parent at a State's parental rights termination proceeding, and, if so, what process is due.

In *Lassiter*, it was "not disputed that state intervention to terminate the relationship between [a parent] and [the] child must be accomplished by procedures meeting the requisites of the Due Process Clause." *Id.*, at 37 (first dissenting opinion); see *id.*, at 24–32 (opinion of the Court); *id.*, at 59–60 (STEVENS, J., dissenting). See also *Little* v. *Streater*, 452 U. S. 1, 13 (1981). The absence of dispute reflected this Court's historical recognition that freedom of personal choice in matters of family life is a fundamental liberty interest protected by the Fourteenth Amendment. *Quilloin* v. *Walcott*, 434 U. S. 246, 255 (1978); *Smith* v. *Organization of Foster Families*, 431 U. S. 816, 845 (1977); *Moore* v. *East Cleveland*, 431 U. S. 494, 499 (1977) (plurality opinion); *Cleveland Board of Education* v. *LaFleur*, 414 U. S. 632, 639–640 (1974); *Stanley* v. *Illinois*, 405 U. S. 645, 651–652 (1972); *Prince* v. *Massachusetts*, 321 U. S. 158, 166 (1944); *Pierce* v. *Society of Sisters*, 268 U. S. 510, 534–535 (1925); *Meyer* v. *Nebraska*, 262 U. S. 390, 399 (1923).

The fundamental liberty interest of natural parents in the care, custody, and management of their child does not evaporate simply because they have not been model parents or have lost temporary custody of their child to the State. Even when blood relationships are strained, parents retain a vital interest in preventing the irretrievable destruction of their family life. If anything, persons faced with forced dissolution of their parental rights have a more critical need for procedural protections than do those resisting state intervention into ongoing family affairs. When the State moves to destroy weakened familial bonds, it must provide the parents with fundamentally fair procedures.[7]

In *Lassiter*, the Court and three dissenters agreed that the nature of the process due in parental rights termination proceedings turns on a balancing of the "three distinct factors" specified in *Mathews* v. *Eldridge*, 424 U. S. 319, 335 (1976): the private interests affected by the proceeding; the risk of error created by the State's chosen procedure; and the countervailing governmental interest supporting use of the challenged procedure. See 452 U. S., at 27–31; *id.*, at 37–48 (first dissenting opinion). But see *id.*, at 59–60 (STEVENS, J., dissenting). While the respective *Lassiter* opinions disputed whether those factors should be weighed against a presumption disfavoring appointed counsel for one not threatened with loss of physical liberty, compare 452 U. S., at 31–32, with *id.*, at 41, and n. 8 (first dissenting opinion), that concern is irrelevant here. Unlike the Court's right-to-counsel rulings, its decisions concerning constitutional burdens of proof have not turned on any presumption favoring any particular standard. To the contrary, the Court has engaged in a straightforward consideration of the factors identified in *Eldridge* to determine whether a particular standard of proof in a particular proceeding satisfies due process.

In *Addington* v. *Texas*, 441 U. S. 418 (1979), the Court, by a unanimous vote of the participating Justices, declared: "The function of a standard of proof, as that concept is embodied in the Due Process Clause and in the realm of factfinding, is to

---

[7] We therefore reject respondent Kramer's claim that a parental rights termination proceeding does not interfere with a fundamental liberty interest. See Brief for Respondent Kramer 11–18; Tr. of Oral Arg. 38. The fact that important liberty interests of the child and its foster parents may also be affected by a permanent neglect proceeding does not justify denying the *natural parents* constitutionally adequate procedures. Nor can the State refuse to provide natural parents adequate procedural safeguards on the ground that the family unit already has broken down; that is the very issue the permanent neglect proceeding is meant to decide.

'instruct the factfinder concerning the degree of confidence our society thinks he should have in the correctness of factual conclusions for a particular type of adjudication.'" *Id.*, at 423, quoting *In re Winship*, 397 U. S. 358, 370 (1970) (Harlan, J., concurring). *Addington* teaches that, in any given proceeding, the minimum standard of proof tolerated by the due process requirement reflects not only the weight of the private and public interests affected, but also a societal judgment about how the risk of error should be distributed between the litigants.

Thus, while private parties may be interested intensely in a civil dispute over money damages, application of a "fair preponderance of the evidence" standard indicates both society's "minimal concern with the outcome," and a conclusion that the litigants should "share the risk of error in roughly equal fashion." 441 U. S., at 423. When the State brings a criminal action to deny a defendant liberty or life, however, "the interests of the defendant are of such magnitude that historically and without any explicit constitutional requirement they have been protected by standards of proof designed to exclude as nearly as possible the likelihood of an erroneous judgment." *Ibid.* The stringency of the "beyond a reasonable doubt" standard bespeaks the "weight and gravity" of the private interest affected, *id.*, at 427, society's interest in avoiding erroneous convictions, and a judgment that those interests together require that "society impos[e] almost the entire risk of error upon itself." *Id.*, at 424. See also *In re Winship*, 397 U. S., at 372 (Harlan, J., concurring).

The "minimum requirements [of procedural due process] being a matter of federal law, they are not diminished by the fact that the State may have specified its own procedures that it may deem adequate for determining the preconditions to adverse official action." *Vitek* v. *Jones*, 445 U. S. 480, 491 (1980). See also *Logan* v. *Zimmerman Brush Co.*, *ante*, at 432. Moreover, the degree of proof required in a particular type of proceeding "is the kind of question which has traditionally been left to the judiciary to resolve." *Woodby* v. *INS*, 385 U. S. 276, 284 (1966).[8] "In cases involving individual rights, whether criminal or civil, '[t]he standard of proof [at a minimum] reflects the value society places on individual liberty.'" *Addington* v. *Texas*, 441 U. S., at 425, quoting *Tippett* v. *Maryland*, 436 F. 2d 1153, 1166 (CA4 1971) (opinion concurring in part and dissenting in part), cert. dism'd *sub nom. Murel* v. *Baltimore City Criminal Court*, 407 U. S. 355 (1972).

This Court has mandated an intermediate standard of proof—"clear and convincing evidence"—when the individual interests at stake in a state proceeding are both "particularly important" and "more substantial than mere loss of money." *Addington* v. *Texas*, 441 U. S., at 424. Notwithstanding "the state's 'civil labels and good intentions,'" *id.*, at 427, quoting *In re Winship*, 397 U. S., at 365–366, the Court has deemed this level of certainty necessary to preserve fundamental fairness in a variety of government-initiated proceedings that threaten the individual involved with "a significant deprivation of liberty" or "stigma." 441 U. S., at 425, 426. See, *e. g.*, *Addington* v. *Texas*, *supra* (civil commitment); *Woodby* v. *INS*, 385 U. S., at 285 (deportation); *Chaunt* v. *United States*, 364 U. S. 350, 353 (1960) (denaturalization);

[8] The dissent charges, *post*, at 772, n. 2, that "this Court simply has no role in establishing the standards of proof that States must follow in the various judicial proceedings they afford to their citizens." As the dissent properly concedes, however, the Court must examine a State's chosen standard to determine whether it satisfies "the constitutional minimum of 'fundamental fairness.'" *Ibid.* See, *e. g.*, *Addington* v. *Texas*, 441 U. S. 418, 427, 433 (1979) (unanimous decision of participating Justices) (Fourteenth Amendment requires at least clear and convincing evidence in a civil proceeding brought under state law to commit an individual involuntarily for an indefinite period to a state mental hospital); *In re Winship*, 397 U. S. 358, 364 (1970) (Due Process Clause of the Fourteenth Amendment protects the accused in state proceeding against conviction except upon proof beyond a reasonable doubt of every fact necessary to constitute the crime with which he is charged).

Schneiderman v. *United States*, 320 U. S. 118, 125, 159 (1943) (denaturalization).

In *Lassiter*, to be sure, the Court held that fundamental fairness may be maintained in parental rights termination proceedings even when some procedures are mandated only on a case-by-case basis, rather than through rules of general application. 452 U. S., at 31–32 (natural parent's right to court-appointed counsel should be determined by the trial court, subject to appellate review). But this Court never has approved case-by-case determination of the proper *standard of proof* for a given proceeding. Standards of proof, like other "procedural due process rules[,] are shaped by the risk of error inherent in the truth-finding process as applied to the *generality of cases*, not the rare exceptions." *Mathews* v. *Eldridge*, 424 U. S., at 344 (emphasis added). Since the litigants and the factfinder must know at the outset of a given proceeding how the risk of error will be allocated, the standard of proof necessarily must be calibrated in advance. Retrospective case-by-case review cannot preserve fundamental fairness when a class of proceedings is governed by a constitutionally defective evidentiary standard.[9]

---

[9] For this reason, we reject the suggestions of respondents and the dissent that the constitutionality of New York's statutory procedures must be evaluated as a "package." See Tr. of Oral Arg. 25, 36, 38. Indeed, we would rewrite our precedents were we to excuse a constitutionally defective standard of proof based on an amorphous assessment of the "cumulative effect" of state procedures. In the criminal context, for example, the Court has never assumed that "strict substantive standards or special procedures compensate for a lower burden of proof . . . ." *Post*, at 773. See *In re Winship*, 397 U. S., at 368. Nor has the Court treated appellate review as a curative for an inadequate burden of proof. See *Woodby* v. *INS*, 385 U. S. 276, 282 (1966) ("judicial review is generally limited to ascertaining whether the evidence relied upon by the trier of fact was of sufficient quality and substantiality to support the rationality of the judgment").

As the dissent points out, "the standard of proof is a crucial component of legal process, the primary function of which is 'to minimize the risk of erro-

III

In parental rights termination proceedings, the private interest affected is commanding; the risk of error from using a preponderance standard is substantial; and the countervailing governmental interest favoring that standard is comparatively slight. Evaluation of the three *Eldridge* factors compels the conclusion that use of a "fair preponderance of the evidence" standard in such proceedings is inconsistent with due process.

A

"The extent to which procedural due process must be afforded the recipient is influenced by the extent to which he may be 'condemned to suffer grievous loss.'" *Goldberg* v. *Kelly*, 397 U. S. 254, 262–263 (1970), quoting *Joint Anti-Fascist Refugee Committee* v. *McGrath*, 341 U. S. 123, 168 (1951) (Frankfurter, J., concurring). Whether the loss threatened by a particular type of proceeding is sufficiently grave to warrant more than average certainty on the part of the factfinder turns on both the nature of the private interest threatened and the permanency of the threatened loss.

Lassiter declared it "plain beyond the need for multiple citation" that a natural parent's "desire for and right to 'the companionship, care, custody, and management of his or her children'" is an interest far more precious than any property

---

neous decisions.'" *Post*, at 785, quoting *Greenholtz* v. *Nebraska Penal Inmates*, 442 U. S. 1, 13 (1979). Notice, summons, right to counsel, rules of evidence, and evidentiary hearings are all procedures to place information *before* the factfinder. But only the standard of proof "instruct[s] the factfinder concerning the degree of confidence our society thinks he should have in the correctness of factual conclusions" he draws from that information. *In re Winship*, 397 U. S., at 370 (Harlan, J., concurring). The statutory provision of right to counsel and multiple hearings before termination cannot suffice to protect a natural parent's fundamental liberty interests if the State is willing to tolerate undue uncertainty in the determination of the dispositive facts.

right. 452 U. S., at 27, quoting *Stanley* v. *Illinois*, 405 U. S., at 651. When the State initiates a parental rights termination proceeding, it seeks not merely to infringe that fundamental liberty interest, but to end it. "If the State prevails, it will have worked a unique kind of deprivation. . . . A parent's interest in the accuracy and justice of the decision to terminate his or her parental status is, therefore, a commanding one." 452 U. S., at 27.

In government-initiated proceedings to determine juvenile delinquency, *In re Winship*, *supra;* civil commitment, *Addington* v. *Texas*, *supra;* deportation, *Woodby* v. *INS*, *supra;* and denaturalization, *Chaunt* v. *United States*, *supra*, and *Schneiderman* v. *United States*, *supra*, this Court has identified losses of individual liberty sufficiently serious to warrant imposition of an elevated burden of proof. Yet juvenile delinquency adjudications, civil commitment, deportation, and denaturalization, at least to a degree, are all *reversible* official actions. Once affirmed on appeal, a New York decision terminating parental rights is *final* and irrevocable. See n. 1, *supra*. Few forms of state action are both so severe and so irreversible.

Thus, the first *Eldridge* factor—the private interest affected—weighs heavily against use of the preponderance standard at a state-initiated permanent neglect proceeding. We do not deny that the child and his foster parents are also deeply interested in the outcome of that contest. But at the factfinding stage of the New York proceeding, the focus emphatically is not on them.

The factfinding does not purport—and is not intended—to balance the child's interest in a normal family home against the parents' interest in raising the child. Nor does it purport to determine whether the natural parents or the foster parents would provide the better home. Rather, the factfinding hearing pits the State directly against the parents. The State alleges that the natural parents are at fault. Fam. Ct. Act § 614.1.(d). The questions disputed and decided are what the State did—"made diligent efforts," § 614.1.(c)—and what the natural parents did not do—"maintain contact with or plan for the future of the child." § 614.1.(d). The State marshals an array of public resources to prove its case and disprove the parents' case. Victory by the State not only makes termination of parental rights possible; it entails a judicial determination that the parents are unfit to raise their own children.[10]

At the factfinding, the State cannot presume that a child and his parents are adversaries. After the State has established parental unfitness at that initial proceeding, the court may assume at the *dispositional* stage that the interests of the child and the natural parents do diverge. See Fam. Ct. Act § 631 (judge shall make his order "solely on the basis of the best interests of the child," and thus has no obligation to consider the natural parents' rights in selecting dispositional alternatives). But until the State proves parental unfitness, the child and his parents share a vital interest in preventing erroneous termination of their natural relationship.[11] Thus,

---

[10] The Family Court Judge in the present case expressly refused to terminate petitioners' parental rights on a "non-statutory, no-fault basis." App. 22–29. Nor is it clear that the State constitutionally could terminate a parent's rights *without* showing parental unfitness. See *Quilloin* v. *Walcott*, 434 U. S. 246, 255 (1978) ("We have little doubt that the Due Process Clause would be offended '[i]f a State were to attempt to force the breakup of a natural family, over the objections of the parents and their children, without some showing of unfitness and for the sole reason that to do so was thought to be in the children's best interest,'" quoting *Smith* v. *Organization of Foster Families*, 431 U. S. 816, 862–863 (1977) (Stewart, J., concurring in judgment)).

[11] For a child, the consequences of termination of his natural parents' rights may well be far-reaching. In Colorado, for example, it has been noted: "The child loses the right of support and maintenance, for which he may thereafter be dependent upon society; the right to inherit; and all other rights inherent in the legal parent-child relationship, not just for [a limited] period . . . , but forever." *In re K. S.*, 33 Colo. App. 72, 76, 515 P. 2d 130, 133 (1973).

Some losses cannot be measured. In this case, for example, Jed Santosky was removed from his natural parents' custody when he was only

at the factfinding, the interests of the child and his natural parents coincide to favor use of error-reducing procedures.

However substantial the foster parents' interests may be, cf. *Smith* v. *Organization of Foster Families*, 431 U. S., at 845–847, they are not implicated directly in the factfinding stage of a state-initiated permanent neglect proceeding against the natural parents. If authorized, the foster parents may pit their interests directly against those of the natural parents by initiating their own permanent neglect proceeding. Fam. Ct. Act § 1055(d); Soc. Serv. Law §§ 384–6.3(b), 392.7.(c). Alternatively, the foster parents can make their case for custody at the dispositional stage of a state-initiated proceeding, where the judge already has decided the issue of permanent neglect and is focusing on the placement that would serve the child's best interests. Fam. Ct. Act §§ 623, 631. For the foster parents, the State's failure to prove permanent neglect may prolong the delay and uncertainty until their foster child is freed for adoption. But for the natural parents, a finding of permanent neglect can cut off forever their rights in their child. Given this disparity of consequence, we have no difficulty finding that the balance of private interests strongly favors heightened procedural protections.

B

Under *Mathews* v. *Eldridge*, we next must consider both the risk of erroneous deprivation of private interests resulting from use of a "fair preponderance" standard and the likelihood that a higher evidentiary standard would reduce that risk. See 424 U. S., at 335. Since the factfinding phase of a permanent neglect proceeding is an adversary contest between the State and the natural parents, the relevant question is whether a preponderance standard fairly allocates the risk of an erroneous factfinding between these two parties.

---

three days old; the judge's finding of permanent neglect effectively foreclosed the possibility that Jed would ever know his natural parents.

In New York, the factfinding stage of a state-initiated permanent neglect proceeding bears many of the indicia of a criminal trial. Cf. *Lassiter* v. *Department of Social Services*, 452 U. S., at 42–44 (first dissenting opinion); *Meltzer* v. *C. Buck LeCraw & Co.*, 402 U. S. 954, 959 (1971) (Black, J., dissenting from denial of certiorari). See also dissenting opinion, *post*, at 777–779 (describing procedures employed at factfinding proceeding). The Commissioner of Social Services charges the parents with permanent neglect. They are served by summons. Fam. Ct. Act §§ 614, 616, 617. The factfinding hearing is conducted pursuant to formal rules of evidence. § 624. The State, the parents, and the child are all represented by counsel. §§ 249, 262. The State seeks to establish a series of historical facts about the intensity of its agency's efforts to reunite the family, the infrequency and insubstantiality of the parents' contacts with their child, and the parents' inability or unwillingness to formulate a plan for the child's future. The attorneys submit documentary evidence, and call witnesses who are subject to cross-examination. Based on all the evidence, the judge then determines whether the State has proved the statutory elements of permanent neglect by a fair preponderance of the evidence. § 622.

At such a proceeding, numerous factors combine to magnify the risk of erroneous factfinding. Permanent neglect proceedings employ imprecise substantive standards that leave determinations unusually open to the subjective values of the judge. See *Smith* v. *Organization of Foster Families*, 431 U. S., at 835, n. 36. In appraising the nature and quality of a complex series of encounters among the agency, the parents, and the child, the court possesses unusual discretion to underweigh probative facts that might favor the parent.[12]

---

[12] For example, a New York court appraising an agency's "diligent efforts" to provide the parents with social services can excuse efforts *not* made on the grounds that they would have been "detrimental to the best interests of the child." Fam. Ct. Act § 614.1.(c). In determining whether

Because parents subject to termination proceedings are often poor, uneducated, or members of minority groups, *id.*, at 833–835, such proceedings are often vulnerable to judgments based on cultural or class bias.

The State's ability to assemble its case almost inevitably dwarfs the parents' ability to mount a defense. No predetermined limits restrict the sums an agency may spend in prosecuting a given termination proceeding. The State's attorney usually will be expert on the issues contested and the procedures employed at the factfinding hearing, and enjoys full access to all public records concerning the family. The State may call on experts in family relations, psychology, and medicine to bolster its case. Furthermore, the primary witnesses at the hearing will be the agency's own professional caseworkers whom the State has empowered both to investigate the family situation and to testify against the parents. Indeed, because the child is already in agency custody, the State even has the power to shape the historical events that form the basis for termination.[13]

---

the parent "substantially and continuously or repeatedly" failed to "maintain contact with . . . the child," § 614.1.(d), the judge can discount actual visits or communications on the grounds that they were insubstantial or "overtly demonstrat[ed] a lack of affectionate and concerned parenthood." Soc. Serv. Law § 384–b.7.(b). When determining whether the parent planned for the child's future, the judge can reject as unrealistic plans based on overly optimistic estimates of physical or financial ability. § 384–b.7.(c). See also dissenting opinion, *post*, at 779–780, nn. 8 and 9.

[13] In this case, for example, the parents claim that the State sought court orders denying them the right to visit their children, which would have prevented them from maintaining the contact required by Fam. Ct. Act. § 614.1.(d). See Brief for Petitioners 9. The parents further claim that the State cited their rejection of social services they found offensive or superfluous as proof of the agency's "diligent efforts" and their own "failure to plan" for the children's future. *Id.*, at 10–11.

We need not accept these statements as true to recognize that the State's unusual ability to structure the evidence increases the risk of an erroneous factfinding. Of course, the disparity between the litigants' re-

The disparity between the adversaries' litigation resources is matched by a striking asymmetry in their litigation options. Unlike criminal defendants, natural parents have no "double jeopardy" defense against repeated state termination efforts. If the State initially fails to win termination, as New York did here, see n. 4, *supra*, it always can try once again to cut off the parents' rights after gathering more or better evidence. Yet even when the parents have attained the level of fitness required by the State, they have no similar means by which they can forestall future termination efforts.

Coupled with a "fair preponderance of the evidence" standard, these factors create a significant prospect of erroneous termination. A standard of proof that by its very terms demands consideration of the quantity, rather than the quality, of the evidence may misdirect the factfinder in the marginal case. See *In re Winship*, 397 U. S., at 371, n. 3 (Harlan, J., concurring). Given the weight of the private interests at stake, the social cost of even occasional error is sizable.

Raising the standard of proof would have both practical and symbolic consequences. Cf. *Addington* v. *Texas*, 441 U. S., at 426. The Court has long considered the heightened standard of proof used in criminal prosecutions to be "a prime instrument for reducing the risk of convictions resting on factual error." *In re Winship*, 397 U. S., at 363. An elevated standard of proof in a parental rights termination proceeding would alleviate "the possible risk that a factfinder might decide to [deprive] an individual based solely on a few isolated instances of unusual conduct [or] . . . idiosyncratic behavior." *Addington* v. *Texas*, 441 U. S., at 427. "Increasing the burden of proof is one way to impress the factfinder with the im-

---

sources will be vastly greater in States where there is no statutory right to court-appointed counsel. See *Lassiter* v. *Department of Social Services*, 452 U. S. 18, 34 (1981) (only 33 States and the District of Columbia provide that right by statute).

portance of the decision and thereby perhaps to reduce the chances that inappropriate" terminations will be ordered. *Ibid.*

The Appellate Division approved New York's preponderance standard on the ground that it properly "balanced rights possessed by the child . . . with those of the natural parents. . . ." 75 App. Div. 2d, at 910, 427 N. Y. S. 2d, at 320. By so saying, the court suggested that a preponderance standard properly allocates the risk of error *between* the parents and the child.[14] That view is fundamentally mistaken.

The court's theory assumes that termination of the natural parents' rights invariably will benefit the child.[15] Yet we have noted above that the parents and the child share an interest in avoiding erroneous termination. Even accepting the court's assumption, we cannot agree with its conclusion that a preponderance standard fairly distributes the risk of error between parent and child. Use of that standard reflects the judgment that society is nearly neutral between erroneous termination of parental rights and erroneous failure to terminate those rights. Cf. *In re Winship*, 397 U. S., at 371 (Harlan, J., concurring). For the child, the likely consequence of an erroneous failure to terminate is preservation of

---

[14] The dissent makes a similar claim. See *post*, at 786–791.

[15] This is a hazardous assumption at best. Even when a child's natural home is imperfect, permanent removal from that home will not necessarily improve his welfare. See, *e. g.*, Wald, State Intervention on Behalf of "Neglected" Children: A Search for Realistic Standards, 27 Stan. L. Rev. 985, 993 (1975) ("In fact, under current practice, coercive intervention frequently results in placing a child in a more detrimental situation than he would be in without intervention").

Nor does termination of parental rights necessarily ensure adoption. See Brief for Community Action for Legal Services, Inc., et al. as *Amici Curiae* 22–23. Even when a child eventually finds an adoptive family, he may spend years moving between state institutions and "temporary" foster placements after his ties to his natural parents have been severed. See *Smith* v. *Organization of Foster Families*, 431 U. S., at 833–838 (describing the "limbo" of the New York foster care system).

an uneasy status quo.[16] For the natural parents, however, the consequence of an erroneous termination is the unnecessary destruction of their natural family. A standard that allocates the risk of error nearly equally between those two outcomes does not reflect properly their relative severity.

C

Two state interests are at stake in parental rights termination proceedings—a *parens patriae* interest in preserving and promoting the welfare of the child and a fiscal and administrative interest in reducing the cost and burden of such proceedings. A standard of proof more strict than preponderance of the evidence is consistent with both interests.

"Since the State has an urgent interest in the welfare of the child, it shares the parent's interest in an accurate and just decision" at the *factfinding* proceeding. *Lassiter* v. *Department of Social Services*, 452 U. S., at 27. As *parens patriae*, the State's goal is to provide the child with a permanent home. See Soc. Serv. Law § 384–b. 1. (a)(i) (statement of legislative findings and intent). Yet while there is still reason to believe that positive, nurturing parent-child relationships exist, the *parens patriae* interest favors preservation, not

---

[16] When the termination proceeding occurs, the child is not living at his natural home. A child cannot be adjudicated "permanently neglected" until, "for a period of more than one year," he has been in "the care of an authorized agency." Soc. Serv. Law § 384–b.7.(a); Fam. Ct. Act § 614.1.(d). See also dissenting opinion, *post*, at 789–790.

Under New York law, a judge has ample discretion to ensure that, once removed from his natural parents on grounds of neglect, a child will not return to a hostile environment. In this case, when the State's initial termination effort failed for lack of proof, see n. 4, *supra*, the court simply issued orders under Fam. Ct. Act § 1055(b) extending the period of the child's foster home placement. See App. 19–20. See also Fam. Ct. Act § 632(b) (when State's permanent neglect petition is dismissed for insufficient evidence, judge retains jurisdiction to reconsider underlying orders of placement); § 633 (judge may suspend judgment at dispositional hearing for an additional year).

severance, of natural familial bonds.[17] § 384–b.1.(a)(ii). "[T]he State registers no gain towards its declared goals when it separates children from the custody of fit parents." *Stanley* v. *Illinois*, 405 U. S., at 652.

The State's interest in finding the child an alternative permanent home arises only "when it is *clear* that the natural parent cannot or will not provide a normal family home for the child." Soc. Serv. Law § 384–b.1.(a)(iv) (emphasis added). At the factfinding, that goal is served by procedures that promote an accurate determination of whether the natural parents can and will provide a normal home.

Unlike a constitutional requirement of hearings, see, *e. g.*, *Mathews* v. *Eldridge*, 424 U. S., at 347, or court-appointed counsel, a stricter standard of proof would reduce factual error without imposing substantial fiscal burdens upon the State. As we have observed, 35 States already have adopted a higher standard by statute or court decision without apparent effect on the speed, form, or cost of their factfinding proceedings. See n. 3, *supra*.

Nor would an elevated standard of proof create any real administrative burdens for the State's factfinders. New York Family Court judges already are familiar with a higher evidentiary standard in other parental rights termination proceedings not involving permanent neglect. See Soc. Serv. Law §§ 384–b.3.(g), 384–b.4.(c), and 384–b.4.(e) (requiring "clear and convincing proof" before parental rights may be terminated for reasons of mental illness and mental retardation or severe and repeated child abuse). New York also demands at least clear and convincing evidence in proceedings of far less moment than parental rights termination proceedings. See, *e. g.*, N. Y. Veh. & Traf. Law § 227.1 (McKinney Supp. 1981) (requiring the State to prove traffic

[17] Any *parens patriae* interest in terminating the natural parents' rights arises only at the dispositional phase, *after* the parents have been found unfit.

infractions by "clear and convincing evidence") and *In re Rosenthal* v. *Hartnett*, 36 N. Y. 2d 269, 326 N. E. 2d 811 (1975); see also *Ross* v. *Food Specialties, Inc.*, 6 N. Y. 2d 336, 341, 160 N. E. 2d 618, 620 (1959) (requiring "clear, positive and convincing evidence" for contract reformation). We cannot believe that it would burden the State unduly to require that its factfinders have the same factual certainty when terminating the parent-child relationship as they must have to suspend a driver's license.

IV

The logical conclusion of this balancing process is that the "fair preponderance of the evidence" standard prescribed by Fam. Ct. Act § 622 violates the Due Process Clause of the Fourteenth Amendment.[18] The Court noted in *Addington:* "The individual should not be asked to share equally with society the risk of error when the possible injury to the individual is significantly greater than any possible harm to the state." 441 U. S., at 427. Thus, at a parental rights termination proceeding, a near-equal allocation of risk between the parents and the State is constitutionally intolerable. The next question, then, is whether a "beyond a reasonable doubt" or a "clear and convincing" standard is constitutionally mandated.

In *Addington*, the Court concluded that application of a reasonable-doubt standard is inappropriate in civil commitment proceedings for two reasons—because of our hesitation to apply that unique standard "too broadly or casually in noncriminal cases," *id.*, at 428, and because the psychiatric evidence ordinarily adduced at commitment proceedings is

[18] The dissent's claim that today's decision "will inevitably lead to the federalization of family law," *post*, at 773, is, of course, vastly overstated. As the dissent properly notes, the Court's duty to "refrai[n] from interfering with state answers to domestic relations questions" has never required "that the Court should blink at clear constitutional violations in state statutes." *Post*, at 771.

rarely susceptible to proof beyond a reasonable doubt. *Id.*, at 429–430, 432–433. To be sure, as has been noted above, in the Indian Child Welfare Act of 1978, Pub. L. 95–608, § 102(f), 92 Stat. 3072, 25 U. S. C. § 1912(f) (1976 ed., Supp. IV), Congress requires "evidence beyond a reasonable doubt" for termination of Indian parental rights, reasoning that "the removal of a child from the parents is a penalty as great [as], if not greater, than a criminal penalty . . . ." H. R. Rep. No. 95–1386, p. 22 (1978). Congress did not consider, however, the evidentiary problems that would arise if proof beyond a reasonable doubt were required in all state-initiated parental rights termination hearings.

Like civil commitment hearings, termination proceedings often require the factfinder to evaluate medical and psychiatric testimony, and to decide issues difficult to prove to a level of absolute certainty, such as lack of parental motive, absence of affection between parent and child, and failure of parental foresight and progress. Cf. *Lassiter* v. *Department of Social Services*, 452 U. S., at 30; *id.*, at 44–46 (first dissenting opinion) (describing issues raised in state termination proceedings). The substantive standards applied vary from State to State. Although Congress found a "beyond a reasonable doubt" standard proper in one type of parental rights termination case, another legislative body might well conclude that a reasonable-doubt standard would erect an unreasonable barrier to state efforts to free permanently neglected children for adoption.

A majority of the States have concluded that a "clear and convincing evidence" standard of proof strikes a fair balance between the rights of the natural parents and the State's legitimate concerns. See n. 3, *supra*. We hold that such a standard adequately conveys to the factfinder the level of subjective certainty about his factual conclusions necessary to satisfy due process. We further hold that determination of the precise burden equal to or greater than that standard is a matter of state law properly left to state legislatures and state courts. Cf. *Addington* v. *Texas*, 441 U. S., at 433.

We, of course, express no view on the merits of petitioners' claims.[19] At a hearing conducted under a constitutionally proper standard, they may or may not prevail. Without deciding the outcome under any of the standards we have approved, we vacate the judgment of the Appellate Division and remand the case for further proceedings not inconsistent with this opinion.

It is so ordered.

JUSTICE REHNQUIST, with whom THE CHIEF JUSTICE, JUSTICE WHITE, and JUSTICE O'CONNOR join, dissenting.

I believe that few of us would care to live in a society where every aspect of life was regulated by a single source of law, whether that source be this Court or some other organ of our complex body politic. But today's decision certainly moves us in that direction. By parsing the New York scheme and holding one narrow provision unconstitutional, the majority invites further federal-court intrusion into every facet of state family law. If ever there were an area in which federal courts should heed the admonition of Justice Holmes that "a page of history is worth a volume of logic,"[1] it is in the area of domestic relations. This area has been left to the States from time immemorial, and not without good reason.

Equally as troubling is the majority's due process analysis. The Fourteenth Amendment guarantees that a State will treat individuals with "fundamental fairness" whenever its actions infringe their protected liberty or property interests. By adoption of the procedures relevant to this case, New

---

[19] Unlike the dissent, we carefully refrain from accepting as the "facts of this case" findings that are not part of the record and that have been found only to be more likely true than not.

[1] *New York Trust Co.* v. *Eisner*, 256 U. S. 345, 349 (1921).

York has created an exhaustive program to assist parents in regaining the custody of their children and to protect parents from the unfair deprivation of their parental rights. And yet the majority's myopic scrutiny of the standard of proof blinds it to the very considerations and procedures which make the New York scheme "fundamentally fair."

I

State intervention in domestic relations has always been an unhappy but necessary feature of life in our organized society. For all of our experience in this area, we have found no fully satisfactory solutions to the painful problem of child abuse and neglect. We have found, however, that leaving the States free to experiment with various remedies has produced novel approaches and promising progress.

Throughout this experience the Court has scrupulously refrained from interfering with state answers to domestic relations questions. "Both theory and the precedents of this Court teach us solicitude for state interests, particularly in the field of family and family-property arrangements." *United States* v. *Yazell*, 382 U. S. 341, 352 (1966). This is not to say that the Court should blink at clear constitutional violations in state statutes, but rather that in this area, of all areas, "substantial weight must be given to the good-faith judgments of the individuals [administering a program] . . . that the procedures they have provided assure fair consideration of the . . . claims of individuals." *Mathews* v. *Eldridge*, 424 U. S. 319, 349 (1976).

This case presents a classic occasion for such solicitude. As will be seen more fully in the next part, New York has enacted a comprehensive plan to *aid* marginal parents in regaining the custody of their child. The central purpose of the New York plan is to reunite divided families. Adoption of the preponderance-of-the-evidence standard represents New York's good-faith effort to balance the interest of parents against the legitimate interests of the child and the State. These earnest efforts by state officials should be given weight in the Court's application of due process principles. "Great constitutional provisions must be administered with caution. Some play must be allowed for the joints of the machine, and it must be remembered that legislatures are ultimate guardians of the liberties and welfare of the people in quite as great a degree as the courts." *Missouri, K. & T. R. Co.* v. *May*, 194 U. S. 267, 270 (1904).[2]

The majority may believe that it is adopting a relatively unobtrusive means of ensuring that termination proceedings provide "due process of law." In fact, however, fixing the standard of proof as a matter of federal constitutional law will only lead to further federal-court intervention in state schemes. By holding that due process requires proof by clear and convincing evidence the majority surely cannot mean that any state scheme passes constitutional muster so long as it applies that standard of proof. A state law permitting termination of parental rights upon a showing of neglect by clear and convincing evidence certainly would not be ac-

---

[2] The majority asserts that "the degree of proof required in a particular type of proceeding 'is the kind of question which has traditionally been left to the judiciary to resolve.' *Woodby* v. *INS*, 385 U. S. 276, 284 (1966)." *Ante*, at 755–756. To the extent that the majority seeks, by this statement, to place upon the federal judiciary the primary responsibility for deciding the appropriate standard of proof in state matters, it arrogates to itself a responsibility wholly at odds with the allocation of authority in our federalist system and wholly unsupported by the prior decisions of this Court. In *Woodby* v. *INS*, 385 U. S. 276 (1966), the Court determined the proper standard of proof to be applied under a *federal* statute, and did so only after concluding that "Congress ha[d] not addressed itself to the question of what degree of proof [was] required in deportation proceedings." *Id.*, at 284. Beyond an examination for the constitutional minimum of "fundamental fairness"—which clearly is satisfied by the New York procedures at issue in this case—this Court simply has no role in establishing the standards of proof that States must follow in the various judicial proceedings they afford to their citizens.

ceptable to the majority if it provided no procedures other than one 30-minute hearing. Similarly, the majority probably would balk at a state scheme that permitted termination of parental rights on a clear and convincing showing merely that such action would be in the best interests of the child. See *Smith* v. *Organization of Foster Families*, 431 U. S. 816, 862–863 (1977) (Stewart, J., concurring in judgment).

After fixing the standard of proof, therefore, the majority will be forced to evaluate other aspects of termination proceedings with reference to that point. Having in this case abandoned evaluation of the overall effect of a scheme, and with it the possibility of finding that strict substantive standards or special procedures compensate for a lower burden of proof, the majority's approach will inevitably lead to the federalization of family law. Such a trend will only thwart state searches for better solutions in an area where this Court should encourage state experimentation. "It is one of the happy incidents of the federal system that a single courageous State may, if its citizens choose, serve as a laboratory; and try novel social and economic experiments without risk to the rest of the country. This Court has the power to prevent an experiment." *New State Ice Co.* v. *Liebmann*, 285 U. S. 262, 311 (1932) (Brandeis, J., dissenting). It should not do so in the absence of a clear constitutional violation. As will be seen in the next part, no clear constitutional violation has occurred in this case.

II

As the majority opinion notes, petitioners are the parents of five children, three of whom were removed from petitioners' care on or before August 22, 1974. During the next four and one-half years, those three children were in the custody of the State and in the care of foster homes or institutions, and the State was diligently engaged in efforts to prepare petitioners for the children's return. Those efforts were unsuccessful, however, and on April 10, 1979, the New York Family Court for Ulster County terminated petitioners' parental rights as to the three children removed in 1974 or earlier. This termination was preceded by a judicial finding that petitioners had failed to plan for the return and future of their children, a statutory category of permanent neglect. Petitioners now contend, and the Court today holds, that they were denied due process of law, not because of a general inadequacy of procedural protections, but simply because the finding of permanent neglect was made on the basis of a preponderance of the evidence adduced at the termination hearing.

It is well settled that "[t]he requirements of procedural due process apply only to the deprivation of interests encompassed by the Fourteenth Amendment's protection of liberty and property." *Board of Regents* v. *Roth*, 408 U. S. 564, 569 (1972). In determining whether such liberty or property interests are implicated by a particular government action, "we must look not to the 'weight' but to the *nature* of the interest at stake." *Id.*, at 571 (emphasis in original). I do not disagree with the majority's conclusion that the interest of parents in their relationship with their children is sufficiently fundamental to come within the finite class of liberty interests protected by the Fourteenth Amendment. See *Smith* v. *Organization of Foster Families*, *supra*, at 862–863 (Stewart, J., concurring in judgment). "Once it is determined that due process applies, [however,] the question remains what process is due." *Morrissey* v. *Brewer*, 408 U. S. 471, 481 (1972). It is the majority's answer to this question with which I disagree.

A

Due process of law is a flexible constitutional principle. The requirements which it imposes upon governmental actions vary with the situations to which it applies. As the Court previously has recognized, "not all situations calling for procedural safeguards call for the same kind of procedure." *Morrissey* v. *Brewer*, *supra*, at 481. See also *Greenholtz* v. *Nebraska Penal Inmates*, 442 U. S. 1, 12 (1979); *Mathews* v. *Eldridge*, 424 U. S., at 334; *Cafeteria Workers* v. *McElroy*, 367 U. S. 886, 895 (1961). The adequacy of a scheme of procedural protections cannot, therefore, be determined merely by the application of general principles unrelated to the peculiarities of the case at hand.

Given this flexibility, it is obvious that a proper due process inquiry cannot be made by focusing upon one narrow provision of the challenged statutory scheme. Such a focus threatens to overlook factors which may introduce constitutionally adequate protections into a particular government action. Courts must examine *all* procedural protections offered by the State, and must assess the *cumulative* effect of such safeguards. As we have stated before, courts must consider "the fairness and reliability of the existing . . . procedures" before holding that the Constitution requires more. *Mathews* v. *Eldridge*, *supra*, at 343. Only through such a broad inquiry may courts determine whether a challenged governmental action satisfies the due process requirement of "fundamental fairness."[3] In some instances, the Court has even looked to nonprocedural restraints on official action in determining whether the deprivation of a protected interest was effected without due process of law. *E. g.*, *Ingraham* v.

[3] Although, as the majority states, we have held that the minimum requirements of procedural due process are a question of federal law, such a holding does not mean that the procedural protections afforded by a State will be inadequate under the Fourteenth Amendment. It means simply that the adequacy of the state-provided process is to be judged by constitutional standards—standards which the majority itself equates to "fundamental fairness." *Ante*, at 754. I differ, therefore, not with the majority's statement that the requirements of due process present a federal question, but with its apparent assumption that the presence of "fundamental fairness" can be ascertained by an examination which completely disregards the plethora of protective procedures accorded parents by New York law.

Wright, 430 U. S. 651 (1977). In this case, it is just such a broad look at the New York scheme which reveals its fundamental fairness.[4]

The termination of parental rights on the basis of permanent neglect can occur under New York law only by order of the Family Court. N. Y. Soc. Serv. Law (SSL) § 384–b.3.(d) (McKinney Supp. 1981–1982). Before a petition for permanent termination can be filed in that court, however, several other events must first occur.

The Family Court has jurisdiction only over those children who are in the care of an authorized agency. N. Y. Family Court Act (FCA) § 614.1.(b) (McKinney 1975 and Supp. 1981–1982). Therefore, the children who are the subject of a termination petition must previously have been removed from their parents' home on a temporary basis. Temporary removal of a child can occur in one of two ways. The parents may consent to the removal, FCA § 1021, or, as occurred in this case, the Family Court can order the removal pursuant to a finding that the child is abused or neglected.[5] FCA §§ 1051, 1052.

---

[4] The majority refuses to consider New York's procedure as a whole, stating that "[t]he statutory provision of right to counsel and multiple hearings before termination cannot suffice to protect a natural parent's fundamental liberty interests if the State is willing to tolerate undue uncertainty in the determination of the dispositive facts." *Ante*, at 758, n. 9. Implicit in this statement is the conclusion that the risk of error may be reduced to constitutionally tolerable levels only by raising the standard of proof—that other procedures can never eliminate "undue uncertainty" so long as the standard of proof remains too low. Aside from begging the question of whether the risks of error tolerated by the State in this case are "undue," see *infra*, at 785–791, this conclusion denies the flexibility that we have long recognized in the principle of due process; understates the error-reducing power of procedural protections such as the right to counsel, evidentiary hearings, rules of evidence, and appellate review; and establishes the standard of proof as the *sine qua non* of procedural due process.

[5] An abused child is one who has been subjected to intentional physical injury "which causes or creates a substantial risk of death, or serious or protracted disfigurement, or protracted impairment of physical or emo-

Court proceedings to order the temporary removal of a child are initiated by a petition alleging abuse or neglect, filed by a state-authorized child protection agency or by a person designated by the court. FCA §§ 1031, 1032. Unless the court finds that exigent circumstances require removal of the child before a petition may be filed and a hearing held, see FCA § 1022, the order of temporary removal results from a "dispositional hearing" conducted to determine the appropriate form of alternative care. FCA § 1045. See also FCA § 1055. This "dispositional hearing" can be held only after the court, at a separate "fact-finding hearing," has found the child to be abused or neglected within the specific statutory definition of those terms. FCA §§ 1012, 1044, 1051.

Parents subjected to temporary removal proceedings are provided extensive procedural protections. A summons and copy of the temporary removal petition must be served upon the parents within two days of issuance by the court, FCA §§ 1035, 1036, and the parents may, at their own request, delay the commencement of the factfinding hearing for three days after service of the summons. FCA § 1048.[6] The fact-finding hearing may not commence without a determination by the court that the parents are present at the hearing and have been served with the petition. FCA § 1041. At the hearing itself, "only competent, material and relevant evidence may be admitted," with some enumerated exceptions

---

tional health or protracted loss or impairment of the function of any bodily organ." FCA § 1012(e)(i). Sexual offenses against a child are also covered by this category. A neglected child is one "whose physical, mental or emotional condition has been impaired or is in imminent danger of becoming impaired as a result of the failure of his parent . . . to exercise a minimum degree of care in supplying the child with adequate food, clothing, shelter or education." FCA § 1012(f)(i)(A).

[6] The relatively short time between notice and commencement of hearing provided by § 1048 undoubtedly reflects the State's desire to protect the child. These proceedings are designed to permit prompt action by the court when the child is threatened with imminent and serious physical, mental, or emotional harm.

for particularly probative evidence. FCA § 1046(b)(ii). In addition, indigent parents are provided with an attorney to represent them at both the factfinding and dispositional hearings, as well as at all other proceedings related to temporary removal of their child. FCA § 262(a)(i).

An order of temporary removal must be reviewed every 18 months by the Family Court. SSL § 392.2. Such review is conducted by hearing before the same judge who ordered the temporary removal, and a notice of the hearing, including a statement of the dispositional alternatives, must be given to the parents at least 20 days before the hearing is held. SSL § 392.4. As in the initial removal action, the parents must be parties to the proceedings, *ibid.*, and are entitled to court-appointed counsel if indigent. FCA § 262(a).

One or more years after a child has been removed temporarily from the parents' home, permanent termination proceedings may be commenced by the filing of a petition in the court which ordered the temporary removal. The petition must be filed by a state agency or by a foster parent authorized by the court, SSL § 384–b.3.(b), and must allege that the child has been permanently neglected by the parents. SSL § 384–b.3.(d).[7] Notice of the petition and the dispositional proceedings must be served upon the parents at least 20 days before the commencement of the hearing, SSL § 384–b.3.(e), must inform them of the potential consequences of the hearing, *ibid.*, and must inform them "of their right to the assistance of counsel, including [their] right . . . to have counsel assigned by the court [if] they are financially unable to obtain counsel." *Ibid.* See also FCA § 262.

As in the initial removal proceedings, two hearings are held in consideration of the permanent termination petition.

---

[7] Permanent custody also may be awarded by the Family Court if both parents are deceased, the parents abandoned the child at least six months prior to the termination proceedings, or the parents are unable to provide proper and adequate care by reason of mental illness or mental retardation. SSL § 384–b.4.(c).

SSL § 384–b.3.(f). At the factfinding hearing, the court must determine, by a fair preponderance of the evidence, whether the child has been permanently neglected. SSL § 384–b.3.(g). "Only competent, material and relevant evidence may be admitted in a fact-finding hearing." FCA § 624. The court may find permanent neglect if the child is in the care of an authorized agency or foster home and the parents have "failed for a period of more than one year . . . substantially and continuously or repeatedly to maintain contact with or plan for the future of the child, although physically and financially able to do so." SSL § 384–b.7.(a).[8] In addition, because the State considers its "first obligation" to be the reuniting of the child with its natural parents, SSL § 384–b.1.(iii), the court must also find that the supervising state agency has, without success, made "*diligent* efforts to encourage and strengthen the parental relationship." SSL § 384–b.7.(a) (emphasis added).[9]

---

[8] As to maintaining contact with the child, New York law provides that "evidence of insubstantial or infrequent contacts by a parent with his or her child shall not, of itself, be sufficient as a matter of law to preclude a determination that such child is a permanently neglected child. A visit or communication by a parent with the child which is of such a character as to overtly demonstrate a lack of affectionate and concerned parenthood shall not be deemed a substantial contact." SSL § 384–b.7.(b).

Failure to plan for the future of the child means failure "to take such steps as may be necessary to provide an adequate, stable home and parental care for the child within a period of time which is reasonable under the financial circumstances available to the parent. The plan must be realistic and feasible, and good faith effort shall not, of itself, be determinative. In determining whether a parent has planned for the future of the child, the court may consider the failure of the parent to utilize medical, psychiatric, psychological and other social and rehabilitative services and material resources made available to such parent." SSL § 384–b.7.(c).

[9] "Diligent efforts" are defined under New York law to "mean reasonable attempts by an authorized agency to assist, develop and encourage a meaningful relationship between the parent and child, including but not limited to:

"(1) consultation and cooperation with the parents in developing a plan for appropriate services to the child and his family;

Following the factfinding hearing, a separate, dispositional hearing is held to determine what course of action would be in "the best interests of the child." FCA § 631. A finding of permanent neglect at the factfinding hearing, although necessary to a termination of parental rights, does not control the court's order at the dispositional hearing. The court may dismiss the petition, suspend judgment on the petition and retain jurisdiction for a period of one year in order to provide further opportunity for a reuniting of the family, or terminate the parents' right to the custody and care of the child. FCA §§ 631–634. The court must base its decision solely upon the record of "material and relevant evidence" introduced at the dispositional hearing, FCA § 624; *In re "Female" M.*, 70 App. Div. 2d 812, 417 N. Y. S. 2d 482 (1979), and may not entertain any presumption that the best interests of the child "will be promoted by any particular disposition." FCA § 631.

As petitioners did in this case, parents may appeal any unfavorable decision to the Appellate Division of the New York Supreme Court. Thereafter, review may be sought in the New York Court of Appeals and, ultimately, in this Court if a federal question is properly presented.

As this description of New York's termination procedures demonstrates, the State seeks not only to protect the interests of parents in rearing their own children, but also to assist and encourage parents who have lost custody of their children to reassume their rightful role. Fully understood, the New York system is a comprehensive program to *aid* parents such as petitioners. Only as a last resort, when "diligent efforts" to reunite the family have failed, does New

---

"(2) making suitable arrangements for the parents to visit the child;

"(3) provision of services and other assistance to the parents so that problems preventing the discharge of the child from care may be resolved or ameliorated; and

"(4) informing the parents at appropriate intervals of the child's progress, development and health." SSL § 384-b.7.(f).

York authorize the termination of parental rights. The procedures for termination of those relationships which cannot be aided and which threaten permanent injury to the child, administered by a judge who has supervised the case from the first temporary removal through the final termination, cannot be viewed as fundamentally unfair. The facts of this case demonstrate the fairness of the system.

The three children to which this case relates were removed from petitioners' custody in 1973 and 1974, before petitioners' other two children were born. The removals were made pursuant to the procedures detailed above and in response to what can only be described as shockingly abusive treatment.[10] At the temporary removal hearing held before the Family Court on September 30, 1974, petitioners were represented by counsel, and allowed the Ulster County Department of Social Services (Department) to take custody of the three children.

Temporary removal of the children was continued at an evidentiary hearing held before the Family Court in December 1975, after which the court issued a written opinion concluding that petitioners were unable to resume their parental responsibilities due to personality disorders. Unsatisfied with the progress petitioners were making, the court also di-

[10] Tina Apel, the oldest of petitioners' five children, was removed from their custody by court order in November 1973 when she was two years old. Removal proceedings were commenced in response to complaints by neighbors and reports from a local hospital that Tina had suffered injuries in petitioners' home including a fractured left femur, treated with a home-made splint; bruises on the upper arms, forehead, flank, and spine; and abrasions of the upper leg. The following summer John Santosky III, petitioners' second oldest child, was also removed from petitioners' custody. John, who was less than one year old at the time, was admitted to the hospital suffering malnutrition, bruises on the eye and forehead, cuts on the foot, blisters on the hand, and multiple pin pricks on the back. Exhibit to Brief for Respondent Kramer 1–5. Jed Santosky, the third oldest of petitioners' children, was removed from his parents' custody when only three days old as a result of the abusive treatment of the two older children.

rected the Department to reduce to writing the plan which it had designed to solve the problems at petitioners' home and reunite the family.

A plan for providing petitioners with extensive counseling and training services was submitted to the court and approved in February 1976. Under the plan, petitioners received training by a mother's aide, a nutritional aide, and a public health nurse, and counseling at a family planning clinic. In addition, the plan provided psychiatric treatment and vocational training for the father, and counseling at a family service center for the mother. Brief for Respondent Kramer 1–7. Between early 1976 and the final termination decision in April 1979, the State spent more than $15,000 in these efforts to rehabilitate petitioners as parents. App. 34.

Petitioners' response to the State's effort was marginal at best. They wholly disregarded some of the available services and participated only sporadically in the others. As a result, and out of growing concern over the length of the children's stay in foster care, the Department petitioned in September 1976 for permanent termination of petitioners' parental rights so that the children could be adopted by other families. Although the Family Court recognized that petitioners' reaction to the State's efforts was generally "nonresponsive, even hostile," the fact that they were "at least superficially cooperative" led it to conclude that there was yet hope of further improvement and an eventual reuniting of the family. Exhibit to Brief for Respondent Kramer 618. Accordingly, the petition for permanent termination was dismissed.

Whatever progress petitioners were making prior to the 1976 termination hearing, they made little or no progress thereafter. In October 1978, the Department again filed a termination petition alleging that petitioners had completely failed to plan for the children's future despite the considerable efforts rendered in their behalf. This time, the Family Court agreed. The court found that petitioners had "failed in any meaningful way to take advantage of the many social and rehabilitative services that have not only been made available to them but have been diligently urged upon them." App. 35. In addition, the court found that the "infrequent" visits "between the parents and their children were at best superficial and devoid of any real emotional content." *Id.*, at 21. The court thus found "nothing in the situation which holds out any hope that [petitioners] may ever become financially self sufficient or emotionally mature enough to be independent of the services of social agencies. More than a reasonable amount of time has passed and still, in the words of the case workers, there has been no discernible forward movement. At some point in time, it must be said, 'enough is enough.'" *Id.*, at 36.

In accordance with the statutory requirements set forth above, the court found that petitioners' failure to plan for the future of their children, who were then seven, five, and four years old and had been out of petitioners' custody for at least four years, rose to the level of permanent neglect. At a subsequent dispositional hearing, the court terminated petitioners' parental rights, thereby freeing the three children for adoption.

As this account demonstrates, the State's extraordinary 4-year effort to reunite petitioners' family was not just unsuccessful, it was altogether rebuffed by parents unwilling to improve their circumstances sufficiently to permit a return of their children. At every step of this protracted process petitioners were accorded those procedures and protections which traditionally have been required by due process of law. Moreover, from the beginning to the end of this sad story all judicial determinations were made by one Family Court Judge. After four and one-half years of involvement with petitioners, more than seven complete hearings, and additional periodic supervision of the State's rehabilitative efforts, the judge no doubt was intimately familiar with this case and the prospects for petitioners' rehabilitation.

It is inconceivable to me that these procedures were "fundamentally unfair" to petitioners. Only by its obsessive focus on the standard of proof and its almost complete disregard of the facts of this case does the majority find otherwise.[11] As the discussion above indicates, however, such a

---

[11] The majority finds, without any reference to the facts of this case, that "numerous factors [in New York termination proceedings] combine to magnify the risk of erroneous factfinding." *Ante*, at 762. Among the factors identified by the majority are the "unusual discretion" of the Family Court judge "to underweigh probative facts that might favor the parent"; the often uneducated, minority status of the parents and their consequent "vulnerab[ility] to judgments based on cultural or class bias"; the "State's ability to assemble its case," which "dwarfs the parents' ability to mount a defense" by including an unlimited budget, expert attorneys, and "full access to all public records concerning the family"; and the fact that "natural parents have no 'double jeopardy' defense against repeated state" efforts, "with more or better evidence," to terminate parental rights "even when the parents have attained the level of fitness required by the State." *Ante*, at 762, 763, 764. In short, the majority characterizes the State as a wealthy and powerful bully bent on taking children away from defenseless parents. See *ante*, at 761–764. Such characterization finds no support in the record.

The intent of New York has been stated with eminent clarity: "the [S]tate's *first obligation* is to *help* the family with services to *prevent* its break-up or to *reunite* it if the child has already left home." SSL § 384–b.1.(a)(iii) (emphasis added). There is simply no basis in fact for believing, as the majority does, that the State does not mean what it says; indeed, the facts of this case demonstrate that New York has gone the extra mile in seeking to effectuate its declared purpose. See *supra*, at 781–785. More importantly, there should be no room in the jurisprudence of this Court for decisions based on unsupported, inaccurate assumptions.

A brief examination of the "factors" relied upon by the majority demonstrates its error. The "unusual" discretion of the Family Court judge to consider the " 'affectio[n] and concer[n]' " displayed by parents during visits with their children, *ante*, at 763, n. 12, is nothing more than discretion to consider reality; there is not one shred of evidence in this case suggesting that the determination of the Family Court was "based on cultural or class bias"; if parents lack the "ability to mount a defense," the State provides them with the full services of an attorney, FCA § 262, and they, like the State, have "full access to all *public* records concerning the family" (emphasis added); and the absence of "double jeopardy" protection simply recognizes the fact that family problems are often ongoing and may in the future

volved a child or children abused by a natural parent over an extended period of time. The difference between the two cases is in the Court's approach to the interests of the child or children involved. *Santosky* was directed toward the best interest of the parent. *DeShaney* concerned the best interest of the child.

Part III of the Article examines the nature of state proceedings involving the termination of parental rights. After providing a detailed account of what occurs in such proceedings, the Article suggests that many state proceedings do not adequately ensure due process protection for the children involved. This part then demonstrates why a preponderance of the evidence standard would provide children with due process protection.

Part IV focuses on the legal status of the child within the changing American family unit. Statistical evidence is offered to show that the child's interest should be considered separately from that of the parents in termination proceedings. Part Four also demonstrates how existing due process analysis supports the best interest of the child. Finally, in Part V, this Article considers the best interest of the child from a federalist perspective and concludes that federalism justifies state autonomy in domestic relations matters.[23]

II. THE LAW OF *SANTOSKY* AND THE FACTS OF *DESHANEY*

Santosky v. Kramer[24] and *DeShaney v. Winnebago Department of Social Services*[25] serve as useful illustrations of the Supreme Court's approach to the best interest of the child. Before examining these cases, however, a brief exposition on the parental presumption is necessary.

(1982). In *DeShaney*, the Court found that the Due Process Clause offered no remedy to a child abused by the parent to whom he was constantly and consistently returned so as to protect that parent's natural rights. "[N]othing in the language of the Due Process Clause itself requires the State to protect the life, liberty, and property of its citizens against invasion by private actors." *DeShaney*, 489 U.S. at 195.

23. This Article supports the proposition that each state be allowed to develop its own standard of proof necessary to terminate parental rights, recognizing that many states will continue to require a higher standard than preponderance of the evidence. Those states legislating a higher standard should then confront the issue of whether that higher standard deprives a child of his or her constitutional guarantees of due process of law, not whether the lower standard deprives a parent of his or her constitutional guarantees of due process.

24. 455 U.S. 745 (1982).

25. 489 U.S. 189 (1989).

focus does not comport with the flexible standard of fundamental fairness embodied in the Due Process Clause of the Fourteenth Amendment.

B

In addition to the basic fairness of the process afforded petitioners, the standard of proof chosen by New York clearly reflects a constitutionally permissible balance of the interests at stake in this case. The standard of proof "represents an attempt to instruct the factfinder concerning the degree of confidence our society thinks he should have in the correctness of factual conclusions for a particular type of adjudication." *In re Winship*, 397 U. S. 358, 370 (1970) (Harlan, J. concurring); *Addington* v. *Texas*, 441 U. S. 418, 423 (1979). In this respect, the standard of proof is a crucial component of legal process, the primary function of which is "to minimize the risk of erroneous decisions."[12] *Greenholtz* v. *Nebraska*

---

warrant action that currently is unnecessary. In this case the Family Court dismissed the first termination petition because it desired to give petitioners "the benefit of the doubt," Exhibit to Brief for Respondent Kramer 620, and a second opportunity to raise themselves to "an acceptable minimal level of competency as parents." *Id.*, at 624. It was their complete failure to do so that prompted the second, successful termination petition. See *supra*, at 781–784 and this page.

[12] It is worth noting that the significance of the standard of proof in New York parental termination proceedings differs from the significance of the standard in other forms of litigation. In the usual adjudicatory setting, the factfinder has had little or no prior exposure to the facts of the case. His only knowledge of those facts comes from the evidence adduced at trial, and he renders his findings solely upon the basis of that evidence. Thus, normally, the standard of proof is a crucial factor in the final outcome of the case, for it is the scale upon which the factfinder weighs his knowledge and makes his decision.

Although the standard serves the same function in New York parental termination proceedings, additional assurances of accuracy are present in its application. As was adduced at oral argument, the practice in New York is to assign one judge to supervise a case from the initial temporary removal of the child to the final termination of parental rights. Therefore,

Penal Inmates, 442 U. S., at 13. See also *Addington* v. *Texas*, *supra*, at 425; *Mathews* v. *Eldridge*, 424 U. S., at 344.

In determining the propriety of a particular standard of proof in a given case, however, it is not enough simply to say that we are trying to minimize the risk of error. Because errors in factfinding affect more than one interest, we try to minimize error as to those interests which we consider to be most important. As Justice Harlan explained in his well-known concurrence to *In re Winship*:

> "In a lawsuit between two parties, a factual error can make a difference in one of two ways. First, it can result in a judgment in favor of the plaintiff when the true facts warrant a judgment for the defendant. The analogue in a criminal case would be the conviction of an innocent man. On the other hand, an erroneous factual determination can result in a judgment for the defendant when the true facts justify a judgment in plaintiff's favor. The criminal analogue would be the acquittal of a guilty man.
>
> The standard of proof influences the relative frequency of these two types of erroneous outcomes. If, for example, the standard of proof for a criminal trial were a preponderance of the evidence rather than proof

---

as discussed above, the factfinder is intimately familiar with the case before the termination proceedings ever begin. Indeed, as in this case, he often will have been closely involved in protracted efforts to rehabilitate the parents. Even if a change in judges occurs, the Family Court retains jurisdiction of the case and the newly assigned judge may take judicial notice of all prior proceedings. Given this familiarity with the case, and the necessarily lengthy efforts which must precede a termination action in New York, decisions in termination cases are made by judges steeped in the background of the case and peculiarly able to judge the accuracy of evidence placed before them. This does not mean that the standard of proof in these cases can escape due process scrutiny, only that additional assurances of accuracy attend the application of the standard in New York termination proceedings.

beyond a reasonable doubt, there would be a smaller risk of factual errors that result in freeing guilty persons, but a far greater risk of factual errors that result in convicting the innocent. Because the standard of proof affects the comparative frequency of these two types of erroneous outcomes, the choice of the standard to be applied in a particular kind of litigation should, in a rational world, reflect an assessment of the comparative social disutility of each." 397 U. S., at 370–371.

When the standard of proof is understood as reflecting such an assessment, an examination of the interests at stake in a particular case becomes essential to determining the propriety of the specified standard of proof. Because proof by a preponderance of the evidence requires that "[t]he litigants . . . share the risk of error in a roughly equal fashion," *Addington* v. *Texas*, *supra*, at 423, it rationally should be applied only when the interests at stake are of roughly equal societal importance. The interests at stake in this case demonstrate that New York has selected a constitutionally permissible standard of proof.

On one side is the interest of parents in a continuation of the family unit and the raising of their own children. The importance of this interest cannot easily be overstated. Few consequences of judicial action are so grave as the severance of natural family ties. Even the convict committed to prison and thereby deprived of his physical liberty often retains the love and support of family members. "This Court's decisions have by now made plain beyond the need for multiple citation that a parent's desire for and right to 'the companionship, care, custody, and management of his or her children' is an important interest that 'undeniably warrants deference and, absent a powerful countervailing interest, protection.' *Stanley* v. *Illinois*, 405 U. S. 645, 651." *Lassiter* v. *Department of Social Services*, 452 U. S. 18, 27 (1981). In creating the scheme at issue in this case, the New York Legislature was expressly aware of this right of parents "to bring up their own children." SSL § 384-b.1.(a)(ii).

On the other side of the termination proceeding are the often countervailing interests of the child.[13] A stable, loving

---

[13] The majority dismisses the child's interest in the accuracy of determinations made at the factfinding hearing because "[t]he factfinding does not purport . . . to balance the child's interest in a normal family home against the parents' interest in raising the child," but instead "pits the State directly against the parents." *Ante*, at 759. Only "[a]fter the State has established parental unfitness," the majority reasons, may the court "assume . . . that the interests of the child and the natural parents do diverge." *Ante*, at 760.

This reasoning misses the mark. The child has an interest in the outcome of the factfinding hearing independent of that of the parent. To be sure, "the child and his parents share a vital interest in preventing *erroneous* termination of their natural relationship." *Ibid.* (emphasis added). But the child's interest in a continuation of the family unit exists only to the extent that such a continuation would not be harmful to him. An error *in the factfinding hearing* that results in a failure to terminate a parent-child relationship which rightfully should be terminated may well detrimentally affect the child. See nn. 14, 15, *infra*.

The preponderance-of-the-evidence standard, which allocates the risk of error more or less evenly, is employed when the social disutility of error *in either direction* is roughly equal—that is, when an incorrect finding of fault would produce consequences as undesirable as the consequences that would be produced by an incorrect finding of *no* fault. Only when the disutility of error in one direction discernibly outweighs the disutility of error in the other direction do we choose, by means of the standard of proof, to reduce the likelihood of the more onerous outcome. See *In re Winship*, 397 U. S. 358, 370–372 (1970) (Harlan, J., concurring).

New York's adoption of the preponderance-of-the-evidence standard reflects its conclusion that the undesirable consequence of an erroneous finding of parental unfitness—the unwarranted termination of the family relationship—is roughly equal to the undesirable consequence of an erroneous finding of parental fitness—the risk of permanent injury to the child either by return of the child to an abusive home or by the child's continued lack of a permanent home. See nn. 14, 15, *infra*. Such a conclusion is well within the province of state legislatures. It cannot be said that the New York procedures are unconstitutional simply because a majority of the Members of this Court disagree with the New York Legislature's weighing of the interests of the parents and the child in an error-free factfinding hearing.

homelife is essential to a child's physical, emotional, and spiritual well-being. It requires no citation of authority to assert that children who are abused in their youth generally face extraordinary problems developing into responsible, productive citizens. The same can be said of children who, though not physically or emotionally abused, are passed from one foster home to another with no constancy of love, trust, or discipline. If the Family Court makes an incorrect factual determination resulting in a failure to terminate a parent-child relationship which rightfully should be ended, the child involved must return either to an abusive home[14] or to the often unstable world of foster care.[15] The reality of these

[14] The record in this case illustrates the problems that may arise when a child is returned to an abusive home. Eighteen months after Tina, petitioners' oldest child, was first removed from petitioners' home, she was returned to the home on a trial basis. Katherine Weiss, a supervisor in the Child Protective Unit of the Ulster County Child Welfare Department, later testified in Family Court that "[t]he attempt to return Tina to her home just totally blew up." Exhibit to Brief for Respondent Kramer 135. When asked to explain what happened, Mrs. Weiss testified that "there were instances on the record in this court of Mr. Santosky's abuse of his wife, alleged abuse of the children and proven neglect of the children." *Ibid.* Tina again was removed from the home, this time along with John and Jed.

[15] The New York Legislature recognized the potential harm to children of extended, nonpermanent foster care. It found "that many children who have been placed in foster care experience unnecessarily protracted stays in such care without being adopted or returned to their parents or other custodians. Such unnecessary stays may deprive these children of positive, nurturing family relationships and have deleterious effects on their development into responsible, productive citizens." SSL § 384–b.1.(b). Subsequent studies have proved this finding correct. One commentator recently wrote of "the lamentable conditions of many foster care placements" under the New York system even today. He noted: "Over fifty percent of the children in foster care have been in this 'temporary' status for more than two years; over thirty percent for more than five years. During this time, many children are placed in a sequence of ill-suited foster homes, denying them the consistent support and nurturing that they so desperately need." Besharov, State Intervention To Protect

risks is magnified by the fact that the only families faced with termination actions are those which have voluntarily surrendered custody of their child to the State, or, as in this case, those from which the child has been removed by judicial action because of threatened irreparable injury through abuse or neglect. Permanent neglect findings also occur only in families where the child has been in foster care for at least one year.

In addition to the child's interest in a normal homelife, "the State has an urgent interest in the welfare of the child." *Lassiter* v. *Department of Social Services*, 452 U. S., at 27.[16] Few could doubt that the most valuable resource of a self-governing society is its population of children who will one day become adults and themselves assume the responsibility of self-governance. "A democratic society rests, for its continuance, upon the healthy, well-rounded growth of young people into full maturity as citizens, with all that implies." *Prince* v. *Massachusetts*, 321 U. S. 158, 168 (1944). Thus, "the whole community" has an interest "that children be both safeguarded from abuses and given opportunities for growth into free and independent well-developed . . . citizens." *Id.*, at 165. See also *Ginsberg* v. *New York*, 390 U. S. 629, 640–641 (1968).

When, in the context of a permanent neglect termination proceeding, the interests of the child and the State in a sta-

---

Children: New York's Definition of "Child Abuse" and "Child Neglect," 26 N. Y. L. S. L. Rev. 723, 770–771 (1981) (footnotes omitted). In this case, petitioners' three children have been in foster care for more than four years, one child since he was only three days old. Failure to terminate petitioners' parental rights will only mean a continuation of this unsatisfactory situation.

[16] The majority's conclusion that a state interest in the child's well-being arises only after a determination of parental unfitness suffers from the same error as its assertion that the child has no interest, separate from that of its parents, in the accuracy of the factfinding hearing. See n. 13, *supra*.

ble, nurturing homelife are balanced against the interests of the parents in the rearing of their child, it cannot be said that either set of interests is so clearly paramount as to require that the risk of error be allocated to one side or the other. Accordingly, a State constitutionally may conclude that the risk of error should be borne in roughly equal fashion by use of the preponderance-of-the-evidence standard of proof. See *Addington* v. *Texas*, 441 U. S., at 423. This is precisely the balance which has been struck by the New York Legislature: "It is the intent of the legislature in enacting this section to provide procedures not only assuring that the rights of the natural parent are protected, but also, where positive, nurturing parent-child relationships no longer exist, furthering the best interests, needs, and rights of the child by terminating the parental rights and freeing the child for adoption." SSL § 384–b.1.(b).

III

For the reasons heretofore stated, I believe that the Court today errs in concluding that the New York standard of proof in parental-rights termination proceedings violates due process of law. The decision disregards New York's earnest efforts to *aid* parents in regaining the custody of their children and a host of procedural protections placed around parental rights and interests. The Court finds a constitutional violation only by a tunnel-vision application of due process principles that altogether loses sight of the unmistakable fairness of the New York procedure.

Even more worrisome, today's decision cavalierly rejects the considered judgment of the New York Legislature in an area traditionally entrusted to state care. The Court thereby begins, I fear, a trend of federal intervention in state family law matters which surely will stifle creative responses to vexing problems. Accordingly, I dissent.

AN ANALYSIS OF REALISTIC DUE PROCESS RIGHTS OF CHILDREN VERSUS PARENTS

Raymond C. O'Brien[*]

I. INTRODUCTION

More often than not, the question presented presupposes the answer. For instance, in the infamous case of *Bowers v. Hardwick*,[1] the Supreme Court was asked to decide whether "the Federal Constitution confers a fundamental right upon homosexuals to engage in sodomy and hence invalidates the laws of the many States that still make such conduct illegal and have done so for a very long time."[2] Even in the relative sexual freedom of the post-*Griswold*[3] era, the answer is quite obvious: No, the Federal Constitution does not confer on homosexuals the fundamental right to engage in sodomy, especially since the states have preemptory jurisdiction over domestic relations;[4] since sodomy is

---

* Professor of Law, The Catholic University of America School of Law; Visiting Professor of Law, Georgetown University Law Center.

1. 478 U.S. 186 (1986) (holding that the due process clause of the Constitution does not confer on homosexuals the right to engage in sodomy in violation of a state statute which prohibits any person, homosexual or heterosexual, from engaging in specifically defined conduct).

2. *Id.* at 190.

3. *See* Griswold v. Connecticut, 381 U.S. 479 (1965) (initiating protection of sexual conduct, albeit for married couples, by holding that specific guarantees in the Bill of Rights have penumbras which, in turn, create zones of privacy to which people are entitled as of right). Subsequent cases extended this zone of privacy to the sexual conduct of single persons. *See, e.g.*, Eisenstadt v. Baird, 405 U.S. 438 (1972) (holding that the Equal Protection Clause prohibits the state from discriminating between married and single persons in the distribution of contraceptives). *Bowers* should have been the next step in this evolutionary process and should have extended privacy rights to homosexuals. *See* Rev. Raymond C. O'Brien, *Discrimination: The Difference With AIDS*, 6 J. CONTEMP. HEALTH L. & POL'Y 93, 102-106 (1990). Indeed, the *Bowers'* dissent took the right of privacy to be the right of "self-definition". *Bowers*, 478 U.S. at 205 (Blackmun, J., dissenting). That is, certain decisions in life are so central to the personal identities of those singled out, that no state regulation should be allowed to hinder them. *See* LAURENCE TRIBE, AMERICAN CONSTITUTIONAL LAW, 943 (1st ed. 1978).

4. *See, e.g.*, Suter v. Artist M., 112 S. Ct. 1360 (1992) (refusing to foster and other dependent children the right to bring suits under the Federal Adoption Assistance and Child Welfare Act of 1980); Planned Parenthood of Southeastern Pa. v. Casey, 112 S. Ct. 2791 (1992) (allowing states to regulate abortions); Ankenbrandt v. Richards, 112 S. Ct. 2206 (1992) (recognizing domestic-relations exception to federal diversity jurisdiction); Barndt v. Barndt, 580 A.2d 320

known to transmit AIDS; since homosexual activity is not a fundamental right;[5] and since the Due Process Clause should not be used to strike down state laws "that may be unwise, improvident, or out of harmony with a particular school of thought."[6] If the question in *Bowers* had inquired as to the right of a person to be accorded equal protection of the law in something so fundamental as consensual, noninjurious sexual conduct in the privacy of his or her home, another answer may have resulted.[7]

So too can the question presuppose the answer in the Solomonic arena of child, parent, and state. For instance, should natural parents have the right to procreate, raise, and enjoy their children? Surely the answer is a resounding yes.[8] And so it was in *Santosky v. Kramer*,[9] where the Supreme Court was asked whether "due process requires that the State support its allegations by at least clear and convincing evidence" before it "may sever completely and irrevocably the rights of parents in their natural child."[10] How could any person justify terminating the rights of a parent in his or her natural child based on anything less than clear and convincing evidence? After all, "[f]or the natural parents . . . the consequence of an erroneous termination is the unnecessary destruction of their natural family."[11] And if the state can-

(Pa. Super. Ct. 1990). The majority in *Santosky* was clearly aware of the need to retain the federal exception to domestic relations jurisdiction. The Court suggested that it will only interfere with "state answers to domestic relations questions" when there are "clear constitutional violations." Santosky v. Kramer, 455 U.S. 745, 768 n.18 (1982) (citation omitted).

5. *See Bowers*, 478 U.S. at 197 (Burger, C.J., concurring). "To hold that the act of homosexual sodomy is somehow protected as a fundamental right would be to cast aside millennia of moral teaching." *Id.*

6. Ferguson v. Skrupa, 372 U.S. 726, 731-32 (1963) (quoting Williamson v. Lee Optical Co., 348 U.S. 483, 488 (1955)).

7. The decision in *Hardwick* was 5-4. A member of the majority, Justice Powell, admitted during a speech in 1990 that he "probably made a mistake" in his vote. He now thinks that the Constitution protects the right to engage in homosexual acts. Stuart Taylor, Jr., *When Judicial Flips Aren't Flops*, LEGAL TIMES, Dec. 17, 1990, at 23.

8. Note that the major Court decisions regarding sexuality have always placed that sexuality in the context of reproduction. *See, e.g.*, Roe v. Wade, 410 U.S. 113 (1973) (woman could decide she did not want to beget a child during pregnancy); Eisenstadt v. Baird, 405 U.S. 438 (1972) (single persons cannot be denied contraceptives if they wish to avoid begetting a child); Griswold v. Connecticut, 381 U.S. 479 (1965) (state may not prohibit distribution of contraceptive devices to married couples who do not wish to beget a child).

9. 455 U.S. 745 (1982).

10. *Id.* at 747-48. New York State, by allowing for preponderance of the evidence, required less proof than most other states at the time: thirty-five states, the District of Columbia, and the Virgin Islands, required either clear and convincing evidence or proof beyond a reasonable doubt. *See infra* text accompanying notes 146-48.

11. 455 U.S. at 766.

not initially meet the clear and convincing standard so as to terminate parental rights the first time, "it always can try once again to cut off the parents' rights after gathering more or better evidence."[12]

The question posed above presents itself in such a way as to evoke a parent versus state confrontation, presupposing an answer that is heavily biased in favor of the parent. The question presumes that the child's best interest subsists within the best interest of the parent. This presupposition, however, is erroneously over-expansive. It does not consider the best interest of the child. At the present time, nevertheless, it is the controlling principle in cases involving efforts by states to terminate parental rights.

The purpose of this Article is to analyze the *Santosky* presupposition and demonstrate why it is misdirected. In particular, the Article posits that the clear and convincing standard adopted by the Court deprives the child of his or her due process rights. The minimum standard should be reduced to at least one of preponderance of the evidence. Such a standard would recognize the so-called parental presumption, i.e. the historical preference given to parents,[13] but give greater recognition to the rights of the child.

This Article examines the due process concerns of parent and child from both a legal and a factual perspective. The legal analysis focuses on the level of proof necessary to terminate parental rights. The factual study examines the rapidly changing portrait of the American family and the efforts of individual states to address the alarming increases in abuse, neglect, and abandonment of children by parents. A synthesis of these factual and legal perspectives serves to illustrate that the best interest of the child is not served by adherence to a constitutional standard that deprives states of their legislative ability to address the significant domestic relations problems within their borders.

A large part of this Article is devoted to providing a statistical look at the plight of children in the United States, especially in geographic areas containing large numbers of single parents and in areas where poverty and persistent social dysfunction are prevalent.[14] The statistics

---

12. *Id.* at 764.

13. *See infra* part II.A.

14. It would be conjecture, a denial of equal protection, and even racist to presume that the family structure is more tenuous in ghettos, cities, and states with higher percentages of minorities, drug use, or poverty. But it would be a denial of due process to ignore the reality that there are differences among the states and that these differences can most often signal vulnerable children. One constantly predictive difference indicating vulnerable children involves single parents: "Nearly 75 percent of all American children growing up in single-parent families expe-

vividly illustrate that it is no longer possible to suggest that the best interest of each and every child subsists within the parent. Government reports such as *Beyond Rhetoric: A New American Agenda for Children and Families* ("*Beyond Rhetoric*"),[15] which was presented to Congress in 1991 by the National Commission on Children, provide factual evidence that supports a lowering of the standard of proof necessary to remove a child from an injurious home. The following excerpts from *Beyond Rhetoric* are worth noting at the outset:

> Today, one in four children in the United States is raised by just one parent, usually a divorced or unmarried mother. Many grow up without the consistent presence of a father in their lives . . . . Each year, half a million babies are born to teenage girls ill prepared to assume the responsibilities of parenthood.[16]
>
> . . . .
>
> Today, children are the poorest Americans. One in five lives in a family with an income below the poverty level. One in four infants and toddlers under the age of three is poor. Nearly 13 million children live in poverty, more than 2 million more than a decade ago. Many of these children are desperately poor; nearly 5 million live in families with incomes less than half the

---

rience poverty for some period during their first 10 years, compared to 20 percent of children in two-parent families. Among children living only with their mothers, sustained poverty for seven or more years is common; among children living with both parents, it is rare." NATIONAL COMMISSION ON CHILDREN, BEYOND RHETORIC: A NEW AMERICAN AGENDA FOR CHILDREN AND FAMILIES 83 (1991) (citations omitted) [hereinafter BEYOND RHETORIC].

15. *Id.* This lengthy report has drawn praise and criticism. In appraising the report, the conservative *National Review* wrote: "In order to achieve a consensus, radically different points of view had to be accommodated, and so the findings are ludicrously inconsistent." Kate Walsh O'Beirne, *Children's Hour; Report by the National Commission on Children and John D. Rockefeller IV's Efforts to Promote Legislation to Protect Children*, NAT'L REV., July 29, 1991, at 34. But the conservative Heritage Foundation found elements to praise in that the report advocates "two-parent families, recognizes the importance of values and morality, endorses school choice, and acknowledges that what families need is not more government programs, but to be allowed to keep more of the money they earn." Wade F. Horn, *Children and Family in America: Challenges for the 1990s*, 345 THE HERITAGE LECTURES 1, 3-4 (1991) (Lecture presented at The Heritage Foundation on July 23, 1991). *See also* David Whitman, *Why Children's Commissions Fail*, 111 U.S. NEWS & WORLD REP., July 8, 1991, at 20 ("Rockefeller's intentions are admirable, but his gift for prophecy is suspect."); Editorial, *Beyond the Pro-Family Rhetoric*, THE CHRISTIAN SCI. MONITOR, July 1, 1991, at 20 (praising the report's efforts to focus on the current needs of the family).

16. BEYOND RHETORIC, *supra* note 14, at 4.

federal poverty level.[17]

. . . While the majority of poor children are white, minority children are much more likely to live in a poor family. About 44 percent of all black children and more than 36 percent of Hispanic children are poor, compared to fewer than 15 percent of white children.[18]

Today, one in four adolescents in the United States engages in high-risk behaviors that endanger his or her own health and well-being and that of others.[19]

. . . [A]pproximately 40 percent of the nation's children are at risk of school failure.[20]

The plight of children in America is not entirely the result of parental neglect, abuse, or abandonment; nor is it entirely the result of a lack of government funding for programs, racism, drugs, or the media. Rather, a combination of factors has led to the current situation. While no single solution will rectify the problems facing America's children, we must ask ourselves one critical question: Is the law concerned with the best interest of the child? The Supreme Court's continued adherence to the parental presumption provides a negative answer.

After giving a brief history of the application of the parental presumption in our legal system, Part II of this Article examines the best interest of the child in the context of two Supreme Court cases: *Santosky* and *DeShaney v. Winnebago County Department of Social Services*.[21] Each case involved the Due Process Clause,[22] and each in-

---

17. *Id.* at 24 (citations omitted).

18. *Id.*

19. *Id.* at xxvii. Disease and unanticipated pregnancy are two consequences of sexual activity that result in high-risk to adolescents. "Early sexual activity, pregnancy, and childbearing are epidemic in this country. Premarital adolescent sexual activity in the United States has been increasing for at least the last two decades. Currently, just over one-half of unmarried women age 15 to 19 have engaged in sexual intercourse at least once. By the time they reach age 19, three-quarters of unmarried women and 86 percent of unmarried men are sexually active." *Id.* at 223 (citations omitted).

20. *Id.* at xxv. Lack of education is high-risk behavior: "In 1988 high school dropouts were nearly twice as likely as high school graduates and five times as likely as college graduates to be unemployed. Students with weak basic academic skills are more than nine times as likely to have a child out of wedlock and more than twice as likely to be arrested as their academically successful peers." *Id.* at 185 (citations omitted).

21. 489 U.S. 189 (1989).

22. The Court in *Santosky* regarded the Due Process Clause as demanding a clear and convincing level of proof so as to protect the interest of the parents. "[A]t a parental rights termination proceeding, a near-equal allocation of risk [preponderance of evidence standard] between the parents and the State is constitutionally intolerable." Santosky v. Kramer, 455 U.S. 745, 768

A. *The Parental Presumption*

The parental presumption is the historical presumption that the child's best interest is served by his or her remaining in the care and custody of a natural parent. As early as 1824, Circuit Justice Story wrote in a child custody decision:

> As to the question of the right of the father to have the custody of his infant child, in a general sense it is true. But this is not on account of any absolute right of the father, but for the benefit of the infant, the law presuming it to be for his interest to be under the nurture and care of his natural protector, both for maintenance and education.[26]

Numerous cases so hold today.[27] The fundamental presumption is that a child and the natural parent should remain together.[28]
Beyond Rhetoric supports this presumption:

> Parents bear the primary responsibility for meeting their children's physical, emotional, and intellectual needs and for providing moral guidance and direction. It is in society's best interest to support parents in their childbearing roles, to enable them to fulfill their obligations, and to hold them responsible for the care and support of their children.[29]

---

26. United States v. Green, 26 F. Cas. 30, 31 (C.C.D.R.I. 1824) (No. 15,256).

27. *See, e.g.*, P.G. v. W.M.T. (*In re* D.B.G.), 590 So.2d 329 (Ala. Civ. App. 1991) (In a custody determination between a parent and third party, the natural parent will be presumed to serve the best interest of the child.). *Accord* Appeal of H.R. (*In re* Baby Boy C.), 581 A.2d 1141 (D.C. 1990); Rose v. Potts, 577 N.E.2d 811 (Ill. App. Ct. 1991); In the matter of the Marriage of Criqui & Criqui, 798 P.2d 69 (Kan. Ct. App. 1990); Westphal v. Westphal, 457 N.W.2d 226 (Minn. Ct. App. 1990); Lewelling v. Lewelling, 796 S.W.2d 164 (Tex. 1990); Mason v. Moon, 385 S.E.2d 242 (Va. Ct. App. 1989); Bancroft v. Bancroft, 578 A.2d 114 (Vt. 1990). *See also* Susan B. Hershkowitz, *Due Process and the Termination of Parental Rights*, 19 FAM. L.Q. 245, 254-55 (1985) (stating that "[c]ourts and commentators generally agree that a child's best interests are most adequately met when the child is in the custody of his parents").

28. *In re* D.G., 583 A.2d 160, 164 (D.C. 1990). For an example of a state statute incorporating the parental presumption, *see* CONN. GEN. STAT. ANN. § 46b-56b (West 1991) (In custody disputes between parents and non-parents, "there shall be a presumption that it is in the best interest of the child to be in the custody of the parent."); *see also* MICH. COMP. LAWS § 722.25 (In dispute between parent and agency or third person, "it is presumed that the best interests of the child are served by awarding custody to the parent or parents, unless the contrary is established by clear and convincing evidence.") (MICH. STAT. ANN. § 25.312(5) (Callaghan 1992)).

29. BEYOND RHETORIC, *supra* note 14, at 65.

. . . .

> Children do best when they have the personal involvement and material support of a father and a mother and when both parents fulfill their responsibility to be loving providers.[30]

Starting in 1923, with its decision in *Meyer v. Nebraska*,[31] the Court began to take the view that the rights of a parent in his or her child are embodied in the Constitution itself. *Meyer* was quickly followed by several other cases, each of which involved the authority of a parent—or a close relative—in a decisional dispute over a child.[32] All flirted with the notion that such authority could be characterized as "fundamental."[33]

The majority opinion in *Santosky v. Kramer* incorporated the fundamental rights notion of these earlier cases. The *Santosky* Court stated that "[t]he fundamental liberty interest of natural parents in the care, custody, and management of their child does not evaporate simply because they have not been model parents or have lost temporary custody of their child to the State."[34]

There was a time when the parental presumption was considered more as a trust, with the state being the dominant party and the parent entrusted with the child only as long as the parent acted in his or her

---

30. *Id.* at 66.

31. 262 U.S. 390 (1923). *See also* Hershkowitz, *supra* note 27, at 252.

32. *See* Wisconsin v. Yoder, 406 U.S. 205, 213-14 (1972) ("[T]he values of parental direction of the religious upbringing and education of their children in their early and formative years have a high place in our society."); Prince v. Massachusetts, 321 U.S. 158, 166 (1944) ("It is cardinal with us that the custody, care and nurture of the child resides first in the parents, whose primary function and freedom include preparations for obligations the state can neither supply nor hinder."); Pierce v. Society of Sisters, 268 U.S. 510, 535 (1925) ("[T]hose who nurture . . . and direct [the child's] destiny have the right, coupled with the high duty, to recognize and prepare [the child] for additional obligations.").

33. Whenever a right is fundamental, it may only be superseded by a state or federal statute when the government has a compelling interest in the statutory objective. For examples of when this issue has arisen, Franz v. United States, 707 F.2d 582 (D.C. Cir. 1983); Sheppard v. Sheppard, 630 P.2d 1121 (Kan. 1981), *cert. denied*, 455 U.S. 919 (1982). *But see* Doe v. Staples, 717 F.2d 953 (6th Cir. 1983), *cert. denied*, 465 U.S. 1033 (1984).

34. Santosky v. Kramer, 455 U.S. 745, 753 (1982). The nature of this fundamental right, however, is elusive and difficult to predict. *See, e.g.*, Hao Thi Popp v. Lucas, 438 A.2d 755 (Conn. 1980) (parent's constitutional right must yield when the child's welfare requires custody to be given to the non-parent); Custody of a Minor, 389 N.E.2d 68 (Mass. 1979) (state may remove child from parental custody only on a showing of unfitness of the parents); Sorentino v. Family & Children's Soc'y of Elizabeth, 378 A.2d 18 (N.J. 1977), *aff'd* 391 A.2d 497 (N.J. 1978); Ellerbe v. Hooks, 416 A.2d 512, 514 (Pa. 1980) (parents have a "prima facie right to custody" which may be forfeited if the child's interests lie in being in the custody of the non-parent) (citation omitted).

proper fiduciary capacity.[35] The state's intervention was considered a "demonstration of the state's benevolence."[36] This attitude was directed more toward the best interest of the child than the rights of the parent. Since the early part of the twentieth century when *Meyer* was decided, however, the parental presumption has become deeply interwoven in American jurisprudence.[37]

Even when the state intervenes on behalf of a child exposed to abuse, neglect, or surrender, for example, the state does so as a substitute parent, i.e. a *parens patriae*.[38] In exercising the power of *parens patriae*, courts frequently deny certain rights to children that are otherwise afforded to adults.[39] For example, states do not have to provide

---

35. In the nineteenth century and early twentieth century, the courts imposed few limitations on the state's ability to intervene in the family relationship. *See* Douglas R. Rendelmen, *Parens Patriae: From Chancery to Juvenile Court*, 23 S.C. L. REV. 205, 213-29 (1971). The early American courts would exercise *parens patriae* authority in private and public custody disputes. Since the parent's rights derived from the state, which delegated control over children to their parents as a trust, failure to discharge faithfully the trust justified state intervention. The lack of modern constitutional interpretation added to the state's authority, with the state's interest at least equal to that of the parent.

36. Hershkowitz, *supra* note 27, at 251-52. State efforts today to remove the child from abusive parents and place the child in a protective setting are often far from benevolent. "For many children, foster care, which is intended to protect them from neglect and abuse at the hands of parents and other family members, becomes an equally cruel form of neglect and abuse by the state." BEYOND RHETORIC, *supra* note 14, at 282; *see also infra* notes 163-73 and accompanying text. The dissent in *Santosky* noted the possible harm that can result to children due to extensive residence in foster care. *Santosky*, 455 U.S. at 789 n.15 (Rehnquist, J., dissenting).

37. *See, e.g.*, Parham v. J.R., 442 U.S. 584, 602 (1979) ("The law's concept of the family rests on a presumption that parents possess what a child lacks in maturity, experience, and capacity for judgment required for making life's difficult decisions. More important, historically it has recognized that natural bonds of affection lead parents to act in the best interests of their children."). *See also* Caban v. Mohammed, 441 U.S. 380 (1979); Stanley v. Illinois, 405 U.S. 645 (1972) (Illinois statute violated the Due Process Clause when it provided for the termination of the parental rights of a father without a determination of his unfitness); Barstad v. Frazier, 348 N.W.2d 479 (Wis. 1984) (court relies upon the parental preference theory in sustaining right of parent to child).

38. *See generally* Hershkowitz, *supra* note 27 (providing historical development of the *parens patriae* right). Even though minors have been extended greater protection under the Constitution, that protection is often limited by judicial decisions. *See* Bellotti v. Baird, 443 U.S. 622, 634 (1979) (constitutional rights of children cannot be equated with those of adults); *see also* Hodgson v. Minnesota, 497 U.S. 417, 435 (1990) ("[T]he constitutional protection against unjustified state intrusion into the process of deciding whether or not to bear a child extends to pregnant minors as well as adult women."); Ohio v. Akron Ctr. for Reprod. Health, 497 U.S. 502 (1990) (upholding Ohio's parental notice requirement for minor women seeking an abortion).

39. For a discussion of the *parens patriae* power, *see* Michael J. Florio, Note, *An Abused Child's Right to Life Liberty, and Property in the Home: Constitutional Approval of State Inac-*

minors with a jury trial in delinquency adjudications;[40] states may prohibit the sale of pornographic material to children;[41] states may deny minors the right to vote; and states may deny minors the right to marry without parental consent.[42] The justification lies in the "peculiar vulnerability of children."[43] Thus, the "State is entitled to adjust its legal system to account for children's vulnerability and their need for concern, . . . sympathy, and . . . paternal attention."[44]

In most cases, the court has the final say, the parent next, and the child last.[45] In *Parham v. J.R.*,[46] for example, the Court invoked the parental presumption to declare that due process does not require a "formal or quasi-formal" preconfinement hearing in cases where children are committed to institutions by their parents.[47] Merely because a child "balks" at hospitalization does not "diminish the parent's authority to decide what is best for the child."[48] Parents are generally seen as acting in the best interest of the child. "Children, by definition, are not assumed to have the capacity to take care of themselves. They are assumed to be subject to the control of their parents, and [failing that, of the state] as parens patriae."[49]

In *Lassiter v. Department of Social Services*,[50] the Court acknowl-

---

tion, 92 W. VA. L. REV. 175, 178 (1989) ("A child's constitutional rights may be either expanded or restricted according to the state's 'parens patriae interest in preserving and promoting the welfare of the child.'") (citation omitted).

40. McKeiver v. Pennsylvania, 403 U.S. 528 (1971).

41. Ginsberg v. New York, 390 U.S. 629 (1968). The Supreme Court has also upheld a statute which prohibited persons from promoting a sexual performance by a child under the age of 16 even if the performance is not obscene. *See* New York v. Ferber, 458 U.S. 747 (1982). The need to protect the physical and psychological well-being of a child is compelling. *See id.* at 756-57.

42. *See, e.g.*, Moe v. Dinkins, 533 F. Supp. 623 (S.D.N.Y. 1981), *aff'd*, 669 F.2d 67 (2d Cir. 1982), *cert. denied*, 459 U.S. 827 (1982) (sustaining New York's requirement of parental consent for marriages of persons between 14 and 18).

43. Bellotti v. Baird, 443 U.S. 622, 634 (1979).

44. *Id.* at 635 (quoting McKeivar v. Pennsylvania, 403 U.S. 528, 550 (1971) (plurality opinion)).

45. *See generally* John D. Goetz, Note, *Children's Rights Under the Burger Court: Concern for the Child But Deference to Authority*, 60 NOTRE DAME L. REV. 1214 (1985).

46. 442 U.S. 584 (1979).

47. *Id.* at 607.

48. *Id.* at 604. *But see In re* Roger S., 569 P.2d 1286 (Cal. 1977) (California commitment statute, very similar to the Georgia statute sustained in *Parham*, was held unconstitutional); *In re* J.C.G., 366 A.2d 733 (Hudson County Ct. 1976) (court would not allow mother access to her daughter's psychiatric records for fear that the mother may seek to have the daughter released when that would not be in the best interest of the child).

49. Schall v. Martin, 467 U.S. 253, 265 (1984).

50. 452 U.S. 18 (1981) (Court engaged in a balancing of competing private and public inter-

edged that the "[s]tate has an urgent interest in the welfare of the child."[51] According to dicta in a prior case, the state has an interest in ensuring that children are safeguarded from abuse which might prevent their "growth into free and independent well-developed men and citizens."[52] Accordingly, the state may require school attendance,[53] compel the vaccination and medical treatment of children,[54] regulate or prohibit child labor,[55] and eventually, may even terminate parental rights under the state's *parens patriae* powers.

Parents, on the other hand, have a right to the care, custody, and management of their children.[56] This encompasses the right to prepare the child for "additional obligations" and to educate the child. The state may not compel a child to attend public school when the parent desires to educate his or her child in a private school;[57] nor may the state compel a child to attend school when the parent chooses to raise the

---

ests, and held that the Due Process Clause does not require appointment of counsel for the parent in every case in which parental rights may be terminated).

51. *Id.* at 27. *See also In re* Ella B., 285 N.E.2d 288 (1972) (holding that counsel must be appointed, at least where there is the possibility of imprisonment).

52. Prince v. Massachusetts, 321 U.S. 158, 165 (1944) (concerning the role that parents play in the education of the child and implying that, while the parental presumption is predominant, the state has an active responsibility to monitor the child's development).

53. *See generally id. But see* Wisconsin v. Yoder, 406 U.S. 205, 213 (1972) (states' interest in assuring education is subject to accommodation/balancing of parents' religious beliefs); Pierce v. Society of Sisters, 268 U.S. 510, 534-35 (1925) (same).

54. *See, e.g.*, Jacqueline Y. Parker, *Dissolving Family Relations: Termination of Parent-Child Relations—An Overview*, 11 U. DAYTON L. REV. 555, 569 (1986) (Parental misconduct alone is not sufficient to justify state intervention without a showing of resultant harm to the child). *See also* Alsager v. District Court, 406 F. Supp. 10 (S.D. Iowa 1975), *aff'd*, 545 F.2d 1137 (8th Cir. 1976) (Before a state can terminate family relationship, the state must prove physical or emotional harm to the child.).

55. *See, e.g., Prince*, 321 U.S. at 166 (upholding the Massachusetts labor laws as they apply to children.)

56. *See, e.g.*, Santosky v. Kramer, 455 U.S. 745, 753 (1982) (holding that "freedom of personal choice in matters of family life is a fundamental liberty interest protected by the Fourteenth Amendment); Lassiter v. Department of Social Servs., 452 U.S. 18, 27 (1981) (The Court's decisions have "made it plain . . . that a parent's desire for and right to 'the companionship, care, custody, and management of his or her children' is an important interest that 'undeniably warrants deference and, absent a powerful countervailing interest, protection.'") (quoting Stanley v. Illinois, 405 U.S. 645, 651 (1972)); *Stanley*, 405 U.S. at 651 ("It is plain that the interest of a parent in the companionship, care, custody, and management of his or her children 'come[s] to this Court with a momentum of respect . . . .' The integrity of the family unit has found protection in the Due Process Clause of the Fourteenth Amendment.") (quoting Kovacs v. Cooper, 336 U.S. 77, 95 (1949) (Frankfurter, J., concurring)).

57. Pierce v. Society of Sisters, 268 U.S. 510 (1925) (An Oregon statute which required all children to attend public school held unconstitutional because it infringed on the parental right to guide the child's education.).

child in accordance with the parent's religious precepts.[58] The state is restrained in these types of actions because the legislated activity infringes upon a perceived "fundamental" parental presumption. Thus, a state may not arbitrarily interfere with the parental presumption merely because the parent's child-raising techniques do not fulfill the state's expectations of ideal parenting. Only a "powerful countervailing interest" of the state would justify interference.[59]

B. Santosky v. Kramer[60]

The Court had little trouble acquiescing to the parental presumption in *Santosky v. Kramer*, a case involving termination of parental rights due to abuse and neglect. In November 1973, nine years before the Supreme Court announced its decision in *Santosky*, the Commissioner of the Ulster County, New York, Department of Social Services initiated a neglect proceeding and removed Tina Apel Santosky from her home.[61] Tina was two-years-old and had suffered numerous injuries while in the care of her parents: a fractured left femur (treated with a homemade splint); bruises on the upper arms, forehead, flank, and spine; and abrasions of the upper leg.[62] The following summer, the Commissioner removed Tina's brother, John, from the Santosky home.[63] John was less than one-year-old at the time. He was suffering from malnutrition, had bruises on the eye and forehead, had cuts and blisters on his hands and feet, and had multiple pin pricks on his

58. Wisconsin v. Yoder, 406 U.S. 205, 234 (1972) (compulsory school attendance law was unconstitutional as applied to Amish children because such law infringed on the parents' right to raise their children in accordance with their Amish beliefs).

59. The extent of this "fundamental" right of the parents is unclear, especially in times of increasing neglect and abuse cases. Nonetheless, see *Stanley*, 405 U.S. at 645. In *Stanley*, the Court held an Illinois dependency statute unconstitutional. Under the statute, children of unwed fathers became wards of the state upon the death of the mother. The statute presumed that unwed fathers were unfit to raise their children. Peter Stanley, the unwed father, had lived with Joan Stanley intermittently for over 18 years. Together they had three children. When Joan Stanley died, however, Stanley's children were declared wards of the state. Stanley challenged the statute on equal protection grounds, alleging that the statute treated unwed fathers differently from married fathers by presuming unmarried fathers were unfit. *Id.* at 646-48. In ruling the statute unconstitutional, the Court emphasized the parent's fundamental right to conceive and raise his or her child and stated that the "private interest here, that of a man in the children he has sired and raised, undeniably warrants deference and, absent a *powerful countervailing interest*, protection." *Id.* at 651 (emphasis added).

60. 455 U.S. 745 (1982).

61. *Id.* at 751.

62. *Id.* at 781 n.10 (Rehnquist, J., dissenting).

63. *Id.*

back.[64] The Commissioner took the third Santosky child from the hospital three days after he was born and likewise placed him in foster care. Although Jed Santosky had not suffered physical abuse, his removal was predicated upon the past abuse suffered by Tina and John.[65]

For over four and one-half years, the state maintained the children in foster care[66] and, at the same time, diligently engaged in efforts to rehabilitate their parents.[67] Annie Santosky was offered training from a mother's aide, a nutritional aide, and a public health nurse. The state

---

64. *Id.*

65. *Id.* The Commissioner found that "immediate removal [of Jed] was necessary to avoid imminent danger to his life or health." *Id.* at 751. In a removal of this sort, without actual neglect, abuse or abandonment, the requisite standard for removal is preponderance of the evidence and removal must be based on actual conditions, not conjecture. *See* Palmore v. Sidoti, 466 U.S. 429 (1984) (mere conjecture that the child will suffer stigma by being raised in an interracial household is insufficient as a basis of custody); Johnson v. Johnson, 564 P.2d 71 (Alaska 1977), *cert. denied,* 434 U.S. 1048 (1978) (conjecture based on affects of religious household, without more, is an insufficient basis of custody); Moye v. Moye, 627 P.2d 799 (Idaho 1981) (mere conjecture that an epileptic parent would be unable to care for a child is not a sufficient ground for a denial of custody).

66. Much of the expense of foster care is borne by the federal government in payments to the state. "If present trends in out-of-home placement continue, the Congressional Budget Office projects that the federal government will spend a total of approximately $9.24 billion between FY 1991 and FY 1996 under Title IV-E to maintain children in foster care." BEYOND RHETORIC, *supra* note 14, at 306. Furthermore, the National Commission on Children currently recommends that, "the federal government . . . require all states to extend foster care to youths up to age 21, conditional on their enrollment in educational or job training programs, and to provide services to prepare them for independent living." *Id.* at 302.

67. The approach utilized by the state was one of "tough-minded compassion." *Id.* at 113. This approach attempts to strike a balance between the view that abuse arises from a lack of personal responsibility and moral strength on the part of the parents, and the view that the problem results from the shortcomings of our social and economic systems. Thus, "[p]arents must be responsible for the health and well-being of their children, but society must enable them to do the job well." *Id.* at 65. Under either a preponderance of the evidence or a clear and convincing standard, the state must provide sufficient support to the family to allow for reunification.

Family support programs are recommended for families under stress but showing no symptoms of disfunction. These programs have common goals:

> First, they attempt to give families the skills and knowledge needed to cope more effectively with the stresses of contemporary life and to care for and nurture their children better. In achieving this goal, programs try to build on family strengths and capacities rather than emphasizing deficits. Second, family support programs are prevention-oriented; that is, they attempt to strengthen families before a crisis occurs. Third, they offer multi-disciplinary services that recognize and address the diverse and interrelated needs of families. Finally, family support programs are community-based and easily accessible to parents in order to be as responsive as possible to the families they serve.

Id. at 275.

family planning clinic offered counseling.[68] The father, John Santosky, was offered psychiatric treatment and vocational training.[69] Despite the considerable efforts of the state on their behalf, Annie and John Santosky refused to avail themselves of the services provided.[70] As a result of the Santoskys' refusal to try to correct the situation that precipitated the abuse of their children, the state initiated termination proceedings in 1978.[71]

By statute, New York permitted the state to terminate parental rights upon a finding of a "fair preponderance of the evidence" that the child had been "permanently neglected."[72] Termination could occur only upon certain conditions being met: First, the child must have already been temporarily removed from the parent's custody and have been in the custody of the state for at least one year.[73] Second, the state must have made "diligent efforts to encourage and strengthen the parental relationship" with the ultimate goal of reunifying the family.[74]

---

68. *Santosky*, 455 U.S. at 782.

69. *Id.*

70. *Id.* at 783.

71. *Id.* at 780.

72. *Id.* at 747. At the time the Court rendered its decision, New York was not the only state using a preponderance of the evidence standard of proof in termination proceedings. *Id.* at 749. The standards of proof varied from state to state. *Id.* at 749 n.3. Thirty-five states used a higher standard of proof than a "fair preponderance of the evidence." *Id.* at 749. Thirty states used the clear and convincing standard: fifteen states (Alaska, California, Georgia, Iowa, Maine, Michigan, Missouri, New Mexico, North Carolina, Ohio, Rhode Island, Tennessee, Virginia, West Virginia and Wisconsin) required the "clear and convincing" standard by statute. *Id.* at 749 n.3. Fifteen different states (Alabama, Arkansas, Florida, Kansas, Minnesota, Montana, Nebraska, New Jersey, North Dakota, Oklahoma, Pennsylvania, Texas, Utah, Washington and Wyoming) plus the District of Columbia and the Virgin Islands required the clear and convincing standard by judicial decisions. *Id.* Two other states, Illinois and New York, required clear and convincing evidence in certain types of parental rights termination proceedings (mental illness or severe child abuse were grounds for termination), but generally required only a preponderance of the evidence. *Id.* Two states, New Hampshire and Louisiana, required the highest standard of proof: beyond a reasonable doubt. *Id.* And one state, South Dakota, required a "clear preponderance" not just a "fair preponderance." *Id.* All other states used the preponderance of evidence standard. *Id.* at 749.

73. Temporary removal of the child could occur in one of two ways. The parents could surrender the child—as is more often the case—or the Family Court could have ordered removal based upon a finding of child abuse or neglect. *Id.* at 776 (Rehnquist, J., dissenting). Neglect was the cause of removal in the *Santosky* case. *Id.* at 751. In 1973, after several incidents suggesting parental abuse and neglect, the Commissioner initiated a neglect proceeding and removed Tina from the home. *Id.* Then, ten months later, the Commissioner procured another Court order to remove John III from the Home because of similar neglect and abuse problems. *Id.* Finally, based on the injuries to the older children, the Commissioner removed Jed from his parents' custody shortly after his birth. *Id.*

74. *Id.* at 779 (Rehnquist, J., dissenting). The greater the efforts of the state to provide reha-

Third, the state had to comply with numerous procedural requirements directed toward the interest of the parents. These included providing notice of the termination hearing and notice of the permissibility of retaining counsel. Finally, the state had the burden of proving that the parents did in fact neglect the child and, because of this neglect, the child's best interest would be served by termination of parental rights.[75]

During the fact-finding hearing, the judge concluded that the state had proven by a preponderance of the evidence that the Santosky children had been "permanently neglected."[76] The judge emphasized that the state had made "diligent efforts" to encourage and strengthen the parental relationship, but that these efforts were to no avail.[77] Annie and John Santosky were not capable of providing for the future of their children in an atmosphere where they could thrive.[78] Thus, it would be in the best interest of the three children to terminate parental rights.[79]

While the children remained in foster care, the parents appealed the decision of the court, arguing that the statute's preponderance of the evidence standard violated their due process rights under the federal Constitution.[80] The New York Supreme Court, Appellate Division, affirmed the Family Court's ruling, holding that the preponderance of the evidence standard was "proper and constitutional."[81] The standard "recognizes and seeks to balance rights possessed by the child . . . with those of the natural parents . . . ."[82] The United States Supreme Court granted certiorari to consider the issue of whether use of the preponderance of the evidence standard in termination proceedings violates the Due Process Clause of the Fourteenth Amendment of the United States Constitution.[83]

On March 24, 1982, four years after the initial termination proceeding was initiated, the Court held that the Santosky's had a fundamental liberty interest in the care and custody of their children,[84] and that the

---

bilitative services, the less the characterization of the state as a bully intent on taking the child from the parents. This is a crucial emphasis.

75. *Id.* at 780.

76. *Id.* at 747.

77. *Id.* at 752.

78. *Id.*

79. *Id.*

80. *Id.*

81. *Id.*

82. *Id.*

83. *Id.*

84. "[The] freedom of personal choice in matters of family life is a fundamental liberty

Due Process Clause required the state to demonstrate by clear and convincing evidence the existence of permanent neglect before terminating that fundamental liberty interest.[85]

The Court ordered a new hearing to determine if sufficient facts warranted termination under the heightened standard of proof.[86] The New York Supreme Court, Appellate Division, reviewed the evidence presented using a clear and convincing standard and affirmed the termination of the Santosky's parental rights.[87]

By framing the issue in terms of the parents' interest rather than that of the children, the *Santosky* Court ignored the factual history of New York's rehabilitative efforts and the length of time the children had spent in foster care. Most importantly, the Court failed to pursue a constitutional analysis that focused on the best interests of the children.[88] The focus of the majority opinion was on the due process rights afforded to the parents of the children. The best interest of the parents, rather than the best interests of the children, was the predominant concern. The Court simply acquiesced in the parental presumption.

C. DeShaney v. Winnebago County Department of Social Services[89]

DeShaney was decided seven years after *Santosky*. "The facts of this case are undeniably tragic."[90] Joshua DeShaney was born in 1979.

---

interest protected by the Fourteenth Amendment." *Id.* at 753.

85. The Court added, somewhat sardonically, that "[w]e cannot believe that it would burden the State unduly to require that its fact-finders have the same factual certainty when terminating the parent-child relationship as they must have to suspend a driver's license." *Id.* at 768. *See* N.Y. VEH. & TRAF. LAW § 227.1 (McKinney Supp. 1981) (requiring the State to prove traffic infractions by clear and convincing evidence).

86. *Id.* at 770.

87. *See In re* John AA, 89 N.Y.S.2d 942 (1982).

88. The decision in *Santosky* may have been due to the Court's concern over the result in Lassiter v. Department of Social Servs., 452 U.S. 18, *reh'g denied*, 453 U.S. 927 (1981), which held that due process gives indigent litigants the right to appointed counsel when such litigants are exposed to deprivation of their physical liberty. *Id.* at 26-27. When the facts of the case present a situation where an indigent parent may lose his or her child, the Court held that the Constitution does not require the appointment of counsel in every parental termination proceeding. *Id.* at 31. Appointment of counsel to represent the child lies within the discretion of the trial court, subject to appellate review. *Id.* at 32. Thus, there is the possibility that the State could amass its forces to deprive an indigent of his or her child without the indigent having an attorney. The State would be a formidable "bully." *See* discussion of *Lassiter* in *Santosky*, 455 U.S. at 752-70 (indicating a significant reliance upon concern over the loss of appointed counsel as a matter of right).

89. 489 U.S. 189 (1989).

90. *Id.* at 191.

In 1980, Joshua's father was awarded custody of his son pursuant to a divorce. The divorce occurred in Wyoming, and Joshua and his father moved to Wisconsin soon thereafter. The father entered into a second marriage, and that, too, ended in divorce.[91] During the divorce proceedings, the second wife complained that the father hit the boy, causing marks.[92] The father denied the accusations. The state Department of Social Services did not investigate.[93]

In 1983, Joshua was admitted to a local hospital. He had multiple bruises and abrasions.[94] The examining physician reported suspected abuse, and Joshua was placed in the temporary custody of the hospital. A child protection team conducted an investigation, but determined that there was insufficient evidence of child abuse to retain Joshua in custody.[95]

Joshua was returned to the custody of his father. One month later, the boy was again treated for suspicious injuries at the hospital emergency room. Again, officials "concluded that there was no basis for action."[96] A social worker began making monthly visits to the DeShaney home. On one such visit, the social worker noticed suspicious injuries on the boy's head. The social worker also learned that the boy was not attending preschool. These circumstances were noted in the file, but the caseworker "did nothing more."[97]

In late 1983, Joshua was again admitted to the emergency room. The hospital notified the Department of Social Services that Joshua had suspicious injuries, but Joshua was sent home. When the social worker visited Joshua's home on two subsequent occasions, "she was told that Joshua was too ill to see her."[98] Finally,

> [i]n March, 1984, Randy DeShaney beat 4-year-old Joshua so severely that he fell into a life-threatening coma. Emergency brain surgery revealed a series of hemorrhages caused by trau-

---

91. *Id.*

92. *Id.* at 192.

93. *Id.*

94. *Id.*

95. *Id.* The Team did, however, decide to recommend several measures to protect Joshua, including enrolling him in a preschool program, providing his father with certain counselling services, and encouraging his father's girlfriend to move out of the home. Randy DeShaney entered into a voluntary agreement with DSS in which he promised to cooperate with them in accomplishing these goals. *Id.*

96. *Id.*

97. *Id.* at 193.

98. *Id.*

> matic injuries to the head inflicted over a long period of time. Joshua did not die, but he suffered brain damage so severe that he is expected to spend the rest of his life confined to an institution for the profoundly retarded.[99]

Joshua and his mother brought suit against the county, its Department of Social Services, and various individuals in the Department. The complaint alleged that Joshua had been deprived of his liberty without due process of law, in violation of his rights under the Fourteenth Amendment, because officials failed to intervene to protect him against a risk of violence at his father's hands of which they knew or should have known.[100]

After a series of lower court proceedings, the Supreme Court granted certiorari due to the

> inconsistent approaches taken by the lower courts in determining when, if ever, the failure of a state or local governmental entity or its agents to provide an individual with adequate protective services constitutes a violation of the individual's due process rights . . . and the importance of the issue to the administration of state and local governments.[101]

The majority found that the Fourteenth Amendment did not provide a remedy of redress against the state for the harm that resulted to Joshua, because the state did not have an affirmative duty under the Fourteenth Amendment to care for Joshua under the circumstances of the case. The Court suggested state remedies in tort[102] under "a system of liability which would place upon the State and its officials the responsibility for failure to act . . . ."[103] The Court concluded that it was up to the

---

99. *Id.*

100. *Id.* The District Court granted summary judgement for the county and its officials, and the Court of Appeals for the Seventh Circuit affirmed. *Id.*

101. *Id.* (citation omitted).

102. *Id.* at 203. "It may well be that, by voluntarily undertaking to protect Joshua against a danger it concededly played no part in creating, the State acquired a duty under state tort law to provide him with adequate protection against that danger." *Id. See, e.g.*, Turner v. District of Columbia, 532 A.2d 662 (D.C. 1987) (the issue was whether the District of Columbia and its officials and agencies may be held liable for the death by starvation of an abused and neglected child and the malnutrition of another child which resulted, in part, from the alleged negligence of an agency of the District of Columbia government).

103. *DeShaney*, 489 U.S. at 203. *See, e.g.*, Suter v. Artist M., 112 S. Ct. 1360, (1992) (holding that the federal Adoption Assistance and Child Welfare Act of 1980 does not create an enforceable right on behalf of children in foster care, but nonetheless containing a strong dissent from Justice Blackmun in which he considers the case a departure from established law);

states to initiate such a system. "[T]hey should not have it thrust upon them by this Court's expansion of the Due Process Clause of the Fourteenth Amendment."[104]

Throughout its opinion, the majority drew attention to the fact that "the harm was inflicted not by the State of Wisconsin, but by Joshua's father."[105] The Court implied that had the boy been within the physical custody of the state, redress against the state would have been available. But since Joshua was at all relevant times in the custody and control of his father,[106] there was no remedy against the state or its agents under the Fourteenth Amendment.

Despite the majority's legal analysis, the Court was moved by the factual dilemma. "Judges and lawyers, like other humans, are moved by natural sympathy in a case like this to find a way for Joshua and his mother to receive adequate compensation for the grievous harm inflicted upon them."[107] It is significant that the majority included the gruesome facts of what happened to the child in its opinion. In so doing, the Court indicated a willingness to reject the presumption that the child's best interest subsists within the parent's best interest.

The facts of *DeShaney* suggest that the best interest of the child is not always subordinate to the interest of the parent. Joshua's father, Randy DeShaney, was not dissimilar to many of the single parents with children today. He was divorced, poor,[108] involved with more than

---

Stoneking v. Bradford Area Sch. Dist., 882 F.2d 720 (3d Cir. 1988), *cert. denied,* 493 U.S. 1044 (1990) (A public school student who alleged that one of her teachers sexually abused her throughout high school, may maintain an action against school officials for their indifferent policies in reporting incidents of abuse).

104. *DeShaney*, 489 U.S. at 203. Such a federalist notion of respect-and-more for state legislative enactments, finds resonance in *Santosky's* dissent, also written by Chief Justice Rehnquist:

> Such a conclusion [to adopt a preponderance of the evidence test rather than a clear and convincing one] is well within the province of the state legislatures. It cannot be said that the New York procedures are unconstitutional simply because a majority of the Members of the Court disagree with the New York Legislature's weighing of the interests of the parents and the child in an error-free fact-finding hearing.

Santosky v. Kramer, 455 U.S. 745, 788 n.13 (1982) (Rehnquist, J., dissenting). This analysis rests in part on the domestic relations exception to federal jurisdiction. This too is reflected in Justice Rehnquist's dissent in *Santosky*: "[The *Santosky* majority] cavalierly rejects the considered judgment of the New York Legislature in an area traditionally entrusted to state care. The Court thereby begins, I fear, a trend of federal intervention in state family matters which surely will stifle creative responses to vexing problems." *Id.* at 791.

105. *DeShaney*, 489 U.S. at 203.

106. *Id.* at 201 n.9.

107. *Id.* at 202-03.

108. "Poverty rates among young families have almost doubled since the mid-1960s, and middle-income families report greater difficulty in making ends meet. For perhaps the first time

one sexual partner, and prone to violence. While being a single parent is not inherently suspect, this, coupled with other factors such as poverty, often has a problematic effect on parenting. "Research on the effects of single parenthood confirms that children who grow up without the support and personal involvement of both parents are more vulnerable to problems throughout childhood and into their adult lives."[109] While the research indicates that Joshua DeShaney may have adapted better in his father-headed household,[110] he was six times more likely to be poor as children who live with both parents, and at most ages, problems seem to be more pronounced for boys in his situation than for girls.[111] The number of single parents is growing rapidly in the United States.[112]

> The divorce rate in the United States has quadrupled in the past three decades: Approximately half of all marriages now end in divorce. Indeed, the United States has the highest divorce rate in the world. Even more alarming than the destruction of these relationships is the high and growing rate of out-of-wedlock childbearing and its connection with poverty and abuse among children.[113]

"Today, approximately one in four children in this country is born outside of marriage, compared to only 1 in 20 in 1960."[114] There is evi-

---

since the Great Depression, American children will no longer routinely surpass their parents' standard of living." BEYOND RHETORIC, *supra* note 14, at 8 (citations omitted).

109. *Id.* at 251.

110. *Id.* at 253.

111. *Id.*

112. Today, one in four children in the United States is raised by just one parent, usually a divorced or unmarried mother. Many grow up without the consistent presence of a father in their lives. One of every five children lives in a family without a minimally decent income. Many of these families are desperately poor, with incomes less than half the federal poverty level. Each year, half a million babies are born to teenage girls ill prepared to assume the responsibilities of parenthood. Most of these mothers are unmarried, many have not completed their education, and few have prospects for an economically secure future.

Id. at 4.

113. Recent studies affirm the growing poverty rate among children. According to the National Center for Children in Poverty, a part of Columbia University's School of Public Health,

> [b]etween 1990 and 1991, the number of poor American children under age 6 rose from 5.3 million to 5.6 million, the highest recorded, and the poverty rate for children under 6 edged up from 23 percent to 24 percent. That is double the poverty rate for Americans 65 and older and more than double the rate for adults ages 18 to 64.

Don Colburn, *Poverty Rate Record Belongs to Children*, WASH. POST, Aug. 31, 1993, at Z5.

114. BEYOND RHETORIC, *supra* note 14, at 252. The statistics suggest that, "more than half of

dence to suggest that laws encourage single parents to remain that way.

> At the federal level, for example, there is a 'marriage penalty' in the tax law; currently, a married couple pays higher taxes than two single adults with the same income who live together. At the state level, Aid to Families with Dependent Children, a public assistance program targeted primarily at single mothers and their children, is available only on a very restricted basis to families where the father is present and both parents are unemployed.[115]

Thus, laws and entitlement programs seem to favor avoiding the kinds of social commitments that are proven to engender better child development. If these laws do in fact contribute to the presence and enlargement of single parent families, they can very well contribute to the kinds of families in which Joshua DeShaney lived when he was brutally beaten by his father.

More attentive diagnosis by hospital personnel may have indicated the presence of battered child syndrome,[116] or perhaps more aggressive custody modification on the part of the mother could have changed the eventual outcome. But the fact remains that Joshua will spend the rest of his life in an institution as a result of parental abuse, abuse that is increasingly common, particularly in geographical areas involved with poverty, drugs or neglect.

Justice Blackmun wrote a separate dissent in *DeShaney*.[117] His

---

all white children and three-quarters of all black children born in the 1970s and 1980s are likely to live for some portion of their formative years with only their mothers." *Id.* at 20. Furthermore,

> Every year, approximately 1 million teenage girls become pregnant; nearly half of them give birth. Approximately half of these births are to young women who have not yet reached their 18th birthday, and most of them occur outside marriage. Until recently, births to adolescent girls had been declining. In 1986, however, the trend reversed, and births to girls age 15 to 17 increased for the first time in nearly two decades. The proportion of teenage births that occur outside marriage has increased steadily since the early 1970s.

Id. at 33 (citations omitted).

115. *Id.*

116. *See generally* Commonwealth v. Rodgers, 528 A.2d 610 (Pa. Super. Ct. 1987) (syndrome is based upon a finding that a child suffers multiple physical injuries, is undernourished, has poor hygiene, and that the severity and type of injury is inconsistent with the explanation offered by the custodial person); Richard J. Gelles, *Child Abuse as Psychopathology: A Sociological Critique and Reformulation*, 43 AM. J. ORTHOPSYCHIATRY 611-21 (1973) (recommends earlier intervention before the child is beaten or killed).

117. *See* DeShaney v. Winnebago County Dep't of Social Serv., 489 U.S. 189, 212 (1989).

opinion is particularly significant because he wrote the majority opinion in *Santosky*, an opinion replete with reference to parental presumptive rights and the intricacies of the Due Process Clause.[118] This is not true in *DeShaney*. Blackmun "would adopt a 'sympathetic' reading, one which comports with dictates of fundamental justice and recognizes that compassion need not be exiled from the province of judging."[119]

While *Santosky* involved the termination of a parent's rights, and *DeShaney* involved a civil rights action against the state and agents of the state, the crucial shift in Blackmun's analysis from *Santosky* to *DeShaney* suggests Blackmun's recognition of the factual reality of the child's plight: "Poor Joshua! Victim of repeated attacks by an irresponsible, bullying, cowardly, and intemperate father . . . ."[120] If there had been a suit by the state to terminate the rights of Randy DeShaney in his son Joshua, would Justice Blackmun still demand clear and convincing proof of the father's neglect and abuse before termination? What if the law demanded the return of Joshua yet again to his father because the father partially cooperated with the state in its rehabilitative efforts and therefore was able to rebut the clear and convincing standard? Indeed, the evidence of abuse present in *DeShaney* was not sufficient to overcome the clear and convincing standard. In order for the state to have satisfied the clear and convincing standard, Randy DeShaney would have had to refuse to cooperate with state efforts at rehabilitation over a long period of time—six months to a year, or perhaps longer.

During this time, what becomes of the child's best interest? This is the crucial question. If Justice Blackmun were serious in wanting to avoid the "sterile formalism" of his due process analysis in *Santosky*, he would have examined the brutal climate in which many children

---

Justices Marshall and Brennan also dissented in *DeShaney*, partly because they interpret the Constitution as providing a remedy for state inaction as well as action, and mostly because of the manner in which the majority presented the question. The two justices accuse the majority of "leading off with a discussion (and rejection) of the idea that the Constitution imposes on the States an affirmative duty to take basic care of their citizens, [and thus] foreshadows—perhaps even preordains—its conclusion that no duty existed even on the specific facts . . . ." *Id.* at 204 (Brennan, J., dissenting). Marshall and Brennan reject such a "stingy scope." *Id.* at 207. For them, "if a State cuts off private sources of aid and then refuses aid itself, it cannot wash its hands of the harm that results from its inaction." *Id.* Furthermore, "a State may be found complicit in an injury even if it did not create the situation that caused the harm." *Id.* Brennan and Marshall found that complicity on the part of the state should be litigated. The fact that Joshua was harmed at the hands of his father was not dispositive for them.

118. *See supra* text accompanying notes 18-21, 90.

119. *DeShaney*, 489 U.S. at 213.

120. *Id.*

exist in America today, and he would recognize that the parent's presumptive interest and the child's best interest increasingly do not coincide.[121]

A preponderance of the evidence standard would still allow consideration of the parent's interest, but would at the same time provide the child with greater due process recognition. Such an approach finds support in *Beyond Rhetoric*:

> Children need strong, stable, one-to-one relationships with their parents. When parents are unable or unwilling to provide consistent care and nurturing, children should have an opportunity to develop stable, trusting relationships with other caring adults. Accordingly, the Commission encourages states to review their judicial policies regarding termination of parental rights and take steps to accelerate the adoption process in cases where babies have been abandoned at birth and where repeated attempts to reunite older children and their parents have been unsuccessful. Some commissioners recommend terminating parental rights for abandoned infants after 90 days, in order to ensure that these very young children are able to be placed in loving homes and to begin the process of bonding with their adoptive parents as early as possible . . . . The Commission further urges the National Conference of Juvenile Court Judges to develop model statutes and administrative procedures to accelerate the termination of parental rights in cases where there is little hope of successfully reuniting children with their biological families and adoption is feasible.[122]

The *DeShaney* majority's suggestion that it was up to the state to provide remedies for the abuse suffered by Joshua reflects a shift in attitude on the part of the Court from *Santosky* to *DeShaney*. The Court

---

121. This position would be in direct opposition to the presupposition of the parental presumption. *See supra* text accompanying notes 47-49.

122. BEYOND RHETORIC, *supra* note 14, at 304-05. Only one other time does the Report refer specifically to termination of parental rights. Again, this was in the context of infants and other young children and the Report again encourages "states to move faster to terminate parental rights, where appropriate. We recognize, however, that termination of parental rights may not be in the best interests of all children." *Id.* at 300-01. But children of all ages are incorporated in the comment: "Until the nation pays substantial attention to building the capacity of communities to support all families in their childrearing roles and provides an array of supportive services to those experiencing problems, the existing child welfare system will continue to be little more than 'an emergency room for troubled families.'" *Id.* at 301.

recognized that the states are the appropriate arenas for resolving family relations matters. In acknowledging the tragic facts of *DeShaney*, the Court may also have finally recognized that states may often have legitimate reasons to depart from a clear and convincing standard of proof in proceedings to terminate the rights of parents like Randy DeShaney.[123]

III. A Portrait of the Termination Process

A. *The Children*

Cases involving the termination of parental rights arise in the context of adoption proceedings or child protection proceedings, the former usually occasioned by voluntary surrender and the latter resulting from abandonment or abuse[124] and neglect.[125] Adoption by someone other

---

123. It is unfair to conclude generally that if termination would be granted through preponderance of the evidence, states would seek to "bully" parents into termination. Santosky v. Kramer, 455 U.S. 745, 784 n.11 (1982). To the contrary, states would still be constitutionally mandated to provide the same kinds of services that were offered to Annie and John Santosky—services that provide for reunification as quickly as possible. There would have to be a showing by a preponderance of the evidence that the parents failed to take advantage of these services, and this finding would of course be subject to appellate review. The distinctive difference between the two standards however, is the factual one that the children would suffer less harm and spend less time in foster care with the lesser of the two levels of proof. The parents would still be given the presumption, but the children would have greater recognition as possessing individual rights.

124. For the difference between abuse and discipline, see State v. Jones, 95 N.C. 588 (1886) (criminal responsibility for abuse arises only when there is infliction of permanent injury or discipline proceeding from malice).

125. Most state statutes clearly define the grounds for involuntary termination resulting from abandonment or abuse and neglect. For example, 23 PA. CONS. STAT. § 2511 (1993) enumerates grounds for involuntary termination as follows:

> (a) General Rule. — The rights of a parent in regard to a child may be terminated after a petition filed on any of the following grounds:
>
> (1) The parent by conduct continuing for a period of at least six months immediately preceding the filing of the petition either has evidenced a settled purpose of relinquishing parental claim to a child or has refused or failed to perform parental duties.
>
> (2) The repeated and continued incapacity, abuse, neglect or refusal of the parent has caused the child to be without essential parental care, control or subsistence necessary for his physical or mental well-being and the conditions and causes of the incapacity, abuse, neglect or refusal cannot or will not be remedied by the parent.
>
> (3) The parent is the presumptive but not the natural father of the child.
>
> (4) The child is in the custody of an agency, having been found under such circumstances that the identity or whereabouts of the parent is unknown and cannot be ascertained by diligent search and the parent does not claim the child within three months after the child is found.

than a biological parent is the anticipated result of termination.[126] This third party could be a state agency, a foster parent, a distant rela-

---

(5) The child has been removed from the care of the parent by the court or under a voluntary agreement with an agency for a period of at least six months, the conditions which led to the removal or placement of the child continue to exist, the parent cannot or will not remedy those conditions within a reasonable period of time, the services or assistance reasonably available to the parent are not likely to remedy the conditions which led to the removal or placement of the child within a reasonable period of time and termination of the parental rights would best serve the needs and welfare of the child.

(6) In the case of a newborn child, the parent knows or has reason to know of the child's birth, does not reside with the child, has not married the child's other parent, has failed for a period of four months immediately preceding the filing of the petition to make reasonable efforts to maintain substantial and continuing contact with the child and has failed during the same four-month period to provide substantial financial support for the child.

(7) The parent is the father of a child who was conceived as a result of a rape.

(b) Other Considerations. — The court in terminating the rights of a parent shall give primary consideration to the needs and welfare of the child. The rights of a parent shall not be terminated solely on the basis of environmental factors such as inadequate housing, furnishings, income, clothing and medical care if found to be beyond the control of the parent. With respect to any petition filed pursuant to subsection (a) (1) or (6), the court shall not consider any efforts by the parent to remedy the conditions described therein which are first initiated subsequent to the giving of notice of the filing of the petition.

Id. (emphasis omitted).

See generally In re N.M.S., 347 A.2d 924 (D.C. 1975) (allowing child to remain with foster parents upon finding by the trial court that it was in the child's best interest); ROBERT H. MNOOKIN, IN THE INTEREST OF CHILDREN (1985); Robert A. Burt, *Forcing Protection on Children and Their Parents: The Impact of* Wyman v. James, 69 MICH. L. REV. 1259 (1971); Robert H. Mnookin, *Foster Care—In Whose Best Interest,* 43 HARV. ED. REV. 599 (1973); Parker, *supra* note 54; Michael S. Wald, *State Intervention on Behalf of "Neglected" Children: Standards for Removal of Children From Their Homes, Monitoring the Status of Children in Foster Care, and Termination of Parental Rights,* 28 STAN. L. REV. 623 (1976). For a discussion of the role of an attorney representing a child, see Sarah H. Ramsey, *Representation of the Child in Protection Proceedings: The Determination of Decision-Making Capacity,* 17 FAM. L.Q. 287 (1983).

126. Adoption is purely a product of statute. The natural parent could surrender the child and consent to the adoption in accordance with the state statute. *See, e.g.,* ARK. CODE ANN. § 9-9-220(b) (Michie 1993) (all rights of a parent to a child may be relinquished and the parent-child relationship terminated by a written agreement signed by the adult parent); CONN. GEN. STAT. § 45a-724(a)(1) (1992) (a statutory parent may, by written agreement, give his or her minor child in adoption). Parental rights may be terminated without consent in states if certain conditions are met. *See, e.g.,* ME. REV. STAT. ANN. tit. 19, § 532(2) (West 1993) (setting forth specific instances when consent to adoption is not required, including those cases where a parent willfully abandoned the child); N.Y. DOM. REL. LAW § 111(2) (McKinney 1993) (also setting forth specific instances when consent to adoption is not required, including parental failure to visit the child for a period of six months when able to do so and parental incompetence due to mental retardation).

tive or friend, or, in some cases, a grandparent.[127]

There is an ever-growing number of children entering the system. Each year there are approximately 1,003,600 cases of child neglect and 675,000 cases of child abuse, resulting in the deaths of 1100 children.[128] Yearly, almost 160,000 children receive serious injuries as a result of maltreatment. These injuries include loss of consciousness, arrested breathing, broken bones, third degree burns, schooling loss, and loss of special education services.[129] Additionally, 952,600 children sustain moderate injuries or impairments. These include bruises, depression, and emotional distress that lasts at least forty-eight hours.[130] These numbers are approximate, but it is ascertainable "that in 1989, 2.4 million reports of suspected child maltreatment were filed in the United States, of which more than 900,000 cases were officially substantiated."[131] The increase in the number of reports of child abuse in recent years has been astronomical.[132]

"In more than [ninety] percent of the cases the child is victimized not by a stranger but by a parent, other family member, or friend known to the child."[133] These children are often removed from the custody of a parent when the parent or another family member is the cause of the abuse. This separation from siblings, school, community

127. Note that the parental presumption arises only in the context of a parent versus the state or some third party. The presumption does not arise in the context of a dispute between two parents; there, the presumption applied in connection with a minor is "primary caretaker presumption." Garska v. McCoy, 278 S.E.2d 357, 363 (W. Va. 1981) (in a custody dispute between a natural mother and a natural father, primary caretaker status arises when one of the parents prepares meals, bathes, disciplines, educates, teaches and arranges for the social agenda of the child).

128. NATIONAL CTR. ON CHILD ABUSE AND NEGLECT, U.S. DEP'T OF HEALTH AND HUMAN SERVS., STUDY OF NATIONAL INCIDENCE AND PREVALENCE OF CHILD ABUSE AND NEGLECT, 3-5 to 3-11 (1988).

129. *Id.* at 3-10 to 3-11.

130. *Id.*

131. DEPARTMENT OF HEALTH AND HUMAN SERVS., CHILD ABUSE AND NEGLECT: CRITICAL FIRST STEPS IN RESPONSE TO A NATIONAL EMERGENCY 15 (1990). These figures do not include child sexual abuse. Nonetheless, these figures have increased as well. For instance, "from 35,000 reports in 1981 to 100,000 in 1984." CHILDREN'S DEFENSE FUND, A CHILDREN'S DEFENSE BUDGET: FY 1988, AN ANALYSIS OF OUR NATION'S INVESTMENT IN CHILDREN 175 (1987). *See generally* Raymond C. O'Brien, *Pedophilia: The Legal Predicament of Clergy*, 4 J. CONTEMP. HEALTH L. & POL'Y 91 (1988); Raymond C. O'Brien & Michael T. Flannery, *The Pending Gauntlet to Free Exercise: Mandating That Clergy Report Child Abuse*, 25 LOY. L.A. L. REV. 1 (1991).

132. CHILDREN'S DEFENSE FUND, *supra* note 131, at 175.

133. *Id.* at 176. The report identifies three groups of children: those abused or neglected, those in the foster home system already, and those suffering emotional problems. There is overlap among the three. *Id.*

and traditional support is acutely painful to the child.

B. *The Bureaucracy*

Once the statutory prerequisites for termination are met, a termination proceeding can be initiated by filing a petition with the court.[134] Upon filing, the clerk of the court sets a time and a place for the hearing and provides notice to the interested parties, including the parents of the child,[135] as well as any legal guardian appointed for the child.[136] The actual termination hearing almost always consists of two

134. *See, e.g.*, ALA. CODE § 26-18-5 (1993) (petition may be filed by public or private licensed child-placing agency, a parent, or with permission of the court, any interested party); ARIZ. REV. STAT. ANN. § 8-533 (1993) (petition may be filed by any person or agency that has a legitimate interest in the welfare of the child, including a relative, foster parent, physician, or child welfare agency); CONN. GEN. STAT. § 17a-112 (1988) (petition may be filed by the Commissioner of Children and Youth Services or, among others, the attorney who represented the child in the prior commitment proceeding); DEL. CODE ANN. tit. 13, §§ 1104(4)-(5) (1993) (petition may be filed by licensed agency or blood relative of the child); FLA. STAT. ch. 39.461 (1993) (petition may be filed by attorney for department or by any person with knowledge of the facts alleged); IDAHO CODE § 16-2004 (1993) (petition may be filed by authorized agency or any other person possessing legitimate interest in the matter); KAN. STAT. ANN. § 38-1581(a) (1992) (petition may be filed by any interested party); MISS. CODE ANN. § 93-15-105(1) (1993) (petition may be filed by any person, agency, or institution); N.H. REV. STAT. ANN. § 170-C:4 (1993) (petition may be filed by an authorized agency or by a guardian or legal custodian of the child); N.C. GEN. STAT. § 7A-289.24 (1993) (petition may be filed by guardian of child, county department of social services, licensed child-placing agency to which the child has been surrendered for adoption, or any person with whom the child has continuously resided for 2 years); 23 PA. CONS. STAT. § 2512(A) (1993) (petition may be filed by "[t]he individual having custody or standing in loco parentis to the child and who has filed a report of intention to adopt"); S.C. CODE ANN. § 20-7-1564 (Law. Co-op. 1991) (petition may be filed by child protective services agency or any interested party).

Some states mandate that intermediary reports be filed in the court in which the petition for adoption is initiated. *See, e.g.*, 23 PA. CONS. STAT. § 2533 (1993), which states:

> Within six months after filing the report of intention to adopt, the intermediary who or which arranged the adoption placement of any child under the age of 18 years shall make a written report under oath to the court in which the petition for adoption will be filed and shall thereupon forthwith notify in writing the adopting parent or parents of the fact that the report has been filed and the date thereof.

In some states, such as Pennsylvania, for example, a report of intention to adopt is not required. The Pennsylvania statute states that "[n]o report shall be required when the child is the child, grandchild, stepchild, brother or sister of the whole or half blood, or niece or nephew by blood, marriage or adoption of the person receiving or retaining custody of physical care." *Id.* at § 2531(c).

135. While some states mandate that a parent is entitled to counsel by statute in the civil termination proceeding, there is no constitutional guarantee to counsel as there is in criminal proceedings under the Sixth Amendment. *See* Lassiter v. Department of Social Servs., 452 U.S. 18, 31 (1981). Few jurisdictions provide counsel for children. *See, e.g.*, *In re* Kapcsos, 360 A.2d 174 (Pa. 1976); Ramsey, *supra* note 125.

136. For statutes providing notice to the guardian of a child, *see, e.g.*, ARIZ. REV. STAT. ANN.

phases.[137] First, the court engages in some type of factfinding process to determine whether the child is in fact abused, dependent, or in some need of aid.[138] Second, a hearing is held to determine if the child's best interest will be served by terminating parental rights or by providing for some other alternative.[139]

---

§ 8-535 (1993); DEL. CODE ANN. tit. 13, § 1107(a) (1993); D.C. CODE ANN. § 16-2357 (1993); FLA. STAT. ch. 39.462 (1993); IDAHO CODE § 16-2007 (1993); IOWA CODE ANN. § 600A.6 (West 1993); ME. REV. STAT. ANN. tit. 22, § 4053 (West 1993); MICH. COMP. LAWS § 712A.19b(2) (1992); NEB. REV. STAT. § 43-291 (1992); NEV. REV. STAT. § 128.060 (1993); N.H. REV. STAT. ANN. § 170-C:7 (1993); N.M. STAT. ANN. § 32A-4-29 (Michie 1993); N.C. GEN. STAT. § 7A-289.29 (1993); OHIO REV. CODE ANN. § 2151.353(D) (2) (Anderson 1993); 23 PA. CONS. STAT. ANN. § 2503(b) (regarding voluntary relinquishment) and § 2513(b) (regarding involuntary termination) (1994); WASH. REV. CODE ANN. § 13.34.070 (West 1994); WIS. STAT. ANN. § 48.42 (West 1994); WYO. STAT. § 14-2-313 (1993).

137. At the fact-finding stage the petitioner must prove the existence of one of the statutory grounds for termination; the disposition stage involves the court's decision as to whether termination is in the best interest of the child. *In re* Montgomery, 316 S.E.2d 246, 252 (N.C. 1984). *See also* COLO. REV. STAT. § 19-11-103 (1986); N.Y. FAM. CT. ACT §§ 622-23 (Consol. 1993). But other states combine the fact-finding and dispositional stage of the proceeding.

Some states, such as Pennsylvania, provide for a fact-finding stage and a separate termination stage. However, grounds for moving toward termination must be presented at the fact-finding stage once the child has been adjudicated dependent. *See* 42 PA. CONS. STAT. ANN. §§ 6301-35 (1994). This is because of statutory requirements that focus on services provided to the family. *See infra* note 164.

138. Even though the statutory grounds for termination vary from state to state, the courts' functions at the fact-finding stage remain similar among the states and the District of Columbia. The essential element is determining if the petitioner has met the statutory grounds for termination: neglect, abuse, surrender or the general sense of dependency. *See* Clemons v. Alabama Dep't of Pensions & Sec., 474 So. 2d 1143, 1145 (Ala. Civ. App. 1985) (trial court must first find from clear and convincing evidence that the child is dependent; once dependency is found, court must determine whether less drastic measures than termination of the rights of the parent would suffice to serve the best interest of the child); ALASKA STAT. § 26-18-7 (1993) (court must determine at the adjudicatory hearing that there is clear and convincing evidence that the child is in need of aid); COLO. REV. STAT. ANN. § 19-3-602 (West 1994) (court must hold a separate hearing and determine if sufficient grounds exist for termination); FLA. STAT. ANN. § 39.467 (West 1994) (court must hold an evidentiary hearing to determine if clear and convincing evidence of the statutory grounds for termination exist); GA. CODE ANN. § 15-11-81 (1993) (court must determine first whether there is clear and convincing evidence of parental misconduct or inability as defined by the statute); KY. REV. STAT. ANN. § 625.080 (Michie/Bobbs-Merrill 1993) (circuit court shall conduct hearing to make findings of fact); MICH. COMP. LAWS ANN. § 712A.19b, annot. 1 (West 1994) (court must determine that there is clear and convincing evidence of one of the statutory grounds for termination); NEV. REV. STAT. § 128.090 (1993) (court shall require the petitioner to establish the facts by clear and convincing evidence); N.Y. FAM. CT. ACT § 622 (Consol. 1994) (court will hold a separate factfinding hearing to determine if the allegations are supported by clear and convincing evidence); N.C. GEN. STAT. § 7A-289.30 (1993) (during the adjudication stage of a termination proceeding, court must determine whether the statutory grounds for termination have been proven by clear and convincing evidence); WIS. STAT. ANN. § 48.424 (West 1994) (purpose of the fact-finding hearing is to determine whether grounds exist for termination of parental rights).

139. In Arizona, for instance, the court may either terminate parental rights or dismiss the pe-

Throughout it all, the state is dependent upon a bureaucratic system often managed and staffed by poorly-paid, over-worked men and women.[140] For instance,

> A nationwide study of salaries in public and private welfare agencies in 1989 found that social workers with master's degrees earned an average of $24,824; those without master's degrees earned between $18,000 and $19,000. A survey of public child welfare staff in more than 40 states found that the median salary for entry-level direct service workers in 1989 was just above $21,000; for top-level direct service workers, it was just above $27,000.[141]

It is not surprising therefore, that "[t]urnover in the field is also quite high. Many experienced social workers leave public service for more lucrative and less stressful positions in private practice, industrial social work, and employee assistance programs."[142]

The social workers currently deployed in the child welfare field "average between 50 and 70 cases at any given time, although some caseworkers report carrying more than 200 cases simultaneously."[143] In addition, because of present budget constraints, many positions are filled by men and women with little professional education or experience in child welfare. "Today, only 25 percent of caseworkers providing direct services in the child welfare system have any social work training; roughly 50 percent have no previous experience working with children and families or in human service agencies."[144] Such deficiencies were brought to the attention of the district court in *Lashawn A. v. Dixon.*[145] The case involved a class action on behalf of children in foster care in the District of Columbia, and children who, although not yet in foster care, were the subject of reports of abuse and neglect. The court found that the foster care system operated by the District of Columbia did not comply with federal law, District law, or the United

---

tition and provide for substitution or supplementation of parental care and supervision, if the best interests of the child so require. ARIZ. REV. STAT. ANN. § 8-538 (1994).

140. For an excellent overview of both the historical and current systems of child dependency actions, see Judith Areen, *Intervention Between Parent and Child: A Reappraisal of the State's Role in Child Neglect and Abuse Cases*, 63 GEO. L.J. 887 (1975).

141. BEYOND RHETORIC, *supra* note 14, at 334.

142. *Id.* at 335 (citation omitted).

143. *Id.* at 335 (citation omitted).

144. *Id.*

145. 762 F. Supp. 959 (D.D.C. 1991).

States Constitution.[146] The court described how the system can deprive the children:

> It is a case about thousands of children who, due to family financial problems, psychological problems, and substance abuse problems, among other things, rely on the District to provide them with food, shelter, and day-to-day care. It is about beleaguered city employees trying their best to provide these necessities while plagued with excessive caseloads, staff shortages, and budgetary constraints. It is about the failure of an ineptly managed child welfare system . . . and the resultant tragedies for District children relegated to entire childhoods spent in foster care drift. Unfortunately, it is about a lost generation of children whose tragic plight is being repeated every day.[147]

While some systems are better than others, for those states with systems similar to the District of Columbia's, the requirement of a clear and convincing level of proof for termination of parental rights prevents states from making their systems more responsive to the child's best interest.

C. *Rehabilitation and Reunification*

Because termination "operates to extinguish all legal rights between parent and child,"[148] termination will occur only as a last resort, after the state has exhausted its statutory prerequisites.[149] Termination pro-

146. *Id.* at 960-61.

147. *Id.*

148. *See* Hershkowitz, *supra* note 27, at 282. Statutes illustrating the finality of termination include: ARIZ. REV. STAT. ANN. § 8-539 (1994) ("An order terminating the parent-child relationship shall divest the parent and the child of all legal rights, privileges, duties and obligations with respect to each other . . . ."). *Accord* COLO. REV. STAT. § 19-3-608 (1993); DEL. CODE ANN. tit. 13, § 1113 (1993); D.C. CODE ANN. § 16-2361 (1993); FLA. STAT. ch. 39.469(2) (b) (1993); GA. CODE ANN. § 15-11-80 (Michie 1993); ILL. ANN. STAT. ch. 705, para. 2-29 (Smith-Hurd 1994); IND. CODE § 31-6-5-6 (1994); KY. REV. STAT. ANN. § 625.100 (Michie/Bobbs-Merrill 1993); MINN. STAT. § 260.241 (1994); MONT. CODE ANN. § 41-3-611 (1993); N.M. STAT. ANN. § 32A-4-29(m) (Michie 1993); N.C. GEN. STAT. § 7A-289.33 (1993); N.D. CENT. CODE § 27-20-46 (1993); 23 PA. CONS. STAT. § 2521 (1994); S.C. CODE ANN. § 20-7-1576 (Law. Co-op. 1991); TEX. FAM. CODE ANN. § 15.07 (West 1994); WASH. REV. CODE § 13.34.200 (1993); WYO. STAT. § 14-2-317 (1993). Some states retain the child's rights to inheritance until a final order of adoption. *See, e.g.*, ARIZ. REV. STAT. ANN. § 8-539 (1988 & Supp. 1991); COLO. REV. STAT. § 19-11-108 (1986).

149. Only Massachusetts and Vermont have no statutes providing for termination of parental rights.

ceedings arise after the state has taken protective custody over a surrendered, abused or neglected child[150] pursuant to a dependency adjudication or care and protection proceeding[151] and then only because state efforts to rehabilitate the parents and provide for reunification of the family have failed.[152]

State efforts at reunification may employ a myriad of services, but those described in *Beyond Rhetoric* are illustrative:

First, they attempt to give families the skills and knowledge

---

150. Absent visible physical abuse, neglect or dependency is difficult to ascertain. The test centers on what a reasonably intelligent person should, by common understanding and practice, realize to be necessary for that particular child. *See* People in Interest of D.K., 245 N.W.2d 644, 651 (S.D. 1976) (statute was sustained in its definition of neglect). *But see* Davis v. Smith, 583 S.W.2d 37, 43 (Ark. 1979) (statute defining parents as unfit if they were unable to provide a "proper home" was unconstitutionally vague). For a case dealing with emotional neglect, see Castorr v. Brundage, 674 F.2d 531 (6th Cir. 1982). For a case dealing with potential neglect, see *In re* East, 288 N.E.2d 343, 346 (Ohio Misc. 1972) ("The law does not require the court to experiment with the child's welfare to see if he will suffer great detriment or harm.").

151. The state's entry into the family unit is predicated on its *parens patriae* authority. Either surrender of the child or a dependency situation will initiate the state action that eventually evolves into the petition of termination. *See* ARK. CODE ANN. § 9-27-341 (Michie 1991) (courts may consider a petition to terminate parental rights after finding by clear and convincing evidence that the juvenile has been adjudicated dependent-neglected); COLO. REV. STAT. § 19-3-602 (1993) (termination of a parent-child relationship shall be considered only after an adjudication of a child as dependent or neglected); CONN. GEN. STAT. ANN. § 17a-112 (West 1994) (court may grant a petition to terminate after a child has been found to be neglected or uncared for in a prior proceeding and parent has not been rehabilitated); HAW. REV. STAT. § 571-61(b) (1) (E) (1993) (involuntary termination proceeding will occur after the child has been removed from parental custody pursuant to judicial proceeding); IND. CODE ANN. § 31-6-5-4 (Burns 1993) (termination involving child in need of services may occur only after the child has been removed from the parent for at least six months under a dispositional decree); N.H. REV. STAT. ANN. § 169-C (1990) (court may terminate when parent fails to correct conditions that led to finding of abuse or neglect); 23 PA. CONS. STAT. ANN. § 2511(a) (1994) (parental rights may be terminated when parent, for period of six months, has demonstrated a settled purpose of relinquishment or failure to perform parental duties). *See generally* Hershkowitz, *supra* note 27, at 281 ("Proceedings to determine dependency are generally a prerequisite to the termination of parental rights"); Parker, *supra* note 54, at 572 (by the time a termination proceeding occurs, the child has already been removed from his parents' home pursuant to a care and protection proceeding).

152. The failure of state rehabilitative efforts is the concrete proof necessary to provide for termination of parental rights. Some state statutes provide for this expressly. *See, e.g.*, CONN. GEN. STAT. § 17a-112(d) (1994); GA. CODE ANN. § 15-11-81(b) (4) (C) (1993); KAN. STAT. ANN. § 38-1583(b) (7) (1993); KY. REV. STAT. ANN. § 625.090(2) (c) (Michie/Bobbs-Merrill 1993); ME. REV. STAT. ANN. tit. 22, § 4055(B) (2) (b) (iv) (West 1993); MINN. STAT. ANN. § 260.221(b) (5) (West 1993); MISS. CODE ANN. § 93-15-103(3) (c) (Supp. 1993); N.M. STAT. ANN. § 32A-4-28(B) (3) (Michie 1993); N.Y. FAM. CT. ACT § 614(1) (C) (Consol. 1993); 23 PA. CONS. STAT. § 2511(a) (5) (1994); R.I. GEN. LAWS § 15-7-7(1) (c) (1993); VA. CODE ANN. § 16.1-283(C) (1) (Michie 1994).

> needed to cope more effectively with the stresses of contemporary life and to care for and nurture their children better. In achieving this goal, programs try to build on family strengths and capacities rather than emphasizing deficits. Second, family support programs are prevention-oriented; that is, they attempt to strengthen families before a crisis occurs. Third, they offer multidisciplinary services that recognize and address the diverse and interrelated needs of families. Finally, family support programs are community-based and easily accessible to parents in order to be as responsive as possible to the families they serve.[153]

Such services are an integral part of the termination process. Their existence rebuts any charge that a state, in initiating a termination proceeding, is depriving the parent of the child through "bullying"[154] or coercion. Indeed, when any childcare agency has custody of a child and brings a proceeding to terminate parental rights, the agency must affirmatively plead and prove, often by clear and convincing evidence, that it has fulfilled its statutory duty to exercise diligent efforts to strengthen the parent-child relationship and reunite the family.[155]

As was noted in *Santosky*, an integral part of the termination equation is the scope of the services offered by the state. If the services designed to bring about termination are not extensive and forthcoming,

---

153. BEYOND RHETORIC, *supra* note 14, at 275. To control obsessive behavior, parents are often required to enroll in programs such as Alcoholics Anonymous, Narcotics Anonymous, or Weight Watchers. Violence clinics or support groups are available to abusive parents and spouses. More traditional programs include the following:

> [1] parent education and support groups for parents;
>
> [2] activities that bring parents and children together to teach parents about child development and strengthen the parent-child relationship;
>
> [3] classes and discussion groups on issues of concern to parents, such as family budgeting, coping with stress, health, and nutrition;
>
> [4] drop in centers, offering unstructured time for families to be with other families and with program staff on an informal basis;
>
> [5] child care while parents are engaged in activities offered by the family support program;
>
> [6] information and referral to other services in the community, including child care, health care, nutrition programs, and counseling services;
>
> [7] home visits, often designed to introduce particularly isolated parents to family resource programs; and
>
> [8] development exams or health screening for infants and children.

Id. at 275-276.

154. Santosky v. Kramer, 455 U.S. 745, 784 n.11 (1982).

155. *In re* Sheila G., 462 N.E.2d 1139, 1140 (N.Y. 1984).

the petition for termination cannot succeed. As Justice Rehnquist noted:

> A plan for providing petitioners with extensive counseling and training services was submitted to the court and approved . . . . Under the plan, petitioners received training by a mother's aide, a nutritional aide, and a public health nurse, and counseling at a family planning clinic. In addition, the plan provided psychiatric treatment and vocational training for the father, and counseling at a family service center for the mother.[156]

When parents refuse to cooperate with such a plan, the state initiates a termination proceeding. Such a proceeding cannot, therefore, succeed under any due process analysis without the state first offering the family services to prevent the break-up of the family or to reunite it if the child has already left home.[157]

In Maine, for example, before termination of parental rights can occur, the social service agency must arrange rehabilitative services for the parents; notify the parents in writing of the child's address when the child is removed from the home; facilitate visitation between the natural parents and the child; and discuss with the parents the reasons for the child's removal from the home and the improvements which must be made before the child is returned.[158]

State requirements on time limits for rehabilitation vary. Some impose a time limit as a prerequisite before parental rights can be terminated. Others require that the child be in the care of an authorized agency for at least one year following the initial adjudication of dependency before termination may be initiated.[159] Statutes with mandated time periods that are not associated with the conduct of the state or with the response of the parents may be invalid as unduly adverse to the best interests of the child under any due process analysis, since the child is most often confined to a foster care facility or an abusive home

156. *Santosky*, 455 U.S. at 781 (Rehnquist, J., dissenting).

157. *Id.* at 784 n.11.

158. ME. REV. STAT. ANN. tit. 22, § 4041 (West 1993).

159. *See, e.g.*, ARIZ. REV. STAT. ANN. § 8-533(B) (6) (1988); ARK. CODE ANN. § 9-27-341(b) (1) (Michie 1987); CAL. FAM. CODE § 7828 (Deering 1994); DEL. CODE ANN. tit. 13, § 1103(5) (1981); HAW. REV. STAT. § 571-61(b) (1) (C) (1988); N.Y. SOC. SERV. LAW § 384-b(7) (a) (Consol. 1987); OR. REV. STAT. § 419.523(3) (1991); TENN. CODE ANN. § 37-1-147 (1991); VA. CODE ANN. § 16.1-283(C) (Michie 1988); WIS. STAT. ANN. § 48.415(2) (c) (West 1988). Generally, states require one year, but some do not. *See, e.g.*, D.C. CODE ANN. § 16-2354(b) (1989) (six months); OKLA. STAT. ANN. tit. 10, § 1130A(3) (West 1991) (imposes a three month period); PA. STAT. ANN. tit. 23, § 2511(a) (5) (1985) (six months); S.C. CODE ANN. § 20-7-1572(2) (Law. Co-op. 1985) (six months).

during this period.[160] Nonetheless, the time periods are meant to add caution to a procedure that seeks to balance the best interests of the child with the parental presumption.

D. *The Problems with Foster Care*

Sometimes the victimized child is placed in the custody of a relative while his or her parents undergo rehabilitation. More often than not, however, the child is placed in foster care. During a termination proceeding, foster care can approximate actual abuse in its injurious effect upon a child.[161]

"Foster care is intended to protect children from neglect and abuse at the hands of parents and other family members, yet all too often it becomes an equally cruel form of neglect and abuse by the state."[162] The number of children in foster care has increased dramatically since early declines in the late 1970s and early 1980s. "Recent estimates project that more than half a million children will be in foster care by 1995."[163]

---

160. *See* Sosna v. Iowa, 419 U.S. 393 (1975), which concerned the validity of a state durational residency requirement for divorce. While the Court sustained the one-year requirement because it was a domestic relations issue and it satisfied the state's need to provide substance to its decrees, *id.* at 396, the dissent lamented the deprivation such statutes cause, *id.* at 418-27. Residence within an injurious environment is sufficient deprivation to warrant close scrutiny of these statutes.

161. [S]ome children linger in foster care or in institutions for extended periods of time; an estimated 14 percent of foster children stay in the system five or more years. Despite widespread knowledge that children do best in settings that provide continuity and stable, caring relationships with adults, they are often moved from one placement to another. Approximately 55 percent of children in foster care experience two or more placements; 8 percent experience six or more placements, in part because there are too few foster parents trained and willing to care for troubled children and children with special needs. In addition, foster children rarely have just one caseworker who tracks their case and monitors their progress. High rates of turnover among caseworkers make it difficult for children to receive continuous personal attention and may amplify their feelings of being lost in an uncaring system.

BEYOND RHETORIC, *supra* note 14, at 287-88 (citations omitted).

162. *Id.* at xxx.

163. *Id.* This high number reflects a reversal of the trend which saw a decline earlier. "In 1977 an estimated 502,000 children were in foster care. By 1980 this number had dropped to 302,000, and it declined further to a low of 275,000 in 1983." *Id.* at 283-84 (citations omitted).

In addition to foster care, "an estimated 91,646 children live in public and private juvenile justice facilities, and another 54,472 receive mental health care as inpatients in hospitals and residential treatment centers." *Id.* at 284 (citations omitted). The increase could be the result of the continued break-up of the family structure, single parent births, homelessness, the continuing recession, drugs, increased reporting requirements, or a pattern of government funding programs that actually provide open-ended out-of-home entitlement, while restricting in-home funds. *See id.* at xxx-xxxi (citing entitlement under Title IV-E of the Child Welfare and Adoption Assistance

Time in foster care is the crucial issue. In cases involving a petition for temporary removal of custody or a petition for permanent termination of parental rights, the state often imposes a time period during which reunification of the family unit is fostered through supportive programs.[164] Nonetheless, if the process is delayed because of bureaucratic reasons, parental insouciance or judicial backlog, the time in which the child remains within foster care lengthens.

If states are required to provide for termination of parental rights through clear and convincing evidence, greater delay than under a preponderance of the evidence standard is likely. That is, either more time will be needed to demonstrate a parental refusal to rectify the situation which has brought on the petition, or greater harm to the child will have to be demonstrated to establish the basis for the petition. In either instance, the best interest of the child is interpreted as less significant than the parental presumption. Although many states have passed legislation to prevent delay in such proceedings, the judicial system is over-

---

Act). *See also id.* at 290 (stating that entitlement for in-home care was $273 million in FY 1991, but $1.8 billion for foster care services for FY 1991, illustrating the difference in priorities). *But see* Editorial, *For Children in Foster Care,* WASH. POST, July 16, 1993, at A18 (editorial recommends the House version of a federal bill that would provide states with $1.5 billion over five years for early intervention with problem families to keep them from needing foster care).

Family income seems to be the single common denominator that predicts the presence of an abusive or neglectful situation. "While poverty does not always or automatically lead to child abuse and neglect, it can contribute to stress and a lack of emotional control that can result in violence or an inability to meet a child's basic daily needs." BEYOND RHETORIC, *supra* note 14, at 284. Drug use, particularly after 1985, is a significant factor, but poverty is the common denominator of abuse and neglect. Although children living apart from their parents come from all racial and ethnic groups—and all income groups—children from minority and single parent families are over-represented. "At the end of fiscal year (FY) 1986, 49 percent of foster children were minority, more than twice the proportion of minority children in the population nationwide. Among black children in foster care, nearly 46 percent were from single-parent families." *Id.* at 284-85.

Drug use among parents is the single greatest reason for the rise in foster care or institutional care among children after 1985. "The growing number of troubled families—largely because of drug use—has overwhelmed the child welfare system." *Id.* at 289.

164. For example, California provides that the child has been abandoned if the child has been left without provision for identification for a period of six months; or by one parent in the care and custody of the other parent for a period of one year without any provision for the child's support; or without communication from the parent or parents, with the intent on the part of the parent or parents to abandon the child. The failure to provide identification, failure to provide support, or failure to communicate shall be presumptive evidence of the intent to abandon. CAL. FAM. CODE § 7822(a)-(b) (Deering 1994). A child is dependent if he or she has been in out-of-home placement under the supervision of the juvenile court, the county welfare department, or other public or private licensed child-placing agency for a one-year period. CAL. FAM. CODE § 7828 (Deering 1994).

burdened, especially in certain geographical areas. The statutes, therefore, even though good-intentioned, are rhetoric.[165]

The fact is that some children linger in foster care or in institutions for extended periods of time. An estimated fourteen percent of foster children stay in the system five years or more.[166] For many of these children, movement from one home to another is the norm, rather than the exception.

> Between 1983 and 1985, the number of children with multiple placements in foster care rose from 16 percent to 30 percent. Recent longitudinal studies of children in foster care found that in New York 27 percent of the children reunited with their families returned to placement some time later; in Illinois, the comparable figure is just under 30 percent.[167]

Children who continually return to the foster care system often lack advantages that have been proven to be absolutely essential to healthy development—a setting that provides continuity, and stable, caring rela-

---

165. *See, e.g.*, CAL. FAM. CODE § 7870 (Deering 1994):

> (a) It is the public policy of this state that judicial proceedings to declare a child free from parental custody and control shall be fully determined as expeditiously as possible.
>
> (b) Notwithstanding any other provision of law, a proceeding to declare a child free from parental custody and control . . . shall be set for trial not more than 45 days after filing notification therefor and completion of service thereon in the manner prescribed by law for service of civil process. The matter so set has precedence over all other civil matters on the date set for trial.
>
> (c) The court may continue the proceeding as provided in Section 7864 or Section 7871.

CAL. FAM. CODE § 7864 (Deering 1994) provides:

> The court may continue the proceeding for not to exceed 30 days as necessary to appoint counsel and to enable counsel to become acquainted with the case.

CAL. FAM. CODE § 7871 (Deering 1994) provides:

> (a) A continuance may be granted only upon a showing of good cause. Neither a stipulation between counsel nor the convenience of the parties is in and of itself a good cause.
>
> (b) Unless the court for good cause entertains an oral motion for continuance, written notice of a motion for a continuance of the hearing shall be filed within two court days of the date set for the hearing, together with affidavits or declarations detailing specific facts showing that a continuance is necessary.
>
> (c) A continuance shall be granted only for that period of time shown to be necessary by the evidence considered at the hearing on the motion. Whenever a continuance is granted, the facts proven which require the continuance shall be entered upon the minutes of the court.

166. BEYOND RHETORIC, *supra* note 14, at 287. Note that the Santosky children were in foster care for four and one-half years. Santosky v. Kramer, 455 U.S. 745, 773 (1982).

167. BEYOND RHETORIC, *supra* note 14, at 288.

tionships with adults.[168] Significant numbers of children never reach this goal, and if they do, it is only after prolonged periods of time have elapsed. As *Beyond Rhetoric* notes:

> Approximately 55 percent of children in foster care experience two or more placements; 8 percent of children experience six or more placements, in part because there are too few foster parents trained and willing to care for troubled children and children with special needs. In addition, foster children rarely have just one caseworker who tracks their case and monitors their progress. High rates of turnover among caseworkers make it difficult for children to receive continuous personal attention and may amplify their feelings of being lost in an uncaring system.[169]

In 1986, of all children leaving foster care, less than sixty percent were either reunited with their families or placed with a parent, relative, or other caregiver. Another seven percent were adopted or relinquished for adoption. Approximately twenty percent either ran away,[170] were incarcerated, got married, died, were discharged to another public agency, or acquired by a legal guardian. Another eight percent reached age eighteen and were no longer eligible for care.[171]

---

168. *Id.* at 287.

169. *Id.* at 288.

170. For an examination of foster care runaways, *see* Kevin M. Ryan, *Stemming the Tide of Foster Care Runaways: Due Process Perspective*, 42 CATH. U. L. REV. 271-311 (1993).

171. BEYOND RHETORIC, *supra* note 14, at 288. No information is available for the remaining six percent of children who left the foster care system in 1986. *Id.* Recommendations have been made to extend foster care beyond age 18 to age 21, so as to redress the negative effects of foster care placement. *See Id.* at 302. "In 1990, recognizing that many foster youth need additional support to complete their high school educations, to pursue postsecondary education and training, and to acquire the necessary skills and knowledge to live successfully on their own, Congress extended federal support for foster care services to youth up to age 21 at state option." *Id.*

Efforts to reduce the number of children who linger in foster care placement are evidenced by some states' codified objectives. *See, e.g.,* 55 PA. CONS. STAT. ANN. § 3130.13 (1991), which states:

> (a) A statewide goal of 1% reduction in the number of children in placement for 2 or more years is established for each of the next 7 years beginning in Fiscal Year 1983-1984 and concluding at the end of Fiscal Year 1989-1990 with a cumulative reduction of 7%. This goal does not apply to individual counties.
>
> (b) The steps taken to achieve this goal will include:
>
> (1) Semiannual judicial or administrative review of the status of children in placement.
>
> (2) Uniform monitoring and enforcement of the case planning and review

E. *Termination: The Final Solution*

The constitutional protections afforded parents in termination proceedings outweigh the protections afforded the child. During the termination proceeding, the child is in a foster care environment that all too often causes further harm to the child.[172] The child is likely to remain in this harmful environment for at least five years pending parental response to state initiatives. The likelihood of adoption decreases as the child grows older.[173] The child is not likely to be represented by legal counsel,[174] and if he or she is represented by counsel, the counsel could be representing the parents as well.[175] The fact of the matter is that a clear and convincing standard places the child at a distinctive disadvantage during the termination process.

In a clash of best interests between the parent and the child, it is difficult to argue that the child is provided due process during termination proceedings. Proceedings subject to a clear and convincing standard simply take too long. The child is traumatized and often suffers irreparable harm, the result of which is often tragic. *Beyond Rhetoric* describes the high rate of suicide among adolescents:

> requirements established in this chapter.
>
> (3) Increased emphasis on the development of adoption resources, including the Adoption Cooperative Exchange (PACE) and the Pennsylvania Adoption Assistance Program.
>
> (4) Increased emphasis on services to children in their own homes.

Id.

172. The dissenting opinion in *Santosky* acknowledged the "often unstable world of foster care." Santosky v. Kramer, 455 U.S. 745, 789 (1982).

173. The parent is provided with complete rights of appeal, and "no petition for adoption may be heard until the appellate rights of the natural parents have been exhausted." CAL. FAM. CODE § 7893(b) (3) (West Spec. Pamphlet 1993).

174. *See, e.g.*, CAL. FAM. CODE § 7861. (West Spec. Pamphlet 1993) "The court shall consider whether the interests of the child require the appointment of counsel. If the court finds that the interests of the child require representation by counsel, the court shall appoint counsel to represent the child, whether or not the child is able to afford counsel." *Id.*

175. *See, e.g.*, *In re* Kapcsos, 360 A.2d 174, 177-78 (Pa. 1976); *In re* D., 547 P.2d 175, 179-80 (Or. Ct. App. 1976) (counsel for the child need not be appointed in all neglect proceedings, only on a case-by-case basis as needed), *cert. denied sub nom.*, C. v. F.F., 429 U.S. 907 (1976); State *ex rel.* Juv. Dep't of Multnomah County v. Wade, 527 P.2d 753, 756 (Or. Ct. App. 1974) (when issue of parental unfitness to be adjudicated, potential for conflict between interests of children and of both parents and state seems manifest), *overruled by In re* D., 547 P.2d 175 (Or. Ct. App. 1976). *But see* CAL. FAM. CODE § 7860 (West Spec. Pamphlet 1993) ("The same counsel shall not be appointed to represent both the child and the child's parent."); CAL. WELF. & INST. CODE § 317 (West Supp. 1994); N.Y. FAM. CT. ACT, §§ 241-49 (McKinney 1983 & West Supp. 1993); KAN. STAT. ANN. § 38-821 (1986 & Supp. 1989).

> During the 1960s and 1970s, the rate at which adolescents took their own lives doubled, from 3.6 to 7.2 deaths per 100,000, while the rate for adults remained steady. By 1986, it had increased another 30 percent, to 10.2 death per 100,000. Suicide is now the second leading cause of death among adolescents, after accidents. Unlike homicide, it is more common among white teens than black teens, and white adolescents are by far the highest-risk group, with a rate of 16 per 100,000.[176]

Even if the child does not fall victim to suicide,

> [i]t requires no citation of authority to assert that children who are abused in their youth generally face extraordinary problems developing into responsible, productive citizens. The same can be said of children who, though not physically or emotionally abused, are passed from one foster home to another with no constancy of love, trust, or discipline.[177]

Surely these statistics support the proposition that in any termination proceeding, the interest of the child is of sufficient importance to allow termination to occur under a preponderance of the evidence standard.

IV. The Current State of Due Process Protection for the Child

Although the parental presumption is deeply imbedded in our system of jurisprudence, courts have recognized the rights of children in some instances. Such recognition has become more widespread over the past quarter century and can be attributed mainly to the changing nature of the American family.

A. *The Expanding Recognition of Childrens' Constitutional Rights*

In 1967, the Court announced for the first time that the Constitution afforded protection to children as well as to adults.[178] Decisions by

---

176. Beyond Rhetoric, *supra* note 14, at 35-36.

177. *Santosky*, 455 U.S. at 789 (Rehnquist, J., dissenting).

178. *In re* Gault, 387 U.S. 1, 13 (1967) ("neither the Fourteenth Amendment nor the Bill of Rights is for adults alone"). *See also* Planned Parenthood of Cent. Mo. v. Danforth, 428 U.S. 52, 74 (1976) ("Constitutional rights do not mature and come into being magically only when one attains the state-defined age of majority. Minors, as well as adults, are protected by the Constitution and possess constitutional rights."); Tinker v. Des Moines Indep. Community Sch.

the Court have established that children have equal protection rights,[179] privacy rights,[180] procedural due process protection,[181] and a right to freedom of speech.[182]

Recent cases have extended guarantees of privacy for individual minors in areas that had been previously considered the inviolate realm of family privacy and the parental presumption. In *Carey v. Population Services International*,[183] for example, the Court found that a statute prohibiting the sale of contraceptives to minors under the age of sixteen was unconstitutional because it intruded into a privacy right that could only be regulated to vindicate a compelling state interest. Abortion is another key area where changing definitions of family and privacy have resulted in the elevated recognition of children's rights. This is particularly true in cases involving parental notification. In all the cases addressing limits on parental notification, the Court has examined three interests: the state's interest in the welfare of the pregnant minor; the interest of the parents; and the interest of the family unit.[184] The deci-

---

Dist., 393 U.S. 503, 511 (1969) (minor students are "persons" under the Constitution).

179. Brown v. Board of Educ., 347 U.S. 483 (1954).

180. Carey v. Population Serv. Int'l, 431 U.S. 678 (1977) (allowing contraceptives to be distributed to persons under the age of sixteen); *see also* Planned Parenthood of Utah v. Matheson, 582 F. Supp. 1001, 1009 (D. Utah 1983) (The absence of a procedure in statute whereby mature minors could demonstrate that parental notification was against their best interests unconstitutionally infringed upon their right to decide whether to bear or beget children.).

181. The Warren Court established the child's right to certain procedural protection in the juvenile context. In *In re* Gault, 387 U.S. 1 (1967), the Court set aside a minor's conviction, holding that even though a juvenile hearing need not "conform with all of the requirements of a criminal trial or even of the usual administrative hearing . . . [it] must measure up to the essentials of due process and fair treatment." *Id.* at 30 (internal quotations and citation omitted).

The Burger Court extended a juvenile's right to due process. In *In Re* Winship, 397 U.S. 358, 368 (1970), the Court held that minors may be found guilty only upon proof beyond a reasonable doubt, and that minors may assert the privilege against compulsory self-incrimination. In Goss v. Lopez, 419 U.S. 565, 581 (1975), the Court recognized that a public school student is entitled to notice and an informal hearing before being suspended from school. In Ingraham v. Wright, 430 U.S. 651, 676 (1977), the Court held that a child has a liberty interest in procedural safeguards that would minimize risk of wrongful punishment. But the Court held further that due process did not require advanced procedural safeguards before a school could administer corporal punishment. *Id.* at 682. *But see* Schall v. Martin, 467 U.S. 253, 273-74, 277, 281 (1984) (Court held that preventive detention of a juvenile pursuant to a state statutory act does not violate the Due Process clause because the detention is limited and serves to keep the juvenile in a more controlled environment than an adult prison).

182. The Court upheld a minor's right to protest the Vietnam war by wearing black arm bands in school, stating that students "may not be confined to the expression of those sentiments that are officially approved." *Tinker*, 393 U.S. at 511.

183. 431 U.S. 678 (1977).

184. Hodgson v. Minnesota, 497 U.S. 417, 444 (1990). In *Hodgson*, the Court held that the state's requirement of notification to both of the pregnant minor's parents was not reasonably

sions are tortuous, but all establish the privacy right of the child *vis-a-vis* the parent.[185]

In *Bellotti v. Baird*,[186] the Court held that a state may not require a minor to obtain her parent's permission to get an abortion in all cases. States are required to provide an alternative procedure by which the minor may obtain an abortion without notifying the parent or receiving consent. The minor must be permitted to convince the court that the abortion is in her best interest, and if successful, must be allowed to obtain the abortion without notifying her parent.

The crux of *Bellotti* is that parental involvement in the decision of whether or not to beget a child interferes with the "unique" nature and "indelible" consequences involved in the fundamental right to choose an abortion.[187] Thus, the Court allowed the child's decision to predominate over that of the parent and nullified the state statute.[188]

---

related to the state's interests. *Id.* at 450.

185. *See, e.g.*, Ohio v. Akron Ctr. for Reprod. Health, 497 U.S. 502 (1990) (upholding a statute requiring notification by the physician to at least one parent, unless the minor could prove her maturity by clear and convincing evidence at a judicial proceeding).

186. 443 U.S. 622 (1979) (Justice Powell wrote for the majority, and was joined by Chief Justice Burger and Justices Stewart and Rehnquist. Justices Stevens, Marshall, Brennan and Blackmun concurred, and Justice White dissented).

187. *Id.* at 642-43; *see also* H.L. v. Matheson, 450 U.S. 398 (1981) (Stevens, J., concurring) (the state has a fundamental and substantial "interest in protecting a young pregnant woman from the consequences of an incorrect abortion decision").

188. *Bellotti*, 443 U.S. at 651 (the Massachusetts statute requiring parental consent was nullified). In Planned Parenthood v. Danforth, 428 U.S. 52 (1976), the Missouri statute, which had required a minor to obtain parental consent before obtaining an abortion, was also nullified. In Akron v. Akron Ctr. for Reprod. Health, Inc., 462 U.S. 416, 441-42 (1983), *overruled by* Planned Parenthood of S.E. Pa. v. Casey, 112 S. Ct. 2791 (1992), the Court found that the local ordinance at issue did not meet constitutional safeguards in protecting minors. The statute required minors seeking an abortion to secure either parental consent or a court order. *Id.* at 439.

Other cases have upheld parental notification statutes. In H.L. v. Matheson, 450 U.S 398 (1981), the Court upheld a Utah statute which required the attending physician to notify parents of a minor, if possible, before performing an abortion. Notification was allowed, in part, because, in the Court's view, parents are counselors to their children and have a guidance responsibility. *Id.* at 410.

Most states that require parental notification for a minor to receive an abortion also have a judicial by-pass, whereby the pregnant minor may petition the court for a hearing in order for the parental consent or notification not to be implemented. California has in place a statutory scheme that requires the minor to receive the consent of one parent in order to get an abortion. However, "[i]f the court finds that the minor is sufficiently mature and sufficiently informed to make the decision on her own regarding an abortion, and that the minor has, on that basis, consented thereto, the court shall grant the petition" for an abortion without parental consent. CAL. HEALTH & SAFETY CODE § 25958 (c) (1) (West 1994).

Some states, like Wyoming, have spelled out the level of proof necessary in order for the

Attention to the child's best interest is not limited to the reproductive context. Other cases have also recognized the child's best interest. These include cases involving the name of the child,[189] interstate travel by the custodial parent,[190] and parental neglect.[191]

The recent change in judicial attitudes concerning the individuality of children results in part from the acknowledgement of changing definitions of family, marriage, privacy, and the nature of "parenthood." The past image of parents as depicted in *The Brady Bunch*, *Leave It to Beaver*, or *I Love Lucy* is simply no longer a reality within a vast segment of the population. For instance, the definition of family as a union of a man and woman united in a contract sanctioned by the state for the purpose of procreation and the raising of children has been affected by a series of cases that allow many of the benefits of marriage with-

---

court to determine whether the minor child has the requisite "maturity" and is adequately informed about the abortion decision. Wyoming uses the clear and convincing standard. WYO. STAT. § 35-6-118 (1993). Some states follow schemes similar to North Dakota's, which requires the consent of both parents, with a judicial bypass. *See* N.D. CENT. CODE § 14-02.1-03.1 (1991); *see also* KY. REV. STAT. ANN. § 311.732 (Baldwin 1993); MASS. GEN. LAWS. ANN. ch. 112, § 12S (West 1983); MISS. CODE. ANN. § 41-41-53 (1993). Other states merely require notification of parents, not consent. *See* ARK. CODE ANN. § 20-16-801 (Michie 1991); GA. CODE ANN. § 15-11-112 (Harrison 1990); MD. HEALTH-GEN. CODE ANN. § 20-103 (1993); MONT. CODE ANN. § 50-20-107 (1993); NEV. REV. STAT. ANN. § 442.255 (Michie 1991); TENN. CODE ANN. § 37-10-301 (1991); UTAH CODE ANN. § 76-7-304 (1990). Still other states require the notification of any adult relative, not necessarily the parents. *See, e.g.*, OHIO REV. CODE ANN. § 2919.12 (Anderson 1993). About half of the states have parental notification and/or consent laws with judicial bypass provisions. *See, e.g.*, 18 PA. CONS. STAT. ANN. § 3206 (1994).

189. Henne v. Wright, 904 F.2d 1208, 1215 (8th Cir. 1990) (upholding, upon rational basis review, a statute providing that a child's welfare is served by bearing surname possessing a connection with at least one legally verifiable parent), *cert. denied*, 498 U.S. 1032 (1991); *In re* D.K.W. v. J.L.B., 807 P.2d 1222, 1224 (Colo. Ct. App. 1990) (best interest of child born out of wedlock served by denying motion by father to change child's surname from mother's to his); Magiera v. Luera, 802 P.2d 6, 7-8 (Nev. 1990) (best interest of child born out of wedlock to keep surname of the parent with whom she lives); Halloran v. Kostka, 778 S.W.2d 454, 456 (Tenn. Ct. App. 1988) (best interest of child of divorced parents to keep father's surname); Rio v. Rio, 504 N.Y.S.2d 959, 961-62 (Sup. Ct. 1986) (providing that the best interest of the child should be the determining factor in what name the child should have).

190. *See, e.g.*, Holder v. Polanski, 544 A.2d 852, 856 (N.J. 1988) (holding that a custodial parent may move with the children of the marriage to another state as long as the move does not interfere with the best interest of the children or the visitation rights of the non-custodial parent).

191. Newmark v. Williams, 588 A.2d 1108 (Del. 1991). Even though the court wrote that any balancing test between the child's condition and state interference must begin with the parental interest, *id.* at 1115, the state can clearly intervene in the parent-child relationship where the health and safety of the child is in jeopardy, *id.* at 1116. The child's interest takes precedence under *parens patriae*.

out the concomitant legal requirements or responsibilities.[192] Explorations into the new world of biology have also affected the definition of family.[193]

While it is certain that "[c]hildren do best when they have the personal involvement and material support of a father and a mother and when both parents fulfill their responsibilities to be loving providers . . . . [M]any children do not have two loving parents."[194] Courts overwhelmingly recognize this and are willing to intervene. Thus,

> when families are so damaged that their children's health and safety are in danger, society must intervene. Through both individual and collective efforts, society must ensure that children's basic needs for food, clothing, shelter, and affection are met when parents are unable to do so alone, and society must protect children who are at serious risk of physical or psychological harm from adults within and outside their families.[195]

In geographical areas where parental surrender, neglect and abuse

---

192. *See, e.g.*, Stanley v. Illinois, 405 U.S. 645 (1971) (marriage is not, in itself, a significant factor in the custody of children); Braschi v. Stahl Assocs. Co., 543 N.E.2d 49, 53-54 (N.Y. 1989) (allowing two unmarried men who had been living in a rent controlled apartment for eleven years to be included in the legislative definition of family); Marvin v. Marvin, 557 P.2d 106, 113 (Cal. 1976) (allowing for the possibility of contractual obligations to arise in a context of non-marital sexual relationship where an express or implied promise is made); Rebecca L. Melton, Note, *Legal Rights of Unmarried Heterosexual and Homosexual Couples and Evolving Definitions of "Family,"* 29 J. FAM. L. 497 (1991); Note, *Looking for a Family Resemblance: The Limits of the Functional Approach to the Legal Definition of Family*, 104 HARV. L. REV. 1640 (1991) (stating the elements of function in a family-like relationship include financial commitment, exclusivity, the reliance members place on each other, the length of the relationship, and presentation to the outside world).

Evidence of this trend is also buttressed by the popularity of domestic partnership legislation and business enactment. *See, e.g.*, Craig A. Bowman & Blake M. Cornish, Note, *A More Perfect Union: A Legal and Social Analysis of Domestic Partnership Ordinances*, 92 COLUM. L. REV. 1164 (1992); Vada Berger, *Domestic Partnership Initiatives*, 40 DEPAUL L. REV. 417 (1991). *But see* Comment, *The Wages of Sin: Discrimination in Housing Against Unmarried Couples*, 25 U.C. DAVIS L. REV. 1055 (1992).

193. *See, e.g.*, Janet L. Dolgin, *Just a Gene: Judicial Assumptions About Parenthood*, 40 UCLA L. REV. 637 (1993). The author describes the conflict between society's definition of family and the emerging biological facts which, more often than not, "presume each individual a separate, autonomous whole, free to negotiate the terms of life." *Id.* at 694. Legal issues touching on sexual orientation have also had an impact on the definition of family. *See Developments in the Law—Sexual Orientation and the Law*, 102 HARV. L. REV. 1508 (1989); Note, *Looking for a Family Resemblance: The Limits of the Functional Approach to the Legal Definition of Family*, *supra* note 192.

194. BEYOND RHETORIC, *supra* note 14, at 66.

195. *Id.* at 71-72.

are rampant, it may seem expedient to dismiss the claims of parents in their children. This would, however, be a denial of due process to parents, just as ignoring the interests of children is a denial of due process. We must, therefore, balance the child's interest with that of the parent. The due process rights of the child, however, always should be the focus of the balance.

B. *The* Santosky *Majority's Flawed Due Process Analysis*

A person has an individual claim to due process protection whenever a state seeks to deprive him or her of life, liberty, or property.[196] In conducting any due process analysis, courts address two issues: First, whether or not the individual possesses a liberty or property interest protected by the Fourteenth Amendment.[197] In making this determination, courts will look to see if an adverse outcome in the proceeding would cause the individual to suffer a "grievous loss."[198] Second, if

---

196. The Fourteenth Amendment of the United States Constitution provides: "No state shall . . . deprive any person of life, liberty, or property, without due process of law . . . ." U.S. CONST. amend. XIV, §1.

197. *See, e.g.*, Morrissey v. Brewer, 408 U.S. 471, 481 (1972) (The applicability of due process depends not on the weight of the interest, but "whether the nature of the interest is one within the contemplation of the 'liberty or property' language of the Fourteenth Amendment."). Property interests include, for example, employment contracts if the public employee had a reasonable expectation of continued employment. *See, e.g.*, Board of Regents v. Roth, 408 U.S. 564, 578 (1972) (holding that an employment contract for a fixed period of only one year does not constitute a property interest). Liberty interests include not only fundamental constitutional rights such as free speech, but also a person's reputation and future employment opportunities. *See Roth*, 408 U.S. at 585 (Douglas, J., dissenting). In Meyer v. Nebraska, 262 U.S. 390, 399 (1923), the Court indicated how expansive the definition of liberty interest could be:

> [Liberty] denotes not merely freedom from bodily restraint but also the right of the individual to contract, to engage in any of the common occupations of life, to acquire useful knowledge, to marry, to establish a home and bring up children, to worship God according to the dictates of his [or her] own conscience, and generally to enjoy those privileges long recognized . . . as essential to the orderly pursuit of happiness by free men [or women].

Id.

198. *See, e.g.*, Joint Anti-Fascist Refugee Comm. v. McGrath, 341 U.S. 123, 168 (1951) (Frankfurter, J., concurring). For an example of a due process claim that did not result in protected conduct, see Bowers v. Hardwick, 478 U.S. 186 (1986) (deciding whether or not the Due Process clause guarantees to homosexuals the right to engage in sodomy), and an article analyzing the case, Jed Rubenfeld, *The Right of Privacy*, 102 HARV. L. REV. 737, 747-52 & *passim* (1989). For an example of a similar case analyzed under an equal protection claim, see Commonwealth v. Wasson, 842 S.W.2d 487 (Ky. 1992) (holding that a criminal statute proscribing consensual homosexual sodomy violates equal protection rights guaranteed by Kentucky Constitution absent showing of rational basis for punishing deviate sexual intercourse solely on basis of sexual preference).

the person possesses a protected property or liberty interest, the court will determine what procedures are constitutionally mandated before the state can deprive him or her of this fundamental interest.[199]

In deciding if the existing state procedures are adequate to provide due process, courts apply the balancing test set forth in *Mathews v. Eldridge.*[200] *Mathews* requires the weighing of three factors: the private interests that will be affected by the state action; the risk of an erroneous deprivation of the private interest caused by the action at issue; and the government's interest as evidenced by the statute.[201]

In *Santosky v. Kramer*, the *Mathews* balancing test was directed toward the rights of the parents, not the child.[202] In applying the first part of the test, the Court focused on the liberty interest of the parents.[203] In applying the second part of the test, the Court emphasized that the case was, in form, a contest between the state and the natural parent.[204] There was no mention of the child. Since the Court had already determined that the child's interest was subordinate to that of the

---

199. *See, e.g.*, Santosky v. Kramer, 455 U.S. 745, 753 (1982) (delimiting two central questions: whether a natural parent is entitled to constitutional due process at a parental rights termination hearing, and if so, what process is due); Morrissey v. Brewer, 408 U.S. 471, 481 (1972) ("Once it is determined that due process applies, the question remains what process is due.")

200. 424 U.S. 319 (1976).

201. *See id.* at 335. In *Mathews*, the Court weighed the three factors and determined that the state was not required to hold an evidentiary hearing before terminating social security benefits. *Id.* at 349. For an explanation of *Mathews*, see Brian A. Cufe, Note, *Methods of Notice in Termination of Parental Rights Hearings*, 5 CONN. PROB. L.J. 317 (1991).

202. In *Santosky*, the Court wrote that "when the State moves to destroy weakened familial bonds, it must provide the parents with fundamentally fair procedures." 455 U.S. at 753-54.

It can be argued that one reason why the Court's attention was directed towards parents rather than towards the child was due to the Court's five-to-four decision in Lassiter v. Department of Social Servs., 452 U.S. 18 (1981), one year earlier. *Lassiter* held that the Due Process Clause does not require the appointment of counsel for indigent parents in every parental status termination proceeding. The majority in *Santosky* mentions that the "disparity between the litigants' resources will be vastly greater in States where there is no statutory right to court-appointed counsel." *Santosky*, 455 U.S. at 763-64 & n.13. The point is clear: Parental rights are a fundamental interest that demand due process consideration. *Id.* at 753. It should be noted, however, that the Court was comfortable with a case-by-case analysis towards due process in *Lassiter*, while *Santosky* adopted a uniform burden of proof upon all states and in every parent-child situation. If *Santosky* was a result of the Court's holding in *Lassiter*, it was a result that imposed a strict and high level of proof that has factually affected the way in which children are provided due process rights.

203. *Id.* at 759. The Court recognized the unique deprivation facing the parents in a termination proceeding. *Id.* If the state prevails, drastic consequences follow: Parental rights will be irrevocably terminated, *id.*, and the parents would also suffer a loss of reputation, *id.* at 759-60.

Throughout the factfinding stage, the focus was on the parents, not the child. The Court emphasized that no separate interest of the child exists at the factfinding stage. *Id.*

204. *Id.* at 762.

parent, it viewed the case as a contest solely between the parent and the state.

In applying the third component of the *Mathews* test, the Court examined the state's interest. The state had two interests in the termination proceeding: its *parens patriae* interest in promoting the welfare of the child and its administrative and fiscal interests in reducing the cost of such a proceeding.[205] The majority found that the state's interest would be better served by a clear and convincing standard.[206] This is because the state's goal in dealing with the child was to find a permanent home with a positive and nurturing environment. The natural home of the child was deemed to be the presumptive place where this could occur.[207] Following this presumption, moreover, would result in decreased costs and thus advance the state's administrative and fiscal interests.

The Court's analysis with respect to the state's fiscal interest was flawed. Raising the level of proof to clear and convincing actually results in an *increased* fiscal and administrative burden.[208] This is due to the fact that the state must amass much more evidence to satisfy the clear and convincing standard. During termination proceedings, the state must bear the cost of foster care and maintain the services that are designed to reunify the family. Consider these facts: Total expenditures by the federal government on child welfare services have increased from $536 million in 1981—one year before *Santosky*—to $2.385 billion in 1991;[209] the estimated costs for state and local services for children was $4.43 billion in 1989;[210] overall, in the 1989 fiscal year, state and local governments spent at least $180.3 billion (approximately thirty-one percent of their budgets) on services and programs for children.[211] Even under a preponderance of the evidence standard, the costs incurred by the state are enormous. The clear and convincing standard increases these costs.

All three components of the *Mathews* test were utilized by the

---

205. *Id.* at 766.

206. *Id.* at 767.

207. *Id.* at 766-67.

208. *See* Hershkowitz, *supra* note 27, at 293 (discussion of the effects of elevated standards of proof on the state's administrative and fiscal resources). The *Santosky* case itself also illustrates the administrative costs: seven proceedings were held concerning the disposition of the children. 455 U.S. at 293 n.352.

209. BEYOND RHETORIC, *supra* note 14, at 308.

210. *Id.* at 315.

211. *Id.* at 316.

majority in such a fashion that the due process rights of the child were ignored. It is not that the due process analysis of *Mathews* itself was applied incorrectly. The problem lies in the fact that the analysis was directed solely toward the parents under the aegis of the parental presumption.

The dissent in *Santosky* reapplied *Mathews* to incorporate the interest of the child. Justice Rehnquist properly recognized the fundamental liberty interest of the parent in the custody and care of his or her child.[212] But he also recognized the private interest of the child in the speedy and proper outcome of the proceeding: "A stable, loving homelife is essential to a child's physical, emotional, and spiritual well-being."[213] This private interest does not automatically subsist within that of the parent.[214] In fact, an error in the proceeding that results in a failure to terminate parental rights has serious repercussions for the child,[215] as the facts of *DeShaney* illustrate. Accordingly, any consideration of the private interest of the child must allow for a separate determination without the parental presumption unduly inhibiting the child's interest. This acknowledgement takes into consideration the factual reality of abuse and neglect in America.

Once the dissent recognized that two private interests were involved in the termination proceeding, it found that due process could be afforded to both the parent and the child by allowing the burden of proof to be borne by each almost equally.[216] Allowing for preponderance of

---

212. *Santosky*, 455 U.S. at 787 (Rehnquist, J., dissenting).

213. *Id.* at 788-89. Emphasis for this is found in BEYOND RHETORIC, *supra* note 14, at 71:

> To grow and thrive, children need order. They need safe homes and neighborhoods, free of violence and drugs. They need to feel confident that the adults in their families and their communities will protect them, not prey upon them. Physical safety and psychological security are essential to children's health, education, and overall development. When their experience teaches them that they cannot depend on the adults in their lives, children often grow hostile, distrustful, and angry. In failing to insulate them from crime and violence, we are jeopardizing the futures of millions of youngsters. Today's young victims are very likely to become tomorrow's armed robbers, drug pushers, and murderers.

Id. (citation omitted).

214. *Santosky*, 455 U.S. at 788 n.13. "This reasoning [subsisting the child's interest within that of the parent] misses the mark. The child has an interest in the outcome of the factfinding hearing independent of that of the parent." *Id.*

215. *Id.* If termination of parental rights does not occur when it rightfully should, the child would suffer abuse and neglect. *See, e.g., id.* at 789 n.14. Or the child could languish in foster care for a period of time too long to allow for adoption by a stable home. *Id.* at 789 n.15.

216. *Id.* at 791. Preponderance of the evidence allows for the burden of proof to be borne almost equally between the two independent private interests. The parent still retains the presumption and also other due process remedies such as void for vagueness statutes that often

the evidence decreased the risk to the child and still safeguarded the parent's rights.

V. FEDERALISM

Implicit within the conflict between state procedures that incorporate a standard of proof to terminate the rights of a parent and the Supreme Court's interpretation of the Constitution rejecting such procedures, is the concept of federalism. It has long been the practice of the federal courts to abstain from interfering with state solutions to domestic relations problems.[217] This is a historical doctrine, more implicit within the constitutional system of government than within any clearly elucidated constitutional provision or federal statute.[218] In his dissent in *Santosky*,[219] Justice Rehnquist addressed this issue: "Even more worrisome, [the majority] cavalierly rejects the considered judgement of the New York legislature in an area traditionally entrusted to state care. The Court thereby begins, I fear, a trend of federal intervention in state family law matters which surely will stifle creative responses to vexing problems."[220]

In mandating a clear and convincing standard in parental termination proceedings, the *Santosky* majority intruded upon the historical ability of states to legislate creative and local solutions to problems such as child abuse. Indeed, any change in the "poverty of hope"[221] will be best brought on by local actors crafting solutions to the particular problems endemic to each community. Federal micro-management

---

arise with termination statutes.

217. *See* Ankenbrandt v. Richards, 112 S. Ct. 2206, 2209-15 (1992) (discussing domestic relations exception to federal diversity jurisdiction); Earl M. Maltz, *The State, the Family, and the Constitution: A Case Study in Flawed Bipolar Analysis*, 1991 B.Y.U. L. REV. 489.

Domestic relations is "an area that has long been regarded as a virtually exclusive province of the States." Sosna v. Iowa, 419 U.S. 393, 404 (1975); *see also* Thompson v. Thompson, 484 U.S. 174, 184-85 (1988); De LaRama v. De LaRama, 201 U.S. 303, 307 (1906); Simms v. Simms, 175 U.S. 162, 167 (1899); Barber v. Barber, 62 U.S. (21 How.) 582, 584 (1858).

218. "Historically, the right to regulate the relationship between parents and children has been one of the most closely-guarded prerogatives of state government; thus, any effort by the Court to restrict local autonomy in this area faces formidable federalism-related obstacles." Maltz, *supra* note 217, at 490-91. The true basis for this exception to federal jurisdiction is stated in a recent decision: "Because we are unwilling to cast aside an understood rule that has been recognized for nearly a century and a half . . . ." *Ankenbrandt*, 112 S. Ct. at 2210 (concerning whether a federal court has jurisdiction over alleged torts committed by a former husband of petitioner against petitioner's children).

219. 455 U.S. 745 (1982) (Rehnquist, J., dissenting).

220. *Id.* at 791.

221. BEYOND RHETORIC, *supra* note 14, at 5.

is not the solution.

Two justifications underlie state autonomy in matters of domestic relations. First, the Court has interpreted the federal statute conferring diversity jurisdiction to exclude federal court jurisdiction over divorce and other cases.[222] "Absent a contrary command of Congress, the federal courts properly should abstain, at least from diversity actions traditionally excluded from the federal courts, such as those seeking divorce, alimony, and child custody."[223] Second, leaving states free from federal control allows them to experiment with different approaches to the same problems. "It is one of the happy incidents of the federal system that a single courageous State may, if its citizens choose, serve as a laboratory; and try novel social and economic experiments without risk to the rest of the country."[224]

Although states have not always risen to the challenge of devising creative solutions to domestic relations problems, "leaving the States free to experiment with various remedies has produced novel approaches and promising progress."[225] States have even "developed specialized courts and institutions in family matters, while Congress and the federal courts generally have not done so."[226] Accordingly, only when a domestic relations statute contains a clear constitutional violation should the federal courts interfere with a state's resolution of domestic relations matters.[227]

---

222. *See* Hershkowitz, *supra* note 27, at 248 n.21. The Judiciary Act of 1789 has been judicially interpreted to include only that subject matter over which the English court of chancery had jurisdiction when the United States became a nation. *Id.* Since the court of chancery did not have jurisdiction over divorce, neither do the federal courts. *Id.* Early cases signaled this approach: "We disclaim altogether any jurisdiction in the courts of the United States upon subject of divorce, or for the allowance of alimony, either as an original proceeding in chancery or as an incident to a divorce *a vinculo*, or to one from bed and board." Barber v. Barber, 62 U.S. (21 How.) 582, 584 (1858). In 1890, however, the Court made it clear that the lack of federal jurisdiction extended to all areas of domestic relations: "The whole subject of the domestic relations of husband and wife, parent and child, belongs to the laws of the States and not to the laws of the United States." *In re* Burrus, 136 U.S. 586, 593-94 (1890).

223. *Ankenbrandt*, 112 S. Ct. at 2221 (Blackmun, J., concurring).

224. New State Ice Co. v. Liebmann, 285 U.S. 262, 311 (1932) (Brandeis, J., dissenting).

225. *Santosky*, 455 U.S. at 771 (Rehnquist, J., dissenting). Examples of state innovations would be: Uniform Premarital Agreement Act, *see, e.g.*, OR. REV. STAT. § 108.725 (1990); goodwill as a marital asset, *see, e.g.*, Thompson v. Thompson, 576 So. 2d 267 (Fla. 1991); the disposition of a cryogenically-preserved product of in vitro fertilization, *see, e.g.*, Davis v. Davis, 842 S.W.2d 588 (Tenn. 1992), *cert. denied*, Stowe v. Davis, 113 S. Ct. 1259 (1993); finding that the state homosexual sodomy statute was unconstitutional under the state constitution, *see, e.g.*, Commonwealth v. Wasson, 842 S.W.2d 487 (Ky. 1992).

226. *Ankenbrandt*, 112 S. Ct. at 2221 (Blackmun, J., concurring).

227. *Santosky*, 455 U.S. at 771. *See also* Hershkowitz, *supra* note 27, at 249; Allan D. Vestal

By imposing a clear and convincing standard, the *Santosky* Court preempted the procedures utilized by numerous states. Many such procedures were enacted by states in an effort to promote "fundamental fairness" to all parties involved—including the interests of the child—in the context of other statutory procedures. In New York, for example, the legislature believed that a preponderance of the evidence standard provided fairness to all the parties: parents, children and the state. The New York scheme did not contain a clear constitutional violation.

As Justice Rehnquist concluded in his dissent in *Santosky*:

> New York's adoption of the preponderance-of-the-evidence standard reflects its conclusion that the undesirable consequences of an erroneous finding of parental unfitness—the unwarranted termination of the family relationship—is roughly equal to the undesirable consequence of an erroneous finding of parental fitness—the risk of permanent injury to the child either

---

& David L. Foster, *Implied Limitations on the Diversity Jurisdiction of Federal Courts*, 41 MINN. L. REV. 1, 23 (1956).

The National Commission on Children has recommended three community-level programs which are essential to the domestic relations exception:

> (1) Promoting child development and healthy family function through locally controlled and coordinated, community-based family support networks that offer access and referrals to a broad range of services, including health and mental health care, education, recreation, housing, parenting education and support, employment and training, and substance abuse prevention and treatment.
>
> . . . .
>
> (2) Assisting families and children in need in order to strengthen and preserve families that voluntarily seek help before their problems become acute. Human service programs, including health and mental health, juvenile services, substance abuse programs, education, and economic and social supports, must collaborate to provide prevention and early intervention services that offer practical solutions to problems faced by families in crisis.
>
> . . . .
>
> (3) Protecting abused and neglected children through more comprehensive child protective services, with a strong emphasis on efforts to keep children with their families or to provide permanent placement for those removed from their homes.

BEYOND RHETORIC, *supra* note 14, at 295-96 (emphasis omitted).

In particular, when babies are abandoned at birth and when repeated attempts to reunify older children and parents have failed, the programs recommend that the adoption process should be streamlined to expedite placement of children in permanent, stable families. *Id.* at 300-01.

As federalism is designed to foster such programs, especially within the geographically diverse economic and cultural fabric of American states, anything less than a clear constitutional violation impedes the recommendations of the National Commission on Children and the best interest of the child. The Court's intrusion into state domestic relations in *Santosky* was unwarranted and not in the best interest of children.

by return of the child to an abusive home or by the child's continued lack of a permanent home. Such a conclusion is well within the province of state legislatures.[228]

The New York scheme in place at the time of *Santosky* incorporated the following requirements to safeguard the rights of the parties involved: (1) that an attorney be appointed to represent the parents; (2) that multiple hearings be held; (3) that there be a determination that the parents are present at the hearings and were served with the petition; (4) that only material and relevant evidence be submitted; (5) that temporary removal be reviewed every eighteen months; (6) that the same judge preside throughout; (7) that parents be notified twenty days before the hearing; (8) that the state make diligent efforts to assist the parents to develop a relationship with the child; (9) that the termination proceeding result in an independent evaluation of the material and relevant evidence; and (10) that the parents be given a right to appeal with the assistance of state appointed counsel.[229] Surely the imposition of such safeguards prevented the possibility of a clear constitutional violation.

In and of itself, the standard of proof necessary to terminate parental rights can not be the reason for a clear constitutional violation. As the *Santosky* dissent noted, "[b]y holding that due process requires proof by clear and convincing evidence the majority surely cannot mean that any state scheme passes constitutional muster so long as it applies that standard of proof."[230] Something more, therefore, must be present before the unique necessity for federal jurisdiction over a matter clearly within the realm of domestic relations is warranted. By imposing a clear and convincing standard, the *Santosky* Court ignored the historical tradition of abstaining from interference in state domestic relations law. In so doing, the Court inflicted a serious blow to our federalist system.

VI. CONCLUSION

The Introduction to this Article suggested that the question presented often presupposes the answer given. If the question presented continues to be whether parents have a clear and convincing due process claim to the custody of their children, the best interest of the child will not merit constitutional, practical, or honest consideration. The present

---

228. *Santosky*, 455 U.S. at 788 n.13 (Rehnquist, J., dissenting) (citation omitted).
229. *Id.* at 776-80.
230. *Id.* at 772.

status of the American family, however, demands that we ask a new question: In a clash between the private interests of parents and the private interests of children, does the Due Process Clause demand that states use a preponderance of the evidence standard in terminating parental rights? The answer is yes, because such a standard of evidence rejects the notion that the best interest of the child subsists within that of the parent.

Within certain easily defined geographical areas of the country, an alarming number of children are being victimized by parents who abuse or neglect them. A rigid adherence to the parental presumption obliterates the rights of these children. While some deference to parental rights is warranted, too much deference translates into suffering on the part of children.

Children suffer because of the delay existent in termination proceedings. Children suffer when they are returned to parents who fail to provide for the child and continue to persist in the abuse and neglect that brought on the termination proceedings. Children suffer from the inability of states to fashion creative approaches to child care due to unwarranted encroachment by the federal government. In order to reduce the suffering of children at the hands of abusive parents, we must reckon with reality and allow states to address the best interest of the child through the use of a preponderance of the evidence standard in termination proceedings.

THE CHILD'S RIGHT TO HUMANE DISCIPLINE UNDER THE U.N. CONVENTION ON THE RIGHTS OF THE CHILD: THE MANDATE AGAINST ALL CORPORAL PUNISHMENT OF CHILDREN

*Susan H. Bitensky**

My father, a professor of social work, said that often the key to understanding an individual's personality is to look at the very things that tend to go unnoticed — seemingly insignificant traits and idiosyncrasies. It has occurred to me that this may be true of humanity in general, that the key to understanding the human condition may be in looking at behaviors which are so much a part of daily life for so many that no one steps back to question them. I believe that one such key behavior is corporal punishment of children. I am not referring to child abuse as is traditionally conceived. Rather, I am referring to spankings and smacks that ordinarily would not be prosecutable in the United States.

As it stands now, about half the states in this country allow school personnel to mete out corporal punishment to students in elementary and secondary schools.[1] All states permit parents or guardians to administer "reasonable" corporal punishment upon their children.[2] A bill was even introduced in Congress that, if enacted, would give parents an express federal right to subject

---

* Professor of Law, Detroit College of Law at Michigan State University. B.A., Case Western Reserve University, 1971; J.D., University of Chicago Law School, 1974.

1. *See* Jerry R. Parkinson, *Federal Court Treatment of Corporal Punishment in Public Schools: Jurisprudence that Is Literally Shocking to the Conscience*, 39 S.D.L. REV. 276, 279 (1994); Scott Bloom, Comment, *Spare the Rod, Spoil the Child? A Legal Framework for Recent Corporal Punishment Proposals*, 25 GOLDEN GATE U. L. REV. 361, 368-69 (1995).

2. *See* Leonard P. Edwards, *Corporal Punishment and the Legal System*, 36 SANTA CLARA L. REV. 983, 984 (1996); Franklin E. Zimring, *Legal Perspectives on Family Violence*, 75 CAL. L. REV. 521, 526 (1987).

their children to "reasonable" corporal punishment.[3] In fact, corporal punishment of children in the family setting is a longstanding and pervasive practice in the U.S. that is taken for granted by many parents as their right and understood by many children as their due.[4]

Disagreement has been developing among sociologists, pediatricians, psychologists, and others with expertise in child development over whether corporal punishment does not do considerably more harm than good.[5] The weight of authoritative expert opinion is that corporal punishment of children is not very effective in promoting long term positive behavior modification.[6] Indeed, there is an empirical and theoretical basis for concluding that the effects of such punishment are not only not helpful, but are profoundly deleterious.[7]

How, you may be wondering, can a few spankings by a loving parent or concerned teacher cause any serious damage? For one thing, corporal punishment may physically injure the child[8] and is often a prelude to full-blown child abuse.[9] Corporal punishment causes other less palpable damage. This sort of damage

---

3. The Parental Rights and Responsibilities Act of 1995, S.984, 104th Cong., 1st Sess. (1995).

4. *See* Edwards, *supra* note 2, at 984.

5. For some of the authorities disfavoring corporal punishment of children, see PHILIP GREVEN, SPARE THE CHILD: THE RELIGIOUS ROOTS OF PUNISHMENT AND THE PSYCHOLOGICAL IMPACT OF PHYSICAL ABUSE *passim* (1991); PENELOPE LEACH, YOUR GROWING CHILD: FROM BABYHOOD THROUGH ADOLESCENCE 224-25 (1995); NANCY SAMALIN, LOVING YOUR CHILD IS NOT ENOUGH: POSITIVE DISCIPLINE THAT WORKS 73-74 (1978); MURRAY A. STRAUS, BEATING THE DEVIL OUT OF THEM: CORPORAL PUNISHMENT IN AMERICAN FAMILIES (1994). For some of the authorities favoring corporal punishment of children, see JAMES DOBSON, THE STRONG-WILLED CHILD: BIRTH THROUGH ADOLESCENCE 34-35 (1978); ROY LESSIN, SPANKING: WHY, WHEN, HOW? (1979); DIANA BAUMRIND, PARENTING: THE DISCIPLINE CONTROVERSY REVISITED, 45 FAM. RELATIONS 405, 409-13 (Oct. 1996).

6. *See* LEACH, *supra* note 5, at 224; WILLIAM SEARS & MARTHA SEARS, THE DISCIPLINE BOOK: EVERYTHING YOU NEED TO KNOW TO HAVE A BETTER-BEHAVED CHILD - FROM BIRTH TO AGE TEN 149-50 (1995).

7. *See* GREVEN, *supra* note 5 *passim*; SEARS & SEARS, *supra* note 6, at 146-54; STRAUS, *supra* note 5 *passim*.

8. *See* LEACH, *supra* note 5, at 224; PETER NEWELL, CHILDREN ARE PEOPLE TOO: THE CASE AGAINST PHYSICAL PUNISHMENT 16-21 (1989); STRAUS, *supra* note 5, at 149-51.

9. *See* NEWELL, *supra* note 8, at 21-31; SEARS & SEARS, *supra* note 6, at 149; STRAUS, *supra* note 5, at 81-87, 90-97.

results from the fact that a child, like any human being, experiences rage and indignation upon being struck, but cannot express these feelings because of the risk that there will be further punishment or withdrawal of adult approval and love.[10] Repression, however, is only a momentary solution. The anger must go somewhere and it does. Time does not permit a full cataloguing of the psychological effects of this repressed anger, but a few of the more pernicious ones are aggressiveness,[11] lack of empathy,[12] and a tendency toward either authoritarianism[13] or blind obedience.[14] The first two symptoms may appear during childhood, and all four symptoms may surface during the teenage years and adulthood.

I have selected these particular psychological effects of corporal punishment of children because they are also human traits that seem to have persisted throughout history and much of the world; they are some of mankind's most troubling traits as well. The traits are certainly not the characteristics of an enlightened and rational citizenry capable of successfully maintaining democracy and a kinder, gentler social order.

Could there be a link between the commonly experienced pain of childhood corporal punishment and the surreal brutality of the Nazis or the Khmer Rouge? From whence comes this capacity, century after century, for mayhem and barbarity on either a societal scale or at the individual criminal level? One of my colleagues has suggested that the answer is simple although

---

10. *See* GREVEN, *supra* note 5, at 132; ALICE MILLER, THE DRAMA OF THE GIFTED CHILD: THE SEARCH FOR THE TRUE SELF 8 (1981); ALICE MILLER, FOR YOUR OWN GOOD: HIDDEN CRUELTY IN CHILD-REARING AND THE ROOTS OF VIOLENCE 7, 61(1990) [hereinafter MILLER, FOR YOUR OWN GOOD].

11. With respect to corporal punishment of children causing aggressiveness during childhood, see SAMALIN, *supra* note 5, at 73; SEARS & SEARS, *supra* note 6, at 153-54. With respect to corporal punishment of children causing lack of empathy during childhood, *see* GREVEN, *supra* note 5, at 126-27; MILLER, FOR YOUR OWN GOOD, *supra* note 10, at 61, 65-66, 115-17, 172; STRAUS, *supra* note 5, at 99, 103, 106, 110, 113-15.

12. With respect to corporal punishment of children causing lack of empathy during childhood, see GREVEN, *supra* note 5, at 127-29. With respect to corporal punishment of children causing lack of empathy during adulthood, see GREVEN, *supra* note 5, at 127-29; MILLER, FOR YOUR OWN GOOD, *supra* note 10, at 79-83, 115.

13. *See* GREVEN, *supra* note 5, at 198-204; ALICE MILLER, BREAKING DOWN THE WALL OF SILENCE: THE LIBERATING EXPERIENCE OF FACING PAINFUL TRUTH 84-85 (1991); NEWELL, *supra* note 8, at 46.

14. *See* GREVEN, *supra* note 5, at 200-04; MILLER, FOR YOUR OWN GOOD, *supra* note 10, at 70; Dean M. Herman, *A Statutory Proposal to Prohibit the Infliction of Violence Upon Children*, 19 FAM. L.Q., 18-20, 37 (1985).

depressing: we are all inherently only one step above ooze.[15] I disagree, not because I am an optimist, but, rather, because there are other explanations. Obviously all of the world's ills cannot and should not be attributed to corporal punishment of children; but, corporal punishment may be one of those little noticed behaviors, of which my father spoke, revealing a contributing factor in man's continuing propensity for carnage and cruelty.

I am not going to represent that all knowledgeable experts would agree with this assessment. There is, as I mentioned before, some disagreement over whether light or moderate corporal punishment of children is harmful. In one sense the wrangling is beside the point if one acknowledges the possibility that physically attacking children's bodies, even in the name of discipline, is inhumane and morally wrong.[16] If your adult neighbor does something really infuriating, you wouldn't swat him to get him to change his behavior. Similarly, if that adult neighbor's child got out of line, you wouldn't feel free to swat the child, either. Our law on assault and battery manifests that we, as a society, have repudiated swatting as a dispute resolution technique. Does that ethical standard change simply because the bottom on the receiving end belongs to a child who is a student or one's own flesh and blood? In light of children's vulnerability and dependency on their parents and teachers, subjecting one's own children or pupils to violence and the dread of violence is perhaps even less defensible than subjecting anyone else to such treatment. This is especially true since alternative disciplinary tactics are available such as time-out, deprivation of privileges, grounding, or reasoning and explaining.

The U.N. Convention on the Rights of the Child[17] reflects these views against corporal punishment. I am currently writing an article which includes a detailed analysis of the many provisions of the Convention that may be interpreted implicitly to prohibit corporal punishment of children.[18] There are, by my

---

15. Assuming that he would appreciate attribution, the comment was made by my colleague Professor Martin L. Kotch several years ago on what I presume was a bad day.

16. *See* NEWELL, *supra* note 8, at 12-16; STRAUS, *supra* note 5, at 10; Herman, *supra* note 14, at 10.

17. Convention on the Rights of the Child, G.A. Res. 44/25, 44 U.N. GAOR, Supp. No. 49, U.N. Doc. A/44/736 (1989) [hereinafter Convention on the Rights of the Child].

18. Susan H. Bitensky, *Spare the Rod, Embrace Our Humanity: Toward a New Legal Regime Prohibiting Corporal Punishment of Children* (forthcoming).

count, at least eleven such provisions. Consider, for example, article 19.1 which provides, in part:

> States Parties shall take all appropriate . . . measures to protect the child from all forms of physical or mental violence, injury or abuse, neglect or negligent treatment, maltreatment or exploitation including sexual abuse, while in the care of parent(s), legal guardian(s) or any other person who has the care of the child.[19]

As a matter of semantics, the conclusion is inescapable that Article 19.1 forbids all corporal punishment of children and not just abuse or punishment which leads to injury. Why else mention "physical . . . violence" separately from "injury or abuse"? Moreover, the Committee on the Rights of the Child, the body which monitors compliance with the Convention, has taken the position that this provision requires States Parties to protect children from all corporal punishment, even in the family context.[20]

Also, consider article 37(a) which declares that, "States Parties shall ensure that no child shall be subjected to torture or other cruel, inhuman, or degrading treatment or punishment."[21] By implication, this language may be construed to obligate States Parties to ensure that no child shall be subjected by anyone to corporal punishment because it is a form of torture or cruel, inhuman or degrading punishment. Indeed, the former Rapporteur of the Committee on the Rights of the Child, Marta Santos Pais, stated last August in reference to this provision that "torture may cover a wide degree of situations," including those which result in "unperceivable mental suffering."[22]

---

19. Convention on the Rights of the Child, *supra* note 17, at art. 19.1.

20. *See, e.g.* Concluding Observations: Spain, CRC/C/15 Add. 28, at para. 10 (Oct. 24, 1994); Concluding Observations: Sri Lanka, CRC/C/15 Add. 40 at para. 32 (June 21, 1995); Concluding Observations: United Kingdom, CRC/C/15 Add. 34, at para. 31 (Feb. 15, 1995).

21. Convention on the Rights of the Child, *supra* note 17, at art. 37(a).

22. Marta Santos Pais, Address at the International Seminar on Worldwide Strategies and Progress Towards Ending All Physical Punishment of Children (Dublin, Ireland, Aug. 22, 1996) (transcript on file with the author).

Finally, article 28, section 2 states, in part: "States Parties shall take . . . measures to ensure that school discipline is administered in a manner consistent with the child's human dignity and in conformity with the present Convention."[23] The Committee on the Rights of the Child has repeatedly advised that article 28, section 2 is intended to outlaw corporal punishment in the schools.[24]

It may be anticipated that insofar as the U.N. Convention on the Rights of the Child aims at banning all corporal punishment of children, it will be highly controversial in the United States. Some will no doubt argue that such a ban would run counter to the U.S. Constitution, especially parents' substantive due process right to rear their children[25] and family privacy rights.[26] This is a bit like arguing that criminalizing child abuse or wife beating violates the Constitution. Such inhumane conduct can be no part of anyone's constitutional right without undermining the Constitution's credibility and mocking its status as one of the world's leading human rights documents.

That the Convention on the Rights of the Child will bring into high relief the dissension in the United States over corporal punishment of children may be both a drawback and an asset. It is a drawback in that this aspect of the Convention may make it more difficult to persuade our country to become a party to the Convention. However, on balance, I believe that the Convention's language against corporal punishment is more of an asset. It is a principled and well-founded stand on a difficult issue. The Convention, as an authoritative expression of the international community, will impel Americans to regard as questionable that which they have accepted as a matter of course. Moreover, because the Convention legitimizes the idea of prohibiting corporal punishment of children, it may be instrumental in the

---

23. Convention on the Rights of the Child, *supra* note 17, at art. 28, para. 2.

24. Concluding Observations: Zimbabwe, CRC/C/15 Add. 55, at para. 18 (June 7, 1996); Concluding Observations: United Kingdom, CRC/C/15 Add. 34, at para. 31 (Feb. 15, 1995); Concluding Observations: Canada, CRC/C/15 Add. 37, at para. 25 (June 20, 1995).

25. *See* Pierce v. Society of Sisters, 268 U.S. 510, 534-35 (1925); Meyer v. Nebraska, 262 U.S. 390, 399-403 (1923).

26. RONALD D. ROTUNDA & JOHN E. NOWAK, TREATISE ON CONSTITUTIONAL LAW: SUBSTANCE AND PROCEDURE § 18.28 (2d ed. 1992); Marsha Garrison, *Child Welfare Decisionmaking: In Search of the Least Drastic Alternative*, 75 GEO. L.J. 1745, 1771 n.116 (1987); Frances E. Olsen, *The Myth of State Intervention in the Family*, 18 J.L. REFORM 835, 847 (1985).

gradual creation of a new norm in the United States disfavoring this form of discipline.[27] The development of a new norm may, in turn, set the stage for domestic legal reform.

This type of dynamic can already be seen in other countries. Five years after the adoption of the Convention, Cyprus became the sixth nation, following Sweden, Norway, Finland, Denmark, and Austria[28], to enact a statute directed at prohibiting all corporal punishment of children.[29] More tellingly, in May 1996, the Italian Supreme Court of Cassation, Italy's highest court, issued a decision forbidding all corporal punishment of children in Italy.[30] The Court relied in significant part on the Convention on the Rights of the Child in deciding the case.[31] As of this writing, efforts have been underway to achieve legislative prohibition in Ireland,[32] Germany,[33] and Croatia.[34] Over the long haul, it is unlikely that the United States can remain totally impervious to and unaffected by these developments, whether or not it finally does the right thing and becomes a party to the Convention.

---

27. With respect to the role of law in norm creation, *see generally* David R. Barnhizer, *Prophets, Priests and Power Blockers: Three Fundamental Roles of Judges and Legal Scholars in America*, 50 U. PITT L. REV. 127, 162-63 (1988); Keith Burgess - Jackson, *Bad Samaritanism and the Pedagogic Function of Law*, 8 CRIM. JUST. J. 1, 3-4, 26 (1985); Philip Soper, *The Moral Value of Law*, 84 MICH. L. REV. 63, 85 (1985).

28. NEWELL, *supra* note 8, at 67-96.

29. Law 147 (1), OFFICIAL GAZETTE OF THE REPUBLIC OF CYPRUS NO. 2886 (June 17, 1994).

30. Judgment of May 16, 1996, Corte Supreme di Cassazione, 6 sezione penale.

31. *Id.*

32. *See* Cian O'Tighearnaigh, Chief Executive, The Irish Society for the Prevention of Cruelty to Children, Address at the International Seminar on Worldwide Strategies and Progress Towards Ending All Physical Punishment of Children (Dublin, Ireland, Aug. 22, 1996).

33. Interview with Paula Honkanen-Schoberth, Regional Manager, German Society for Children, Aachen Region, in Dublin, Ireland (Aug. 20, 1996).

34. *See* Letter from Darija Remeta, Department Head, Department of the Disabled, Croation Office of Victims of War (Sept. 4, 1996) (on file with author).

ARTICLE

SPANKING AND OTHER CORPORAL PUNISHMENT OF CHILDREN BY PARENTS: OVERVALUING PAIN, UNDERVALUING CHILDREN

*David Orentlicher**

Table of Contents

I. INTRODUCTION 148

II. THE DEFINITION OF CORPORAL PUNISHMENT 149

III. PREVALENCE OF CORPORAL PUNISHMENT BY PARENTS 151

IV. THE LAW ON CORPORAL PUNISHMENT BY PARENTS 151

V. CONCERNS ABOUT CORPORAL PUNISHMENT 155

VI. ALTERNATIVES TO CORPORAL PUNISHMENT 161

VII. THE LEGAL FRAMING OF CORPORAL PUNISHMENT 166

VIII. EXPLAINING THE LEGAL FRAMEWORK 173

IX. CONCLUSION 185

---

* Visiting DeCamp Professor of Bioethics, Princeton University; Associate Professor of Law and Co-Director, Center for Law and Health, Indiana University School of Law-Indianapolis. B.A., Brandeis, 1977; M.D., Harvard, 1981; J.D., Harvard, 1986. I am grateful for the contributions of Judy Failer.

I. INTRODUCTION

For generations, parents have viewed spanking and slapping as important, though perhaps regrettable, methods of discipline for ensuring the appropriate social development of their children. As the proverbial dictum warns, to spare the rod is to spoil the child.[1] To be sure, some parents abjure corporal punishment entirely, and other parents employ it as an infrequent and last resort, but corporal punishment of children has wide and deep roots in American society.[2]

This broad social imprimatur of corporal punishment is reflected in the law. Court decisions regularly show a good deal of tolerance for corporal punishment of children.[3] Indeed, in the absence of significant bruising or worse, corporal punishment by parents does not run afoul of prohibitions against child abuse.[4] Yet, when we compare the legal acceptability of corporal punishment with the view of medical and other experts in child rearing and family violence, we see a substantial gap.[5] Child-rearing experts are far less tolerant of corporal punishment than is the law.[6] In the view of professionals in the field, corporal punishment has serious disadvantages, and its advantages can be

1. *See generally* Timothy A. Carey, Spare the Rod and Spoil the Child. *Is This a Sensible Justification for the Use of Punishment in Child Rearing?*, 18 CHILD ABUSE & NEGLECT 1005, 1005-06 (1994) (examining the validity of the well-known proverb).

2. *See* Murray A. Straus et al., *Spanking by Parents and Subsequent Antisocial Behavior of Children*, 151 ARCHIVES OF PEDIATRICS & ADOLESCENT MED. 761, 761 (1997) (indicating that nearly 100% of parents used corporal punishment on toddlers in the 1950s and more than 90% do so today).

3. *See, e.g., In re* Coleen "P," 538 N.Y.S.2d 361, 362-63 (N.Y. App. Div. 1989) (finding no child neglect in a case in which a parent shook her child, causing the child's head to strike the pavement twice, because there was no "impairment of the child's physical, mental or emotional condition"); *In re* Rodney C., 398 N.Y.S.2d 511, 516 (N.Y. Fam. Ct. 1977) (declining to find abuse in a case in which a seven-year-old boy with emotional difficulties was found with 26 visible marks on his back three days after receiving a beating because the punishment was not "life threatening or likely to cause permanent disfigurement").

4. Refer to note 37 *infra* and accompanying text (discussing instances in which convictions were upheld).

5. Refer to notes 6, 26-36 *infra* and accompanying text (comparing the law's view of corporal punishment with commentators' views).

6. *See, e.g.*, T. BERRY BRAZELTON, TOUCHPOINTS 260 (1992) (noting that "physical punishment has very real disadvantages"); Murray A. Straus, *Corporal Punishment By Parents*, *in* DEBATING CHILDREN'S LIVES 195, 197-203 (Mary Ann Mason & Eileen Gambrill eds., 1994) (arguing that the use of corporal punishment is child abuse and that spanking a child should be illegal). *See generally* BENJAMIN SPOCK, DR. SPOCK ON PARENTING 151-52 (1988) (disapproving of physical punishment); MURRAY A. STRAUS & DENISE A. DONNELLY, BEATING THE DEVIL OUT OF THEM (1994).

achieved through less harmful, alternative means of discipline.[7] Accordingly, experts see little, if any, role for corporal punishment in child rearing.[8]

This gap between the law and professional expertise needs to be explained. Why does the law permit much more corporal punishment than can be justified in terms of the purposes of discipline? The gap might reflect a distrust of professional expertise, but, in other areas of the law, particularly medical malpractice, the legal standard expressly incorporates a deference to professional expertise.[9] The gap might also reflect some important legal principle, but, as discussed at greater length in this Article, consideration of legal principle indicates that this explanation is not adequate either.[10] In this Article, I will argue that the legal-professional disjunction reflects a combination of our society's views about pain and about children—we overvalue pain, and we undervalue children.

The tolerance of corporal punishment, then, is highly problematic. It fails to serve the legitimate social goal of enhancing child rearing, but instead reinforces misguided views about children and pain. Corporal punishment also undermines social efforts to curtail violence, especially family violence. To the extent that society tells children that hitting others has a legitimate role, children are more likely to adopt physical force as a means of resolving disputes with others. A better approach for children and society would be for this country to follow the lead of those countries, like Sweden, whose laws show little tolerance for corporal punishment.

II. THE DEFINITION OF CORPORAL PUNISHMENT

What do I mean by corporal punishment? I follow the definition articulated by Murray Straus, a sociologist who has studied and written extensively on the topic.[11] He defines corporal punishment as

---

7. Refer to Part VI *infra* (suggesting alternative means of discipline).

8. Refer to note 6 *supra* (giving examples of this intolerance for corporal punishment).

9. *See, e.g.*, W. PAGE KEETON ET AL., PROSSER AND KEETON ON THE LAW OF TORTS § 32, at 189 (5th ed. 1984).

10. Refer to Part VII *infra* (considering legal principle as an explanation for the gap).

11. *See, e.g.*, STRAUS & DONNELLY, *supra* note 6, at 4-5; MURRAY A. STRAUS & RICHARD J. GELLES, PHYSICAL VIOLENCE IN AMERICAN FAMILIES (1990); Murray A. Straus et al., *supra* note 2, at 761; Murray A. Straus, *Discipline and Deviance: Physical Punishment of Children and Violence and Other Crime in Adulthood*, 38 SOC. PROBS. 133 (1991) [hereinafter Straus, *Discipline and Deviance*]; Murray A. Straus & Glenda Kaufman Kantor, *Corporal Punishment of Adolescents by Parents: A Risk Factor in the Epidemiology of Depression, Suicide, Alcohol Abuse, Child*

"the use of physical force with the intention of causing a child to experience pain, but not injury, for the purpose of correction or control of the child's behavior."[12] Frequent forms of corporal punishment are "spanking, slapping, grabbing or shoving a child roughly . . . , and hitting with certain objects such as a hair brush, belt, or paddle."[13]

Under this definition, restraining a child to prevent the child from running into the street or from touching a hot stove would not constitute corporal punishment. Such restraint is used only to prevent impending undesirable behavior, not to also cause pain and not as a punitive response to undesirable behavior.

States typically do not define corporal punishment, but define instead the line between reasonable and excessive corporal punishment.[14] However, several states do define corporal punishment in their public education statutes.[15] In Florida, for example, corporal punishment "is the moderate use of physical force or physical contact by a teacher or principal as may be necessary to maintain discipline or to enforce school rule."[16] In Michigan, corporal punishment "means the deliberate infliction of physical pain by hitting, paddling, spanking, slapping, or any other physical force used as a means of discipline."[17]

Abuse and Wife Beating, 29 ADOLESCENCE 543 (1994).

12. STRAUS & DONNELLY, *supra* note 6, at 4.

13. *Id.* at 5.

14. Refer to Part IV *infra* (analyzing the law on corporal punishment).

15. *See, e.g.*, CAL. EDUC. CODE § 49001 (West 1993) (defining corporal punishment as the "willful infliction of, or willfully causing the infliction of, physical pain on a pupil" and prohibiting the use of such punishment on pupils); FLA. STAT. ANN. § 228.041(27) (West Supp. 1998); MICH. STAT. ANN. § 15.41312 (Law. Co-op. 1996); MINN. STAT. ANN. § 127.45 (West 1994) (defining corporal punishment as "(1) hitting or spanking a person with or without an object; or (2) unreasonable physical force that causes bodily harm or substantial emotional harm"); MONT. CODE ANN. §20-4-302 (1997) (defining corporal punishment as "knowingly and purposely inflicting physical pain on a pupil as a disciplinary measure").

16. FLA. STAT. ANN. § 228.041(27). The statute also provides that corporal punishment "does not include the use of such reasonable force by a teacher or principal as may be necessary to protect himself or other students from disruptive students." *Id.*

17. MICH. LAWS ANN. § 15.41312. Corporal punishment is also defined in some child and family services statutes. *See, e.g.*, IOWA CODE ANN. § 234.40 (West 1994) (defining corporal punishment for purposes of foster care as "the intentional physical punishment of a foster child," but stating that "[a] foster parent's physical contact with the body of a foster child shall not be considered corporal punishment if the contact is reasonable and necessary under the circumstances and is not designed or intended to cause pain or if the foster parent uses reasonable force").

III. PREVALENCE OF CORPORAL PUNISHMENT BY PARENTS

Corporal punishment of children by parents is common. In national surveys of families that looked at the prevalence of family violence, researchers found in both 1975 and 1985 that more than sixty percent of parents reported using corporal punishment in the preceding twelve months and that more than ninety percent of parents reported using corporal punishment at some point in raising their children.[18] Corporal punishment was most common with children between the ages of three and six.[19] More than eighty percent of parents reported using corporal punishment on children of those ages.[20] The likelihood that parents would spank or slap their children did not drop below fifty percent unless the children were younger than age two or older than age twelve.[21]

Data on parental approval and use of corporal punishment since 1968 suggest that support for corporal punishment has decreased.[22] When asked in 1968 whether there is sometimes a role for corporal punishment in child rearing, ninety-three percent of parents expressed their approval.[23] By 1986, parental approval of corporal punishment had declined to eighty-three percent, and, by 1994, parental approval had dropped to sixty-nine percent.[24] In a series of national surveys conducted between 1988 and 1992, there was a decline over the five year period from sixty-four to fifty-three in the percentage of parents reporting that they spanked or hit their child in the past year.[25]

IV. THE LAW ON CORPORAL PUNISHMENT BY PARENTS

Legislatures and courts employ a high threshold before deeming corporal punishment unacceptable.[26] Children are therefore subject to substantial levels of physical punishment that risk serious harm, but promise little benefit. The degree to which the law permits corporal punishment is not apparent from the formal

18. *See* STRAUS & DONNELLY, *supra* note 6, at 23, 26-27.

19. *See id.* at 23.

20. *See id.*

21. *See id.*

22. *See* Murray A. Straus & Anita K. Mathur, *Social Change and Trends in Approval of Corporal Punishment by Parents from 1968 to 1994* (visited Mar. 8, 1998) <http://www.unh.edu/frl/cp27f.htm>.

23. *See id.*

24. *See id.*

25. *See* Deborah Daro & Richard J. Gelles, *Public Attitudes and Behaviors with Respect to Child Abuse Prevention*, 7 J. INTERPERSONAL VIOLENCE 517, 521 (1992).

26. Refer to note 29 *infra* and accompanying text (discussing lawmakers' and courts' treatment of the issue).

legal standards.[27] Rather, it is in the application of those standards that the permissiveness of the law becomes clear.[28]

The predominant approach by legislatures and courts across the fifty states is to allow "reasonable and timely corporal punishment" by parents.[29] The punishment must be delivered for purposes of behavioral modification rather than to express the anger of the parent.[30] More specifically, corporal punishment must be employed for the "proper training or education of the child or for the preservation of discipline."[31] In addition, what counts as reasonable varies "in relation to the sensitivity and character of the child, the child's age, sex, physical condition, as well as in relation to the particular offense for which punishment is to be meted out."[32] Thus, for example, the graver the misbehavior, the more severe may be the punishment.[33] In addition, since corporal punishment is permitted only for appropriate behavioral modification, it is tolerated less for children who are too young to "have the capacity to understand or appreciate the correction" and on whom "the value of the training, education or discipline is [therefore] lost."[34] Other relevant factors in determining the reasonableness of corporal punishment include the child's mental condition, the child's motive for committing the misbehavior, and the influence of the misbehavior on the child's siblings.[35] Accordingly, harsher punishments are permitted if the children's offenses are intentional rather than the result of misjudgment or inattention and if children are "ringleaders" or otherwise likely to encourage siblings to follow their example of misconduct.[36]

On its face, this standard seems perfectly appropriate. After all, how could a requirement that corporal punishment be "reasonable and timely" not be a reasonable approach? In addition, it

27. Refer to notes 29-36 *infra* and accompanying text (analyzing the standards).

28. Refer to notes 37-41 *infra* and accompanying text (discussing the application of the standards).

29. 59 AM. JUR. 2D *Parent and Child* § 22 (1987).

30. *See, e.g.*, State v. Arnold, 543 N.W.2d 600, 603 (Iowa 1996) (defining punishment meted out for such purposes as "corrective" punishment that is acceptable under the law).

31. RESTATEMENT (SECOND) OF TORTS § 151 (1965).

32. State v. Thorpe, 429 A.2d 785, 788 (R.I. 1981); *see also Arnold*, 543 N.W.2d at 603; Carpenter v. Commonwealth, 44 S.E.2d 419, 424-25 (Va. 1947).

33. *See* RESTATEMENT (SECOND) OF TORTS § 150 cmt. c (1965).

34. *In re* Rodney C., 398 N.Y.S.2d 511, 515 (N.Y. Fam. Ct. 1977).

35. *See* RESTATEMENT (SECOND) OF TORTS § 150 (1965).

36. *See id.* § 150 cmt. c. For further discussion of current legal standards, see Mary Kate Kearney, *Substantive Due Process and Parental Corporal Punishment: Democracy and the Excluded Child*, 32 SAN DIEGO L. REV. 1, 33-34 (1995) (discussing the scope of reasonable corporal punishment).

seems appropriate to permit weightier punishments for older children and for more serious misconduct.

The problem is in how the courts and legislatures have fleshed out the standard of reasonableness. Parents usually do not get into trouble unless they engage in serious abuse, such as when they beat a child repeatedly with paddles, belts, or other implements and cause at least marked bruising, if not more serious injury like broken bones or burns.[37] In Iowa, corporal punishment becomes unreasonable only if the parent "[k]nowingly acts in a manner that creates a substantial risk to a child or minor's physical, mental or emotional health or safety."[38] In Pennsylvania, corporal punishment is permitted as long as "the force used is not designed or known to create a substantial risk of death, serious bodily injury, disfigurement, extreme pain or mental distress or gross degradation."[39] In North Dakota, corporal punishment does not amount to abuse unless it causes "serious physical harm or traumatic abuse."[40] In Rhode Island, corporal punishment by parents becomes unreasonable if the parent "ceases to act in good faith and with parental affection and acts immoderately, cruelly, or mercilessly with a malicious desire to inflict pain."[41] Under all of these approaches, children do not receive the protection of the state until corporal punishment becomes quite severe.

To be sure, given the implications for criminal or child custody proceedings, one might expect the law to employ a high

37. *See, e.g.*, Carson v. United States, 556 A.2d 1076, 1081 (D.C. 1989) (upholding a conviction for cruelty to children because of multiple bruises, lacerations, and abrasions in several places on the children's bodies); People v. Rogers, 432 N.E.2d 975 (Ill. App. 1982) (upholding a conviction for child endangerment in a case in which a parent broke several bones and caused a cigarette burn on the eyelid of her infant child); *Arnold*, 543 N.W.2d at 601-03 (upholding a conviction for child endangerment on the basis of multiple bruises that led the child abuse investigator to conclude "'rarely do you see bruising to the magnitude that [the child] had on her buttocks'"); *In re* Coleen "P," 538 N.Y.S.2d 361, 362-63 (N.Y. App. Div. 1989) (finding no child neglect in a case in which parent shook her child, causing the child's head to strike the pavement twice, because there was no "impairment of the child's physical, mental or emotional condition"); *Rodney C.*, 398 N.Y.S.2d at 516 (finding neglect in a case in which a seven-year-old boy with emotional difficulties had 26 marks visible on his back three days after a beating was administered, but not finding abuse because the punishment was not "life threatening or likely to cause permanent disfigurement").

38. IOWA CODE ANN. § 726.6(1)(a) (West Supp. 1997); *see also Arnold*, 543 N.W.2d at 602 (delineating the statutory standard of child endangerment).

39. Boland v. Leska, 454 A.2d 75, 78 (Pa. Super. Ct. 1982).

40. N.D. CENT. CODE § 50-25.1-02(2) (Supp. 1995); *see also* Raboin v. North Dakota Dept. of Human Servs., 552 N.W.2d 329, 334 (N.D. 1996) (finding no evidence of child abuse due to the absence of serious physical harm or traumatic abuse in disciplinary parental spankings).

41. State v. Thorpe, 429 A.2d 785, 788 (R.I. 1981).

threshold before finding abuse. We do not want to convict people or to deprive them of their fundamental rights of parenting for all conduct that is unacceptable, just as we do not revoke a driver's license simply because a person violates the speed limit. However, it is also problematic when the law sends a strong message to parents that they have a good deal of freedom to employ corporal punishment. Parents are essentially told that they may employ physical violence against their children that is harsh and that unquestionably would not be tolerated if employed against others.[42] Indeed, as one court observed, "'[t]he control and proper discipline of a child by the parent may justify acts which would otherwise constitute assault and battery.'"[43]

The law's tolerance for corporal punishment is even greater under the United States Constitution than under state common or statutory law. The Constitution does not limit parental use of corporal punishment because the Constitution applies only to state action.[44] Rather, the Constitution is invoked in cases involving corporal punishment in the public schools because such punishment involves a governmental actor.[45] However, the Supreme Court has held that corporal punishment of students does not violate the Eighth Amendment's prohibition against cruel and unusual punishment and that the Eighth Amendment was adopted to protect individuals convicted of crimes, not children paddled by teachers.[46] Because schools, unlike prisons, are open institutions at which students are in the presence of classmates and teachers "who may witness and protest any instances of mistreatment" and because students are free at the end of the day to return home, the Court has concluded that public school students do not need the protection of the Eighth Amendment.[47]

---

42. *See* Straus, *Discipline and Deviance*, *supra* note 11, at 134 (noting that parents have a legal right to hit their children, an act that would be criminal if carried out by someone with a noncustodial relationship to a child).

43. *Arnold*, 534 N.W.2d at 603 (quoting 59 AM. JUR. 2D *Parent and Child* § 22 (1987)).

44. *See* JOHN E. NOWAK & RONALD D. ROTUNDA, CONSTITUTIONAL LAW § 12.1, at 470 (5th ed. 1995) (explaining that the constitutional protections for individual rights and liberties apply only to the activities of state or federal governments).

45. *See id.* (stressing that actions of any governmental entity, including any subdivision of a state, constitute state actions for constitutional purposes).

46. *See* Ingraham v. Wright, 430 U.S. 651, 664, 671 (1977) (adhering to the Eighth Amendment's longstanding application only to convicted criminals and holding that the Eighth Amendment is inapplicable to corporal punishment in public schools).

47. *See id.* at 670-71. The Court held that the right to procedural due process under the Fourteenth Amendment applies to corporal punishment in public schools, but that due process does not require that the student receive a hearing before the administration of corporal punishment. *See id.* at 672, 682.

While some of the federal courts of appeals have held that the Fourteenth Amendment's guarantee of substantive due process protects school children from excessive corporal punishment, there is often little protection for students.[48] The Fifth Circuit Court of Appeals has held that corporal punishment of students does not violate substantive due process.[49] Other appellate courts have applied the same standard as developed for police brutality cases.[50] In the Fourth and Tenth Circuits, the issue is

> "whether the force applied caused injury so severe, was so disproportionate to the need presented, and was so inspired by malice or sadism rather than a merely careless or unwise excess of zeal that it amounted to a brutal and inhumane abuse of official power literally shocking to the conscience."[51]

The Third and Eighth Circuits are somewhat more protective of students, holding that we should look at the need for corporal punishment, the relationship between the need and the amount of force used, the extent of injury caused, and the extent to which the punishment was administered "in a good faith effort to maintain discipline or maliciously and sadistically for the very purpose of causing harm."[52]

V. CONCERNS ABOUT CORPORAL PUNISHMENT

The law's tolerance of corporal punishment is problematic not only because of the high threshold before such punishment becomes unacceptable, but also because the law's tolerance cannot be justified in terms of the benefits and harms from corporal punishment. There may be some benefits from spanking,[53] but those benefits can be realized by alternative methods of discipline.[54] In addition, there is evidence suggesting a link between

---

48. *See* David Orentlicher, *Corporal Punishment in the Schools*, 267 JAMA 3205, 3205 (1992) (observing that lower federal courts have examined the substantive due process right to liberty in corporal punishment cases while emphasizing that few limitations have been imposed under such right).

49. *See* Coleman v. Franklin Parish Sch. Bd., 702 F.2d 74, 76 (5th Cir. 1983) (per curiam).

50. *See* Orentlicher, *supra* note 48, at 3205.

51. Garcia v. Miera, 817 F.2d 650, 655 (10th Cir. 1987) (quoting Hall v. Tawney, 621 F.2d 607, 613 (4th Cir. 1980)).

52. Wise v. Pea Ridge Sch. Dist., 855 F.2d 560, 564 (8th Cir. 1988); *see also* Metzger v. Osbeck, 841 F.2d 518, 520 (3d Cir. 1988).

53. The benefits, however, may be short-lived. Many parents can think of cases in which corporal punishment stopped an undesirable behavior at the time, but there is some question about its effectiveness in changing behavior over time. *See* PETER NEWELL, CHILDREN ARE PEOPLE TOO 16-21 (1989).

54. Refer to Part VI *infra* (discussing the effective alternatives to corporal

corporal punishment and serious problems for the child later in life, harms that can be avoided by the use of alternative methods of discipline.[55]

There are several potential harms from corporal punishment.[56] The most obvious risk is that of physical injury to the child.[57] Injuries may be inadvertent, as when the child trips or falls while trying to escape punishment or when the parent strikes an infant without taking into account the infant's vulnerability to injury.[58] If corporal punishment is ineffective at first, the parent may resort to more severe punishment, thereby increasing the risk of injury.[59] Indeed, children often become inured to mild or moderate spankings after sufficient repetition such that parents must resort to increasingly harder spankings to achieve the desired response.[60] As the discussion of case law involving corporal punishment indicates, many children suffer serious injury from parental discipline, and academic research suggests that corporal punishment may escalate into frank child abuse.[61]

There also appears to be a significant risk of psychological injury to the child. Corporal punishment is associated with a loss

---

punishment).

55. *See The Role of the Pediatrician in Violence Prevention: Findings, Recommendations, and Action Steps*, 94 PEDIATRICS 577, 580 (1994) (contending that corporal punishment increases the probability of and acceptance of violent behavior as an adult).

56. This is not to suggest that corporal punishment is the only kind of discipline harmful to children. Children are also harmed by yelling or other verbal assault. *See* Yvonne M. Vissing et al., *Verbal Aggression by Parents and Psychosocial Problems of Children*, 15 CHILD ABUSE & NEGLECT 223, 225, 235 (1991) (demonstrating that verbal aggression adversely affects a child's psychosocial development and finding that verbal aggression increases the probability of physical aggression, delinquency, and interpersonal problems); *see also* Donileen R. Loseke, *Reply to Murray A. Straus: Readings on "Discipline and Deviance"*, 38 SOC. PROBS. 162, 165 (1991) (observing that people can also be dominated by others through non-corporal means of control). Still, verbal assault appears to be used in concert with physical assault rather than as a substitute for it. *See* David Hemenway et al., *Child-Rearing Violence*, 18 CHILD ABUSE & NEGLECT 1011, 1016 (1994) (observing that physical and verbal punishment tend to coexist).

57. *See* STRAUS & DONNELLY, *supra* note 6, at 81.

58. *See* NEWELL, *supra* note 53, at 31.

59. *See* Carey, *supra* note 1, at 1007 (asserting that when corporal punishment fails, punishment increases over time and child abuse often results).

60. *See* Robert D. Needlman, *Growth and Development*, in NELSON TEXTBOOK OF PEDIATRICS 30, 56 (Waldo E. Nelson et al. eds., 15th ed. 1996).

61. *See* Barbara A. Wauchope & Murray A. Straus, *Physical Punishment and Physical Abuse of American Children: Incidence Rates by Age, Gender, and Occupational Class*, in PHYSICAL VIOLENCE IN AMERICAN FAMILIES 133, 147 (Murray A. Straus & Richard J. Gelles eds., 1990) (revealing that physical abuse usually begins as ordinary corporal punishment).

of self-esteem and increased anxiety.[62] There is a correlation between being hit by one's parents and becoming depressed later in life—the more a child is hit, the more likely it is that the child will develop depression.[63] Moreover, this correlation persists after controlling for other important variables like sex of the child, socioeconomic status, alcohol abuse by the child later in life, and violence between the child's parents.[64]

Corporal punishment also appears to promote violent behavior by children contemporaneously and/or later in life.[65] Many, but not all, studies have found that children subjected to corporal punishment are at higher risk for becoming users of violence themselves, whether against their siblings or playmates while young,[66] or against spouses and children when older.[67] These

---

62. *See* Straus et al., *supra* note 2, at 761 (noting that studies have found a link between corporal punishment and behavioral problems such as depression, low self-esteem, and aggressive/delinquent behavior).

63. *See* STRAUS & DONNELLY, *supra* note 6, at 71-77 (showing that adults who were hit by their parents as adolescents are more likely to be depressed than those whose parents did not use physical punishment); Robert H. DuRant et al., *Exposure to Violence and Victimization and Depression, Hopelessness, and Purpose in Life Among Adolescents Living in and Around Public Housing*, 16 J. DEVELOPMENTAL & BEHAVIORAL PEDIATRICS 233, 236 (1995) (demonstrating intrafamilial violence as a strong correlate of psychological distress, including adult depression and hopelessness); Sandra J. Holmes & Lee N. Robins, *The Role of Parental Disciplinary Practices in the Development of Depression and Alcoholism*, 51 PSYCHIATRY 24, 31 (1988) (finding a strong relationship between reports of harsh or unfair punishment during childhood and alcohol abuse and depression as an adult); Straus & Kantor, *supra* note 11, at 550-51 (finding corporal punishment in adolescence results in an increased probability of depression as an adult).

64. *See* STRAUS & DONNELLY, *supra* note 6, at 77-78; Straus & Kantor, *supra* note 11, at 550.

65. *See* Leopold Bellak & Maxine Antell, *An Intercultural Study of Aggressive Behavior on Children's Playgrounds,* 44 AM. J. ORTHOPSYCHIATRY 503, 508 (1974) (finding a correlation between parental aggressiveness toward their children and aggressiveness by the children toward others); Straus & Kantor, *supra* note 11, at 555-56 (stressing that the use of corporal punishment on a child increases the probability that the subject will abuse a spouse or child as an adult).

66. *See* Bellak & Antell, *supra* note 65, at 508 (showing an association between parental aggressiveness toward their children and child aggressiveness toward other playmates); Robert H. DuRant et al., *Factors Associated with the Use of Violence Among Urban Black Adolescents*, 84 AM. J. PUB. HEALTH 612, 614-15 (1994) (noting a correlation between violent activity of urban black adolescents and their having experienced corporal punishment at home); Zvi Strassberg et al., *Spanking in the Home and Children's Subsequent Aggression Toward Kindergarten Peers*, 6 DEV. & PSYCHOPATHOLOGY 445, 445 (1994) (finding that children who were spanked at home were more aggressive toward their classmates and that the most aggressive children were those who received violent discipline); Straus, *Discipline and Deviance*, *supra* note 11, at 142 (finding that children who are physically punished are three times as likely as other children to assault their siblings);. *But see* Marjorie Lindner Gunnoe & Carrie Lea Mariner, *Toward a Developmental-Contextual Model of the Effects of Parental Spanking on Children's Aggression*, 151 ARCHIVES OF PEDIATRICS & ADOLESCENT MED. 768, 773-74 (1997) (indicating that spanking fosters aggression only for 8-to 11-year-old Caucasian boys being raised by a single

harmful consequences may reflect the fact that corporal punishment sends an inappropriate message from the people on whom children model their behavior.[68] Corporal punishment tells children that the way to deal with anger or to resolve disputes is through the imposition of physical force, *i.e.*, "might makes right."[69] It also tells children that love and hitting go together. To the child, the parent employing corporal punishment is saying that the people who love you the most, your parents, are the most likely people, and possibly the only people, to hit you.[70]

Children who are corporally punished may be prone not only to physical aggression but also to other kinds of misbehavior, including cheating, lying, bullying, disobedience, and breaking things deliberately.[71] They may also be more likely to show callous disregard for the feelings of others and to engage in truancy, drug abuse, and

---

mother).

67. *See* Hemenway et al., *supra* note 56, at 1013 (observing that parents who were spanked at least weekly as a child are much more likely to spank their children than are parents who were spanked less often than once a week); Straus & Kantor, *supra* note 11, at 555-56 (finding that the likelihood of abuse against children or spouses by a person increases with the frequency of corporal punishment experienced by the person as a child); Murray A. Straus & Carrie L. Yodanis, *Corporal Punishment by Parents: Implications for Primary Prevention of Assaults on Spouses and Children*, 2 U. CHI. L. SCH. ROUNDTABLE 35, 44, 58 (1995) (finding a link between corporal punishment and later violence against spouses and children); *see also* Robert T. Muller et al., *The Intergenerational Transmission of Corporal Punishment: A Comparison of Social Learning and Temperament Models*, 19 CHILD ABUSE & NEGLECT 1323, 1324, 1332 (1995) (finding that use of corporal punishment is better explained by individuals learning their parenting techniques from their own parents rather than by the temperament of the individuals).

However, as critics have noted, the evidence demonstrating a link between corporal punishment of children and violence as an adult is open to question. *See* Demie Kurz, *Corporal Punishment and Adult Use of Violence: A Critique of "Discipline and Deviance,"* 38 SOC. PROBS. 155, 156 (1991) (denoting that efforts by social scientists to explain why physical punishment as a child results in adult violence are disappointing).

68. *See* Muller et al., *supra* note 67, at 1332 (discussing the probability that use of physical punishment is socially learned from the parents). There is disagreement among experts as to whether physical punishment by parents promotes aggression by children because the children imitate the behavior of their parents or because children who are abused or neglected, whether through physical punishment or other means, become antisocial. *See* Joan McCord, *Questioning the Value of Punishment*, 38 SOC. PROBS. 167, 167-68 (1991) (arguing for the antisocial theory to explain why punishment leads to violent behavior).

69. *See* Kim J. Overby, *Pediatric Health Supervision, in* RUDOLPH'S PEDIATRICS 1, 27 (Abraham M. Rudolph et al. eds., 20th ed., Appleton & Longe 1996).

70. *See* Straus & Yodanis, *supra* note 67, at 37-38.

71. *See* Straus et al., *supra* note 2, at 762, 766 (explaining that use of corporal punishment increases the risk of antisocial behavior).

criminal conduct.[72] In addition, rather than promoting respect toward parents, corporal punishment tends to promote fear[73] and anger.[74]

There is some evidence for the view that corporal punishment per se is not harmful, but that parents who employ corporal punishment are more likely to be deficient in parenting skills.[75] For example, one study found that, if parents accompanied their spanking with discussion to resolve conflict with the child, the association between spanking and aggressiveness by the child toward the parents disappeared.[76] Another study suggested that the harmful effects of corporal punishment can be mitigated if parents make consistent demands on their children.[77] There is also evidence, however, suggesting that physical punishment is effective only if it is used under conditions that are difficult to satisfy and that are likely to be unacceptable to most parents. Some studies indicate that, for physical punishment of humans to be effective, it should be employed frequently and harshly.[78]

---

72. *See* Patricia Cohen & Judith S. Brook, *The Reciprocal Influence of Punishment and Child Behavior Disorder, in* COERCION AND PUNISHMENT IN LONG-TERM PERSPECTIVES 154, 156-58 (Joan McCord ed., 1995) (documenting a link between corporal punishment and childhood conduct disorder, as defined in the American Psychiatric Association's third edition-revised of the *Diagnostic and Statistical Manual of Mental Disorders* ("DSM-III-R")). According to DSM-III-R, childhood conduct disorder includes truancy, drug abuse, and criminal conduct. *See* AMERICAN PSYCHIATRIC ASSOCIATION, DIAGNOSTIC AND STATISTICAL MANUAL OF MENTAL DISORDERS: DSM-III-R, §§ 312.20, 312.00, 312.90, at 53-56 (3d ed., rev. 1987).

73. *See* Lawrence A. Vitulano & Jacob Kraemer Tebes, *Child and Adolescent Behavior Therapy, in* CHILD AND ADOLESCENT PSYCHIATRY 815, 819 (Melvin Lewis ed., 2d ed. 1996) (indicating that physical punishment may elicit fear conditioned to the situation or the punisher).

74. *See* Susan Crockenberg, *Predictors and Correlates of Anger Toward and Punitive Control of Toddlers by Adolescent Mothers*, 58 CHILD DEV. 964, 971-73 (1987) (relating that child anger is associated with maternal anger).

75. *See* Mary Lou Kelley et al., *Acceptability of Positive and Punitive Discipline Methods: Comparisons Among Abusive, Potentially Abusive, and Nonabusive Parents*, 14 CHILD ABUSE & NEGLECT 219, 219 (1990).

76. *See* Robert E. Larzelere, *Moderate Spanking: Model or Deterrent of Children's Aggression in the Family?*, 1 J. FAM. VIOLENCE 27, 32 (1986). However, the use of discussion did not reduce the association between spanking and aggressiveness of the child toward siblings. *See id.* at 33; *see also* Robert E. Larzelere et al., *Relations of Spanking and Other Parenting Characteristics to Self-Esteem and Perceived Fairness of Parental Discipline*, 64 PSYCHOL. REP. 1140, 1141 (1989) (finding that the negative effects of spanking disappeared when parents used positive communication).

77. *See* Robert Agnew, *Physical Punishment and Delinquency*, 15 YOUTH & SOC'Y 225, 231-34 (1983).

78. These studies suggest that corporal punishment should be employed after each occurrence of the undesirable behavior and with fairly high intensity. *See* NEWELL, *supra* note 53, at 17-19; Carey, *supra* note 1, at 1006 (discussing important factors affecting corporal punishment's effectiveness); Kenelm F. McCormick, *Attitudes of Primary Care Physicians Toward Corporal Punishment*, 267 JAMA 3161, 3161 (1992) (citing J.M. Johnston, *Punishment of Human Behavior*, 27 AM. PSYCHOL. 1033, 1033-54 (1972)). Some data, however, suggest that increasing the

It is important to recognize that the empirical evidence on corporal punishment is not definitive.[79] There is disagreement as to whether the problems with physical punishment are problems with frequent and/or harsh punishment or whether problems also exist with infrequent and mild levels of punishment.[80] In addition, the studies generally have not controlled for the direction of the cause and effect relationship.[81] It may be that children with behavioral problems are more likely to be punished rather than that children who are punished are more likely to end up with behavioral problems. Some recent research suggests that it is the punishment that causes the behavioral problems, while other recent research casts doubt on the link between corporal punishment and behavioral problems.[82]

Despite uncertainties in the data, the existence of the evidence suggesting harm gives us good reason to be concerned about corporal punishment. Moreover, there are two other important considerations. First, even if we believe it to be effective, corporal punishment violates basic values of human dignity and respect. As a society, we no longer condone, or even tolerate, the hitting of other persons.[83] Only children are still viewed as proper objects of corporal punishment. Second, there are alternatives to corporal punishment that make it unnecessary.

---

intensity of corporal punishment will decrease its effectiveness. *See* Carey, *supra* note 1, at 1007 (citing Marie T. Balaban et al., *Orienting and Defense Responses to Punishment: Effects on Learning*, 30 BIOLOGICAL PSYCHOL. 203, 215 (1990) (noting a disagreement among researchers on this issue)).

79. *See* Gunnoe & Mariner, *supra* note 66, at 774 (recognizing that additional research is needed to reconcile the competing interpretations offered on the effectiveness of corporal punishment).

80. *See* Robert E. Larzelere, *Corporal Punishment by Parents, in* DEBATING CHILDREN'S LIVES, *supra* note 6, at 204, 204 (attempting to distinguish between abusive and beneficial corporal punishment).

81. *See* Straus et al., *supra* note 2, at 763-64 (disclosing that no studies were found that controlled for the child's initial aggression level). Because ethical and practical problems prevent direct experimental studies from being performed, data about causal direction must most likely come from longitudinal research. *See id.*

82. *Compare id.* at 765-66 (finding that, after controlling for behavioral problems initially, a child's behavior grew worse the more the child was spanked), *with* Gunnoe & Mariner, *supra* note 66, at 774 (finding little evidence that spanking children at young ages leads to aggression and other anti-social behavior by those children).

83. Even in the context of professional sports, society does not condone violence outside the playing arena. *See* Erik Brady & Gary Mihoces, *Crossing the Line: Player-Coach Battle Stirs Debate,* U.S.A. TODAY, Dec. 5, 1997, at C1 (discussing the public's intolerance of off-field violent incidents involving players and coaches). "A sports league does not have to accept or condone behavior that would not be tolerated in any other segment of society," announced NBA Commissioner David Stern regarding the suspension of a player for physically assaulting his coach. *See id.* at C1.

VI. ALTERNATIVES TO CORPORAL PUNISHMENT

Perhaps the strongest argument against corporal punishment is the availability of nonviolent alternatives for disciplining children.[84] Several of these alternatives are measures to prevent the need for punishment. If a child misbehaves by biting, fighting with siblings, going into the street or other dangerous locations, sulking, or using foul language, the child often is acting that way to elicit attention from parents.[85] Accordingly, much misbehavior can be avoided if parents ensure that they are adequately attending to the child.[86] For example, young children often seek assurance by looking to or coming over to their parents for contact.[87] The child's need can be satisfied by brief responses to these bids for contact.[88] It is also useful to set aside special time for undivided attention in which the parent shows interest in what the child is doing but is nonjudgmental and nondirective.[89] This special time is experienced by the child as unconditional love.[90] It is important for parents to acknowledge good behavior with verbal praise, smiles, and occasional small rewards (*e.g.*, reading a story, stickers, or extra privileges), especially for children who are prone to disruptive behaviors, and to ignore minor or harmless transgressions by the child (*e.g.*, tantrums, whining, or sulking).[91] Acknowledging the good behavior reinforces it, and ignoring the minor, bad behavior avoids feelings for the child that the parent is supervising and criticizing.[92] Ignoring bad behavior also avoids the creation of secondary gain for the child from the behavior.[93]

---

84. *See* Irwin A. Hyman, *Corporal Punishment, Psychological Maltreatment, Violence, and Punitiveness in America: Research, Advocacy, and Public Policy*, 4 APPLIED & PREVENTIVE PSYCHOL. 113, 119 (1995).

85. *See* Barbara J. Howard, *Discipline in Early Childhood*, 38 PEDIATRIC CLINICS N. AM. 1351, 1353 (1991) (noting that children learn that such behavior elicits attention from parents).

86. *See id.* (opining that for the ignored child "[e]ven negative attention from parents is better than none at all").

87. *See id.* at 1353-54.

88. *See id.* at 1354 (noting that providing attention to the child for as little as one to two seconds is usually sufficient to satisfy the child's need for attention).

89. *See id.*

90. *See id.*

91. *See id.* at 1355-56; Overby, *supra* note 69, at 26-27; Martin T. Stein, *Difficult Behavior: Temper Tantrums to Conduct Disorders*, *in* RUDOLPH'S PEDIATRICS, *supra* note 69, at 128, 132.

92. *See* Howard, *supra* note 85, at 1355-56 (observing that positive reinforcement has the effect of increasing the frequency of good behavior).

93. *See id.* at 1356 (adding that ignoring behavior also helps eliminate it).

Misbehavior can also be prevented by appropriate verbal responses.[94] When encouraging or discouraging certain behaviors, for example, it is important to label the behavior, rather than the child, as good or bad.[95] Similarly, verbal feedback should be specific and terse (*e.g.*, "I like this clean room; you put away all the blocks and cars").[96] If feedback is too elaborate, the point can get lost or be seen as not credible (as with elaborate praise), and the parent comes across as overbearing.[97] Communications to the child must be consistent with the parent's emotions and feelings.[98] If parents say one thing but convey something different with their tone or facial expressions, then the child receives a mixed message that is confusing and reinforcing of the child's lack of self-control.[99] Comparison to other children can be demoralizing and should be avoided.[100] If done routinely and kindly, correcting behavior is important not only in shaping future behavior but also in preparing the child for correction in school and elsewhere in life.[101]

Misbehavior can also be prevented by conveying to the child a sense of being capable.[102] This can be achieved by employing routines for the child's schedule (*e.g.*, regular times and rituals for meals, chores, and sleeping), by modeling appropriate behavior (*e.g.*, thanking or apologizing to the child when indicated), by giving clear instructions, by having progressive and realistic expectations for the child (*i.e.*, having the child move on to more demanding tasks but also recognizing the need for repetition to master new tasks), and by offering the child choices that are simple and therefore manageable.[103]

---

94. *See id.* at 1357 (opining that verbal communication is "central to a child's developing sense of being lovable").

95. *See id.*; Alexander K.C. Leung et al., *Counseling Parents About Childhood Discipline*, 45 AM. FAM. PHYSICIAN 1185, 1187 (1992) (stressing the importance of directing punishment toward the behavior rather than the child); Overby, *supra* note 69, at 27 (recommending that verbal disapproval be coupled with positive instruction).

96. *See* Howard, *supra* note 85, at 1357 (remarking that young children also need feedback about their behavior approximately every five minutes).

97. *See id.* (noting that specificity fosters learning by the child).

98. *See id.* at 1358.

99. *See id.* (attributing the confusion to "the primacy of nonverbal communication"); *see also* BRAZLETON, *supra* note 6, at 260.

100. *See* Howard, *supra* note 85, at 1358.

101. *See* Overby, *supra* note 69, at 26-27.

102. *See* Howard, *supra* note 85, at 1359.

103. *See id.* at 1359-60 (discussing how using routines, models, instructions, progressive expectations and allowing children the opportunity to make choices, helps convey to the child a sense of being capable); *see also* BRAZLETON, *supra* note 6, at 259-60 (noting that modeling behavior for the child helps him or her develop ways to deal with situations through the use of examples); Overby, *supra* note 69, at 27 (noting that allowing a child to make choices from acceptable options allows the

Finally, it is important for parents to anticipate situations in which misbehavior can arise and take action to avoid such scenarios.[104] For example, parents might schedule shopping trips when their children are rested, bringing along the child's toys to avoid boredom.[105] Children typically have little control over their activities, so they often respond with disruptive behavior to changes in their routine.[106] It is therefore helpful for parents to give their children some notice (*e.g.*, "five more minutes of play time before a bath, nap, or bedtime") in advance of changes to assist the transitions.[107] It is also helpful when parents give their children clear and unequivocal directions (*e.g.*, "it's time to go to bed" rather than, "would you like to go to bed?"),[108] and parents should engage in active listening, whereby they verbally reflect and express their child's emotions, to show that the child is being understood (*e.g.*, "you seem to be really angry").[109] Sometimes disruptive behavior results from frustrating features of the child's physical environment, and parents can avoid the problem by rearranging or otherwise restructuring the home.[110]

Even with the best parenting, children will misbehave, and there are ways for parents to respond without employing corporal punishment. In some cases, parents can let the child suffer the natural consequences of their action.[111] If children are late for dinner, they can be given their meal in its current cold state; if they spill a cup or jar, they can be expected to help clean up the spill; and if they mishandle a toy, the toy can be taken away.[112] Other important responses to misbehavior include verbal or nonverbal expressions of disapproval,[113] diversion of the child to another activity or another room,[114] loss of a treat or privilege,[115] and

---

child an outlet to express in a positive manner the child's need for control and independence).

104. *See* Overby, *supra* note 69, at 27 (noting that by appropriately structuring an environment, the parent will help minimize the temptation of misadventure).

105. *See* Stein, *supra* note 91, at 131.

106. *See* Howard, *supra* note 85, at 1358.

107. *See id.* at 1358; Overby, *supra* note 69, at 27; Stein, *supra* note 91, at 131.

108. *See* Stein, *supra* note 91, at 131.

109. *See* Howard, *supra* note 85, at 1356-57; Stein, *supra* note 91, at 131-32 (suggesting also a moment of silence after verbal reflections to allow the child to absorb the experience).

110. *See* Stein, *supra* note 91, at 131.

111. *See* Howard, *supra* note 85, at 1361.

112. *See* Overby, *supra* note 69, at 27.

113. *See* BRAZELTON, *supra* note 6, at 257.

114. *See* Stein, *supra* note 91, at 132.

115. *See id.* (stating that loss of privileges usually gives a strong message to the child that disruptive behavior will not be tolerated); *see also* Overby, *supra* note 69, at 27 (noting that "[d]elaying privileges until other less pleasurable tasks are com-

"time out" (*i.e.*, requiring the child to sit quietly for a specified and brief period of time).[116] Because sensitive children may be devastated by discipline that would be appropriate for other children, the specific discipline used should be adjusted to the child.[117] With all of these alternative methods of discipline, parents can achieve the same goal that they would hope to achieve with corporal punishment—the fostering of appropriate social development of their children.[118]

Given the disadvantages of corporal punishment and the availability of alternative methods of discipline, many experts in pediatrics either strongly discourage the use of corporal punishment or call for its elimination entirely.[119] According to a leading textbook in pediatrics,

> [t]he argument against physical punishment focuses on two issues. First, there are other effective methods for managing disruptive behaviors that teach children self-regulation, provide alternatives to uncontrolled anger, and assist in the attainment of self-esteem. Second, physical punishment models an adult method of conflict resolution that children should not be taught to use. It is a form of behavior modification that cannot be internalized in the child's quest for learning to regulate feelings and conflicts. In fact, it may be experienced as a form of resolving unpleasant situations that is counterproductive to their emerging sense of self-worth. Child-oriented advocacy that focuses on anticipatory guidance, behavior modification, improved

---

pleted" is an effective method of discipline).

116. *See* Edward R. Christophersen, *Anticipatory Guidance on Discipline*, 33 PEDIATRIC CLINICS N. AM. 789, 794-96 (1986); Howard, *supra* note 85, at 1363-65; Overby, *supra* note 69, at 27; Stein, *supra* note 91, at 132.

117. *See* BRAZELTON, *supra* note 6, at 259.

118. *See* Overby, *supra* note 69, at 26-27 (noting that parents can best shape their child's behavior and conscience by showing interest and caring, complimenting good behavior, providing consistent, appropriate limits, and setting good examples).

119. *See* BRAZELTON, *supra* note 6, at 260 (explaining that physical punishment has real disadvantages in that it lets the child see you lose control and act physically aggressive); Howard, *supra* note 85, at 1365 (contending that physical punishment, at best, has short term effectiveness and should only be a small part of the structure of discipline for children); Overby, *supra* note 69, at 27 (attacking the use of physical punishment and proclaiming that "[c]orporal punishment is not only less effective than positive reinforcement but is also potentially harmful and teaches children that physical aggression is an acceptable means of dealing with anger"); Stein, *supra* note 91, at 132 (advocating discipline based on anticipatory guidance, behavior modification, improved parent-child communication skills, and effective limit setting rather than physical punishment).

parent-child communication skills, and effective limit-setting is more appropriate for pediatric counseling.[120]

Similarly, T. Berry Brazelton, a leading pediatric authority on child development and the "Dr. Spock"[121] for the current generation of parents, has written, "*Physical punishment has very real disadvantages.* Remember what it means to a child to see you lose control and act physically aggressive. It means you believe in power and physical aggression."[122]

Finally, a task force on violent prevention in pediatrics concluded:

> Finding: Corporal punishment has many adverse side effects, including increased probability of violent behavior and acceptance of violent behavior later in life; furthermore, it is no more effective than other modes of discipline in the short-term and less effective in the long-term.
>
> Recommendation: *Pediatricians should work toward the ultimate goal of ending corporal punishment in homes and schools.*[123]

---

120. Stein, *supra* note 91, at 132. *But see* Needlman, *supra* note 60, at 56 (observing that there are more effective techniques for disciplining children than corporal punishment and that pediatricians should help parents "renounce spanking or at least reserve it for extreme circumstances" but that "[t]here is no evidence that spanking per se is harmful").

Although experts in childhood discipline oppose corporal punishment, there is considerable support for corporal punishment among primary care physicians. In one statewide survey, the researcher found support for corporal punishment among 70% of family physicians and 59% of pediatricians. *See* McCormick, *supra* note 78, at 3163 (revealing that most family physicians support corporal punishment even though evidence suggests it can be harmful).

121. The reference is to Dr. Benjamin Spock, whose classic book, BABY AND CHILD CARE, had a 40th Anniversary Edition in 1985. *See* BENJAMIN SPOCK & MICHAEL B. ROTHENBERG, BABY AND CHILD CARE (40th Anniversary ed. 1985). While Dr. Spock was a reluctant advocate of limited corporal punishment for many years, he ultimately has come to disapprove of its use in child rearing. *See* BENJAMIN SPOCK, DR. SPOCK ON PARENTING 151-52 (1988) (stating that he originally avoided completely coming out against physical punishment due to his belief that it would disturb parents if a professional person implied he knew how to treat children better than the parents).

122. BRAZELTON, *supra* note 6, at 260.

123. *The Role of the Pediatrician in Violence Prevention*, *supra* note 55, at 580; *see also* Lawrence S. Wissow & Debra Roter, *Toward Effective Discussion of Discipline and Corporal Punishment During Primary Care Visits: Findings From Studies of Doctor-Patient Interaction*, 94 PEDIATRICS 587, 587 (1994) (discussing the harms from corporal punishment of children and methods for physicians to use in order to guide parents toward alternative methods of discipline).

The American Academy of Pediatrics "strongly opposes striking a child." *See* American Academy of Pediatrics, *Physical Punishment*, CHILD HEALTH MONTH, Oct. 1997 (visited Mar. 10, 1998) <http://www.aap.org/advocacy/childhealthmonth/spank.htm>.

These experts all emphasize an important point: whatever the benefits of corporal punishment in shaping childhood behavior, those benefits can be achieved with other methods of discipline.[124] Moreover, the other methods can provide their benefits without posing the risks of corporal punishment to the welfare of children immediately and later in life.[125]

VII. THE LEGAL FRAMING OF CORPORAL PUNISHMENT

Given the problems with corporal punishment, we might expect the law to show little tolerance for it. Indeed, a few countries forbid corporal punishment by parents entirely. In 1979, the International Year of the Child, Sweden became the first country to prohibit corporal punishment of children.[126] Between 1983 and 1987, Finland, Denmark, and Norway also banned corporal punishment.[127] In these four countries, parents are not ordinarily prosecuted simply for a mild spanking—the bans were incorporated into the countries' civil codes and carry no penalties.[128] Rather, the Scandinavian countries have relied primarily on education about the dangers of corporal punishment and the availability of alternative methods of discipline to change behavior.[129] Instead of leading to greater intervention by the state into the family, the laws have apparently been followed by lower rates of intervention.[130] In 1989, Austria became the fifth country to ban corporal punishment of children.[131]

Despite the example of the Scandinavian countries and Austria, the law in this country has remained quite permissive of corporal punishment,[132] and the permissiveness reflects the way

124. Refer to notes 86-110 *supra* and accompanying text (providing a number of effective alternatives to and ways to avoid the need for corporal punishment).

125. Refer to Part V *supra* (discussing the potential harmful effects of corporal punishment).

126. The ban on corporal punishment also includes a ban on "other injurious and humiliating treatment." NEWELL, *supra* note 53, at 70-73. The societal move against corporal punishment in Sweden began much earlier than 1979; by 1966, the law expressly permitting corporal punishment by parents had been repealed. *See id.* at 70-71.

127. *See id.* at 67-96.

128. Nevertheless, because corporal punishment of children is no longer an accepted exception to prohibitions on assault, occasional prosecutions for spanking are possible. *See id.* at 81 (reporting that in 1984, a Swedish father was fined a nominal amount for spanking his son).

129. *See id.* at 69; Joan Senzek Solheim, *A Cross-Cultural Examination of Use of Corporal Punishment on Children: A Focus on Sweden and the United States*, 6 CHILD ABUSE & NEGLECT 147, 152 (1982).

130. *See* NEWELL, *supra* note 53, at 70.

131. *See id.* at 67-69.

132. Refer to Part IV *supra* (discussing the law in the United States on corporal

we have chosen to conceptualize the issue. While we might consider corporal punishment from the perspective of the child, we have chosen instead to consider it from the perspective of the parents. Or, to put it another way, corporal punishment is viewed as an issue of parental rights rather than as an issue of children's rights. Either framework is plausible, but they lead to very different results.

From the parental perspective, corporal punishment implicates the fundamental right of parents to direct the upbringing of their children. The State may protect children from abuse and neglect and, therefore, may ensure that parents feed, educate, and secure health care for their children. Nevertheless, parents enjoy a broad range of discretion to decide how children should be raised. The constitutional dimension of this parental right was first enunciated by the Supreme Court in two cases in the 1920s. In *Meyer v. Nebraska*,[133] the Court discussed parental rights in the context of childhood education.[134] Robert Meyer was convicted of unlawfully teaching a ten-year old pupil in a parochial school to read German.[135] By teaching German to the student, Mr. Meyer violated a Nebraska law that prohibited the teaching of languages other than English to students who had not passed the eighth grade.[136] The law also required that classes in subjects other than language be taught exclusively in English.[137] The Supreme Court struck down the law, which was designed to weaken the ties of immigrant families to their native countries, on the grounds that it interfered with the freedom of teachers to pursue their occupations of choice and the freedom of parents to bring up their children, including the authority to determine the education of their children.[138]

---

punishment by parents).

133. 262 U.S. 390 (1923).

134. *See id.* at 398-401 (stating that "the legislature ha[d] attempted materially to interfere . . . with the power of parents to control the education of their own [children]").

135. *See id.* at 396-97.

136. *See id.* at 397 (setting forth the relevant sections of the statute violated by Mr. Meyer).

137. *See id.*

138. *See id.* at 401-03 (affirming that the state has a right to promote public safety by attempting to inhibit American-born children from following foreign ideals, but that this right must be subject to certain fundamental rights of individuals). The Court acknowledged that the freedom of parents to control the education of their children is not infringed by state laws requiring compulsory attendance at some school and state curricular requirements for schools that the state supports. *See id.* at 402-03 (noting that those matters were not at issue).

The constitutional rights of parents were reaffirmed by the Court two years later in another case involving childhood education. In *Pierce v. Society of Sisters*,[139] a sectarian school and a military academy challenged an Oregon statute requiring education of children in public schools through at least the eighth grade.[140] According to the Court, the law

> unreasonably interfere[d] with the liberty of parents and guardians to direct the upbringing and education of children under their control. . . . The child is not the mere creature of the State; those who nurture him and direct his destiny have the right, coupled with the high duty, to recognize and prepare him for additional obligations.[141]

In recent years, when explaining the scope of the Fourteenth Amendment's guarantee of liberty and/or privacy, the Court has repeatedly cited *Meyer* and *Pierce* as establishing a right of parents "to direct the education and upbringing of one's children."[142]

The right of parents to raise their children without governmental interference reflects a number of considerations. As the Supreme Court recognized in *Skinner v. Oklahoma*,[143] procreation is one of our fundamental rights.[144] For many persons, becoming a parent is the most important role they can assume, both in terms of expressing their individuality and in terms of making their contribution to society.[145] All of us will leave our legacy in different ways, and many people see their offspring as the core of their legacy.[146] Procreation is also an important way for people to express their love and commitment to another person. For many people, the ultimate intertwining of two individuals is their creating

139. 268 U.S. 510 (1925).

140. *See id.* at 530-32 (describing the purpose of the Act and the nature of the schools challenging said Act).

141. *Id.* at 534-35.

142. Washington v. Glucksberg, 117 S. Ct. 2258, 2267 (1997); *see also* Planned Parenthood v. Casey, 505 U.S. 833, 849 (1992) (discussing the right of a person to make "basic decisions about family and parenthood"); Parham v. J.R., 442 U.S. 584, 602 (1979) (noting that the Court's "jurisprudence historically has reflected Western civilization concepts of the family as a unit with broad parental authority over minor children"); Roe v. Wade, 410 U.S. 113, 153 (1973) (observing that the individual's right of privacy extends to activities relating to "child rearing and education").

143. 316 U.S. 535 (1942).

144. *See id.* at 541 (describing procreation as "one of the basic civil rights of man").

145. *See* W. Penn Handwerker, *Politics and Reproduction: A Window on Social Change, in* BIRTHS AND POWER 1, 1 (W. Penn Handwerker ed., 1990) (noting that parents tend to perceive childbirth and the surrounding events as statements of individuality).

146. *See* A. F. ROBERTSON, BEYOND THE FAMILY 7 (1991) (explaining that because children raise their own children, they extend reproductive credit to the next generation).

and giving birth to a unique, new person. If procreation is to have its fullest meaning, people must not only be able to bear children, but also must be able to raise the children they have borne. Procreation would lose much of its meaning if children could be taken away immediately after birth and raised by the State.

Parental rights in child rearing also reflect the inability of children to exercise their own rights and our sense that we can trust parents most to look out for the interests of children.[147] Parental love leads people to undertake great sacrifices for their children, sacrifices that other people would likely not make.[148]

Finally, we defer to parental authority because we do not want the State making decisions about the raising of children. Family (and individual) autonomy reflects both the desire to rest important decisions in the hands of the family (or the individual) as well as the desire to take those same decisions out of the hands of the State.[149]

Given all of the strong reasons for parental authority, we defer to parents on matters of child rearing as long as the parental decisions are not clearly unreasonable.[150] Accordingly, parental choices for discipline are accepted as long as the discipline is not clearly harmful.[151] Because we cannot say that spanking is clearly unreasonable, at least when applied with mild force, we do not prohibit corporal punishment of children.[152] As discussed, empirical

147. *See Parham*, 442 U.S. at 602 (noting that "natural bonds of affection lead parents to act in the best interests of their children"); Francis Barry McCarthy, *The Confused Constitutional Status and Meaning of Parental Rights*, 22 GA. L. REV. 975, 1017-18 (1988).

148. *See* Catherine L. Leone, *The Politics of Parenthood: Fairness, Freedom, and Responsibility in American Reproductive Choices, in* BIRTHS AND POWER 113, 117-18 (W. Penn Handwerker ed., 1990) (listing sacrifices made in the name of parenthood such as loss of freedom, "driving more carefully, curtailment of drinking alcohol, retiring from dangerous sports, deleting profanity from the vocabulary, and coming home earlier from social events").

149. *See* Jed Rubenfeld, *The Right of Privacy*, 102 HARV. L. REV. 737, 782-84 (1989). Although concerns about governmental control play an important role in parental authority, it is important to note that the parental right is not simply a right against the State; it is also a right against private persons. If a child psychologist observed a misbehaving child in the park and felt that the child's parent was unable to control the child or that the parent was not around, the psychologist would not be free to spank the child to stop the misbehavior without the parent's consent.

150. *See* Prince v. Massachusetts, 321 U.S. 158, 165-67 (1944) (explaining that society's interest in protecting the welfare of children acts as a limitation on parental rights).

151. *See* Sweaney v. Ada County, 119 F.3d 1385, 1391-92 (9th Cir. 1997) (noting that, under *Prince*, parental rights are subject to limitation when parental decisions appear to jeopardize the health or safety of the child).

152. *See, e.g.*, Clark v. Clark, 683 N.E.2d 800, 803 (Ohio Ct. App. 1996) (finding that although appellant's corporal punishment of his daughter was "unwarranted and clearly excessive under the circumstances, . . . it did not create a substantial risk of physical harm" and, thus, did not constitute child abuse).

evidence suggests that corporal punishment provides no benefit over alternative methods of discipline and that corporal punishment is always harmful.[153] Nevertheless, our understanding of the effects of corporal punishment remains sufficiently uncertain that courts might reasonably conclude they lack a firm enough basis to overcome the presumption in favor of parental autonomy in child rearing.[154]

An alternative to the parental perspective on corporal punishment is the child's perspective.[155] Instead of viewing the right at stake as the right of parents to discipline their children as they see fit, we could view the right at stake as the right of children to be free of unwanted touchings (*i.e.*, unwanted bodily contact).[156] This right is also of fundamental importance.[157] In all states, unwelcome touchings by another person constitute a battery, both under tort law and criminal law,[158] and the touching need not be harsh to amount to a battery.[159] Similarly, the Supreme Court has recognized that people are protected under the Constitution from unwelcome touchings committed by the State.[160]

The right to be free of unwanted touchings reflects our society's deep concern with the individual's need for bodily integrity.[161] Interferences with bodily integrity are profoundly violative of a person, and they compromise the freedom of individuals to

153. Refer to Parts V & VI *supra*.

154. Refer to notes 79-82 *supra* and accompanying text.

155. *See* Patrick Henigan, Note, *Is Parental Authority Absolute? Public High Schools Which Provide Gay and Lesbian Youth Services Do Not Violate the Constitutional Childrearing Right of Parents*, 62 BROOK. L. REV. 1261, 1282-83 (1996) (detailing the growth in the constitutional rights of children as a limit on parental control).

156. *See* Vacco v. Quill, 117 S. Ct. 2293, 2301 (1997) (referring to the rights of bodily integrity and freedom from unwanted touching as "well established, traditional rights").

157. *See id.*

158. *See* KEETON ET AL., *supra* note 9, § 9 (describing the elements of a tortious battery); WAYNE R. LAFAVE & AUSTIN W. SCOTT, JR., CRIMINAL LAW § 7.15 (1986) (identifying the elements of a criminal battery).

159. Under tort law, any unwanted physical contact is a battery, although slight contact may yield little in damages. *See* KEETON ET AL., *supra* note 9, § 9. In most states, a criminal battery requires a physical injury or an unwanted sexual advance, but a minority of states do not require a physical injury for a nonsexual battery. *See* LAFAVE & SCOTT, *supra* note 158, § 7.15.

160. *See* Cruzan v. Missouri Dep't of Health, 497 U.S. 261, 269-79 (1990) (discussing the history of the common law doctrine of informed consent and the view that it generally encompasses a competent person's right to refuse life sustaining medical treatment).

161. *See* Union Pac. Ry. Co. v. Botsford, 141 U.S. 250, 251 (1891) (observing that "[n]o right is held more sacred, or is more carefully guarded . . . than the right of every individual to the possession and control of his own person, free from all restraint or interference of others").

control their destiny.[162] As the Supreme Court has observed, the right to be free of unwanted physical invasions of privacy is "'basic to a free society.'"[163] Unwanted touchings are also a sign of disrespect for the person. Accordingly, unwanted bodily invasions are prohibited even if designed to save the person's life.[164] From this perspective, there is no need to demonstrate that corporal punishment has harmful physical or psychological effects on the child.[165] The punishment itself is a serious harm.[166]

We might conclude that the child's perspective is less appropriate for corporal punishment than the parent's perspective, because children typically enjoy fewer rights and privileges than adults.[167] Children may not drive,[168] vote,[169] or purchase firearms.[170] However, the reasons why we limit children's rights[171] do not carry over very well to the right to be free of physical assault. We ordinarily limit children's rights because they do not have the maturity to exercise those rights on their own.[172] A two-year-old is

---

162. *Cf.* DeShaney v. Winnebago County Dep't of Soc. Servs., 489 U.S. 189, 191-93 (1989) (chronicling the abuse a four-year-old boy endured, which resulted in permanent brain damage and severe mental retardation).

163. Schmerber v. California, 384 U.S. 757, 767 (1966) (quoting Wolf v. Colorado, 338 U.S. 25, 27 (1949), for the proposition that the Fourth Amendment protects one's privacy against "'arbitrary intrusions by the police'").

164. Thus, individuals have a right to refuse life-sustaining medical treatment. *See generally Cruzan*, 497 U.S. at 279 (noting that the Constitution grants a competent person the protected right to refuse lifesaving hydration and nutrition).

165. Refer to Part V *supra* (reviewing the potential for damage connected to corporal punishment).

166. *See* NEWELL, *supra* note 53, at 15.

167. For a thoughtful analysis of children's rights, see generally LAURA M. PURDY, IN THEIR BEST INTEREST? (1992).

168. *See, e.g.*, ALA. CODE § 32-5-64 (1989) (prohibiting minors under 16 years old to drive, unless the minor is enrolled in a state approved driver training program); GA. CODE ANN. § 40-5-24 (1997) (allowing 15-year-olds to apply for an instruction permit); LA. REV. STAT. ANN. § 416.1 (West Supp. 1997) (making it unlawful for anyone under 17 years of age to drive between the hours of 11:00 p.m. and 5:00 a.m. Monday through Thursday, and between midnight and 5:00 a.m. Friday through Sunday); N.H. REV. STAT. ANN. § 263:16 (1993) (forbidding persons under 18 years of age to obtain a driver's license, with few exceptions).

169. *See* U.S. CONST. amend. XXVI, § 1 (guaranteeing U.S. citizens over 18 years of age the right to vote).

170. Many state statutes prohibit the selling of firearms to persons under 18 years of age. *See, e.g.*, FLA. STAT. ANN. § 790.17 (West Supp. 1998); 720 ILL. COMP. STAT. § 5/24-3 (Michie Supp. 1997); MASS. GEN. LAWS ANN. ch. 140, § 131E (West 1991); N.J. STAT. ANN. § 2C:58-3(c)(4) (West 1995); OHIO REV. CODE ANN. § 2923.211 (Anderson 1996); R.I. GEN. LAWS § 11-47-35.2 (Supp. 1997).

171. *See* Bob Franklin, *Children's Political Rights, in* THE RIGHTS OF CHILDREN 24, 25-29 (Bob Franklin ed., 1986) [hereinafter RIGHTS OF CHILDREN II] (considering and rejecting paternalistic reasons for limiting children's rights); M.D.A. FREEMAN, THE RIGHTS AND WRONGS OF CHILDREN 1-2 (1983) (analyzing the reasons why children are not allowed to vote, which include incompetence, lack of experience, and irrationality).

172. *See* Franklin, *supra* note 171, at 27-28; FREEMAN, *supra* note 171, at 1-2.

simply not able to cast an informed ballot or even to cast a ballot at all.[173] With the right to be free of unwanted touchings, on the other hand, the child's immaturity, vulnerability, and lack of power all suggest the need for greater protection than for adults. It is precisely because children often cannot understand why they are being hit, because they are susceptible to serious injury, and because they cannot protect themselves that we should be especially reluctant to tolerate physical assaults of children.

From this perspective, the burden should lie with proponents of corporal punishment to demonstrate a real need for its use. If there is to be a role for corporal punishment, that role must be justified by some substantial benefit in order to overcome the presumption that people must not be assaulted without their consent.

We might try to justify corporal punishment on the ground that it is an important component of parental discipline, but that case has not yet been made. The evidence about the harms of corporal punishment may be open to question, but so is the evidence in support of a role for corporal punishment.[174] There are studies suggesting some benefit from spanking,[175] but, in the words of a leading proponent of corporal punishment, the data is "sketchy."[176] Moreover, the evidence supporting corporal punishment suggests a very limited role for its use, a role that is sharply at odds with what is permitted under state law.[177] The studies in support of corporal punishment suggest a benefit from spanking only when the child "is between ages 2 and 6," and the spanking "is limited to a maximum of two slaps to the buttocks with an open hand, . . . is used to supplement positive parenting, not to replace it, . . . [and] is used primarily to back up less aversive discipline responses, such as verbal correction or time-out."[178]

173. Refer to note 169 *supra*.

174. Refer to Part V *supra*.

175. *See generally* Anthony M. Graziano & Karen A. Namaste, *Parental Use of Physical Force in Child Discipline*, 5 J. INTERPERSONAL VIOLENCE 449, 456 (1990) (reporting findings from their study in which a majority of the respondents thought their use of spankings was usually "helpful" to "very helpful").

176. Larzelere, *supra* note 80, at 204.

177. *See* Murray A. Straus & Carrie L. Yodanis, *Corporal Punishment in Adolescence and Physical Assaults on Spouses in Later Life: What Accounts for the Link?*, 58 J. MARRIAGE & FAM. 825, 826 (1996) (observing that corporal punishment is legal in all 50 states).

178. Larzelere, *supra* note 80, at 204 (advocating these conditions as the distinctions between abusive and beneficial forms of corporal punishment); *see also* Robert E. Larzelere, *Response to Oosterhuis: Empirically Justified Uses of Spanking: Toward a Discriminating View of Corporal Punishment*, 21 J. PSYCHOL. & THEOLOGY 142, 142-43 (1993). *But See id.* at 143 (observing that the combination of noncorporal punishment and reasoning is as effective as corporal punishment together with reasoning); Murray A. Straus, *Corporal Punishment by Parents*, *in* DEBATING

Finally, even if there is some benefit from spanking, we have already seen that alternatives are available to ensure appropriate discipline of children that avoid the potential harms of corporal punishment.[179]

As I have observed, how we come down on corporal punishment depends very much on how we frame the issue. If we frame it as an issue of parental rights,[180] with the burden on opponents of corporal punishment to demonstrate its harm convincingly, then that burden has not been met. If we frame the issue as one of children's rights, with the burden on proponents of corporal punishment to demonstrate its benefits convincingly, then that burden has also not been met.

Each of the two ways to frame the issue are plausible. Why, then, have we chosen to frame the issue as one of parental rights?

VIII. EXPLAINING THE LEGAL FRAMEWORK

The choice of the parental perspective likely reflects two important features of our society. First, we undervalue children.[181] Second, we overvalue pain.[182]

Our society's undervaluation of children has been well documented. At one time, children were considered the chattel of their fathers.[183] Fathers were permitted to exploit the labor of their children by removing them from school and hiring them out to others.[184] They could also determine their children's marital

---

CHILDREN'S LIVES, *supra* note 6, at 197, 219-20 (responding to and disagreeing with Larzelere).

179. Refer to Part VI *supra*.

180. Refer to notes 133-42 *supra* and accompanying text (discussing two Supreme Court decisions affirming constitutional rights of parents to raise their children as they deem necessary). *See also* GARY B. MELTON, CHILD ADVOCACY 5-6 (1983) (reviewing court cases which traditionally have supported parental rights to raise their children as they deem necessary).

181. *See* Patricia Hewitt, *Foreword* to THE RIGHTS OF CHILDREN II, *supra* note 171, at vii, vii (describing the lack of attention given to children's rights).

182. Refer to notes 217-54 *infra* and accompanying text (analyzing society's notions about pain and suffering).

183. *See* Robert E. Shepherd, Jr., *The Abused Child and the Law, in* THE RIGHTS OF CHILDREN 174, 177 (Albert E. Wilkerson ed., 1973) (noting that under Roman law, fathers had absolute power over their children's lives, while old English law gave fathers the right to reasonably discipline their children); Barbara Bennett Woodhouse, *"Who Owns the Child?": Meyer and Pierce and the Child as Property*, 33 WM. & MARY L. REV. 995, 1036-50 (1992) (describing the numerous rights fathers maintained over their children).

184. *See* Bob Franklin, *Introduction* to RIGHTS OF CHILDREN II, *supra* note 171, at 10, 10 (detailing the young age at which children were sent out to serve apprenticeships); Woodhouse, *supra* note 183, at 1046 (explaining the paternal right to

partners.[185] There has been considerable change in how we treat children.[186] Child labor laws have been passed, all children can receive a public education through the twelfth grade, and children are allowed to reach adulthood and choose their spouses themselves.[187] Nevertheless, we still do not see children fully as people who are entitled to the same rights as others.[188]

Indeed, even with some of our most fundamental rights—the provisions of the Bill of Rights—children receive short shrift.[189] The courts have seriously curtailed children's First Amendment rights of expression, including the core right of freedom in political expression.[190] For example, the Supreme Court gives school officials broad latitude in regulating the political speech of their students.[191] In a case involving speech in student government, the Court wrote that "[t]he determination of what manner of speech in the classroom or in school assembly is inappropriate properly rests with the school board."[192] Similarly, the Sixth Circuit upheld

---

transfer children to others for child labor).

185. *See* Woodhouse, *supra* note 183, at 1046. Society's undervaluation of children has a long and disturbing pedigree. For a discussion of the treatment of children in Europe and North America from antiquity through the nineteenth century, see generally THE HISTORY OF CHILDHOOD (Lloyd deMause ed., 1974).

186. *See* FREEMAN, *supra* note 171, at 16 (commenting that children are freer today than they were a century ago).

187. An Iraqi-American man in Lincoln, Nebraska was recently charged with child abuse for marrying his 13-and 14-year-old daughters to Iraqi-Americans in the local community. *See* Don Terry, *Cultural Tradition and Law Collide in Middle America*, N.Y. TIMES, Dec. 2, 1996, at A10.

188. *See* Franklin, *supra* note 171, at 15 (contending that children are denied many rights which are considered by adults as essential for living a full, free life).

189. *See, e.g.*, Ingraham v. Wright, 430 U.S. 651, 669-71 (1977) (holding that the Eighth Amendment's ban against cruel and unusual punishment does not apply to school children who are paddled).

190. *See* S. Elizabeth Wilborn, *Teaching the New Three Rs—Repression, Rights, and Respect: A Primer of Student Speech Activities,* 37 B.C. L. REV. 119, 120 (1995) (observing that "core political speech is no more protected in the public schools than a dirty limerick scrawled in a bathroom stall").

191. *See* Bethel Sch. Dist. No. 403 v. Fraser, 478 U.S. 675, 685 (1986) (upholding the suspension of a student for using sexual innuendo in the context of political discourse).

192. *Id.* at 683. In *Bethel*, the student had nominated a friend for a student government position by describing the friend as "firm in his pants," as someone who goes to "the climax" for everyone, and as someone who does not "come between" his fellow students and what is best for the school. *See id.* at 687 (Brennan, J., concurring). In addition to the suspension, the school disqualified the student as a candidate for graduation speaker. *See id.* at 678. In contrast, the state is restricted in the way it limits the content of the political speech of adults unless it can show that the speech is likely to incite or produce "imminent lawless action," Brandenburg v. Ohio, 395 U.S. 444, 447 (1969), is "inherently likely to provoke violent reaction," Cohen v. California, 403 U.S. 15, 20 (1971), is defamatory, *see* New York Times Co. v. Sullivan, 376 U.S. 254 (1964), or is obscene, *see* Miller v. California, 413 U.S. 15 (1973).

the disqualification of a high school student's candidacy for his student council presidency because of a campaign speech, on the ground that school officials must have freedom to decide which pedagogical values to emphasize and how best to promote those values.[193]

The First Amendment right to freedom from censorship of the press has also been eviscerated for students.[194] In its leading case on the issue, the Supreme Court upheld a high school principal's decision to ban student newspaper articles discussing student pregnancy and the impact of parental divorce on students, employing the undemanding standard that the censorship be "reasonably related to legitimate pedagogical concerns."[195] Freedom of religious expression carries over weakly to children as well.[196] When the Supreme Court recognized the right of the Amish to stop the formal education of their children after the eighth grade in *Wisconsin v. Yoder*,[197] only Justice Douglas, in dissent, believed that if the children exhibited sufficient maturity

---

193. *See* Poling v. Murphy, 872 F.2d 757, 762 (6th Cir. 1989). In *Poling*, the student was disqualified because he mocked the stutter of an assistant principal. *See id.* at 759-60. The student said in his campaign speech that "[t]he administration plays tricks with your mind and they hope you won't notice. For example, why does Mr. Davidson stutter while he is on the intercom? He doesn't have a speech impediment." *Id.* at 759.

To be sure, the Supreme Court has also limited the freedom of public employees to speak about matters that are not of "public concern" in the workplace. *See* Connick v. Myers, 461 U.S. 138, 146-49 (1983) (upholding the dismissal of an assistant district attorney after she circulated a questionnaire challenging the office's transfer policy).

194. *See* Hazelwood Sch. Dist. v. Kuhlmeier, 484 U.S. 260, 274 (1988) (concluding that a principal acted reasonably in deleting two articles from a student newspaper).

195. *Id.* at 273. In contrast, censorship of newspapers outside the schools is highly disfavored. *See* Near v. Minnesota, 283 U.S. 697, 716 (1931) (observing that prior restraint of the press is limited to "exceptional cases," including obstructions of a war effort, incitements to acts of violence, and publication of obscenity).

Under the *Hazelwood* standard, a lower court upheld a school's one-day suspension of a student for wearing a T-shirt with the words "Drugs Suck!" imprinted on the front, noting that the school's action served the legitimate educational goal of "teaching students the boundaries of socially appropriate behavior." Broussard v. School Bd., 801 F. Supp. 1526, 1535 (E.D. Va. 1992). This standard leaves student speech with less protection than "a commercial for Hostess Twinkies." Wilborn, *supra* note 190, at 122. The government may not limit commercial speech unless its regulation "directly advances" a "substantial" government interest, and the regulation "is not more extensive than is necessary to serve that interest." Central Hudson Gas & Elec. Corp. v. Public Serv. Comm'n, 447 U.S. 557, 566 (1980) (declaring unconstitutional a New York law prohibiting electric utilities from advertising to promote the use of electricity).

196. *See* Wisconsin v. Yoder, 406 U.S. 205, 234 (1972) (holding that the Free Exercise Clause of the First Amendment, as made applicable to the States by the Fourteenth Amendment, prevents Wisconsin from requiring public education of Amish children until the age of 16).

197. 406 U.S. 205 (1972).

to choose for themselves, they should be heard as to their own preferences.[198]

The Supreme Court has gutted other provisions of the Bill of Rights when applying them to children, including the right to a trial by jury when children are prosecuted in juvenile court.[199] Due process rights for children being committed to mental institutions are virtually nonexistent—parents may commit their children without a hearing or any other kind of legal scrutiny, and children may not petition for discharge until they reach an adult age.[200] Fourth Amendment protections have been limited such that school officials can search the purses of children, even without suspicion of any violation of the law.[201] The official need only suspect a breach of a school rule.[202] Moreover, the Court has dispensed with the requirement of probable cause, requiring only a reasonable suspicion that the student violated a school rule.[203]

To the extent that we recognize the interests of children, we often do so not because we value children so much, but because we serve the interests of adults by recognizing children's interests.[204] A minor's right to an abortion ensures that fewer children will become dependent on the state for financial support. Rehabilitation of juvenile offenders spares society the costs of future dangerous criminals.[205] Child labor laws reduce the pool of available workers, thereby driving up the wages of adult employees.[206]

198. *See id.* at 243-46 (Douglas, J., dissenting in part) (discussing the contexts in which the Court has granted children constitutional protection over their actions, and the need for a child to be heard from when a decision on the child's educational future is being made).

199. *See* McKeiver v. Pennsylvania, 403 U.S. 528, 545 (1971) (determining that a trial by jury is not a constitutional requirement in a juvenile adjudication). To be sure, it would not be feasible for children to be tried by a jury of peers, but there are benefits to a jury trial other than being judged by one's peers (*e.g.*, the benefit of having multiple decision makers reach a consensus instead of a single decision maker deciding on his or her own).

200. *See* James W. Ellis, *Due Process for Adolescents*, *in* DEBATING CHILDREN'S LIVES, *supra* note 6, at 272, 278.

201. *See* New Jersey v. T. L. O., 469 U.S. 325, 345 (1985).

202. *See id.* at 341-42.

203. *See id.* at 341.

204. *See* Martha Minow, *Rights for the Next Generation: A Feminist Approach to Children's Rights*, 9 HARV. WOMEN'S L.J. 1, 5-6 (1986) (indicating that powerful social goals, such as control of crime and regulation of abortion, are the real focus of laws that affect children).

205. *See* Wendy Anton Fitzgerald, *Maturity, Difference, and Mystery: Children's Perspectives and the Law*, 36 ARIZ. L. REV. 11, 17 (1994) (emphasizing that rehabilitating juvenile offenders is actually geared towards utility for adults).

206. *See* Minow, *supra* note 204, at 6 (noting that child labor laws came about after organized labor realized their increased bargaining power with a smaller labor pool).

The undervaluation of children pervades not only the law but also other aspects of social policy. In a number of respects, we do not ensure a decent life for children.[207] For example, children are the most likely people to be living in poverty.[208] According to recent data, more than twenty percent of children live in poverty, a rate that is one-and-one-half to eight times higher than rates in other industrialized countries.[209] Furthermore, millions of children go hungry for some part of a typical month.[210] Inadequate education also plagues this country's youth.[211] We permit many of our urban public schools to be overrun by violence, to have overcrowded classrooms, to maintain low graduation rates, to suffer crumbling infrastructures, and to use inadequate textbooks and supplies.[212] In addition, we tolerate student achievement levels in mathematics and science that put American children behind children in most other industrialized countries in international comparisons.[213]

Because children are undervalued, we are insufficiently sensitive to potential harms to them. As we have seen, despite the fact that corporal punishment poses serious risks of psychological and behavioral problems for the child, the law gives parents considerable rein to employ corporal punishment as they see fit.[214]

The law's tolerance for corporal punishment reflects not only the undervaluation of children, but also an overvaluation of pain and other kinds of suffering. In the United States, pain is seen as

---

207. *See id.* at 6-8 (giving the examples of child poverty, neglect of foster care, child suicide, and nutrition deficiency).

208. *See* U.S. BUREAU OF THE CENSUS, U.S. DEP'T OF COMMERCE, STATISTICAL ABSTRACT OF THE UNITED STATES 1997, at 8 tbl.2, 15 tbl.14, 476 tbl.739 (117th ed. 1997) (indicating that 21.4% of children under 18 were living in poverty, whereas only 12.1% of adults were living in poverty).

209. *See* CHILDREN'S DEFENSE FUND, THE STATE OF AMERICA'S CHILDREN YEARBOOK 1996, at 2, 6 (1996).

210. *See id.* at 18.

211. *See generally* JONATHAN KOZOL, SAVAGE INEQUALITIES (1991) (documenting the educational shortcomings of cities such as St. Louis, New York, Chicago, San Antonio, Camden, and Washington, D.C.).

212. *See* Peter Applebome, *Enrollments Soar, Leaving Dilapidated School Buildings Bursting at the Frayed Seams*, N.Y. TIMES, Aug. 25, 1996, at 24 (discussing the fiscal strife that has led to inadequate educational facilities for America's youth); Jane Gross, *Los Angeles Schools: Hobbled and Hurting*, N.Y. TIMES, Feb. 16, 1993, at A1 (exposing the harsh realities of an education system that is not conducive to learning).

213. *See* OFFICE OF POLICY & PLANNING, U.S. DEP'T OF EDUCATION, INTERNATIONAL EDUCATION COMPARISONS 22-23 (1992); Chester E. Finn, Jr., *Why America Has the World's Dimmest Bright Kids*, WALL ST. J., Feb. 25, 1998, at A22 (describing data from a 1995 international comparison of students in mathematics and science in which U.S. twelfth-graders finished 19th out of 21 in mathematics and 16th out of 21 in science).

214. Refer to Parts IV & V *supra* (analyzing the relevant law).

playing an important role in character development, and this belief has deep roots in American culture.[215] Punishment—and fear of punishment—have traditionally played a strong role in Christianity, the dominant American religion.[216] Accordingly, punishment of children is often seen as consonant with Biblical teachings.[217] In seventeenth and eighteenth century America, Puritan thought was influential in child rearing, and strict discipline, including public whippings, was thought to ensure eternal salvation by promoting obedience to the child's parents.[218] This perspective had a strong influence on parenting in the United States through the early nineteenth century.[219] The role of punishment in Christianity is particularly striking in evangelical and fundamentalist Protestant theology in which there is an emphasis on humility and the breaking and conquering of a child's will.[220] Many Christian theologians believe that the infliction of pain fosters the important value of obedience to parent and God.[221] In their view, corporal punishment plays a substantial role in child rearing.[222]

The experience of other kinds of suffering has also been important in Christianity.[223] Jesus set a profound example with his

---

215. *See* Judge Leonard P. Edwards, *Corporal Punishment and the Legal System*, 36 SANTA CLARA L. REV. 983, 988-90 (1996) (demonstrating that corporal punishment has its roots in the Colonial period, and still remains an integral part of American family life).

216. *See* PHILIP GREVEN, SPARE THE CHILD 55-60 (1990) (expounding on external punishment as the root of fear and pain for over 200 years). Punishment and fear are important in other religions; I single out Christianity because of its dominant place in American society.

217. *See id.* at 46-54 (detailing the Biblical justifications of more than 2000 years of violence and assaults against children). At its extreme, the Bible calls for *capital* punishment of the disobedient child, *see Deuteronomy* 21:18-21, or the child who curses a parent, *see Exodus* 21:17.

218. *See* Toni M. Massaro, *Shame, Culture, and American Criminal Law*, 89 MICH. L. REV. 1880, 1915 (1991) (describing the harsh treatment of Puritan children, based on original sin, leading to an adult that is extremely sensitive to shame).

219. *See* Rex Forehand & Britton McKinney, *Historical Overview of Child Discipline in the United States: Implications for Mental Health Clinicians and Researchers*, 2 J. CHILD & FAM. STUD. 221, 222-23 (1993).

220. *See* GREVEN, *supra* note 216, at 65-72 (considering the breaking of a child's will as the focal point of Protestant child rearing).

221. *See id.* at 72-81 (stating that Christian advocates believe pain and punishment should begin early and continue until children learn obedience and submission to parental authority).

222. *See id.* This is not to say that corporal punishment is strongly endorsed throughout Protestant theology—it is common to see preferences for alternative methods of discipline, with corporal punishment being reserved for children who do not respond to the alternatives. *See id.* at 82-96 (reflecting on the moderate Christian belief in corporal punishment as a last resort).

223. *See* MARGARET PABST BATTIN, THE LEAST WORST DEATH 233-34 (1994) (interpreting Christian values on suffering as a means "to the beatific world beyond death").

concern for the suffering of others; he also set an important example with his own deep suffering, which culminated in his crucifixion and which he overcame in his resurrection.[224] Identification with Jesus therefore means not only avoiding behavior that would cause suffering for others and taking action to relieve the suffering of others; it also includes experiencing and overcoming suffering.[225] In this view, just as Jesus's suffering ultimately was for the salvation of others, so a person's suffering today can benefit others.[226] By volunteering for a task that involves suffering, for example, we can spare others from that task and the suffering it may cause.[227] Suffering can also be explained in terms of its role in facilitating moral or spiritual development.[228] By enduring a trial of suffering, the individual is able to achieve a higher stage of personal development.[229] To a large extent, finding value in suffering is a necessary corollary to the belief in the infinite goodness of God.[230] A good God, it is believed, would not subject innocent persons to senseless suffering.[231] Accordingly, there must be value in their suffering.[232]

The belief in a salutary role for pain and suffering is manifest in many other aspects of American society.[233] Consider for example the maxims "spare the rod and spoil the child"[234] and "no pain, no gain." These common phrases send the message that progress and self-improvement cannot be achieved without hardship,

---

224. *See* JOHN BOWKER, PROBLEMS OF SUFFERING IN RELIGIONS OF THE WORLD 46-47 (1970) (relating Jesus's suffering and concern for others' suffering to the foundation of the Christian response to suffering).

225. *See id.* at 72-73 (stating the Christian premises upon which suffering is based).

226. *See id.*

227. *See id.* at 74.

228. *See id.* at 45-46.

229. *See* Mary C. Rawlinson, *The Sense of Suffering*, 11 J. MED. & PHIL. 39, 59 (1986) (asserting that suffering is essential to personal growth and development).

230. *See id.* at 51, 53-54 (examining the tendency to search for value in human suffering to support the belief in a benevolent God).

231. *See id.* at 51 (relating Nietzsche's belief that suffering helps to restore the appropriate divine order and, thus, the "suffering of the innocents" is justified).

232. *See id.* at 54 (exploring the need for Christians to find value in suffering to sustain their belief in God's goodness).

233. *See* BATTIN, *supra* note 223, at 234 (discussing the ideal that personal growth results from physical and mental suffering).

234. While this phrase is attributed to the Bible, it actually comes from a poem, "Hudibras," by Samuel Butler, written in 1664. SAMUEL BUTLER, HUDIBRAS 143 (London, Frederick Warne & Co. 1880) (1664) ("Love is a boy, by poets styl'd, Then spare the rod, and spoil the child."). In Proverbs, it is written that "he who spares his rod hates his son, But he who loves him disciplines him diligently." *Proverbs* 13:24. For further discussion of this passage, see Carey, *supra* note 1, at 1005-06 (noting that the Bible says only that a loving parent should discipline his child, but observing that the Bible does not mention the *effect* of a lack of discipline).

that pain helps build character.[235] Similarly, our society tends to be critical of people who seek "easy outs" for the relief of pain and suffering or who try to achieve their goals with the assistance of drugs.[236] For example, we are critical of people who use medications like diazepam (Valium) to relieve anxiety instead of "toughing it out" or undertaking therapy to grapple with the psychological causes of their anxiety, and we are suspicious of people who try to lose weight with drugs that suppress appetite instead of through exercise and greater self-control at the dining table.[237] We are also critical of athletes who use drugs to enhance their performances, often citing the health risks from the drugs,[238] despite the fact that we encourage athletes to take much greater health risks as part of their participation in sports. Professional football players are not supposed to take anabolic (tissue-building) steroids for greater muscle bulk because of the potential harms from doing so, but they are expected to play a violent game in which players are routinely, often seriously, injured.[239]

---

235. *See* BATTIN, *supra* note 223, at 234 (noting that a variety of cultural truisms reflect a societal belief that physical or mental pain builds character).

236. *See id.* at 233-34 (revealing that Christians believe suicide is a cowardly attempt to avoid suffering).

237. *See* Robert Dunlop, *Physician's Perspective on Suffering, in* SUFFERING 143, 150 (Betty Rolling Ferrell ed., 1996) (asserting that physicians avoid recognizing and responding to suffering by "relabeling" patients as anxious rather than as actually suffering from pain). It turns out that obesity is probably better viewed as a chronic disease like diabetes or hypertension, for which long-term drug use is necessary for treatment, rather than simply as a failure of will power. *See* David E. Schteingart, *Phenylpropanolamine in the Management of Moderate Obesity, in* OBESITY 220, 220 (Theodore B. VanItallie & Artemis P. Simopoulos eds., 1995) (concluding that treatment for moderate obesity should include the use of drugs as well as diet, exercise, and behavioral therapy). To be sure, some drugs for obesity have caused serious side effects and have been pulled off the market. These instances demonstrate the need for safer drugs, not a need to abandon drug treatment for obesity altogether.

238. *See* Thomas H. Murray, *The Coercive Power of Drugs in Sports*, HASTINGS CENTER REP., Aug. 1983, at 24, 29-30 (advocating sanctions for the use of performance-enhancing drugs because they are harmful and lack any corresponding social benefit).

239. *See* Norman Fost, *Banning Drugs in Sports: A Skeptical View*, HASTINGS CENTER REP., Aug. 1986, at 5, 6 (reporting that the prohibition on steroid use due to health concerns is at odds with the reality that football itself is eminently more dangerous than the drugs). Indeed, football players are expected to play even when they have suffered previous injuries that cause substantial pain and put them at an increased risk for permanent injury. *See* Stewart E. Niles, Jr., & Roderick K. West, *In Whose Interest? The Return of the Injured Athlete to Competition*, 25 SPG Brief 8, 12 (1996) (commenting that athletes tend to play injured out of concern for their job security). Not surprisingly, many retired football players cannot run, or even walk, without limping. *See* Fost, *supra*, at 6 (noting that professional football players are frequently permanently disabled by the sport).

Opponents of drug use by athletes make other arguments, but those arguments also are not persuasive. For example, it is sometimes argued that drug use injects an unnatural element into sports, but we tolerate other unnatural additions, like the replacement of the bamboo pole with a fiberglass pole in pole-vaulting or the

Because pain is perceived as a virtue, it is not surprising that physicians have given insufficient attention to pain relief.[240] The debate over physician-assisted suicide has shed considerable light on the failure of the medical profession to treat pain aggressively in their patients, even if the patients are dying and addiction is not a concern.[241] In the SUPPORT study, a major study of medical care for seriously ill patients, family members reported that in fifty percent of cases of patients who died in the hospital and who were conscious before their death, the patients had complained of suffering moderate to severe pain at least half of the time during their last three days of life.[242]

The failure of physicians to treat pain properly is especially prevalent in the treatment of children.[243] The use of anesthesia for infants and children has lagged greatly behind its use in adults.[244] Indeed, as recently as 1992, researchers reported that infants undergoing cardiac surgery did better if they were deeply anesthetized rather than only lightly anesthetized as was the common practice.[245] To some extent, the withholding of anesthesia reflects fears of adverse effects of anesthetic drugs on fragile infants,

---

development of special nutritional aids in the laboratory, like Gatorade. *See id.* at 7. In the end, arguments against drug use often rest on the idea that drug use by athletes is at odds with the essence of athletic competition, but that is just another way of saying that we think it is wrong when we see people looking for painless ways to succeed.

240. *See* Betty Rolling Ferrell, *Humanizing the Experience of Pain and Illness*, *in* SUFFERING, *supra* note 237, at 211, 215 (questioning why the United States' advanced and highly technological healthcare system has historically and consistently undertreated patients' pain); DAVID B. MORRIS, THE CULTURE OF PAIN 21-22 (1991) (discussing the long tradition of physicians' neglecting pain). *See generally* Symposium, *Appropriate Management of Pain: Addressing the Clinical, Legal, and Regulatory Barriers*, 24 J.L. MED. & ETHICS 285 (1996) (discussing barriers to better pain control and efforts to overcome those barriers).

241. *See* David Orentlicher, *The Legalization of Physician-Assisted Suicide*, 38 B.C. L. REV. 443, 453-54, 459 (1997).

242. *See* The SUPPORT Principal Investigators, *A Controlled Trial to Improve Care for Seriously Ill Hospitalized Patients: The Study to Understand Prognoses and Preferences for Outcomes and Risks of Treatments (SUPPORT)*, 274 JAMA 1591, 1594 (1995).

243. *See* Mark C. Rogers, *Do the Right Thing: Pain Relief in Infants & Children*, 326 NEW ENG. J. MED. 55, 55 (1992) (observing that infants and children commonly receive inadequate pain relief).

244. *See id.* (urging that children should be provided the same pain-free intraoperative care that adult patients are provided).

245. *See* K.J.S. Anand & P.R. Hickey, *Halothane-Morphine Compared with High-Dose Sufentanil for Anesthesia and Postoperative Analgesia in Neonatal Cardiac Surgery*, 326 NEW ENG. J. MED. 1, 8 (1992) (warning that the results of the experiment were inconclusive, but revealing that the results showed that neonates might benefit from deeper anesthesia during cardiac surgery).

but it also reflects insensitivity to the pain of the children.[246] In an editorial accompanying the study of anesthesia of infants during cardiac surgery, the author observed that infants and children were still often receiving insufficient or even no treatment for pain during minor surgical procedures and after major surgical procedures, practices that would not be tolerated for adults.[247] Insensitivity to pain in infants persists.[248] Only last year, researchers reported on a new approach for preventing pain during circumcision of newborn boys,[249] and an accompanying editorial noted that circumcision was still being performed without analgesia in the usual case.[250] While it is commonly believed that there is no harm to the infant from the pain of circumcision, there is evidence of alterations in sleeping, feeding, and crying patterns as well as increased sensitivity to painful experiences for several months after circumcision.[251]

To be sure, there has been a strong push by the medical profession for more aggressive treatment of pain, even to the point of sedating dying patients into unconsciousness,[252] and inadequate

---

246. *See* Rogers, *supra* note 243, at 56 (remarking that doctors are more concerned with the potential adverse effects of pain-relieving drugs on children than they are about the adverse effects of exposing the children to pain unnecessarily).

247. *See id.* at 56 (reporting that minor surgical procedures, such as bone marrow aspiration, are routinely performed on children with little or no pain medication even though the same is not true for adult patients).

248. *See id.* at 55-56 (asserting that it is common practice to perform minor and major surgical procedures on infants and children without the benefit of adequate anesthesia or other pain relief).

249. *See* Anna Taddio et al., *Efficacy and Safety of Lidocaine-Prilocaine Cream for Pain During Circumcision,* 336 NEW ENG. J. MED. 1197, 1200 (1997) (reporting that the use of lidocaine-prilocaine cream safely and efficiently reduces the pain of circumcision and recommending that doctors use the cream during such a painful surgical procedure).

250. *See* Thomas E. Wiswell, *Circumcision Circumspection,* 336 NEW ENG. J. MED. 1244, 1244 (1997) (noting that infants undergoing circumcision are not usually given analgesics to ease the pain of the procedure because it is erroneously believed that infants do not feel, localize, or remember pain); *see also* Janice Lander et al., *Comparison of Ring Block, Dorsal Penile Nerve Block, and Topical Anesthesia for Neonatal Circumcision: A Randomized, Controlled Trial,* 278 JAMA 2157, 2157 (1997) (reporting that in some areas, 64% to 96% of neonatal circumcisions are done without anesthesia).

251. *See* Taddio et al., *supra* note 249, at 1201 (recounting that physicians do not utilize analgesics during neonatal circumcision because they believe the pain associated with the procedure is "inconsequential," but noting, however, that untreated pain from circumcision has been linked to abnormal sleeping, feeding, and crying patterns and to increased pain during routine vaccinations at 4 to 6 months of age).

252. *See* Nathan I. Cherny & Russell K. Portenoy, *Sedation in the Management of Refractory Symptoms: Guidelines for Evaluation and Treatment,* J. PALLIATIVE CARE, Summer 1994, at 31, 31 (describing the dying patient's desire for deep sedation to alleviate the intolerable pain associated with terminal cancer notwithstanding the concomitant decrease in interactional awareness).

relief of pain reflects a number of concerns, including fears of legal liability.

Nevertheless, an important factor in the failure to treat pain properly is a sense among many physicians that suffering has value and that patients and their families benefit from having endured a trial of pain.[253] Consider, for example, the following description of the death of a young child from a brain disease by Dr. Ira Byock, a physician who is a prominent proponent and practitioner of hospice care:

> Michael's dying formed a crucible in which people were purified and forever altered. As he lay dying, his family was transformed from a collection of related people to a process. . . . And those of us on the periphery of the family circle contributed to transforming "community" into a coordinated process of committed caring.
>
> One of the early lessons of Michael's dying had to do with the nature of tragedy. At first glance, his dying appeared to be a horrible tragedy: A little boy with no childhood or future was suffering and dying from something totally beyond anyone's control. But his own and his family's suffering and devastation shrank compared with the joy and growth he engendered.[254]

In discussing the death of another patient, a young man with AIDS, Dr. Byock addresses the concern about the family's burdens in taking care of a dying patient:

> Sometimes, more than dying, people dread becoming dependent on caregivers and making them feel responsible for both financial and physical needs as well as the inevitable emotional demands. . . .
>
> However, to speak of this time solely as a "burden" misrepresents the nature of the experience. Although a patient may feel that this care and attention is unduly taxing or unpleasant, caregivers frequently tell me that they regard this time as precious. The burden is rarely too heavy. Far more often, they say it feels like a sacred responsibility that they want to shoulder—that they *need* to shoulder. . . . Allowing a spouse or grown child to care for one becomes a final gift from the person dying.[255]

253. *Cf.* Dunlop, *supra* note 237, at 150-51 (maintaining that physicians inadequately treat their patients' pain because they lack first-hand experience with suffering and training in pain control is minimal).

254. IRA BYOCK, DYING WELL 175 (1997).

255. *Id.* at 159-60. While there is some truth to what Dr. Byock writes, he makes a small part of the picture into a very big part. Nessa Coyle, a supportive care

As mentioned earlier, this tendency by Dr. Byock to glorify the experience of suffering has strong religious roots.[256] In the words of a Catholic priest active in the healing ministry:

> The purpose of suffering is growth. . . . All suffering experiences can be growth experiences. Suffering often forces us to let go of situations, jobs, or people. It also opens the door to receiving a lot more as well. Adversity builds character. Crisis gives human beings a proof of their abilities that they probably wouldn't even try to use unless they were forced to. . . .
>
> Suffering changes our perspective on life. . . Suffering puts important things in focus. . . . When you're faced with accepting some type of permanent change that you can't avoid—even death—you start paying attention to the things that really are important in life. . . .
>
> People who are suffering become much more sensitive, much more caring, and much more aware. Maybe it's the depth of pain that makes a person much more sensitive to others. When you are suffering, you empathize with everybody's suffering in the world.[257]

---

nurse at the Memorial Sloan-Kettering Cancer Center in New York City, provides a more realistic appraisal of the family's burden. In reporting typical comments by family members, she writes:

> Families become exhausted by attempting to meet both the needs of the patient and the needs of the family as a whole. These statements reflect the resultant irritability and stress.
>
> > Everything's such a production. Everything takes so long. To eat, to dress, everything.
> >
> > . . .
> >
> > Others look forward to the weekend[s], but I dread them.
> >
> > . . .
> >
> > This is all such a burden on me. I can't sleep, can't eat. I feel I'm cracking up. I can't cope. I'm the one who is here all the time. Had to do the income tax, have to dash out to shop and dash home. His brothers stay for a while and then say good-bye, good luck. My niece has her own life to lead. Everyone is getting tired. They have their own lives to lead.

Nessa Coyle, *Suffering in the First Person, in* SUFFERING, *supra* note 237, at 29, 44.

256. Refer to notes 217-32 *supra* and accompanying text (exploring the religious roots of the search for value in human suffering). *See also* Father Robert Smith, *Theological Perspectives, in* SUFFERING, *supra* note 237, at 159, 165-66 (observing that the "mystery of suffering" is a common theme in religious scriptures and literature).

257. Edward B. Pritchard, *"What Am I Learning from This Suffering?", in* WHEN THE WORST THAT CAN HAPPEN ALREADY HAS 78, 79-80 (Dennis Wholey ed., 1992).

I do not disagree that some people gain much from suffering. My concern begins when people generalize such gains to other persons who are suffering or when people cite the benefits from suffering as arguments against efforts to diminish suffering (*e.g.*, as arguments against proposals to reduce corporal punishment of chil-

Because we overvalue pain and suffering, we are inclined to see greater virtue in corporal punishment than is justified by its actual benefits and harms. Indeed, we end up mistakenly viewing the pain caused by spanking as salutary to a child's social development rather than more appropriately as harmful to the child's psychological and behavioral well-being.

IX. CONCLUSION

If, as I have argued, we view corporal punishment from the perspective of parents rather than that of children because we undervalue children and overvalue pain, it follows that we need to reconsider our choice of perspective. By shifting to the child's perspective and rejecting *any* use of corporal punishment—even to the point of prohibiting corporal punishment as in Scandinavia and Austria—we would bring social policy more in line with the appropriate valuations of children and pain. We would also bring about at least two important social benefits. First, by reducing the use of corporal punishment, we would enhance the quality of childhood discipline. With the substitution of alternative means of discipline for corporal punishment, parents would be relying on disciplinary methods that appear to be more effective and less harmful to children. Second, shifting to the child's perspective would send an important message about the necessity of ending violence against children. It is difficult for society to send a clear message against the use of physical violence when it sanctions corporal punishment of children.

---

dren or to permit assisted suicide for dying patients).

MEDICAL DECISION MAKING FOR AND BY CHILDREN: TENSIONS BETWEEN PARENT, STATE, AND CHILD†

*Walter Wadlington**

The conflict between parental desire to maintain control over the upbringing of their children and the government's interest in ensuring that various aspects of children's lives are not subject to unfettered discretion and parental whim arises frequently within the context of education, religion, or any other of a broad host of social issues. This conflict is seldom more dramatically presented, however, than in situations where parents wish to withhold, for whatever reason, potentially life-saving medical procedures from their children. In this article, originally presented as a David C. Baum Memorial Lecture at the University of Illinois College of Law, Professor Walter Wadlington surveys the history of ever-increasing legislative and judicial intervention in parental choice of their child's medical treatment. He further assesses the complex constitutional issues with which courts are presented when parental justification for declining life-saving treatment stems from the tenets of the parents' religion. Professor Wadlington concludes that the current societal debate over the proper scope of "children's rights" in many respects mirrors the often contradictory responses of legislatures and courts to parental refusal of medical treatment for their children. The conflict between parental autonomy and governmental protection of children does not promise to be easily resolved.

Debate over state involvement in decision making for medical treatment of minors has spanned more than a century, but many issues remain unresolved, and new issues continue to surface. The most publicized and controversial area involves a state's attempts to overrule parents who refuse consent to special medical procedures for de-

---

† *This article was originally presented on September 26, 1991, as the first 1991-92 lecture of the David C. Baum Memorial Lectures on Civil Liberties and Civil Rights at the University of Illinois College of Law.*

* *James Madison Professor of Law, University of Virginia. A.B. Duke University, 1951; LL.B. Tulane University, 1954.*

fective newborns.[1] This lecture will focus on an area of even greater importance: the state's role in ensuring that necessary medical care is not withheld from children beyond the neonatal period because of parental refusal to give consent to specific medical procedures necessary to attain or maintain a minimal level of care.

Part of the recent increase in court challenges regarding medical care for minors may be attributed to a general societal movement toward increased participation in medical decision making by patients or their legal representatives. This shift in societal values helps explain the development of a negligence-based doctrine of informed consent which imposes a duty on physicians to offer patients information about risks and alternatives so that the patient can participate effectively in the decision process.[2] Public awareness and debate about patients' rights increased following extensive media coverage of the *Cruzan v. Director, Missouri Department of Health*[3] decision and the Supreme Court's discussion of the possible constitutional sources of an individual's right to choose the course of treatment or care when suffering from a terminal illness. Although these parallel developments are significant, the new cycle of litigation involving children reflects an additional pattern of greater state involvement in protecting children, an intervention which can pose a significant intrusion into family life. In response to this increased governmental intrusion, many litigants seek to drape with a constitutional mantle their challenges to state intervention in the parental decision making process.

Professor Homer Clark explained in an earlier lecture in this series that "there is nothing in the Constitution about children, minors or infants, or parents for that matter."[4] Despite the lack of any explicit constitutional mention of parents and children, however, a movement toward significant "constitutionalization" of family law dates from the U.S. Supreme Court's mid-1960s decisions in *Griswold v. Connecticut*[5] and *Loving v. Virginia*,[6] which addressed issues of reproductive rights, marital privacy, and the validity of state restrictions on interracial marriage. Before *Griswold* and *Loving*, domestic relations had been the major remaining bastion of state's rights. Only after these cases did a sizeable body of litigation seeking to apply the

1. State intervention in cases involving defective neonates presents special problems dealing with issues of possible discrimination based on disability. In recent years specific government regulations have attempted to address these problems, but continue to undergo court challenges and legislative modification. *See, e.g.*, LA. REV. STAT. ANN. § 40:1299.36.1 (West 1992), *repealed by* 1991 La. Acts 235; Bowen v. American Hosp. Ass'n, 476 U.S. 610 (1986); 42 U.S.C.A § 5102 (West 1983); American Academy of Pediatrics v. Heckler, 561 F. Supp. 395 (D.D.C. 1983).

2. *See* Walter Wadlington, *Breaking the Silence of Doctor and Patient*, 93 YALE L. J. 1640 (1984) (reviewing JAY KATZ, THE SILENT WORLD OF DOCTOR AND PATIENT (1984)).

3. 497 U.S. 261 (1990).

4. Homer H. Clark, Jr., *Children and the Constitution*, 1992 U. ILL. L. REV. 1, 1.

5. 381 U.S. 479 (1965).

6. 388 U.S. 1 (1967).

Fourteenth Amendment to allegedly arbitrary state regulation in the domestic relations sphere begin to accumulate. The amount of litigation that followed *Griswold* and *Loving* was actually not as great as many commentators had anticipated, however, because the decisions induced states to reexamine and revise or eliminate some constitutionally vulnerable state law provisions, no doubt in many cases obviating the need for judicial challenges.

Two cases decided long before the 1960s loom large when considering a state's ability to override a parent's decision regarding a minor's health, even though these cases did not directly involve medical care. In 1923, the U.S. Supreme Court in *Meyer v. Nebraska*[7] invalidated a state law, enacted during World War I when anti-German feelings were strong, which banned the teaching of foreign languages in public schools. The Court provided a "laundry list" of liberties protected by the Fourteenth Amendment, including a right to marry and a right to "establish a home and bring up children."[8] These rights, according to *Meyer*, "may not be interfered with, under the guise of protecting the public interest, by legislative action which is arbitrary or without reasonable relation to some purpose within the competency of the State to effect."[9] With regard to the particular statute before them, the Court added that "there seems no adequate foundation for the suggestion that the purpose was to protect the child's health by limiting his mental activities."[10]

Destined to become even more significant was a 1944 decision, *Prince v. Massachusetts*,[11] in which the Supreme Court upheld the conviction of a parent for permitting a child to sell religious tracts on the streets in violation of Massachusetts's child labor law. Rejecting arguments that the statute invalidly encroached on the First Amendment right to religious freedom, the court incorporated into its opinion a brief statement that has since been widely used, often with little or no detailed explanation,[12] in response to religious objections against state involvement in parental decision making about children's medical care. After noting that "[w]hat may be wholly permissible for adults . . . may not be so for children, either with or without their parents' presence,"[13] the Court added:

> Parents may be free to become martyrs themselves. But it does not follow that they are free, in identical circumstances, to make martyrs of their children before they have reached the age of full

7. 262 U.S. 390 (1923).
8. *Id.* at 399.
9. *Id.* at 399-400. *Meyer*'s statement regarding marriage was subsequently used as a tenuous basis for asserting that states were subject to some constitutional limitations when regulating marriage, at least before the decision in Loving v. Virginia, 388 U.S. 1 (1967).
10. *Meyer*, 262 U.S. at 403.
11. 321 U.S. 158 (1944).
12. *See infra* text accompanying note 31.
13. *Prince*, 321 U.S. at 169.

and legal discretion when they can make that choice for themselves.[14]

Pithy quotes of this sort in the bodies of judicial opinions, as well as verbal time bombs tucked into footnotes,[15] have had great impact on domestic relations jurisprudence. This perhaps reflects the paucity of deeply reasoned cases in the field.[16]

I. A Step Back in Time

A good starting point for an historical review of how the law on medical decision making for children developed is the case of Tony Tuttendario, which reached a Pennsylvania court in 1912.[17] Tony, age seven, suffered from rickets which had caused his legs to be badly misshapen. Medical testimony indicated that an operation could remedy the problem, but that without it Tony probably would be "a cripple all his life and unable to provide for himself."[18] Despite that dire prospect, his parents refused to consent to the operation. This refusal presented a dilemma to Tony's doctors. Because a minor is legally incompetent to consent to medical care or enter into contracts, a parent, guardian or other legally authorized person must give consent to any medical procedure. Otherwise, a physician performing nonemergency surgery risks a tort action for battery based on an unauthorized violation of a protected bodily interest. Because of this potential liability, judicial approval or designation of a new legal representative to give consent has long been sought in such cases.[19]

After complaints from school authorities, the Society for the Prevention of Cruelty to Children[20] asked that Tony be committed to them in order to receive proper medical treatment. The court reviewed existing legislation, some of it dating from 1860, which attempted to protect children whose lives or health were endangered, including an 1893 Act specifically authorizing judicial commitment of such minors to charitable societies. The court next stated the question it considered to be before it:

14. *Id.* at 170.

15. Perhaps the most celebrated example of this in domestic relations cases is footnote nine in Stanley v. Illinois, 405 U.S. 645, 657 n.9 (1972), which dealt with the provision of notice to fathers of illegitimate children before termination of paternal rights through adoption.

16. Such a shortage may reflect not only the relatively small number of decisions on the issue before the 1960s, but what might be euphemistically described as a low level of sensitivity to the precedential potential at the initial stages of building up a constitutional jurisprudence of family law.

17. *In re* Tuttendario, 21 Pa. D. 561 (Q.S. Phila. 1912).

18. *Id.* at 561.

19. For more general discussion, see Walter Wadlington, *Consent to Medical Care for Minors: The Legal Framework*, *in* Children's Competence to Consent 57, 58 (Gary B. Melton et al. eds., 1983).

20. The SPCC was a benevolent society established in the late 1800s, a few years after the Society for Prevention of Cruelty to Animals was founded.

> We are . . . asked to supersede the child's natural guardians on the sole ground that their judgement is impaired by natural love and affection, and that we should substitute for them a humane society whose judgment is untainted by such emotions.[21]

The court concluded:

> We see no warrant in the statutes for granting this request. We have not yet adopted as a public policy the Spartan rule that children belong, not to their parents, but to the state. . . . Even if the law had advanced so far as to consider defective judgment of parents in a critical case a good reason for depriving them of their guardianship, we would not be prepared to say that a clear case of defective judgment has been here made out. The science of medicine and surgery, notwithstanding its enormous advances, has not yet been able to insure an absolutely correct diagnosis in all cases, and still less an absolutely correct prognosis. There is always a residuum of the unknown, and it is this unknown residuum which scientists, by a necessary law for the development of science, disregard, but which parents, in their natural love for their children, regard with apprehension and terror.[22]

One important consideration underlying the court's refusal to displace the natural parents from their decisional role was that the child's present condition involved "no danger to its life." The court also seemed to believe that under existing law it could otherwise intervene only on the ground of cruelty.[23]

Given the state of medicine in 1912, the decision may have been appropriate from a practical standpoint. But, in following the progression of legal responses in subsequent cases, we should remember that the *Tuttendario* court made a forceful statement in favor of parental decision making (almost a cry of "parents *uber alles*"), laying the groundwork for what later was dubbed a "life threatening exception" which endured for half a century.

The typical cases invoking the "life threatening exception" involved requests for surgical intervention to obviate almost certain death for a minor whose parents refused consent to a blood transfusion. These cases posed special legal concerns because parental objections typically were based on religious beliefs.[24] Because of the

21. *Tuttendario*, 21 Pa. D. at 563.

22. *Id.*

23. *Id.*

24. Genesis 9:4 ("I give you everything, with this exception: you must not eat flesh with life, that is to say blood, in it."); Leviticus 17:14 ("For the life of all flesh is its blood, and I have said to the sons of Israel: You must not eat the blood of any flesh, for the life of all flesh is in its blood, and anyone who eats it shall be outlawed from his people."); and Acts 15:19-20 (James's speech to the Pharisees at Jerusalem) ("I rule, then, that instead of making things more difficult for pagans who turn to God, we send them a letter telling them merely to abstain from anything polluted by idols, from fornication, from the meat of strangled animals and from blood.") are the most frequently cited sources of Biblical support for religious objections to transfusion of whole blood.

urgency in such situations, operations were often performed before appeals could be heard. Although the cases were therefore technically moot, appellate courts were sufficiently concerned with providing guidelines for the future that appeals were heard under exceptions to the mootness doctrine.[25]

In 1952, the Illinois Supreme Court[26] upheld such an intervention for an eight-day-old girl with erythroblastosis after two physicians testified that the child would certainly die without transfusions. A third physician said that although there was a slim chance the child might live, she would suffer permanent mental impairment without the transfusion. The court upheld the constitutionality of the statute permitting intervention, as well as the trial judge's decision in applying it. The determination that the statute was constitutional was important because by the early 1950s the requirements and procedures for state intervention to protect children had been more completely specified in legislation. Although courts in medical intervention cases were (and still are) wont to explain that they are acting for the state in the role of *parens patriae*, intervention is usually specifically predicated on a child protection statute. Under these statutes, the sanctions or remedies available to the court may range from appointing a guardian with limited powers to removing a child from parents temporarily, or even permanently.

In determining that the parents' First Amendment rights were not violated, the Illinois Supreme Court relied heavily on both the U.S. Supreme Court's 1878 *Reynolds*[27] decision, which upheld the bigamy conviction of a man who asserted that his acts were in furtherance of his religious beliefs, and, not surprisingly, the 1944 *Prince* decision.[28] Similar cases reaching other state supreme courts around

25. As the Illinois Supreme Court explained in People *ex rel.* Wallace v. Labrenz, 411 Ill. 618, 622-23, 104 N.E.2d 769 (Ill. 1952) (citations omitted):

> [W]hen the issue presented is of substantial public interest, a well-recognized exception exists to the general rule that a case which has become moot will be dismissed upon appeal. Among the criteria considered in determining the existence of the requisite degree of public interest are the public or private nature of the question presented, the desirability of an authoritative determination for the future guidance of public officers, and the likelihood of future recurrence of the question.
>
> Applying these criteria, we find that the present case falls within that highly sensitive area in which governmental action comes into contact with the religious beliefs of individual citizens. Both the construction of the statute under which the trial court acted and its validity are challenged. In situations like this one, public authorities must act promptly if their action is to be effective, and although the precise limits of authorized conduct cannot be fixed in advance, no greater uncertainty should exist than the nature of the problems makes inevitable. In addition, the very urgency which presses for prompt action by public officials makes it probable that any similar case arising in the future will likewise become moot by ordinary standards before it can be determined by this court. For these reasons the case should not be dismissed as moot.

26. *Id.*

27. Reynolds v. United States, 98 U.S. 145 (1878).

28. The other major authorities cited by the Illinois Supreme Court, albeit with minimal explanation, were Meyer v. Nebraska, 262 U.S. 390 (1923), West Virginia Board of Education v. Barnette, 319 U.S. 624 (1943), and Jacobson v. Massachusetts, 197 U.S. 11 (1905). *Meyer* and

this time met with like results.[29] Sixteen years later a three-judge federal court, in a case initiated under 42 U.S.C.A. § 1983, upheld the constitutionality of a Washington state law construed to authorize judges to provide consent for a minor's necessary blood transfusions over a parent's refusal.[30] The U.S. Supreme Court upheld the decision in a one- sentence opinion, citing *Prince v. Massachusetts*.[31]

Two cases during this period illustrate the outer limits of the scope of the "life threatening exception." In 1942, an adult sibling of an eleven-year-old complained to a Washington juvenile court that her younger sister was not receiving adequate medical care.[32] The child was born with a congenitally oversized arm that was functionally useless and posed increasing danger to her system, although there was no suggestion that it would cause imminent death. Physicians recommended amputation, and there was evidence that the child agreed to such a procedure. Her mother refused,[33] explaining that she had no religious objection but "thought there was 'too much of a chance on [the daughter's] life.' "[34] The Supreme Court of Washington declined to overrule the parental objection, holding that there was no basis for intervention unless the refusing parent was found unfit. The court explained:

> At the common law no court had jurisdiction, there is no authority granted by statute or constitution to any court, nor has a court of equity inherent power, to deprive a natural guardian of custody and control of his or her minor child in the absence of a determination, after a hearing that such parent is unfit to have custody of the child.[35]

The opinion discloses a very limited view of a court's *parens patriae* powers: in cases involving child protection, courts may not intervene

Barnette dealt with the rights of parents to care for and train their children, while *Jacobson* upheld the constitutionality of a compulsory vaccination ordinance. *Jacobson* seems strained as an authority because it refers to protecting the *public* health under the police power, rather than protecting the health of a specific individual. On the other hand, there was not much else in the way of U.S. Supreme Court decisions available for the Illinois court to cite.

29. *See, e.g.*, State v. Perricone, 181 A.2d 751 (N.J. 1962).

30. Jehovah's Witnesses v. King County Hosp. Unit No. 1, 278 F. Supp. 488 (W.D. Wash. 1967).

31. Jehovah's Witnesses v. King County Hosp. Unit No. 1, 390 U.S. 598 (1968). The Court simply stated that "[t]he judgment is affirmed," relying without comment on its previous decision in Prince v. Massachusetts, 321 U.S. 158 (1944). Justice Douglas and Justice Harlan noted probable jurisdiction and would have set the case for oral argument.

32. *In re* Hudson, 126 P.2d 765 (Wash. 1942).

33. The child lived with her mother and her invalid father. According to the court, the father,

> inappreciative of his paternal right of guardianship and unmindful of the obligation imposed upon him by virtue of that sacred right, bowed to the will of his wife and testified, in effect, that while he would not of his own volition approve amputation of his child's left arm, he would like to shirk his responsibility as a father and leave the entire matter to the court.

Id. at 768.

34. *Id.*

35. *Id.* at 783.

independent of some clear statutory mechanism authorizing intervention. I doubt that this view is widely prevalent among judges today. Even if a court holds such a view, however, there is now ample authority for judicial intervention in cases involving medical care for children under child protection, neglect, or abuse statutes.

In another boundary-defining case, *In re Seiferth*,[36] the New York Court of Appeals refused to authorize a state agency to intervene[37] and overrule a father's refusal to consent to corrective surgery for his fourteen-year-old son's cleft palate and harelip.[38] The only risk of mortality in the surgical procedure, the court noted, was a possible adverse reaction to anesthesia. The father professed belief "in mental healing by letting 'the forces of the universe work on the body'" although he regarded these beliefs more as an expression of his particular philosophy than as part of any organized religion. Torn by its concern with the need for cooperation by both child and parent, the court refused to intervene. In a dissenting opinion, Judge Fuld noted that the Children's Court Act defined a neglected child as one "whose parent, guardian or custodian neglects or refuses, when able to do so, to provide necessary medical, surgical, institutional or hospital care for such child," and expressed the view that the court had a duty to uphold in the case before it.[39]

By the late 1950s, the rules regulating state intervention may have seemed fairly clear, at least to the extent that rules can be discerned from judicial opinions. At this time, however, courts began to see major increases in constitutional litigation contesting state regulation of the family, as well as an ensuing spate of legislative reform. Although much of the latter focused on areas such as divorce and marital property, the scheme for child protection was also expanded. In retrospect, further disputes over medical neglect should have seemed almost inevitable.

36. 127 N.E.2d 820 (N.Y. 1955).

37. The agency sought to have custody transferred to the local Commissioner of Social Welfare for the specific purpose of consenting to whatever medical, surgical, and dental services might be deemed necessary to remedy the problem. *Id.* at 821.

38. The court explained that the condition called for three operations followed by an extended period of concentrated speech therapy. *Seiferth*, 127 N.E.2d at 821.

39. Judge Fuld further explained that:

> Neither by statute nor decision is the child's consent necessary or material, and we should not permit his refusal to agree, his failure to co-operate, to ruin his life and any chance for a normal, happy existence; normalcy and happiness, difficult of attainment under the most propitious conditions, will unquestionably be impossible if the disfigurement is not remedied.

Id. at 824 (Fuld, J., dissenting).

II. A Period of Transition

A. *Key Transitional Cases*

Two cases in the early 1970s reflect both a change in judicial attitudes and the expansion of state activity to protect children in situations that might fit within a category soon to be labeled "medical neglect." The first, *In re Sampson*,[40] went to trial in 1970 and reached the New York Court of Appeals the following year.[41] A County Health Commissioner instituted a neglect petition because the mother of Kevin Sampson, a fifteen-year-old boy with neurofibromatosis (now popularly known as "elephant man's disease"), would not consent to surgical excision of a bag-like, benign growth that had caused one side of Kevin's face to be twice the size of the other. Kevin was functionally illiterate, in large part because he had left school at an early age in response to taunts from his peers. It is fraught with irony that Kevin had to reach this advanced stage of physical deformity before the public finally took an interest in him, seemingly motivated as much by the prospect of being visually offended by Kevin's presence as by concern about his health. Physicians knew that Kevin's condition could not be cured, but surgery offered at least temporary aid in improving his grotesque appearance. Kevin's mother did not object to the operation, but she refused to consent to a blood transfusion on religious grounds. Without her consent, the operation could not be performed.[42]

The Family Court judge decided that intervention to overrule the mother's consent was both permissible and appropriate. Although the judge recognized that his decision to authorize surgical intervention over the mother's objection might be difficult to distinguish from the earlier decision of the New York Court of Appeals in *Seiferth*, he stated that:

> [T]his court's authority to deal with the abused, neglected or physically handicapped child is not limited to "drastic situations" or to those which constitute a "present emergency", . . . the Court has a "wide discretion" to order medical or surgical care and treatment for an infant even over parental objection, if in the Court's judgment the health, safety or welfare of the child requires it.[43]

The court explained that in the particular case

40. 317 N.Y.S.2d 641 (1970).

41. *In re* Sampson, 278 N.E.2d 918 (N.Y. 1972).

42. The case provides an early illustration of the sensitivity of members of the medical community to such problems. The physicians first tried to see if the surgery could be performed without requiring a blood transfusion, in such a fashion that only plasma extenders would be used to remedy blood loss during surgery. *Sampson*, 317 N.Y.S.2d at 645. This option was not feasible because the child was so small. *Id.* at 655.

43. *Id.* at 654.

> if this court is to meet its responsibilities to this boy it can neither shift the responsibility for the ultimate decision onto his shoulders nor can it permit his mother's religious beliefs to stand in the way of attaining through corrective surgery whatever chance he may have for a normal, happy existence, which . . . is difficult of attainment under the most propitious circumstances, but will unquestionably be impossible if the disfigurement is not corrected.[44]

The *Sampson* case, which passed through each level of the New York court system without a dissenting vote,[45] constituted a dramatic breakaway from previous rigid application of the "life threatening" exception. In *Sampson*, only the operation, not the underlying medical condition, could fairly be considered to pose a significant threat to the child's life. Furthermore, the best possible outcome from any surgical procedure would only partially remedy the condition. One response to *Sampson* might be to realize that the particular disease involved in the case raised special factual issues (perhaps almost as special as those in *Yoder*[46]), but it nevertheless seems clear that one can read *Sampson* as recognizing that quality of life, as distinct from physical survival, can serve as a criterion for intervention in at least some instances.

The Family Court was careful to explain that it used the word *neglected* in its limited legal sense within the meaning of the Family Court Act, but that this "in no way imports a finding that the mother failed in her duty to the child in any other respect."[47] This statement exemplifies how courts began to distinguish many instances of medical neglect by characterizing the operative conduct as an error in judgement which did not carry the moral opprobrium often associated with other types of neglect.

The second of the key transitional decisions was *In re Green*,[48] a latter-day reworking of *Tuttendario* that also took place in Pennsylvania. Ricky Green, a fifteen-year-old boy suffering from paralytic

44. *Id.* at 657.

45. *In re* Sampson, 317 N.Y.S.2d 641 (1970), *aff'd per curiam*, 278 N.E.2d 918 (1972).

46. In Wisconsin v. Yoder, 406 U.S. 205 (1971), the U.S. Supreme Court upheld the Wisconsin Supreme Court's decision that the First and Fourteenth Amendments prevented the state from compelling Old Order Amish parents to cause their children to attend high school until age sixteen. While recognizing the history of the Amish in American society, the court nevertheless sought to limit the scope of the decision, stating that:

> Nothing we hold is intended to undermine the general applicability of the State's compulsory school-attendance statutes or to limit the power of the State to promulgate reasonable standards that, while not impairing the free exercise of religion, provide for continuing agricultural vocational education under parental and church guidance by the Old Order Amish or others similarly situated.

Id. at 236.

47. *Sampson*, 317 N.Y.S.2d at 658. Though it might be deemed revisionist history, the per curiam opinion of the Court of Appeals in *Sampson* explained that the result was not at odds with the *Seiferth* decision because in that case the court "did not limit to drastic or mortal circumstances the statutory power of the Family Court or like court in neglect proceedings to order necessary surgery." *Sampson*, 278 N.E.2d at 918.

48. 292 A.2d 387 (Pa. 1972).

scoliosis, was the subject of a neglect petition brought by the Director of the State Hospital for Crippled Children. The petition sought appointment of a guardian to consent to corrective surgery to prevent Ricky from being bedridden for the remainder of his life. The operation was potentially dangerous, and Ricky's condition was not life threatening. For religious reasons, the boy's mother refused to consent to the whole blood transfusions required for surgery. The court refused to follow *Sampson*. Describing the potential problems that could stem from *Sampson* as "endless," the Supreme Court of Pennsylvania refused to appoint a guardian on the ground that "as between a parent and the state, the state does not have an interest of sufficient magnitude outweighing a parent's religious beliefs when the child's life is *not immediately imperiled* by his physical condition."[49]

Despite the court's unwillingness to expand the "life threatening" exception,[50] the *Green* decision can be described as transitional because it took a cue from Justice Douglas's dissent in *Wisconsin v. Yoder*.[51] Following Douglas's suggestion, the *Green* court remanded the case so that the views of the child whose health was at stake could be heard.[52] Although it was ultimately determined on remand that the child would adhere to the parent's decision, *Green* may have sowed some seeds for a subsequent movement toward permitting or seeking participation by minor children in decisions affecting their own health. An even more important manifestation of this movement, arising at about the same time, was the judicial development of a so-called mature minor doctrine which allowed older minors to consent to some forms of medical care for themselves. Admittedly, however, the mature minor doctrine was based less on concern about children's rights than on the desire to negate a battery action against

49. *Id.* at 392.

50. In a strong dissent, Judge Eagen took issue with the court's adherence to the life threatening exception and pointed out that the pertinent statute referred to neglect or refusal "to provide *proper or necessary* subsistence, education, *medical or surgical care, or other care necessary for his or her health* . . . ." *Id.* at 395 (Eagen, J., dissenting) (citing 11 PA. CONS. STAT. § 243(5)(c)).

51. 406 U.S. 205, 246 (1972). The Pennsylvania court noted that in *Yoder*

> The majority opinion as well as the concurring opinion of Mr. Justice Stewart did not think it wise to reach this point for two principal reasons: (1) it was the parents, not the children, who were criminally prosecuted for their religious beliefs; and (2) the record did not indicate a parent-child conflict . . . . While the record before us gives no indication of Ricky's thinking, it is the child rather than the parent in this appeal who is directly involved which thereby distinguishes *Yoder's* decision not to discuss the beliefs of the parents vis-a-vis the children.

292 A.2d at 392 (1972).

The Pennsylvania court also noted that in *Sampson*, the trial judge felt that "foisting" the decision on the boy was unreasonable (a view which the court recognized had been expressed also by Judge Fuld in his dissent in *Seiferth*). Nevertheless, the court determined that Ricky Green should be heard. *Id.*

52. In an evidentiary hearing after remand, Ricky indicated that he did not wish to submit to the surgery. His view ostensibly was not simply on religious grounds; he said he had been going to the hospital for a long time and no one had told him that " 'it is going to come out right.' " *In re* Green, 307 A.2d 279, 280 (Pa. 1973).

medical personnel if an older minor consented in near-emergency situations or when a parent was unavailable.[53]

B. Some Important Legislative Developments During the Period

Several noteworthy legislative developments during this "transition" period included (1) the rapid adoption of child abuse reporting statutes during the 1960s, along with further expansion in the 1970s; (2) the enactment of statutes providing clearer rules and procedures for emancipation of older minors, with other statutes authorizing unemancipated minors to consent to medical treatment for certain illnesses or conditions; and (3) the proliferation of religious exemption statutes intended to insulate parents from criminal prosecution premised on providing only religious or spiritual assistance rather than medical treatment for their children.

1. The Child Abuse Reporting Statutes

The primary purpose of the initial child abuse reporting statutes was to protect children from harm through physical violence by their parents or other family members.[54] These laws required certain persons (typically physicians, hospitals, teachers or school officials) to report to law enforcement officials, the juvenile court, or a protective services agency instances of such abuse coming to their attention through their official duties. Many statutes utilized positive reinforcement measures such as offering protection from civil liability for good faith reporting, rather than penalties for not reporting, in order to encourage professionals (such as physicians) to report probable abuse. The statutes were well received following their introduction in the mid-1960s, and the scope of these laws has been considerably expanded in many states since their initial adoption. For example, some jurisdictions have established free "hot lines" to facilitate reporting, and others use central registries to collect records of child abuse reports.[55]

The child abuse reporting statutes have special relevance to children's medical care for two reasons. First, the ways in which the stat-

53. *See, e.g.*, Younts v. St. Francis Hosp. & Sch. of Nursing, Inc., 469 P.2d 330 (Kan. 1970) (upholding hospital's decision to perform minor surgery on a 17-year-old girl's finger, with her consent, while her mother was under the effects of anesthesia and the father's whereabouts were unknown); Angela R. Holder, *Minors' Rights to Consent to Medical Care*, 257 JAMA 3400 (1987); Walter Wadlington, *Minors and Health Care: The Age of Consent*, 11 OSGOODE HALL L.J. 115, 117-20 (1973). Professor Holder points out that there have been very few cases in which a physician has been sued for nonnegligent care of an adolescent without parental consent.

54. For a contemporary discussion of the development of child abuse reporting statutes, see Monrad Paulsen et al., *Child Abuse Reporting Laws—Some Legislative History*, 34 GEO. WASH. L. REV. 482 (1966).

55. This has produced civil liberties concerns based on the possible misuse of such records, as well as court actions seeking to expunge records of past reports. *See, e.g.*, Crawford/Sebastian County SCAN v. Kelly, 778 S.W.2d 219 (Ark. 1989).

utes encourage the reporting of potential abuse illustrate a very strong public policy regarding the need to protect children from some parental conduct. "Informer" statutes are never popular in the United States, in part because of special concerns which arose in the family context in Nazi Germany. That legislatures have been willing to resort to "informer" provisions demonstrates society's overwhelming concern with shielding children.

The second relevant facet of the child abuse reporting laws is that the definition of what qualifies as reportable conduct has increasingly been extended to cases of medical neglect. This expansion has resulted either from specific language in the reporting statutes, or through adoption of basic definitions from abuse, neglect, or endangerment laws as the operative key to what should be reported. The practical effect is an increase in the likelihood of disputes about medical decision making reaching the courts. One can ask, quite justifiably, whether a physician today would be required to report Tony Tuttendario as medically neglected.

2. *Emancipation and Minor Medical Consent Laws*

Emancipation was for many years a legal morass, often requiring courts to make a factual determination in each case.[56] Considering that even experienced lawyers could find it difficult to know whether a minor was in fact emancipated, it seems absurd that a physician should have been expected to make such a determination when assessing a minor's capacity to consent. Modern statutes providing formal procedures and the necessary criteria for emancipation, as well as the effects which follow emancipation, offer a degree of certainty previously unknown in the medical care context. These statutes also make the emancipated minor financially responsible.[57] Nonetheless, only a limited number of persons can qualify for emancipation under them.[58]

Even more important than the general emancipation statutes have been provisions allowing minors to consent to treatment for specific illnesses or conditions.[59] Some laws provided no specific age floor,[60] while others set a much lower minimum age than that required for general emancipation. Although one might assume that these laws were based on the concept of assuring greater personal autonomy for minors, they were in fact largely rooted in expediency. Parental consent is not needed for certain selective conditions such as crisis coun-

56. *See* Comment, *The Uncertain Status of the Emancipated Minor: Why We Need a Uniform Statutory Emancipation of Minors Act (USEMA)*, 15 U.S.F. L. REV. 473, 475-79 (1981).

57. *See, e.g.*, CONN. GEN. STAT. ANN. § 46b-150d (West 1988 & Supp. 1993).

58. One reason for this is that emancipation statutes generally provide a minimum age only a year or two below the age of majority.

59. *See, e.g.*, VA. CODE ANN. § 54.1-2969(D) (Michie 1991 & Supp. 1993).

60. *Id.*

seling, substance abuse, contagious disease, and birth control. These are situations where legislatures feared that minors would be unwilling to seek assistance or consent from their parents. If minors could not personally consent to treatment, they might not obtain medical care—to the detriment of themselves, their families, and society. The statutes provide an example of legislative recognition of the disturbing changes that have occurred in the counseling and consultative relationship between many parents and their children.

A further variation is the statutory codification of the "mature minor" doctrine, sometimes in a fashion which enlarges the judicially created exception. For example, Arkansas authorizes consent to treatment by "[a]ny unemancipated minor of sufficient intelligence to understand and appreciate the consequences of the proposed surgical or medical treatment or procedures . . . ."[61]

These statutes did not completely resolve all potential problems, however. For example, neither the limited "minor consent" statutes nor those codifying a "mature minor" rule address the problem of obtaining informed consent. As a general rule, informed consent requirements usually dictate that medical personnel disclose risks and alternatives in language that the consenting individual can understand. Whether this calls for special care and wording when advising a minor, and whether at some level a minor's comprehension might be below that normally expected for a decision maker, could lead to future litigation notwithstanding the existence of the statutes.

3. *Religious Exemptions in Neglect or Endangerment Statutes*

Another frequently occurring type of legislative provision in the transition period was statutory exceptions to child medical care requirements when parents chose to use spiritual treatment or care. These provisions varied significantly in language depending on whether they were included in a basic neglect or child endangerment law, a child abuse reporting statute, a criminal provision for failure to secure medical attention for an injured child, or a statute combining these elements. Some provisions specifically refer to spiritual or faith healing or use of prayer, while others make reference to a specific religious group.[62] Statutory exceptions for religious healing received a boost in 1974 when the federal government adopted the Child Abuse and Prevention Act,[63] an example of the modern federal attempt to shape certain aspects of family law by offering financial incentives to the states to participate in joint federal-state programs. To receive federal funds under the Child Abuse and Prevention Act, a state must

61. *See* Ark. Code Ann. § 20-9-602(7) (Michie 1987). Mississippi has a similar provision. Miss. Code Ann. § 41-41-3(h) (1993).

62. Va. Code Ann. § 18.2-314 (Michie 1988), for example, refers to "Christian Science treatment by a duly accredited Christian Science practitioner . . . ."

63. 42 U.S.C. § 5101 (1988 & Supp. III 1991).

enact a child abuse reporting law meeting federally established guidelines. Although the initial guidelines established by the supervising federal agency (in 1974, the Department of Health, Education and Welfare) did not require that states include medical neglect in their definitions of child abuse, the guidelines included a model provision for religious accommodation.[64] In 1987 the Department of Health and Human Services redefined the definition of neglect to include failure to provide medical care,[65] but the religious accommodation provision was eliminated from the model clause in the guidelines.[66] By that time, however, many states had adopted such a provision in their statutes.

III. Time Present

Roughly a decade ago, things again might have seemed fairly well settled. Legislative and administrative structures for child protection had been expanded to recognize medical care as a necessity for children. The concept of medical neglect was well established. Although the exact parameters of medical neglect had not been fully litigated, state authority to intervene to protect children in need of medical care, enforceable through the courts without a finding of general parental unfitness, seemed unassailable. Usually, a guardian would be appointed for the limited purpose of consenting to medical treatment. Many courts tried hard to avoid undue stigmatization of an otherwise effective parent who "fell short" in this single area.

States also seemed to have the clear authority to intervene in appropriate cases in the face of religious objections. Judicial opinions affirming state legislative and judicial authority to act under such circumstances may not have been masterpieces of conceptualization (as we have seen, some opinions did no more than cite to *Prince*), but their message seemed unequivocal. Although some statutes included religious exceptions, they were usually qualified by language to the effect that receiving religious or spiritual treatment would not "for that reason alone" amount to violation of the requirements to obtain medical care for children.

Given that most legal issues appeared to be resolved, it may seem surprising that the past decade marked an increase in litigation focusing on various aspects of decision making, independent of abortion and pregnancy, about children's medical care. In part, the increase in litigation arose as a result of increased child protection initiatives by the states. There are several explanations for this renewed activity.

---

64. 45 C.F.R. § 1340.1-2(b)(1) (1975).
65. *See* 45 C.F.R. § 1340.2(d)(2)(i) (1993).
66. For further discussion of the history and background of these steps, see Christine A. Clark, *Religious Accommodation and Criminal Liability*, 17 Fla. St. U. L. Rev. 558, 562-66 (1990).

One explanation emphasizes the popular belief that courts are the best place to go in seeking redress for perceived grievances regarding the family. Furthermore, litigants may have anticipated that the recent First Amendment gloss in other areas would make courts reconsider older decisions on children's medical care. Finally, even though improved technology has provided greater potential for effective medical care in many situations, the "residuum of the unknown" described by the court in *Tuttendario*[67] has also grown because these advances in medical technology presented new risks as well. What sorts of challenges have courts recently faced, and what further challenges might be expected?

A. *Issues of Religious Freedom*

In the typical blood transfusion case, courts still seem willing to follow past practice and make a "tip of the wig" to *Prince*.[68] In many ways, this fact situation is the easiest to resolve, because these cases usually involve a single decision which presents a high probability of a successful outcome, as opposed to the potentially grave consequences of not allowing the transfusion. But, as modern medicine progresses, not all problems are so easy to define—particularly in situations involving dangerous, long-term therapies. Some cases presenting less clear-cut situations have ostensibly been decided not on the parents' asserted religious objection, but on whether the facts called for intervention in the particular case. I suspect, however, that parental religious objections may be an unstated factor for some courts in resolving especially difficult or "long shot" cases.

Several shifts in state litigation and enforcement strategies have been influential. One such shift is a seemingly greater willingness to prosecute parents when a child has died as a result of the parents' failure to secure necessary treatment. Application and interpretation of the aforementioned religious exceptions in neglect and other statutes have been the center point of several such recent prosecutions.

In *Walker v. Superior Court (People)*,[69] the Supreme Court of California upheld the state's authority to bring a prosecution for felony child endangerment and involuntary manslaughter against the mother of a child who had died from meningitis after receiving treatment by prayer rather than medical care. The mother based her decision on her religious beliefs as a Christian Scientist, and she contended that the prosecution violated free exercise and due process guarantees of both the United States and California constitutions. She also asserted that California Penal Code section 270, which contained criminal sanctions for child neglect, provided her with a com-

67. *See supra* note 22 and accompanying text.
68. *See* Prince v. Massachusetts, 321 U.S. 158 (1944).
69. 763 P.2d 852 (Cal. 1988), *cert. denied*, 491 U.S. 905 (1989).

plete defense. That provision enumerated the necessities that parents must furnish to their children, including "medical attendance, or other remedial care," and made willful failure to provide them, without lawful excuse, a misdemeanor. In 1976, section 270 was amended to provide that "treatment by spiritual means through prayer alone" constitutes "other remedial care." However, neither a separate provision on involuntary manslaughter[70] nor another on felony child endangerment[71] was amended to include this exception.

After carefully reviewing the language and legislative background of the three statutes, the court concluded that "[t]he plain language, purpose, and legislative history of section 270 . . . fail to establish a discernible legislative intent to exempt prayer treatment, as a matter of law, from the reach of the manslaughter and felony child-endangerment statutes."[72] The court emphasized the gravity of the state's interest in protecting children's health and, indeed, in saving lives. It also recognized the severity of the imposition on the mother's religious beliefs. As to the latter, the court quoted the language from *Prince*. Although finding that a compelling state interest justified imposing felony liability for failure to seek medical care for a seriously ill child, the court determined that to survive a First Amendment challenge "the policy must also represent the least restrictive alternative available to the State."[73]

The defendant contended that civil dependency proceedings would advance the governmental interest in a less intrusive manner. The court responded that:

> First, we have already noted the profoundly intrusive nature of such proceedings; it is not clear that parents would prefer to lose custody of their children pursuant to a disruptive and invasive judicial inquiry than to face the prospect of criminal liability. Second, child dependency proceedings advance the governmental interest only when the state learns of the child's illness in time to take protective measures . . . . Finally, the imposition of criminal liability is reserved for the actual loss or endangerment of a child's life and thus is narrowly tailored to those instances where government intrusion is absolutely compelled.[74]

Subsequent to the *Walker* decision, the Supreme Courts of Florida and Massachusetts confronted similar issues. Each state's statutory scheme included religious exceptions in neglect or endangerment statutes, but not in other provisions under which successful prosecutions had been brought. In each instance, one or both parents had been convicted for failing to secure medical attention for a child who

70. Cal. Penal Code § 192(b) (West 1988).
71. *Id.* § 273a(1).
72. *Walker*, 763 P.2d at 862.
73. *Id.* at 870.
74. *Id.* at 870-71.

died after receiving only spiritual or religious assistance. In the Florida case, *Hermanson v. State*,[75] the court overturned the conviction because the statutory scheme was so vague as to make it unclear what conduct was prohibited. In *Commonwealth v. Twitchell*,[76] the Massachusetts Supreme Court set aside a conviction and remanded the case for a new trial at the prosecutor's discretion. The parents had evidently relied on a manual incorporating language from a State Attorney General's opinion later established to have been incorrect. The court held that the child neglect statute containing the religious exception and the second-degree manslaughter statute were not *in pari materia*; thus, the exception for spiritual treatment and prayer in the child neglect statute did not exempt parents from all criminal prosecutions. However, the court also found that the indictment violated the parents' due process rights because the statute failed to give fair notice of the prohibited conduct. The lesson to be learned from *Walker*, *Hermanson*, and *Twitchell* is the need for clarity in any statutory scheme providing a religious exemption from prosecution. These cases do not declare that statutes without a religious exemption are invalid. Nor do they hold that there is a common-law religious exemption.

Religious exemptions have been the most attractive topic for law review commentary addressing health care decisions for children,[77] perhaps indicating that there is greater interest in First Amendment scholarship than family law. But despite this attention in the scholarly literature, exemption laws still pose several unresolved constitutional issues. One question is whether these provisions are vulnerable under the Establishment Clause, especially when such statutes refer to a specific religious group. Because of the manner in which the cases usually arise,[78] this issue will not necessarily be raised at the trial level, and appellate courts may be able to uphold intervention without

75. 604 So. 2d 775 (Fla. 1992). *Compare* Lybarger v. People, 807 P.2d 570 (Colo. 1991) (invalidating conviction because jury instructions improperly eliminated prosecution's burden to prove that parents had not established the affirmative defense to a child abuse charge of "treatment by spiritual means").

76. 617 N.E.2d 609 (Mass. 1993).

77. *See, e.g.*, Christine A. Clark, *Religious Accommodation and Criminal Liability*, 17 FLA. ST. U. L. REV. 558, 562 (1990); John D. Ingram, *State Interference With Religiously Motivated Decisions on Medical Treatment*, 93 DICK. L. REV. 41 (1988); David H. Bamberger, Comment, Mercy Hospital, Inc. v. Jackson: *A Recurring Dilemma for Health Care Providers in the Treatment of Jehovah's Witnesses*, 46 MD. L. REV. 514 (1987); Wesley M. Frye, Comment, *When Rights Clash: The Conflict Between a Parent's Right To Free Exercise of Religion Versus His Child's Right to Life*, 19 CUMB. L. REV. 585 (1989); JoAnna A. Gekas, Note, *California's Prayer Healing Dilemma*, 14 HASTINGS CONST. L. Q. 395 (1987); Donna K. LeClair, Comment, *Faith-Healing and Religious-Treatment Exceptions to Child-Endangerment Laws: Should Parental Religious Practices Excuse the Failure to Provide Necessary Medical Care to Children?*, 13 U. DAYTON L. REV. 79, 95 (1987); Geraldine K. Russell & Donald Wallace, Note, *Jehovah's Witnesses and the Refusal of Blood Transfusions: A Balance of Interests*, 33 CATH. LAW. 361 (1991).

78. In the typical case, a defendant seeks not to challenge but instead to rely upon the basic validity of a religious exemption, and perhaps even to extend the scope of the exemption's coverage.

reaching this constitutional argument. At least one trial court has declared such a provision constitutionally invalid,[79] while Justice Mosk, concurring in *Walker*,[80] raised the same issue with regard to California's statute, although the majority of the court did not reach the question. The Delaware Supreme Court also devoted some attention to the Establishment Clause issue, but the court noted that neither side had raised the issue and it would have to be left for another day.[81]

B. Providing Greater Autonomy for Children

A separate group of cases can be categorized as falling within the rubric of assuring children's autonomy. To some extent, these cases build on the previously described doctrines of general emancipation, minor consent, and "mature minor" laws. An important set of issues stemming from minor consent statutes that remains unresolved in many, if not most, jurisdictions is whether a minor who can consent to treatment for certain conditions or illnesses is entitled to the same privacy and confidentiality rights as an adult patient. More specifically, can minors who consent to treatment bar their physicians from revealing information regarding the treatment to their parents? Most statutes are silent on this, although drafters of the Juvenile Justice Standards on the Rights of Children attempted to establish a model using a balancing test that would vary the amount of disclosure to parents according to the need for parental involvement or cooperation.[82]

One of the most controversial issues that courts have been called on to decide is whether a minor on life support measures can authorize withdrawal. This question raises special concerns, because minors are not included in the coverage of most natural death acts which allow a competent individual to predetermine and declare what sort of treatment he or she wants in the event of subsequent incompetence and terminal illness.[83]

79. State v. Miskimens, 490 N.E.2d 931, 933-36 (Ohio Ct. Com. Pl. 1984). An account of a subsequent unreported trial court decision in Ohio following the reasoning of *Miskimens* can be found in LeClair, *supra* note 77, at 95.

80. Walker v. Superior Court (People), 763 P.2d 852, 875 (Cal. 1988).

81. Newmark v. Williams, 588 A.2d 1108, 1114 (Del. 1990). For further discussion, see *infra* text accompanying notes 104-08.

82. *See* INSTITUTE OF JUDICIAL ADMIN. & AM. BAR ASS'N, JUVENILE JUSTICE STANDARDS: STANDARDS RELATING TO RIGHTS OF MINORS § 4.1 (1980).

83. A challenge by a minor might be one way to effectively raise a constitutional challenge based on age classification, particularly in a state that already has lowered age requirements for other medical decision making. On the other hand, what little case law exists suggests that courts may be reluctant to hear on the merits cases challenging these types of statutes. *See, e.g.*, Dinino v. State *ex rel.* Gorton, 684 P.2d 1297 (Wash. 1984) (suit challenging state statute permitting adults to authorize discontinuance of life-saving treatment dismissed for want of a justiciable controversy on grounds that party did not exhibit any of the medical conditions required for the statute *not* to apply).

The situations discussed thus far have usually involved one or more parents disagreeing with the state about the course of medical care. In *In re* Doe, 418 S.E.2d 3 (Ga. 1992), the Supreme

A 1973 medical case study focused on the process through which a sixteen-year-old girl was permitted to withdraw from dialysis after rejecting a kidney transplant.[84] No legal intervention was involved, and the discussion centered on ethical issues. Today, courts are forced to resolve cases with similar fact patterns. In 1989, the Illinois Supreme Court held in *In re E.G.*[85] that a seventeen-year-old with leukemia who needed blood transfusions was a "mature minor" who could refuse that procedure based on her right to freely exercise her religion. She had not been formally emancipated, but the court noted that Illinois's Consent by Minors to Medical Operations Act allows persons over age twelve to seek medical attention for venereal disease or substance addiction, while another Illinois statute permits persons under eighteen who are pregnant or married to consent to treatment. The court also noted the "mature minor doctrine" adopted by the U.S. Supreme Court in cases of abortion decision making, although it recognized that choosing an abortion involved the exercise of a constitutional right. The *E.G.* court also mentioned numerous other cases extending protection of constitutional rights ranging from privacy in the use of contraceptives,[86] freedom of expression in schools,[87] and procedural due process in juvenile courts.[88] The court also pointed to the judicial development of the "mature minor" doctrine in tort actions.[89] Relying on this mass of precedent, the court concluded that the common-law right to control one's health care should extend to mature minors and explained that "[t]he State's *parens patriae* power pertaining to minors is strongest when the minor is immature . . . to make these decisions on her own. The *parens patriae* authority fades, however, as the minor gets older and disappears upon her reaching adulthood."[90] *E.G.* holds special procedural interest because the trial court found the child to be medically neglected and appointed a guardian to consent to the transfusions. However, by the time the case reached the Illinois Supreme Court, the child had become an

Court of Georgia was forced to determine whether a hospital could provide less treatment to a terminally ill child in the face of parental disagreement. *Id.* at 4. The court held that the state statute required both parents to agree to the lessened treatment if both parents were actively participating in the decision making process. *Id.* at 7. Although a Georgia statute permits "any parent" to consent to a DNR ("do not resuscitate") order, it also allows "any parent" to revoke such consent. *Id.* Unless both parents consent, the statutory presumption that a patient wishes to be resuscitated will be followed. *Id.*

84. John E. Schowalter et al., *The Adolescent Patient's Decision to Die*, 51 PEDIATRICS 97 (1973).

85. *In re* E.G., 133 Ill. 2d 98, 549 N.E.2d 322, 139 Ill. Dec. 810 (1989).

86. Carey v. Population Serv. Int'l, 431 U.S. 678 (1977).

87. Tinker v. Des Moines Indep. Community Sch. Dist., 393 U.S. 503 (1969).

88. *In re* Gault, 387 U.S. 1 (1967).

89. In *E.G.*, the Illinois Supreme Court noted with approval the Tennessee Supreme Court's decision in Cardwell v. Bechtol, 724 S.W.2d 739 (Tenn. 1987), upholding the right of a 17-year-old to consent to medical care and thus obviate a battery action against the treating physician. 133 Ill. 2d at 109-10, 549 N.E.2d at 326-27, 139 Ill. Dec. at 814-15.

90. *Id.* at 103, 549 N.E.2d at 327, 139 Ill. Dec. at 815.

adult, and the case was technically moot. Noting that a finding of neglect by the mother would be improper if the trial court had ruled that the child was a mature minor, the case was remanded to expunge such a finding. The court also pointed out that the determination that the child was a mature minor made it unnecessary to reach constitutional issues regarding either the child's or the mother's religious objections to the transfusions.

At about the same time, the Supreme Court of Maine allowed premajority statements of a terminally ill patient in a vegetative state to be used as evidence of his wishes not to be kept alive in such a condition.[91] A Texas Court of Appeals, however, refused to apply the rationale of *E.G.* in the case of a sixteen-year-old who signed a form which refused consent to a transfusion and also released his physician from all liability.[92] In appointing a conservator to consent to blood transfusions opposed on religious grounds by the minor and his parents, the court opined that Texas had no mature minor doctrine and that no authority had been cited to show that the action infringed on state or federal rights of privacy, or free exercise of religion.

C. *Deciding About Intervention in Today's Complex Medical World*

Modern courts, applying modern statutes, have largely moved away from the hyper-strict rule that state intervention is permitted only in life threatening cases. The standards for determining which circumstances justify overruling parental decisions, and the burden of proof for establishing the case for intervention, however, are not necessarily clear. A California appellate court articulated a decade ago one set of criteria for the former:

> The state should examine the seriousness of the harm the child is suffering or the substantial likelihood that he will suffer serious harm; the evaluation for the treatment by the medical profession; the risks involved in medically treating the child; and the expressed preferences of the child. Of course, the underlying consideration is the child's welfare and whether his best interests will be served by the medical treatment.[93]

As to the burden of proof, some courts apply a clear and convincing standard,[94] whether or not they feel such a standard is constitu-

---

91. *In re* Swan, 569 A.2d 1202, 1205 (Me. 1990).

92. O.G. v. Baum, 790 S.W.2d 839, 841-42 (Tex. Ct. App. 1990).

93. *In re* Phillip B., 156 Cal. Rptr. 48, 51 (Cal. Ct. App. 1979). The *Phillip B.* court did not really address the policy underlying the decision of the trial judge, stating that the appellate court's role "ends with a determination as to whether there is any substantial evidence, contradicted or uncontradicted, which will support the conclusion of the trier of fact." *Id.*

94. *See, e.g., id.* The court further noted, however, that such a heightened standard applied only to the trial court. The power of the appellate court was limited to reviewing whether the facts adduced at trial supported the lower court's decision. *Id.*

tionally required. Is this appropriate? In paternity cases initiated by individuals rather than the state, the U.S. Supreme Court has upheld a statute using a preponderance of the evidence standard.[95] But, when states attempt to terminate parental rights, the Supreme Court has required the state to prove its case by clear and convincing evidence, in large measure because of a perceived disparity in the adversaries' litigation options and resources.[96] Even so, then Justice Rehnquist's dissent in *Santosky v. Kramer*, in which the majority of the Court announced the clear and convincing standard, makes a persuasive argument that the higher burden of proof may not be appropriate even in termination cases. Justice Rehnquist noted that when a judge makes an erroneous decision in not terminating a parent-child relationship, "the child involved must return either to an abusive home or the often unstable world of foster care,"[97] and went on to add that:

> When, in the context of a permanent neglect termination proceeding, the interests of the child and the State in a stable, nurturing homelife are balanced against the interests of parents in the rearing of their child, it cannot be said that either set of interests is so clearly paramount as to require that the risk of error be allocated to one side or the other.[98]

Santosky involved an allegation of severe child abuse. One can similarly ask whether the problem of balancing a policy of nonintervention in family medical decision making is so important as to be weighed more heavily than the interest of a child in receiving medical care that is clearly needed for his or her health and growth. Is the concern with the state's superior litigation resources sufficient to justify the higher burden of proof?

Some courts have rationalized giving greater weight to the interest in protecting parental decision making by citing Blackstone's comment that "natural bonds of affection lead parents to act in the best interests of their children."[99] Citing Blackstone for such a proposition seems anomalous today, considering that in Blackstone's time only the father had parental rights, and children were valued specially for their economic potential. Nor was English law in 1765 known for its kindness or gentleness toward children. We should instead ask whether any such presumption in favor of parents is justified at a time of widespread child abuse reporting statutes and minor consent laws. One might even raise potential concerns about conflict of interest,

95. Rivera v. Minnich, 483 U.S. 574, 575 (1987).

96. Santosky v. Kramer, 455 U.S. 745, 747-48 (1982).

97. *Id.* at 789.

98. *Id.* at 790-91.

99. *See, e.g.*, Parham v. J.R., 442 U.S. 584, 602 (1979) (examining what process is constitutionally due a child when parents or a legal guardian seek state-administered institutional mental health care).

based on the high cost of medical care and the lack of a universal access health care program for children.[100]

Some of the more difficult and celebrated cases have involved life threatening conditions in which death was not imminent and chances of recovery were not so strong as in many of the blood transfusion cases. Several key cases have involved the question whether to overrule parental decisions against chemotherapy for their children. In some, the alternatives proposed by the parents were medically unrecognized (or even repudiated) treatments.[101] Although courts in these cases have sometimes been accused of "practicing medicine," this condemnation fails to recognize that cases typically get to court because physicians or hospitals have initiated some sort of child protection action. An example of great judicial restraint in passing on the merits of a particular procedure is shown in *Matter of Hofbauer*,[102] in which the New York Court of Appeals refused to consider whether laetrile was appropriate treatment for a child with Hodgkin's disease. Instead, the court held that the parents had fulfilled their duty by taking the child to a licensed physician, even though the doctor might have used a treatment which other physicians considered inappropriate, or even dangerous.[103]

Newmark v. Williams,[104] a recent Delaware case, illustrates the difficulties that courts regard themselves as facing when determining whether to overrule parental decisions not to undergo complex medical treatment when the odds of success are less than even. *Newmark* might have been further complicated by the fact that the parents were Christian Scientists who initially had taken their child for medical examination because of concern for their potential criminal liability if they did not do so.[105] The court noted, but did not reach, the issue of whether a statutory religious exemption from the requirement of obtaining medical care was constitutional. The judges purported to primarily base their decision on factors other than religion, although this underlying concern is continuously noted throughout the opinion.

Newmark involved a three-year-old who had been diagnosed as being in an advanced stage of Burkett's lymphoma, a particularly aggressive pediatric cancer which is fatal without treatment. By the time

100. In this regard, it seems noteworthy that virtually all cases following *Tuttendario* have largely ignored issues of cost. An historical explanation for this may have been the judicial desire to avoid the addition of any further complicating issues.

101. *See, e.g.*, Custody of a Minor, 393 N.E.2d 836 (Mass. 1979).

102. In the Matter of Hofbauer, 393 N.E.2d 1009 (N.Y. 1979).

103. The father's comments after his 10-year-old child died illustrate the potential strength of parental opposition to state intervention. He described his son as "a pioneer whose purpose was to establish the right of parents to make these decisions for their children and to keep [New York] Governor Carey and his faceless bureaucrats out of the family." Walter H. Waggoner, *Boy, 10, in Laetrile Case Dies*, N.Y. TIMES, July 18, 1980, at D13.

104. 588 A.2d 1108 (Del. 1990).

105. This was stipulated by the parties. *Id.* at 1110.

the case reached the Delaware Supreme Court, the condition was no longer localized, and doctors advised intensive chemotherapy for at least six months. Testimony indicated that this course of treatment offered the child no more than a forty percent chance of survival, and it was not possible to predict whether other tumors would develop in the future.[106] The basic issue before the court was whether to declare the child neglected because of the parents' refusal of further medical care under the circumstances and award temporary custody to the Delaware Division of Child Protective Services to authorize chemotherapy.

The court proceeded to engage in what it described as a balancing test in which many different interests were described. Key factors included preserving the integrity of the family (the essential element of which was described as "maintaining the autonomy of the parent-child relationship"[107]), protecting the health and safety of children in jeopardy (the *parens patriae* role, underlied by the state's interest in preserving life), and the right of a child to enjoy a full and healthy life. Next considering the invasiveness of the treatment, and the probability of its effectiveness, the court stated that

> No American court, even in the most egregious case, has ever authorized the State to remove a child from the loving, nurturing care of his parents and subject him, over parental objection, to an invasive regimen of treatment which offered, as [the treating doctor] defined the term, only a forty percent chance of "survival".[108]

After reviewing the odds of success in other cases, the court concluded that it would be in the best interests of the child to permit the parents to retain custody of the child and make the treatment decisions.

I do not mean to detract in any way from the sincerity of the court and the agonizing way in which it reached a decision. The *Newmark* decision, however, leaves serious questions about whether it produced any workable criteria for the future. To many, a forty percent chance of survival when the alternative is near-term death is not bad odds. And in some cases, one could equally dramatize both the agonies of treatment and nontreatment for a patient. Certainly the situation in *Newmark* was far different from the typical blood transfusion case, even though it clearly involved a life-threatening condition. Perhaps the bottom line is whether in such cases a court can do any more than try to evaluate the seriousness and sincerity of the parents.

---

106. *Id.* at 1119. According to the court, the doctor "ultimately admitted that there was a real possibility that the chemotherapy could kill Colin." *Id.*

107. *Id.* at 1115 (quoting Quilloin v. Walcott, 434 U.S. 246, 255 (1978)).

108. *Id.* at 1119.

IV. Closing Observations

I have described a slow movement toward defining and implementing the state's role in assuring that children are not deprived of necessary medical care by the decisions of their parents or other guardians. In any movement, there can be important jockeying by competing interests to obtain control of the catchiest or most potentially popular tag. For example, one can plausibly argue that *Fair Trade* should signify free price competition for a product. But, the persons who wanted the term to refer to price fixing by a manufacturer or a limited group of contractors garnered the name first. Similarly, the label *children's rights* is used by advocates who see it as embracing what can be vastly different concepts or goals. In this case, however, no single group has as yet gained a corner on the tag.

One group of "children's rights" proponents has the goal of increasing autonomy for children in many or all aspects of decision making. Another group wishing to march under the same banner promotes expanded state involvement to protect children against their parents and themselves, as well as the rest of the world. Yet another group asserts that children's rights should be fungible with family rights, which is often another way of saying that children should have few rights and that the state should protect parental decision making in all but dire instances.[109] These conflicting views are evident in the area of children's medical decision making. In a simplistic way, the political conflict illustrates the problems courts face in developing an adequate approach to balancing the competing interests that society today seeks to protect.

In 1916 Dean Roscoe Pound described one of the factors that continues to play a key role in the movement toward greater state involvement in areas such as family decision making. He explained that:

> It must not be forgotten that family law in general is one of the earliest branches of the law to become fixed and hence preserves traces of an archaic condition in which group interests rather than individual interests were secured. Tenderness of the individual interests of parents, since legal interference in family relations touches individuals in a peculiarly sensitive spot, has induced hesitation in changing the established rules, even where reasons for change were evident.[110]

109. Other arguments can obviously be made to support abstaining from interference in parental decision making. Professor Joseph Goldstein has provided an eloquent expression of the argument against most forms of state intervention, contending that intervention interferes with the continuity necessary to ensure a child's physical and psychological wellbeing. *See* Joseph Goldstein, *Medical Care for the Child at Risk: On State Supervision of Parental Autonomy*, 86 Yale L.J. 645 (1977).

110. Roscoe Pound, *Individual Interests in the Domestic Relations*, 14 Mich. L. Rev. 177, 187 (1916).

This lecture has covered a period beginning around the time that Dean Pound made the preceding observation, which provides at least one important reason why courts long were reluctant to utilize their authority to intervene in family decision making for medical care to minors. And although the rules of the legal game have changed, judicial reluctance remains in many quarters despite other changes in familial and parent-child relationships that have prompted such drastic measures as child abuse reporting statutes.

Given the movement toward recognizing the need for child protection in securing medical care, and legislative and judicial recognition of state authority to overrule parental decisions, the next round of questions receiving the most attention in this area may be different. Courts might be forced to determine whether the judicial system is an appropriate mechanism for resolving medical decision making issues in light of its adversarial approach and the length of time courts take to reach decisions. Another important issue might well be whether child abuse reporting statutes, at present one of the few formal measures for channeling medically deprived children into the health-care system, are the appropriate approach either in terms of effectiveness or timing. In resolving questions such as these, we always fear that a new bureaucracy might be created, perhaps one that is insensitive to the "residuum of the unknown" or its modern counterpart. However, we also hope that while it will be quick to respond to the health needs of children, it will nevertheless remain sensitive to the needs of parents, relying less on the threat of criminal sanctions. A system for universal access to health care might well be the catalyst for the development of such an approach.

SPIRITUAL TREATMENT EXEMPTIONS TO CHILD MEDICAL NEGLECT LAWS: WHAT WE OUTSIDERS SHOULD THINK

*James G. Dwyer**

There are strongly opposing views as to whether parents should be exempted from the normal legal responsibility to secure medical treatment for sick or injured children when the parents have religious objections to medical care. There are some who advocate an absolute exemption,[1] even in life-threatening situations, and some who argue that no exemption whatsoever should exist.[2] Still others take an inter-

---

* Assistant Professor, College of William & Mary, Marshall-Wythe School of Law.

1 *See* John Dwight Ingram, *State Interference with Religiously Motivated Decisions on Medical Treatment*, 93 DICK. L. REV. 41, 41 (1988) (arguing that "[t]he constitutional protections of religious freedom prohibit the state from interfering with religiously motivated decisions regarding the rendering of medical care").

2 *See* Henry J. Abraham, *Abraham, Isaac and the State: Faith-Healing and Legal Intervention*, 27 U. RICH. L. REV. 951, 977 (1993) (arguing for repeal of spiritual treatment exemptions because this "would send the unambiguous message that, in the context of a medical emergency, prayer and faith-healing efforts, however laudable, caring and arguably efficacious they may be, are acceptable to the state only if a child's life or safety is also protected by the provision of any needed medical treatment"); Elizabeth A. Lingle, *Treating Children by Faith: Colliding Constitutional Issues*, 17 J. LEGAL MED. 301, 330 (1996) (opposing exemptions); Ann MacLean Massie, *The Religion Clauses and Parental Health Care Decisionmaking for Children: Suggestions for a New Approach*, 21 HASTINGS CONST. L.Q. 725, 739 (1994) (arguing that spiritual treatment exemptions violate the Establishment Clause); Paula A. Monopoli, *Allocating the Costs of Parental Free Exercise: Striking a New Balance Between Sincere Religious Belief and a Child's Right to Medical Treatment*, 18 PEPP. L. REV. 319, 322 (1991) (arguing that lifting spiritual treatment exemptions would not abridge parents' rights to free exercise of religion); Rita Swan, Ph.D., *On Statutes Depriving a Class of Children of Rights to Medical Care: Can This Discrimination be Litigated?*, 2 QUINNIPIAC HEALTH L.J. 73, 92–94 (1998) (positing that spiritual treatment exemptions are unconstitutional); Jennifer Trahan, *Constitutional Law: Parental Denial of a Child's Medical Treatment for Religious Reasons*, 1989 ANN. SURV. AM. L. 307, 340 (1990) (proposing medical neglect statute that expressly precludes exemption on the grounds of religious belief); *see also* American Academy of Pediatrics, *Religious Objections to Medical Care*, 99 PEDIATRICS 279, 279 (1997) (stating AAP opposition to spiritual treatment exemptions); Andrew Skolnick, *Religious Exemptions to Child Neglect Laws Still Being Passed Despite Convictions of Parents*, 264 JAMA 1226, 1233 (1990)

mediate position—for example, that there should be an exemption in all but life-threatening situations.[3] The division of opinion is not simply between the members of religious groups who want such an exemption for themselves and the rest of the world. There is division even among us "outsiders," we who are not members of a religious group with beliefs opposed to medical care and who therefore have no personal stake in the issue. I will discuss in this Essay only what position outsiders should take on the issue. I assume nearly all members of the legal academic community are outsiders, and I believe we who are outsiders come at the issue from a perspective that is to a large extent similar as amongst ourselves, yet fundamentally different from that of the parents whose legal obligations are in question. In addition, the relevant legal question—whether the State should decide to confer a particular legal power on certain people—is necessarily one that must be addressed from the State's perspective, and the State's perspective is also an outsider perspective, since the State does not hold the religious beliefs of those who request that legal power.

I. Why We Outsiders Disagree Amongst Ourselves

Outsiders on both sides of the issue are motivated primarily, I think, by compassion for the insiders in these religious groups—the parents, the children, perhaps even the group as a whole, which is striving to preserve its way of life. Why is it, then, if outsiders have no personal stake in the issue, but rather take an interest out of concern

---

(stating opposition of American Medical Association to spiritual treatment exemptions).

3 *See* Janna C. Merrick, Ph.D., *Christian Science Healing of Minor Children: Spiritual Exemption Statutes, First Amendment Rights, and Fair Notice*, 10 Issues in L. & Med. 321, 341–42 (1994) (arguing for abrogation of spiritual treatment exemptions but cautioning that courts should order treatment over the objection of parents "only in cases of very serious illness where reliable and proven therapies can effectively manage the disease"); Barry Nobel, *Religious Healing in the Courts: The Liberties and Liabilities of Patients, Parents and Healers*, 16 U. Puget Sound L. Rev. 599, 603 (1993) (taking the position that "[c]ourts should refrain from interfering with the parent-child relationship absent life-threatening circumstances accompanied by the probability—rather than the possibility—of medical cure"); LaDonna DiCamillo, Comment, *Caught Between the Clauses and the Branches: When Parents Deny Their Child Nonemergency Medical Treatment for Religious Reasons*, 19 J. Juv. L. 123, 157 (1998) ("The state's interest is sufficiently compelling only when the risk associated with foregoing medical treatment is at a point when the child's life is immediately endangered, and the proposed treatement offers probable cure with minimal risk."); Jennifer L. Hartzell, Comment, *Mother May I . . . Live? Parental Refusal of Life-Sustaining Medical Treatment for Children Based on Religious Objections*, 66 Tenn. L. Rev. 499, 528 (1999) (proposing that spiritual treatment exemptions be permitted except in cases where "the child's life may be threatened" or "the child's condition may result in a permanent disability").

for the experience of people inside these minority religious communities, that there is such a sharp division of opinion? Is it simply because we disagree about empirical issues so that differing assumptions about relevant facts lead us to translate our common concern into disparate legal and policy recommendations? I do not think so. I do not think we outsiders disagree significantly amongst ourselves regarding the facts.

There is, for instance, no real dispute among us outsiders about the efficacy of modern medicine. *We* all believe that it is quite effective for certain things, though less so for others, that its efficacy is simply uncertain for some conditions, and that certain kinds of evidence reliably inform conclusions about efficacy. And when *our* children become seriously ill or injured, we take them to a doctor. We do not do that because it is some sort of cultural ritual we just happen to have been brought up to perform, without reflection or without subjecting the practice to rigorous empirical scrutiny. We do it because we have good reason to believe that for many physical problems it works better than any available alternative. We have no doubt, for example, that if a child has diabetes, the most effective treatment available is administration of insulin.

There is, additionally, no disagreement among us outsiders about the usefulness of positive thinking, about the ability of the mind to support physical responses to disease and injury, and about the possibility of using prayer and religious teaching as one form of such positive thinking.[4] But there is also no disagreement among us that positive thinking alone is not sufficiently efficacious for many physical problems, particularly with children too young for their mental processes to work in this way. We outsiders all agree that medical care *coupled with* positive thinking, where that is possible, is the most effective approach, generally much more effective than positive thinking alone. Thus, we all try to comfort our children when they are seriously ill and assure them that they will soon be better, but we also give them medicine, if there is medicine with demonstrated ability to cure the disease or ameliorate suffering without causing negative side effects that outweigh the benefits.

Finally, there is no disagreement among us outsiders about the potential psychological consequences of one legal rule or another on

4 I am not suggesting here that people who pray for healing believe they are simply engaging in positive thinking. Rather, I assume that the State, from its secular perspective, may view prayer as efficacious in healing because of the positive psychological states it entails, but may not assume prayer is efficacious because God responds to it. The latter assumption would involve the State deciding religious questions.

the adults and children in these religious groups. Parents may experience great anxiety, fear, and anger if forced to secure medical treatment for their children in violation of their sense of religious obligation and contrary to what they believe to be best for their children. Other adult members of the religious community may also be affected by compelled medical treatment, perhaps by experiencing a sense of threat to, or violation of, their chosen way of life by the outside world. And children, too, might experience some anxiety, fear, and/or anger as a result of the State preventing their parents from fulfilling religious commands.

Importantly, though, adults and children in these religious communities may also experience great anxiety and fear if the State *does not* compel medical care and if the child's condition does not improve. I doubt that members of the Church of Christ Scientist watch their children suffer and die with equanimity, and the children themselves might be terrified, in addition to suffering physical pain. Sometimes people are relieved to be compelled to do things their religion precludes them from doing voluntarily. And sometimes religious groups adapt doctrinally to the legal environment in which they live by excusing adherents from moral responsibility for doing that which the State commands.[5] The psychological effects of compelled medical care are therefore complex, cutting in both directions.

There may be other categories of relevant facts, but those are the major ones. If, then, there is no real disagreement among us outsiders as to factual issues, why is there such disagreement among us as to what the law should be? One explanation is that we sometimes fail to give proper consideration to all the interests at stake. We focus on just a subset of all the affected interests and ignore or under-value others. Some might think only about the affront to parents and to religious groups and the anxiety that members of a family or community might experience as a result of compelled medical care. They may give insufficient attention or weight to the physical and mental suffering of the children who fail to receive medical care for their illness or injury. That is clearly inappropriate. Others might think

5 *See, e.g.*, *In re* President of Georgetown Coll., Inc., 331 F.2d 1000, 1007 (D.C. Cir. 1964) (relating view of adult Jehovah's Witness patient that if a court ordered a blood transfusion, "it would not then be her responsibility"); United States v. George, 239 F. Supp. 752, 753 (D. Conn. 1965) (relating statement by an adult patient that his "conscience was clear" because the responsibility for receiving medical care would be "upon the Court's conscience"); *In re* E.G., 515 N.E.2d 286, 289 (Ill. App. Ct. 1987), *aff'd in part and rev'd in part*, 549 N.E.2d 322 (Ill. 1989) (noting an assertion by the State that the patient's church would view the transfusion as "the court's transgression, not her own, and would support rather than punish her").

only about the suffering and danger that the children might incur as a result of not receiving medical care, having little sympathy for the parents and other members of the religious group and disregarding the potential psychological consequences for children of compelling medical care. This is also deficient, at least in terms of personal moral outlook, though I will offer reasons below for thinking that it is appropriate for the State to disregard the adults' interests in its decision making process.

Perhaps the greatest cause of the disagreement among outsiders, however, is confusion about the significance of the insiders' perspective.[6] Supporters of exemptions point out that the insiders' perspective differs from ours in at least two ways. First, insiders perceive certain spiritual interests, of their own and of their children, that we outsiders do not perceive because we do not share their religious beliefs.[7] Those spiritual interests count against medical care for their children, and insiders assign great weight to those spiritual interests. Second, some groups disagree with us outsiders on the relative efficacy of medical treatment in general. They think prayer is more effective in curing illness or healing injury and may even believe medical treatment to be counter-productive, because seeking it makes them less able to secure, or less worthy of, divine healing assistance.[8] Many outsiders who support religious exemptions believe insider parents are entitled to act on the basis of their beliefs or that the State ought to defer to the insiders' perspective.[9]

Disagreement among us outsiders thus stems principally from two sources—a disparity as to whose interests we emphasize and a disparity as to what role we assign to the insiders' perspective. The remainder of this Essay will support the following two positions: first, the interests

---

6 For description of the beliefs of particular religious groups that oppose medical care and the effects these beliefs have had on children, see generally Seth M. Asser, M.D. & Rita Swan, Ph.D., *Child Fatalities from Religion-Motivated Medical Neglect*, 101 PEDIATRICS 625 (1998); Rita Swan, *Children, Medicine, Religion, and the Law*, 44 ADVANCES IN PEDIATRICS 491 (1997).

7 *See, e.g.*, Ingram, *supra* note 1, at 62; DiCamillo, *supra* note 3, at 143–44; Anne D. Lederman, Note, *Understanding Faith: When Religious Parents Decline Conventional Medical Treatment for Their Children*, 45 CASE W. RES. L. REV. 891, 918 (1995).

8 *See, e.g.*, Lederman, *supra* note 7, at 892–93 (1995); Deborah Sussman Steckler, Note, *A Trend Toward Declining Rigor in Applying Free Exercise Principles: The Example of State Courts' Consideration of Christian Science Treatment for Children*, 36 N.Y.L. SCH. L. REV. 487, 488, 502 (1991) (describing beliefs of Christian Scientists).

9 *See, e.g.*, Ingram, *supra* note 1, at 65 ("The first amendment prohibits the state from prescribing that physical life on earth is more important than life hereafter. Every person has the right to make that critical decision. Similarly, parents have the right to make that decision for their children . . . ."); *see also infra* Parts II.B.2, II.C.

of the children involved should be decisive; second, the State must not defer to the insiders' perspective as to what the children's interests are, but rather must decide what the legal rule will be on the basis of the State's own judgment regarding the children's interests. These two positions support a conclusion that if it is ever permissible for parents to fail, for religious reasons, to secure medical care for a sick or injured child, it is only in cases of illness or injury that are so minor that failure to provide medical treatment ordinarily would not trigger state action anyway, even in the absence of a spiritual treatment exemption. Because spiritual treatment exemptions would operate in practice only in cases where, I conclude, the State should not permit parents to deny children medical care, spiritual treatment exemptions to medical neglect laws are unwarranted.

I will preface my brief arguments for these two positions by emphasizing that what is at issue in this debate is state decision-making. Supporters of spiritual treatment exemptions, and of religious exemptions to parental legal responsibilities in other contexts, tend to overlook the facts that the State makes legal rules (laws do not fall out of the sky) and that asking for an exemption from the usual parental legal responsibilities therefore means asking the State to make a certain decision. Consequently, they also overlook the fact that any argument for an exemption must appeal to considerations the State may properly take into account in its decision making. This means, most importantly, that supporters of exemptions cannot appeal to the truth of certain religious beliefs, since the State may not assume that any particular religious beliefs are true.[10] It also means, for the same reason, that supporters of exemptions cannot expect the State itself to *adopt* the insiders' perspective, insofar as it is based on religious beliefs.

10 *See* County of Allegheny v. ACLU, 492 U.S. 573, 593–94 (1989) ("The Establishment Clause, at the very least, prohibits government from appearing to take a position on questions of religious belief."); Kathleen M. Sullivan, *Parades, Public Squares and Voucher Payments: Problems of Government Neutrality*, 28 CONN. L. REV. 243, 258 (1996) ("Government itself may espouse any viewpoint a democratic majority wishes *except* a religious viewpoint."). In *McGowan v. Maryland*, Justice Frankfurter stated:

> The Establishment Clause withdrew from the sphere of legitimate legislative concern and competence a specific, but comprehensive, area of human conduct: man's belief or disbelief in the verity of some transcendental idea and man's expression in action of that belief or disbelief. Congress may not make these matters, as such, the subject of legislation, nor, now, may any legislature in this country.

McGowan v. Maryland, 366 U.S. 420, 465–66 (1961) (Frankfurter, J., concurring).

II. How the State Should Go About Deciding

The first question that must be answered, then, is how the State should go about deciding whether to grant some parents an exemption from the normal legal responsibility to secure medical care for a sick or injured child. The two leading theories of state decision making favor a utilitarian approach or a rights-based approach. Below is a brief sketch of how those two approaches would apply to the matter of spiritual treatment exemptions.

A. *A Utilitarian Approach*

Under this approach, the State would take into account the interests of every person who might be affected by its decision, assigning relative weights to the various interests and balancing them to reach its decision. In favor of exemptions, from the State's perspective, would be principally the interest of adult members of the religious group in having their preferences for the children's lives satisfied and in avoiding all the bad feelings mentioned above—anxiety, fear, anger, offense, and sense of threat to their way of life. Also counting in favor of the exemptions would be the children's interest in avoiding whatever bad feelings compelled medical care might produce in them. This interest of children would vary considerably, depending on the children's ages and on the extent to which their parents attempted to insulate them from such effects, as one might expect loving parents to do. Counting against exemptions would be the anxiety and fear the adults might experience as a result of the children's continued suffering and, most importantly, the interests of the children in receiving medical care—interests in avoiding not merely anxiety and fear, but also pain and other forms of physical discomfort, loss or impairment of functioning body parts, and heightened risk of death.

Balancing those competing interests would most likely lead the State to establish guidelines requiring parents to secure medical care for some illnesses and injuries but not for others. For very minor ailments—a cold, perhaps, or a small cut—the State might rationally conclude that compelling violation of religious commands would cause more harm than it prevented, when everyone's interests are taken into account. At the other extreme, where life-threatening, but treatable, problems arise—meningitis or a serious accident—the state would rationally conclude that it would do more good than harm, when everyone's interests are taken into account, to require parents to secure medical care.[11]

11 I speak here of requiring parents to secure medical care, but if there were some alternative way to ensure a child receives medical care that is just as effective and that avoids some of the religious conflict for the parent, then I see no reason not to take that approach—for example, if there might be some way to ensure the State is notified whenever a child is sick or injured, so that it could assume a temporary and limited guardianship for purposes of authorizing treatment. What is important is that the children receive the care, not how exactly that is made to happen. Several commentators have proposed a reporting requirement as an alternative to civil and criminal neglect proceedings. *See, e.g.*, Abraham, *supra* note 2, at 977; Stephen L. Carter, *The Free Exercise Thereof*, 38 WM. & MARY L. REV. 1627, 1653–54 (1997); Jennifer L. Rosato, *Putting Square Pegs in a Round Hole: Procedural Due Process and the Effect of Faith Healing Exemptions on the Prosecution of Faith Healing Parents*, 29 U.S.F. L. REV. 43, 117 (1994); Daniel J. Kearney, Note, *Parental Failure to Provide Child with Medical Assistance Based on Religious Beliefs Causing Child's Death—Involuntary Manslaughter in Pennsylvania*, 90 DICK. L. REV. 861, 885 (1986); Eric W. Treene, Note, *Prayer-Treatment Exemptions to Child Abuse and Neglect Statutes, Manslaughter Prosecutions, and Due Process of Law*, 30 HARV. J. ON LEGIS. 135, 171–76 (1993). However, imposing a reporting duty on parents and "faith healers" has proven ineffective as a means of accomplishing this purpose, because members of these religious groups flout reporting requirements just as readily as they flout the basic duty to secure medical care for a child themselves. *See, e.g.*, Walker v. Superior Court, 763 P.2d 852, 871 (Cal. 1988) ("Under ordinary circumstances, . . . the case of a true believer in faith healing will not even come to the attention of the authorities, unless and until someone dies."); Christine A. Clark, *Religious Accommodation and Criminal Liability*, 17 FLA. ST. U. L. REV. 559, 566, 576, 580 (1990) (describing a case in Florida in which parents and Christian Scientist practitioners allowed a child to die of a treatable medical condition without notifying state officials of her illness despite the existence of a state statute requiring Christian Science practitioners to notify a state agency when a sick child is being treated only with prayer); Kearney, *supra*, at 885–86 (same); Lederman, *supra* note 7, at 923 (explaining why threat of legal punishment has little deterrent effect on Christian Science parents). For some religious groups, such as the Christian Science church, it is just as wrong to acknowledge the existence of a disease as it is to get medical treatment for it. "It is no more Christianly scientific to see disease than it is to experience it." MARY BAKER EDDY, SCIENCE AND HEALTH WITH KEY TO THE SCRIPTURES 421 (First Church of Christ, Scientist 1994) (1875).

> If it becomes necessary to startle mortal mind to break its dream of suffering, vehemently tell your patient that he must awake. Turn his gaze from the false evidence of the senses to the harmonious facts of Soul and immortal being. Tell him that he suffers only as the insane suffer, from false beliefs.
>
> . . . .
>
> . . . There is *no disease.*

Id. at 420–21.

Moreover, even if parents do report that their child is sick, their religious views may lead them to grossly mischaracterize the child's condition, with the result that state child protective workers are led to believe the illness is much less serious than it really is. Currently, statutory child neglect reporting requirements in many states also contain a spiritual treatment exemption making it more likely that the State will not

More refined empirical analysis would be necessary to figure out where exactly the line should be drawn between the very minor and the very serious cases.[12] I am not aware that anyone has done such an empirical analysis, least of all the legislatures that enacted spiritual treatment exemptions. I *suspect* the line would not be far above the most minor cases, because it seems likely that in any case where there is a substantial risk to the child of either substantial short-term suffering or significant long-term impairment, the child's interests in favor of receiving medical attention outweigh all other interests, which are for the most part—from the State's perspective—simply unpleasant psychological states. Additionally, the very minor cases are ones that medical neglect laws would not cover anyway—that is, ones in which

become aware of a child's illness, if at all, until after the child is dead. *See* Rosato, *supra*, at 52 n.44; Treene, *supra*, at 143. Eliminating these exemptions would be a step in the right direction, but would not be sufficient to protect the children.

It is not clear how the State can effectively compel parents to secure medical care for their children; if they are determined to follow their religious beliefs regardless of what the law is. Two possible means of doing so are (1) to eliminate all existing exemptions in civil neglect laws, so that no parent is led to believe the State tolerates this form of neglect to any degree, and (2) to impose stiff sentences under criminal neglect and involuntary manslaughter laws for parents who flout their legal responsibilities, something courts have been—as insider parents well know—reluctant to do. *See* Kearney, *supra*, at 866 ("[J]udicial recognition of the harshness of imposing criminal liability has resulted in the imposition of moderate sentences . . . ."); Edward Egan Smith, Note, *The Criminalization of Belief: When Free Exercise Isn't*, 42 HASTINGS L.J. 1491, 1511 (1991) (noting that a "number of convictions of faith healing parents . . . have been overturned on technical grounds unrelated to the underlying charge" and suggesting judicial sympathy for these parents); Treene, *supra*, at 171–76 (discussing the conflicting messages parents receive from civil neglect laws that contain a spiritual treatment exemption and criminal neglect and involuntary manslaughter laws that do not); *id.* at 197–98 (noting the lenient sentence in a criminal conviction of parents who caused a child to die by neglecting to secure medical care).

12 In theory, the legal obligation might best be stated in terms of what response from parents is required when certain symptoms are present, rather than (or perhaps in addition to) stating it in terms of what parents must do when a child has a particular disease or when a substantial risk is present, since the latter would require parents to make medical judgments they likely are not prepared to make. In practice, though, specifying which symptoms should trigger action might be quite difficult. The practical difficulty of precisely identifying the symptoms that signal a serious or potentially serious problem provides an additional reason for excusing failure to secure medical care only in the most minor cases. *See* Clark, *supra* note 11, at 585–86, 589 (describing cases in which illnesses that appeared on the surface to be less serious turned out to be life-threatening); *cf. id.* at 589 ("Families who rely on spiritual healing need a more certain standard to guide their daily decisions."). Clark also notes that the religious beliefs of Christian Scientist parents would make them less able to identify signs of serious illness, because those beliefs include the view that disease is an illusion. *See id.* at 586.

failure to secure medical care ordinarily would not trigger action by a state agency even when the failure is not motivated by religious objection to medical care, simply because any harm to the children is slight. As such, a religious exemption would serve no legitimate purpose. That said, if a balancing of interests is a proper approach to drawing the line, it really ought to be done by people more suited to the task than are legal academics.

That is a quick take on a utilitarian approach. I know of no one who takes such an approach to this issue, at least not self-consciously and rigorously. As noted above, outsiders who speak to the issue tend to focus just on a subset of all interests. This might be reasoning with blinders on, or it might be that they favor more of a rights-based approach, which shortcuts the decision making process somewhat by honing in on the people who have such great interests at stake that they might be said to have a right to protection of their interests. This right trumps consideration of the non-right protected interests of others. A rights-based approach is certainly a defensible one, and it is the approach typically taken to medical decision making by or for adults, so let us see what the State should conclude if it applied that approach.

B. *A Rights-Based Approach*

Who is the *best* candidate for being a right-holder in this context? The answer to that question is so obvious that it is bewildering how little attention is paid to these persons by supporters of exemptions. The sick or injured child is, of course, the best candidate for being a right-holder. It is the child's body and the child's life that are the subject of discussion. Imagine having legal decisions and scholarly arguments regarding the medical treatment of elderly, incompetent persons turn on the rights of family members, while largely ignoring the rights of the elderly person. We would regard that as not merely improper, but also morally offensive. Yet that is what routinely happens with children in this context (and many others).

I am not aware that any supporter of exemptions has ever explicitly denied that children have the most important interests and rights at stake in this matter, and I cannot imagine anyone doing so. Instead, many simply ignore the children, treating the conflict as one involving only parents, religious communities, and the State;[13] perhaps suspecting that it is not possible to articulate a plausible argument that children have a right to spiritual treatment exemptions.

13 *See, e.g.*, Ingram, *supra* note 1, at 65; Smith, *supra* note 11, at 1510; Steckler, *supra* note 8, at 514–15.

Ignoring the welfare and rights of the children is clearly inappropriate. Other supporters of exemptions have a different strategy for dealing with children's rights, which is to argue that the State should defer to parents' views about what the content of their children's rights is, just as they argue that the State must defer to parents' views of what their children's interests are. I address that deference argument in Section C.

1. Giving Content to Children's Rights

To say that children are the best candidates for being right-holders is not to demonstrate the correctness of any ultimate conclusion; it is necessary first to give content to the rights of the children. So what content should our legal system give to children's rights in this context?[14] A comparison with the rights of adults who have never been competent is instructive. Never-competent adults, many of whom are still in the care of their parents, are entitled to have decisions about their medical care based on their interests and not on the interests of their caretakers.[15] Requests by parents of mentally retarded women to have them sterilized are a case in point. For such a procedure to be undertaken, guardians must show that the benefits of the procedure for the woman outweigh its costs for her.[16] The guardian's own inter-

14 I pose this primarily as a moral, rather than doctrinal, legal question, and for the purpose of critiquing existing doctrine, which gives little recognition to the rights of children in religious child-rearing contexts. *See* James G. Dwyer, *Parents' Religion and Children's Welfare: Debunking the Doctrine of Parents' Rights*, 82 CAL. L. REV. 1371, 1379–405 (1994). The argument here that analogizes children's situations to that of incompetent adults could, however, be couched in terms of legal doctrine interpreting the Equal Protection Clause of the Fourteenth Amendment. One could argue that children are similarly situated to never-competent adults and so should receive the same legal protections for their physical well-being. Further below, I advance a different sort of equal protection argument, one that argues against discrimination among groups of children based on the religious beliefs of their parents. *See infra* notes 18–19 and accompanying text.

15 *See* John E. Donaldson, *Reform of Adult Guardianship Law*, 32 U. RICH. L. REV. 1273, 1291–93 (1998) (describing the law of guardianship in Virginia); Hal Fliegelman & Debora C. Fliegelman, *Giving Guardians the Power To Do Medicaid Planning*, 32 WAKE FOREST L. REV. 341, 349–51 (1997).

16 *See, e.g.*, *In re* C.D.M., 627 P.2d 607, 612–13 (Alaska 1981); *In re* Debra B., 495 A.2d 781, 782–83 (Me. 1985); *In re* Wirsing, 573 N.W.2d 51, 55 (Mich. 1998); *In re* Grady, 426 A.2d 467, 474–75 (N.J. 1981); Estate of C.W., 640 A.2d 427, 428 (Pa. Super. Ct. 1994); *see also* Elizabeth S. Scott, *Sterilization of Mentally Retarded Persons: Reproductive Rights and Family Privacy*, 1986 DUKE L.J. 806, 817–23 (explaining the current sterilization laws in different states, and finding that a court generally may authorize sterilization for an incompetent woman only if it finds clear and convincing evidence that sterilization would be in the woman's best interests).

ests do not factor into the determination.[17] There is no good reason why children should not have the same right, a right to have decisions about their medical care based on *their* interests rather than on the interests of their caretakers—that is, their parents.

In practice, this would mean that the children in these religious groups have a right to medical care whenever the benefits for them of receiving care outweigh whatever costs such care might entail *for them*, all things considered. In other words, in establishing guidelines for parental responsibility to secure medical care, the State should balance only the children's interests. From the State's perspective, the costs of compelled medical care would include any effects on children's psychological well being from seeing their parents' wishes thwarted or from believing that such treatment will violate God's will and perhaps even harm them, if they are old enough to have such thoughts. The costs would not include a threat to the children's chances for salvation or damage to their relationship with God, since the State may not make judgments about those things. Guidelines based on a balancing of the costs the State can recognize against the psychological and physical benefits of medical care might still exclude some truly minor cases from compulsory medical care, but presumably fewer than when the interests of adults were in the mix. And as noted above, truly minor illnesses or injuries would not be covered by medical neglect laws anyway, so there would be no warrant for including a religious exemption in neglect statutes. Again, it does not appear that anyone has done such a balancing of costs and benefits in a rigorous way, and legal academics—including myself—would not appear particularly well-equipped to do it. What I aim to establish here is the moral position that children of the members of these religious groups possess a right to have decisions about their health care made solely on the basis of their interests.

Importantly, the right of incompetent adults to have decisions based on what is best for them is not affected by the religious beliefs

17 *See, e.g.*, *In re* Debra B., 495 A.2d at 782 (noting that the purpose of state legislation concerning sterilization of incompetent adults is "to ensure that no person who is incapable of informed consent may be sterilized unless the operation is necessary to that person's best interests"); *In re* Terwilliger, 450 A.2d 1376, 1382 (Pa. Super. Ct. 1982) ("[I]n making the decision of whether to authorize sterilization, a court should consider only the best interest of the incompetent person, not the interests or convenience of the individual's parents, the guardian or of society . . . ."); *see also* Scott, *supra* note 16, at 821–22 (stating that current law excludes consideration of parents' interests from the sterilization decision).

of their caretakers.[18] In fact, it would be unconstitutional for a State to diminish or eliminate an incompetent adult's rights because of the religious beliefs of her caretaker. The State would be affording certain incompetent adults lesser protection of the laws than it gives to others, for reasons not tied to *their* well being, and would therefore violate the Equal Protection Clause of the Fourteenth Amendment. There is no good reason why children of Christian Scientists should not have a similar equal protection right to the same legal protection of their welfare that other children receive. If spiritual treatment exemptions compromise their welfare, they violate the Equal Protection Clause.[19] An Ohio court struck down the religious exemption in that state's child medical neglect laws for precisely this reason. In doing so, the court explained:

> [I]f the real purpose of [the neglect law] is to protect children from parental defalcation, then the prayer exception creates a group of children who will never be so protected, through no fault or choice of their own. . . . Why . . . should children not be afforded special protection by our laws, each child on an equal basis with every other child, where the denial of that protection may injure or cripple the child for life or even result in that child's premature death? This special protection should be guaranteed to all such children until they have their own opportunity to make life's important religious decisions for themselves upon attainment of the age of reason. After all, given the opportunity when grown up, a child may someday choose to reject the most sincerely held of his parents' religious beliefs, just as the parents on trial here have apparently grown to reject some beliefs of their parents. Equal protection should not be

18 *See, e.g., In re* Quinlan, 355 A.2d 647, 661–62 (N.J. 1976) (rejecting a claim by the parents of an adult in a persistent vegetative state that they had a right based on their religious beliefs to decide that life support would be terminated and stating, "[w]e do not recognize an independent parental right of religious freedom to support the relief requested").

19 For an extended argument that spiritual treatment exemptions in child neglect laws violate the equal protection rights of children who are consequently denied necessary medical care, see generally James G. Dwyer, *The Children We Abandon: Religious Exemptions to Child Welfare and Education Laws as Denials of Equal Protection to Children of Religious Objectors*, 74 N.C. L. Rev. 1321 (1996). *See also* Massie, *supra* note 2, at 731–32 (noting that, although children have never been defined as a suspect class under the equal protection doctrine, courts have traditionally "regarded governmental actions specifically affecting the welfare of children with special care"); Monopoli, *supra* note 2, at 348–49 (1991) (regardless of how children whose parents practice spiritual healing are classified under the equal proection doctrine, the court must at least find the exception rationally related to the statute's purpose for enactement); Swan, *supra* note 2, at 92–94 (referring to four state court cases that hold a religious exemption statute pertaining to children violates the Fourteenth Amendment).

denied to innocent babies, whether under the label of "religious freedom" or otherwise.[20]

To avoid the imputation of unconstitutionality, a State would need a *valid* reason for treating these children differently, and a valid reason would only be one that rested on the interests of the children themselves.[21] To the extent that these children are similarly situated to other children—that is, have the same interests as other children—spiritual treatment exemptions cannot be saved from the equal protection charge. Children of insiders are *somewhat* differently situated, because their psychological interests are shaped to some degree by their parents' religious beliefs, but otherwise the State must regard these children as having the same interests as other children have in avoiding pain, disfigurement, impairment, and death. If the State fails to accord the same weight to the interests of insiders' children that it gives to the interests of outsiders' children, it violates the right of insiders' children to equal protection.[22]

In sum, a comparison with never-competent adults suggests that children in general have a substantive moral right to medical decision making based on their interests and that children of "religious objectors" have a formal legal right to equal protection of the laws—in particular, to the protection afforded by laws guarding children's fundamental interest in physical health. A spiritual treatment exemption violates those rights unless the State can demonstrate that the exemption is really in the children's best interests, as the State sees

20 Ohio v. Miskimens, 490 N.E.2d 931, 935–36 (Ohio Ct. Com. Pl. 1984); *see also* Brown v. Stone, 378 So. 2d 218, 223 (Miss. 1979) (invalidating a religious exemption to Mississippi's child immunization law as a violation of children's right to equal protection of child welfare laws).

21 For an explanation of why parents' rights and interests cannot provide a legitimate basis for such discrimination, see Dwyer, *supra* note 19, at 1423–33.

22 *See* Ronald Dworkin, A Matter of Principle 191 (1985) ("[T]here is broad agreement within modern politics that the government must treat all its citizens with equal concern and respect . . . ."); Ronald Dworkin, *What is Equality? Part 3: The Place of Liberty*, 73 Iowa L. Rev. 1, 7 (1987) ("[W]e are now united in accepting the abstract egalitarian principle: government must act to make the lives of those it governs better lives, and it must show equal concern for the life of each."); Gregory Vlastos, *Justice and Equality*, *in* Theories of Rights 41, 41–42 (Jeremy Waldron ed., 1984) (noting that this notion of formal equality of consideration has been embedded in the concept of justice since its origins in Ancient Greece); *cf.* FCC v. Beach Communications, Inc., 508 U.S. 307, 323 n.3 (1993) (Stevens, J., concurring) ("[W]hen Congress imposes a burden on one group, but leaves unaffected another that is similarly, though not identically, situated, . . . we should inquire whether the classification is rationally related to 'a legitimate purpose that we may reasonably presume to have motivated an impartial legislature.'" (quoting U.S. R.R. Ret. Bd. v. Fritz, 449 U.S. 166, 181 (1980) (Stevens, J., concurring))).

them. I am not aware that any supporter of exemptions has made that case. The "as the State sees them" modifier still requires support, and this is coming in Section C, but first I must say something about parents' rights, which preoccupy the courts and supporters of exemptions.

2. Parents' Rights

Supporters of exemptions typically assert that parents in these religious groups have a prima facie right to withhold medical care from their children, a right that is outweighed by other considerations, if ever, only in the most extreme cases.[23] They typically do not claim the same right for other parents—that is, those for whom it is not a matter of religious principle. Rather, they conceive of the right as primarily one of religious freedom.[24] There is in our constitutional scheme a general right to religious freedom, though today it does not by itself support claims for exemptions from generally applicable legal obligations.[25] The general right is founded upon the liberal principle of self-determination, which holds that people are better off in the long run and receive the respect they are due as moral agents when the

23 *See, e.g.*, Ingram, *supra* note 1, at 60, 65; Nobel, *supra* note 3, at 636; DiCamillo, *supra* note 3, at 143–44; Lederman, *supra* note 7, at 907 (arguing that parents' free exercise right is never outweighed by the interests of their children); Shelli Dawn Robinson, Comment, Commonwealth v. Twitchell: *Who Owns the Child?*, 7 J. CONTEMP. HEALTH L. & POL'Y 413, 431 (1991); Smith, *supra* note 11, at 1510; Steckler, *supra* note 8, at 519.

24 *See, e.g.*, Clark, *supra* note 11, at 587–89; Nobel, *supra* note 3, at 636 ("To promote religious liberty and family integrity, judges should rarely second-guess consensual family healthcare decisions based on religious considerations."); *id.* at 660 (describing judicial rejection of parental claims to a free exercise right to provide "religious treatment alone" as an "aberration of free exercise jurisprudence"); Kearney, *supra* note 11, at 889; Lederman, *supra* note 7, at 894–95, 898; Robinson, *supra* note 23, at 425–29; Steckler, *supra* note 8, at 519; *cf.* Lainie Friedman Ross & Timothy J. Aspinwall, *Religious Exemptions to the Immunization Statutes: Balancing Public Health and Religious Freedom*, 25 J.L. MED. & ETHICS 202, 205 (1997) (arguing in favor of religious exemptions to child immunization laws, on the basis of parents' right to religious freedom). *But see* Robinson, *supra* note 23, at 431 (asserting that parents should be excused for medical neglect regardless of the reason for their failure to secure medical care—or in other words, that there should be no such thing as medical neglect of children).

25 *See* Employment Div. v. Smith, 494 U.S. 872, 881–82 (1990) (holding that facially neutral and generally applicable laws that incidentally burden religious practice do not violate the Free Exercise Clause, but distinguishing cases—such as religious parenting—that involve an additional constitutional right, such as a substantive due process right, by suggesting that the second right somehow enhances the free exercise claim).

State lets them live their own lives by their own lights.[26] The greatest restriction on the right is the harm principle—religious freedom, like freedom more generally, is properly curtailed when it threatens significant harm to other persons, as the State sees it.[27]

The Supreme Court, in its important 1990 free exercise decision, *Employment Division v. Smith*,[28] treated parental free exercise rights differently from ordinary free exercise rights, as it should have. However, the Court got things backwards. The case before the Court involved claims by Native American adults, on behalf of themselves, that Oregon law prohibiting use of peyote violated their free exercise rights.[29] The Court held that generally applicable laws that are neutral as to religion, as Oregon's drug laws were, do not violate the Free Exercise Clause even if they incidentally burden religious practice.[30] Such laws do not trigger the strict scrutiny sometimes applied in the past in free exercise cases. In dictum, *Smith* suggested that parental free exercise rights are *stronger* than free exercise rights in non-child rearing contexts—specifically, that they might still trigger strict scrutiny.[31] But clearly, the case for attributing rights is *weaker* when a person seeks protection of action directed at controlling the lives of *other* persons than when the right-holder is engaging in *self*-determination. Surely any right I have to direct my children's lives should be weaker than the right I have to control my own life, not vice versa. At best, the parental free exercise right should be a relatively weak one, insufficient to block state action that promotes the health of children.

Decisions of the Supreme Court in which child rearing was directly at issue support this conclusion. In only two of those cases—*Prince v. Massachusetts*[32] and *Jehovah's Witnesses v. King County Hospital*[33]—was the record deemed to support a finding that parents'

26 *See* JOHN LOCKE, A LETTER CONCERNING TOLERATION 38 (James H. Tully ed., Hackett Pub. Co. 1983) (1689); JOHN STUART MILL, ON LIBERTY 53–73 (Elizabeth Rapaport ed., Hackett Pub. Co. 1978) (1859); JOHN RAWLS, A THEORY OF JUSTICE 543–44 (1971); *see also* Cruzan v. Mo. Dep't of Health, 497 U.S. 261, 287 (1990) (O'Connor, J., concurring) ("[O]ur notions of liberty are inextricably entwined with our idea of physical freedom and self-determination.").

27 *See* 1 JOEL FEINBERG, THE MORAL LIMITS OF THE CRIMINAL LAW: HARM TO OTHERS 10–12 (1985); MILL, *supra* note 26, at 9. Legal decisions concerning refusal of medical care by competent adults are consistent with this description of rights and their limitations. *See* Nobel, *supra* note 3, at 616–20.

28 494 U.S. 872 (1990).

29 *See id.* at 874.

30 *See id.* at 882.

31 *See id.*

32 321 U.S. 158 (1944).

33 278 F. Supp. 488 (W.D. Wash. 1967), *aff'd per curiam*, 390 U.S. 598 (1968).

choices would harm the children at issue, and in both cases the Court rejected the parents' free exercise claim. In *Prince*, the Court held that simply allowing a child to distribute religious pamphlets in the streets posed sufficient danger to the child's welfare as to justify a restriction on the parents' child-rearing freedom.[34] In *King County Hospital*, the Court affirmed without opinion[35] a lower court decision to order blood transfusions for a child who needed surgery over the religious objection of the child's Jehovah's Witness parents.[36]

In fact, the State arguably should not assign any *right*—that is, any legal *entitlement*—to protect choices and actions that are not a matter of self-determination. Such a right finds no support in general liberal political principles. To view religiously-motivated child medical neglect as a First Amendment issue is as much a conceptual mistake as it would be to view religiously-motivated wife-beating as a First Amendment issue. Additionally, this right directly conflicts with a principle that is basic to our legal and moral culture—namely, that no one is *entitled* to control the life of another person in accordance with their own preferences. This principle is manifest not only in the abolition of slavery and in the demise of the coverture regime in domestic relations law, but also in the legal rules governing caretaking for incompetent adults.[37] Guardians for incompetent adults are not deemed entitled to direct the life of the ward in a way that furthers the guardians' own interests, nor to have a right to decide what the ward's interests are, to the exclusion of efforts by the State to constrain a guardian's discretion. Rather, they are deemed to occupy a fiduciary role as a matter of legal privilege.

This same principle supports the conclusion that parents, too, should not be deemed right-holders in this situation at all, but rather should be viewed as fiduciaries occupying a caretaking role as a matter

34 *See* 321 U.S. at 170. The Court also indicated in dictum that parental free exercise rights were inadequate to support a claim for exemption from child immunization laws, stating that a parent "cannot claim freedom from compulsory vaccination for the child more than for himself on religious grounds. The right to practice religion freely does not include liberty to expose the community or the child to communicable disease or the latter to ill health or death." *Id.* at 166–67 (citation omitted); *see also* Brown v. Stone, 378 So. 2d 218, 223 (Miss. 1979) (rejecting parental free exercise challenge to child immunization requirement and stating, "To the extent that [immunization] may conflict with the religious beliefs of a parent, however sincerely entertained, the interests of the school children must prevail").

35 *See* 390 U.S. at 598.

36 *King County Hosp.*, 278 F. Supp. at 504–05.

37 For an extended exposition of this point, see Dwyer, *supra* note 14, at 1405–23.

of legal privilege.[38] The Ohio court that invalidated that state's spiritual treatment exemption to medical neglect laws on equal protection grounds recognized this limitation on rights to self-determination when it stated:

> [I]t is not the personal religious practices of these parents which are sought to be regulated. An important line must be drawn between the right of an individual to practice his religion by refusing medical treatment for his own illness and that of a parent to practice his religion by refusing to obtain or permit medical treatment for another person, i.e., his child. This court, as with any governmental entity, can neither know nor care whether someone who relies solely on faith healing for his own affliction is religiously or scripturally "correct." But the right to hold one's own religious beliefs, and to act in conformity with those beliefs, does not and cannot include the right to endanger the life or health of others, including his or her children.[39]

At a minimum, then, parents should not be deemed holders of rights that have greater force than the rights of their children. The children's rights should therefore be dispositive.

Academic supporters of parental rights often echo the courts in reciting the syllogism that because parents have a fundamental interest in raising their children, parents should have child-rearing rights.[40] Neither these academics nor the courts seem to have much understanding of what makes an interest fundamental. It surely is not the subjective importance people assign to having their wishes fulfilled. A fundamental interest is a *basic* component of well being, fulfillment of which is prerequisite to pursuing any higher aims in life.[41] Health and elementary and secondary education are interests of that sort. Child rearing is not; it is, rather, one of the higher aims that

38 For an extended argument along these lines, see *id.* For an explanation of the distinction between a right and a privilege, see *id.* at 1374–75.

39 Ohio v. Miskimens, 490 N.E.2d 931, 934 (Ohio Ct. Com. Pl. 1984) (emphasis added).

40 *See, e.g.*, William Galston, *Expressive Liberty, Moral Pluralism, Political Pluralism: Three Sources of Liberal Theory*, 40 WM. & MARY L. REV. 869, 874 (1999); Stephen G. Gilles, *On Educating Children: A Parentalist Manifesto*, 63 U. CHI. L. REV. 937, 940 (1996); *see also* Santosky v. Kramer, 455 U.S. 745, 753 (1982) (describing the ability to make decisions regarding child rearing as a "fundamental liberty interest"); Wisconsin v. Yoder, 406 U.S. 205, 232 (1972) (conferring on Amish parents a constitutional right to keep their high school age children out of school by relying on "the fundamental interest of parents . . . to guide the religious future and education of their children").

41 *See* FEINBERG, *supra* note 27, at 37–38.

some of us choose to pursue.[42] In any event, what is under consideration in the debate over spiritual treatment exemptions is not the prospect of denying some adults *any* opportunity to raise children, but rather simply denying parents the power to effectuate one particular choice regarding their children's lives. Surely, having that power is not fundamental to any adult's well being.[43]

In sum, both a utilitarian approach and a rights-based approach tentatively support the conclusion that spiritual treatment exemptions are morally and legally impermissible. A more definite conclusion would require empirical investigation and analysis of a kind that has yet to be done. But it is plausible to think that if a child is likely to incur substantial suffering or significant long-term harm as a result of not receiving medical care, then the child's interests in receiving care outweigh all competing interests. When that is the case, the State should require medical care regardless of what the child's parents believe, because the child is entitled to protection of his or her basic welfare.

C. *Should the State Defer to the Insiders' Perspective?*

Some supporters of spiritual treatment exemptions recognize that they cannot simply ignore the welfare and rights of the children involved and adopt an alternative strategy to supporting the conclusion that parents in these religious groups should be able to deny their children medical care. They ask, "Who determines what a child's interests are?" and answer this question by asserting that parents have a right to do so and the State does not.[44] They then point out that the parents in these religious groups have a different perspective on human welfare and that, from the parents' perspective, the children are better off not receiving medical care.[45]

42 *See id.* at 37 (including "successfully raising a family" among those human interests that are "ulterior" rather than fundamental).

43 *Cf.* Kendall v. Kendall, 687 N.E.2d 1228, 1236 (Mass. 1997) (holding that restriction on non-custodial parent's exposure of children to his religion's beliefs and services did not violate his parental or free exercise rights and concluding that "requiring only that he limit sharing certain aspects of his beliefs with his children" imposed only a minimal burden on those rights and was justified by a finding that the restriction was in the best interests of the children).

44 *See, e.g.*, Ingram, *supra* note 1, at 65 ("The first amendment prohibits the state from prescribing that physical life on earth is more important than life hereafter. . . . [P]arents have the right to make that decision for their children . . . ."); DiCamillo, *supra* note 3, at 157; Robinson, *supra* note 23, at 415–16, 431.

45 *See, e.g.*, Ingram, *supra* note 1, at 58, 62–65; Lederman, *supra* note 7, at 923.

This brings us, then, to the final issue—whether the State should defer to the insiders' perspective. Essentially, what most supporters of spiritual treatment exemptions to medical neglect laws argue is not that extensive exemptions are compelled by a proper balancing of interests *as the State sees them,* but rather that the State's view of what a child's interests are should not be controlling. They contend that the parents' view of what a child's interests are and of how best to promote them should instead be controlling in children's lives.[46]

This is distinct from a claim simply for parental freedom, for noninterference with actions motivated by personal belief. I considered that claim above and concluded that it is, at best, very weak in this context, where the freedom for which protection is sought is freedom to control the lives of other persons rather than to engage in self-determination. The claim here is about spheres of authority. It is essentially a claim about the proper domain of the State. It is a claim that parental control over children's lives is primordial, outside the public realm, and no business of the State.

Curiously, though, most proponents of this sort of "spheres of authority" position allow for state control over child rearing at the margins. The State may step in to prevent death.[47] But they provide no real explanation for this qualification of the separate spheres position, for ceding some authority to the State. Instead, they may talk of bounds of reasonableness; parents' choices should control unless they are unreasonable, and a choice that will lead to a child's death is unreasonable.[48] However, not only do supporters of exemptions fail to offer a coherent account of what "reasonable" means, but they also never explain why this or any other standard should limit parental authority within the private domain. If it is truly a separate domain, then how can the State *ever* legitimately intrude into child rearing? They do not tell us. Nor do they provide an argument for postulating separate spheres in the first place. Nor an explanation of why the "family as separate sphere" position would not also apply in non-religious child-rearing contexts, and indeed to relations between spouses. Should domestic violence laws contain a religious exemption on the theory that abusive husbands are entitled to determine what their

46 *See, e.g.*, Ingram, *supra* note 1, at 65; DiCamillo, *supra* note 3, at 143–44.

47 *See, e.g.*, Nobel, *supra* note 3, at 651, 710; Kearney, *supra* note 11, at 885. Several courts have also taken this position, drawing the line of permissible court intervention between life-threatening and other conditions. *See* Dwyer, *supra* note 19, at 1356.

48 *See, e.g.*, Smith, *supra* note 11, at 1523–25 (arguing that courts should judge parents' conduct in denying medical care to children by a subjective rather than objective standard of reasonableness); Steckler, *supra* note 8, at 517 (same).

wives' best interests are, at least so long as their wives do not object?[49] If not, then supporters of spiritual treatment exemptions need to explain why not.

In any event, the reality is that the family is not a separate, primordial sphere that is or can be cordoned off from the power of the State. The law creates the family, and things could not be otherwise.[50] The State assigns legal custody to particular adults for each and every child at the time of birth, reassigns custody at later points in the lives of a large percentage of children (for example, in connection with a divorce), and attaches to custody numerous legal rights and powers. Without the law creating and protecting parent-child relationships in this way, chaos would reign. So the separate spheres argument, in addition to being theoretically ungrounded, is out of touch with reality. It therefore fails as a basis for the position that the State should defer to the views of religious parents as to what constitutes the interests and rights of their children. The State does and must establish the rules for parental control over children's lives and, in doing so, must rest its judgment on assumptions about children's interests and rights as it sees them. In doing so, the State might justifiably conclude that parents should have presumptive authority to make decisions for children in many aspects of their lives, because the State has good reason to believe that it is, in general, best for children that their par-

49 For a description and critique of cases in which criminal defendants have based a defense to charges of rape, kidnap, and other crimes against adult (usually female) victims on the defendant's holding non-western cultural beliefs, see generally Doriane Lambelet Coleman, *Individualizing Justice Through Multiculturalism: The Liberals' Dilemma*, 96 COLUM. L. REV. 1093 (1996). Coleman points out that arguments for a cultural defense in such adult contexts have numerous problems: they overlook the fact that the primary function of the criminal law is to protect victims and the public generally from harmful conduct; excusing conduct on the basis of cultural beliefs sends the message that such conduct is acceptable, and so persons inclined to engage in such behavior have no reason to conform to majoritarian norms; basing culpability on the culture of the victim amounts to a violation of equal protection guarantees and sends a message to subordinate members of cultural minorities that they are not worthy of the protection of our laws and cannot hope to escape the oppressive practices of the culture of their upbringing; and condoning practices motivated by values and attitudes that we as a society have rejected erodes the progress we have made toward eliminating injustice and the treatment of certain classes of persons as less worthy human beings. *See id.* at 1136–44. All of these problems also afflict arguments for religious exemptions to child neglect laws.

50 *See generally* Frances E. Olsen, *The Myth of State Intervention in the Family*, 18 U. MICH. J.L. REFORM 835 (1985) (demonstrating that what is generally viewed as state non-intervention in the family is actually just another kind of state intervention—namely, state creation and enforcement of legal rights for the dominant person in family relationships).

ents have that presumptive authority. What supporters of spiritual treatment exemptions need to argue is that the State has good reason to believe that it is best for children that their parents have authority to deny them medical care that the State deems necessary for the children's physical well-being whenever such care conflicts with the parents' religious beliefs. They have yet to offer any such reason.

III. Responses to Objections

Certain objections arise with some regularity to the position that children are entitled to greater restrictions on parental child rearing freedom than currently exist. Many of these are variants on a few core ideas. I have responded above to certain variants of these ideas, but want to address other variants more explicitly here. They are the claims that (1) parents are, as an empirical matter, best positioned to decide what is best for their children, (2) parents have a greater moral claim than the State to make decisions about children's lives, (3) the State has insufficient interest in child rearing absent extreme harm to children, and (4) the State may not assume that parents' religious beliefs are false.

A. *Parents Are in the Best Position to Decide*

A common refrain among those who endorse plenary parental control over children's lives, in this and other contexts, is that parents are in a better position than the State to decide what is best for children.[51] The claim is often stated in very broad terms; in any area of a child's life—medical care, education, discipline, et cetera—parents know best.[52] What is the basis for that assertion? It is really a deductive argument rather than a conclusion drawn from empirical evidence. The syllogism goes like this: Parents love their children more than anyone else loves them and know their children better than anyone else knows them. Therefore, parents are the best decisionmakers.[53]

This is clearly inadequate as an argument for parental authority in any aspect of children's lives. One could respond by challenging the premise that all parents know and love their children best, by

51 *See, e.g.*, Gilles, *supra* note 40, at 953–57; Ingram, *supra* note 1, at 58–59; *cf.* Parham v. J.R., 442 U.S. 584, 602 (1979) ("The law's concept of the family . . . historically . . . has recognized that natural bonds of affection lead parents to act in the best interests of their children." (citations omitted)).

52 *See, e.g.*, Ingram, *supra* note 1, at 58–59.

53 Stephen Gilles argues for plenary parental control over children's education along these lines. *See* Gilles, *supra* note 40, at 953–60.

pointing out that far too many parents give far too little love and attention to their children.[54] One could also point out that in religious contexts, such as that of spiritual treatment exemptions or that of religious objections to school curriculum, there is the problem of competing motivations. Parents motivated by a sense of religious obligation to oppose mainstream child-rearing norms might be, by virtue of that motivation, less likely to make decisions and act in a manner consistent with their children's welfare, even as they view their children's welfare from their own perspective. Because religious commands regarding child rearing are not necessarily dictated by what is best for children, even as seen from within the religious perspective from which the command emanates, a parent's sense of religious obligation might detract from or override the motivation, which a parent otherwise has, to do what is best for a child. The Old Testament story of Abraham preparing to stab to death and burn his son Isaac at God's command illustrates the potential conflict quite well.[55] In light of this fact about religious obligation, it is ironic that this argument from parental motivation usually appears in support of special exemptions from legal child-rearing responsibilities for parents who oppose mainstream child-rearing norms on religious grounds.[56] One might think that parents have a stronger claim for an exemption when motivated by an alternative secular view of what is best for children—for example, by a scientifically-based view that certain vaccines create risks of harm that outweigh potential benefits for individual children, or that some illnesses, such as the flu, are best treated by letting the body develop and deploy its own defenses, rather than by administering drugs that a doctor might prescribe.

A larger problem with this objection, though, is that even if it *were* true that all parents were perfectly loving and whole-heartedly committed to parenting, the implicit major premise in the syllogism above—that this is all it takes to be a good parent or to make the best decisions for a child—is clearly false. Many factors go into making good decisions for one's children. Loving concern is just one such factor. Also critical are competence and knowledge, and merely living with a child does not supply much of either.

54 *Cf.* BRUCE A. CHADWICK & TIM B. HEATON, STATISTICAL HANDBOOK ON THE AMERICAN FAMILY 135–36 (2d ed. 1999) (indicating that there were over one million child victims of substantiated maltreatment—including emotional abuse, sexual abuse, physical abuse, and neglect—in the United States in 1995 and almost three million children reported to be victims of parental abuse or neglect in that year).

55 *Genesis* 22:1–14. There is no indication in this biblical story that Abraham believed killing Isaac would be good for Isaac.

56 *See supra* note 22.

Living with a child makes one more aware than other people of what a child's unique interests and temperament are, but that is not sufficient to inform a decision regarding proper nutrition, health care, education, et cetera. There is a great deal to know about children's development that is more general in nature, that is not unique to one's own child, and that is not apparent simply from looking at and interacting with a child. If that were not the case, there would be no point in having medical schools train pediatricians or having schools of education train teachers. I am certain that my wife and I love our two daughters more than anyone else does and that we know better than anyone else what our daughters' personalities are like, what makes them laugh and what upsets them. But I am also certain that on almost any significant decision we have to make about their lives, there are people who have made a career of studying that aspect of child rearing who could tell us a lot we would not otherwise know about what is generally best for children in that regard. Simply loving and interacting with our children tells us little about how to make such decisions.

That competence and knowledge are critical, and that many parents make little effort to acquire them, is evident from the bad choices that parents in this country make on a routine basis. Listening to proponents of the "parents know best" mantra, one might suppose that few parents in this country feed their children junk food on a regular basis, that few parents in this country allow their children to watch garbage television or play shoot-and-kill video games for most of their time outside of school, and that few parents in this country do such a poor job of instilling self-discipline and self-respect that their children become teen delinquents or school dropouts. I am not suggesting here that state officials are all-knowing or that the State should be legislating what children eat for breakfast and what children do at home after school, but rather that "parents know best" is not a particularly credible response to an argument for increased restriction of parental freedom in hardly any area of children's lives. Parents vary tremendously in their competence to make good choices for their children, and the number of parents whose ability is quite low is not trivial.[57]

---

57 *Cf.* CHADWICK & HEATON, *supra* note 54, at 118 (showing that 49% of parents say they do not restrict the amount of television their five to seventeen year-old children watch and that 19% say they do not restrict the content of what their children watch); *id.* at 117 (showing that 94% of parents allow their children to be home alone after school, at night, and even overnight); *id.* at 115 (showing that 10% of children have been suspended or expelled from school and that 2.4% drop out of school); *id.* at 113 (showing that 10% of parents *give themselves* a grade of C or worse for the

Talk about competence, however, is really beside the point in the present context. In religious child-rearing contexts, there is a more fundamental problem with the "parents know best" position that its proponents overlook. It does not make sense to argue that parents know better than the State how to promote children's welfare when parents have an entirely different view of what constitutes a child's welfare, or have a view as to how to promote their child's temporal welfare that is based on faith rather than on the kinds of empirical evidence on which the State must rely. If parents believe their children's welfare consists principally in eternal salvation and temporal well-being should be sacrificed whenever necessary to secure that ultimate good, then comparing their ability to act in their children's best interests with the State's ability is comparing apples and oranges. The State does not aim to secure salvation for any of us; it aims at promoting temporal well-being. Likewise, if some parents are convinced that prayer is sufficient treatment for meningitis and that also administering penicillin would be counter-productive, what separates them from doctors and state health officials is not a degree of competence but rather religious belief. Their greater love for and familiarity with their children is irrelevant to the question the State must answer—whether their children should receive penicillin.

What opponents of restrictions on parenting in religious contexts, such as the spiritual treatment debate, need to argue is that parents are entitled to define what the aims are for their children and what sources of instruction on healing are authoritative. They must argue that parents have a right to preclude the State from deciding that the proper aim for the child, until the child grows up and decides for herself wherein her welfare resides, is temporal well-being or from deciding that the best conclusions of the scientific community are authoritative. Relative motivation and competence have nothing to do with those issues. Asserting that parents love most and know best is simply talking around the real issue in these religious child-rearing cases.[58]

---

quality of their parenting); *id.* at 124 (reporting the results of a survey of parents showing that 29% seldom or never have calm discussions with their children about serious disagreements between them); *id.* at 104 (showing that 20% of parents report almost never talking with their children about things that worry the children and that 62% report almost never talking with their children about things that excite the children); JOSEPH P. VITERITTI, CHOOSING EQUALITY: SCHOOL CHOICE, THE CONSTITUTION, AND CIVIL SOCIETY 9 (1999) (noting the great disparity among parents in their ability to make intelligent choices about their children's education).

58 Stephen Gilles, addressing authority over children's education, appears to take the position that the State should conclude that parents, at least when motivated by

B. *Parents Have a Greater Moral Claim to Decide for Children*

More relevant to the issue of who gets to define the ends of child rearing is the assertion that parents have a superior moral claim to that power than the State does.[59] Some liberals—so called "liberal statists"—do appear to take the position that the State has a superior moral claim to that power in some areas of children's lives. Amy Gutmann has argued, for example, that society as a whole, acting through the instrumentality of the State, is entitled to control children's education to a substantial degree in order to serve certain collective ends—principally the reproduction of democratic culture from one generation to the next.[60] But that is certainly not the only logical alternative

religious belief, are entitled to plenary control of this aspect of children's lives because parents have greater incentive to further their children's interests *as they perceive them* than the State has to further children's interests *as it perceives them. See* Gilles, *supra* note 40, at 940. He adds as an important proviso, though, that parents must be acting within bounds of reasonableness and he appears to presume that the State will define what those bounds are (who else would do it?). *See id.* But for the State to reach the conclusion Gilles urges regarding parental entitlement, the State would have to assume that, from *its* perspective, it is good for children to have promoted their interests as their parents perceive them. This in turn would require the State to regard the parents' perception as accurate, or at least plausible, based on the State's own criteria for children's welfare. The State could not rationally conclude from the fact of high parental motivation that parental control is best if the parents' view of what is best for their children entails, from the State's perspective, great physical harm, educational deprivation, or other harm. In fact, the high motivation of such parents would be reason to give them *less* control. Thus, the fact that parents have a different worldview cannot carry any independent weight; the State must define the permissible range of parental choices, based on its own standards and empirical assumptions, and afford parents only the freedom to choose within that range. The critical question is simply how broad the range should be, or how much freedom the State should give parents to depart from the State's judgments. In Gilles's theory, "reasonableness" ends up doing all the heavy lifting, but he never gives material form to that phantom concept. As noted above in the text, this is par for the course among proponents of extensive parental religious freedom. Gilles offers no reason why the State should not conclude that parents act unreasonably, regardless of what motivates them, if they act significantly contrary to what the State regards as in children's best interests.

59 *See, e.g.*, Robinson, *supra* note 23, at 431; *cf.* Parham v. J.R., 442 U.S. 584, 602 (1979) ("[O]ur constitutional system long ago rejected any notion that a child is 'the mere creature of the State' and, on the contrary, asserted that parents generally 'have the right, coupled with the high duty, to recognize and prepare [their children] for additional obligations.'" (citations omitted)).

60 *See* AMY GUTMANN, DEMOCRATIC EDUCATION 14 (rev. ed. 1999). Courts, too, when acting to restrict parenting practices deemed harmful, often do so to serve interests of society as a whole rather than for the sake of the individual child at issue. *See, e.g.*, Walker v. Superior Court, 763 P.2d 852, 870 (Cal. 1988) ("Imposition of felony liability for endangering or killing an ill child by failing to provide medical care

to the position that parents are entitled to decide what the aims are for their children's lives. In my view, neither parents *nor* the State have any moral claim on their own behalf, any *entitlement* to decide what the ends of a child's life are. Rather, only children themselves have any moral claim or entitlement in connection with their upbringing, and we adults should be deliberating about how best to fulfill our obligation to them, not about which adults are entitled to determine how children's lives will go. Talk of superior moral claims of this sort effectively treats children and children's lives instrumentally, as means for satisfying the interests of one or another group of adults, and that is morally inappropriate. I have suggested in this Essay that the best way to fulfill the rights of children is to protect and promote their healthy development into adults, who can decide for themselves the aims for their lives.

C. *The State Has Insufficient Interest Absent Extreme Harm*

Related to the assertion of superior parental moral claim is the position that, except in life-threatening situations, the State does not have sufficient reason to restrict parental decision making. As noted above, most supporters of spiritual treatment exemptions concede that the State may step in to prevent death. In such extreme cases, they are willing to allow the child's interests to prevail. But when they discuss less extreme cases, supporters of exemptions are unable to maintain a focus on the child's interests and rights; they shift to a discussion of state interests and parental rights. They characterize the problem as one of deciding who "owns" the child.[61] Putting the matter in those terms makes it easier to say that parental choices should prevail; no one would seriously maintain that children are owned by the State. But insofar as the State's interest is in promoting the child's welfare, in its *parens patriae* role, rather than in avoiding negative consequences for the rest of society, the contest is really between the child's welfare and parental preferences. In saying that parental rights prevail in intermediate cases, supporters of exemptions are really saying that parental preferences should trump children's welfare. If that is not what they believe, but believe instead that in intermediate

furthers an interest of unparalleled significance: the protection of the very lives of California's children, upon whose 'healthy, well-rounded growth . . . into full maturity as citizens' our 'democratic society rests, for its continuance.'" (quoting Prince v. Massachusetts, 321 U.S. 158, 168 (1944))).

61 *See, e.g.*, Robinson, *supra* note 23, at 431 (identifying as "the fundamental principle at stake: Who 'owns' the child and who will determine what (including religion) is in the child's best interest. Will it be the state or the parents?").

cases religious exemptions best serve children's interests, then why do they not say so? If they were truly concerned about the children and intent on always doing what is best for the children, why would they slip into a "parents' rights versus state interests" mode? One begins to suspect that the concession of state intervention to prevent death is merely a gesture designed to ward off the charge of ignoring children and not evidence of real commitment to children's welfare.

D. *The State May Not Assume That Parents' Religious Beliefs Are False*

I noted in Part I above that the State in our society may not assume the truth of religious beliefs. The principle of church-state separation embodied in the Establishment Clause precludes it from doing so.[62] Some supporters of religious exemptions to medical neglect laws counter that the State also may not assume that parents' religious beliefs are *false*, and they infer from this premise that the State may not override parental choices that are based on religious beliefs.[63]

The premise itself is subject to challenge. Arguably, the State must routinely assume that a multitude of possible or actually held religious beliefs are false, in order for it to carry on at all. Some people might have the religious belief, for example, that if the State attempts to tax citizens then God will wipe out human civilization. Given the magnitude of the threatened divine punishment, it would be irrational for the State to impose taxes unless the possibility of that belief being true were zero or very close to zero. Thus, to carry on, the State must assume that the belief is false, or at least exceedingly unlikely to be true. One can easily imagine other examples of beliefs that state officials must routinely treat as false.

The greater problem with this line of argument, though, is that it reflects a fundamental confusion about principles of liberal government. The argument essentially transports the argument for protection of self-determination to the child-rearing context, which, as noted above, is not a matter of self-determination. When adults have religious beliefs that lead them to direct *their own* lives in ways contrary to secular or common views of human welfare, liberalism holds that the State may not, on the basis of an assumption that the persons' religious beliefs are false, try to coercively change the persons' beliefs or prohibit them from directing their own lives in accordance with those beliefs, absent threat of harm to others. Thus, if my religious beliefs tell me I should not accept medical care for myself if I become

62 *See supra* note 6.

63 *See, e.g.*, Ingram, *supra* note 1, at 63; Lederman, *supra* note 7, at 921; Steckler, *supra* note 8, at 514–15.

sick or injured, liberal principles require the State to forbear from trying to convince me that my religious beliefs are false and from compelling me to accept medical care for myself, absent threat of harm to others (for example, if I might spread infectious disease).

But that is all that anyone is due in a liberal society with respect to their religious beliefs. Liberal principles do not preclude the State from overriding religiously-motivated choices that affect *other* people in order to protect other people from what the State regards as harm.[64] In other words, liberal protections do not extend beyond self-determination. A contrary rule, that the State must forbear from restricting any religiously-motivated conduct, no matter who it will affect, because the State may not assume that the motivating beliefs are false, would lead to chaos and mayhem. Under such a rule, I could stone my neighbor with impunity if my religious beliefs told me that doing so would help to save his soul. Yet that is essentially what is being advocated when supporters of spiritual treatment exemptions argue that the State may not restrict religiously-motivated parenting choices, because it may not assume that any religious beliefs are false.[65] Generalizing the argument to religiously-motivated conduct

64 *Cf.* Ohio v. Miskimens, 490 N.E.2d 931, 934 (Ohio Ct. Com. Pl. 1984). In rejecting a parental free exercise claim to a religious exemption to medical neglect laws, the court stated:

> [T]his court, as with any governmental entity, can neither know nor care whether someone who relies solely on faith healing for his own affliction is religiously or scripturally "correct." But the right to hold one's own religious beliefs, and to act in conformity with those beliefs, does not and cannot include the right to endanger the life or health of others, including his or her children.

Id.

65 Some have couched the argument against the State assuming the falsity of religious beliefs in terms of the religious beliefs of the children themselves. *See, e.g.*, Ingram, *supra* note 1, at 63. With respect to very young children, that argument depends upon a prediction about children's beliefs at some point in the future. Even if any predictions were reliable, determining what the relevant future point in time would be—for example, when the child is old enough to speak, when the child is old enough to think independently, when the child reaches adulthood—would be a difficult task that proponents of the argument have not undertaken. With respect to older children—for example, teenagers—complex questions regarding the appropriateness of deferring to children's expressed wishes arise, and proponents of this argument have not undertaken to answer those questions either. *But cf.* Jennifer L. Rosato, *The Ultimate Test of Autonomy: Should Minors Have a Right to Make Decisions Regarding Life-Sustaining Treatment?*, 49 RUTGERS L. REV. 1, 49–51 (1996) (arguing that young children should not have a right to refuse medical care but that "mature minors" with terminal illnesses should have a right to reject life-sustaining treatment in limited circumstances). As Rosato notes, current law is largely opposed to the view that minors should have the power to refuse medical care for themselves when they

affecting any other person—and its proponents offer no reason why it need not be—reveals its lack of principled foundation and its unacceptable implications.

CONCLUSION

When parents seek to direct their children's lives in ways otherwise prohibited by law, they are necessarily asking the State to make a decision about their children's lives. They are asking the State to change the rules for them. There may be good reasons for doing so in some cases, but they must be reasons the State can endorse, from its perspective. I have argued that, from the State's perspective, there is no good reason to include spiritual treatment exemptions in medical neglect laws and strong reasons—the welfare and rights of children—not to include such exemptions.

I close with an observation about the style of argument in debates over state regulation of religious child rearing, including debates in the realm of education as well as in the realm of medical care. There is a great deal of ad hoc "reasoning" in debates about state restrictions on parental freedom. The rhetoric one typically hears would suggest many people believe that the situation of children is entirely unique, that there are no commonalities between children and other people, and no general principles can be called on to reason about allocation of authority over children's lives. If that were true, though, there would be little point in debating child-rearing issues. If competing positions could not be justified by appeal to general principles, then participants in the debate could do no more than shout at one another, with no prospect of anyone demonstrating that others should agree with him.

To the best of my knowledge, no one has ever demonstrated that the situation of children is entirely *sui generis*. Simply acknowledging

---

are seriously ill. *See id.* at 17. For an argument against creating a mature minor doctrine in these cases, see Jessica A. Penkower, Comment, *The Potential Right of Chronically Ill Adolescents to Refuse Life-Saving Medical Treatment—Fatal Misuse of the Mature Minor Doctrine*, 45 DEPAUL L. REV. 1165 (1996). Compare *Prince v. Massachusetts*, where the Court stated:

> [T]he mere fact a state could not wholly prohibit this form of adult activity . . . does not mean it cannot do so for children. . . . The state's authority over children's activities is broader than over like actions of adults. . . . A democratic society rests, for its continuance, upon the healthy, well-rounded growth of young people into full maturity as citizens, with all that implies. It may secure this against impeding restraints and dangers within a broad range of selection.

321 U.S. 158, 168 (1944).

that children are persons, as everyone appears willing to do these days, implies that *some* general principles are relevant to decision making about their lives. There are widely shared moral beliefs and legal rules about how we should treat people simply by virtue of their personhood. In addition, what at first blush seems to make children's situation factually unique, at least to those who ordinarily think only about relations among autonomous adults—namely, their dependence and relative lack of autonomy—are actually characteristics they share with many adults. This suggests that certain additional principles—namely, those generally applicable to dependent, non-autonomous persons—should apply to children's lives.

Yet rarely do participants in debates over state regulation of child rearing consider whether and to what extent general principles regarding treatment of dependent, non-autonomous persons, or general principles regarding treatment of individuals in light of their personhood, should govern decision making about children's lives. That is a major shortcoming of the debates. In this Essay, I have suggested ways in which the issue of spiritual treatment exemptions might be informed by appeal to general principles regarding the respect due individuals as persons and by comparison to our beliefs about the proper approach to medical decision making on behalf of non-autonomous adults. Both approaches support the conclusion that spiritual treatment exemptions are unlawful and immoral to the extent they cannot be justified in terms of what is best, from the State's perspective, for the children whose welfare is at stake.

AFFIRMATIVE DUTIES, SYSTEMIC HARMS, AND THE DUE PROCESS CLAUSE

*Barbara E. Armacost**

Introduction

A woman suffers permanent injury when she is shot during a robbery. She brings suit under the Due Process Clause alleging that municipal police failed to protect her from the injury. Plaintiff challenges the city's policy of disregarding calls for assistance unless and until a crime actually has been committed and alleges that the city has failed to provide adequate police protection in a high-crime area.[1]

A mother brings suit under the Due Process Clause to recover for injuries to her young son who suffered permanent brain damage when his caseworker failed to remove the child from the custody of his abusive father. The social worker's notes indicate that she was worried about the child's safety, but she apparently failed to monitor the situation closely enough.[2]

Police officers arrest an intoxicated driver, impound his car, and leave his female companion stranded in a dangerous section of the city. The woman brings suit under the Due Process Clause for injuries sustained when she is mugged and raped while walking to a local convenience store to call for a ride home.[3]

* * *

The scenarios above have a number of things in common: in each of them, the immediate cause of the injury was a *nongovernmental* actor. Also in each, the plaintiff sought to bring suit not against the private tortfeasor but against the government, on the theory that state or local officials deprived the plaintiff of a liberty

* Assistant Professor of Law, University of Virginia. B.S. 1976, University of Virginia; M.T.S. 1984, Regent College, University of British Columbia; J.D. 1989, University of Virginia. — Ed. I thank Lillian BeVier, Clay Gillette, Jack Goldsmith, John Jeffries, Glen Robinson, George Rutherglen, Bob Scott, Elizabeth Scott, Mike Seidman, Bill Stuntz, and Judge J. Harvie Wilkinson III for helpful comments on earlier drafts. I also thank the participants in a workshop at the University of Virginia and Tom Beshere, Victoria Corke, and Chris Gacek for research assistance.

1. *See* Reiff v. City of Philadelphia, 471 F. Supp. 1262 (E.D. Pa. 1979).
2. *See* DeShaney v. Winnebago County Dept. of Social Servs., 489 U.S. 189 (1989).
3. *See* Hilliard v. City of Denver, 930 F.2d 1516 (10th Cir. 1991).

interest by failing to prevent the injuries from occurring. The other commonality is that none of these scenarios ultimately resulted in governmental liability. The rationale for nonliability as expressed by the Supreme Court in *DeShaney v. Winnebago County Department of Social Services*[4] is that the Due Process Clause

> is phrased as a limitation on the State's power to act, not as a guarantee of certain minimal levels of safety and security. It forbids the State itself to deprive individuals of life, liberty, or property without "due process of law," but its language cannot fairly be extended to impose an affirmative obligation on the State to ensure that those interests do not come to harm through other means.[5]

In the oft-repeated words of Judge Richard Posner, "[T]he Constitution is a charter of negative rather than positive liberties."[6] Under the Supreme Court's jurisprudence, the only context in which it is *certain* that the government has an affirmative duty to protect citizens from harm by third parties is where the plaintiff is in the government's custody.[7]

The *DeShaney* holding has engendered a scholarly response that is impassioned and unequivocally negative.[8] The facts of *DeShaney*, which in part drive much of the criticism, are "undeniably tragic":[9] social workers followed a four-year-old child's case,

---

4. 489 U.S. 189 (1989).

5. 489 U.S. at 195.

6. Jackson v. City of Joliet, 715 F.2d 1200, 1203 (7th Cir. 1983), *cert. denied,* 465 U.S. 1049 (1984).

7. Prisoners, pretrial detainees, and involuntarily committed psychiatric patients enjoy a right to be free from unreasonable risk of harm while in governmental custody. *See* Estelle v. Gamble, 429 U.S. 97 (1976) (holding that the Eighth Amendment requires the government to provide medical care to incarcerated prisoners); City of Revere v. Massachusetts Gen. Hosp., 463 U.S. 239 (1983) (holding that the Fourteenth Amendment requires the government to provide medical care to pretrial detainees); Youngberg v. Romeo, 457 U.S. 307 (1982) (holding that the Fourteenth Amendment requires the government to provide for the reasonable safety of involuntarily committed mental patients).

8. *See, e.g.,* Akhil Reed Amar, *Remember the Thirteenth,* 10 CONST. COMMENTARY 403 (1993); Susan Bandes, *The Negative Constitution: A Critique,* 88 MICH. L. REV. 2271 (1990); Jack M. Beermann, *Administrative Failure and Local Democracy: The Politics of* DeShaney, 1990 DUKE L.J. 1078; Theodore Y. Blumoff, *Some Moral Implications of Finding No State Action,* 70 NOTRE DAME L. REV. 95 (1994); Thomas A. Eaton & Michael Wells, *Governmental Inaction as a Constitutional Tort:* DeShaney *and Its Aftermath,* 66 WASH. L. REV. 107 (1991); Steven J. Heyman, *The First Duty of Government: Protection, Liberty and the Fourteenth Amendment,* 1991 DUKE L.J. 507; Laura Oren, DeShaney*'s Unfinished Business: The Foster Child's Due Process Right to Safety,* 69 N.C. L. REV. 113 (1990); Laura Oren, *The State's Failure to Protect Children and Substantive Due Process:* DeShaney *in Context,* 68 N.C. L. REV. 659 (1990) [hereinafter Oren, DeShaney *in Context*]; Louis Michael Seidman, *The State Action Paradox,* 10 CONST. COMMENTARY 379 (1993); Aviam Soifer, *Moral Ambition, Formalism, and the "Free World" of* DeShaney, 57 GEO. WASH. L. REV. 1513 (1989); David A. Strauss, *Due Process, Government Inaction, and Private Wrongs,* 1989 SUP. CT. REV. 53; Laurence H. Tribe, *The Curvature of Constitutional Space: What Lawyers Can Learn from Modern Physics,* 103 HARV. L. REV. 1 (1989).

9. *DeShaney,* 489 U.S. at 191.

documented evidence of abuse by the child's father, but ultimately failed to remove him from his father's custody before he suffered beatings that left him permanently brain damaged.[10] The majority's reminder that Joshua's father inflicted the injury and that "[t]he most that can be said of the state functionaries in this case is that they stood by and did nothing"[11] is normatively unappealing; one might argue that the government exists, at least in part, to protect us from certain harms, and it should not be *permitted* to stand by and do nothing. Moreover, it is not wholly accurate to say that the government simply did nothing with regard to Joshua: in both general ways, by establishing a department of social services and passing laws regulating marriage and the family, and specific ways, by awarding custody of Joshua to his father and assigning a caseworker to follow him, the government took positive action with regard to Joshua and indeed may have discouraged potential private rescuers from taking action to prevent the harm.[12]

Although no one is inclined to object to the Supreme Court's holdings that those in custody have the right to receive some measure of protection from injury[13] — no one argues that the government can throw you in jail and take no responsibility for providing your basic needs — it is hard to articulate exactly why, as a constitutional matter, custody is special. The *DeShaney* Court reasoned that the government's duty to protect is triggered when it restrains an individual's ability to act on her own behalf or plays a part in creating or increasing the danger of harm.[14] That reasoning appeals to powerful and widely shared normative intuitions about appropriate governmental behavior; and certainly custody is the most dramatic example of the government limiting one's ability to care for oneself. But it is not clear how the normative intuitions captured in the Court's reasoning are derived from the Due Process Clause and — to the extent they are — why the same reasoning would not apply to a case like *DeShaney*. It is disingenuous to say that the government did not shape and constrain Joshua's ability to protect himself, even if less so than in the custodial setting.

10. *See* 489 U.S. at 191-93, 208-09; *see also infra* notes 27-31 and accompanying text.

11. 489 U.S. at 203.

12. *See* 489 U.S. at 208-10 (Brennan, J., dissenting).

13. *See supra* note 7.

14. *See DeShaney*, 489 U.S. at 200-01.

In light of the nearly universal condemnation of *DeShaney*,[15] it might come as a surprise that "failure-to-protect"[16] claims in the broader legal context *only rarely result in liability. DeShaney* is not an outlier in the judicial landscape: in numerous cases spanning more than a decade prior to *DeShaney*, the lower federal courts were uniformly reluctant to hold the government liable for failures to protect and did so only in very narrow circumstances. In addition, there is a whole universe of ordinary tort cases virtually identical to the cases that have been brought under the Due Process Clause. In the tort context — contrary to a strong, general trend toward increased governmental liability — the overwhelming presumption *against* liability for failure to protect has held fast.

Critics of *DeShaney* have not given adequate consideration to this broader legal landscape and the clues it offers for understanding the Supreme Court's rejection of constitutional failure-to-protect claims. This article suggests that the constitutional cases are better explained, not by constitutional text or history, but by judicial reluctance to second-guess legislative decisions about budgetary matters, the same concerns that account for the presumptive rule of nonliability in tort. This rationale for the nonliability rule makes *DeShaney* a much harder case on its facts and goes a long way toward a more satisfying positive account of the Supreme Court's approach to this line of cases. It also provides a plausible counterargument to the moral and constitutional objections to nonliability in cases like *DeShaney*.

Part I of the article lays out the major academic criticisms of *DeShaney*. Part II describes the contours of liability for failure to protect in tort. Part III offers a positive explanation for the strong presumption against governmental liability[17] in failure-to-protect

---

15. *See supra* note 8. Indeed, I have not found a single article purporting to offer a positive rationale for nonliability.

16. By "failure to protect," for purposes of this article, I am referring to situations in which the immediate, physical cause of the injury was a nongovernmental actor or entity and the claim is that the government had a duty to prevent that injury. I understand that in many such instances governmental behavior could be described as either act or omission. The terminology is not important; the question in these cases is the extent of the government's obligation to take precautions against injuries by third parties.

17. By "governmental liability," I mean liability against states or localities or against state or local officers. In tort, the extent of governmental liability is determined by common law and statutory rules governing sovereign immunity. *See infra* notes 94-98 and accompanying text. In the constitutional context, 42 U.S.C. § 1983 (1988), which provides a cause of action for deprivations of constitutional rights, permits suits against municipalities for actions that execute a governmental "policy or custom," *see* Monell v. Department of Social Servs., 436 U.S. 658 (1978), as well as against local officials in their individual capacities. The Eleventh Amendment bars § 1983 suits for damages against states and state officers in their official capacities. Injunctive relief, however, may be obtained against state officials — and so as a

cases: permitting broad liability for failure to protect would involve the courts in second-guessing political decisions about the use of limited community resources. This explanation has two parts. First, as a matter of institutional competence, budgetary decisions about the appropriate level and distribution of public services are better suited to political rather than judicial resolution. Second, failure-to-protect claims are more likely to involve the courts in budgetary review than other kinds of claims against the government. One may question exactly where the line between political and judicial action ought to be, but the notion that there is a line somewhere — and that judges are seeking to draw such a line in these cases — resonates in many areas of the law. Part IV demonstrates that the resource-allocation rationale has significant explanatory power in constitutional failure-to-protect cases. To the extent these considerations are a significant part of what is driving the results in failure-to-protect cases, they have not been addressed adequately by *DeShaney*'s critics.

I. The "Duty-To-Protect" in the Constitutional Context

The Due Process Clause of the Fourteenth Amendment provides that no state shall "deprive any person of life, liberty, or property, without due process of law."[18] The text of the Clause has been interpreted to create certain substantive rights as well as to guarantee the right to adequate process. That is, there are certain things the government may not do, regardless of how much process it provides.[19] Perhaps the most well known of the substantive due process rights is the right to privacy.[20] The Due Process Clause also has been construed to forbid a category of tortlike deprivations of life, liberty, or property. For example, under certain circumstances,[21] a prison official who deliberately — or recklessly[22] —

practical matter against the state itself — through the "fiction" of suing state officials in their individual capacities. *See Ex parte* Young, 209 U.S. 123 (1908).

18. U.S. Const. amend. XIV, § 1.

19. *See* Rochin v. California, 342 U.S. 165 (1952).

20. *See* Roe v. Wade, 410 U.S. 113 (1973).

21. The Supreme Court has held that there can be no deprivation within the meaning of the Due Process Clause if there are adequate state postdeprivation remedies. *See* Parratt v. Taylor, 451 U.S. 527 (1981), *overruled in part on other grounds by* Daniels v. Williams, 474 U.S. 327 (1986).

22. The Due Process Clause requires more than negligence, *see Daniels*, 474 U.S. at 327, but the Supreme Court has not opined on exactly what level of intent — between negligence and willfulness — is required to make out a claim. *See* 474 U.S. at 334 n.3. The courts of appeals are divided on the issue. *See, e.g.*, Webber v. Mefford, 43 F.3d 1340 (10th Cir.) (recklessness); Fagan v. City of Vineland, 22 F.3d 1283 (3d Cir.), *affd. on rehg.*, 22 F.3d 1296 (3d Cir. 1994) ("shock the conscience"); Temkin v. Frederick County Commr., 945 F.2d 716 (4th

lost[23] or damaged[24] a prisoner's personal effects could be charged with unlawful deprivation of property; an official who acted with deliberate indifference toward a serious threat of illness or injury could be found to have violated a liberty interest.[25] Although many of these tortlike cases have involved prisoners, a number of courts have permitted suits for such injuries outside the custodial setting, for example, injuries resulting from the reckless or intentional actions of police officers.[26]

In *DeShaney*, petitioners, four-year-old Joshua DeShaney and his mother, sought to extend the reasoning of these tortlike due process cases by arguing that the Winnebago County Social Services Department had deprived Joshua of "his liberty interest in 'free[dom] from . . . unjustified intrusions on personal security,' by failing to provide him with adequate protection against his father's violence."[27] For the two years prior to the serious injuries that gave rise to this suit, the Winnebago County Social Services Department had been monitoring Joshua, who had been in the official custody of his father since his parents' divorce when Joshua was still an infant, for suspected abuse by his father Randy Deshaney.[28] During these two years of monitoring, there were numerous incidents suggesting possible child abuse, including three emergency-room visits for suspicious injuries, reports of suspected abuse by neighbors and the father's second wife, and visits by a social worker who observed a number of suspicious injuries.[29] Although the social worker "du-

---

Cir. 1991) (same); Roach v. City of Fredericktown, 882 F.2d 294 (8th Cir. 1989) (same); Jones v. Sherrill, 827 F.2d 1102 (6th Cir. 1987) (gross negligence or recklessness).

23. *See Parratt*, 451 U.S. at 527. In *Parratt*, officials who lost a prisoner's hobby kit were found to have deprived him of property but not without "due process of law" because there were adequate state postdeprivation remedies. *See* 451 U.S. at 543-44.

24. *See* Hudson v. Palmer, 468 U.S. 517 (1984). The claim in *Hudson*, alleging intentional destruction of property, ultimately failed because adequate state postdeprivation remedies were available. *See* 468 U.S. at 533-36.

25. *See* Davidson v. Cannon, 474 U.S. 344 (1986). The Court denied the prisoner's claim in *Davidson* because he had not made a showing that prison officials were more than merely negligent. *See* 474 U.S. at 347-48; *see also supra* note 22.

26. *See, e.g.*, Grandstaff v. City of Borger, 767 F.2d 161 (5th Cir. 1985) (holding that plaintiff whose decedent was killed when police officers mistook him for a fugitive and recklessly shot into his truck could recover under Due Process Clause); Ragusa v. Streator Police Dept., 530 F. Supp. 814 (N.D. Ill. 1981) (holding that due process claim for intentional deprivation of property arising out of impoundment of plaintiff's truck by the police survived motion to dismiss).

27. DeShaney v. Winnebago County Dept. of Social Servs., 489 U.S. 189, 195 (1989) (quoting Ingraham v. Wright, 430 U.S. 651, 673 (1977)).

28. *See* 489 U.S. at 191-93.

29. *See* 489 U.S. at 192-93, 208-09. At one point when Joshua was admitted to a local hospital with multiple injuries, the examining physician notified the Winnebago Social Services Department that he suspected child abuse. The Department obtained a court order plac-

tifully recorded these incidents in her files, along with her continuing suspicions that someone in the DeShaney household was physically abusing Joshua,"[30] no action was taken to remove him from his home. In 1984, Randy DeShaney beat Joshua so savagely that he suffered a series of cerebral hemorrhages, leaving him profoundly retarded and likely to spend the rest of his life in an institution.[31]

The Supreme Court rejected Joshua's due process claim. The Court concluded that neither the language of the Due Process Clause itself nor its history support the "expansive reading"[32] that would permit petitioner's claims. The Court reasoned that

> nothing in the language of the Due Process Clause itself requires the State to protect the life, liberty, and property of its citizens against invasion by private actors. The Clause is phrased as a limitation on the State's power to act, not as a guarantee of certain minimal levels of safety and security. It forbids the State itself to deprive individuals of life, liberty, or property without "due process of law," but its language cannot fairly be extended to impose an affirmative obligation on the State to ensure that those interests do not come to harm through other means.[33]

The Court also noted that, as a historical matter, the purpose of the Due Process Clause "was to protect the people from the State, not to ensure that the State protected them from each other."[34]

At the same time, the Court affirmed its prior holdings involving affirmative duties owed to persons in governmental custody on the ground that the government's "act of restraining the individual's freedom to act on his own behalf — through incarceration, institutionalization, or other similar restraint of personal liberty" triggers a duty to "assume some responsibility for his safety and general well-being."[35] Such duties arise when, as in the custodial

---

ing Joshua in the temporary custody of the hospital. The hospital convened a "Child Protection Team," consisting of physicians and other hospital personnel, social workers, police, and the county's lawyer, which ultimately determined that there was insufficient evidence of child abuse to retain custody of Joshua. The Child Protection Team, however, did recommend a number of measures to protect Joshua, and Joshua's father entered into a voluntary agreement to cooperate with the Team in accomplishing these goals. Based on the Team's recommendation, the juvenile court dismissed the child-protection case and returned Joshua to his father's custody, where the abuse apparently continued. *See* 489 U.S. at 192.

30. 489 U.S. at 193.

31. *See* 489 U.S. at 193.

32. *See* 489 U.S. at 195.

33. 489 U.S. at 195.

34. 489 U.S. at 196.

35. 489 U.S. at 200.

setting, the government by the use of its power "so restrains an individual's liberty that it renders him unable to care for himself."[36]

Scholars have criticized *DeShaney*[37] on a number of grounds, all of which lead them to conclude that there should be liability under the facts of *DeShaney* or, at the very least, broader liability than the Supreme Court's holding appears to permit. Many of the criticisms are driven, at least in part, by the compelling and ultimately tragic story behind the case. The facts suggest that governmental officials may have acted irresponsibly in the face of significant evidence that harm was likely to occur. The government's failure to protect a helpless child from a known abuser conflicts with widely held norms requiring minimally reasonable behavior. It also bumps up against common expectations about how we think the *government,* in particular, ought to behave: many people would consider it "wrong" for a police officer to fail to respond to a call for help or for a social worker to ignore evidence that a child was being abused[38] and perhaps would be surprised if they found that there were no legal sanction for doing so.[39]

Another source of criticism is the *DeShaney* Court's rationale for, on the one hand, rejecting petitioners' claim that the Due Process Clause creates a general duty to protect and, on the other hand, affirming the existence of such a duty in the custodial context.[40] As David Currie and others have pointed out, constitutional cases have found affirmative governmental obligations in many

36. 489 U.S. at 200. The Court explicitly left open the possibility that government-ordered foster care might be sufficiently analogous to custody to give rise to a duty to protect. *See* 489 U.S. at 201 n.9.

37. *See supra* note 8 (citing articles).

38. *See* Eaton & Wells, *supra* note 8, at 128.

39. Ordinary citizens, of course, have no legally enforceable duty, except in narrow circumstances, to rescue their fellow citizens or protect them from threatened or impending harm. For articles critical of the no-liability rule for private rescuers, see, e.g., James Barr Ames, *Law and Morals,* 22 HARV. L. REV. 97 (1908); Steven J. Heyman, *Foundations of the Duty to Rescue,* 47 VAND. L. REV. 673 (1994); Jay Silver, *The Duty to Rescue: A Reexamination and Proposal,* 26 WM. & MARY L. REV. 423 (1985); and Daniel B. Yeager, *A Radical Community of Aid: A Rejoinder to Opponents of Affirmative Duties to Help Strangers,* 71 WASH. U. L.Q. 1 (1993); see also Saul Levmore, *Waiting for Rescue: An Essay on the Evolution and Incentive Structure of the Law of Affirmative Obligations,* 72 VA. L. REV. 879 (1986).

40. *See DeShaney,* 489 U.S. at 200 ("[W]hen the State by the affirmative exercise of its power so restrains an individual's liberty that it renders him unable to care for himself, and at the same time fails to provide for his basic human needs — *e.g.* food, clothing, shelter, medical care, and reasonable safety — it transgresses the substantive limits on state action set by the . . . Due Process Clause."); City of Revere v. Massachusetts Gen. Hosp., 463 U.S. 239 (1983) (holding that the Fourteenth Amendment requires the government to provide medical care to pretrial detainees); Youngberg v. Romeo, 457 U.S. 307 (1982) (holding that the Fourteenth Amendment requires the government to provide for the reasonable safety of involuntarily committed mental patients).

"negatively phrased provisions."[41] Indeed, the Due Process Clause itself has been construed to create certain positive duties in addition to the affirmative duties of protection owed to individuals in custody.[42] Moreover, as a purely linguistic matter, the operative word "deprive" certainly could support the more passive meaning urged by the *DeShaney* petitioners; it could mean, for instance, "to keep [a person from] what he would otherwise have."[43]

A number of scholars have sought to defend a broader reading of the Due Process Clause by attacking the Court's account of constitutional history and seeking to demonstrate that the historical meaning of the Clause included a general duty to provide protection against private harms.[44] These accounts may call into question the Court's conclusion that Fourteenth Amendment history *forecloses* a more broadly defined duty to protect. They do not, however, offer an explanation of the scope of liability in failure-to-protect cases prior to *DeShaney* nor do they provide a basis for deciding what the proper limits of such a right might be.[45]

The Court's identification of custody as the only context that gives rise to a duty to protect has also been the subject of strong criticism. The Court's logic for permitting liability in the custodial context seems to be that, although private action was not the immediate cause of the injury, "state action [was] present in the background; the state's action placed the victim in a position where he

41. David P. Currie, *Positive and Negative Constitutional Rights,* 53 U. CHI. L. REV. 864, 886 (1986). *See generally id.* at 872-86; Eaton & Wells, *supra* note 8, at 122-23. Cases finding affirmative obligations in "negatively phrased provisions" include, for example: Richmond Newspapers v. Virginia, 448 U.S. 555, 579-80 (1980) (holding that the government must provide access to certain information); Cruz v. Beto, 405 U.S. 319 (1972) (holding that a prisoner must be provided reasonable opportunity to pursue his religion); and Gideon v. Wainwright, 372 U.S. 335 (1963) (holding that the government must provide counsel to indigent defendants).

42. *See* Boddie v. Connecticut, 401 U.S. 371 (1971) (holding that a state may not deny, solely because of inability to pay, access to state-controlled divorce proceeding); Truax v. Corrigan, 257 U.S. 312 (1921) (holding that a state must provide a remedy against picketing by striking workers on employer's property).

43. 4 THE OXFORD ENGLISH DICTIONARY 490 (2d ed. 1989), *quoted in* Eaton & Wells, *supra* note 8, at 116 (alteration in original). For example, it seems perfectly natural to conclude, in the context of a schoolyard fight, that those who prevent a student's buddies from intervening to protect him from the school bully have "deprived" him of the opportunity to avoid a bloody nose.

44. *See, e.g.,* Eaton & Wells, *supra* note 8, at 118-21; Heyman, *supra* note 8, at 546-54, 557-63, 566-70; Oren, DeShaney *in Context, supra* note 8, at 687-92; Seidman, *supra* note 8, at 382-83; Soifer, *supra* note 8, at 1521-26. *But see* Currie, *supra* note 41, at 865-66 ("The Framers would have been astounded to hear it contended that by adopting the Bill of Rights they had managed to make mandatory the exercise of a Congressional power to help needy citizens . . . .").

45. *See* Heyman, *supra* note 8, at 512.

or she could be injured."[46] The intuition for finding affirmative duties in the custodial situation is undoubtedly strong: "When the state is obviously, visibly responsible for a person's vulnerability to private violence, no court has denied that the state ought to provide some protection against the private wrongs that the person suffers."[47] But, as David Strauss points out, the Court's logic could be extended to other, noncustodial situations in which governmental action has compromised an individual's ability to protect herself: "[S]tate action is always present in the background" in the sense that it "contributes to the condition in which all members of society . . . find themselves."[48] The Court gives no clear explanation — constitutional or otherwise — for halting liability at the prison door.

A related criticism focuses on the Court's characterization of the facts of *DeShaney* as a governmental failure to act — to which the Due Process Clause has nothing to say — rather than as governmental action. As the dissent in *DeShaney* pointed out, the distinction between action and inaction may simply depend upon how broadly in time one defines the injuring event:[49] Is the appropriate starting point for analysis the *action* of governmental officials in establishing a social services department and taking on the task of monitoring Joshua DeShaney for suspected child abuse but doing it badly?[50] Or is the case better characterized as governmental *failure to act* to prevent purely private harm, where the government had no role in creating the risk of harm in the first place and so has no duty to prevent it from occurring?

Along the same lines, Professor Beermann criticizes the very limited liability permitted under *DeShaney* as inconsistent with governmental responsibility in the modern welfare state.[51] He argues

46. Strauss, *supra* note 8, at 67.

47. *Id.*

48. *Id.*

49. *See* DeShaney v. Winnebago County Dept. of Social Servs., 489 U.S. 189, 205-11 (1989) (Brennan, J., dissenting).

50. *See* 489 U.S. at 208-11. An even broader temporal view would argue that the establishment of laws applicable to marriage and family, which by definition limit the possibilities of rescue from certain harms, is the starting point for analyzing governmental liability. *See* Strauss, *supra* note 8, at 64-65 (arguing that the state's role is not limited to the custody award to Joshua's father; the family unit itself is largely the product of state regulation).

51. *See* Beermann, *supra* note 8, at 1089; *see also* Bandes, *supra* note 8, at 2311 ("The welfare state, with its proliferation of government regulation and subsistence programs, little resembles the polity with which the Framers were familiar."); Tribe, *supra* note 8, at 9-14 (calling for "circumspection and questioning in assessing how the distribution and direction of all public powers — including those of judges — define the legal space through which we all move").

that the government's extensive involvement in modern society "creates dependencies that give rise to further responsibility."[52] The existence of "[g]overnment[al] institutions invite[s] people to rely on their programs," and, "[w]hen government fails to act as individuals legitimately anticipated, it is as if government has yanked a chair out from under a person as she settled into the chair."[53] Thus, citizens who rely on the existence of agencies that fail to deliver are made worse off because the existence of such entities discourages intervention by alternative private entities.[54] Building on the *DeShaney* dissent, Beermann argues that "the existence of a social services department . . . strengthens the case for judicial intervention by raising the possibility that absent the local agency, people in the community might have aided Joshua on their own."[55]

All of these criticisms seek to undermine the Court's nearly categorical rejection of duty-to-protect liability and provide a starting point for permitting broader liability, including liability under the facts of *DeShaney*. While almost no one seriously argues that the government should be liable for *all* external harms,[56] *DeShaney's* critics argue for much broader liability than is currently available. A number of proposals have been offered for identifying what kinds of governmental behavior should give rise to liability for failure to protect.

Thomas Eaton and Michael Wells have proposed a framework for analyzing constitutional duty-to-protect claims which seeks to

52. Beermann, *supra* note 8, at 1089.

53. *Id.* at 1096.

54. *See id.* David Strauss makes the similar point that governmental failure to act, like a negligently performed rescue, "may have worsened the victim's situation by causing the victim to forgo other sources of aid or by discouraging other potential rescuers from coming to the victim's aid." Strauss, *supra* note 8, at 62; *see also DeShaney*, 489 U.S. at 210 (Brennan, J., dissenting) ("Wisconsin's child-protection program . . . effectively confined Joshua DeShaney within the walls of Randy DeShaney's violent home until such time as DSS took action to remove him."); Oren, DeShaney *in Context, supra* note 8, at 695-97, 703-05 ("Having actively put the child in an isolated position and knowing of the specific danger that he faced, the state should not then escape all constitutional accountability."); Soifer, *supra* note 8, at 1518-20 ("The idea that the state did not worsen Joshua's situation by appearing to protect him, that it is absolved because it did not affirmatively erect an obstacle, is belied by the record.").

55. Beermann, *supra* note 8, at 1096. *But see* Seidman, *supra* note 8, at 386 (arguing that Justice Brennan's claim rests on "sheer speculation").

56. Jack Beermann appears to argue — astonishingly in my view — that the Due Process Clause *should* be understood to create a general duty to protect citizens from all civil harm of which governmental actors are aware. Beermann ultimately concedes that his argument taken to its logical stopping point "may even point toward unlimited government responsibility for all private misfortune and private misconduct — a plainly unacceptable result." Beermann, *supra* note 8, at 1089.

work within the boundaries set by *DeShaney,* while taking the broadest possible reading of its rationale.[57] They argue that liability for failure to protect should rest on two factors. First, liability should attach whenever the state's involvement in producing the plaintiff's plight is sufficiently egregious that it "imping[es] a plaintiff's constitutionally protected right to respectful treatment by government officers."[58] This factor would be satisfied when the state has "imposed limitations on self-help and private rescue,"[59] when the state affirmatively has contributed to the danger that caused the harm,[60] or when the government's actions have worsened the plaintiff's situation.[61] Second, government officials whose actions satisfy the first factor would be liable only if their actions amount to "deliberate indifference" to the risk of harm.[62] Eaton and Wells argue that the presence of these two factors identifies failures to act that are sufficiently "egregious and abusive"[63] to amount to constitutional violations.

Similarly, David Strauss argues that the Court's distinction between custodial and noncustodial situations should be abandoned and proposes that liability should attach whenever the government's withholding of protection constitutes an "abuse of power."[64] Envisioning the government as a "fiduciary," Strauss argues that governmental officials abuse their power whenever they fail to act with "the degree of prudence that an ordinary person would show in conducting his or her own affairs."[65] Under this approach, merely negligent actions or omissions would trigger liability under

57. *See* Eaton & Wells, *supra* note 8. Although Eaton and Wells have chosen to craft their proposal to fit within the rationale of the *DeShaney* holding, in a world of their own creation, they apparently would support significantly broader liability. *See id.* at 166 ("The only firm rule laid down in *DeShaney* is that officials owe no duty to help a person unless the state played at least some part in creating a peril or in rendering the victim more vulnerable to it. . . . Hopefully, the Court will someday reconsider this rule in light of considerations of justice and the pervasive role of government in modern life.").

58. *Id.* at 144.

59. *Id.* at 147-49.

60. *See id.* at 149-55.

61. *See id.* at 155-58. Eaton and Wells suggest that these situations are ones that would comprise a common law "special relationship." *See id.* at 147. The tort-law special relationship giving rise to a duty to rescue by governmental officials is, however, significantly narrower than Eaton and Wells envision. *See infra* notes 83-90 and accompanying text.

62. *See* Eaton & Wells, *supra* note 8, at 159-65.

63. *See id.* at 159.

64. *See* Strauss, *supra* note 8, at 79-80. The underlying interest being deprived, according to Strauss, is the property interest in having governmental decisions made in a nonarbitrary and nonabusive way: the establishment of a governmental program "creates an interest, protected by the Due Process Clause, in a decision based on the government's agenda rather than the private agenda of the responsible official." *Id.* at 81.

65. *Id.* at 83-84.

the Due Process Clause.[66] Strauss's analysis would increase significantly the universe of tortlike due process claims — including those not involving failure-to-protect claims — permitted under current law.[67]

* * *

The above criticisms point out the difficulties inherent in seeking to understand the Supreme Court's holding entirely on the basis of constitutional text and history. They also give expression to the normative objections raised by a rule that appears to permit governmental officials to behave irresponsibly. At the very least, these criticisms substantially undermine the Court's arguments for nonliability in cases like *DeShaney*.

The great amount of attention and criticism that followed the *DeShaney* decision has, however, left the mistaken impression that the Court's approach to liability for governmental failure to protect was unprecedented or without legal "pedigree." Those who push for expansive due process liability for failure to protect have not considered adequately that such claims are generally and strongly disfavored in the broader legal context, for example, in tort.[68] The

66. *See id.* at 84.

67. Strauss concedes that his proposal threatens to turn a "variety of ordinary torts by state officials" into "federal constitutional claims." *Id.* at 84. He proposes to remedy that problem by: (1) requiring plaintiffs with procedural claims to look to adequate state remedies and (2) requiring "[m]any wrongs now viewed as violations of the Due Process Clause" — for example, "physical abuse by a state official . . . an unreasonable seizure of the person" — "[to be seen] as violations of more specific constitutional provisions." *Id.* at 84-85. It seems clear, however, that Strauss's proposal would substantially increase the scope of tortlike claims that could be litigated in federal court. Under current law, a plaintiff who alleges a tortlike substantive due process claim is precluded from bringing a federal claim if state remedies are available and adequate. *See* Parratt v. Taylor, 451 U.S. 527 (1981). Strauss's framework apparently would eliminate that requirement except where the claim is procedural. *See* Strauss, *supra* note 8, at 84-85. On Strauss's second point, it is unclear exactly what universe of due process claims *could* be litigated under more specific constitutional provisions if the current boundaries of those provisions were respected. For example, physical abuse by a state official would not be a seizure under the Fourth Amendment unless intentionally applied. *See* Brower v. County of Inyo, 489 U.S. 593 (1989). That means that anything less than "intentional" physical deprivation — which presumably is what interests Strauss — would continue to fall into a residual category of tortlike claims that could be litigated under the Due Process Clause.

68. Eaton and Wells recognize and briefly discuss the implications of "tort policy" in formulating their paradigm for analyzing failure-to-protect cases. *See* Eaton & Wells, *supra* note 8, at 110, 127-33, 142-43. However, they fail to appreciate the explanatory power of tort policies in accounting for the existing pattern of liability in this class of cases, and — perhaps for that reason — they do not take seriously enough the rationales behind the tort policies they identify. *See also* Beermann, *supra* note 8, at 1093 ("Because imposing positive duties on government raises questions about allocation of governmental resources, these problems may be somewhat less amenable to judicial resolution than other constitutional problems."); Michael Wells & Thomas A. Eaton, *Affirmative Duty and Constitutional Tort,* 16 U. MICH. J.L. REF. 1 (1982) (noting, in a pre-*DeShaney* analysis of failure-to-protect cases, that such cases are best viewed as a blend of constitutional and tort principles).

puzzle, then, is whether there is a sensible explanation for the rule of nonliability, which appears to conflict with powerful normative intuitions about governmental behavior but has a solid and long-standing legal pedigree. The pattern of liability in tort provides insights into a possible rationale for nonliability in the constitutional context.

II. The Tort-Law Pedigree of Nonliability for Failure To Protect

As a preliminary matter, one might question the relevance of tort law in analyzing constitutional damages claims. The simplest response is that section 1983,[69] which in two sentences of text provides the cause of action in damage suits for constitutional violations, simply leaves unresolved many basic issues, such as rules for determining causation and computing damages, the role of governmental immunities, and what statutes of limitations should apply. In adjudicating section 1983 claims, the federal courts have a long-standing practice of borrowing tort rules to fill those "gaps," reasoning that the drafters legislated against the background of common law rules applicable to analogous cases.[70] The kinship between section 1983 claims and common law civil-damages claims is so well accepted that the former have become known as "constitutional torts."[71]

More specifically, many section 1983 claims alleging deprivations of life, liberty, and property under the Due Process Clause are

---

69. Section 1983 provides, in pertinent part:

> Every person who, under color of any statute, ordinance, regulation, custom, or usage, of any State or Territory or the District of Columbia, subjects, or causes to be subjected, any citizen of the United States or other person within the jurisdiction thereof to the deprivation of any rights, privileges, or immunities secured by the Constitution and laws, shall be liable to the party injured in an action at law, suit equity, or other proper proceeding for redress.

42 U.S.C. § 1983 (1988).

70. *See, e.g.*, Carey v. Piphus, 435 U.S. 247, 257-59 (1978) (stating that the common law applicable to tort damages is the starting point for a damages inquiry under § 1983); Pierson v. Ray, 386 U.S. 547, 553-54 (1967) (stating that there is no reason to believe that the common law immunity applicable to judges was abolished by § 1983). Once adopted by the federal courts, the common law rules have evolved into a form that is distinctively federal, constituting a body of "federal common law" applicable to § 1983 claims. *See, e.g., Carey*, 435 U.S. at 258 (noting that the common law damage rules must be adapted to provide fair compensation for constitutional injuries); Imbler v. Pachtman, 424 U.S. 409, 420-29 (1976) (discussing common law prosecutorial immunity and considering whether "the same considerations of public policy that underlie the common law rule likewise countenance absolute immunity under § 1983").

71. The term "constitutional tort" first appears in the scholarly literature in Marshall Shapo, *Constitutional Tort:* Monroe v. Pape *and the Frontiers Beyond*, 60 Nw. U. L. Rev. 277, 323-24 (1965).

factually indistinguishable from garden-variety tort actions against the government. Indeed, in many cases, the same underlying fact pattern and resulting injury could give rise to both constitutional and tort claims, and litigants often attempt to bring claims under both federal and state law.[72] It is not surprising, then, that courts adjudicating these tortlike injuries under the Due Process Clause have looked to tort law and policies in setting the boundaries of liability for constitutional damage claims.

Claims of governmental failure to protect in tort typically involve injuries by nongovernmental actors or instrumentalities, that governmental service providers — such as police, firefighters, social workers, and so on — failed to prevent. The most common fact pattern in these cases is that the government received a call for help or had knowledge of a particular risk of harm and failed to respond quickly or adequately in order to prevent the injury from occurring. When analyzing such cases, an overwhelming majority of jurisdictions start with a presumption that the government generally is not liable for failing to protect people from injuries by nongovernmental sources, even when governmental officials have been informed or are aware of the risk of harm.[73]

The doctrine that is most often invoked for denying liability in such cases is the so-called public duty rule. That rule provides that, in situations involving certain services such as police and fire protection, the government "has a duty to the general public, as opposed to [any] particular individual," and thus the breach of that duty does not give rise to a private damage claim.[74] The purpose of the public duty rule is to "protect[ ] municipalities from liability for

72. Plaintiffs may prefer to bring the federal claim, if possible, in order to gain access to a federal forum and take advantage of attorneys' fee awards available to prevailing plaintiffs under 42 U.S.C. § 1988 (1988). Section 1983 claims, of course, also may be litigated in state court. The elements of the constitutional claim, however, will differ in important respects from the elements of an analogous tort claim. For example, although § 1983 itself has no intent requirement, damage liability under the Due Process Clause requires that the actions giving rise to the deprivation be more than negligent. *See* Daniels v. Williams, 474 U.S. 327 (1986). In addition, the Supreme Court has held that the existence of an adequate state postdeprivation remedy forecloses many tortlike due process claims on the grounds that the plaintiff has received all the process that is due. *See* Parratt v. Taylor, 451 U.S. 527 (1981). Liability against the governmental unit itself under § 1983 also requires a showing that the deprivation resulted from a governmental "custom or policy." *See* Monell v. Department of Social Servs., 436 U.S. 658 (1978).

73. *See generally* W. Page Keeton et al., Prosser and Keeton on the Law of Torts § 131, at 1047-50 (5th ed. 1984); 18 Eugene McQuillin, The Law of Municipal Corporations § 53.04.50 (James Perkowitz-Solheim et al eds., 3d ed. 1993); Horace B. Robertson, Jr., *Municipal Tort Liability: Special Duty Issues of Police, Fire, and Safety,* 44 Syracuse L. Rev. 943, 946-52 (1993).

74. 18 McQuillin, *supra* note 73, § 53.04.25, at 165; *see also* Moch Co. v. Rensselaer Water Co., 159 N.E. 896 (N.Y. 1928).

failure to adequately enforce general laws and regulations, which were intended to benefit the community as a whole."[75] So, for example, state or local governments may be required by law to *establish* and *operate* police, fire, social services, and other similar departments.[76] But their responsibility in doing so is to provide general protection to the public at large,[77] and, in most cases, no individual has a cause of action in damages if those services fail to prevent a particular injury from occurring.[78]

The general rule is illustrated in the well-known case of *Riss v. City of New York.*[79] In that case, a young woman, Linda Riss, had sought the arrest of Burton Pugach, a rejected suitor, who allegedly had threatened her repeatedly with death or bodily harm over a period of six months. When she became engaged to another man, Pugach again threatened her, and she notified the police. The following day, a thug hired by Pugach threw lye in Riss's face, causing disfigurement and serious vision loss. In affirming dismissal of the claim, the Court of Appeals of New York reasoned that to proclaim a general duty of protection based on a "showing of probable need for and request for protection"[80] would rearrange legislative-

75. 18 McQuillin, *supra* note 73, § 53.04.25, at 165.

76. The public duty itself is generally understood to derive from state or municipal law. *See, e.g.*, Steitz v. City of Beacon, 64 N.E.2d 704, 705 (N.Y. 1945) (city charter provided that the city " 'may construct and operate a system of waterworks' " and that " 'it shall maintain fire, police, school and poor departments.' "). Such laws, however, are construed to require only that the government establish and operate certain services and departments. These provisions are not understood to provide a cause of action running in favor of any particular individual or group. *See, e.g.*, 64 N.E.2d at 706 ("[P]rovisions [of the city charter] were not in terms designed to protect the personal interest of any individual and clearly were designed to secure the benefits of well ordered municipal government enjoyed by all as members of the community.").

77. *See* Riss v. City of New York, 240 N.E.2d 860 (N.Y. 1968); 18 McQuillin, *supra* note 73, § 53.04.25, at 165; *see also* Warren v. District of Columbia, 444 A.2d 1, 8 (D.C. 1981) ("A person does not, by becoming a police officer, insulate himself from any of the basic duties which everyone owes to other people, but neither does he assume any greater obligation to others individually. The only additional duty undertaken by accepting employment as a police officer is the duty owed to the public at large.").

78. Courts at times have articulated the nonliability rule for failure to protect in terms of immunity for "discretionary" functions. *See, e.g.*, Crouch v. Hall, 406 N.E.2d 303 (Ind. Ct. App. 1980) (finding no liability for failure to apprehend rapist who subsequently raped and murdered the plaintiff's decedent). Alternatively, courts have reasoned that the provision of certain protective services, such as inspections required by municipal building or fire codes, was intended for the protection generally from particular hazards, rather than as a service to any particular individual. *See, e.g.*, Green v. Irwin, 570 N.Y.S.2d 868 (N.Y. App. Div. 1991) (finding a town not liable for negligent issuance of a building permit simply because the issuance was shown to be in violation of the building code). The terminology is not important to my argument. My point is simply that such cases ordinarily do not give rise to governmental liability, whatever the doctrinal explanation for the result.

79. 240 N.E.2d 860 (N.Y. 1968).

80. 240 N.E.2d at 861.

executive decisions about how the community's limited resources should be allocated and result in liability "without predictable limits."[81] The court distinguished cases where "police authorities undertake responsibilities to particular members of the public and expose them, without adequate protection, to the risks which then materialize into actual losses."[82]

As noted in *Riss,* there is a limited doctrinal category of failure-to-protect cases — the so-called special relationship cases — that may give rise to liability. These cases represent an exception to the public duty rule in cases where "there was a 'special relationship' between a public official and a particular individual that [gives] rise to a duty to that individual separate from the official's duty to the general public."[83] The special relationship exception, according to the courts, permits liability for failure to protect when the plaintiff was injured while in government custody[84] or when government officials have given assurances or acted in a way that induced the victim reasonably to rely to his detriment on the promise of protection.[85] A finding of liability requires significantly more than a call for help;[86] the courts have required a showing that the gov-

81. 240 N.E.2d at 860-61.

82. 240 N.E.2d at 861 (citing Schuster v. City of New York, 154 N.E.2d 534 (N.Y. 1958)). In *Schuster,* a witness who had supplied information to the police leading to the arrest of a dangerous fugitive received threats to his life and subsequently was shot to death. His estate sued on the grounds that the police negligently had failed to provide him with a requested bodyguard or other protection. The court held the government liable on the ground that the police owe a special duty to protect those "who have collaborated . . . in the arrest or prosecution of criminals, once it reasonably appears that they are in danger due to their collaboration." 154 N.E.2d at 537.

83. 18 McQuillin, *supra* note 73, § 53.04.25, at 166.

84. *See, e.g.,* Ashby v. City of Louisville, 841 S.W.2d 184 (Ky. Ct. App. 1992) (declining to find a special relationship when victim was not in state custody); Breaux v. State, 326 So. 2d 481 (La. 1976) (finding a state liable for the death of a prisoner when officials reasonably should have anticipated attack); Daniels v. Andersen, 237 N.W.2d 397 (Neb. 1975) (finding a state liable to an intoxicated victim who was locked up in a "drunk tank" where he was beaten by another drunk).

85. *See* Cuffy v. City of New York, 505 N.E.2d 937, 938 (N.Y. 1987). There also may be liability for governmental failure to protect against harm by dangerous persons who are released from custody, when such persons have threatened harm to *particular* individuals. *Compare* Johnson v. State, 447 P.2d 352 (Cal. 1968) (finding liability for failure to warn when specific person is threatened) *with* Thompson v. County of Alameda, 614 P.2d 728 (Cal. 1980) (finding no liability for failure to warn neighbors when prisoner's threat to kill was not directed toward identifiable individual).

86. *See, e.g.,* Hartzler v. City of San Jose, 120 Cal. Rptr. 5 (Ct. App. 1975) (finding no liability for failure of the police to respond to a plea made 45 minutes before homicide); Antique Arts Corp. v. City of Torrance, 114 Cal. Rptr. 332 (Ct. App. 1974) (finding no liability for police radio dispatcher who delayed broadcasting burglary in progress for 10 minutes after alarm triggered); McCarthy v. Frost, 109 Cal. Rptr. 470 (Ct. App. 1973) (finding no liability when the police negligently failed to find a motorist who required medical aid); Hines v. District of Columbia, 580 A.2d 133 (D.C. 1990) (finding no liability for alleged failure to dispatch emergency medical care); Warren v. District of Columbia, 444 A.2d 1

ernment officer gave the plaintiff specific assurances of protection, that she relied on those assurances, and that the claimed injury resulted from the plaintiff's reliance on the promise to protect.[87] Thus, for example, a claim that police officers failed to protect a particular individual from injury by nongovernmental actors is generally not cognizable; a successful claim would require sufficient prior contacts between police and the individual to indicate a specific undertaking or promise by the police to provide protection and detrimental reliance by the individual. Absent such facts, there is generally no liability for failure to enforce laws and regulations in-

(D.C. 1981) (finding no liability in a suit against the police by women assaulted in their homes by intruders); City of Rome v. Jordan, 426 S.E.2d 861 (Ga. 1993) (finding no liability for failure to respond to a call by the assault victim's sister-in-law informing the police that the perpetrator was at the victim's house); Lewis v. City of Indianapolis, 554 N.E.2d 13 (Ind. Ct. App. 1990) (finding no liability for failure to timely answer 911 call); Trezzi v. City of Detroit, 328 N.W.2d 70 (Mich. Ct. App. 1982) (finding no liability for 90-minute delay in sending police to the scene after 911 call when the behavior at most was negligent); Doe v. Hendricks, 590 P.2d 647 (N.M. Ct. App. 1979) (finding no liability for allegedly slow police response to a call for help by the neighbor of a child who was abducted and dragged into an abandoned house); Merced v. City of New York, 551 N.E.2d 589 (N.Y. 1990) (finding a municipality not liable for injuries resulting from failure reasonably to investigate a 911 call by the victim's neighbor when there was no evidence that the victim relied on assurances of assistance); Kircher v. City of Jamestown, 543 N.E.2d 443 (N.Y. 1989) (finding no liability when a police officer failed to act on a citizen report of abduction that resulted in the victim being raped and locked in a trunk for 12 hours); Sawicki v. Village of Ottawa Hills, 525 N.E.2d 468 (Ohio 1988) (finding no liability to family of a crime victim alleging negligent response to an emergency call); Steiner v. City of Pittsburgh, 509 A.2d 1368 (Pa. Commw. Ct. 1986) (finding no liability to a rape victim who sued the city for failure to respond to her emergency call). *But see* Barth v. Board of Educ., 490 N.E.2d 77 (Ill. App. Ct. 1986) (finding the municipality liable to an injured student for misconduct of a 911 operator); Schear v. Board of County Commrs., 687 P.2d 728 (N.M. 1984) (finding a municipality may be liable when a police department failed to respond to an emergency call for assistance from a woman who subsequently was raped).

87. *See, e.g.*, Delong v. Erie County, 455 N.Y.S.2d 887 (N.Y. App. Div. 1982); Chambers-Castanes v. King County, 669 P.2d 451 (Wash. 1983). The court in *Cuffy* laid out the factors to be established in order to prove the existence of a special relationship:

> (1) an assumption by the municipality, through promises or actions, of an affirmative duty to act on behalf of the party who was injured; (2) knowledge on the part of the municipality's agents that inaction could lead to harm; (3) some form of direct contact between the municipality's agents and the injured party; and (4) that party's justifiable reliance on the municipality's affirmative undertaking.

505 N.E. at 940. In *Cuffy*, although police had given assurances that they would arrest the individual who allegedly posed a threat to plaintiffs, their injuries were not caused by reliance on these assurances. *See* 505 N.E. at 941.

tended to benefit the community as a whole,[88] failure to provide police or fire protection,[89] or failure to inspect.[90]

Significantly, the public duty rule as applied to failure-to-protect claims has remained the law in a substantial majority of jurisdictions,[91] despite criticism in the literature[92] and in the courts[93] and despite an overwhelming trend toward abrogation of sovereign im-

---

88. *See, e.g.*, O'Connor v. City of New York, 447 N.E.2d 33 (N.Y. 1983) (finding no liability for negligence of a building inspector who certified that a new gas pipe conformed to city regulations despite an open gas pipe and the absence of a shut-off valve at the connection to the main line at the street).

89. *See, e.g.*, Frye v. Clark County, 637 P.2d 1215 (Nev. 1981) (finding no governmental liability for an alleged failure to respond to an emergency call reporting a fire); Steitz v. City of Beacon, 64 N.E.2d 704 (N.Y. 1945) (finding no governmental liability for failure to maintain adequate fire-fighting equipment and failure adequately to maintain the water pressure and flow-regulating valve near the plaintiff's property). *See generally* Robertson, *supra* note 73, at 946-50; *supra* note 86.

90. *See, e.g.*, Motyka v. City of Amsterdam, 204 N.E.2d 635 (N.Y. 1965) (finding no governmental liability for property damage and deaths resulting from a fire caused by a defective oil-heating stove even though the fire-department official had failed to report the defective stove after it had caused a previous fire). In some safety inspection cases, courts have found a special relationship based on the particular facts of the case. *See, e.g.*, Gordon v. Holt, 412 N.Y.S.2d 534 (App. Div. 1979). Other courts impliedly or explicitly have abrogated the public duty rule with regard to negligent fire inspections, holding that such inspections are for the benefit of the occupants of the inspected buildings, a "special identifiable group of persons." Robertson, *supra* note 73, at 953; *see, e.g.*, Wilson v. Nepstad, 282 N.W.2d 664 (Iowa 1979).

91. *See generally* 18 McQUILLIN, *supra* note 73, § 53.04.25, at 165. For cases purporting to abandon the public duty rule, see, e.g., Adams v. State, 555 P.2d 235, 241 (Alaska 1976); Leake v. Cain, 720 P.2d 152 (Colo. 1986); Commercial Carrier Corp. v. Indiana River County, 371 So. 2d 1010 (Fla. 1979); Wilson v. Nepstad, 282 N.W.2d 664 (Iowa 1979); Stewart v. Schmieder, 386 So. 2d 1351 (La. 1980); Schear v. Board of County Commrs., 687 P.2d 728 (N.M. 1984); Brennen v. City of Eugene, 591 P.2d 719 (Or. 1979); Catone v. Medberry, 555 A.2d 328 (R.I. 1989); and Wood v. Milin, 397 N.W.2d 479 (Wis. 1986). In a number of these jurisdictions, however, the state legislatures have responded by passing statutes exempting particular emergency services from liability for failures to protect. *See, e.g.*, ALASKA STAT. § 09-65.070 (1994); IOWA CODE ANN. § 670.4 (West Supp. 1993); LA. REV. STAT. ANN. § 9:2793.1 (West 1991). In addition, many jurisdictions have other immunity rules that protect municipalities from liability. *See* 18 McQUILLIN, *supra* note 73, § 53.04.25, at 167; *see also* Gordon v. Bridgeport Hous. Auth., 544 A.2d 1185 (Conn. 1988) (finding a city immune from liability under discretionary-function exception for assault that occurred in public housing project). Other jurisdictions employ ordinary tort doctrines — such as the requirements of foreseeability and causation — to limit the scope of municipal liability. *See* 18 McQUILLIN, *supra* note 73, § 53.04.25, at 167.

92. *See, e.g.*, Stewart F. Hancock, Jr., *Municipal Liability Through a Judge's Eyes,* 44 SYRACUSE L. REV. 925 (1993); Albert J. Harno, *Tort Immunity of Municipal Corporations,* 4 ILL. L.Q. 28 (1921); Daniel C. Kramer, *The Governmental Tort Immunity Doctrine in the United States: 1790-1955,* 1966 U. ILL. L.F. 795; *see also* James T.R. Jones, *Battered Spouses' State Law Damage Actions Against the Unresponsive Police,* 23 RUTGERS L.J. 1 (1991).

93. In New York, for example, after an extensive and impassioned debate in majority and dissenting opinions over a number of years, the rule ultimately was reaffirmed. *See* O'Connor v. City of New York, 447 N.E.2d 33 (N.Y. 1983). *See generally* Hancock, *supra* note 92. Similarly, when the Arizona state courts moved to abrogate the public duty rule, the legislature stepped in to reestablish the narrow limits of affirmative-duty liability in that state. *See* Bird v. State, 821 P.2d 287 (Ariz. Ct. App. 1991) (dismissing a negligence claim against a state on the ground that the earlier common law rule imposing liability had been overruled by state legislature).

munity for much negligent harm-causing behavior by governmental officials.[94] As a historical matter, both states[95] and municipalities[96] were largely immune from suit. In recent times, an increasing number of jurisdictions have abrogated or modified state sovereign immunity by statute.[97] Similarly, the modern trend is toward abrogation of traditional distinctions that protected municipalities from liability in certain circumstances — such as liability for proprietary functions but not governmental ones — and toward a general doctrine of liability for negligent actions.[98] Despite the general trend toward broader liability, the nonliability rule for governmental failure to protect has remained largely intact.[99] Indeed, a number of jurisdictions that have substantially abrogated municipal immunity by statute have carved out specific immunities disallowing failure-to-protect claims against police, firefighters, 911 and other protective-service providers.[100]

---

94. *See generally* 5 Fowler V. Harper et al., James and Gray on The Law of Torts §§ 29.6, 29.11, at 620-22, 691-92 (2d ed. 1986).

95. States are generally immune from suit without their consent. *See generally 5 id.* § 29.2-29.4, at 599-600, 603-05.

96. Traditionally, municipalities were immune from suit for "governmental functions" — functions they performed as agents or representatives of the state — but not for other "proprietary functions." *See generally 5 id.* § 29.6, at 622-39. The tests most commonly invoked for distinguishing governmental from proprietary functions are: "(1) whether the function is allocated to the municipality for its profit or special advantage or whether for the purpose of carrying out the public functions of the state without special advantage to the city, and (2) whether the function is one historically performed by the government." *5 Id.* § 29.6, at 627.

97. *See generally 5 id.* § 29.11, at 690-95.

98. *See generally* Note, *Municipal Tort Liability in Virginia*, 68 Va. L. Rev. 639, 639 n.2 (1982) (noting that 43 jurisdictions have abolished or limited the scope of immunity for governmental functions); *see also generally* 5 Harper et al., *supra* note 94, § 29.6, at 622-39; 18 McQuillin, *supra* note 73, § 53.02.05, at 130.

99. The public duty rule is a judicially created rule. However, courts have continued to apply the rule even after legislative abrogation of municipal sovereign immunity.

100. These statutes generally provide immunity from liability for failure to provide certain protective services or for harms done by third parties that city employees allegedly failed to prevent. *See, e.g.*, Alaska Stat. § 09.65.070 (1994) (providing that fire departments and 911 services have immunity for failed response); Ariz. Rev. Stat. Ann. §§ 12-820.01 to -820.05 (1992 & Supp. 1994) (providing immunity for police for failure to arrest or prevent a crime); Cal. Govt. Code §§ 845, 846, 850 (West 1995) (providing no liability for failure to provide police protection, fire protection, or failure to arrest); Ill. Ann. Stat. ch. 745, para. 10/4-103 to 10/4-107 (Smith-Hurd 1993) (providing immunity for failure to provide police protection or failure to arrest); Iowa Code Ann. § 670.4 (West Supp. 1995) (providing immunity for failure to act if damage is caused by a third party and for failure of a 911 service to respond); La. Rev. Stat. Ann. § 9:2793.1 (West 1991) (providing immunity for damage caused by a crime or fire unless "grossly negligent"); Miss. Code Ann. § 11-46-9 (1995) (providing that police and fire fighters are immune unless exercising "reckless disregard"); Tex. Civ. Prac. & Rem. Code Ann. § 101.055 (West 1986) (providing immunity for failure to provide police and fire protection and failure to respond to emergencies); Utah Code Ann. § 63-30-10 (1993) (providing immunity for failure to provide emergency medical assistance or fire service); W. Va. Code § 29-12A-5 (1992 & 1995 Supp.) (providing immunity for failure to provide police and fire services).

The fact that the public duty rule has survived against the tide of increasingly broad governmental liability does not prove, of course, that courts have good or coherent reasons for invoking it.[101] I consider the question of what might explain the courts' line between liability and nonliability in Part III below. My purpose here is simply to point out that the strongly held presumptive rule in this class of tort cases is that there is generally no liability for governmental failure to protect. At the very least, the tenacity of that rule suggests that there may be a coherent rationale behind the courts' seeming reluctance to find liability in failure-to-protect cases.

III. Rationale for the Nonliability Rule

In the preceding section I made an important — and, I believe, neglected — observation: contrary to what one might have predicted, at least from the overwhelmingly negative reaction to *DeShaney,* the ordinary rule in a whole universe of cases involving failure to protect in tort is that the government generally has no duty to protect from third-party harm. The observation itself is significant: *DeShaney*'s critics have tended to treat the case as a legal outlier and — perhaps as a result — have found little reason to consider whether there may be a plausible or persuasive explanation for it. The pattern of limited liability observed in tort is also important in another way: it mirrors the pattern found in the constitutional cases. That observation suggests that the primary driving force behind *DeShaney* and similar constitutional cases may not be constitutional text or history but the same kinds of considerations that have led to the rejection of such claims in the tort context. If so, it would go a long way toward explaining why the Court's constitutional analysis in *DeShaney* has proved so unsatisfying.

A standard rationale offered by the state courts for the so-called public duty rule in tort is that permitting liability for inadequate protection would make the courts the arbiters of decisions about how to allocate finite public resources and manpower that are best left to the political branches. The level of protection that the government plausibly can provide is determined, in large part, by the amount of resources the legislature has allocated to particular serv-

101. The mere longevity of a rule or pattern of liability does not, of course, prove that the rule or pattern has a coherent or normatively defensible explanation. On the other hand, one ought at least to entertain the possibility that a rule for handling certain kinds of cases that endures over time — in this case against a legal environment moving in the opposite direction — could reflect a defensible, if not normatively satisfying, rationale. That is especially true when the general pattern of liability has been repeated, as we shall see, in two different legal contexts in which different patterns might have been predicted.

ices.[102] Permitting individuals to bring failure-to-protect claims would require the courts to review resource-allocation decisions and permit judges to mandate a level of protection different from the level determined by the political branches.[103]

The above rationale has two parts: first, it takes the view that resource-allocation decisions are political ones and that permitting judges to review them is inappropriate. Second, to the extent this explanation is used to defend nonliability for duty-to-protect claims — as opposed to other kinds of claims against the government — it assumes that duty-to-protect claims are significantly more likely to implicate judicial second-guessing of budgetary decisions. This Part fleshes out these two propositions in more detail in order to explore whether or not some version of the resource-allocation rationale for retaining sovereign immunity in this class of cases is defensible.

A. *Resource Allocation and Institutional Competence*

In our governmental system, it is uncontroversial that budgetary decisions are ordinarily political decisions. That is, judgments about what combination of goods and services will be provided by the government, how much money is required to supply such services, and how available funds will be allocated ordinarily are made by citizens through their elected representatives. To the extent that failure-to-protect cases involve the judiciary in second-guessing such decisions (an issue I discuss in the next section), they raise the question whether these cases are appropriate for judicial resolution.

As a matter of institutional design, budgetary decisions generally are thought to be political decisions rather than judicial ones, at least in part, because they involve a kind of decisionmaking that courts do not do well. Courts specialize in resolving disputes between two parties, each of whom can represent its interests before the court, "by declaring victory for one and a loss for the other."[104] They are not, however, well-suited to resolving what have been called "polycentric"[105] problems. "Polycentricity" is "the property

102. *See* Riss v. City of New York, 240 N.E.2d 860, 860 (N.Y. 1968).

103. *See* 240 N.E.2d at 860; *see also* Mann v. State, 139 Cal. Rptr. 82, 85 (Ct. App. 1977) (Statutory immunity for failure to protect "was designed to prevent political decisions of policy-making officials of government from being second-guessed by judges and juries . . . . In other words, [the] essentially budgetary decisions of these officials were not to be subject to judicial review in tort litigation.").

104. Clayton P. Gillette, Local Government Law 396 (1994).

105. *See* William A. Fletcher, *The Discretionary Constitution: Institutional Remedies and Judicial Legitimacy*, 91 Yale L.J. 635, 645-49 (1982); Lon L. Fuller, *The Forms and Limits of Adjudication*, 92 Harv. L. Rev. 353, 394 (1978). The concept of polycentricity apparently

of a complex problem with a number of subsidiary problem 'centers,' each of which is related to the others, such that the solution to each depends on the solution to all the others."[106] To illustrate, consider the task of deciding how one million dollars in research funds should be allocated among many competing scientific projects: the decision is never one of

> Project *A* v. Project *B*, but rather of Project *A* v. Project *B* v. Project *C* v. Project *D* . . . bearing in mind that Project *Q* may be an alternative to Project *B*, while Project *M* supplements it, and that Project *R* may seek the same objective as Project *C* by a cheaper method, though one less certain to succeed, etc.[107]

The less the dispute at issue resembles the winner-takes-all model and the more polycentric elements it contains, the less amenable it is to judicial resolution.[108]

The budgetary process that allocates public money among governmental goods and services is polycentric in a way that makes judicial resolution problematic.[109] Budgetary decisions involve balancing the interests and preferences of individuals and groups with divergent demands for a finite "pot" of public monies. In a world of limited resources, every budgetary decision involving a particular good or service requires adjustment and readjustment of allocations applicable to other goods and services. For example, more resources for police protection means less for education or fire protection or public parks; more money for public parks or schools requires more money for infrastructure to service them; less money for police might affect the mix of other services that depend on police and so on. Thus, the point is not only that more of a particular service "x" means less of "y" and "z" but that the levels of x, y, and

---

was derived from MICHAEL POLANYI, THE LOGIC OF LIBERTY: REFLECTIONS AND REJOINDERS 171 (1951).

106. Fletcher, *supra* note 105, at 645. Lon Fuller compares a polycentric situation to a spiderweb: "A pull on one strand will distribute tensions after a complicated pattern throughout the web as a whole. Doubling the original pull will, in all likelihood, not simply double each of the resulting tensions but will rather create a different complicated pattern of tensions." Fuller, *supra* note 105, at 395.

107. Fuller, *supra* note 105, at 401.

108. As Fuller points out, polycentricity is a matter of degree; almost all problems presented for adjudication involve *some* polycentric elements. There is, however, a point at which the polycentric elements so dominate a problem that attempting to resolve it in a judicial forum may exceed the "proper limits of adjudication." *Id.* at 398-99. Legal scholars disagree as to where the dividing line ought to be drawn between functions that are appropriate for judicial resolution and those that are so polycentric as to exceed the capabilities of the judicial process. But the debate itself presupposes widespread agreement that there is — or ought to be — such a line and that the relative polycentricity of legal problems is relevant to the line-drawing process.

109. *See generally* GILLETTE, *supra* note 104, at 394-96.

z are intertwined such that effectuating a workable arrangement among them after increasing the level of x requires a number of interrelated adjustments and readjustments in order to reach a new, workable equilibrium. Courts are not institutionally equipped to make the adjustments and readjustments necessary to resolve budget-allocation issues.[110]

These kinds of decisions are best handled in a forum where all the affected interests can appear before the decisionmaking body and the "multiple centers can engage in exchange and consider the claims of others,"[111] a forum that looks much more like a legislative committee or other political entity than a court. Legislatures, unlike courts, have access to both the information and the deliberative processes necessary to permit that kind of exchange. Legislators are in contact with both the wide variety of citizen demands for and views about certain distributions of public resources and the administrative and fiscal realities faced by those who administer various public programs. They can gather information, hold public hearings, and promote negotiation and debate among affected interests in order to analyze various alternatives and consider the broader ramifications of those alternatives. Indeed, the legislative process is the consummate forum for this kind of multidimensional deliberation.[112]

The traditional judicial role, on the other hand, is to adjudicate particular cases involving the specific legal rights and interests of the parties before the court. While judges are clearly aware of — and, in some cases, influenced by — the broader consequences of their decisions, their ability to consider such consequences is quite limited. For example, courts generally do not permit nonparties to

110. In the words of William Fletcher, resolution of such interlocking disputes requires

> mutual spontaneous adjustment by the constituent parts of the problem itself — rather like the bees in a hive finding their appropriate space and function by their sense of the bees around them, with each bee individually adjusting to its neighbors, and each neighboring bee in turn adjusting to the other's adjustment until a stable equilibrium is reached.

Fletcher, *supra* note 105, at 647 (citing POLANYI, *supra* note 105); *see also* HENRY M. HART & ALBERT M. SACKS, THE LEGAL PROCESS: BASIC PROBLEMS IN THE MAKING AND APPLICATION OF LAW 669 (tentative ed. 1958) (noting that polycentric problems "present so many variables as to require handling by the method either of *ad hoc* discretion or of negotiation or of legislation").

111. GILLETTE, *supra* note 104, at 396.

112. It is, of course, open to debate how well legislatures function in their deliberative capacity: whether they actually reflect the preferences of their various constituencies or whether they have been captured by special interests and lobbyists. That question is beyond the scope of this article. My only point is that, as a matter of institutional competence, there is reason to believe that legislatures are in a better position than courts to handle these sorts of questions.

argue the broader ramifications of the case at bar for other situations or issues not before the court.[113] Moreover, unlike legislatures, courts cannot hold hearings to gather information that might be relevant to the polycentric aspects or broader context of their decisions. They are limited to the facts and information made available by the parties before them. To make the point in the budgetary context, a court holding that a municipality must increase the level of a particular governmental service, such as police or fire protection, would not — unlike the legislature that made the initial allocation decisions — have sufficient information to consider the complicated effects of its ruling on other, interrelated budget allocations.[114]

The rise of structural-reform litigation has, of course, posed a challenge to the traditional judicial role described above. In structural-reform cases, the litigants seek, not so much to resolve a binary dispute between two or more parties, but to make systemic changes in governmental institutions, operations, or procedures.[115] For example, desegregation cases seek not simply to remedy specific instances of unlawful discrimination but rather to reverse the effects of years of enforced segregation through structural remedies such as busing and magnet schools. Structural-reform remedies involve the courts in such nontraditional functions as running the day-to-day operations of schools and prisons and even intervening to permit the taxation necessary to fund such activities.[116] Significantly, however, the farther such cases have moved away from the more traditional judicial role — for example, from prohibiting de

113. Under certain circumstances, nonparties may be able to file amicus curiae briefs in order to bring additional information before the court, assure presentation of the complete factual scenario, or point out the broader implications of the court's decision. Such participation, however, is limited, and the rules regarding the participation of amicii curiae differ among various federal and state jurisdictions. *See generally* Michael K. Lowman, Comment, *The Litigating Amicus Curiae: When Does the Party Begin After the Friends Leave?*, 41 AM. U. L. REV. 1243 (1992); Randy S. Parlee, *A Primer on Amicus Curiae Briefs*, WIS. LAW., Nov. 1989, at 14.

114. *See generally* Ann Judith Gellis, *Legislative Reforms of Governmental Tort Liability: Overreacting to Minimal Evidence*, 21 RUTGERS L.J. 375 (1990). Gellis states:

> A government decision to provide a good which is either unavailable in, or inadequately supplied by, the private sector involves various sub-decisions relating to the provision of that good: how much to produce, who should receive the good, how to finance it, and how to structure delivery of the good. These decisions are complicated political decisions, quite apart from the political nature of the budgetary process. . . . [T]he complexity of the decision-making process as to the entire output makes it far less certain that the judiciary has the information necessary to second guess as to any one decision.

Id. at 386.

115. *See* PETER W. LOW & JOHN C. JEFFRIES, JR., CIVIL RIGHTS ACTIONS: SECTION 1983 AND RELATED STATUTES 721 (2d ed. 1991).

116. *See* Missouri v. Jenkins, 495 U.S. 33 (1990).

jure discrimination to busing and requiring capital expenditures on magnet schools — the more they have been subject to criticism on institutional competence grounds.[117] That is because these broad remedies — the *exact* contours of which are not constitutionally compelled[118] — require judges to entertain such questions as what specific educational facilities and programs a locality should provide to its students[119] and what constitutes a well-run prison.[120] These kinds of decisions are not only highly polycentric, but they look more legislative or executive than judicial, in part, because there is very little in the way of legal norms to guide the discretion of the decisionmaker.[121] Scholars endorsing judicial intervention in structural-reform cases have found it necessary to defend the legitimacy of such cases against those who attack them on institutional competence grounds.[122] Moreover, the Supreme Court's restrictions on such remedies can be seen as an effort to cabin judicial discretion in order to address the nontraditional aspects of these cases.[123]

---

117. *See generally* Fletcher, *supra* note 105, at 640-41.

118. In structural-reform cases, there are generally a number of permissible ways in which a constitutional violation could be remedied. For example, in a prison-overcrowding case the judge could order the release of prisoners, improvement of existing facilities, or the building of new facilities. *See id.* at 646-47.

119. For example, one district court decree required

> high schools in which every classroom will have air conditioning, an alarm system, and 15 microcomputers; a 2,000-square-foot planetarium; green-houses and vivariums; a 25-acre farm with air-conditioned meeting room for 104 people; a Model United Nations wired for language translation; broadcast capable radio and television studios with an editing and animation lab; a temperature controlled art gallery; movie editing and screening rooms; a 3,500-square-foot dust-free diesel mechanics room; 1,875-square-foot elementary school animal rooms for use in a zoo project; swimming pools; and numerous other facilities.

Missouri v. Jenkins, 495 U.S. 33, 77 (1990) (Kennedy, J., concurring in part and concurring in the judgment).

120. Decrees in prison and mental hospital cases may specify, among other things, "precise staffing ratios, the temperatures in rooms or cells, the types and quantities of food to be served, [and] the manner of determining types of and times for isolation or solitary confinement." Fletcher, *supra* note 105, at 639.

121. *See generally id.* at 645-49. Fletcher argues that courts called upon to formulate broad structural remedies are dealing with nonlegal-polycentric problems that call into question their institutional authority because courts have "no guidance from legal norms as to the appropriate values to be served by the solution[s]." *Id.* at 647. Even when judicial intervention is itself "triggered by the violation of a legal standard," the court reaches beyond the limits of the judicial role when the remedy calls on the court to "reorganize the governmental functions of a political branch of [the government]." *Id.*

122. *See, e.g.,* Owen M. Fiss, *The Supreme Court, 1978 Term — Foreword: The Forms of Justice,* 93 HARV. L. REV. 1, 28-44 (1979); Fletcher, *supra* note 105, at 641-49, 692-97; David Rudenstine, *Institutional Injunctions,* 4 CARDOZO L. REV. 611, 624-37 (1983).

123. Examples of the Supreme Court's efforts to limit the potential reach of structural reform remedies are the requirement that the remedy be closely tailored to the constitutional violation, *see* Milliken v. Bradley, 418 U.S. 717, 744 (1974), and the enforcement of standing

To illustrate the problem in the budgetary context, imagine, for example, a claim by city residents whose property has been damaged in a fire that the city's one fire station is inadequate to provide reasonable fire protection to their neighborhood. Suppose further that remedying the situation would require the city to build a new fire station to serve that part of the city. The remedy would not only require the city substantially to increase the part of the budget allocated to fire protection, it would also affect other parts of the budget: the increase in money allocated to fire protection would have to come out of the funds originally allocated for some other service. But the requirement that more money be spent for fire protection — for example, by decreasing the budget for police services — would also involve deciding how the increase in fire protection and decrease in police protection would affect the mix of other services. Thus, the resolution of the one issue — the alleged need for more fire protection services — would require not just a substitution of funds from one service to another but a reallocation of a large part of the municipal budget.[124]

A court called upon to adjudicate the claim described above, unlike the political process that formulated the original budget, would not have before it the whole range of tradeoffs and interlocking budgetary issues that would be affected by its resolution of the claim. The court's view is limited to the parties before it (in this case, the injured plaintiff and the city as defendant) and consideration of one governmental service (fire protection) as if it existed in a vacuum. But fire protection does not exist in a vacuum; it is inextricably intertwined with many other items in the budget that originally were determined by balancing all manner of individual and collective preferences.

Given the institutional limitations of the judicial process, there is no reason to think that the court is likely to make a better allocation than the legislature that made the initial budgetary decisions. For example, how do we know whether more fire protection and less police protection — or perhaps more of both and higher taxes — would make citizens better off, even in the narrow sense of less lives and property being lost? Moreover, once we broaden the "better off" question and begin to weigh less police protection against less education or less sanitation, the question of "correct-

requirements, *see* City of Los Angeles v. Lyons, 461 U.S. 95, 105-10 (1983); *see also infra* notes 229-231 and accompanying text.

124. *See generally* GILLETTE, *supra* note 104, at 394-95.

ness" seems impossible to answer as a legal matter.[125] To borrow a garden metaphor: In order "[t]o preserve some substance for the form of adjudication you have to judge pumpkins against pumpkins, not pumpkins against cucumbers, especially when there are some relevant cucumbers not entered in the show."[126] The point here is not that politicians do a perfect job at making these sorts of decisions but that there is no reason to think courts would do it better. It seems clear that courts have no apparent institutional advantage over the political processes in decisionmaking of this sort.

The notion that courts are not institutionally well suited to second-guessing certain kinds of decisions is not a new or particularly controversial idea; it resonates in many areas of the law. My point here is to show that it has great explanatory power in failure-to-protect cases. I turn, then, to the question whether failure-to-protect claims are more likely than other kinds of claims against the government to involve the court in second-guessing resource-allocation decisions.

B. *Special Concerns Raised by Failure-To-Protect Claims*

As noted above,[127] the strong trend in tort law is toward increasingly broad governmental liability. Against that general trend, however, courts and legislatures have continued to adhere to a rule of nonliability for governmental failure to protect. The rationale that has been given for this special treatment is that these sorts of claims involve the courts in second-guessing resource-allocation decisions.[128] This Part explores whether the courts' distinction between failure-to-protect claims and other kinds of claims against the government is defensible.

---

125. There are, of course, some judicially enforceable legal restraints on the *relative* distribution of goods and services, such as constitutional prohibitions against discrimination on the basis of race or sex. *See* U.S. CONST. amend. XIV, § 1; Thurman v. City of Torrington, 595 F. Supp. 1521 (D. Conn. 1984).

126. Fuller, *supra* note 105, at 403.

127. *See supra* notes 91-98 and accompanying text.

128. Available state legislative history confirms that the rationale for statutes disallowing failure-to-protect claims is legislators' view that decisions about whether and at what level to provide certain protective services lies properly within the purview of the political process rather than the courts. *See, e.g., Sovereign Immunity Study*, 5 CAL. L. REVISION COMMN. REPORTS 11, 464 (1963) (noting that the decision of whether to provide fire protection was primarily political and "quite unfitted to the processes of judicial administration"); *Tort Liability of Public Entities and Public Employees: Recommendation*, 4 CAL. L. REVISION COMMN. REPORTS 807, 860-861 (1963) ("To permit review of these decisions [whether to provide police or fire protection] by judges and juries would remove the ultimate decisionmaking authority from those politically responsible for making the decisions.").

To begin, consider a claim of failure to protect brought by a city resident whose children were burned to death in a house fire.[129] Prior to the time of the fire, the city, for financial reasons, had begun closing a number of firehouses on a random, rotating basis. Plaintiff alleges that the firehouse nearest to her home was closed on the day of the fire, that the closure constituted negligence on the part of the city, and that this negligence was the proximate cause of her children's deaths. Plaintiff's theory of liability under these facts raises the specter of judicial budgetary review in a dramatic form: first, it seems clear that the government's failure to respond in this situation resulted from conscious policy decisions about how to manage municipal resources. Governmental officials apparently found it necessary to cut the level of services in order to remain within the budget that the legislature had allocated for the service. In addition, officials made resource-allocation decisions at the operational level when they decided to close firehouses on a rotating basis rather than, for example, closing one firehouse permanently or decreasing staffing at all fire stations. A court entertaining plaintiff's claim would be required to review these decisions based on the court's independent judgment as to whether the city's decision to cut services and its method for doing so were reasonable. For the reasons laid out above,[130] there is no reason to think that state courts are better equipped than members of the political branches to get the resource-allocation issues right.[131]

Of course, not all failure-to-protect cases raise resource-allocation issues so starkly as the fire protection example. Imagine, for example, claims by two different plaintiffs who are beaten by thugs in a city metro station and bring suit against the municipal police department for failure to prevent these injuries.[132] The first plaintiff alleges that police officers who arrived on the scene during the beating failed to intervene before he was seriously injured. In the second incident, police officers failed to arrive at all. The sec-

129. These facts are drawn from Chandler v. District of Columbia, 404 A.2d 964 (D.C. 1979).

130. *See supra* notes 104-26 and accompanying text.

131. Of course, not all such cases would result in liability. Plaintiff would have to demonstrate that the government was at fault and that its actions were the legal and proximate cause of the injury; she ultimately may be unable to do so. But the argument against liability is that even *entertaining* cases that challenge resource allocations necessarily would involve the court in reviewing political decisions and raise institutional competence concerns.

132. The facts are based, with modifications, on Crosland v. New York City Transit Authority, 498 N.E.2d 143 (N.Y. 1986). I am indebted to Clay Gillette for the comparison of *Chandler* with *Crosland,* which appears in GILLETTE, *supra* note 104, at 714-18, and which he discussed with me at some length.

ond plaintiff alleges that the city was negligent in not having one or more police officers available or permanently assigned to this particular station because there had been a number of previous incidents of violent crimes there. The first claim is more likely to go forward and could lead to liability assuming that the plaintiff can make out the elements of the claim. The second claim will virtually never succeed because, as explained by one court, it "alleges a failure to properly allocate police resources."[133]

In what sense does the second claim involve the court in reviewing resource-allocation decisions that the first claim does not? Both claims *implicate* budgetary matters in that liability could require the government to spend more of its available resources on police services: permitting liability for failure to have enough officers at particular locations ultimately would force the city to hire more police officers, which would obviously require greater expenditures for police protection.[134] On the other hand, liability based on the theory that officials on the scene failed to intervene might also require more resources to be devoted to police services, for example, to provide better training and supervision or to hire more competent police officers.[135]

These two claims differ significantly, however, in the way they implicate underlying political decisions. In considering the first claim, the court is being called upon simply to enforce the decision of the political branches to provide a certain level of police protection to the public. That is, once the decision has been made to fund a police department and police officers are actually on the scene, liability simply requires them to do the job they were intended to

133. *Crosland,* 498 N.E.2d at 145.

134. In the first instance, the police department could respond to liability for its failure to post officers at the metro station by shifting available officers from other locations, rather than by hiring additional officers. But the police department's ability to cover all locations where third-party harms are likely to occur is obviously limited by the number of available officers. It seems likely that, over time, liability based on the theory that *more* officers ought to have been stationed at *more* locations would put significant pressure on the city to hire substantially more police officers.

135. *See* Riss v. City of New York, 240 N.E.2d 860, 865 (N.Y. 1968) (Keating, J., dissenting). There is, however, a plausible argument that these two kinds of claims would differ significantly in the *degree* to which liability would affect the municipal budget. In many instances, one could expect that increasing the level of services — hiring more police officers, building more firehouses — would be more expensive than reasonably maintaining the level of services one already has. This difference in degree surely matters if we are concerned about liability that implicates resource allocation. Claims that would have an incidental effect on the municipal budget by requiring the government to spend more money on supervision and training are at one end of the spectrum, and claims that would require the reallocation of enough resources to increase the level of services, plausibly requiring resources to be moved from one service "box" to another, are at the other.

do in a reasonable manner. By permitting liability in this situation, the court is not requiring the government to do anything more than it already has committed itself to do. In essence, the court is enforcing the political bargain: the legislative decision to have a reasonably functioning police department.[136] Permitting such cases to go forward may have an effect on the budget — in that it may cost money — but it does not involve the court in reviewing the legislative allocations themselves.[137]

The second claim, however, would involve the court in quite a different kind of review: the number of police officers that are available to answer calls — the size of the police force and the level of police services that plausibly can be provided — is a direct function of the level of resources that the legislature has devoted to police services. Liability for failure to have more officers at particular locations would redefine the politically determined level of service by requiring a more extensive police force. Moreover, the very process of determining whether there *ought* to have been more police officers stationed at this or that place — or whether police should have been available to answer this or that call — inevitably requires the court to ask the resource-allocation questions: Was the level of police services that the government chose to provide adequate, or, at the very least, was the city's operational allocation of existing police services appropriate? It is hard to imagine what the legal standard for such review would be: What constitutes an appropriate level of any particular service? Further, how can that question sensibly be answered without knowing how an increase in the service at issue would affect the allocation of resources for other services? Permitting these sorts of claims to go forward means that the courts, rather than the political branches, are deciding what level and distribution of protective services the community will have.[138]

136. This assumes, not implausibly, that the legislature intended to establish and fund a police force that would act nonnegligently in its interactions with the public.

137. In this regard, these sorts of failure-to-protect claims are very like governmental liability in situations not involving intervening third-party harm. For example, imagine a claim against the government for police brutality in which the plaintiff alleges that the police officers who arrested him on drug charges caused him to sustain a concussion and two broken arms. It is unlikely that these police actions were determined or limited *in principal part* by resource constraints, except in the limited sense that training and supervision costs money. Resolution of the claim would not involve the court in reviewing the kind of resource-allocation decisions implicated by the inadequate-fire-protection claim; the court simply would determine whether police officers used a reasonable amount of force under the circumstances, the sort of question courts are accustomed to resolving.

138. To give another illustration of the same idea, consider the difference between a claim for injuries due to a defective sidewalk and a claim for injuries resulting from failure to lay a sidewalk in the first place. The first claim will result in liability if the municipality had notice of a significant defect and failed to remedy it. *See, e.g.*, Livings v. City of Chicago, 326

There is not, of course, as clear a line as I have drawn between claims that raise resource-allocation concerns and those that do not. For example, it is at least possible that the police officers who stood by and did nothing to aid our hypothetical plaintiff did so because the city lacked the money to arm and train them to intervene against violent third-party assaults or because they lacked sufficient "back-up." Conversely, perhaps there were, in fact, enough available police officers to patrol the metro station and the surrounding area. But, my point is that claims involving general failures to protect — claims that directly implicate the level of services — are more likely than other kinds of claims against the government to bump up against the realities of resource limitations. Furthermore, because courts are reluctant to interfere with political decisions, the likelihood that they will intervene in failure-to-protect cases will be quite low when the level of care or services in question is limited by scarce public resources.

Interestingly, while there is a strong argument that courts are not very good at monitoring claims involving the "level" of services, as opposed to the "quality" of services, there is reason to believe that the situation is exactly the opposite when it comes to political monitoring: the political process may be better at monitoring the *level* of services than it is at monitoring their *quality*. It is a well-accepted justification for permitting certain governmental immunities that the political process can also serve as an effective check against governmental misbehavior. For example, when governmental officials or employees in their agencies or departments cause harm — particularly in these days of extensive media coverage — the public can exert considerable pressure for offending officials to step down or be fired, and elected officials can be voted out of office.[139] This kind of political pressure would presumably be effective in controlling harms resulting from both level and quality of services.

N.E.2d 170 (Ill. App. Ct. 1975). *See generally* 19 McQuillin, *supra* note 73, §§ 54.80-54.80d, at 256-68. Liability would require the city reasonably to implement a prior decision by the political branches to have a sidewalk in a particular location. Indeed, cities are required to close defective public ways if they cannot maintain them nonnegligently, for example, due to lack of funding. *See id.* § 54.23, at 75. By contrast, the second claim would involve the court in evaluating political decisions about how much money should be available for sidewalk construction (resource allocation at the legislative level) and how those resources ought to be allocated among all the possible locations where sidewalks might be needed (resource allocation at the operational level). Such claims virtually never succeed. *See, e.g.*, Arvel v. City of Baton Rouge, 234 So. 2d 458 (La. Ct. App. 1970); Braithwaite v. West Valley City Corp., 860 P.2d 336 (Utah 1993).

139. A full discussion of the strengths and weaknesses of the political process in monitoring the behavior of governmental officials is beyond the scope of this paper.

There is, however, evidence that politicians — particularly elected officials — get considerably more mileage out of promises to *increase* goods and services than promises to *better maintain* existing ones.[140] Promises to put more cops on the street or hire more teachers for overcrowded public schools are more politically salient than simple assurances that existing police officers and teachers will do a better job. Similarly, there is empirical evidence that governmental agencies tend to neglect maintenance of existing services precisely because it is politically less rewarding.[141] Agencies have greater incentive to add new facilities or programs than to improve existing ones because the former is more likely to enable them to enlarge their budgets.[142] Failure adequately to maintain and supervise existing facilities has been shown to be linked to increased liability costs.[143]

Thus, along with the institutional-competence arguments against liability in situations that implicate the level of services, damage liability may also be less important in those situations than in situations involving negligent delivery of existing services because the political process is more likely to serve as an effective monitor against governmental misbehavior in the former than in the latter.

---

140. *See generally* Gellis, *supra* note 114, at 389-90; *see also* Larry Kramer & Alan O. Sykes, *Municipal Liability Under § 1983: A Legal and Economic Analysis,* 1987 SUP. CT. REV. 249, 279 (arguing that because officials are confronted both with demands for increased public services and calls for lower taxes, they are under pressure to provide higher levels of public service at minimum cost).

141.

> Maintenance is a low visibility service, and empirical evidence supports the theory that when a bureau is forced to reduce costs, maintenance will be at the top of its list. Maintenance is an operating expense funded out of the current budget for which the short-term political rewards are likely to be viewed as less compelling compared with those associated with adding new facilities or new programs.

Gellis, *supra* note 114, at 390 (footnotes omitted). *See generally* FRANK LEVY ET AL., URBAN OUTCOMES: SCHOOLS, STREETS, AND LIBRARIES 48, 59, 137, 185 (1974) (noting that a study of public services — primarily schools and streets — in Oakland, California found that routine maintenance was the first to suffer when funding cutbacks were made); *see also generally* HERMAN B. LEONARD, CHECKS UNBALANCED: THE QUIET SIDE OF PUBLIC SPENDING 169-75 (1986) (explaining why maintenance of infrastructure is a "no-reward" expenditure for public officials).

142. *See generally* ANTHONY DOWNS, INSIDE BUREAUCRACY 195-99 (1967) (giving reasons for expansionist tendency of agencies and bureaus); WILLIAM A. NISKANEN, JR., BUREAUCRACY AND REPRESENTATIVE GOVERNMENT (1971) (arguing that, unlike a private firm, the survival of a public bureau depends on the size of its budget, rather than on the efficiency of its operations).

143. *See* Gellis, *supra* note 114, at 390 (citing BETTY VAN DER SMISSEN, THE LEGAL LIABILITY OF CITIES AND SCHOOLS FOR INJURIES IN RECREATION AND PARKS § 4.2, at 192 (1968) (showing the connection between maintenance and liability costs)).

C. *The Rationale Applied*

The notion that failure-to-protect cases uniquely involve the courts in reviewing resource-allocation decisions provides a theoretical rationale for the presumptive rule of nonliability, the so-called public duty rule: state courts invoke the public duty rule when liability would involve the court directly in second-guessing political decisions about budgetary matters or when the facts or context strongly suggest that the level of care that was provided resulted from the realities of limited public resources. In other words, courts generally decline to entertain individual claims that challenge the level or distribution of services or complain that a different level or distribution would have prevented some particular harm. Implicit in the notion of public duty is the recognition that the higher level of services that may have prevented a particular harm could mean less of something else and a different — though not necessarily superior — distribution of harms. Rather than involving themselves in second-guessing whether the political branches got it "right" when they chose a particular use of resources, the courts have chosen to defer to the legislature on such matters.

Thus, the more a plaintiff's theory of liability resembles the first claim in *Crosland*[144] — where police officers were on site but failed to perform reasonably — the *less* likely adjudicating the claim would involve the court in second-guessing budgetary decisions and the *more* likely liability could result. In doctrinal terms, courts are most likely to find a "special relationship" giving rise to liability when the government has involved itself in a particular situation to such an extent that resource decisions have already been made and resources have already been assigned.[145] On the other hand, the more governmental defendants plausibly can argue that the level of care afforded the plaintiff resulted from resource constraints — *Chandler*-like cases[146] — the less likely the claim will lead to liability.

The notion that courts are not institutionally competent to handle failure-to-protect claims is *most powerful* in explaining why

144. *See supra* notes 132-33 and accompanying text.

145. *See, e.g.*, Kircher v. City of Jamestown, 543 N.E.2d 443, 446 (N.Y. 1989) ("[W]here a municipality voluntarily undertakes to act on behalf of a particular citizen who detrimentally relies on an illusory promise of protection offered by the municipality, we have permitted liability because in such cases the municipality has by its conduct determined how its resources are to be allocated in respect to that circumstance and has thereby created a 'special relationship' with the individual seeking protection.").

146. *See supra* notes 129-31 and accompanying text.

courts are strongly disinclined to permit liability in most failure-to-protect cases. It provides a persuasive and normatively defensible justification for a rule that is, for other reasons, unappealing. On the other hand, resource-allocation concerns only roughly predict when the courts will depart from the nonliability rule. As noted above, the special relationship cases are less likely to involve the courts in reviewing budgetary decisions. But the fact is that failure-to-protect cases implicate resource-allocation decisions along a continuum. Thus, while one can predict that claims like the one in *Chandler* will virtually never result in liability and claims like the first one in *Crosland* are more likely to lead to liability, the exact boundary line between liability and nonliability remains predictably fuzzy.

IV. Implications for Failure To Protect Under the Due Process Clause

Claims alleging a governmental duty to protect under the Constitution appear to be relatively new.[147] For over a decade prior to the Court's holding in *DeShaney,* however, such cases had been percolating in the lower federal courts. Significantly, the pattern that emerges from the lower court cases is strikingly similar to the way state courts have treated analogous cases in tort. The presumptive rule in the constitutional cases as in the tort context is that there is no liability for governmental failure to protect.

This Part outlines the range of failure-to-protect claims that have been brought under the Due Process Clause and how the courts have handled such claims. A discussion of each category shows how concerns about resource allocation help to explain the courts' approach to liability.

147. Constitutional duty-to-protect cases trace their roots back to the 1976 case of Estelle v. Gamble, 429 U.S. 97 (1976), in which the Supreme Court held that the government owes a duty under the Eighth Amendment to protect prisoners from certain injuries while in custody. Later, in Youngberg v. Romeo, 457 U.S. 307 (1982), and City of Revere v. Massachusetts General Hospital, 463 U.S. 239 (1983), the Court held that the government owes a similar duty of protection under the Fourteenth Amendment to involuntarily committed mental patients and pretrial detainees, respectively. The Court first considered a claim of failure to protect outside the custodial setting in Martinez v. California, 444 U.S. 277 (1980), a case against the government for the release of a parolee who subsequently killed plaintiff's decedent. The Court dismissed the case on the grounds that there was no causation but left open the possibility that, under other circumstances, such a Fourteenth Amendment right might be upheld. *See* 444 U.S. at 284-85. Lower court cases prior to *DeShaney* involving noncustodial failure-to-protect claims under the Fourteenth Amendment relied on *Martinez*. *See generally* Jensen v. Conrad, 747 F.2d 185, 190-94 (4th Cir. 1984), *cert. denied,* 470 U.S. 1052 (1985).

The claims fall along a continuum roughly correlated with the extent of governmental involvement in the events giving rise to the harm: at one end of the spectrum are situations in which the government allegedly had reason to know of a particular risk of injury but no ongoing relationship with the potential victim. There is almost never liability in such cases. At the other end are cases in which the plaintiff was injured — for example, by another prisoner — while in custody, the one situation where liability is clearly permitted under *DeShaney*. A middle category of claims, where failure to protect may or may not lead to liability, involves situations in which governmental actors arguably have contributed in some way to the risk of harm.

A. *General Failures To Protect — No Liability*

Claims at one end of the continuum involve allegations that governmental actors failed to provide protection against a risk of harm that they knew or should have known existed. The cases take a variety of forms from a general allegation of failure to enforce the laws to a single, unaddressed call for help, to a claim of reliance on explicit or implicit governmental assurances of help. Such claims almost never give rise to liability.

There are relatively few cases seeking damages for general failures to enforce the law or general failures to protect from the risk of harm. Such cases raise issues of resource allocation in the starkest form. For example, in *Reiff v. City of Philadelphia,*[148] plaintiff was shot during a robbery at a store where she was shopping. Plaintiff alleged that the government had failed to protect her by its policy of responding only when a crime actually had been committed[149] and by providing inadequate police protection in a high crime area. This case is just another version of *Chandler*;[150] litigation of the claim would require the court to consider both whether the total number of police officers was adequate for the city's needs (resource allocation at the legislative level) and whether the city's allocation of officers among the various needs in the community was appropriate (resource allocation at the operational level). As noted above, the courts have no institutional ad-

148. 471 F. Supp. 1262 (E.D. Pa. 1979).

149. The facts recited by the district court suggest that the police never actually received a call for help from plaintiff or anyone else. *See* 471 F. Supp. at 1264.

150. *See supra* notes 129-31 and accompanying text.

vantage over the political process in assessing how available resources ought to be allocated.[151]

There are any number of such cases in which resource-allocation issues are even closer to the surface: for example, in *Dollar v. Haralson County,*[152] plaintiff, whose children drowned while she was attempting to cross a rain-swollen ford, brought suit against the county for failing to build a bridge across the ford.[153] The County Commissioner testified at trial that building a bridge over that particular ford was one of his "top priorities."[154] According to the Commissioner, however, it was county policy to wait for a state contract rather than spend local revenue on bridges.[155] The thrust of plaintiff's claim was that the county was negligent in failing to spend local funds to build the bridge.[156] It is hard to imagine a clearer case of judicial review of budgetary decisions.

Cases involving injuries allegedly caused by governmental failures to enforce state or local laws raise similar issues. For example, in *California First Bank v. State,*[157] plaintiffs alleged that injuries they sustained in an automobile accident resulted from police failure to enforce liquor control laws and drunk driving laws at certain "Indian Bars" that were notorious for excessive drinking. The intoxicated driver of the automobile that collided with plaintiffs' car had been drinking at one of the unregulated bars on the night in

151. In a case raising similar issues, Jackson v. Byrne, 738 F.2d 1443 (7th Cir. 1984), plaintiffs sought damages for governmental failure to prevent their children's deaths in an apartment fire. The deaths occurred during a firefighters' strike in which the city had closed a firehouse near plaintiffs' apartment building. *See* 738 F.2d at 1444-45. Thirteen minutes after the fire was detected a fire truck from a manned firehouse arrived and extinguished the blaze. *See* 738 F.2d at 1445. The case differs from *Chandler* in that picketing fire fighters who detected the fire were prevented by police guarding the nearby firehouse from gaining access to fire-fighting equipment. The decision to prevent access to certain firehouses was, however, clearly part of the city's strategy for conserving resources and protecting public property during the strike. (There was no evidence that police obstructed the efforts of rescuers to reach the burning building.) The court held the government not liable for the children's deaths. *See* 738 F.2d at 1448; *see also* McKee v. City of Rockwall, 877 F.2d 409, 416 (5th Cir. 1989) (finding no liability for failure to arrest a third party who subsequently injured plaintiff), *cert. denied,* 493 U.S. 1023 (1990); Wright v. City of Ozark, 715 F.2d 1513, 1516 (11th Cir. 1983) (finding no liability when a rape victim claimed that the city had failed to protect her by suppressing information about the number of rapes that had occurred in the city); Bowers v. DeVito, 686 F.2d 616, 618 (7th Cir. 1982) (finding no governmental liability to family of a victim killed by a mental patient who was released despite having committed an earlier killing and having been adjudicated not guilty by reason of insanity).

152. 704 F.2d 1540 (11th Cir.), *cert. denied,* 464 U.S. 963 (1983).

153. *See* 704 F.2d at 1541.

154. *See* 704 F.2d at 1542.

155. *See* 704 F.2d at 1542.

156. The Court of Appeals reversed a jury verdict finding the county negligent on plaintiff's theory. *See* 704 F.2d at 1544.

157. 801 P.2d 646 (N.M. 1990).

question.[158] This claim is obviously problematic from a resource perspective: the level of law enforcement that is possible, like the level of police protection in *Reiff,* is a direct function of the amount of resources allocated to the agency responsible for that function. A court called upon to answer the question whether there has been adequate enforcement of the laws cannot escape the necessity of reviewing the level and distribution of law-enforcement resources.[159]

A large number of cases in this category involve unanswered calls for help rather than general failures to protect. For example, the courts consistently have denied claims of failure to respond to a call or request for fire[160] or police protection[161] or for other emergency services.[162] Even when governmental officials have had

158. *See* 801 P.2d at 648.

159. *See, e.g.,* Jones v. City of Carlisle, 3 F.3d 945, 947, 950 (6th Cir. 1993) (finding no liability when plaintiff who sustained injuries in an accident caused by an epileptic driver sued the government for alleged failure to investigate and report accidents with epileptic drivers), *cert. denied,* 114 S. Ct. 1218 (1994); Edwards v. Johnston County Health Dept., 885 F.2d 1215, 1225 (4th Cir. 1989) (finding no liability for governmental failure to enforce state and federal migrant-housing statutes); Hull v. City of Duncanville, 678 F.2d 582, 585 (5th Cir. 1982) (finding no liability for failure to enforce train-speed ordinance); Baugh v. City of Milwaukee, 823 F. Supp. 1452, 1466-67 (E.D. Wis. 1993) (finding no liability for deaths by fire when city allegedly failed properly to inspect apartment building for smoke alarms), *affd.,* 41 F.3d 1510 (7th Cir. 1994); Crosby v. Luzerne County Hous. Auth., 739 F. Supp. 951, 952, 956 (M.D. Pa.) (finding no liability for injuries to plaintiff's son, who was unable to escape from third floor of burning building, when local officials had inspected premises and permitted use of "fire ladder" that did not meet requirements under applicable state regulations), *affd.,* 919 F.2d 134 (3d Cir. 1990); Wright v. Bailey, 611 So. 2d 300, 302, 306 (Ala. 1992) (finding no liability for death of plaintiff's wife in a two-car accident when government allegedly permitted the other driver, who was intoxicated, to get into his car and drive in order to enhance the charges against him).

160. *See, e.g.,* Shortino v. Wheeler, 531 F.2d 938, 939 (8th Cir. 1976) (finding no liability for alleged inadequate fire protection throughout Kansas City, Missouri); Westbrook v. City of Jackson, 772 F. Supp. 932, 942-43 (S.D. Miss. 1991) (finding a municipality not liable for failure to provide fire protection due to inadequate water supply to property recently annexed to city); Wooters v. Jornlin, 477 F. Supp. 1140, 1148-50 (D. Del. 1979) (rejecting the argument that certain state and county laws had created a property interest in the provision of governmental services), *affd.,* 622 F.2d 580 (3d Cir.), *cert. denied,* 449 U.S. 992 (1980); Reedy v. Mullins, 456 F. Supp. 955, 957-58 (W.D. Va. 1978) (finding no general right to adequate fire protection and rejecting the argument that vague contract with city based on payment of taxes created property right in adequate fire protection).

161. *See, e.g.,* Bryson v. City of Edmond, 905 F.2d 1386, 1392-94 (10th Cir. 1990) (finding no liability for police failure to protect when gunman entered a post office and started shooting); Wells v. Walker, 852 F.2d 368, 370 (8th Cir. 1988) (finding that members of general public have no constitutional right to be protected by the state against harm inflicted by third parties); McClary v. O'Hare, 786 F.2d 83, 88 (2d Cir. 1986) (finding no liability for failure to act); Beard v. O'Neal, 728 F.2d 894, 899 (7th Cir. 1984) (finding no duty to intervene when general public is imperiled); Hynson v. City of Chester, 731 F. Supp. 1236, 1240 (E.D. Pa. 1990) (finding that a state's Protection from Abuse Act did not create property interest under the Due Process Clause).

162. *See, e.g.,* Archie v. City of Racine, 847 F.2d 1211, 1221 (7th Cir. 1988) (finding that failure of the city to send an ambulance driver to the home of a hyperventilating woman who later died did not violate due process), *cert. denied,* 489 U.S. 1065 (1989); Wideman v. Shal-

ongoing contact with an individual through repeated calls for help or prior responses to such calls, courts — well before *DeShaney* — denied liability for governmental failure to prevent injury-causing behavior. For example, prior to *DeShaney,* only one court had held social workers liable for injuries to a child not in state-sponsored foster care.[163] On the other hand, in the domestic violence context, the results — both before and after *DeShaney* — are more mixed; cases permitting liability for failure to protect have generally involved repeated complaints of threatened or actual violence coupled with the failure to enforce a restraining order against the abusive spouse.[164]

---

lowford Community Hosp., 826 F.2d 1030, 1036 (11th Cir. 1987) (finding no liability when ambulance drivers refused to take pregnant woman to certain hospital); Handley v. City of Seagoville, 798 F. Supp. 1267, 1272 (N.D. Tex. 1992) (finding no liability for failure to provide ambulance service when requested); Hendon v. DeKalb County, 417 S.E.2d 705, 712 (Ga. Ct. App. 1992) (finding no liability to stroke victim for failure to respond to 911 call); Doe v. Calumet City, 609 N.E.2d 689, 694 (Ill. App. Ct. 1992) (finding no liability for failure to respond to 911 call); Culver-Union Township Ambulance Serv. v. Steindler, 629 N.E.2d 1231, 1234 (Ind. 1994) (finding no municipal liability for actions of city ambulance service in response to emergency call).

163. *See* Estate of Bailey *ex rel.* Oare v. County of York, 768 F.2d 503, 511 (3d Cir. 1985); *see also* Jensen v. Conrad, 747 F.2d 185, 194-95 (4th Cir. 1984) (finding no clearly established right of protection owed to children not in foster care but noting that special relationship could arise under certain circumstances), *cert. denied,* 470 U.S. 1052 (1985). *But see* Milburn v. Anne Arundel County Dept. of Social Servs., 871 F.2d 474, 479 (4th Cir. 1989) (finding no liability for alleged failure to report abuse and to remove child from abusive foster home); Harpole v. Arkansas Dept. of Human Servs., 820 F.2d 923 (8th Cir. 1987) (finding no liability for injuries to child being monitored by social services). Cases after *DeShaney* have denied governmental liability for failure to prevent the abuse of children being followed by social services but not in foster care. *See, e.g.,* McComb v. Wambaugh, 934 F.2d 474 (3d Cir. 1991); Doe v. Milwaukee County, 903 F.2d 499 (7th Cir. 1990); Edwards v. Johnston City Health Dept., 885 F.2d 1215 (4th Cir. 1989); Sapp v. Cunningham, 847 F. Supp. 893 (D. Wyo. 1994); Burke v. Sheboygan County Human Servs., 790 F. Supp. 194 (E.D. Wis. 1992); Chrissy F. v. Mississippi Dept. of Pub. Welfare, 780 F. Supp. 1104 (S.D. Miss. 1991), *cert. denied sub nom.* Chrissy F. v. Dale, 114 S. Ct. 1336 (1994); *see also* Griffith v. Johnston, 899 F.2d 1427 (5th Cir. 1990), *cert. denied,* 498 U.S. 1040 (1991) (finding no liability for failure to provide adequate information to adoptive parents). Some courts have held the government liable for injuries to children in state-sponsored foster care. *See infra* note 198.

164. *See, e.g.,* Balistreri v. Pacifica Police Dept., 855 F.2d 1421 (9th Cir. 1988), *revd. in light of* DeShaney, 901 F.2d 696 (9th Cir. 1990); Dudosh v. City of Allentown, 629 F. Supp. 849 (E.D. Pa. 1985). Most failure-to-protect claims involving domestic violence after *DeShaney* have not resulted in liability, even when the claim alleged failure to enforce a protective order. *See, e.g.,* Losinski v. County of Trempealeau, 946 F.2d 544 (7th Cir. 1991); Dawson v. Milwaukee Hous. Auth., 930 F.2d 1283 (7th Cir. 1991); Brown v. Grabowski, 922 F.2d 1097 (3d Cir. 1990), *cert. denied,* 501 U.S. 1218 (1991); Coffman v. Wilson Police Dept., 739 F. Supp. 257 (E.D. Pa. 1990); Hynson v. City of Chester, 731 F. Supp. 1236 (E.D. Pa. 1990); Duong v. County of Arapahoe, 837 P.2d 226 (Colo. Ct. App. 1992); Ashby v. City of Louisville, 841 S.W.2d 184 (Ky. Ct. App. 1992). *But see* Freeman v. Ferguson, 911 F.2d 52, 55 (8th Cir. 1990) (finding liability when defendant police officer was friend of attacker); Pinder v. Commissioners of Cambridge, 821 F. Supp. 376, 395 (D. Md. 1993) (finding liability when the government promised plaintiff that defendant-attacker would remain in jail but then released him); Siddle v. City of Cambridge, 761 F. Supp. 503 (S.D. Ohio 1991) (finding that protective order created property right in abused spouse to be protected from domestic vio-

Cases involving unanswered calls for help are more difficult because they implicate two possible underlying stories, one of which appears not to raise resource-allocation concerns.[165] To illustrate, imagine a version of *Reiff*[166] in which a store employee called the police to report that he had seen a suspicious individual enter the store with what looked like a gun hidden under his coat. The police fail to respond to the call, and plaintiff is injured in the ensuing robbery. She brings a due process claim against the municipality for its failure to respond to the call for assistance in a timely manner. Plaintiff also challenges the police department's policy not to respond to calls for assistance unless or until a crime actually has been committed.

Police failure to respond here implicates two possible stories of governmental behavior or misbehavior: one possibility is that the failure to respond resulted from shirking by individual governmental actors. For example, maybe police officers failed to respond because the police dispatcher neglected to communicate information to the appropriate persons or gave responding officers the wrong address. An equally plausible story, however, is that the officers' failure to respond resulted from institutional constraints or choices. For example, suppose police officers were unable to follow up on the call because they were compelled to place their priorities on other, more serious reports or to choose among many calls for assistance. In turn, the officers' need to set priorities is traceable to the realities of limited resources, budgetary constraints, and resulting institutional-level decisions about staffing and workloads. In that regard, it is quite likely that the police department's policy of placing first priority on calls for assistance when a crime has been committed is its way of responding to the reality of more calls than available officers can accommodate. Moreover, when the claim is simply that government officials failed to respond to a known risk of harm, it may be difficult or impossible to determine whether the injury resulted from individual behavior or systemic constraints or, most likely, a combination of the two.

The notion that there are two plausible stories behind these sorts of injury-producing failures to protect — and that one story

lence but that police did not violate this right because they made reasonable efforts to protect her).

165. Cases involving general failures to protect theoretically could implicate two stories as well; but the "misbehavior" story is more difficult to make out when no identifiable governmental agent has been involved with the injured plaintiff.

166. *See supra* notes 148-51 and accompanying text.

involves the realities of institutional limitations — has important implications for liability. If the government's account strongly suggests that a resource-allocation story is behind an injury-causing failure to protect, the courts will be reluctant to entertain a claim against the government.[167]

To see why this makes *DeShaney* a harder case, consider again the facts of that case: plaintiff, the mother of a child who is being followed by a social worker, sues the government for failure to remove her child from the custody of her abusive ex-husband. Plaintiff argues that the social worker ignored evidence of child abuse contained in the child's file. At first glance, this case looks a lot like the metro-station hypothetical in which governmental officials were already "on the scene" and failed to intervene: the social worker apparently had committed the government's resources to following this particular child. She had made multiple visits to the child's home, taken copious notes about his situation, and indicated her clear impression that he was at risk. Yet the social worker failed to act in the face of significant evidence suggesting child abuse. Viewing these facts in isolation, *DeShaney* seems to be wrongly decided; it appears that the social worker acted negligently, if not recklessly, toward the risk of harm to this child.

It would be misleading, however, to view the social worker's behavior in isolation; her actions as to this child cannot fairly be assessed without reference to the whole range of serious cases she was currently monitoring. One can imagine what the social worker might say if she were called upon to defend her actions: she explains that, at the same time she was following Joshua DeShaney, she had 100 other children in her caseload. By definition, *all* of these children were at some significant risk of serious injury; the differences among them were only a matter of degree. Of these 100 children, she estimates that at least twenty had situations at least as serious as Joshua's.[168]

167. It is not necessary to distinguish entity liability from individual-officer liability in this regard. In the event that injured victims pursue a judgment against the individual officer rather than the "deep pocket" governmental defendant, most states provide some form of indemnification against adverse judgments or settlements. *See generally* Peter H. Schuck, Suing Government 85-88 (1983). Thus, the burden of liability will ultimately fall upon the governmental entity.

168. These numbers are not unrealistic. Many caseworkers are required to carry much higher caseloads than they realistically can manage. In a District of Columbia case, one social worker testified that she was responsible for 69 families and 251 children, down from a high of 131 families and over 300 children. *See* LaShawn A. v. Dixon, 762 F. Supp. 959, 978 (D.D.C. 1991). To comply with state and federal law applicable to the District of Columbia, a social worker should have a maximum of only 20-40 families.

The social worker's defense is that she did the best she could — indeed, that she acted nonnegligently — given the range of her caseload and the resources available to her. Determining when to remove children from abusive homes is not an exact science; it may not be clear whether or not interventions short of removal are bringing about change and when the risk of injury has reached a crucial point. In addition, monitoring such situations is incredibly resource intensive, involving multiple visits, consultations, family counseling, and intermediate interventions. Moreover, a decision to separate a child from parental custody obviously has its own costs. Given that context, the level of care that plausibly can be tendered to any individual child by the social worker is significantly limited by the demands her total caseload places upon her, which in turn is a function of the resources allocated to child-protective services by the political process. What looks on its face like gross negligence or worse may look quite different when the social worker's broader responsibilities are considered.

But why couldn't the court consider whether the social worker acted reasonably *in light of these resource constraints?* A judge sensitive to budgetary issues could use qualified immunity or the due process requirement that defendant's actions be more than negligent to separate out cases with a plausible resource-allocation story.[169] Indeed, it is implicit in my argument here that courts *were* able to get to the "proper" results in resource-allocation terms even before the Supreme Court's categorical rejection of failure-to-protect claims in *DeShaney*. If so, why have a blanket rule against failure-to-protect claims?

I address that question more fully in discussing the Supreme Court's narrow holding in *DeShaney*.[170] One possible difficulty with a "resource-allocation defense," however, is that it would not entirely avoid judicial second-guessing. For example, the social worker with a resource-allocation story would have to explain her interventions and noninterventions in her other cases in order to justify her actions in the situation giving rise to the suit. We might worry that such an inquiry gets the court right back into the business of reviewing decisions about resource allocation and distribu-

169. There is also reason to think that the "custom or policy" analysis applicable to municipal liability could be sensitive to resource-allocation issues. *See* City of Canton v. Harris, 489 U.S. 378, 392 (1989) (holding that claims against a municipality for inadequate training require a showing of deliberate indifference in order to avoid judicial "second-guessing [of] municipal employee-training programs").

170. *See infra* notes 196-236 and accompanying text.

tion,[171] the very inquiry it is seeking to avoid. Similarly, it is not clear that a threshold fault standard — something like "deliberate indifference" — is well-suited to separate out cases involving resource constraints. For example, suppose the court adopted an objective fault standard: the operative question could be whether the risk of serious harm to a particular individual was *so great* that the social worker's failure to intervene should be considered blameworthy, notwithstanding her caseload. That standard would not necessarily identify governmental behavior constrained by resource limitations: by definition, the conscientious-but-overworked social worker likely would have files evidencing substantial risks of serious harm to children but be unable, through no fault of her own, to address all such cases.[172]

Putting aside for the moment the question why the Supreme Court apparently chose a categorical rule rather than case-by-case adjudication, my point here is that *DeShaney* is a much harder case than its critics acknowledge. Because the social-work context, almost by definition, will involve more cases of possible child abuse or neglect than plausibly can be addressed, the line between claims that raise resource-allocation concerns and those that do not is difficult to draw. That is exactly what makes *DeShaney* hard. It is, on the one hand, not an "easy" case for *nonliability,* as if it had involved a single report of child abuse that went uninvestigated or a claim that more social workers should have been assigned to a particular neighborhood. As noted earlier, these sorts of claims rarely result in liability because they raise the most serious resource-allocation issues. But *DeShaney* is also not simply a case where social workers "on the scene" stood by and failed to intervene. The picture is much more complicated. The social worker was "on the scene," so to speak, of many potentially abusive situations involving many at-risk children. In order to evaluate the reasonableness of her behavior toward one child, one would want to know more

171. Judicial reluctance to do this kind of review seems to have influenced the doctrine of absolute prosecutorial immunity in suits alleging malicious prosecution: it would be difficult or impossible to show malice in such cases without reviewing the prosecutor's decisionmaking process, including past cases that she chose *not* to prosecute. Although this idea does not often appear in the literature, colleagues who teach criminal procedure have identified this notion as one strand of the rationale for prosecutorial immunity. *See, e.g.,* United States v. Redondo-Lemos, 955 F.2d 1296, 1299-300 (9th Cir. 1992).

172. One could defend the objective fault rule on normative grounds as simply a way of defining the minimal standard necessary to satisfy the demands of the Constitution, regardless of resulting budgetary implications. Indeed, courts are fond of saying that lack of funds is no excuse for unconstitutional governmental actions. That begs the question, however, of what exactly the Constitution requires in this class of cases.

about her obligations and behavior in connection with these other cases as well.

My point, then, is that cases like *DeShaney,* which might seem clear when viewed in isolation, are more difficult when viewed in the broader context in which there are countless demands on governmental resources, and street-level officials must make choices among them.

B. *Failures To Protect in the Noncustodial Setting — Liability?*

In contrast to the cases cited above, there is a category of cases in which the lower federal courts — both before and after *DeShaney*[173] — have been willing to entertain duty-to-protect claims, whether or not governmental officials ultimately are found to have violated that duty. These cases arise out of a wide variety of fact patterns. But what they have in common is that they are less likely to require the courts to engage in a review of resource-allocation decisions than the general failure-to-protect cases discussed above.

Consider, for example, the following pair of cases alleging governmental failure to protect from death by drowning. In *Ross v. United States,*[174] plaintiffs brought a due process claim against the City of Waukegan and the County of Lake City, Illinois in connection with the death of their twelve-year-old son who had fallen off a breakwater into Lake Michigan and drowned. Plaintiffs alleged that a deputy county sheriff had deprived their son of a liberty interest by preventing available private divers from attempting a rescue.[175] County divers who were authorized to carry out the rescue did not arrive until twenty minutes after the private rescuers had made themselves available.[176] The Court of Appeals permitted the due process claim to go forward against the County and the Deputy

173. After *DeShaney* — and despite language that could be read to foreclose failure-to-protect liability except in the custodial setting — courts have continued to permit liability in a subset of noncustodial cases. Courts have relied on the *DeShaney* Court's rationale for finding *no liability* in that case — that the government had played no part in creating the dangers that caused Joshua's injuries or in rendering him any more vulnerable to them, *see* DeShaney v. Winnebago County Dept. of Social Servs., 489 U.S. 189, 201 (1989) — to justify *liability* when governmental officials allegedly have played a part in creating or increasing the risk of injury to plaintiff. *See, e.g.,* Reed v. Gardner, 986 F.2d 1122, 1125 (7th Cir. 1993); Dwares v. City of New York, 985 F.2d 94, 98-99 (2d Cir. 1993); Wood v. Ostrander, 879 F.2d 583, 589-90 (9th Cir. 1989).

174. 910 F.2d 1422 (7th Cir. 1990).

175. The Deputy Sheriff apparently was following an explicit county policy prohibiting civilians from attempting rescues under any circumstances. *See* 910 F.2d at 1425.

176. *See* 910 F.2d at 1425.

Sheriff. In *Andrews v. Wilkins,*[177] plaintiffs sued the U.S. Park Police[178] in connection with the drowning death of their son, who had plunged into the Potomac River in an attempt to flee from officials threatening to arrest him for urinating in public. Police officers made several attempts to toss the young man a life ring and directed a private boat to go alongside him, but they also directed the occupants of the boat — who apparently were trained swimmers — not to go in after the young man.[179] The court rejected plaintiffs' due process claim that the Park Police had a duty to rescue their son from drowning.[180] The court apparently deemed cognizable plaintiffs' claim that officials had interfered with private rescuers, but it ultimately concluded that park officials had acted reasonably under the circumstances.[181]

What is significant about these two cases is that the claims the courts permitted do not implicate the kinds of resource-allocation concerns raised by general failure-to-protect claims: plaintiffs claimed that governmental officials on the scene behaved badly by restraining private rescuers from giving aid. Adjudicating that claim does not require the court to evaluate either the adequacy of the overall level of services (resource allocation at the legislative level) or the appropriateness of the distribution of those services among competing uses (resource allocation at the operational level). Rather, it calls upon the court to assess the appropriateness of governmental behavior after officials on the scene had undertaken certain actions toward the respective plaintiffs. That is exactly the kind of judgment that courts are accustomed to making. In *Ross*, the court concluded that the officials had behaved recklessly in the face of an obvious risk of danger,[182] while the court in *Andrews* concluded that those officials had behaved reasonably under the circumstances.[183]

177. 934 F.2d 1267 (D.C. Cir. 1991).

178. Plaintiffs' claim was brought against federal officials under 42 U.S.C. § 1983 (1988) on the theory that they were acting under color of state law at the time of the injury. *See* 934 F.2d at 1269.

179. *See* 934 F.2d at 1269.

180. *See* 934 F.2d at 1270.

181. *See* 934 F.2d at 1271.

182. In *Ross,* the court noted that county officials failed to inquire whether the private rescuers were qualified to attempt a rescue, even when it became apparent that the governmental rescuers were not going to arrive in time to save the child's life. *See* Ross v. United States, 910 F.2d 1422, 1433 (7th Cir. 1990).

183. The *Andrews* court distinguished *Ross* on the grounds that both the officers' behavior and the underlying circumstances were materially different in the two cases. For example, the court noted that, in *Andrews*, police officers were reasonable in discouraging the private rescuers because the officers had no way of assessing the rescuers' level of skill, and — given

The largest category of cases that has given rise to liability involves situations where, according to the courts, the government recklessly or willfully has exposed plaintiffs to an increased risk of danger. For example, there are a number of cases involving injuries to passengers after traffic stops in which police arrest or detain the driver. In the seminal pre-*DeShaney* case, *White v. Rochford*,[184] the court entertained a due process claim for injuries to child passengers who suffered injury when they were left alone in a car on a busy highway after the driver was arrested for drag racing. Similarly, in *Wood v. Ostrander*,[185] a post-*Deshaney* case, the court permitted a claim by a plaintiff who was raped when police allegedly left her stranded in a high-crime district after the companion with whom she had been riding was arrested for driving while intoxicated, and the car was impounded.[186] Like the claims in *Ross* and *Andrews*, abandoned-passenger claims permit the court to consider the limited question of whether governmental officials acted reasonably in their actual encounter with the later-injured plaintiff; they do not require the court to inquire into the level and distribution of governmental services.[187]

---

the victim's bizarre behavior — police reasonably thought he could have been dangerous. *See Andrews*, 934 F.2d at 1271; *see also* Franklin v. City of Boise, 806 F. Supp. 879, 888 (D. Idaho 1992) (finding police officers acted reasonably in prohibiting an intoxicated private rescuer from diving after an individual who fell into a pond and drowned while resisting arrest).

184. 592 F.2d 381 (7th Cir. 1979). Even judges who are generally hostile to duty-to-protect claims have indicated their agreement with *White*. *See, e.g.*, Archie v. City of Racine, 847 F.2d 1211, 1223 (7th Cir. 1988) (Judge Easterbrook), *cert. denied*, 489 U.S. 1065 (1989); Jackson v. City of Joliet, 715 F.2d 1200, 1204 (7th Cir. 1983) (Judge Posner), *cert. denied*, 465 U.S. 1049 (1984).

185. 879 F.2d 583 (9th Cir. 1989), *cert. denied*, 498 U.S. 938 (1990).

186. A number of jurisdictions have rejected such claims after *DeShaney*. For example, in Hilliard v. City of Denver, 930 F.2d 1516 (10th Cir.), *cert. denied*, 502 U.S. 1013 (1991), the court found no liability when a woman was robbed and sexually assaulted by a third party after the intoxicated driver of the car in which she had been traveling was arrested, and his car was impounded. *Hilliard* cannot readily be distinguished from *Ostrander* on factual grounds nor on grounds that it raises greater concerns about resource allocation. The court found *DeShaney* controlling and held that no duty to protect in that situation was "clearly established." *See* 930 F.2d at 1520. In two other cases, the courts apparently concluded that governmental officials behaved reasonably under clear law. *See* Walton v. City of Southfield, 995 F.2d 1331, 1339 (6th Cir. 1993) (finding that no clearly established law was violated when police officers permitted a fifteen-year-old and a two-year-old to find their own way home after officers arrested their grandmother, who had been driving the car); Sewell v. Van Buren Township Police Dept., 806 F. Supp. 1315, 1320-21 (E.D. Mich. 1992) (finding no clearly established law violated when plaintiff, who was suffering from delusions, was arrested, released, and later injured while wandering down the median of an interstate highway as she attempted to walk home).

187. *See, e.g.*, Reed v. Gardner, 986 F.2d at 1122 (7th Cir. 1993) (permitting liability when police left intoxicated passenger in car after arresting driver, after which passenger drove off and caused an accident that injured plaintiff); Russell v. Steck, 851 F. Supp. 859 (N.D. Ohio 1994) (permitting a due process claim when police officers insisted that plaintiff, who had

Another group of cases in which the courts have permitted liability for failure to protect includes ones loosely characterized by the fact that governmental officials are *actually* and *purposefully* on the scene before the injury-causing events take place. For example, in *Dwares v. City of New York,*[188] the court upheld a due process claim by an individual who was injured by skinheads while participating in a flag-burning demonstration. The court noted that, although police had no general duty to protect plaintiff based on past incidents of violence by skinheads, a duty arose where the attack occurred in the presence of police officers who had promised the skinheads that they would not intervene unless things "got out of control."[189] The court permitted only plaintiff's claim that governmental officials *on the scene* willfully failed to intervene to prevent ongoing harm. That claim did not involve the court in reviewing the level or distribution of police services; it merely required the court to consider the behavior of officers who were already on the scene performing the duties of their governmental offices.

Not all officer-on-the-scene cases, however, have resulted in governmental liability. For example, in *Tucker v. Callahan,*[190] the court did not permit a due process claim against a police officer who sat in his police car while a man was beaten in a hotel parking lot across the street. The court held that the officer was entitled to qualified immunity because the mere fact that the officer was on the scene and observed the beating did not create a duty under clearly established law.[191] Under my positive analysis of failure-to-protect cases, this result seems clearly wrong: the case does not appear to raise resource-allocation concerns. Plaintiff does not allege that there should have been more officers on hand, and there is no suggestion that the officer failed to intervene because he was engaged in other police activities. Moreover, unlike in many such cases,

become disorderly at a hotel, get into his car and exit the premises despite evidence — and over his objections — that he was too intoxicated to drive); Estate of Tittiger v. Doering, 678 F. Supp. 177 (E.D. Mich. 1988) (permitting a due process claim for death of passenger who was killed when police stopped the car in which he had been riding, gave the teenage driver a number of sobriety tests, and then insisted that the intoxicated passenger ride his bicycle home at night with no lights rather than ride home with his intoxicated friend). *But see* Gregory v. City of Rogers, 974 F.2d 1006 (8th Cir. 1992) (finding no liability when police detained "designated driver" on outstanding traffic warrant, and passengers — who unbeknownst to police were also intoxicated — were injured when they attempted to drive themselves home), *cert. denied,* 113 S. Ct. 1265 (1993).

188. 985 F.2d 94 (2d Cir. 1993).

189. *See* 985 F.2d at 97, 99.

190. 867 F.2d 909 (6th Cir. 1989).

191. *See* 867 F.2d at 914.

there is no factual discussion in *Tucker* suggesting that the officer's nonliability turned on a lack of the requisite intent; the court simply fails to inquire into the "misbehavior" story at all.[192]

On the other hand, *Tucker* may illustrate the difficulty of making case-by case determinations on resource-allocation grounds. The court apparently was reluctant to open the door to such inquiries by holding that the mere observation of harm-causing behavior automatically gives rise to a duty to protect: an officer who happens to arrive on the scene where an injury is occurring — as opposed to being there by design as in *Dwares* — may not be much different from an official who receives a call for help or has knowledge of possible harm.[193] At the very least, one would want more information about what the officer in *Tucker* was doing while the beating was going on and what reasons he may have had for his failure to intervene.[194]

In sum, concerns about judicial review of resource allocations are most powerful in accounting for the strong presumptive rule against liability in failure-to-protect cases. The question whether adjudicating particular claims would involve the courts in such review is also useful in predicting what *sorts* of failure-to-protect claims are most likely to result in governmental liability.[195]

---

192. By contrast, in Losinski v. County of Trempealeau, 946 F.2d 544 (7th Cir. 1991), the court found no liability when plaintiff's decedent was murdered in the presence of a deputy sheriff who had accompanied her to a meeting with her estranged husband. Although the court's analysis, citing *DeShaney,* centers around the absence of a duty to protect, it appears from the court's detailed presentation of the facts that the deputy's actions at most were grossly negligent. *See* 946 F.2d at 550.

193. *See supra* notes 160-66 and accompanying text; *see also* Jackson v. City of Joliet, 715 F.2d 1200, 1204 (7th Cir. 1983) (finding a police officer not liable for failing to determine whether anyone was still inside a burning automobile when the officer arrived at the scene of an accident), *cert. denied,* 465 U.S. 1049 (1984).

194. *Cf.* Rogers v. City of Port Huron, 833 F. Supp. 1212 (E.D. Mich. 1993) (finding no liability for injuries to an intoxicated man who was hit by a car after police left him on a grassy area of lawn by the curb). Courts have avoided *Tucker*-like claims on a number of grounds: for example, that plaintiffs failed to show causation, *see, e.g.,* Beard v. O'Neal, 728 F.2d 894 (7th Cir. 1984) (holding FBI informant who was with a police officer when he carried out a contract killing not liable for failing to prevent the murder), or failed to prove that governmental officials had the requisite intent. *See, e.g.,* Escamilla v. City of Santa Ana, 796 F.2d 266 (9th Cir. 1986) (finding undercover police officers, who happened to be in a bar when a fight broke out, not liable for failure to prevent a shooting).

195. It might be objected that what really explains the line between liability and nonliability in failure-to-protect cases is that courts permit liability when governmental officials act in bad faith. That explanation would mean that none of the general failure-to-protect cases, including cases involving unanswered calls for help, involves bad faith. But there is no reason to think that general failures to protect *never* involve some element of bad faith. Rather, courts appear unwilling even to *consider* the question of bad faith where resource-allocation issues are significantly implicated.

C. *Failure To Protect in the Custodial Setting — Liability*

Virtually every court of appeals that has considered the issue has held that there is a duty under the Due Process Clause to protect individuals whom the government has placed in custody,[196] and the Supreme Court reaffirmed that conclusion in *DeShaney.*[197] One reading of *DeShaney* would preclude liability *except* in the custodial setting and perhaps in circumstances closely analogous to custody, such as foster care.[198] As noted above, however, the lower courts have continued to permit liability in situations not remotely custodial.[199] I have argued that courts have allowed these cases to

196. *See, e.g.,* Ryan v. Burlington County, 889 F.2d 1286 (3d Cir.), *cert. denied sub nom.* Fauver v. Ryan, 490 U.S. 1020 (1989) (finding that a pretrial detainee has clearly established right to safe environment and not to be housed with dangerous inmate); Withers v. Levine, 615 F.2d 158 (4th Cir.) (finding a duty to protect prison inmates from a known risk of harm from sexual assaults by other inmates), *cert. denied,* 449 U.S. 849 (1980); Spence v. Staras, 507 F.2d 554 (7th Cir. 1974); Merideth v. Grogan, 812 F. Supp. 1223 (N.D. Ga. 1992) (finding a duty to protect a person in custody with known suicidal tendencies from risk of suicide), *affd.,* 985 F.2d 579 (11th Cir. 1993); Simmons v. City of Philadelphia, 728 F. Supp. 352 (E.D. Pa. 1990) (finding that an intoxicated pretrial detainee was entitled to at least the same level of care as a convicted prisoner), *affd.,* 947 F.2d 1042 (3d Cir. 1991), *cert. denied,* 503 U.S. 985 (1992); Gann v. Delaware State Hosp., 543 F. Supp. 268 (D. Del. 1982) (finding that the state has a duty to provide for the reasonable safety of an involuntarily committed patient in a state mental hospital); *see also* Strauss, *supra* note 8, at 67.

197. *See* DeShaney v. Winnebago County Dept. of Social Servs., 489 U.S. 189, 200 (1989).

198. *See* 489 U.S. at 201 n.9. A number of lower courts, both before and after *DeShaney,* have permitted liability for injuries to children in government-mandated foster care when governmental officials were "deliberately indifferent" to the risk of harm to the child. *See, e.g.,* Norfleet v. Arkansas Dept. of Human Servs., 989 F.2d 289 (8th Cir. 1993); Yvonne L. v. New Mexico Dept. of Human Servs., 959 F.2d 883 (10th Cir. 1992); K.H. v. Morgan, 914 F.2d 846 (7th Cir. 1990); Meador v. Cabinet for Human Resources, 902 F.2d 474 (6th Cir.), *cert. denied,* 498 U.S. 867 (1990); Taylor *ex rel.* Walker v. Ledbetter, 818 F.2d 791 (11th Cir. 1987), *cert. denied sub nom.* Ledbetter v. Taylor, 489 U.S. 1065 (1989); Doe v. New York Dept. of Social Servs., 709 F.2d 782 (2d Cir.), *cert. denied sub nom.* Catholic Home Bureau v. Doe, 464 U.S. 864 (1983); Eric L. v. Bird, 848 F. Supp. 303 (D.N.H. 1994); Baby Neal v. Casey, 821 F. Supp. 320 (E.D. Pa. 1993); LaShawn A. v. Dixon, 762 F. Supp. 959 (D.D.C. 1991); B.H. v. Johnson, 715 F. Supp. 1387 (N.D. Ill. 1989). After *DeShaney,* some courts have disposed of the cases on qualified immunity grounds, holding that a right to protection while in foster care was not clearly established. *See, e.g.,* Estate of Cooper *ex rel.* Cotturo v. Montgomery County Office of Children & Youth, 1993 WL 477084 (E.D. Pa. 1993), *affd.,* 30 F.3d 1485 (3d Cir. 1994); Eugene D. *ex rel.* Olivia D. v. Karman, 889 F.2d 701 (6th Cir. 1989), *cert. denied,* 496 U.S. 931 (1990); Doe v. Bobbitt, 881 F.2d 510 (7th Cir. 1989), *cert. denied,* 495 U.S. 956 (1990); Coker *ex rel.* Coker v. Henry, 813 F. Supp. 567 (W.D. Mich. 1993), *affd.,* 25 F.3d 1047 (6th Cir. 1994); Lintz v. Skipski, 807 F. Supp. 1299 (W.D. Mich. 1992), *affd.,* 25 F.3d 304 (6th Cir.), *cert. denied,* 115 S. Ct. 485 (1994). A few courts have distinguished cases involving *voluntary* foster care as not giving rise to a governmental duty of protection. *See, e.g.,* Milburn v. Anne Arundel County Dept. of Social Servs., 871 F.2d 474 (4th Cir. 1989); Pfoltzer v. County of Fairfax, 775 F. Supp. 874 (E.D. Va. 1991), *affd.,* 966 F.2d 1443 (9th Cir. 1992).

199. *See supra* notes 173-89 and accompanying text. A large number of jurisdictions have considered and rejected the claim that students in public schools are in custody within the meaning of the Due Process Clause. *See, e.g.,* Graham v. Independent Sch. Dist., 22 F.3d 991 (10th Cir. 1994) (finding school officials not liable for injuries to students by fellow students); Dorothy J. v. Little Rock Sch. Dist., 7 F.3d 729 (8th Cir. 1993) (finding school officials not liable for sexual assault of mentally retarded boy by another student in the boys' shower);

go forward because they tend not to involve judicial second-guessing of budgetary decisions. But how shall we understand the Supreme Court's focus on *custody* as the determining factor in failure-to-protect cases?

When *DeShaney* came before the Supreme Court, the Court already had recognized in *Revere*[200] and *Youngberg*[201] a duty to protect pretrial detainees and involuntary mental patients, respectively, under the Due Process Clause. These cases extended the duty of protection owed to prisoners under the Eighth Amendment[202] to individuals in other custodial settings. In the wake of these holdings and relying on certain language from the Court's analysis in *Martinez v. California*,[203] a number of jurisdictions had begun to extend the duty to protect to certain noncustodial situations. In particular, one line of cases held that, once the government learns a third party poses a particular danger to an identified victim and indicates its intention to protect against that danger, a "special relationship"[204] arises between the government and the potential victim, creating a duty to protect enforceable under the Due Process Clause.[205] The Supreme Court in *DeShaney* rejected the

Maldonado v. Josey, 975 F.2d 727 (10th Cir. 1992) (finding school officials not liable for choking death of child in cloakroom of school), *cert. denied,* 113 S. Ct. 1266 (1993); D.R. v. Middle Bucks Area Vocational Technical Sch., 972 F.2d 1364 (3d Cir. 1992) (finding compulsory school attendance is not analogous to custody, and state did not create or increase the danger giving rise to the injury), *cert. denied,* 113 S. Ct. 1045 (1993). *But see* Waechter v. School Dist., 773 F. Supp. 1005 (W.D. Mich. 1991) (denying dismissal of due process claim when student died of cardiac arrhythmia following "gut run" imposed by teacher as punishment); Pagano v. Massapequa Pub. Schs., 714 F. Supp. 641 (E.D.N.Y. 1989) (denying motion to dismiss when plaintiff had suffered 17 incidents of physical and mental injury by other students, and school officials failed to end the abuse).

200. *See* City of Revere v. Massachusetts Gen. Hosp., 463 U.S. 239 (1983).

201. *See* Youngberg v. Romeo, 457 U.S. 307 (1982).

202. *See* Estelle v. Gamble, 429 U.S. 97 (1976).

203. 444 U.S. 277, *rehg. denied,* 445 U.S. 920 (1980). In *Martinez,* the Court ultimately rejected a claim seeking to hold the government liable under the Due Process Clause for the death of a citizen at the hands of a parolee. The Court decided the case on causation grounds without facing the constitutional issue. The Court, however, left open the question whether a parole officer could, under some circumstances, be held liable for the injury-causing behavior of a parolee. The Court noted that in the extant case "the parole board was not aware that [the victim] faced any special danger." 444 U.S. at 285.

204. The scope of liability in the constitutional "special relationship" cases was significantly broader than the scope of liability defined by common law special relationships. In the leading case, Jensen v. Conrad, 747 F.2d 185 (4th Cir. 1984), *cert. denied,* 470 U.S. 1052 (1985), the court noted that a "special relationship" could arise if, for example, the government had expressly indicated its intent to protect, or the government merely had knowledge of the risk of harm. *See* 747 F.2d at 194 n.11.

205. *See, e.g.,* Balistreri v. Pacifica Police Dept., 855 F.2d 1421, 1425-26 (9th Cir. 1988), *revd. in light of* DeShaney, 901 F.2d 696 (9th Cir. 1990); Estate of Bailey *ex rel.* Oare v. County of York, 768 F.2d 503, 510-511 (3d Cir. 1985); *Jensen,* 747 F.2d at 190-94 & 194 n.11 (dicta). *But see* Wideman v. Shallowford Community Hosp., 826 F.2d 1030, 1034-37 (11th Cir. 1987); Harpole v. Arkansas Dept. of Human Servs., 820 F.2d 923, 926-27 (8th Cir. 1987);

special-relationship analysis, purporting to limit liability to custodial or custody-like situations.[206]

The Supreme Court's approach in *DeShaney* is best understood as a way to cabin liability in a potentially troubling category of cases by restricting liability to an easily defined and relatively less troubling context. If general failure-to-protect claims are at one end of the spectrum of cases raising resource-allocation concerns, custody cases are clearly at the other. When the government has placed an individual in custody, it has already undertaken the task of providing — and paying for — that person's most basic needs: food, shelter, clothing, and so on. These expenditures have already been included in the budget allocated to prisons or other custodial institutions. Whatever extra expenditures are required to provide basic medical care and protection from injury are merely adjustments at the margin;[207] the basic allocations already have been made. Moreover, unlike society at large, the prison context is a limited environment in which governmental officials have a tremendous amount of control. That control gives them many more options for providing protection — options less likely to implicate resource allocation at the macro level — than are available outside the prison context. For example, prisoners can be prevented from harming one another by rearranging, separating, or isolating them from each other. In addition, even the total number of individuals who are subject to incarceration — and are thus guaranteed some minimal level of protection — is itself under the control of governmental officials; legislatures determine lengths of incarceration for various crimes, parole boards determine when prisoners will be paroled, and judges determine when alternatives to incarceration — for example, for juvenile offenders — might be warranted. All of these factors make the scope of liability for failure to protect in the custodial setting both more predictable and more limited. They also make it less likely that liability for failure to protect would involve the courts in reviewing resource-allocation decisions at the macro level.

DeShaney v. Winnebago County Dept. of Social Servs., 812 F.2d 298 (7th Cir. 1987), *affd.*, 489 U.S. 189 (1989); Estate of Gilmore v. Buckley, 787 F.2d 714, 720-23 (1st Cir.), *cert. denied*, 479 U.S. 882 (1986).

206. *See DeShaney*, 489 U.S. at 197-98 & n.4.

207. The duty of protection in this context is quite modest. The lower courts have held that prison officials are not liable for mere negligence; liability attaches only if they are "deliberately indifferent" to the risk of injury. In addition, the responsibility to provide medical treatment is limited to "serious medical needs." *See, e.g.*, Murphy v. Walker, 51 F.3d 714, 717, 719 (7th Cir. 1995).

Thus, permitting liability in the custody setting is defensible from the standpoint of resource allocation.[208]

Perhaps more importantly, in *DeShaney*, the Supreme Court fastened upon a "bright-line" rule that permitted liability in the clearly defined context of custody, without inviting the more troubling variety and volume of such claims in the noncustodial setting.[209] The Court specifically disapproved a line of lower court cases that would have permitted broader liability in such contexts as social services[210] and police protection,[211] based on the broadly defined theory of "special relationship."[212] Further, despite certain statements made by the *DeShaney* Court that have led lower courts to extend the duty to protect beyond the custodial context,[213] the majority declined to cite with approval *any* case finding liability outside that setting. The Supreme Court's approach apparently was intended to avoid the difficult line-drawing problems occasioned by a more broadly defined duty to protect.

The Court's approach reflects its continuing concern that all manner of garden-variety torts not be turned into constitutional claims under the generic language of the Due Process Clause.[214] Given that the affirmative right to protection urged upon the Court in *DeShaney* has a very limited reach even in tort, it is not surprising that the Court sought to limit such liability under the Due Process Clause. Halting liability at the jailhouse door provides the obvious benefit of a clear rule with no danger of a "slippery slope"

208. There is also a sense in which the custody cases do not *need* a resource-allocation rationale: the duty to protect in custodial settings has the normatively powerful rationale, captured in cases like City of Revere v. Massachusetts General Hospital, 463 U.S. 239 (1983), and Youngberg v. Romeo, 457 U.S. 307 (1982), that the government may not restrain an individual's ability to care for herself and then fail to provide her most basic human needs. But, when that rationale is pushed outside the custodial setting, as the plaintiffs in *DeShaney* tried to do, there is the need for a theory to explain why some cases result in liability and some do not.

209. *See DeShaney,* 489 U.S. at 199-200.

210. *See, e.g.*, Estate of Bailey *ex rel.* Oare v. County of York, 768 F.2d 503, 510-11 (3d Cir. 1985); Jensen v. Conrad, 747 F.2d 185, 190-94 & n.11 (4th Cir. 1984), *cert. denied*, 470 U.S. 1052 (1985).

211. *See, e.g.*, Balistreri v. Pacifica Police Dept., 855 F.2d 1421, 1425-26 (9th Cir. 1988), *revd. in light of* DeShaney, 901 F.2d 696 (9th Cir. 1990).

212. *See DeShaney,* 489 U.S. at 197-98.

213. *See supra* notes 173-89 and accompanying text.

214. *See* Paul v. Davis, 424 U.S. 693, 701 ("[A] reading" that would regard every injury perpetrated by the government as a violation of Due Process "would make of the Fourteenth Amendment a font of tort law . . . ."), *rehg. denied,* 425 U.S. 985 (1976); *see also* Daniels v. Williams, 474 U.S. 327, 332-33 (1986) (holding that due process claims require more than negligence); Parratt v. Taylor, 451 U.S. 527, 538 (1981) (holding that the existence of an adequate state remedy forecloses certain substantive due process claims).

toward generalized liability for failure to protect or failure to provide aid, a result that the Court obviously wished to avoid.[215]

To appreciate the full extent of the "risk" that clearly troubled the Court, consider the sheer volume of claims that could potentially be brought under a broader reading of the Due Process Clause: virtually every tort committed by a private individual that the government potentially could have prevented could give rise to a federal claim. The sheer number of such cases that would appear in the federal courts is truly staggering, especially when one considers that such liability could arise over virtually the whole range of public services. It seems likely that the deep pocket of governmental liability would encourage any individual who plausibly could claim the failure of protective services as a cause of her injuries to do so.[216] Even if many of these cases ultimately did not result in liability — for example, on grounds of causation, failure to show fault, or qualified immunity — the litigation burden on government entities and public officials would be enormous. It has been suggested, for example, that requiring a showing of "deliberate indifference" or "bad faith" would sufficiently limit liability. However, allegations of bad faith are easy to make but difficult and costly to litigate because they require fact-intensive inquiry into the mental processes of governmental officials.[217] Again, even if many such cases were ultimately dismissed, they would expose the governmental defendant to the burdens of broadranging discovery and the costs of trial.[218] The Court apparently took the view that given its

215. The *DeShaney* opinion states:

> [T]he Due Process Clauses generally confer no affirmative right to governmental aid, even where such aid may be necessary to secure life, liberty, or property interests of which the government itself may not deprive the individual. . . . If the Due Process Clause does not require the State to provide its citizens with particular protective services, it follows that the State cannot be held liable under the Clause for injuries that could have been averted had it chosen to provide them.

See DeShaney, 489 U.S. at 196-97. Judge Posner, who wrote the lower court opinion in *DeShaney*, expressed the "slippery slope" concern in an earlier case, Jackson v. City of Joliet, 715 F.2d 1200, 1204 (7th Cir. 1983) ("The next case if this one succeeds will be one where the police and fire departments, maybe because of budget cuts, do not arrive at the scene of the accident at all."), *cert. denied*, 465 U.S. 1049 (1984).

216. A similar argument has been made in the context of prosecutorial immunity. *See* Imbler v. Pachtman, 424 U.S. 409, 425 (1976) ("[S]uits [for malicious prosecution] could be expected with some frequency, for a defendant often will transform his resentment at being prosecuted into the ascription of improper and malicious actions to the state's advocate. . . . Moreover, suits that survived the pleadings would pose substantial danger of liability even to the honest prosecutor.").

217. This is one reason for the Court's move away from subjective bad faith as an element of the qualified immunity defense. *See* Harlow v. Fitzgerald, 457 U.S. 800, 815-19 (1982).

218. *See Imbler*, 424 U.S. at 424-25.

slippery-slope concerns and the high cost of identifying meritorious claims not implicating budgetary issues, the game was not worth the candle.

Thus, the best way to understand the Supreme Court's decision to limit affirmative-duty claims to the custodial setting is as a rights-defining solution to the specter of a very intrusive remedy: the Court apparently chose to define the scope of the due process right narrowly in order to avoid liability that would intrude upon political decisions.[219]

This is not the first time the Supreme Court has responded to the troubling remedial implications of section 1983 liability by narrowing the scope of the underlying right. The Court seems to have taken a similar approach in the structural-reform cases. These cases are characterized by the grant of detailed affirmative injunctions requiring governmental defendants to take specific steps to eliminate unconstitutional behaviors or conditions.[220] The Supreme Court has sanctioned such broad relief in a very limited set of contexts, including school desegregation, prison reform, and voting reapportionment.[221] Once the courts find a constitutional violation in these contexts, they are understood to have broad powers to craft detailed affirmative remedies governing the specifics of how the offending institutions are to be run. It is not hard to see that such remedies are extremely intrusive into what are ordinarily highly discretionary executive and legislative decisions. One way the Supreme Court has responded to the remedial implications of these suits is to limit the scope of the right that can give rise to the remedy in the first place.[222] So, for example, in prison-reform cases the Court has upheld structural-reform decrees under the Eighth Amendment only when prison conditions are egregious under the

219. A number of scholars have argued that the Supreme Court's general approach to tortlike due process claims has been to narrow the scope of the right in order to limit the reach of the remedy. *See, e.g.*, Henry Paul Monaghan, *Of "Liberty" and "Property,"* 62 CORNELL L. REV. 405 (1977).

220. *See supra* notes 115-23 and accompanying text.

221. The federal courts also have granted structural-injunctive relief guaranteeing minimally adequate treatment to involuntarily confined mental patients. *See, e.g.*, Welsch v. Likins, 550 F.2d 1122 (8th Cir. 1977); Donaldson v. O'Connor, 493 F.2d 507 (5th Cir. 1974), *revd. on other grounds*, 422 U.S. 563 (1975); Wyatt v. Stickney, 325 F. Supp. 781 (M.D. Ala. 1971), *affd. in part sub nom.* Wyatt v. Aderholt, 503 F.2d 1305 (5th Cir. 1974). At least one court has intervened in the foster care context. *See* LaShawn A. *ex rel.* Moore v. Kelly, 990 F.2d 1319 (D.C. Cir. 1993), *cert. denied*, 114 S. Ct. 691 (1994).

222. *See generally* Fletcher, *supra* note 105, at 683-91.

"totality of the circumstances"[223] but not on the basis of an isolated, questionable practice.[224] Similarly, the Supreme Court has indicated its hostility toward a claimed Fourteenth Amendment "right to treatment" owed to patients in state mental hospitals in cases where finding such a right implicated a broad structural remedy.[225]

Faced with the specter of another, potentially intrusive remedy — this time under the Due Process Clause — with implications for a wide range of governmental services including prisons, social services, police departments, fire departments, ambulance, and 911 services, the Supreme Court opted for a bright-line rule. As in the structural-reform context, the Court apparently sought to confine a category of cases with potentially troubling and intrusive remedial implications by narrowly defining the right.

It might be objected that the very existence of structural-reform litigation undermines the argument that courts are not institutionally competent to handle claims that implicate political decisions, such as the allocation of public resources: If courts are deemed competent to craft and administer intrusive structural remedies that impinge upon the prerogatives of the executive and legislative branches — and even to open the way for tax increases necessary to pay for such remedies[226] — then why not in the context of failure-to-protect claims? One answer is that, after nearly fifty years of experience with structural-reform litigation, it is not at all clear that courts *are,* in fact, good at micromanaging the decisions of the political branches. There is a significant literature questioning both whether courts ultimately are competent to craft and administer

223. *See* Hutto v. Finney, 437 U.S. 678, 687 (1978) (permitting a district court order limiting to 30 days the time spent in punitive "isolation" in light of the "long and unhappy history of the litigation" and as a way of insuring "against the risk of inadequate compliance").

224. *See* Rhodes v. Chapman, 452 U.S. 337, 341, 347-50 (1981) (reversing a district-court order that would have prohibited double-celling in an otherwise "topflight, first-class facility"); Bell v. Wolfish, 441 U.S. 520 (1979) (reversing a detailed remedial order that would have required a four-year-old prison to change a number of its practices). In *Bell,* the Court warned that the judiciary should not become "enmeshed in the minutiae of prison operations" and noted that the "wide range of 'judgment calls' that meet constitutional and statutory requirements are confided to officials outside of the Judicial Branch of Government." 441 U.S. at 562.

225. *See* Pennhurst State Sch. & Hosp. v. Halderman, 451 U.S. 1, 16 n.12 (1981) (dismissing a class action suit brought on behalf of mentally retarded residents of a state institution without reaching the constitutional question and noting that "this Court has never found that the involuntarily committed have a constitutional 'right to treatment,' much less the voluntarily committed"). *See generally* Fletcher, *supra* note 105, at 688-91.

226. *See* Missouri v. Jenkins, 495 U.S. 33 (1990) (affirming a circuit court holding that the district court supervising a desegregation remedy may authorize a school board to submit a levy to the state tax-collection authorities and enjoin the operation of state laws hindering the school district from adequately funding the remedy).

structural-reform decrees[227] and whether such remedies are effective in bringing about their desired result.[228] Moreover, the trend in the Supreme Court is to constrain, if not contract, the reach of structural remedies. In addition to limiting the contexts in which such remedies are permitted,[229] the Court increasingly has reserved structural injunctions for extraordinary circumstances[230] and has continued to enforce the requirement that their scope not exceed the scope of the violation.[231] Thus, the mere existence of structural-reform litigation does not negate that such remedies are reserved for narrow circumstances, and they continue to be controversial on institutional competence grounds.

More importantly, whatever the merits or demerits of structural-reform litigation — and the more activist judiciary it represents — as a positive matter, courts adjudicating constitutional failure-to-protect claims largely have rejected the expanded judicial role represented by structural-reform cases and embraced a more traditional one. Those who broadly defend the propriety of structural-reform remedies may, for similar reasons, disagree with the courts' dispositions of failure-to-protect claims. That, however, suggests that a significant component of the controversy over

227. For critical or cautionary views of structural reform litigation, see generally DONALD L. HOROWITZ, THE COURTS AND SOCIAL POLICY (1977); Colin S. Diver, *The Judge as Political Powerbroker: Superintending Structural Change in Public Institutions,* 65 VA. L. REV. 43 (1979); Gerald E. Frug, *The Judicial Power of the Purse,* 126 U. PA. L. REV. 715 (1978); Paul J. Mishkin, *Federal Courts as State Reformers,* 35 WASH. & LEE. L. REV. 949 (1978); and Robert F. Nagel, *Separation of Powers and the Scope of Federal Equitable Remedies,* 30 STAN. L. REV. 661 (1978). For more favorable views, see generally Abram Chayes, *The Role of the Judge in Public Law Litigation,* 89 HARV. L. REV. 1281 (1976); Abram Chayes, *The Supreme Court, 1981 Term — Foreword: Public Law Litigation and the Burger Court,* 96 HARV. L. REV. 4 (1982); Fiss, *supra* note 122; Fletcher, *supra* note 105; Rudenstine, *supra* note 122; David Rudenstine, *Judicially Ordered Social Reform: Neofederalism and Neonationalism and the Debate over Political Structure,* 59 S. CAL. L. REV. 449 (1986).

228. *See generally* GERALD ROSENBERG, THE HOLLOW HOPE: CAN COURTS BRING ABOUT SOCIAL CHANGE? (1991); *see also generally* HOROWITZ, *supra* note 227.

229. In this regard, it is worth noting that in the one context where the Supreme Court has clearly permitted failure-to-protect liability — the custodial setting — it also has permitted structural relief. But in the law-enforcement context, where the Supreme Court disallowed structural remedies, *see* City of Los Angeles v. Lyons, 461 U.S. 95 (1983); Rizzo v. Goode, 423 U.S. 362 (1976), the federal courts also have eschewed failure-to-protect claims. The courts' reasoning for disallowing both kinds of relief in the latter context was to avoid micromanaging political decisions about the allocation and distribution of state and local law-enforcement resources. *See, e.g., Lyons,* 461 U.S. at 113 (holding that federal courts should avoid using structural injunctions to "oversee the conduct of law enforcement authorities on a continuing basis"); Jackson v. City of Joliet, 715 F.2d 1200, 1204 (7th Cir. 1983) ("The next case if this one succeeds will be one where the police and fire departments, maybe because of budget cuts, do not arrive at the scene of the accident at all."), *cert. denied,* 465 U.S. 1049 (1984).

230. *See supra* notes 223-24 and accompanying text.

231. *See, e.g.,* Missouri v. Jenkins, 115 S. Ct. 2038 (1995); Milliken v. Bradley, 433 U.S. 267 (1977).

DeShaney and similar cases may involve a broader disagreement between those who embrace a more traditional view of courts as adjudicators of concrete disputes and those who view the courts as architects of broader political and social change.

Finally, it might be objected that whatever the restraints or policies applicable to tort claims, they are wholly irrelevant to the question of what standard of behavior is required by the Constitution: the operative question is what the Constitution requires, and, once determined, that is the end of the inquiry. As Thomas Eaton and Michael Wells have argued: "[T]here is nothing distinctly constitutional about a judicial policy favoring the preservation of executive and legislative discretion [to allocate public resources]."[232] To the extent that objection is a normative assertion about what considerations *ought* to be part of the inquiry in these cases, I do not purport to answer it in this article; my purpose here is to offer a positive rationale for the pattern of liability in this class of cases rather than primarily to defend the rationale on normative grounds. That having been said, Eaton and Wells are simply wrong in their assertion. Although the notion of judicial deference to the political branches appears in many legal contexts, it has particular salience in the task of analyzing constitutional claims: structural constitutional considerations, such as separation-of-powers and federalism, are surely implicated when contemplated judicial action could trench upon the prerogatives of the legislative and executive branches or involve micromanaging certain affairs of the states.

Moreover, the proper scope for failure-to-protect liability is not simply a question of constitutional *law* but a question of constitutional *remedies;* it is well-accepted that determining the scope of remedies under section 1983 involves legal and policy considerations that are not wholly constitutional.[233] Not every constitutional violation gives rise to a damages remedy; for example, governmental officials whose conduct is reasonable under clear law receive qualified immunity from damages even if their conduct violated constitutional norms.[234] Qualified immunity is justified on largely

232. Eaton & Wells, *supra* note 8, at 129.

233. *See supra* notes 69-72 and accompanying text (discussing influence of common law on § 1983 jurisprudence). The Supreme Court could perhaps be faulted, in this regard, for discussing cases such as *DeShaney* in terms of constitutional rights rather than constitutional remedies.

234. *See* Anderson v. Creighton, 483 U.S. 635 (1987); Harlow v. Fitzgerald, 457 U.S. 800 (1982). *See generally* Richard H. Fallon, Jr. & Daniel J. Meltzer, *New Law, Non-Retroactivity, and Constitutional Remedies,* 104 HARV. L. REV. 1731 (1991) (arguing that qualified immunity, like other doctrines based on the jurisprudence of "new law," is best located within the law of remedies).

nonconstitutional grounds, such as avoiding overdeterrence and preventing unfair surprise.[235] Similarly, the rationales for eschewing respondeat superior liability against governmental units — and embracing a "custom or policy" requirement — but also denying them qualified immunity rely heavily on policy considerations about the relative importance of compensation, deterrence, and risk spreading.[236] It is not surprising, then, that the scope of section 1983 liability for failure to protect also should be determined, in part, by broader policy considerations implicated by damage liability against the government.

CONCLUSION

I have argued that the strong presumption against liability in constitutional failure-to-protect cases is largely the result of judicial reluctance to get involved in second-guessing political decisions. This notion that certain kinds of decisions should be left to the political branches rather than the courts reflects strongly held and normatively powerful beliefs about how our governmental system should operate. It is grounded in the separation of powers and includes the familiar idea that the various branches have different areas of institutional competence. This idea resonates in many areas of the law and can be seen in a number of doctrines, from the political question doctrine, to institutional constraints on judicial interpretation of statutes, to the granting of prosecutorial immunity.

Critics of *DeShaney* and other failure-to-protect cases have pointed out the possible moral and constitutional objections to *nonliability*, but they have not adequately considered objections to *liability* bottomed on the notion that failure-to-protect claims raise resource-allocation issues better left to the political branches. To the extent that failure-to-protect cases raise such issues, the call for broader liability is also a challenge to a conception of government — adhered to by the courts in these cases — that leaves to the legislative judgment how to arrange the relative spheres of public and private activities. Individuals might differ on exactly *where* the line ought to be drawn between political versus judicial action and, indeed, between governmental versus private responsibility. But the important point is that the line drawing in these cases may have less to do with constitutional law and more to do with judgments

235. *See Harlow*, 457 U.S. at 813-817.

236. *See* Owen v. City of Independence, 445 U.S. 622 (1980); Monell v. Department of Social Servs., 436 U.S. 658 (1978).

about who should decide the limits of governmental responsibility and what those limits should be.

Proponents of broader liability who have couched the issues primarily in constitutional and moral terms have missed an important dimension of the debate; they have not acknowledged — or adequately defended — the broader, institutional implications of their proposals. Yet only adequate consideration of the institutional concerns raised by failure-to-protect claims can make sense of the strong presumption against liability in constitutional failure-to-protect cases.

Child Law **Practice**

Vol. 19 No. 5 July 2000 *Helping Lawyers Help Kids*

Protecting Children's Relationships with Extended Family: The Impact of *Troxel v. Granville*

by Barbara Bennett Woodhouse

On June 5, the Supreme Court decided its first family law case of the new Millennium. The Troxels sought visitation with the children of their deceased son under a Washington statute giving any person at any time standing to seek court-ordered visitation. The mother, Tommie Granville, objected to the order as an unconstitutional state intervention in her parental autonomy. The Washington Supreme Court agreed with Granville, and invalidated the statute as unconstitutional.

Troxel was quickly labeled "the grandparents' rights case" by the media. In fact, the Troxels did not claim a constitutional right, nor were any claims raised by the children. The child welfare and family law bars, however, recognized that the case had potentially broad implications for the power of states and family courts to protect children's relationships with kin, extended family, and de facto caretakers. The case was hard fought by the parties, and vigorously debated in a dozen hefty amicus briefs.

As Justice O'Connor remarked from the bench in announcing her plurality opinion, the Court was as divided as the family in this case. The Court delivered no fewer than six separate opinions—a plurality (four votes to affirm based on Justice O'Connor's reasoning), two concurrences in the judgment (these are votes to affirm but for different reasons than those given by the plurality), and three dissents (voting to reverse and remand, but disagreeing on the reason why). This case will occupy the scorekeepers for decades. Remember, it takes five votes to make a "majority," so when the Court decides a case by a "plurality," the law of the case is limited to whatever concurring opinion most narrowly supports the result. Despite this principle, advocates pay close attention to each justice's opinions, as a barometer of future weather patterns and directions.

The Plurality

The plurality, written by Justice O'Connor and joined by Chief Justice Rehnquist and Justices Breyer and Ginsburg, concluded that the Washington statute, "as applied" in this case, violated the mother's constitutional right to decide how to rear her children. By using an "as applied" analysis, O'Connor carefully confined the scope of the discussion. As she framed the case, it was unnecessary to decide whether the Washington statute would be unconstitutional in all circumstances, or even to decide whether the Washington Court got its constitutional analysis exactly right. While she noted that the statute's "any person at any time" approach was "breathtakingly broad," she expressed doubt that this statute or other states' visitation statutes should be treated as "per se" unconstitutional or unconstitutional on their face (as would be, for example, laws that prohibited racial groups from intermarrying). Instead, she confined her opinion to critiquing how the Washington law was applied to *this* family.

She began by affirming that parents enjoy a constitutional liberty interest, under the substantive due process doctrines of the Fourteenth Amendment case law, to control the upbringing of their children. A long line of cases, beginning with *Meyer v. Nebraska* and *Pierce v. Society of Sisters*, firmly established this principle. In a paragraph that is already being

(Continued on page 70)

What's Inside:

66 CASE LAW UPDATE

72 FROM THE FIELD
New School, New Problems: Foster Children Struggle in U.S. Schools

76 BETTER LAWYERING
Advocating for Teen Clients Outside the Courtroom

77 NEED TO KNOW
Adoption Myths and Facts

78 VIEWPOINT
Turning Law into Practice: A National Snapshot of MEPA/IAP

80 Resources for Parents

E-mail: childlawpractice@staff.abanet.org • Internet: http://www.abanet.org/child

(Troxel, continued from page 65)
quoted out of context, she summarized current doctrine as follows:

> Accordingly, so long as a parent adequately cares for his or her children (i.e., is fit), there will *normally* be no reason for the state to inject itself into the private realm of the family to further question the ability of that parent to make the best decisions concerning the rearing of that parent's children (emphasis added).

Some in the media instantly seized on this sentence and concluded that grandparent visitation orders may never be entered against the wishes of a fit parent. In context, the opinion clearly does not stand for this proposition, which would cast doubt on a host of state statutes and family court practices. The plurality goes on to explain, that

> [t]he problem here is not that the Washington Supreme Court intervened, but that when it did so, it gave no material weight at all to Granville's determination of her daughters' best interests.

In short, there was no deference to the parent and no showing of facts or circumstances that took this particular case outside the "norm" of nonintervention.

O'Connor identified several fatal flaws in the Washington family court's analysis. For one, the judge seemed to adopt the view that grandparent visitation was presumptively in every child's best interest. Instead, O'Connor reasoned, parents' choices about intergenerational relationships must be accorded deference by the state (here, in the guise of a judge) and presumed to be in the child's best interest unless there is a showing to the contrary. Furthermore, the judge ignored the fact that the mother had not foreclosed all contact but merely wanted to limit contact to one day per month, while the grandparents wanted far more. As the opinion implied, the state (as well as the child and the grandparents) may have had a weightier interest in avoiding a complete severance of the grandparent-grandchild relationship than in second guessing a parent's decisions about the time, place and manner of such contacts.

What many media accounts missed in analyzing the plurality opinion was its purposeful narrowing of the issues. O'Connor took a common law approach to the task, examining the case before her and leaving other issues to future decisions. Noting that each of the 50 states has a visitation statute, she used comparisons with these statutes to suggest the variety of situations in which "third parties" seek visitation and the many ways state legislatures have found to protect children while respecting the parent's autonomy. These include imposing burdens of proof, heightening evidentiary standards, or requiring various elements, such as harm to the child or unreasonable denial of all contact, and due deference to parental authority. Rather than deciding whether a given approach was constitutionally mandated, the plurality opinion left all of these statutes intact to be addressed on a case-by-case basis.

The plurality also refused to decide whether (as the Washington Court believed) the Constitution mandated a showing of "harm" to the child. O'Connor's approach, consistent with her concern for federalism, stressed that constitutional protections in this area are best "elaborated with care"(quoting the concurrence of Justice Kennedy). The opinion also gave deference to the roles of judges, noting that "the constitutionality of any standard for awarding visitation turns on the specific manner in which that standard is applied," and that "much of the adjudication in this context occurs on a case by case basis."

The core of the plurality opinion was quite simple and limited: given that parents enjoy constitutional protection of their child-rearing decisions, the state may not intervene without giving "some special weight" to a fit parent's decision. That was precisely what the Washington court failed to do for Tommie Granville, and no more need or should be said. Questions of how to balance various rights and interests are left for another day. In this sense, the plurality opinion was judicially "conservative," as many in the world of child welfare and family law had hoped it would be. When the Court decides to enter an area as alien to its docket as family law, it runs a heightened risk of leaving behind misguided dicta, like land mines that take years to defuse. The plurality approach also recognized the needs of these parties for closure. By declining to remand, it permitted Tommie Granville to get on with her life. Because it analyzed the statute "as applied," it left room for the gradual development of the law of third party visitation, as new cases presenting new facts come before the courts. While some will criticize the plurality for leaving too much unsaid, others will applaud it for declining to dictate specific standards and parameters, beyond those necessary to decide this case.

The Concurrences

Justices Souter and Thomas provided the fifth and sixth votes for the outcome, but they did not endorse O'Connor's approach. Justice Souter concurred in the judgment but not the plurality's reasoning because he believed the Court should have affirmed and "say no more." He disagreed with O'Connor's adoption of an "as applied" analysis, given that the Washington Court had found its own statute invalid on its face and at least one constitutional ground it cited (overbreadth) supported this finding.

Justice Thomas, also concurring in the judgment, accepted the "as applied" approach, but seemed torn between two radically different, all-or-nothing directions. On one hand, he seems sympathetic to Scalia's critique (discussed below) of substantive due process. But since the parties did not raise this issue, the Court must rely on its precedents and Thomas insisted the appropriate standard was "strict scrutiny." This is the most stringent measure of oversight of state action, and requires that the state show a "compelling interest" and prove that its intervention is narrowly tailored to advance only that interest. Clearly, it was no accident that the plurality opinion spoke vaguely of "heightened" scrutiny, and of the need to give "some special weight" or "material weight" to the parent's decisions. Family law cases are too complex for a one-size-fits-all constitutional standard. Strict scrutiny may be appropriate when a lone individual's rights are pitted against the awesome powers of the state. As Justice Stevens explained, however, where courts are called upon to mediate competing rights and interests of parents, children and other family members, the Constitution will surely allow a more nuanced balancing.

The Dissents

Parting ways with both O'Connor and Souter on procedural issues, Justice Kennedy would remand for reconsideration. Stressing the diversity of family forms, he argued the Washington Court misinterpreted the federal Constitution, and erred in holding that "the best interest of the child standard is never [constitutionally] appropriate in third-party visitation cases." But he believed the Washington high court should be given another crack at the task of interpreting its own statute.

Justice Stevens' dissent, like Justice Kennedy's, argued for a remand based on concerns about the Washington Court's sweeping language. Stevens also objected to O'Connor's "as applied" approach. Of all the opinions, Stevens' was most explicit in discussing the interests of other members of the family constellation, including children. He charged Justice O'Connor with suggesting that "children are so much chattel" when she referred to an "independent third party interest" in them. She countered that, in adopting such terminology, she was simply recognizing that visitation statutes may pose questions of constitutional magnitude. Given O'Connor's narrow approach, addressing only those issues raised in this case, her silence on whether children have separate interests in family relationships can hardly be interpreted as rejecting the notion.

The only radical voice in this case was Justice Scalia's. He rejected the venerable line of substantive due process cases that identified various "unenumerated rights" in the Fourteenth Amendment, including those of parents to raise their children. In his view, while such rights may be "inalienable" as a matter of political theory, it is the province of the states under the Ninth Amendment to protect them, and the federal courts should stay away. At least Scalia is consistent, opposing federal court intervention to protect parenting decisions of all kinds, whether in the context of abortion or visitation.

What do the two concurrences, and the dissents of Kennedy, Stevens and Scalia, tell us about how the Court is likely to decide future cases involving state intervention to protect children's contacts with third parties such as grandparents, kin and partners or de facto parents? What do they add or subtract from the plurality?

By my count, at least seven justices (Rehnquist, O'Connor, Breyer, Ginsburg, Souter, Thomas, and Kennedy) agreed that a statute granting visitation to "any person at any time" based on a pure best interest standard could lead to unconstitutional interventions. At least seven Justices (Rehnquist, O'Connor, Breyer, Ginsburg, Souter, Kennedy, and Stevens) also appeared to accept that, under certain circumstances, states may be justified in ordering third party visitation against the wishes of a fit parent. And at least six Justices (Rehnquist, O'Connor, Breyer, Ginsburg, Souter, and Thomas) saw a clear infringement in this case. The crucial issue that divided the Court was actually more procedural than substantive, and first surfaced at oral argument. The justices startled the parties by grilling them about the procedural posture of the case: what should the Court do when faced with a state court judgment striking down a statute as facially invalid, when the statute is unconstitutional in some but not all possible applications? It was clear, even then, that the justices sharply disagreed over a complex and arcane point of Supreme Court procedure.

What Troxel *Means in Practice*

What does all this mean for children and their advocates? *Troxel* definitely does *not* mean that courts are powerless to protect children's extended family relationships in the face of a fit parent's objections. While parents' do have a protected liberty interest that must be given due deference, this may be accomplished in a number of ways. For now, experimenting with the proper balance between the state's interests, those of parents, and those of other family members, is left to the laboratory of state legislatures and state courts, with the Supreme Court patrolling the boundaries as the case law evolves.

Just as *Stanley v. Illinois* opened a continuing discussion about the rights of unwed fathers, *Troxel v. Granville* will be the opening gambit in a series of decisions about children's relationships with extended family. In *Troxel*, the Court avoided the trap it fell into in *Stanley*, where it painted biological fathers' rights with such a broad brush that it threw adoption and child welfare law into disarray, and was forced to backtrack step by step. Instead, the Court has started cautiously, indicating that some deference must be shown to parental autonomy, but leaving the precise balance of state and private interests to be elaborated in future cases.

A bonus for children's advocates: Justice Stevens' opinion provides a fine roadmap for arguing, in future cases, that children possess constitutionally protected interests in family relationships.

Barbara Bennett Woodhouse is Professor of Law and Co-Director of the Center for Children's Policy Practice & Research at the University of Pennsylvania Law School.

NONPARENT VISITATION RIGHTS v. FAMILY AUTONOMY: AN ABRIDGEMENT OF PARENTS' CONSTITUTIONAL RIGHTS?

Elizabeth Weiss

I. INTRODUCTION

The United States Supreme Court has long recognized the fundamental right of parents to raise their children as they see fit. Dating back to 1923, in *Meyer v. Nebraska*,[1] the Court proffered that parents' rights to direct the upbringing of their children are protected under the "liberty" guaranteed by the Fourteenth Amendment.[2] Since that time, courts have developed further protections for parents' and children's rights. Recently, the United States Supreme Court addressed the tension that exists between parents' rights, the interests of third parties, and the best interests of children.[3]

Notwithstanding the consistent recognition of parents' rights, these rights are currently under attack by third parties seeking a role in a child's life. Recently, and in growing numbers, nonparents are challenging the traditional notions of family law by seeking visitation rights with children with whom they have formed a bond. The current state of our nation's family structures have a portion of the population up in arms, calling for the state legislatures and courts to enforce visitation orders for nonparents, such as grandparents and other relatives, step parents, or third parties, some of whom may have fulfilled the role of a psychological parent at a previous time. This growing phenomena, the pursuit by nonparents to have the courts award orders of child visitation, forces the courts and legislatures to determine whether parents' rights are contingent upon their marital status and whether their rights can be infringed by the demands of outsiders.

This Comment addresses the issues implicated by the increase in petitions for nonparent child visitation rights. Part II of this Comment explores in detail the

---

[1] 262 U.S. 390 (1923).

[2] *See id.* at 399. "Nor shall any State deprive any person of life, liberty, or property, without due process of law . . ." U.S. CONST. amend. XIV, § 1.

[3] *See* Troxel v. Granville, 120 S. Ct. 2054 (2000).

history of the constitutional rights of parents, children, and family autonomy. Part III of this Comment surveys various theories on the origination of the traditional nuclear family. Further, Part IV examines the derivation and development of visitation rights. Part V contains a more thorough analysis of the current, principal types of nonparent visitation statutes. More specifically, in Part VI, the approaches of different states are detailed, including the approaches of New York, New Jersey, and Washington. Additionally, Part VI explores the United States Supreme Court's review of Washington's visitation statutes in *Custody of Smith v. Stillwell*,[4] currently before the United States Supreme Court. The approaches are also delineated in Part VI. Finally, Part VII of this Comment consists of the author's analysis, addressing the threat to the constitutional rights of parents in nontraditional family structures.

II. HISTORY OF THE CONSTITUTIONAL RIGHTS OF PARENTS, CHILDREN, AND FAMILY AUTONOMY

With the exception of the sporadic family law case accepted by the United States Supreme Court that presents a constitutional challenge, family law is governed by the states.[5] Within the context of family law, parents have the constitutionally protected rights to free association,[6] privacy,[7] and interstate travel.[8]

---

[4] 969 P.2d 21 (Wash. 1998), *cert. granted sub nom.* Troxel v. Granville, 120 S. Ct. 11 (1999).

[5] *See* Katharine B. Silbaugh, Comment, Miller v. Albright: *Problems of Constitutionalization in Family Law*, 79 B.U.L. REV. 1139, 1139 (1999).

[6] *See* 3 CHILD CUSTODY & VISITATION LAW & PRACTICE § 16.02[1][a], at 16-11 (John P. McCahey ed. 1983); Michael v. Hertzler, 900 P.2d 1144, 1147 (Wyo. 1995) ("The right to associate with one's family is a fundamental constitutional right").

[7] *See id.* (citing Planned Parenthood of Southeastern Pa. v. Casey, 505 U.S. 833, 926 (1992) ("Throughout this century, this Court also has held that the fundamental right of privacy protects citizens against governmental intrusion in such intimate family matters as procreation, childrearing, marriage, and contraceptive choice.") (citation omitted)). The Fifth Circuit opined that "[t]he rights to conceive and to raise one's children have been deemed essential, basic civil rights of man." Morris v. Dearborne, 181 F.3d 657, 667 (5th Cir. 1999) (quoting Stanley v. Illinois, 405 U.S. 645, 651 (1972)). "[T]his circuit recognized the most essential and basic aspect of familial privacy—the right of the family to remain together without the coercive interference of the awesome power of the state." *Id.* (quoting Hodorowski v. Ray, 844 F.2d 1210, 1216 (5th Cir. 1988) (citation omitted)); "The parental interest in direction and control of a child's education is central to the family's constitutionally protected privacy rights." Brantley v. Surles, 718 F.2d 1354, 1358 (5th Cir. 1983) (citing Meyer v. Nebraska, 262 U.S. 390, 401 (1923)).

[8] *See* CHILD CUSTODY & VISITATION LAW & PRACTICE, *supra* note 6, § 16.02[1][a], at

When it comes to issues of family life, freedom of personal choice is a fundamental right protected by the "liberty" guarantee of the Fourteenth Amendment.[9] A more recent phenomenon is the courts' acknowledgement of the rights of children.[10] Children are entitled to the "right and privilege of getting to know, love and respect both parents,"[11] "the right to the love, companionship and guidance of both parents,"[12] "the right to a stable home,"[13] and "the right to effective and proper parental control and care."[14] Any limit placed upon parents' or children's constitutionally protected rights raises questions of the constitutionality of such constraints.[15]

A brief examination of the development of parents' rights commences with *Meyer v. Nebraska*, when parents' rights were first acknowledged by the United States Supreme Court.[16] The Court acknowledged that the liberty guaranteed by

---

16-11. The Fifth Amendment provides that no person shall be "deprived of life, liberty, or property, without due process of law." U.S. CONST. amend. V. An individual can not be deprived of the right to travel without due process of the law. *See, e.g.*, Kent v. Dulles, 357 U.S. 116, 125 (1958) (declaring the right to travel to be within the "liberty" of the Fifth Amendment of the federal Constitution); Murnane v. Murnane, 552 A.2d 194, 198 (N.J. Super. Ct. App. Div. 1989) (addressing the constitutional protection of the right to travel).

[9] *See* Santosky v. Kramer, 455 U.S. 745, 753 (1982) (citing Quilloin v. Walcott, 434 U.S. 246, 255 (1978); Smith v. Organization of Foster Families, 431 U.S. 816, 845 (1977); Moore v. East Cleveland, 431 U.S. 494, 499 (1977) (plurality opinion); Cleveland Board of Education v. LaFleur, 414 U.S. 632, 639-40 (1974); Stanley v. Illinois, 405 U.S. 645, 651-52 (1972); Prince v. Massachusetts, 321 U.S. 158, 166 (1944); Pierce v. the Society of the Sisters of the Holy Names of Jesus & Mary, 268 U.S. 510, 534-35 (1925); Meyer v. Nebraska, 262 U.S. 390, 399 (1923)).

[10] *See* CHILD CUSTODY & VISITATION LAW & PRACTICE, *supra* note 6, § 16.02[1][b], at 16-12. *See generally* John E. Coons and Robert H. Mnookin, *Toward a Theory of Children's Rights, in*, THE CHILD AND THE COURTS 391 (Ian F.G. Baxter & Mary A. Eberts eds., 1978).

[11] CHILD CUSTODY & VISITATION LAW & PRACTICE, *supra* note 6, § 16.02[1][b], at 16-12 to 16-13 (citing *In re* Marriage of Wahl, 246 N.W.2d 268 (Iowa 1976)).

[12] *Id.* § 16.02[1][b], at 16-13 (citing Warren v. Warren, 528 P.2d 1088, 1089 (Or. App. 1974)).

[13] *Id* (citing *In re* Male L., 369 N.Y.S.2d 273, 276 (Surr. Ct. 1975)).

[14] *Id.* (citing *In re* Appeal in Maricopa County, Juvenile Action No. J 75482, 536 P.2d 197, 199 (Ariz. 1975)).

[15] *See id.* § 16.02[1][a], at 16-11.

[16] 262 U.S. 390 (1923). The plaintiff challenged his conviction under a Nebraska law prohibiting the teaching of foreign languages to students prior to their successful completion

the Fourteenth Amendment[17] represents more than mere freedom from bodily restraint.[18] In *Meyer*, a school teacher was convicted of unlawfully teaching the German language to a student who had not yet completed the eighth grade, a misdemeanor crime under Nebraska law.[19] The pertinent act in Nebraska, concerning the teaching of foreign languages, condoned the teaching of a language other than English only to students that had successfully completed the eighth grade.[20] While the State Supreme Court held the law to be a proper exercise of the state's police power, the United States Supreme Court declared Nebraska's law unconstitutional under the Fourteenth Amendment.[21] The Court enumerated that liberty, protected under the Fourteenth Amendment, includes the right "to marry, establish a home and bring up children . . . and generally to enjoy those privileges long recognized at common law as essential to the orderly pursuit of happiness by free men."[22] Accordingly, the Court held that the right of parents to retain the plaintiff to instruct their children in a foreign language was protected under the liberty of the Fourteenth Amendment.[23]

The principle proclaimed in *Meyer* was unequivocally reaffirmed in *Pierce v. Society of Sisters*.[24] In *Pierce*, an Oregon law that required children between the ages of eight and sixteen who have not completed the eighth grade be sent to public school was challenged.[25] The Court in *Pierce* followed the doctrine established in *Meyer* by holding that Oregon's Compulsory Education Act of 1922 "unreasonably interfere[d] with the liberty of parents and guardians to direct the

---

of the eighth grade. *See id.* at 396-97.

[17] *See* U.S. CONST. amend. XIV, § 1 ("Nor shall any State deprive any person of life, liberty, or property, without due process of law . . .").

[18] *See Meyer*, 262 U.S. at 399.

[19] *See id.* at 396-97.

[20] *See id.* at 397.

[21] *See id.* at 403.

[22] *Id.* at 399.

[23] *See id.*

[24] *See* John DeWitt Gregory, *Blood Ties: A Rationale for Child Visitation by Legal Strangers*, 55 WASH. & LEE L. REV. 351, 383-84 (1998) (citing Pierce v. the Society of the Sisters of the Holy Names of Jesus & Mary, 268 U.S. 510 (1925)).

[25] *See* Pierce v. Society of Sisters, 268 U.S. 510, 529-30 (1925).

upbringing and education of children under their control."[26] In so holding, the Court further stated that "[t]he child is not the mere creature of the state; those who nurture him and direct his destiny have the right, coupled with the high duty, to recognize and prepare him for additional obligations."[27] Parents are free to control where their children are educated, be it private or public schools.

Family autonomy and parental authority were further bolstered when the United States Supreme Court reaffirmed these principles in *Wisconsin v. Yoder.*[28] In *Yoder*, Amish parents convicted of violating Wisconsin's compulsory school attendance law challenged the law's constitutionality under the Free Exercise Clause of the First Amendment.[29] Wisconsin's law mandated school attendance until the age of sixteen.[30] However, belonging to the Old Order Amish religion, the respondents refused to send their children to school after they completed the eighth grade, believing it to be disagreeable with their religion and the Amish way of life.[31] Invalidating the parents' convictions under the First and Fourteenth Amendments, the *Yoder* Court stated that the "history and culture of Western civilization reflect a strong tradition of parental concern for the nurture and upbringing of their children. This primary role of the parents in the upbringing of their children is now established beyond debate as an enduring American tradition."[32]

III. ORIGINATION THEORIES OF THE TRADITIONAL

[26] *Id.* at 534-35.

[27] *Id.* at 535.

[28] *See* Gregory, *supra* note 24, at 383 (citing Wisconsin v. Yoder, 406 U.S. 205 (1972)).

[29] *See Yoder*, 406 U.S. at 208-09.

[30] *See id.* at 207.

[31] *See id.* at 207, 209.

[32] *Id.* at 232. However, while autonomy in family life is protected by the Constitution, it is not an absolute right. *See* Hurndon v. Tuhey, 857 S.W.2d 203, 207 (Mo. 1993) (citing Ginsberg v. New York, 390 U.S. 629, 639 (1968) (noting the state's authority to regulate the well-being of children); Prince v. Massachusetts, 321 U.S. 158, 166-67 (1944) (recognizing the state's ability to limit parental freedom by mandating school attendance and regulating child labor)). Moreover, the Court declared in *Stanley v. Illinois* that parents have a right to "the companionship, care, custody, and management of his or her children." Stanley v. Illinois, 405 U.S. 645, 651 (1972) (addressing an unwed father's right to a hearing on his parental fitness before his children could be deemed dependents of the state after the death of the children s mother).

"NUCLEAR" FAMILY

The popularity of nonparent visitation rights among some courts and legislatures stems from a desire to compel non-traditional families to conform as closely as possible to the historical family norm. The prevalent notion in society that there is a crisis in the structure of our country's families has developed from the ideal and nostalgia for the traditional two-parent family. Notions of "family" have traditionally consisted of a mother, father, and those related by blood. Not surprisingly, the 1981 White House Conference on Families adopted the National Pro-Family Coalition's definition of family, consisting solely of "persons who are related by blood, marriage or adoption."[33]

The traditional "nuclear" family is comprised of a heterosexual married couple living as a family unit under one roof with their biological or adopted children.[34] While multiple theories have struggled to explain the origination of the traditional nuclear family,[35] this comment is not capable of thoroughly portraying the vast literature on this topic. Nonetheless, an attempt to outline a few salient hypotheses follows. One of the earliest prominent arguments was that each child requires extensive caretaking and thereby mandates an identifiable mother and father.[36] It was hypothesized that the subsequent pairing of men and women to determine paternity of offspring and responsibility for children was a naturally occurring phenomenon resulting in family units.[37] Opposing theories hypothesized that the traditional family developed in response to capitalistic needs.[38] Under this theory, instead of fulfilling emotional or material needs, the nuclear

---

[33] Kris Franklin, Note, "*A Family Like Any Other Family:" Alternative Methods of Defining Family Law*, 18 N.Y.U. REV. L. & SOC. CHANGE 1027, 1029 (1990/1991) (citing *National Pro-Family Coalition on the White House Conference on Families*, *in* NATIONAL ORGANIZATIONS RESOURCE BOOK (1981)). Under this definition of family, heterosexuality is intrinsically implied in marriage. *See id.* at 1078 n.7.

[34] *See id.* at 1031.

[35] *See id.* at 1033-1039.

[36] *See id.* at 1034 (citing Keller, *Does the Family Have a Future?*, *in* FAMILY IN TRANSITION: RETHINKING MARRIAGE, SEXUALITY, CHILD REARING, AND FAMILY ORGANIZATION 520 (A. Skolnick & J. Skolnick, 5th ed. 1986) at 8-9 [hereinafter FAMILY IN TRANSITION]; B. Malinowski, A SCIENTIFIC THEORY OF CULTURE 91-119 (1944)).

[37] *See id.* at 1034-35 (citing Skolnick & Skolnick, *Introduction: Family in Transition*, *in* FAMILY IN TRANSITION, *supra* note 36, at 8-9).

[38] *See id.* at 1034 (discussing theories on the development of the nuclear family by Karl Marx & Frederick Engels).

family was designed to protect private property interests by promoting monogamy and thereby ensuring the paternity of children and the proper descent of property through the generations.[39]

Alternative theories attributed the development of the nuclear family to the shift from agrarian life, dominated by the extended family,[40] to the industrial revolution.[41] Villages in seventeenth-century New England were composed of self-sufficient family units, where survival depended upon cooperation and each member was interdependent upon the other.[42] Men, women, and children farmed the land, while the home was a workplace for processing raw farm materials into food for the family, clothing, soap, and other necessities.[43] As wage labor became more prevalent in the nineteenth century through capitalism and trading of goods, the self-sufficient household dissipated into a capitalist system of free labor.[44]

Adding to these analyses, functional theories of the family emerged, proclaiming that the contemporary nuclear family was inevitable due to separate gender roles.[45] The functionalists agreed that the nuclear family evolved from the extended family with the introduction of industrialization.[46] Additionally, the functionalist theory proposed a shift in the purpose and function of the family, maintaining that the home is a place to raise children and to prepare them for life outside the home, as well as a place for caring for the adults employed in the

---

[39] *See* Franklin, *supra* note 33, at 1034.

[40] *See id.* at 1035 (citing *See, e.g.*, J. SHAFFER, FAMILY AND FARM: AGARIAN CHANGE AND HOUSEHOLD ORGANIZATION IN THE LOIRE VALLEY, 1500-1900, at 4-12 (1982) (land-tenure system mandated the joint family system).

[41] *See id.* at 1035-36 (citing M. GORDON, THE NUCLEAR FAMILY IN CRISIS: THE SEARCH FOR AN ALTERNATIVE 2 (1972)). Large family units were not necessary for work within industry. *See id.* (citing Hareven, *American Families in Transition: Historical Perspectives on Change*, *in* FAMILY IN TRANSITION, *supra* note 36, at 44-46).

[42] *See* John D. Emilio, *Capitalism and Gay Identity*, *in* POWERS OF DESIRE: THE POLITICS OF SEXUALITY 100, 102-106, 108-109 (Ann Snitow *et al.* eds., 1983).

[43] *See id.*

[44] *See id.*; *see also* Franklin, *supra* note 33, at 1036.

[45] *See* Franklin, *supra* note 33, at 1036 (citing T. PARSONS & R. BALES, FAMILY, SOCIALIZATION AND INTERACTION PROCESS (1955)).

[46] *See id.* at 1037.

industrial world.[47]

In response to the numerous theories of the development of the nuclear family, multiple criticisms have surfaced, most notably within the province of feminism.[48] Regardless of its inception, the idea that everyone should conform to the construct of the nuclear family is prevalent in our society.[49]

IV. VISITATION

A. Derivation and Development of Visitation Rights

Faced with the decline of the traditional family unit and the desire to retain some semblance of the nuclear family, visitation rights evolved from within the constitutional body of parental rights, specifically, from the right of custody.[50] Though not absolute, natural parents have a constitutionally-protected right to the custody of their minor children.[51] In a further attempt to preserve the parent-child bond in the aftermath of divorce, visitation rights developed in response to the separate households and the division of the child's time between parents who no longer lived together. In both custody and visitation determinations, courts consider the same legal principles: the best interests and welfare of the child.[52]

Parental visitation rights will be granted to parents who are denied custody of their children ("noncustodial parents") unless it is against the best interests of the child[53] or it would jeopardize the welfare of the child.[54] Accordingly, a parent's

---

[47] *See id.* (citing PARSONS, THE AMERICAN FAMILY: ITS RELATIONS TO PERSONALITY AND TO THE SOCIAL STRUCTURE, in id. at 3-9).

[48] *See generally* THE FEMINIST PAPERS: FROM ADAMS TO DE BEAUBOIR (1973); C. GILMAN, WOMEN AND ECONOMICS: A STUDY OF THE ECONOMIC RELATION BETWEEN MEN AND WOMEN AS A FACTOR IN SOCIAL EVOLUTION (1989); *see also* Elizabeth B. Clark, *Matrimonial Bonds: Slavery and Divorce in Nineteenth-Century America*, 8 LAW & HIST. REV. 25 (1990)

[49] *See* Franklin, *supra* note 33, at 1032.

[50] *See* 59 AM. JUR. 2D *Parent and Child* 36 (1987) (citing Jackson v. Fitzgerald, 185 A.2d 724, 726 (D.C. 1962); Julien v. Gardner 628 P.2d-1165, 1166 (Okla. 1981)).

[51] *See In re* Jeffrey, 435 S.E.2d 162, 170 (W. Va. 1993) (citing *In re* Carlita B., 408 S.E.2d 365, 376 (1991); *In re* Scottie D., 406 S.E.2d 214, 218 (1991); Nancy Viola R. v. Randolph W., 356 S.E.2d 464, 466 (1987); *In re* Darla B., 331 S.E.2d 868, 870 (1985)).

[52] *See* 59 AM. JUR. 2D, *supra* note 50 (citing Lo Presti v. Lo Presti, 355 N.E.2d 372 (N.Y. 1976) (citations omitted)).

[53] *See id.* (citing *In re* Two Minor Children, 173 A.2d 876, 879 (Del. 1961); Raysor v.

visitation rights may only be denied if the noncustodial parent has relinquished his or her right of visitation by some action or if the parent's visitation would be adverse to the child's welfare.[55] Determining whether a noncustodial parent's visitation should be limited or denied involves the evaluation of numerous factors.[56] These factors include violence by the parent, the visitation's effect upon the emotional development of the child, the child's preference, parental interference with the child's relationship with the other parent, sexual misconduct, mental illness of the parent, drug and alcohol abuse, and if the parent maintains minimal contact with the child.[57]

In contrast, nonparent visitation rights are less firmly established in our judicial system. At common law, parents were afforded the right to control with whom their children associated[58] and nonparents were infrequently granted visitation rights over parental objections.[59] The courts were reluctant to infringe upon a parent's right "to exclusive custody and control of minor children"[60] and

---

Gabbey, 395 N.Y.S.2d 290, 295 (N.Y. App. Div. 1977)).

[54] *See id.* (citing Griffin v. Griffin, 75 S.E.2d 133 (N.C. 1953); Petraglia v. Petraglia, 392 N.Y.S.2d 697 (N.Y. App. Div. 1977)).

[55] *See* CHILD CUSTODY & VISITATION LAW & PRACTICE, *supra* note 6, § 16.01[1], at 16-4.

[56] *See id.*

[57] *See id.* at § 16.02[3][a]-[3][i], at 16-21 to 16-37.

[58] *See* Michael v. Hertzler, 900 P.2d 1144, 1146 (Wyo. 1995); CHILD CUSTODY & VISITATION LAW & PRACTICE, *supra* note 6, § 16.03[1], at 16-49 (presupposing that the parents properly perform their duties to the child).

[59] *See* CHILD CUSTODY & VISITATION LAW & PRACTICE, *supra* note 6, § 16.03[2], at 16-50; *See* 59 AM. JUR. 2D, *supra* note 50 (citing Ross v. Powell, 359 So. 2d 803 (Ala. Civ. App. 1978); Odell v. Lutz, 177 P.2d 628 (Cal. Dist. Ct. App. 1947); Jackson v. Fitzgerald, 185 A.2d 724 (D.C. 1962) (citations omitted)). However, at times grandparent visitation has been awarded over a custodial parent's objection. *See In re* Marriage of Spomer, 462 N.E.2d 724 (Ill. App. Ct. 1984) (by statute); Krieg v. Glassburn, 419 N.E.2d 1015 (Ind. Ct. App. 1981); Looper v. McManus, 581 P.2d 487 (Okla. Ct. App. 1978). Visitation rights have also been extended to people other than natural parents or grandparents. *See* Gotz v. Gotz, 80 N.W.2d 359 (Wis. 1957) (blood relatives); Carter v. Brodrick, 644 P2d 850 (Alaska 1982) (citations omitted) (stepparents); Wills v. Wills, 399 So. 2d 1130 (Fla. Dist. Ct. App. 1981) (citations omitted) (interested third parties).

[60] CHILD CUSTODY & VISITATION LAW & PRACTICE, *supra* note 6, § 16.01[2], at 16-5.

many courts denied requests for nonparent visitation for a number of reasons.[61]

Today however, many courts have rejected the common law rule and have awarded nonparent visitation rights in the name of the child's best interests, even over the objections of a fit parent. This judicial departure from common law, permitting third parties to petition for visitation rights, centers around the best interests of the child standard.[62] While the standard for permitting visitation rights of nonparents is less stringent than the standard used in custody determinations,[63] the child's best interests remains the deciding factor.[64] Third parties

---

[61] *See id.* § 16.03[1], at 16-50. Requests for grandparent visitation, in particular, have been denied under various rationales, such as:

> 1. Ordinarily the parents' obligation to allow the grandparent to visit the child is moral, and not legal;
>
> 2. The judicial enforcement of grandparent visitation rights would divide proper parental authority, thereby hindering it;
>
> 3. The best interests of the child are not furthered by forcing the child into the midst of a conflict of authority and ill feelings between the parent and grandparent;
>
> 4. Where there is a conflict as between grandparent and parent, the parent should be the judge without having to account to anyone for the motives in denying the grandparent visitation; and
>
> 5. The ties of nature are the only efficacious means of restoring normal family relations and not the coercive measures which follow judicial intervention.

Id.

[62] *See* CHILD CUSTODY & VISITATION LAW & PRACTICE, *supra* note 6, § 16.03[2], at 16-51. "Courts have found that where exceptional circumstances exist, they have the inherent authority to order visitation for a nonparent where such visitation is in the child's best interests." *Id.*

[63] *See Visitation Rights of Persons Other than Natural Parents or Grandparents*, 1 A.L.R.4th 1270, § 2 (1980).

[64] *See id.*; Primary consideration in any determination involving a visitation dispute is the child s best interests. *See* CHILD CUSTODY & VISITATION LAW & PRACTICE, *supra* note 6, § 16.01[1], at 16-4. Controlling consideration in both visitation and custody cases are best interest and welfare of the child. *See* 59 AM. JUR. 2D, *supra* note 50 (1987) (citations omitted)

seeking child visitation rights must demonstrate sufficient reasons to subjugate the *prima facie* parental right to uninterrupted custody.[65] For an award of visitation rights, a third party generally needs to show only that it is in the child's best interest to allot a portion of the child's time to visits with the petitioner, whereas in a custody case, the third party must persuade the court that it is in the child's best interest to remove custody from a parent completely and award it to a third party.[66] Factors considered by the courts when granting visitation rights under principles of equityinclude prior continuous contact,[67] death of a parent,[68] and *in loco parentis* status.[69]

As our nation's core definition of "family" is stretched to embrace the modern reality of divorced households, single parents, and alternative lifestyles, statutes

---

[65] *See Visitation Rights of Persons Other than Natural Parents or Grandparents*, *supra* note 63, § 2.

[66] *See id.* (citing Commonwealth *ex rel.* Williams v. Miller, 385 A.2d 992 (Pa. Super. Ct. 1978)).

[67] *See id.* § 16.03[2][a], at 16-51 (instructing that it is the grandparents' burden to prove the child's best interests are served by continuing contact between the grandparents and the child.) Grandparents who have provided a home to the child are favored, though evidence of this is not dispositive. *See id.* Courts often require a showing that the grandparent and child share a close and loving relationship, or that the grandparents' house is considered home to the child. *See id.* (citing Michael L. Allen, Note, *Visitation Rights of a Grandparent Over the Objection of a Parent: The Best Interests of the Child*, 15 J. Fam. L. 51, 63-63 (1976-77)). *See also id.* § 16.03[2][b], at 16-51 to 16-52.

[68] *See id.* § 16.03[2][b], at 16-51 (John P. McCahey ed. 1983). Grandparent visitation rights have been granted over a custodial parent's objections after the grandparent's child is deceased. *See id.* Some courts have the sole requirement that visitation be found in the child's best interests. *See id.* However, other courts have required more compelling justifications, such as an existing close relationship between the grandparent and child, evidence that a denial of visitation rights would eliminate the child's contact with one side of the family, that the child may gain financially or emotionally from visitation with the grandparents, or the possibility that the child's custodian may no longer be capable of taking care of the child. *See id.* (footnotes omitted). *See also id.* § 16.03[2], at 16-54 to 16-56.

[69] *See id.* § 16.03[2][c], at 16-51. Both grandparents and other nonparents have been granted visitation rights after the nonparent has shown 1) an *in loco parentis* relationship to the child, and 2) that visitation between the child and the nonparent serves the child's best interests. *See id.* (citing *In re* Melissa M., 421 N.Y.S.2d 300 (Fam. Ct. 1979)). *In loco parentis* status entails both the assumption of parental status as well as the performance of parental duties. *See id.* (citing Spells v. Spells, 378 A.2d 879 (Pa. Super. 1977)). After a nonparent establishes *in loco parentis* status, a hearing is usually held to determine whether it is in the best interests of the child to award visitation rights. *See id.* (footnote omitted). *See also id.* § 16.03[2][c], at 16-54 to 16-56.

have been enacted in all fifty states to provide nonparents, particularly grandparents, with visitation rights.[70] These changes in modern society, such as the increase in the number of divorces,[71] geographical expansion between family members, and the increasing scarcity of the traditional family unit,[72] are reflected in the increase in number of visitation disputes.[73] Furthermore, the growing

---

[70] *See id.* § 16.03[3], at 16-51. The trend since the 1970 s has been for the majority of states to enact legislation permitting nonparent visitation. *See id.* Proposed reasons for the legislative action include the rising divorce rate, the growing number of children born out-of-wedlock, and the resulting distortion of the traditional nuclear family. *See id.* (citing Howard G. Zaharoff, *Access to Children: Towards a Model Statute for Third Parties,* 15 Fam. L.Q. 165 (1981)). Additionally, some courts have considered the benefits derived from the unique relationship between grandparents and their grandchildren. *See id.* (citing Mimkon v. Ford, 332 A.2d 199 (N.J. 1975)). *See also id.* 16.03[3], at 16-56 to 16-57. *See* Erica L. Strawman, *Grandparent Visitation: The Best Interests of the Grandparent, Child, and Society*, 30 U. TOL. L. REV. 31, 33-34 (1998). In addition to statutes granting grandparents visitation rights, some statutes have granted visitation rights to nonparents, including blood relatives, *see* Gotz v. Gotz, 80 N.W.2d 359 (Wis. 1957), stepparents, *see* Carter v. Brodrick, 644 P2d 850 (Alaska 1982) (citations omitted), and interested third parties, *see* Wills v. Wills, 399 So. 2d 1130 (Fla. Dist. Ct. App. 1981) (citations omitted).

[71] There are many proposed harbingers to the increase in divorces, such as the rise of feminism, the late 1960 s to mid 1970's "sexual revolution," and the division of sex and marriage, and the increased acceptance of homosexuality. *See* Franklin, *supra* note 33, at 1043. As a result of the increase in divorces, often followed by remarriage, new families of "husbands, wives, ex-husbands, ex-wives, step-children, half-siblings, and other variations on this theme have exploded the previously uniform membership of the nuclear family." *Id.* at 1044 (citing W. BEER, RELATIVE STRANGERS: STUDIES OF STEPFAMILY PROCESSES ix-x (1988) (finding a 75% remarriage rate of divorced persons and that 50% of those who remarry have children less than 18 years of age)).

[72] In addition to the increase in divorce rate and mothers who opt for single parenthood, even women who enter traditional nuclear families may continue to work after marriage in order to contribute monetarily to the home, to secure financial independence for herself should the marriage end in divorce, and for the fulfillment and independence associated with a career. *See id.* (citing Sokoloff, *Motherwork and Working Mothers, in* FEMINIST FRAMEWORKS: ALTERNATIVE THEORETICAL ACCOUNTS OF THE RELATIONS BETWEEN WOMEN AND MEN 262 (2d ed. 1984)). Additionally, as the divorce rate increases, many people have opted to live together without marrying, having lost faith in the institution of marriage and its purported stability. *See id.* at 1045.

[73] *See* Naomi Karp, *Introduction, in* GRANDPARENT VISITATION DISPUTES: A LEGAL RESOURCE MANUAL.1, 1 (Ellen C. Segal & Naomi Karp eds., 1989). Adding to the increasing number of controversies, the United States Supreme Court extended the protection of family privacy in *Moore v. City of East Cleveland*, 431 U.S. 494 (1977), when a housing ordinance was held unconstitutional for its limitation upon the definition of family. Hawk v. Hawk, 855 S.W.2d 573, 578-79 (Tenn. 1993). The Court protected the right of families to define its members, restating that "the Constitution protects the sanctity of family." *Id.* at 579 (quoting Moore, 431 U.S. at 503).

prominence of the issue of grandparent visitation may also reflect demographic and political changes.[74] Influencing factors include America's aging population and the increased articulation of issues of concern to the senior population which are recognized by legislators and policy makers.[75] However, these visitation statutes do not provide grandparents with an absolute right to visit their grandchildren, but rather a possibility that a court will order visitation privileges if it is determined to be in the best interests of the children.[76]

B. PREDOMINANT FRAMEWORKS OF NONPARENT VISITATION STATUTES

Throughout the country, most visitation statutes embody variations of a few main statutory constructions. The two fundamental issues in visitation legislature concern whether there must be a showing of harm prior to permitting interference with parental autonomy and whether this consideration is altered when the child is no longer part of a traditional nuclear family. The latter concern presents itself as a threshold distinction among various nonparent visitation statutes and can be phrased as a question of whether there must be an initial showing of a disruption to the family unit. Some state statutes require a showing of family unit disruption, such as a divorce or the death of a parent, before the state may intrude by granting nonparent visitation rights.[77]

---

[74] *See* Karp, *supra* note 73, at 1.

[75] *See id.*

[76] *See* Ellen C. Segal & Jody George, *State Law on Grandparent Visitation: An Overview of Current Statutes, in* GRANDPARENT VISITATION DISPUTES: A LEGAL RESOURCE MANUAL 1, 5 (Ellen C. Segal & Naomi Karp eds., 1989).

[77] *See, e.g.*, 59 AM. JUR. 2D, *supra* note 50 (citing Barry v. Barrale, 598 S.W.2d 574 (Mo. Ct. App. 1980); Globman v. Globman, 386 A.2d 390 (N.J. Super. Ct. App. Div.), *cert. denied*, 391 A.2d 507 (N.J. 1978)); *In the United States Supreme Court*, 11 DIVORCE LITIG. 206, 206-07 (1999) (recognizing that many grandparent visitation statutes permit grandparents to seek a visitation order from the courts after "the parents have divorced, one parent has died, or the parent-child relationship has otherwise been affected or established, as by adoption, termination of parental rights, or by paternity proceedings"). While some statutes provide for grandparent visitation rights only upon the death of the grandparent's child, others also provide for visitation where any divorce or custody proceeding has been heard by the court. *See* CHILD CUSTODY & VISITATION LAW & PRACTICE, *supra* note 6, § 16.03[3][a], at 16-57. *See also* Strawman, *supra* note 63, at 37 (enumerating three types of family disruptions that may lead to an award of grandparent visitation: divorce, death, and adoption). However, even when the family is disrupted, a number of state statutes have denied visitation when both parents voiced objections. *See* Steward v. Steward, 890 P.2d 777, 780 (Nev. 1995) (citing IND. CODE § 31-1-11.73 (1993); MISS. CODE ANN. § 93-16-1 (1993); VT. STAT. ANN. tit. 15 § 1012 (1993); W. VA. CODE § 48 48-2B-2 (1993)).

However, even when the family unit has been disrupted by divorce, some visitation statutes have been interpreted to deny grandparents visitation rights when the divorced parents objected to the visitation request because they believed it was not in the child's best interests.[78] In *Steward v. Steward*, the court held that absent clear and convincing evidence to the contrary, allowing a statute to grant visitation rights to a nonparent over the objection of divorced parents retaining legal rights to their children "would have the absurd result of permitting the state to intrude solely because the parties are divorced, regardless of the fact that both parents are in agreement as to what was in the best interests of their child."[79] Courts have also denied grandparent visitation within the setting of a disrupted family when the grandparent's child, the noncustodial parent, had visitation rights.[80] The court reasoned that it would "seldom, if ever, be in the best interests of the child to grant visitation to the grandparents when their child, the parent, has such rights. . . . otherwise the child might have four, or even six people competing for his company: father, mother, paternal grandparents and maternal grandparents."[81]

Contrasting the visitation statutes that have a threshold requirement of family disruption, some statutes are drafted broadly with a more expansive reach, permitting nonparents[82] to attain visitation rights even when the child's family is intact.[83] This breed of statute contains no prerequisite of family disruption and

---

[78] *See* Steward v. Steward, 890 P.2d 777, 782 (Nev. 1995) (interpreting statute to contain a presumption against granting visitation to grandparents over the objection of divorced parents who possess full legal rights to their children). The legislative intent behind statutes that do not address the effect of parental objections have been interpreted by several states not to provide visitation rights when there is an objection by both parents or an objection is made by the grandparent's child. *See id.* at 780 (citing Olds v. Olds, 36 N.W.2d 571, 574 (Iowa 1984)).

[79] *Id.* at 782.

[80] *See In re* Adoption of a Child by M., 355 A.2d 211, 213 (N.J. Super. Ct. Ch. Div. 1976).

[81] *Id.*

[82] Standing may be limited to grandparents, depending on the particular statute. *Compare* KY. REV. STAT. ANN. § 405.021 (Michie 1999) (granting standing for visitation rights to grandparents only), *with* WASH. REV. CODE ANN. § 26.09.240 (West 1997) (permitting any "person other than a parent" to petition for visitation rights).

[83] *See* Herndon v. Tuhey, 857 S.W.2d 203, 209 (Mo. 1993) (holding statutes granting grandparent visitation rights where the sole criteria was the best interests of the child constitutional since the infringement on parents constitutional rights was "less than substantial encroachment on a family"); King v. King, 828 S.W.2d 630 (Ky.), *cert. denied*, 506 U.S. 941

permits a court to grant visitation rights with the sole inquiry being the child's best interests.[84] These statutes rely upon the assumption that maintaining contact with grandparents serves the best interests of children.[85] However, such legislation has been deemed unconstitutional by some courts under state and Federal Constitutions.[86]

Moving beyond the threshold distinction and focusing on the issue of harm, current approaches to nonparent visitation differ on what standards should be used when determining whether or not to grant nonparent visitation. Two distinctions appear in the forefront. Numerous courts have interpreted state statutes to require a showing of harm, a threat of harm to the child, or parental unfitness prior to permitting state interference in family life.[87] These courts cite a line of

---

(1992)). Courts have even granted visitation rights to nonparents over the objections of both parents of an intact family. *See also* King, 828 S.W.2d at 632. *But cf., e.g.*, Beagle v. Beagle, 678 So. 2d 1271 (Fla. 1996) (finding the imposition of grandparent visitation over the objection of a parent of an intact family to be impermissible absent a showing of harm to the child).

[84] For example, section 405.021 of the Kentucky Revised Statutes provides in part: "REASONABLE VISITATION RIGHTS TO GRANDPARENTS. (1) The Circuit Court may grant reasonable visitation rights to either the paternal or maternal grandparents of a child and issue any necessary orders to enforce the decree if it determines that it is in the best interests of the child to do so." KY. REV. STAT. ANN. § 405.021 (Michie 1999).

[85] *See* 59 AM. JUR. 2D, *supra* note 50 (citing Globman v. Globman, 386 A.2d 390 (N.J. Super. Ct. App. Div.), *cert. denied*, 391 A.2d 507 (N.J. 1978)). *But see In re* Griffiths, 353 N.E.2d 884, 887 (Ohio Ct. App. 1975) (denying grandparents visitation rights provided by statute due to intense resentment and dislike by child of grandparents.)

[86] *See In the United States Supreme Court*, 11 DIVORCE LITIG. 206, 207 (1999); Brooks v. Parkerson, 454 S.E.2d 769, 774 (Ga. 1995) (declaring statute unconstitutional under both state and federal constitutions since it was not clear that it furthered the welfare or health of the child and did not require evidence of harm prior to permitting state interference with the family); Steward v. Steward, 890 P.2d 777, 782 (Nev. 1995) (concluding that if the state statute were interpreted to permit grandparent visitation rights over the objections of divorced parents with full legal rights, it would infringe upon the parents' constitutional right to the care and custody of their children); Hawk v. Hawk, 855 S.W.2d 573, 575 (Tenn. 1993) (holding Tenn. Code Ann. 36-6-301, which permits courts to award grandparent visitation if within the best interests of the child, unconstitutional under the privacy rights guaranteed by the Tennessee Constitution).

[87] *See Hawk*, 855 S.W.2d at 579 (holding that "without a substantial danger of harm to the child, a court may not constitutionally impose its own subjective notions of the "best interests of the child" when an intact, nuclear family with fit, married parents is involved"); Jackson v. Fitzgerald, 185 A.2d 724, 725 (D.C. 1962) ("In the absence of any charge of unfitness or misconduct, there was plainly no basis for disturbing the father's right to custody. And, logically, the same must be said as to the claim for visitation rights.").

cases from the United States Supreme Court to support this requirement. In *Meyer v. State of Nebraska*, the Court pointed to the fact that teaching a foreign language is "not injurious to the health, morals or understanding of the ordinary child" when it struck down a law prohibiting foreign languages to be taught to children who have not yet completed the eighth grade, finding that the law infringed upon parental rights.[88] Additionally, in *Wisconsin v. Yoder*, the Court rejected the state's allegation that it properly exercised its *parens patriae*[89] power to require secondary education for children irrespective of parents' wishes.[90] The Court specified that the case involved no "harm to the physical or mental health of the child or to the public safety, peace, order, or welfare."[91]

In contrast, some state statutes have been interpreted to merely require a demonstration that the visitation would be in the best interest of child, finding that this alone serves a compelling state interest, without a showing of harm or unfitness.[92] How a state legislature comes out on these principal issues will determine the permissible degree of infringement upon parental rights. The best interests of the child standard, existing alone without the additional requirement that there be a threat of harm to the child or parental unfitness, condones the greatest intrusion upon the family unit. Moreover, conditioning standing to petition for nonparent visitation upon a family disruption, in essence, uses the marital status of a parent to determine third parties' abilities to petition the court for visitation rights and unfairly disadvantages single parents. Absent a showing of harm, a threat of harm to the child, or parental unfitness, the state should not be authorized to intrude upon family autonomy, regardless of whether there has been a disruption of the traditional family structure or not.

V SPECIFIC STATE STATUTORY APPROACHES TO NONPARENT VISITATION

Throughout the country, nonparent visitation statutes vary amongst jurisdictions. Prior to the recent United States Supreme Court ruling, states independently enacted legislation to govern child visitation rights within their respective

---

[88] 262 U.S. 390, 402 (1923).

[89] *See infra* text accompanying notes 119-122.

[90] *See* Wisconsin v. Yoder, 406 U.S. 205, 222 (1972).

[91] *Id.* at 229.

[92] Some courts consider severing the grandparent-grandchild relationship as a harm in and of itself. *See* Strawman, *supra* note 70, at 38-39 (citing Parks v. Crowley, 253 S.W.2d 561 (Ark. 1952)).

borders. Subsection A of this Part of the comment will identify the current state of law in New York concerning nonparent visitation with children. New Jersey's approach to nonparent visitation is explicated in Subsection B. Subsection C will delve into the Washington State statutes and the case recently granted *certiorari* by the United States Supreme Court. Finally, the Court's recent examination of the Washington State case is explored in Part D.

A. New York Nonparent Visitation Statutory Law

New York visitation law for nonparents extends only to grandparents and requires a threshold determination of standing prior to applying the best interest of the child standard. Historically, New York common law did not recognize the rights of grandparents to petition for visitation over objections of a custodial parent.[93] Legislation was first enacted in New York in 1966 to allow grandparents standing to petition for visitation rights.[94] This initial version of section 72 of the Domestic Relations Law[95] only extended to grandparents whose child had died.[96] The statute was amended in 1975 to extend standing to grandparents whenever "equity would see fit to intervene" based upon the present circumstances, regardless of whether a parent was deceased.[97] Thus, the current state of law in New York enables grandparents to apply to the court for forced visitation with a child when the child's parent is deceased or when circumstances show that equity demands intervention.[98]

New York courts have interpreted the statute to require a showing of "a sufficient existing relationship with [the] grandchild, or in cases where that has been frustrated by the parents, a sufficient effort to establish one" such that "equity would see fit to intervene."[99] Courts are granted the discretion to examine the

---

[93] *See* Emanuel S. v. Joseph E., 577 N.E.2d 27, 28 (N.Y. App. Div. 1991) (finding that grandparents have standing to petition for visitation rights with a grandchild over the objections of parents of an intact family) (citing Lo Presti v. Lo Presti, 355 N.E.2d 372, 375 (N.Y. 1976) (citations omitted)).

[94] *See id.*

[95] N.Y. Dom. Rel. Law 72 (McKinney 1966) (amended 1988).

[96] *See Emanuel S.*, 577 N.E.2d at 28. The grandparents' rights were not independent, existing only by way of the deceased parent. *See id.* at 28-29.

[97] *See id.* (quoting N.Y. Dom. Rel. Law 72 (McKinney 1966) (L. 1975, ch. 431, § 1, as amended)).

[98] *See id.*

[99] *Id.* at 30; Wenskoski v. Wenskoski, 699 N.Y.S.2d 150, 151 (N.Y. App. Div. 1999); Lo

relevant facts in making a determination on standing. Considerations include the basis for parental objection if the child's family is intact, "the nature and extent" of the relationship between the child and grandparent, or the presence of a good faith effort to establish a relationship.[100]

After the court determines that a grandparent has standing, New York courts must then evaluate whether it is in the best interests of the child to grant visitation rights to the grandparent.[101] This determination requires the courts to apply a totality of the circumstances approach and to weigh all relevant factors of the case.[102]

New York's approach to visitation permits grandparents to petition for visitation without explicitly requiring any showing of harm to the child or parental unfitness. However, New York does require the court to find that equity demands intervention before commencing its analysis of the best interest of the child. Unfortunately, the court's interpretation of circumstances that warrant state intervention and the granting of visitation rights leaves the door open for intruding upon the family even when the facts do not rise to the level of a threat of harm to the child or parental unfitness.

While grandparents in New York may petition for visitation irrespective of whether the child's family is intact or disrupted, this may be taken into consideration under the statute's terminology granting standing whenever "equity would see fit to intervene."[103] On its face, New York's approach does not distinguish on the basis of whether the traditional nuclear family remains intact, but in practice, this still plays a role under the broad discretion granted to the

---

Presti v. Lo Presti, 355 N.E.2d 372, 375 (N.Y. 1976)). Grandparents will be unable to show circumstances where "equity would see fit to intervene" if they have not previously established a relationship with the child notwithstanding available opportunities. *Emanuel S.*, 78 N.Y.2d at 182-83. However, if a grandparent's efforts to visit have been thwarted by the child s parents the lack of an established relationship with the child should not be held against the petitioner. *See* Agusta v. Carousso, 617 N.Y.S.2d 189, 190 (N.Y. App. Div. 1994) (finding an immediate and concerted effort by the grandparent to contact his grandchild through means of letters, gifts, telephone calls, visits, and the help of third parties weighed in the grandparent's favor and created standing).

[100] *Emanuel S.*, 577 N.E.2d at 29-30.

[101] *See id.* at 29. *See e.g.*, Hanna v. Hanna, 700 N.Y.S.2d 532, 533 (N.Y. App. Div. 1999) ("It is axiomatic that in adjudicating custody and visitation rights, the most important factor to be considered is the best interest of the child.") (citation omitted); Coulter v. Barber, 632 N.Y.S.2d 270, 270 (N.Y. App. Div. 1995).

[102] *See Hanna*, 700 N.Y.S.2d at 533 (citations omitted).

[103] *Emanuel S.*, 577 N.E.2d at 29.

courts.[104]

B. NEW JERSEY NONPARENT VISITATION STATUTORY LAW

In New Jersey, visitation rights have been granted to persons other than natural parents under the authority of both the New Jersey Legislature[105] and general principles of equity.[106] New Jersey's current visitation statute grants standing to grandparents and siblings to petition the court for an order of child visitation.[107] This statute places a preponderance of the evidence burden on the petitioner to show that it is in the child's best interests to grant visitation and provides a list of factors that the court must consider when making its determination.[108] Furthermore, the statute declares that if a petitioner shows that he or she was a full-time caretaker for the child then it is *prima facie* evidence that the best interest of the child would be served by awarding visitation.[109]

Even absent statutory authority, New Jersey courts have permitted nonparents who are neither a grandparent nor a sibling to petition for visitation rights if they have performed the role of a parent.[110] Again, the standard for determining

---

[104] *See id.* at 30.

[105] *See* N.J. STAT. ANN. 9:2-7.1 (West 1999) (establishing visitation rights for grandparents and siblings).

[106] *See V.C.*, 725 A.2d at 22 (citing Klipstein v. Zalewski, 553 A.2d 1384, 1386 (N.J. Super. Ct. Ch. Div. 1988)).

[107] *See* § 9:2-7.1.

[108] *See* § 9:2-7.1 a - b. Factors included within the list are the relationship between the applicant and child, the relationship between the custodian and the applicant, the length of time since applicant last had contact with the child, as well as the effect the visitation will have upon the relationship between the custodian and the child. *See* § 9:2-7.1.b.(1) - (8). Other factors include the existing time arrangements between the child and the parents if they are separated or divorced, the good faith of the applicant, any history of abuse or neglect, as well as any other factors relevant to determining the best interests of the child. *See id.*

[109] *See* § 9:2-7.1 c.

[110] *See* Watkins v. Nelson, 729 A.2d 484, 491 (N.J. Super. Ct. App. Div. 1999). To determine whether a true parent-type relationship exited between a third party and the child for purposes of determining visitation rights when there is no statutory authority, New Jersey adopted the test established in *In Custody of H.S.H-K. v. Knott*, 533 N.W.2d 419, 421 (Wis. 1995). *H..S.H.-K.* laid out four elements that petitioner must prove:

that the biological or adoptive parent consented to, and fostered, the petitioner's for-

whether to grant visitation is the best interests of the child.[111] Interestingly, New Jersey's statutory definition of "parent" includes "*when not otherwise described by the context*, ["parent"] means a natural parent or parent by previous adoption."[112] Accordingly, when a third party establishes a parental relationship to the child, the standard applied for determining both custody and visitation rights should be the child's best interest.[113] This flexible definition is consistent with the diverse family structures that exist in modern society.[114]

New Jersey courts have recognized that "[w]hen social mores change, governing statutes must be interpreted to allow for those changes in a manner that does not frustrate the purposes behind their enactment."[115] The approach adopted by New Jersey places a strong emphasis on whether the petitioning non-parent fulfilled the role of a parent in the child's life, acknowledging the modern structures of many families. Recognizing the crucial role contemporary relationships can serve in children's lives helps balance the interests and rights of both the child and the parent by narrowing the breadth of standing granted to potential petitioners.

> mation and establishment of a parent-like relationship with the child; (2) that the petitioner and the child lived together in the same household; (3) that the petitioner assumed obligations of parenthood by taking significant responsibility for the child's care, education and development, including contributing towards the child's support, without expectation of financial compensation; and (4) that the petitioner has been in a parental role for a length of time sufficient to have established with the child a bonded, dependent relationship parental in nature.

Id.

[111] *See id.* at 490.

[112] *See* N.J. STAT. ANN. 9:2-13(f) (West 1999) (emphasis added); *Watkins*, 729 A.2d at 491 (quoting V.C. v. M.J.B., 725 A.2d 13, 19 (N.J. Super. Ct. App. Div. 1999) (Wecker, J., concurring and dissenting)). The Legislature conceded that someone other than a natural parent might fall within the category of "parent" depending upon the context. *Id.*

[113] *See Watkins*, 729 A.2d at 492 (quoting Zack v. Fiebert, 563 A.2d 58, 62 (N.J. Super. Ct. App. Div. 1989)).

[114] *See id.* at 491-92 (quoting V.C., 725 A.2d at 27 (Wecker, J., concurring and dissenting)).

[115] V.C., 725 A.2d at 19 (quoting Adoption of Two Children by H.N.R., 666 A.2d 535, 540 (N.J. Super. Ct. App. Div. 1995) (quoting Adoptions of B.L.V.B. and E.L.V.B., 628 A.2d 1271, 1275 (Vt. 1993)).

C. WASHINGTON STATE NONPARENT

VISITATION LAW: THE *STILLWELL* DECISION

The issue of nonparent visitation rights was recently addressed by the United States Supreme Court in *Troxel v. Granville.*[116] This Washington Supreme Court case, previously named *Custody of Smith v. Stillwell,* consolidated three cases to examine Washington State statutes, sections 26.10.160(3)[117] and former 26.09.240[118] of the Revised Code of Washington, to determine 1) whether petitioners had standing under the statutes[119] and 2) whether the statutes violated parents' constitutionally protected right to raise their children without state interference.[120] The Washington Supreme Court held that the statutes violated the constitutionally protected interests of the parents because the statutes, as written, permit "any person, at any time, to petition for visitation without regard to relationship to the child, without regard to changed circumstances, and without regard to harm."[121] The first of the three consolidated cases[122] involved a nonpar-

---

[116] Custody of Smith v. Stillwell, 969 P.2d 21, 23 (Wash. 1998), *cert. granted sub nom.* Troxel v. Granville, 120 S. Ct. 11 (1999).

[117] Section 26.10.160(3) of the Washington Revised Code provides that: "Any person may petition the court for visitation rights at any time including, but not limited to, custody proceedings. The court may order visitation rights for any person when visitation may serve the best interest of the child whether or not there has been any change of circumstances." WASH. REV. CODE ANN. § 26.10.160(3) (West 1997).

[118] Until the 1996 amendment, section 26.09.240 of the Washington Revised Code provided:

> The court may order visitation rights for a person other than a parent when visitation may serve the best interest of the child whether or not there has been any change of circumstances. A person other than a parent may petition the court for visitation rights at any time. The court may modify an order granting or denying visitation rights whenever modification would serve the best interests of the child.

Stillwell, 969 P.2d at 24 (quoting former WASH. REV. CODE ANN. § 26.09.240 (West 1997)).

[119] *See id.* at 23. The court held that petitioners had standing. *See id.* at 27 (Due to length constraints, this aspect will not be discussed further in this Comment.)

[120] *See Stillwell*, 969 P.2d at 23.

[121] *Id.*

ent who sought visitation rights under section 26.10.160(3)[123] after having lived with the child and the child's mother for four years prior to his relationship ending with the mother.[124] The second consolidated case[125] concerned the rights of paternal grandparents to visit their grandchildren born out-of-wedlock.[126] The last of the consolidated cases addressed the visitation rights of the family of a deceased parent.[127]

Writing for the majority, Justice Madsen initiated the inquiry of the constitutionality of the state's nonparent visitation statutes[128] by acknowledging that parents have an undisputed "fundamental right to autonomy in child rearing decisions" without interference from the state.[129] The majority noted that this constitutionally protected interest was defined in *Stanley v. Illinois*[130] and has

---

[122] Clay v. Wolcott, 933 P.2d 1066 (Wash. Ct. App. 1997).

[123] WASH. REV. CODE ANN. 26.10.160(3) (West 1997).

[124] *See Stillwell*, 969 P.2d at 23 (case dismissed because petitioner "lacked standing to seek visitation because he is not related to [the child] and no custody action was pending").

[125] *In re* the Visitation of Troxel, 940 P.2d 698 (Wash. Ct. App. 1997).

[126] *See Stillwell*, 969 P.2d at 23-24. After parents who never married separated, the father moved in with his parents, the Troxels, and the children visited there. *See id.* The father committed suicide and shortly thereafter the mother limited the children's visitation with the paternal grandparents. *See id.* The court held that "nonparents lack standing to seek visitation unless a custody action is pending." *Id.*

[127] *See id.* at 24. The child, Sara, was conceived through artificial insemination using donor sperm other than Brian Smith's, the parent. *See id.* The mother sought to end the marriage and both parents sought custody. *See id.* The maternal grandmother shot Smith at his home and was killed herself when Smith shot back at her. *See id.* Subsequently, Smith's surviving family petitioned for visitation rights with Sara. *See id.* The trial court awarded visitation and established a schedule. *See id.* The mother appealed and her motion to transfer the case to the Supreme Court of Washington was granted. *See id.*

[128] WASH. REV. CODE ANN. § 26.10.160(3) (West 1997); former WASH. REV. CODE ANN. 26.09.240 (prior to 1996 amendments).

[129] *Stillwell*, 969 P.2d at 27 (citing Meyer v. Nebraska, 262 U.S. 390, 399 (1923); Pierce v. the Society of the Sisters of the Holy Names of Jesus & Mary, 268 U.S. 510, 534 (1925); Prince v. Massachusetts, 321 U.S. 158, 166 (1944); Wisconsin v. Yoder, 406 U.S. 205, 235-36 (1972); Santosky v. Kramer, 455 U.S. 745, 753 (1982)).

[130] 405 U.S. 645, 651 (1972) (declaring a presumption that fathers of illegitimate children are unfit to have custody of their children after the death of the children's mother was deemed a violation of equal protection under the Fourteenth Amendment). The court noted that "[t]he State's interest in caring for Stanley's children is de minimis if Stanley is shown to

been accepted as a fundamental "liberty" interest deriving its protections from the Fourteenth Amendment and from privacy rights inherent in the Constitution.[131] Accordingly, the court recognized that state interference with the fundamental right of parents to rear their children is subject to strict scrutiny, mandating that the state put forth a compelling interest and show that the interference is narrowly drawn to achieve only that compelling state interest.[132]

The majority commenced its strict scrutiny analysis by focusing on whether the State of Washington had a compelling interest to justify interfering in family life.[133] The court enumerated two possible sources of state power.[134] First, Justice Madsen addressed the state's police power that provides the authority to protect the health and safety of its citizens, in addition to protecting citizens from injuries imposed by third parties.[135] The justice stressed that within the realm of family life, states may override parental decisions that would harm a child.[136] Justice Madsen identified that a second source of state authority exists in its *parens patriae* power.[137] In the role of *parens patriae*, the court explained that the state acts "from the viewpoint and in the interests of the child."[138] The majority reasoned that under both police power and *parens patriae* power, the state has authority to act on behalf of children who lack "the guidance and protection of fit parents of their own,"[139] but only when a child has suffered harm or is subject to

---

be a fit father." *Id.* at 657-58.

[131] *See Stillwell*, 969 P.2d at 28.

[132] *See id.* (citations omitted).

[133] *See id.*

[134] *See id.*

[135] *See id.* For example, States have the power to mandate vaccination of children against communicable diseases, regardless of parent's objections. *See* Prince v. Massachusetts, 321 U.S. 158, 166-67 (1944).

[136] *See Stillwell*, 969 P.2d at 28. In *Prince*, the Supreme Court acknowledged an exception to parents' constitutional right to child-rearing autonomy and held legislation prohibiting parents from permitting minor children to sell merchandise on public streets held valid. *See Prince*, 321 U.S. at 168-69.

[137] *See Stillwell*, 969 P.2d at 28.

[138] *Id.*

[139] *Id.*

a threat of harm.[140] The court pointed to *Yoder*, where the United States Supreme Court held that states could not mandate that Amish children be sent to public school after the eighth grade.[141] The *Yoder* Court contrasted the facts of its case to those that were present in *Prince v. Massachusetts*, noting that *Yoder* was "not one in which any harm to the physical or mental health of the child or the public safety, peace, order, or welfare has been demonstrated or may be properly inferred."[142]

In an effort to promote the best interests of the child standard, petitioners in *Stillwell* argued that a compelling interest exists when visitation with nonparents serves the best interests of the child, whether or not there are allegations of parental unfitness, a threat of harm, or actual harm to the child.[143] The Washington Supreme Court rejected this argument, citing a line of United States Supreme Court cases that support state interference only "if it appears that parental decisions will jeopardize the health or safety of the child, or have a potential for significant social burdens."[144] The majority acknowledged that Washington courts have followed the lead of the United States Supreme Court by tolerating state interference with parental rights to rear children only when it is to prevent harm to a child or a risk thereof.[145] In contrast, Justice Madsen found no such com-

---

[140] *See id.* (citing Wisconsin v. Yoder, 406 U.S. 205, 206 (1972)).

[141] *See id.* at 28-29.

[142] *See id.* at 29 (quoting *Yoder*, 406 U.S. at 230; discussing Prince v. Massachusetts, 321 U.S. 158 (1944)). In *Prince*, the state was authorized to protect children from the harm associated with child labor. *See id.*

[143] *See Stillwell*, 969 P.2d at 29.

[144] *Id.* (quoting *Yoder*, 406 U.S. at 234; citing Pierce v. the Society of the Sisters of the Holy Names of Jesus & Mary, 268 U.S. 510, 534 (1952) (state interference not permitted since parents' decisions to school their children in private schools was not inherently harmful); Meyer v. Nebraska, 262 U.S. 390, 402-03 (1923) (state's interest in fostering a homogeneous population was not a sufficiently compelling interest to justify state interference since teaching a foreign language was "not injurious to the health, morals or understanding of the ordinary child."); Stanley v. Illinois, 405 U.S. 645, 645 (1972) (parental neglect must be shown prior to revoking parental rights of unwed father); Prince v. Massachusetts, 321 U.S. 158, 170 (1944) (court upheld conviction of parent who permitted her child to sell magazines and approved state interference aimed at preventing "psychological or physical injury to the child.")).

[145] *See Stillwell*, 969 P.2d at 29-30 (citing *In re* the Welfare of Sumey, 621 P.2d 108 (Wash. 1980)). The *Sumey* court held that the state acted within its parens patriae power under the former Washington Revised Code section 13.32 when it temporarily denied custody to the parents. *See Sumey*, 622 P.2d at 111-12. The statute was enacted to protect "the mental and emotional health of the child by removing him or her from a situation of family conflict that is so extreme that the parents and child are unable to live together even with the aid of counsel-

pelling state interest in *Stillwell* because the statutes involved did not contemplate harm or a threat of harm to children as a requirement for granting third party visitation.[146] In fact, the court found no justification under the statutes for state interference with parental rights under either state police or *parens patriae* powers.[147] The majority further admonished that "[t]he requirement of harm is the sole protection that parents have against pervasive state interference in the parenting process."[148]

Justice Madsen did acknowledge that there could be situations where the denial of visitation of third parties with a substantial relationship to the child would result in severe psychological harm to the child.[149] However, the court took issue with the fact that the Washington statutes permitted any person to petition at any time for visitation, provided that it was in the best interest of the child.[150] Specifically, Justice Madsen found no statutory requirement that a petitioner must show that harm would result if the visitation petition was denied.[151] The majority further reasoned that without requiring, at a minimum, a demonstration of potential harm, the best interests standard would permit the state to interfere with families solely by determining what the court believes to be "better" for the children.[152] Justice Madsen asserted that the best interests of the child standard

---

ing." *Id.* at 111 (citations omitted).

[146] *See Stillwell*, 969 P.2d at 30.

[147] *See id.*

[148] *Id.* (quoting Hawk v. Hawk, 855 S.W.2d 573, 580 (Tenn. 1993)). The court further stated that:

> For the state to delegate to the parents the authority to raise the child as the parents see fit, except when the state thinks another choice would be better, is to give the parents no authority at all. "You may do whatever you choose, so long as it is what I would choose" also does not constitute a delegation of authority.

Hawk, 855 S.W.2d at 580 (quoting Kathleen Bean, *Grandparent Visitation: Can the Parent Refuse?*, 24 U. LOUISVILLE J. FAM. L. 393, 441 (1985-86)).

[149] *See Stillwell*, 969 P.2d at 30.

[150] *See id.*

[151] *See id.* Unless the best interest of the child was shown to be to prevent harm, the standard is insufficient and does not rise to the level of a compelling state interest that would justify overruling parental rights. *See id.*

[152] *See id.* at 30-31.

is an insufficient justification for overriding parents' fundamental rights and does not rise to the level of a compelling state interest.[153] Additionally, the court admonished that the statutes created an increased possibility of frivolous claims for visitation and disapproved of the lack of protections afforded to families under the statute.[154] Concluding that Washington's visitation statutes were unconstitutional, the court held that the statutes "impermissibly interfere[d] with a parent's fundamental interest in the 'care, custody and companionship of the child.'"[155]

Separately concurring and dissenting, Justice Talmadge agreed that petitioners had standing under Washington law, yet diverged from the majority's holding to find that visitation would not constitutionally infringe parental rights.[156] The justice proclaimed that preventing the statute from providing limited visitation rights to nonparents would have "cruel and far-reaching effects on loving relatives."[157] Attributing the majority's error to two underlying flaws, the justice proffered that parents' rights to autonomy in raising their children are not absolute and that the State's *parens patriae* power can be used to protect children's welfare absent any evidence of harm.[158] While conceding that the care and custody of children is a well established right of parents, Justice Talmadge pointed out that it is equally well-established that the right is not absolute.[159] Suggesting that the majority's reliance on *Prince*, when stating that the "custody, care and nurture of the child reside first in parents" was askew, the justice focused on additional statements in *Prince* that "the family itself is not beyond regulation in the public interest . . . [a]nd neither rights of religion nor rights of parenthood are beyond limitation."[160] The justice put forth that the constitutional issue before

---

[153] *See id.* at 30.

[154] *See id.* at 31. The court specifically noted that there was no requirement that petitioner show a substantial relationship with the child and that the statutes do not instruct courts to consider parents' reasons for limiting visitation. *See id.*

[155] *Stillwell*, 969 P.2d at 31 (quoting *In re* the Welfare of Sumey, 621 P.2d 108, 111 (Wash. 1980) (citation omitted)).

[156] *Stillwell*, 969 P.2d at 32 (Talmadge, J., concurring /dissenting). Justice Talmadge concurred with the majority's holding that petitioners had standing under Washington Revised Code section 26.10.160(3) and former section 26.09.240 to seek a visitation order. *See id.*

[157] *Id.*

[158] *See id.*

[159] *See id.*

[160] *Id.* (quoting Prince v. Massachusetts, 321 U.S. 158, 166-67 (1944)).

the court requires addressing and balancing the rights of the child and the state, as well as those of the parents.[161]

Justice Talmadge first cited *In re the Welfare of Sumey*,[162] where the Washington Supreme Court previously addressed the parameters of a state's *parens patriae* powers and parental rights.[163] Under a broad interpretation of the state's *parens patriae* power, the *Sumey* court held that temporary residential placement of a child under the direction of a state statute was constitutional.[164] The *Sumey* court heralded the need to obtain a proper balance between the constitutional rights of parents and the constitutionally protected state interest in protecting the best interests of children under the doctrine of *parens patriae*.[165]

In the dissenting portion of the opinion, Justice Talmadge articulated that the essential consideration of the balancing test in *Sumey* was "the degree of abridgment of parental rights."[166] The court in *Sumey* contrasted the residential placement issue that was before the court with the severity of abridgment of rights that resulted when a termination of parental rights was sought.[167] When an extreme abridgment of parental rights is being contemplated, the *Sumey* court discerned that there must be a "commensurately grave circumstance of harm (physical, mental or emotional) to the child resulting from the parent's conduct."[168] Justice Talmadge compared the *Sumey* court's analysis of temporary residential placement to the issue of awarding visitation to nonparents.[169] Finding the granting of visitation to be a lesser abridgment of parental rights than temporary residential placement out of the home, Justice Talmadge reasoned that when granted under the statutes in question, visitation is a minor and permissible infringement on pa-

---

161 *See id.*

162 621 P.2d 108 (1980).

163 *See Stillwell*, 969 P.2d at 32 (Talmadge, J., concurring /dissenting).

164 *See id.* (citing WASH. REV. CODE ANN. § 13.32 (West 1999)).

165 *See id.* at 33 (Talmadge, J., concurring /dissenting) (quoting *In re* the Welfare of Sumey, 621 P.2d 108, 110 (Wash. 1980)).

166 *Id.*

167 *See id.*

168 *Id.*

169 *See Stillwell*, 969 P.2d at 33 (Talmadge, J., concurring /dissenting) (noting that the *Sumey* court found that temporary residential placement did not to infringe as severely upon constitutional rights as a termination of parental rights).

rental rights.[170]

The justice further noted that in the cases relied upon by the majority, greater infringements of constitutional rights were involved.[171] Distinguishing those cases from the lesser infringement associated with visitation awards, Justice Talmadge pointed to the substantial threats involved in the cases relied upon by the majority,[172] such as parents' free exercise of religion,[173] parents' ability to raise their children and select whether to send them to religious or military school,[174] and a presumption that allowed the termination of an unwed father's parental rights.[175] Justice Talmadge proposed that, under *Sumey*, the minor abridgment of parental rights associated with the Washington statutes is permissible.[176]

Justice Talmadge next focused on the state's *parens patriae* power.[177] The justice challenged the majority's claim that there must be evidence of parental unfitness or harm to the child before the state may exercise its *parens patriae* power.[178] Supporting this challenge, Justice Talmadge again underscored the *Sumey* case, emphasizing that while there was no claim of harm or parental unfitness, a child's temporary residential placement by the state outside of the home was deemed a permissible exercise of *parens patriae* power.[179] Moreover, the

---

[170] *See id.* These statutes authorize visitation to be granted if in furtherance of the best interests of the child. *See id.*

[171] *See Stillwell*, 969 P.2d at 33-34 (Talmadge, J., concurring /dissenting).

[172] *See Stillwell*, 969 P.2d at 34 (Talmadge, J., concurring /dissenting).

[173] *See id.* (citing Wisconsin v. Yoder, 406 U.S. 205 (1972)).

[174] *See id.* (citing Pierce v. Society of Sisters, 268 U.S. 510 (1925)).

[175] *See id.* (citing Stanley v. Illinois, 405 U.S. 645 (1972)).

[176] *See id.* Justice Talmadge quoted the Indiana Appellate Court s response to the same argument as made by the current majority, where that court upheld a grandparent visitation act: Unlike these significant infringements, visitation rights by grandparents as defined by the Act are less than a substantial encroachment on the parent's fundamental rights or the autonomy of the nuclear family. *Id.* (quoting Sightes v. Barker, 684 N.E.2d 224, 230 (Ind. Ct. App.), *transfer denied*, 690 N.E.2d 1187 (Ind. 1997)).

[177] *See id.*

[178] *See Stillwell*, 969 P.2d at 34 (Talmadge, J., concurring /dissenting).

[179] *See id.* (citing *In re* the Welfare of Sumey, 621 P.2d 108, 111 (Wash. 1980)).

justice recounted that the Washington Supreme Court previously held that even in a dependency proceeding, threatening a more severe abridgment of constitutional rights, it is not necessary to find unfitness prior to making a determination.[180] Furthermore, Justice Talmadge noted a previous Washington custody case and again urged that parental unfitness is not a prerequisite for the state to act under its *parens patriae* authority and emphasized that the best interest of the child is also the governing standard in child custody cases where the court's determination significantly infringes upon at least one parent's constitutional rights.[181] Instead of using parental unfitness as a threshold requirement for the state to exercise its *parens patriae* power, the justice proposed that a showing of parental unfitness or harm to a child relates to the extent that the state may infringe upon parental rights.[182]

Justice Talmadge criticized the majority's claim that the United States Supreme Court cases support the proposition that the state may only interfere with parental rights to rear their children if there is a threat of harm to the child or the potential for substantial social burden.[183] The justice intimated that the cases cited by the majority stand for principles different from what the majority has portrayed.[184] In *Wisconsin v. Yoder*,[185] compulsory school attendance law was barred from being applied to the Older Order Amish under the First Amendment's Free Exercise Clause.[186] *Yoder* is based on a claim of free exercise of religion by the Amish and the case's unique facts.[187] Under those circumstances,

---

180 *See Stillwell*, 969 P.2d at 35 (Talmadge, J., concurring /dissenting) (citing *In re* the Welfare of Key, 836 P.2d 200, 206 (Wash. 1992), *cert. denied*, 507 U.S. 927 (1993)).

181 *See id.* (citing *In re* Marriage of Allen, 626 P.2d 16 (Wash. Ct. App. 1981) (awarding custody to a nonparent requires more than a showing of the best interests of a child, but less than parental unfitness)). "Precisely what might outweigh parental rights must be determined on a case-by-case basis. But unfitness of the parent need not be shown." *Allen*, 626 P.2d at 23.

182 *See id.*

183 *See id.*

184 *See Stillwell*, 969 P.2d at 35-36 (Talmadge, J., concurring /dissenting).

185 406 U.S. 205 (1972).

186 *See Stillwell*, 969 P.2d at 35 (Talmadge, J., concurring /dissenting) (citing *Yoder*, 406 U.S. at 215). "Congress shall make no law respecting an establishment of religion, or prohibiting the free exercise thereof; . . ." U.S. CONST. amend. I.

187 *See Stillwell*, 969 P.2d at 36 (Talmadge, J., concurring /dissenting).

the *Yoder* Court required a compelling state interest, but warned that parental rights would be limited even when there was a free exercise claim if there was a threat of harm to the child or the potential for substantial social burdens.[188] Justice Talmadge explained that the Supreme Court did not require that harm be established prior to interference with parental rights, as proposed by the majority's assertion in the case at bar.[189] To the contrary, Justice Talmadge clarified that *Yoder* denoted that even when heightened protections exist for parental rights,[190] interference would be justified under the extreme circumstances of harm to a child.[191]

Justice Talmadge also found error with the majority's reliance on *Prince* to support the view that there must be evidence of harm before the state can interfere with parental rights.[192] The justice repeated the *Prince* Court's holding, stating that when the child labor law at issue was upheld against challenges under the First Amendment and parents' right to raise their children, the Court held that "the rightful boundary of [the state's] power has not been crossed in this case" and that "[o]ur ruling does not extend beyond the facts the case presents."[193] While the majority interpreted *Prince* to establish a requirement that harm must be present before state interference is permissible, Justice Talmadge construed *Prince* in a more narrow fashion.[194] The justice explained that when the state sought to prevent harm to a child, state interference with parental rights was appropriate.[195] Justice Talmadge suggested that evidence of harm was not necessary in all circumstances of state interference in family life.[196]

---

188 *See id.* (quoting *Yoder*, 406 US. at 233-34).

189 *See id.*

190 In *Yoder*, the parents' claims of constitutional protection as parents were magnified by their claims under the Free Exercise clause of the First Amendment. *See Yoder*, 406 U.S. at 207.

191 *See Stillwell*, 969 P.2d at 36 (Talmadge, J., concurring /dissenting).

192 *See id.* (citing Prince v. Massachusetts, 321 U.S. 158, 170 (1944)).

193 *See id.* (quoting *Prince*, 321 U.S. at 170-71). Justice Talmadge proposed that while Prince shows that state interference in religious practices or parental authority is proper to protect a child from harm, the case does not indicate that harm is a threshold requirement for state interference in all circumstances. *Id.*

194 *See id.*

195 *See id.*

196 *See id.*

Justice Talmadge examined, but dismissed, the two cases cited by the majority, addressing the constitutionality of grandparent visitation statutes in light of their intrusion on parental rights.[197] The justice noted that the first case mentioned by the majority was *Hawk v. Hawk*, where the visitation statute was held unconstitutional under a state constitution.[198] Justice Talmadge argued the inapplicability of *Hawk* to the present case in view of the fact that *Hawk* was decided under Florida's Constitution, which provides greater privacy protection than the Federal Constitution.[199] The justice warned of the slight precedential value of *Hawk* in the state of Washington since Washington's constitution provides no greater protection than that offered by the Federal Constitution, outside of search and seizure matters.[200] The justice conceded that the second case addressed by the majority, *Brooks v. Parkerson*, concerned a grandparent visitation statute that was held unconstitutional under both state and federal constitutions.[201] However, Justice Talmadge stressed that the *Brooks* court rested its holding upon the premise that any infringement upon parental rights, however slight, was unconstitutional.[202] The justice repeated that such approach was rejected in *Sumey*.[203]

Moreover, Justice Talmadge found fault with the majority for only addressing the minority view and failing to acknowledge that the majority of states uphold grandparent visitation statutes.[204] Quoting the Utah Court of Appeals which upheld Utah's Grandparent Visitation Statute as constitutional, Justice Talmadge stressed that "the vast majority of courts that have addressed the constitutionality of grandparent visitation statutes authorizing visitation if in the best interest of the child, have upheld those statutes as constitutional."[205] As additional evidence

---

197 *See Stillwell*, 969 P.2d at 36 (Talmadge, J., concurring/dissenting) (citing Hawk v. Hawk, 855 S.W.2d 573 (Tenn. 1993); Brooks v. Parkerson, 454 S.E.2d 769 (Ga.), *cert. denied*, 516 U.S. 942 (1995)).

198 *See id.* (citing *Hawk*, 855 S.W.2d at 582).

199 *See id.*

200 *See id.* (citing Ramm v. City of Seattle, 830 P.2d 395 (Wash. Ct. App. 1992)).

201 *See Id.* at 37 (Talmadge, J., concurring /dissenting) (citing *Brooks*, 454 S.E.2d at 774 n.6).

202 *See id.* (citing *Brooks*, 454 S.E.2d at 774 n.6).

203 *See Stillwell*, 969 P.2d at 37.

204 *See id.*

205 *Id.* (quoting Campbell v. Campbell, 896 P.2d 635, 644 n.18 (Utah App. 1995) (citations within quotation omitted). "To date, only Georgia has declared a statute permitting

of the constitutionality of these statutes, the justice highlighted the denial of *certiorari* by the United States Supreme Court to hear the Kentucky case, *King v. King.*[206] In *King*, a statute permitting visitation in the best interest of the child by nonparents was held constitutional under a Federal Constitution challenge.[207] Justice Talmadge alluded to the fact that the denial of *certiorari* suggested that the Kentucky case was decided correctly and therefore the statute did not impermissibly infringe upon parental rights under the Federal Constitution.[208] Correspondingly, the justice argued that since the Washington Constitution affords the same protection as the Federal Constitution in this area,[209] the Washington statute presently under consideration should similarly withstand a constitutional challenge.[210]

Justice Talmadge next turned to cases where the courts, as an instrumentality of the state, have awarded visitation rights under an exercise of *parens patriae* power, even absent specific statutory authority.[211] The justice recounted the rationale in *Roberts v. Ward*[212] where, under the court's equitable powers, grandparents were awarded visitation rights over the objections of a natural parent.[213] The justice quoted the *Roberts* court's analysis of parental rights and the modern family, when it submitted:

> [p]arental autonomy is grounded in the assumption that natural parents raise their own children in nuclear families, consisting of a married couple and their children . . . .The realities of modern living, however, demon-

court-ordered grandparent visitation, if in the best interest of the child, to be unconstitutional under the United States Constitution." *Id.*

[206] 828 S.W.2d 630 (Ky.), *cert. denied*, 506 U.S. 941 (1992).

[207] *See Stillwell*, 969 P.2d at 37 (Talmadge, J., concurring /dissenting).

[208] *See id.*

[209] *See id.* (citing Ramm v. City of Seattle, 830 P.2d 395, 402 (Wash. Ct. App.), *review denied*, 844 P.2d 437 (1992)).

[210] *See Stillwell*, 969 P.2d at 37-38 (Talmadge, J., concurring /dissenting).

[211] *See Stillwell*, 969 P.2d at 38-39 (Talmadge, J., concurring /dissenting) (citing Roberts v. Ward, 493 A.2d 478 (N.H. 1985) (awarding visitation rights to grandparents despite a parent s objection)).

[212] 493 A.2d 478 (N.H. 1985).

[213] *See Stillwell*, 969 P.2d at 38 (Talmadge, J., concurring /dissenting).

> strate that the validity of according almost absolute judicial deference to parental rights has become less compelling as the foundation upon which they are premised, the traditional nuclear family, has eroded . . . .[214]

Justice Talmadge continued to quote the *Roberts* court's opinion, finding that due to the decline of the traditional nuclear family, children are more likely to become attached to people not within their immediate families and to have non-parents perform the role of psychological parents when the family is not intact.[215] The justice pointed to the necessity, as suggested by the court in *Roberts*, to acknowledge the intricacy of the modern family and to recognize that children have the right to maintain close relationships formed with people outside the family when their family lacks the traditional nuclear family structure.[216] Justice Talmadge transcribed a portion of the *Roberts* holding, articulating that the court must accept that it is the child's right to know her grandparents that is being protected and not the grandparents' interests.[217]

Justice Talmadge next addressed the majority's denouncement of the best interest standard.[218] The justice clarified that the Washington statute's standard of the best interests of the child embodies the very items the majority found lacking in the statutes.[219] Enumerating factors such as a relationship between the petitioner and the child and any incidents of abuse in the past, the justice explained that such factors are considered in the case-by-case approach inherent in the best interests standard.[220] Justice Talmadge maintained that case law concerning the welfare of children in Washington supports the use of a best interests standard.[221] Declaring that the standard of best interests of the child "lacks nothing in its brevity," the justice underscored the flexibility retained by the standard to ad-

---

214 *Id.* (quoting *Roberts*, 493 A.2d at 481 (citations omitted)).

215 *See id.* (quoting *Roberts*, 493 A.2d 478, 481 (citations omitted)).

216 *See Stillwell*, 969 P.2d at 38-39 (Talmadge, J., concurring /dissenting) (quoting *Roberts*, 493 A.2d 478, 481) (citations omitted)).

217 *See Stillwell*, 969 P.2d at 39 (Talmadge, J., concurring /dissenting).

218 *See id.*

219 *See id.*

220 *See id.* Justice Talmadge explicated that statutes containing enumeration of such best interest factors are often included only as examples and are not exclusive. *See id.* at 39 n 5.

221 *See Stillwell*, 969 P.2d at 41 (Talmadge, J., concurring /dissenting).

dress the myriad of circumstances that must be considered when making determinations that concern a child's welfare, such as visitation rights.[222] Justice Talmadge highlighted that this standard "remain[s] the touchstone by which all other rights are tested and concerns addressed in various contexts dealing with children."[223]

Similarly, Justice Talmadge dismissed the majority's concern that the statutes in question lacked protection against frivolous visitation petitions as unfounded.[224] The justice was confident that courts are sufficiently capable of deterring such abuses through means of sanctions and by awarding attorney fees and costs.[225]

Justice Talmadge concluded by restating an objection to the majority's holding that parental rights are impermissibly infringed when visitation is awarded based upon a determination of the best interests of a child.[226] Justice Talmadge found the majority's conclusion unsound and irreconcilable with previous decisions that held abridgments of parental rights of greater magnitude to be constitutional.

Statutes analogous to those addressed in *Stillwell* are found throughout the country. The United States Supreme Court granted certiorari and forayed into the area of family law, offering some direction to state legislatures and courts for deciding the permissible reach of the state's authority into family life.

D. THE UNITED STATES SUPREME COURT'S VOICE: *TROXEL V. GRANVILLE*

The United States Supreme Court released a plurality decision on June 5, 2000 limiting its holding to the Washington State statute's validity as applied to the facts of the case before it.[227] Justice O'Connor was joined by Chief Justice Rehnquist, Justice Ginsburg, and Justice Breyer in announcing the Court's judgment affirming the Washington State Supreme Court's holding.[228] The Court reviewed the procedural history, noting that the Washington Court of Appeals re-

---

222 *Id.*

223 *Id.* (footnote omitted).

224 *See Stillwell*, 969 P.2d at 42 (Talmadge, J., concurring /dissenting).

225 *See id.* (citations omitted).

226 *See id.*

227 *See Troxel v. Granville*, 120 S. Ct. 2054 (2000).

228 *See id.* at 2057, 2059.

versed the Superior Court's order of visitation and dismissed the petition for visitation under the belief that "nonparents lack standing to seek visitation under § 26.10.160(3) unless a custody action is pending."[229] While the Washington Supreme Court affirmed the Court of Appeals, it did so on different grounds, finding that the Troxels did have standing under the plain language of the Washington statute, but that the statute was an unconstitutional infringement upon fundamental rights of parents to raise their children.[230]

In affirming the Washington State Supreme Court's judgment, the plurality took notice of the changing demographics of the average American family.[231] Justice O'Connor reasoned that the universal enactment of nonparent visitation statutes is an acknowledgment of the changing structures of the modern family.[232] Appreciating that a price is paid in exchange for the expansion of statutory rights to nonparents, the Plurality identified that a "substantial burden [can be placed] on the traditional parent-child relationship" and that constitutional questions may be raised.[233] Justice O'Connor next defined narrowly the question before the Court: whether section 26.10.160(3) of the Revised Code of Washington violates the Federal Constitution as it was applied to the Granville family.[234]

Discussing the Due Process guarantees of the Fourteenth Amendment, the Plurality proclaimed the existence of a substantive component protecting certain fundamental rights.[235] Justice O'Connor identified the fundamental liberty interest implicated in the case to be a parents' interest in the "care, custody, and control of their children" and recognized it as being one of the oldest liberty interests recognized by the United States Supreme Court.[236] Declaring the Washington

---

229 *Id.* at 2058.

230 *See id.*

231 *See id.* at 2059 (remarking on the increased number of children being raised in single-parent households or by grandparents).

232 *See id.*

233 *Troxel*, 120 S. Ct. at 2059.

234 *See id.*

235 *See id.* at 2059-60 (quoting Washington v. Glucksberg, 521 U.S. 702, 719-20 (1997))

236 *Id.* at 2060 (citing Meyer v. Nebraska, 262 U.S. 390 (1923); Pierce v. Society of Sisters, 268 U.S. 510 (1925); Prince v. Massachusetts, 321 U.S. 158 (1944)). The plurality also noted that this fundamental right of parents has been recognized more recently, as well. See id. (citing Stanley v. Illinois, 405 U.S. 645 (1972); Wisconsin v. Yoder, 406 U.S. 205 (1972); Quilloin v. Walcott, 434 U.S. 246 (1978)).

statute "breathtakingly broad," Justice O'Connor clearly stated that section 26.10.160(3), as applied to the present case, is an unconstitutional infringement upon the parent's, Tommie Granville's, fundamental right to make decisions pertaining to the care, custody and control of her children.[237]

The Plurality first examined the breadth of the statute before applying the law to the facts of the case.[238] The language of the statute "effectively permits any third party seeking visitation to subject any decision by a parent concerning visitation of the parent's children to state-court review."[239] The Plurality posited that once a parent's decision was before a judge, it was accorded no deference and the determination of the child's best interests would rest solely with the judge.[240]

Significantly, Justice O'Connor declared that the Washington Supreme Court declined to read section 26.10.160(3) narrowly.[241] The Plurality pointed to the Superior Court's holding as evidence that a broad interpretation of the statute results in outcomes based on mere disagreements in opinions between parents and judges on what is in the child's best interests.[242] Justice O'Connor continued on, noting that there were no special factors justifying the state's interference with the fundamental right of a parent to direct the rearing of her children.[243]

Again proclaiming that section 26.10.160(3), as applied to the facts of the case, violated the Due Process Clause, Justice O'Connor delineated factors supporting this finding.[244] The Plurality first posited that there were no allegations or findings of parental unfitness on the part of Granville, stressing the import of

---

[237] *Id.* at 2060-61.

[238] *See id.* at 2061.

[239] *Troxel*, 120 S. Ct. at 2061. "According to the statute's text, '[a]ny person may petition the court for visitation rights at any time,' and the court my grant such visitation rights whenever 'visitation may serve the best interest of the child.'" *Id.* (citing WASH. STAT. § 26.10.160(3)).

[240] *See id.*

[241] *See id.* To the contrary, the Washington Supreme Court interpreted the statute to permit "any person, at any time, to petition for visitation without regard to relationship to the child, without regard to changed circumstances, and without regard to harm." *Id.* (citing *Custody of Smith v. Stillwell*, 969 P.2d 21, 30 (Wash. 1998)).

[242] *See id.* at 2061.

[243] *See id.*

[244] *See id.* at 2061-64.

this due to the existing presumption that "fit parents act in the best interests of their children."[245] The second factor considered by the Plurality is that the Superior Court gave no special weight to Granville's opinion regarding the best interest of her children.[246] To the contrary, Justice O'Connor stressed that the Superior Court judge's comments were indicative of a presumption in opposition to the traditional approach.[247] The Plurality interpreted the lower court judge's comments as a presumption that requests for grandparent visitation should be awarded unless the fit custodial parent showed there would be an adverse impact on the children, placing the burden upon the fit parent.[248] Justice O'Connor criticized the Superior Court's failure to provide protection for a parent's fundamental right to direct the rearing of her children.[249] Finding this particularly troublesome since the statute was interpreted to subject parental decisions to judicial review, the Plurality reiterated that the courts must attach some modicum of special weight to parents' determinations.[250]

Addressing the last factor that lead the Plurality to find that the statute unconstitutionally infringed Tommie Granville's fundamental rights, Justice O'Connor noted that Granville never tried to eliminate visitation completely.[251] Once again, the Plurality commented on the fact that the court gave no weight to the fact that Granville agreed to permit visitation before the grandparents petitioned the court, and instead the court ordered a visitation schedule that it considered to be middle ground, rejecting Granville's proposal.[252] Justice O'Connor implied

---

245 *Id.* at 2061.

246 *See Troxel*, 120 S. Ct. at 2062.

247 *See id.* The Plurality quoted the Superior Court's explanation that "[the burden is to show that it is in the best interest of the children to have some visitation and some quality time with their grandparents. I think in most situations a commonsensical approach [is that] it is normally in the best interest of the children to spend quality time with the grandparent, unless the grandparent, [sic] there are some issues or problems involved wherein the grandparents, their lifestyles are going to impact adversely upon the children. . . . I think [visitation with the Troxels] would be in the best interest of the children and I haven't been shown it is not in [the] best interest of the children." *Id.* (citation omitted).

248 *See id.*

249 *See id.*

250 *See id.*

251 *See id.* at 2062-63.

252 *See Troxel*, 120 S. Ct. at 2063. The Superior Court ordered "one weekend of visitation per month, one week in the summer, an time on both the petitioning grandparents' birth-

that there is another statutory option that exists, namely statutes that prohibit visitation "unless a parent has denied (or unreasonably denied) visitation to the concerned third party."[253]

Reiterating its finding that the court's visitation order unconstitutionally infringed upon Granville's fundamental right to decide upon the care, custody and control of her children, the Plurality repeated that this case merely concerned a disagreement between Granville and the Washington Superior Court in determining the best interests of her children and that the Due Process Clause does not entitle a state "to infringe on the fundamental right of parents to make childrearing decisions simply because a state judge believes a 'better' decision could be made."[254]

Justice O'Connor concluded by acknowledging the limited guidance provided by the United States Supreme Court, and that the constitutional question of whether the Due Process Clause mandates nonparent visitation statutes to require a showing of "harm or potential harm to the child" prior to awarding visitation rights was not addressed.[255] Furthermore, the Plurality affirmed the Washington Supreme Court and declined to remand the case due to the disruptive nature of litigating domestic relations proceeding, both on the parent-child relationship and on the finances of Granville.[256]

While concurring in the judgment, Justice Souter would have affirmed the Washington Supreme Court's invalidation of the statute and declined to review and limit the holding to the specific application of the statute to the facts of the case.[257] Justice Souter found no error with one of the Supreme Court of Washington's grounds for invalidating the statute, namely that the statute is too broad and therefore unconstitutional since visitation rights could be petitioned by any person at any time under the statute, subject only to the best interests of the child standard.[258]

---

days," as opposed to Granville's suggestion proposal of one short visit per month and special holidays.

[253] *Id.* (citing Miss. Code Ann. § 93-16-3(2)(a) (1994); Ore. Rev. Stat. § 109.121(1)(a)(B) (1997); R.I. Gen. Laws § 15-5-24.3(a)(2)(iii)-(iv) (Supp. 1999)).

[254] *Id.* at 2063-64.

[255] *Id.* at 2064 ("We do not, and need not, define today the precise scope of the parental due process right in the visitation context.")

[256] *See id.* at 2065.

[257] *See id.* at 2065 (Souter, J., concurring)

[258] *See Troxel*, 120 S. Ct. at 2065-66 (Souter, J., concurring).

Accordingly, Justice Souter did not find it necessary to consider the Supreme Court of Washington's other ground for invalidating the statute, that the statute failed to require harm prior to entertaining a visitation request.[259] The Justice's concurrence recognized the protection afforded parents in "the nurture, upbringing, companionship, care and custody of children."[260]

In addition, Justice Souter warned that this principle would be a "sham" without protecting parents from "judicially compelled visitation by 'any party' at 'any time' a judge believed he 'could make a 'better' decision."[261] The Justice concluded by recognizing that a state's highest court has the power to interpret its own domestic statute and to utilize a demanding standard when determining its constitutionality.[262]

Separately concurring in the judgment, Justice Thomas opined that the standard of review to be applied to infringements of fundamental rights was strict scrutiny.[263] The Justice deciphered that Washington lacked a mere legitimate governmental interest "to say nothing of a compelling one – in second-guessing a fit parent's decision regarding visitation with third parties."[264]

Leading the multiple dissenting opinions, Justice Stevens posited that certiorari should never have been granted.[265] However, since the case is before the Court, the Justice proposed that the federal questions be examined.[266] Justice Stevens agreed with Justice Souter's opinion that a review of the Superior Court's application of the statute to the facts of the case at bar is unwarranted.[267]

---

[259] *See id.*

[260] *Id.* at 2066 (Souter, J., concurring) (citing Meyer v. Nebraska, 262 U.S. 390, 399 (1923); Pierce v. Society of Sisters,, 268 U.S. 510 535 (1925); Stanley v. Illinois, 405 U.S. 645, 651 (1972); Wisconsin v. Yoder, 406 U.S. 205, 232 (1972); Quilloin v. Walcott, 434 U.S. 246, 255 (1978); Parham v. J.R., 442 U.S. 584, 602 (1979); Santosky v. Kramer, 455 U.S. 745, 753 (1982); Washington v. Glucksberg, 521 U.S. 702, 720 (1997)).

[261] *Id.* at 2066-67 (Souter, J., concurring).

[262] *See id.* at 2067 (Souter, J., concurring).

[263] *See id.* at 2068 (Thomas, J., concurring).

[264] *Troxel*, 120 S. Ct. at 2068 (Thomas, J., concurring).

[265] *See id.* at 2068 (Stevens, J., dissenting) (noting the troublesome character of the Superior Court's decision and the uniqueness of the statute at issue).

[266] *See id.*

[267] *See id.* Justice Stevens determined that in light of the Washington Supreme Court s

Finding the Washington Supreme Court's reasoning flawed, Justice Stevens recommended that the Court correct the errors and remand the case for proper review of the Superior Court's determinations.[268]

First, the Justice viewed the State Supreme Court's basis for invalidating the statute insufficient under federal constitutional analysis.[269] According to Justice Stevens, neither the provision granting "any person" standing to petition nor the absence of a requirement that harm be shown invalidates the statute in all its applications.[270] Therefore, the Justice disagreed with the State Supreme Court's conclusion that the statute "would invariably run afoul of the Fourteenth Amendment" since within the scope of the statute lies circumstances where the statute would be constitutional.[271] Second, Justice Stevens declared the that Washington Supreme Court was unsupported in its interpretation that the Federal Constitution requires a finding of harm or potential harm prior to granting visitation over a parent's objection.[272]

While assenting to the Plurality's analysis of parents' fundamental right under the Fourteenth Amendment to maintain the parent-child relationship, Justice Stevens articulated that this right exists within limits and is not absolute.[273] Moreover, the Justice expanded his analysis to contemplate children's interests in preserving intimate relationships.[274] Balancing the child's interest as an addi-

---

invalidation based upon the Federal Constitution, the state court of appeals did not have the opportunity to review the Superior Court's finding, and as such, the United States Supreme Court should not be doing so. *See id.*

[268] *See id.* at 2070 (Stevens, J., dissenting).

[269] *See id.*

[270] *See Troxel*, 120 S. Ct. at 2070 (Stevens, J., dissenting).

[271] *Id.*

[272] *See id.* Justice Stevens recognized that the parent-child relationship is protected by the Constitution from arbitrary State interference. *See id.* at 2070-71 (Stevens, J., dissenting). However, the Justice clarified that this parental right is not so absolute that a "rigid constitutional shield" exists to protect every parental decision from challenges where a showing of harm is lacking. *Id.* at 2071 (Stevens, J., dissenting).

[273] *See id.* at 2071-72 (Stevens, J., dissenting). For example, Justice Stevens discussed *Lehr v. Robertson*, 463 U.S..258 (1983), where a parent-child relationship was required before a biological parent is afforded constitutional protections as a parent. *See id.* at 1072 (Stevens, J., dissenting). However, this Court has held that both biology and an established relationship was insufficient to instill parental rights and overcome a state statutory presumption that a child's father is the husband of the child's mother. *See id.*

[274] *See id.* at 1072 (Stevens, J., dissenting).

tional factor, Justice Stevens proposed that the protection of parental rights against arbitrary state interference should not prevent the protection of children from the "arbitrary exercise of parental authority that is not in fact motivated by an interest in the welfare of the child."[275] The required balancing of interests, the Justice instructed, should be tackled by the states, not federal courts applying a national standard.[276] Justice Stevens concluded by proclaiming that the states have the ability to evaluate the "impact on a child of possibly arbitrary parental decisions that neither serve nor are motivated by the best interests of the child" under the Due Process Clause of the Fourteenth Amendment.[277]

Separately dissenting, Justice Scalia suggested that he supported the argument that states should not have the power to interfere with parental rights to direct the rearing of their children.[278] However, since this right remains unenumerated, the Justice did not find support in the Constitution to invalidate a law contrary to this interest.[279] Furthermore, Justice Scalia believed the diversity of opinions on parental rights diminished any argument for the application of stare decisis or the expansion upon its underlying theory.[280] Admonishing the protection of the unenumerated parental right under the auspices of the Federal Constitution, the Justice forecasted the need for judicial initiative to define "parents," "other persons" who may qualify to petition for visitation, and "harm to the child."[281] Justice Scalia cautioned that the result would be judicially and federally prescribed family law.[282]

Justice Kennedy prepared the last dissent in response to the Plurality's opinion. Justice Kennedy commenced by criticizing the Washington Supreme Court's decision that it was an error for the statute not to require a showing that

---

275 *Id.*

276 *See Troxel*, 120 S. Ct. at 2073 (Stevens, J., dissenting).

277 *Id.* at 2074 (Stevens, J., dissenting).

278 *See id.* at 2074 (Scalia, J., dissenting).

279 *See id.*

280 *See id.*

281 *Id.*

282 *See Troxel*, 120 S. Ct. at 2075 (Scalia, J., dissenting). Justice Scalia took issue with subjecting family law to a federal regime since the federal judiciary is no better suited that the state legislatures to shape this area of the law. Additionally, the Justice found reason to keep this area for the states since any harm would be more limited in scope and more easily corrected at the state level, not to mention the peoples' ability to remove the legislators. *See id.*

harm to the child would result if visitation were to be denied.[283] Positing that the state supreme court's theory was too broad, the Justice interpreted it to imply that the best interests of the child standard would be inappropriate in any visitation case.[284] Under this view, Justice Kennedy proposed that the appropriate recourse is to vacate and remand, in order to allow the Washington Supreme Court to reconsider the case and correct its overly broad formulation of a harm requirement.[285]

Justice Kennedy initially analyzed whether a showing of harm must be present in every visitation petition by recognizing the constitutional right of parents to determine "without undue interference by the state, how best to raise, nurture, and educate" their children.[286] The Justice clarified that the Washington State Supreme Court's attempted to further define this parental right by requiring third parties petitioning for visitation to establish that harm would result to the child if visitation was denied.[287] Justice Kennedy questioned whether the State Supreme Court's reasoning rested on an underlying assumption that parents objecting to visitation requests were the child's primary caregiver and that third parties petitioning for visitation were without established relationships with the child.[288] Finding this assumption to rest upon the concept of the conventional nuclear family, the Justice articulated that this is not the predominant structure in many families today.[289]

Justice Kennedy challenged the State Supreme Court's rationale and predicted that cases will arise in which an absolute parental veto would be inappropriate due to a third party's substantial role in the child's life, such as a third party who fulfills the role of a caregiver.[290] Contrary to the State Supreme Court's conclusion that use of the best interests of the child standard is prohibited

[283] *See id.* at 2075 (Kennedy, J., dissenting).

[284] *See id.*

[285] *See id.* at 2075-76 (Kennedy, J., dissenting).

[286] *Id.* at 2076 (Kennedy, J., dissenting).

[287] *See id.* The Washington Supreme Court viewed the best interests of the child standard to be an inadequate reason for the state to override parents' fundamental rights.

[288] *See Troxel*, 120 S. Ct. at 2076.

[289] *See id.* Justice Kennedy recognized that many children are raised without two parents regardless of whether their upbringing consisted of tragedy or happiness. *Id.*

[290] *See id.*

under the Constitution in visitation proceedings, the Justice argued that when dealing with certain relationships, states should be permitted to utilize the best interests of the child standard in order to avoid harm.[291] Moreover, as a result of the limited history of cases granting third parties visitation,[292] and in light of the "almost universal adoption of the best interests standard for visitation disputes," Justice Kennedy considered it unlikely that there is any right to be free in all cases from courts applying the best interests standard.[293] Instead, Justice Kennedy suggested that the decision whether the application of the best interests standard is constitutional should be decided after examining the specific facts of the case.[294] Agreeing with Justices Stevens and Scalia, Justice Kennedy identified the state courts as being best qualified to sort through the issues arising in family law cases.[295]

Finding that the Washington Supreme Court did not evaluate the specific visitation order in this case due to its "sweeping ruling" that the best interest standard always results in an unconstitutional ruling, Justice Kennedy determined that the proper recourse is to vacate the judgment and remand the case for further consideration.[296]

VI ANALYSIS

Faced with the deterioration of the "nuclear" family and motivated by the desire to insure a proper environment consisting of the close ties attributed to the traditional nuclear family, our judiciary has been forced to consider whether children's needs and rights should trump parental rights. When we contemplate

---

291 *See id.* at 2078 (Kennedy, J., dissenting). Justice Kennedy pointed to other methods of protecting parents from excessive third-party visitation petitions, such as statutory limitations on who has standing to petition, such as grandparents, or by requiring the third party to demonstrate that a substantial relationship exists with the child. *See id.*

292 *See id.* at 2076-77 (Kennedy, J., dissenting). "The consensus among court and commentators is that at least through the 19th century there was no legal right of visitation; court-ordered visitation appears to be a 20th century phenomenon." *Id.* at 2077 (citations omitted).

293 *Id.* at 2079 (Kennedy, J., dissenting).

294 *See Troxel*, 120 S. Ct. at 2079 (Kennedy, J., dissenting). The court's conclusion would vary depending upon whether a stranger is petitioning for visitation over a fit parent's objection as opposed to determining visitation for another parent or someone fulfilling the role of a parent. *Id.*

295 *See id.*

296 *Id.*

the best interests of the child, it is tempting to conclude that they are paramount to parents' rights to privacy and autonomy in raising their children. Indeed, some courts have held this to be so.[297] However, both the welfare of children and parents' rights will be protected if, prior to the inquiry of the child's best interests, there is a required showing of harm to a child, a threat of harm, or parental unfitness. Permitting the sole criteria for state interference to be the court-decided best interests of the child, absent a finding of harm or parental unfitness, condones the diminution of parents' rights and family autonomy without requiring any compelling state interest.

Constitutional rights of parents[298] are threatened by two aspects of the nonparent visitation case law. First, the level of protection afforded to parental rights should not be dependent upon marital status. As the face of the traditional "nuclear" family changes, we must decide whether this equates to a dilution of parents' constitutional rights. Case law shows that in some jurisdictions, standing for nonparents to petition for visitation is contingent upon whether the child's family is disrupted.[299] Statutes permitting state intrusion more easily upon disrupted families than upon intact families should not be tolerated.

Allowing the state to intrude more easily upon parental rights simply because the traditional family unit is no longer intact is an impermissible infringement upon parents' Constitutional rights to raise their children. Statutes that distinguish between disrupted and intact families send a message that parents must choose between staying in an unhappy marriage or loosing their constitutional rights as parents.

Whether a man or woman chooses to leave a marriage, chooses to bring a child into the world as a single parent, is left by a spouse or becomes widowed, the same protections should be afforded under the Constitution as to parents who are fortunate enough to maintain a marriage that comports with society's traditional definition of "family." When the United States Supreme Court enunciated that "[t]his Court has long recognized that freedom of personal choice in matters of marriage and family life is one of the liberties protected by the Due Process Clause of the Fourteenth Amendment,"[300] they did not limit the freedom to mar-

---

[297] Two states have held the valid state interest in the welfare of children is paramount to the rights of the parent to direct the upbringing of his or her child. *See* CHILD CUSTODY & VISITATION LAW & PRACTICE, *supra* note 6, § 16.02[1][a], at 16-11 to 16-12 (citing See Simmons v. Sheridan, 414 N.Y.S.2d 83 (N.Y. Sup. Ct. 1979); DeWeese v. Crawford, 520 S.W.2d 522 (Tex. Civ. App. 1975)).

[298] Women are particularly affected by this issue since in the majority of custody battles, the children are awarded to the mother.

[299] *See infra* note 78 and accompanying text.

[300] Moore v. City of East Cleveland, 431 U.S. 494, 499 (1977).

ried individuals, but specifically stated that it was a *personal* freedom. Moreover, the Due Process Clause of the Fourteenth Amendment, under which parental rights are derived, states that "[n]o State shall . . . deprive any *person* of life, liberty or property, without due process of law."[301] An individual's rights are not contingent upon his or her marital status. It is undeniable that as a society we must be concerned with protecting children's safety and well-being, but absent a showing of at least a threat of such harm, a parent's liberty must not be truncated.

The second threat to parents' constitutional rights arises when the sole criteria used for determining visitation rights of nonparents is the best interests of the child standard. Whether a family is intact or disrupted, courts should require petitioners to establish a more compelling reason for ordering visitation than merely submitting that visitation would be in the child's best interests. Relying on the best interests standard alone permits the courts, grandparents, and other third parties to propose what they believe is "better" for a child and impermissibly interferes with family autonomy as established under the Constitution. Irrespective of whether there is a disruption to the traditional family unit, a showing of harm or parental unfitness should be required prior to any state interference with parental rights.

While noble in heart, court attempts to "strengthen familial bonds" [302] by granting nonparent visitation rights result in judges substituting their own judgment in personal family relations with a limited understanding of the circumstances and the ramifications of state intrusion upon that particular family. This is evidenced by the court's reasoning in *King v. King*, where the court denied the wishes of married parents that their children not be visited by their grandparents.[303] The court rationalized that "[t]here is no reason that a petty dispute between a father and son should be allowed to deprive a grandparent and grandchild of the unique relationship that ordinarily exists between those individuals. One of the main purposes of the statute is to prevent a family quarrel of little significance to disrupt a relationship which should be encouraged rather than destroyed."[304] To have courts with demanding dockets and little personal knowledge of the parties involved dictating when and how disagreements may occur within families is a far cry from family autonomy. As quoted previously:[305]

---

301 U.S. CONST. amend. XIV, § 1 (emphasis added).

302 King v. King, 828 S.W.2d 630, 632 (Ky.), *cert. denied*, 506 U.S. 941 (1992)).

303 *See id.*

304 *Id.*

305 *See supra* note 130 and accompanying text.

> For the state to delegate to the parents the authority to raise the child as the parents see fit, except when the state thinks another choice would be better, is to give the parents no authority at all. 'You may do whatever you choose, so long as it is what I would choose also does not constitute a delegation of authority.'"[306]

The best interests standard leaves open questions as to what is in the "best interest" of the child and who defines the best interest of the child. More is needed than a belief or "feeling" that another alternative would best serve the child's interests. Unless parental unfitness is established, a child's parent has always been considered to be in the best position to make such decisions. Parents' rights enable them to restrict visitation of nonparents with their children and "the law's concept of the family rests 'on a presumption that parents possess what a child lacks in maturity, experience, and capacity for judgment . . . .'"[307]

Without a showing of harm or the presence of such a threat, the state has no compelling interest to justify an intrusion upon family autonomy.[308] As stated in *Stillwell*, "[s]tate intervention to better a child's quality of life through third party visitation is not justified where the child's circumstances are otherwise satisfactory."[309] If the best interests of the child is the sole criteria used to determine whether state interference is warranted, then the family autonomy may be challenged repeatedly by third parties purporting to know what is best or even better for the child. Not only will third parties trespass upon parental rights, but the courts will enter the business of determining what is "better" for children. Absent at least a threat of harm, it is not within the state's province to base decisions affecting family life upon a belief they could "make a 'better' decision."[310] While a shocking suggestion, the *Stillwell* court warned that "[t]o suggest otherwise would be the logical equivalent to asserting that the state has the authority to break up stable families and redistribute its infant population to provide each

---

[306] Custody of Smith v. Stillwell, 969 P.2d 21, 30 (Wash. 1998) *cert. granted sub nom.* Troxel v. Granville, 120 S. Ct. 11 (1999) (quoting Hawk. v. Hawk, 855 S.W.2d 573, 580 (Tenn. 1993) (quoting Bean, *supra* note 148, at 441)).

[307] *Id.* at 31 (quoting Brooks v. Parkerson, 454 S.E.2d 769, 772 (Ga. 1995)(citation omitted)).

[308] *See id.* at 31; *Hawk*, 855 S.W.2d at 582 (quoting *King*, 828 S.W.2d at 633-34 (Lambert, J., dissenting)).

[309] *Stillwell*, 969 P.2d at 30.

[310] *Id.* at 31.

child with the 'best family.'"[311] Ultimately, for the courts to impose an order of visitation based upon its own determination of the child's best interests, the court merely "impose[s] its own notion of the children's best interests over the shared opinion of the[ir] parents, stripping them of their right to control in parenting decisions."[312]

Equal protection of the constitutional rights of parents, whether part of an intact or disrupted family, will protect the sanctity of the family and the ability of parents to be the primary authority in raising their children and protecting their children's welfare. Furthermore, by requiring an initial showing of harm or parental unfitness before the best interests standard is evoked, parents' childrearing decisions will be subject to minimal judicial second-guessing[313] and the family autonomy protected by the Constitution will retain its intended integrity.

While the United States Supreme Court's decision in *Troxel v. Granville* is helpful in securing parental rights, it stops short of addressing instrumental questions within the area of third party visitation rights. The plurality's concern with the lack of special weight afforded to parents' determinations on what is in a child's best interest may help strengthen support for parents' decisions in the raising of their children. Additionally, the plurality keenly recognized the petty disagreements that may arise in the future between parents, third parties, and the courts as to what is "better" for a child.[314] However, the plurality's failure to address whether a showing of harm is required under the Due Process Clause provides little instruction to state legislatures and courts. Furthermore, in declining to define the scope of rights within the visitation context and instead leaving the determination of whether a visitation order unconstitutionally infringes upon parental rights to case-by-case analysis, the Court leaves the door open to great variation in decisions on visitation and room for abuse of discretion by the state courts.

---

311 *Id.* at 30-31.

312 *Hawk*, 855 S.W.2d at 582 (concerning the scenario of an intact family).

313 *See id.* at 581.

314 *See id.* at 2061.

GRANDPARENT VISITATION: THE BEST INTERESTS OF THE GRANDPARENT, CHILD, AND SOCIETY

*Erica L. Strawman**

> Grandparents who are not required by law to care for their grandchildren are doing so because they love them and believe that it is the right thing to do. They just need help doing the best job possible.[1]

INTRODUCTION

A. Case Study 1

ROBERT and Dorothy Smith are grandparents seeking visitation rights[2] for their seven-year-old granddaughter, Jennifer. Robert and Dorothy are a relatively affluent, retired couple in their early sixties. Robert was a former college professor who still does a small amount of business consulting, and Dorothy teaches piano lessons and organizes musical activities for children in their community. The couple has always loved young people despite being able to only have one child of their own. Jennifer's parents were married and divorced at a young age, and Jennifer rarely sees her father. The Smiths are the parents of Jennifer's mother (maternal grandparents), and did not approve of the marriage at the time it occurred. They have since accepted Peggy's past decisions, and wish to reconcile with her, but she is not nearly as forgiving as her parents.

Peggy works several jobs to support she and Jennifer, thus Jennifer and her mother spend very little time together. There is very little money left over at the end of the month for the two of them. As a result, Jennifer's mother cannot afford to pay for Jennifer to participate in any extracurricular activities. An older neighbor watches Jennifer after school until her mother gets home from work in the evening. Jennifer does not have any brothers and sisters, nor does she have any aunts and uncles. Jennifer never had much contact with her paternal grandparents. Jennifer has not had much contact with her maternal grandparents because of their estrangement with Peggy, and although she is somewhat ambivalent of the situation because of her age, she seems comfortable with the idea of spending time with the Smiths.

---

* B.A., University of Michigan; J.D., Ohio State College of Law. Ms. Strawman is an attorney with the firm of Keating, Muething & Klekamp, P.L.L., in Cincinnati, Ohio. The author would like to thank her immediate family, John, Debbie and Brittany Strawman, for their love and support with her career, as well as her grandparents.

1. FAITH MULLEN, A TANGLED WEB: PUBLIC BENEFITS, GRANDPARENTS, AND GRANDCHILDREN at i (1995).

2. The author uses the terms "rights of companionship" and "grandparent visitation rights" interchangeably.

B. Case Study 2

Todd Peterson was orphaned at age nine when his parents were killed in a tragic automobile accident. The Treegers, his mother's brother and his wife, were appointed as his legal guardians after the accident. Unfortunately, the Treegers live in a rural area of southeastern Ohio and Todd had spent his entire life in urban Cleveland, Ohio. Todd's paternal grandparents, the Peterson's, have decided to petition for grandparent visitation rights. The Peterson's have a very large extended family with many aunts, uncles, and cousins whom he used to see almost on a daily basis, as his parents placed a high value on family. The Treegers have never had any contact with Todd's paternal relatives, but feel that visitation with Todd's other relatives would be of great inconvenience to them.

C. Case Study 3

Tony Johnson is an eleven-year-old boy who was adopted by his stepfather following the divorce of his parents and the remarriage of his mother. Tony's paternal grandfather, Mr. Block, had taken care of Tony for an extended period of time while his biological parents were in Africa doing government work. Tony's stepfather and stepgrandparents have been more than accommodating in welcoming him into their family, but Mr. Block greatly misses the time he used to spend with his grandson. Mr. Block's doctor even thinks the physical and mental well-being of his patient has deteriorated as a result of not seeing his young grandson nearly as much. Tony's father has since moved to Eastern Europe and spends very little time in the United States, so he is not available to plan events for the three of them. Mr. Block has decided to petition for grandparent visitation rights with Tony.

Each of the three previous case studies presents a variety of different fact patterns. However, all three family situations include an event in the family that resulted in a disruption of the grandparent-grandchild relationship. As the law exists now, the primary consideration behind family law is the best interest of the child.[3] Grandparents must petition for visitation rights with their grandchildren in order to see them if the parents do not make the child accessible. However, despite the obvious desire of a grandparent who files a petition to establish this right, the courts put the wishes of the grandparent to the side, and apply a very amorphous test in order to make their decision. This paper addresses the area of family law which involves grandparent visitation rights. Part I presents the background and expansion of grandparent visitation rights. Part II differentiates the categories of disruptions in the family situation that generally give rise to rights of companionship for grandparents. Part III gives a brief overview of the aging population in the United States. Parts IV and V present the benefits of an intergenerational relationship from both the perspective of the grandparent as well as that of the grandchild. Sociological studies on the grandparent-grandchild relationship as it affects the grandparent may

3. The best interest of the child is the general principle that the right to visit with a child depends upon whether such visitation would be in the child's best interest. *See generally* 59 AM. JUR. 2d *Parent and Child* § 45 (1987).

be the driving force to expand rights of companionship for grandparents from the point at which the law currently exists. Part VI puts forth the idea of combining sociological information with the "best interests" test in order to determine rights of companionship for grandparents. Part VII concludes with thoughts on the future of grandparent visitation rights.

I. THE EXPANSION OF RIGHTS OF COMPANIONSHIP AS APPLIED TO GRANDPARENTS

Common law does not allow grandparents legal rights of communication or access to their grandchildren.[4] Parents had complete autonomy in raising their children,[5] and judges could not intrude upon the family unit in order to oblige parents to extend their familial boundaries to include grandparent visitation.[6] In response to the changing American family,[7] family law has seen the enactment of statutes in all fifty

4. There are several rationales as to why visitation rights were disallowed under common law. First, judicially enforced grandparent visitation infringes upon a parents fundamental right to raise their child as they see fit. Second, the disruption a legal battle can cause in determining grandparent visitation rights is contrary to the child's best interest. Third, as the law currently exists, a parent's obligation to allow a grandparent visitation rights is moral, not legal. Finally, family communication and negotiation is more effective and meaningful than a mandate from the legal system. *See* Anne Marie Jackson, Comment, *The Coming of Age of Grandparent Visitation Rights*, 43 AM. U. L. REV. 563, 573-74 (1994). *See generally* Sara Simrall Rorer, Comment, *Grandparents' Visitation Rights in Ohio: A Procedural Quagmire*, 56 U. CIN. L. REV. 295 (1987); Judith L. Shandling, Note, *The Constitutional Constraints on Grandparents' Visitation Statutes*, 86 COLUM. L. REV. 118 (1986).

5. The right to privacy in the family relationship has been given protection as a fundamental right under the Fourteenth Amendment by the Supreme Court. *See* Pierce v. Society of Sisters, 268 U.S. 510, 534-35 (1925). In *Pierce*, two private schools challenged an Oregon statute requiring students to attend public schools. *Id.* at 530-32. The Court determined the statute was an unreasonable interference on the parent's right "to direct the upbringing and education of children under their control." *Id.* at 534-35. *Meyer v. Nebraska* was also a case contesting a statute regulating education. Meyer v. Nebraska, 262 U.S. 390 (1923). In *Meyer*, the Court found that liberty under the Fourteenth Amendment "[w]ithout doubt . . . denotes . . . the right of the individual to . . . establish a home and bring up children." *Id.* at 399. Subsequent cases and comments have recognized *Pierce* and *Meyer* for the broader proposition that the Fourteenth Amendment constitutionally protects the parent-child relationship. *See, e.g.*, Wisconsin v. Yoder, 406 U.S. 205, 232 (1972) (stating that Amish parents may now avoid law requiring them to send their children to school beyond the eighth grade); Prince v. Massachusetts, 321 U.S. 158, 166 (1944) ("[The] custody, care and nurture of the child reside first in the parents . . . . [I]t is in recognition of this that [our] decisions have respected the private realm of family law which the state cannot enter."). *Cf.* Bellotti v. Baird, 443 U.S. 662, 638 (1979) (ruling that while "the parental role implies a substantial measure of the authority over one's children," a mature minor is nonetheless entitled to obtain an abortion without parental consent); Parham v. J.R., 442 U.S. 584, 602 (1979) ("Our jurisprudence historically has reflected Western civilization concepts of the family as a unit with broad parental authority over minor children.").

6. "[T]he obligation ordinarily to visit grandparents is moral, and not legal." *See* Shandling, *supra* note 4, at 118 (quoting Succession of Reiss, 15 So. 151, 152 (La. 1894)).

7. Grandparent visitation statutes have been enacted as a product of the disrupted family. *See* Shandling, *supra* note 4, at 121; Rorer, *supra* note 4, at 296. The rising number of divorced or unmarried parents, combined with the existence of step-families, changing concepts of child custody and visitation, the estrangement of extended family members, and a decrease in the number of grandchildren have all contributed to the growing trend toward allowing grandparents to have visitation rights under statutory law. *Id.*

states that provide grandparents with a vehicle to enforce visitation rights.[8] The growing trend toward allowing grandparent visitation is due largely to the well-organized efforts of the "gray lobby"[9] to ensure that the law preserves the unique relationship between grandparents and grandchildren.[10]

Twenty years ago, "rights of companionship" statutes were virtually nonexistent.[11] Yet, even with the statutory enactment of visitation rights by the states,[12] the issue has

---

8. *See* ALA. CODE § 30-3-4 (Supp. 1998); ALASKA STAT. § 25.24.150 (Michie 1996); ARIZ. REV. STAT. ANN. § 25-409 (West Supp. 1998); ARK. CODE ANN. § 9-13-103 (Michie 1998); CAL. CIV. CODE § 3102 (West Supp. 1998); COLO. REV. STAT. § 19-1-117 (Supp. 1995); CONN. GEN. STAT. ANN. § 46b-59 (West 1995); DEL. CODE ANN. tit. 10, § 1031 (Supp. 1997); FLA. STAT. ANN. § 752.01 (West 1997); GA. CODE ANN. § 19-7-3 (Supp. 1998); HAW. REV. STAT. § 571-46(7) (1993); IDAHO CODE § 32-719 (1996); 750 ILL. COMP. STAT. ANN. 5/607(b)(1) (West Supp. 1993); IND. CODE ANN. § 31-17-5-1 (West Supp. 1993); IOWA CODE ANN. § 598.35 (West Supp. 1998); KAN. STAT. ANN. § 38-129 (Supp. 1997); KY. REV. STAT. ANN. § 405.021 (Banks-Baldwin 1991); LA. CIV. CODE ANN. art. 136(B) (West Supp. 1998); ME. REV. STAT. ANN. tit. 19A, §§ 1801-1805 (West 1998); MD. CODE ANN., FAM. LAW § 9-102 (Supp. 1997); MASS. ANN. LAWS ch. 119, § 39(d) (Law. Co-op. Supp. 1992); MICH. STAT. ANN. § 25.312(7b) (Law. Co-op. Supp. 1979); MINN. STAT. ANN. § 257.022 (West 1992); MISS. CODE ANN. § 93-16-3 (Supp. 1998); MO. ANN. STAT. § 452.402 (West 1997); MONT. CODE ANN. § 40-9-102 (1997); NEB. REV. STAT. § 43-1802 (1988); NEV REV. STAT. § 125A.340 (1996); N.H. REV. STAT. ANN. § 458-17-d (1992); N.J. STAT. ANN. § 9:2-7.1 (West Supp. 1999); N.M. STAT. ANN. § 40-9-2 (Michie 1994); N.Y. DOM. REL. LAW § 72 (McKinney Supp. 1998); N.C. GEN. STAT. § 50-13.2 (1995); N.D. CENT. CODE § 14-09-05.1 (1997); OHIO REV. CODE ANN. §§ 3109.051, 3109.11 (Anderson 1996); OKLA. STAT. ANN. tit. 10, § 5 (West 1998); OR. REV. STAT. § 109.121 (1995); 23 PA. CONS. STAT. ANN. §§ 5311-12 (1991); R.I. GEN. LAWS § 15-5-24.1 to -24.3 (1996); S.C. CODE ANN. § 20-7-420(33) (Law. Co-op. Supp. 1997); S.D. CODIFIED LAWS §§ 25-4-52 to 25-4-54 (Michie 1992); TENN. CODE ANN. § 36-6-302 (Supp. 1997); TEX. FAM. CODE ANN. § 153.433 (West Supp. 1998); UTAH CODE ANN. § 30-5-2 (Supp. 1998); VT. STAT. ANN. tit. 15, §§ 1011 to 1016 (1989); VA. CODE ANN. §§ 20-107.2, 20-124.1 (Michie Supp. 1998); WASH. REV. CODE ANN. § 26.09.240 (West 1997); W.VA. CODE § 48-2B (Supp. 1998); WIS. STAT. ANN. § 767.245 (West Supp. 1997); WYO. STAT. ANN. § 20-7-101 (Michie 1995).

9. The gray lobby is a coalition of more than a dozen groups of senior citizens and older Americans that exert their influence in the Washington, D.C. political arena. W. ANDREW ACHENBAUM, SHADES OF GRAY 119 (1983). The groups work both together and independently on issues in the areas of service, labor, professional, fraternal, and community interests in order to raise the status of the elderly in America. *Id.* Three organizations dominate the gray lobby: The National Retired Teachers Association/American Association of Retired Persons (NRTA/AARP), The National Council on Aging (NCOA), and The National Council of Senior Citizens (NCSC). *Id.* at 119 n.2.

10. *See Grandparents Rights: Preserving Generational Bonds: Hearing Before the Subcomm. on Human Services of the House Select Comm. on Aging*, 102d Cong. 3 (1991) [hereinafter *Grandparents Rights*] (statement of Rep. Thomas Downey) (remarking that senior citizens are "the most active lobby in this country, and when it comes to grandparents there is no one group more united in their purpose"); Edward M. Burns, *Grandparent Visitation Rights: Is It Time for the Pendulum to Fall?*, 25 FAM. L.Q. 59, 59 (1991) (remarking that older Americans have taken a more vocal stance than in the past); Andre P. Derdeyn, *Grandparent Visitation Rights: Rendering Family Dissension More Pronounced?*, 55 AM. J. ORTHOPSYCHIATRY 277, 282 (1985); Katrine Ames, *Grandma Goes to Court*, NEWSWEEK, Dec. 2, 1991, at 67.

11. Elaine D. Ingulli, *Grandparent Visitation Rights: Social Policies and Legal Rights*, 87 W. VA. L. REV. 295-98 (1984-85).

12. While a federally mandated statute would seem to be ideal for vindicators of grandparent visitation rights, this is technically impossible under the Constitution. Article 1, Section 8 of the Constitution enumerates the areas in which Congress may legislate, and family matters, including grandparents' rights, do not fall within the confines of Congress' enumerated powers. The Tenth Amendment of the Constitution explicitly delegates all powers outside of Congress to the States.

still not fully been resolved.[13] The state visitation provisions are far from uniform. Some statutes are drawn broadly,[14] while other statutes have a very narrow reading.[15] Moreover, the Supreme Court has traditionally shown great deference to state courts and legislatures in matters of family law.[16] The decision by the Court to deny certiorari to cases addressing grandparent visitation has furthered the ambiguities in this area of the law.[17] As a result, the legal entitlement of grandparents to see and interact with their grandchildren remains in a continual state of change. Thus, under the current state of the law, what is conferred upon grandparents in granting visitation would seem to be a privilege and not a full-fledged right.

In Ohio it is clear the grandparent-grandchild relationship per se does not give rise to a legally protected interest.[18] However, grandparents may exercise rights of companionship as interested third parties under Ohio Revised Code sections 3109.05(B) and 3109.11.[19] The Ohio provisions are part of a narrowly drawn

---

Therefore, grandparent visitation rights are in the domain of state control. Since Congress cannot create one national statute, it can either precondition the receipt of federal funding on a compliance with federal standards, or pass a resolution or model statute addressing this area of the law. Yet, according to a CRS report for Congress, Congress could not precondition federal funds in the area of grandparent visitation because there is no federal program relating to visitation to which to link funds. *See Grandparents Rights*, *supra* note 10, at 16. The uniformity of a resolution would provide a starting point for all states to insure grandparent visitation rights. *See* Jackson, *supra* note 4, at 592-93.

13. *See generally* Sarah Norton Harpring, Comment, *Wide-Open Grandparent Visitation Statutes: Is the Door Closing?*, 62 U. CIN. L. REV. 1659 (1994); Jackson, *supra* note 4; Rorer, *supra* note 4; Shandling, *supra* note 4; Annotation, *Grandparents' Visitation Rights*, 90 A.L.R.3d 222 (1996) [hereinafter *Grandparents' Visitation Rights*].

14. Several state statutes are broadly written to the extent of permitting grandparent visitation rights even in an intact family. *See, e.g.*, ALA. CODE § 30-3-4(c) (1989); CONN. GEN. STAT. ANN. § 46b-59 (West 1995); KY. REV. STAT. ANN. § 405.021 (Banks-Baldwin 1991).

15. In some states, visitation laws for grandparents extend only to disrupted or unstable families. *See* Jackson, *supra* note 4, at 577. *See, e.g.*, ARIZ. REV. STAT. ANN. § 25-409(A) (West Supp. 1997-1998); ARK. CODE ANN. § 9-13-103(a)(1) (Michie 1998); 750 ILL. COMP. STAT. ANN. 5/607(b)(1) (West Supp. 1998); MD. CODE ANN., FAM. LAW § 9-102 (1991).

16. There are two types of interests in family law cases that have been granted certiorari before the Supreme Court. *See* Shandling, *supra* note 4, at 128. First, the right of child rearing which has been established for parents as the autonomy to raise their child as they see fit. *Id.* Second, the right of family definition which, for relevant purposes, encompasses the individual's decisions about family structure. *Id.* The Supreme Court articulated in *Moore v. City of East Cleveland*, that where the traditional extended family is involved, the Due Process Clause of the Fourteenth Amendment prohibits the state from dictating family organization. Moore v. City of East Cleveland, 431 U.S. 494 (1977). Thus, the door is open for states to permit, or even legislate, the visitation rights of grandparents.

17. The Supreme Court has elected to deny certiorari to two recent cases upholding grandparents' visitation rights. King v. King, 828 S.W.2d 630, 630-33 (Ky. 1992), *cert. denied*, 506 U.S. 941 (1992); H.F. v. T.F., 483 N.W.2d 803, 804-07 (Wis. 1992), *cert. denied*, 506 U.S. 953 (1992).

18. *In re* Schmidt, 496 N.E.2d 952, 958 (Ohio 1986).

19. OHIO REV. CODE ANN. § 3109.051(B) (Anderson 1996) provides that in divorce actions, the court may grant visitation rights to "any other person having an interest in the welfare of the child." OHIO REV. CODE ANN. § 3109.11 (Anderson 1996) provides in full:

> If either the father or mother of an unmarried minor child is deceased, the relatives of such deceased person may be granted reasonable companionship or visitation rights to the minor child during its minority by a court of competent jurisdiction upon a finding that such companionship or visitation rights would be in the best interests of the minor child.

legislative scheme, which requires a disruption in the family before a grandparent can bring an action seeking rights of companionship. The Ohio Supreme Court has not disturbed the statutes.[20] However, the Court has addressed the significance of the special relationship between grandparent and grandchild on more than one occasion, which may open the door for future expansion of grandparent visitation rights.[21]

OHIO REV. CODE ANN. § 3109.11 (Anderson 1996).

20. *In re* Martin, 626 N.E.2d 82, 83 (Ohio 1994).

> [T]his court has observed that at common law, grandparents had no legal rights of access to their grandchildren. In addition we have held that grandparents have no constitutional right of association with their grandchildren. This court has also stated that if grandparents are to have visitation rights, they must be provided for by statute, and that the Ohio statutes allow visitation only if it is in the grandchildren's best interest.

Id. (internal citations omitted).

21. The Ohio Supreme Court in *In re Whitaker* addressed the benefits of a healthy grandparent-grandchild relationship stating:

> A very special relationship often arises and continues between grandparents and grandchildren. The tensions and conflicts which commonly mar relations between parents and children are often absent between those very same parents and their grandchildren. Visits with a grandparent are often a precious part of a child's experience and there are benefits which devolve upon the grandchild from the relationship with his grandparents which he cannot derive from any other relationship. Neither the Legislature nor this Court is blind to human truths which grandparents and grandchildren have always known.

In re Whitaker, 522 N.E.2d 563, 567 (Ohio 1988) (quoting Mimkon v. Ford, 332 A.2d 199, 204-05 (N.J. 1975)). The Ohio Supreme Court has also recognized the sociological importance of the grandparent-grandchild relationship on more than one occasion by stating the following:

> Sociological literature has documented and analyzed the benefits children receive from a healthy relationship with their grandparents. Contact with grandparents produces children who are rooted in and proud of their family and culture, emotionally secure, and highly socialized. Additionally, 'interaction between grandparents and grandchildren mitigates ageism in children because older people love them, mitigates sexism because grandmothers and grandfathers do essentially the same thing, and eliminates fear of old age because grandparents serve as ancestor role models. Finally, grandparents can give grandchildren an emotional sanctuary from the everyday world.' These findings are consistent with those of other experts on child development who generally agree that it is important for children to maintain ongoing meaningful relationships.

See In re Adoption of Ridenour, 574 N.E.2d 1055, 1062 (Ohio 1991) (quoting Peter A. Zablotsky, *To Grandmother's House We Go: Grandparent Visitation After Stepparent Adoption*, 32 WAYNE L. REV. 1, 46 (1985)); *In re* Whitaker, 522 N.E.2d 563, 567 n.3 (Ohio 1988) (same). *See also In re* Adoption of Ridenour (proposing more discretion to the trial judge as to the determination of grandparent visitation rights):

> I agree in essence, then, that grandparents have no statutory rights in an adoption proceeding. However, I am not convinced, as the majority of my colleagues apparently are, that the trial court, while considering the best interests of the child, has no discretionary jurisdiction to review the familial input of the grandparents of the subject child or children, and to determine that the best interests of the children would be best served by continued association, to some degree, with

II. CATEGORIES OF VISITATION RIGHTS

There is no legal right to grandparent visitation until a precipitating event has caused a disruption in the family, thus necessitating interaction by the legal system.[22] There are primarily three types of disrupting family situations in which the courts and legislatures will award or permit grandparent visitation rights: death of a parent, divorce, and adoption, which is further dependent on whether a stranger or non-stranger (stepparent or family member) adopts the minor child.[23] Although the Ohio courts and courts throughout the United States have enforced grandparent visitation rights on numerous occasions for each of the aforementioned family patterns,[24] the courts have also found grandparent visitation not to be in the best interest of the parties involved.[25] One of the theories in family law is the best interest of the child. Hence, rights of companionship will not be granted if the child's interests do not prevail.[26] Clearly, the consensus has been to examine each case independently, based upon its own unique set of facts.

> their grandparents.
>
> In light of the multifarious benefits which a child may derive from a healthy relationship with a grandparent, it would contravene the general policy of the adoption and visitation laws—that the best interests of the child must remain paramount—for this court to hold that, in all cases, adoption automatically terminates preexisting grandparent visitation rights. . . . [T]ermination of visitation will permanently deprive the child of the grandparental influence. . . .

Ridenour, 574 N.E.2d at 1064 (Holmes, J., concurring in part and dissenting in part). *See also* Farley v. Farley, 619 N.E.2d 427, 429 (Ohio Ct. App. 1992) ("We are impelled by the specific language of R.C. 3107.15 and the rationale of Ridenour to conclude that relatives of parents whose parental rights are terminated have no standing in any Ohio court to assert visitation rights. In many instances this conclusion works a disservice to both the child and the grandparents. . . . [T]he remedy, however, lies with the legislature . . . .").

22. Roberta Kotkin, Note, *Grandparents Versus the State: A Constitutional Right to Custody*, 13 HOFSTRA L. REV. 375, 385-87 (1985) (parental autonomy may be trespassed "when some parental act of omission triggers the interest and concern of the state").

23. *See generally* Harpring, *supra* note 13; Jackson, *supra* note 4; Rorer, *supra* note 4, Shandling, *supra* note 4; *Grandparents' Visitation Rights, supra* note 13.

24. Some courts grant grandparent visitation where a child's parents are living apart, where a child's parents are living and divorced, or where a child is adopted after divorce. *See generally* Brock v. Brock, 205 So.2d 903 (Ala. 1968); Minge v. Minge, 289 S.W.2d 189 (Ark. 1956); Parks v. Crowley, 253 S.W.2d 561 (Ark. 1952); Bookstein v. Bookstein, 86 Cal. Rptr. 495 (Cal. Ct. App. 1970); Benner v. Benner, 248 P.2d 425 (Cal. Ct. App. 1952); *In re* Marriage of Davisson, 797 P.2d 809 (Colo. Ct. App. 1990); George v. Sizemore, 233 S.E.2d 779 (Ga. 1977); Scott v. Scott, 115 S.E. 2 (Ga. 1922); Lingwall v. Hoener, 483 N.E.2d 512 (Ill. 1985); Solomon v. Solomon, 49 N.E.2d 807 (Ill. App. Ct. 1943); Baker v. Perkins, 774 S.W. 2d 129 (Ky. Ct. App. 1989); *In re* Adoption of A.M.R., 527 N.W.2d 565 (Minn. Ct. App. 1995); Layton v. Foster, 460 N.E.2d 1351 (N.Y. 1984); Beers v. Beers, 632 N.Y.S.2d 257 (N.Y. App. Div. 1995); Anonymous v. Anonymous, 269 N.Y.S. 2d 500 (N.Y. Fam. Ct. 1966); Bishop v. Piller, 581 A.2d 670 (Pa. Super. Ct. 1990).

25. *In re* Griffiths, 353 N.E.2d 884 (Ohio Ct. App. 1975) (holding where a 13-year-old grandchild disliked his grandparents to such a degree that the court determined that the enforcement of visitation rights would only result in an intensification of his resentment, and that the best interests of the child required the court to deny visitation rights to the grandparents).

26. *See supra* note 3.

While remedies are available for grandparents who want to obtain visitation rights with their grandchildren, the party must know the breadth of their jurisdiction's statute in order to determine whether they may have a cause of action for their particular situation.[27] In a jurisdiction that does not have a visitation statute applicable to the facts of the case, the appropriate procedure is to file an action in the domestic relations division of the court for a declaratory judgment.[28] On the other hand, in a jurisdiction with a visitation statute applicable to the grandparents' immediate situation, the proper remedy is to file a motion to modify the custody decree in the domestic relations division of the court system.[29]

The establishment of grandparent companionship rights is generally simplified by a family situation that does not involve adoption of the minor child.[30] Grandparent visitation rights have been awarded or held permissible in cases of minor children whose parents were living apart.[31] First, courts have found grandparent visitation to be in the best interest of the child based on an unhappy family situation.[32] Second, courts have awarded grandparent visitation in cases where the minor children had previously lived with their grandparents.[33]

Where a minor child's parents are living, but divorced,[34] the courts have also seen fit to award a grandparent rights of companionship[35] because the minor child previously lived with the grandparents or upon finding that visitation would be in the best interests of the child.[36] In the case of divorce,[37] the courts have further extended

---

27. *See Grandparents' Visitation Rights*, *supra* note 13, at 228 (attorney practice considerations).

28. *Id.*

29. OHIO REV. CODE ANN. § 3105.65 (Anderson 1996); OHIO R. CIV. P. 75(I).

30. *But see Grandparents' Visitation Rights*, *supra* note 13, at 236-37 ("[G]randparents must sometimes pay the heavy penalty wrought by the lack of domestic harmony between parents, and that a broken home almost always penalizes not only the descendants, but also . . . the ancestors.").

31. *See id.* at 235-36. *See also* Baker v. Perkins, 774 S.W.2d 129 (Ky. Ct. App. 1989); Beers v. Beers, 632 N.Y.S.2d 257 (N.Y. App. Div. 1995); Bishop v. Piller, 581 A.2d 670 (Pa. Super. Ct. 1990). *But cf. Grandparents' Visitation Rights*, *supra* note 13, at 236-37 (stating that although the parents of minor children were living apart, it was not in the best interest of the child to award rights of companionship to the grandparents).

32. Anonymous v. Anonymous, 269 N.Y.S.2d 500 (N.Y. Fam. Ct. 1966).

33. Perry v. Perry, 7 Pa. D. 240, 7 Pa. C. 245 (1897).

34. In *Hollingsworth v. Hollingsworth*, the Franklin County Court of Appeals held that section 3109.05(B) of the Ohio Revised Code is constitutional and the state has a compelling government interest in enforcing it.

> [T]he state has a compelling interest in assuring that the child or children of a broken marriage or home receive that attention, care, and concern it is presumed they would have received had the marriage and family life not been drastically altered by the divorce action. Accordingly, R.C. 3109.05(B) does not violate equal protection by differentiating between divorced and non-divorced situations.

516 N.E.2d 1250, 1253 (Ohio Ct. App. 1986); OHIO REV. CODE ANN. § 3109.05(B) (Anderson 1996).

35. *Grandparents' Visitation Rights*, *supra* note 13, at 237-44. *But cf. id.* at 244-45 (stating divorce situations where, in the absence of court and special circumstances, visitation cannot be awarded to grandparents because it would seldom, if ever, be in a minor child's best interest to grant visitation to grandparents).

36. Brock v. Brock, 205 So. 2d 903, 910 (Ala. 1968).

37. Statistics show that the divorce rate in 1970 was 3.5 per 1000; in 1980 the rate increased to

their rationale toward granting grandparent visitation rights because the children might be emotionally harmed if the relationship was severed.[38] The courts often receive statutory guidance when divorce is the precipitating event, as provided in section 3109.05(B) of the Ohio Revised Code.

In the event that one or both of the minor child's parents dies, rights of companionship have also been held permissible between the child and grandparent.[39] Trial judges have more discretionary authority in these matters. Judges ordinarily do not abuse their power in granting custody, although when less is at stake in granting rights of companionship, the personal opinions of the judge may filter into his legal decision.[40] For the most part, courts have found where there is love and affection in a grandparent-grandchild relationship, and where a parent has died, it would be incredibly unkind to isolate the minor child from her or his grandparents.[41] Visitation could even be awarded absent a showing that the surviving parent is unfit if it is in the best interests of the child.[42]

It is more difficult for grandparents to petition for visitation rights when an adoption has taken place following a separation, divorce, or death. In the event of an adoption by a non-stranger, such as a stepparent or relative, it is a question of fact for the court to determine on a case by case basis.[43] Courts will grant grandparents companionship rights if it is determined the best interests of the minor child are involved and the adoptive relationship would not be hindered by the grandparent's interaction.[44] On the other hand, grandparent visitation generally is not granted to

---

5.2 per 1000; by 1990 the rate had decreased to 4.7 per 1000. BUREAU OF THE CENSUS, U.S. DEP'T OF COMMERCE, STATISTICAL ABSTRACT OF THE U.S. 102 (1995). Additionally, the remarriage of divorced women increased 7.3 per 1000 in 1970 to 11.4 per 1000 in 1990. *Id.* The number of births to unmarried women took a staggering leap from 399 in 1970 to 1225 in 1992. *Id.* at 76.

38. Parks v. Crowley, 253 S.W.2d 561 (Ark. 1952).

39. *Grandparents' Visitation Rights*, *supra* note 13, at 252-59. *But cf. id.* at 260-67 (stating situations when visitation was denied or held impermissible for grandparents where one or both of the parents of minor children have died because it was not in the best interest of the child).

40. *See* Shandling, *supra* note 4, at 123 which offers:

> Judges seldom use "best interests" analysis so blatantly as a vehicle for imposing their own values on their decisions. In grandparent visitation suits, however, where the stakes are far lower than in custody suits, "best interests" are especially slippery, and there is great potential that judges will decide on the basis of their own values, rather than on what is truly appropriate for the child.

Id.

41. Gary v. Hauschildt, 528 N.W.2d 271 (Minn. Ct. App. 1995).

42. Graziano v. Davis, 361 N.E.2d 525 (Ohio Ct. App. 1976) (relatives of the deceased parent granted reasonable companionship or visitation rights with the minor child upon the finding that it would be in the best interests of the child); *In re* Zahoransky, 488 N.E.2d 944 (Ohio Ct. App. 1985) (visitation rights are inherent in guardianship for paternal grandparents where maternal grandparents and father were co-guardians because the mother had been slain by the father); Holley v. Higgins, 620 N.E.2d 251 (Ohio Ct. App. 1993) (visitation granted to maternal grandmother whose relationship to her granddaughter was that of a loving, caring parent where the mother died of a drug overdose); *In re* Coons, 11 Ohio Cir. Dec. 208 (1899) (best interest of the child to continue visitation with her maternal grandparents with whom she had lived subsequent the death of her mother).

43. *Grandparents' Visitation Rights*, *supra* note 13, at 267-71.

44. Grandparents in Ohio may be granted visitation rights as a third party interested in the welfare

biological grandparents following a stranger adoption.[45] There is a different policy consideration embedded in an adoption by a stranger which "seeks to transform the child's collection of relationships, and in effect, give the child a new identity."[46] There are no cases in Ohio in which any court, at its discretion, elected to grant the biological grandparents visitation rights in a stranger adoption. This is purely in line with Ohio statutory law that "terminate[s] all legal relationships between the adopted person and his relatives, including his biological or other legal parents, so that the adopted person thereafter is a stranger to his former relatives."[47]

The courts have consistently recognized families are affected by a wide range of circumstances. As state legislatures have enacted visitation statutes, so too have courts increasingly given latitude to grandparents pursuing an action for visitation rights with their grandchildren.[48] Many individuals take on grandparenting as their primary role later in life. However, courts have yet to factor the grandparents' wants and needs into the family equation.[49] Senior citizens as a group are increasing at an extraordinary rate.[50] As a profession mandated by the laws of democracy, and majority rule, it is contrary to public policy to ignore the wants and needs of our senior population which is most affected by rights of companionship.

III. THE AGING POPULATION

It is anticipated in the next thirty years, the older population will double in size. By 2030, there will be about seventy million older persons, which is more than twice

---

of the minor child, but not solely based upon their ancestral history. *See* OHIO REV. CODE ANN. § 3109.05(B) (Anderson 1996); OHIO REV. CODE ANN. § 3109.11 (Anderson 1996).

45. Farley v. Farley, 619 N.E.2d 427, 429 (Ohio Ct. App. 1992). On August 6, 1992, this court heard two cases involving similar issues where grandparents sought visitation rights after the minor child was adopted. Although reviewed in dicta, the Court stated:

> Unfortunately, we read R.C. 3107.15 as clearly and unequivocally denying standing (and hence potential relief) to grandparents, where their bloodline descendant has had his or her parental rights terminated by adoption. The statute can mean nothing other than that the bloodline relatives of the child whose parent has had parental rights eliminated are, as relatives, likewise terminated. Note that in addition to specifically including relatives among those whose rights are terminated, the statute also terminates rights of inheritance from such natural grandparents. *By contrast* the legislature has seen fit to preserve grandparental rights in adoption proceedings where the parent in the same bloodline is deceased.

Id. (internal citation omitted) (emphasis added).

46. *In re* Adoption of Ridenour, 574 N.E.2d 1055, 1062 (Ohio 1991).

47. OHIO REV. CODE ANN. § 3107.15 (Anderson 1996).

48. *See, e.g.*, Frances E. v. Peter E., 479 N.Y.S.2d 319 (N.Y. Fam. Ct. Aug. 9, 1984) (granting rights of companionship to grandparents who had never seen their two grandchildren because their parents refused to allow them to do so, relying on a visitation statute that permits courts to grant visitation rights in situations where "equity would see fit to intervene"); N.Y. DOM. REL. LAW § 72 (McKinney Supp. 1999).

49. *Ridenour*, 574 N.E.2d at 1062. The Court found that grandparents have no right to visitation after adoption by a stranger. The Court duly noted, "In fact, it seems that in denying the adoptions, the judge elevated the rights of the grandparents over the best interests of the children." *Id.* at 1059.

50. American Ass'n of Retired Persons, *Profile of Older Americans* (Dec. 1996) (visited May 17, 1999) http://research.aarp.org/general/profile97.html>.

their number in 1996.[51] People age 65 and older are projected to represent 13% of the population in the year 2000, but will be 20% by the year 2030.[52] Moreover, the population over eighty years of age is predicted to increase by 64.3%.[53] The shift in the proportions of elderly to youth can be attributed to the combination of people living longer, the baby boomers aging, and lower fertility rates. Thus, as the population ages, the legislature ages, and public policy favors statutes and rights for senior citizens, including grandparents.

More than 75% of older Americans are grandparents.[54] The number continues to grow, with estimates of roughly ninety-eight million grandparents by the year 2001.[55] In 1994, every state with the exception of the District of Columbia had at least one statute dealing with grandparent visitation.[56] The voice of senior citizen lobbying groups has grown louder with their growing numbers and in reaction to the decreasing numbers of grandchildren. Certainly, if the statutory trend continues, aging legislators may chip away at the visitation exceptions until a law emerges that expressly grants grandparent visitation rights.

IV. THE BENEFITS TO GRANDPARENTS FROM GRANDCHILDREN AND FAMILY INTERACTION

Most courts agree the impetus behind grandparent visitation rights is to maintain existing relationships, not force new ones.[57] Grandparent visitation as a statutory right focuses on the past relationship between the grandparents and the minor grandchild.[58] The relationship, however, can play an important part in the life of the grandparent, and functions in many positive ways. A healthy relationship between the grandparent and grandchild may improve the physical health of the grandparent.[59] In addition to the grandparent's physical well-being, there is a high correlation between social support provided by the family, including grandchildren, and the mental well-being of the elderly.[60] Grandchildren can provide incentive for grandparents to live long and prosperous lives.[61] A University of Michigan study

---

51. *Id.*

52. *Id.*

53. *Id.*

54. *Grandparents Rights*, *supra* note 10, at 1 (opening statement of Thomas J. Downey, Chairman, Subcommittee on Human Services, House Select Committee on Aging).

55. *See* Harpring, *supra* note 13, at 1659 & n.2 (citing Megan Rosenfeld, *Grandparents' Rights; Activists Turn to Court to Protect Their Ties to Grandchildren*, WASH. POST, Oct. 16, 1991, at Z12). The numbers have also been expressed as 58 million in 1992 and 98 million projected by 2020. SUBCOMM. ON HUMAN SERVS. OF THE HOUSE SELECT COMM. ON AGING, 102D CONG., 2D SESS. GRANDPARENTS: NEW ROLES AND RESPONSIBILITIES 1 (Comm. Print 1992) (opening statement of Thomas J. Downey, Chairman, Subcommittee on Human Services, House Select Committee on Aging).

56. *See* statutes cited *supra* note 8.

57. *See* Jackson, *supra* note 4, at 568.

58. *Id. See also* Longwell v. White, No. 7-95, 1996 Ohio App. LEXIS 707, at *7 (Ohio Ct. App. Jan. 5, 1996) (holding that "matter is remanded . . . in order to determine whether visitation with appellant is in the child's best interest, *not the grandparent's interest*") (emphasis added).

59. Marshall J. Graney, *Interpersonal Support and Health of Older People*, *in* SOCIAL BONDS IN LATER LIFE 294 (Warren A. Peterson & Jill Quadagno eds., 1985).

60. *See* U.S. SENATE SELECT COMMITTEE ET AL., AGING IN AMERICA 295 (1991).

61. ARTHUR KORNHABER, GRANDPARENT POWER! 58 (1994).

supports the idea that optimism is extremely material to the well-being of grandparents.[62] "[D]ata show[s] that people who stay young at heart are very focused on the future, in a hopeful way, but not with unrealistic expectations. [T]hey recognize their potential as well as their limitations, and they keep striving for new goals. They go after what they want."[63] Clearly, for older people, family ties are of primary importance for socialization as well as informal support.[64] Furthermore, a stable family life can also ease the transition into later life.[65] A healthy relationship between the grandparent and grandchild can provide continuity for changes that may occur later in life and ease the transition between those changes.[66]

While legal authors have claimed the role grandparents play is not universally enjoyed, there are other sociological studies showing quite the contrary.[67] For many older people, being a grandparent is the most significant aspect of their life.[68] Grandchildren bring inexpressible joy and meaning.[69] Moreover, their lives are fulfilled by the unconditional love a child offers to them.[70] While studies have been more ambivalent with respect to younger grandchildren, one study has shown having grandparents has a notable impact on an individual as an adult.[71] In evaluating the relationship, respondents to the study also stated that over the years many had become closer to their grandparents.[72] The same respondents reported reciprocal visiting and calling on a regular basis, not necessarily for a holiday or special occasion.[73] More often than not, communication between grandparents and grandchildren is in person.[74] Additionally, a healthy rapport and good communication can influence one to be a successful grandparent in later years. Along the same lines, the grandparent and grandchild relationship may have a unique significance for grandfathers and grandmothers.[75]

Grandparents currently find themselves in a difficult position. Grandparents in Western society lack the respect their Eastern counterparts receive.[76] While grandparents recognize their role[77] has changed greatly throughout the century, it

---

62. *Id.*

63. *Id.*

64. Lynne Gershenson, *Adult Grandchildren and Their Grandparents: The Enduring Bond, in* TIES OF LATER LIFE 155 (Jon Hendricks ed., 1995).

65. Ida Harper Simpson & John C. McKinney, *Preface* to SOCIAL ASPECTS OF AGING at v (Ida Harper Simpson & John C. McKinney eds., 1966).

66. *See* Graney, *supra* note 59, at 297.

67. *See* KORNHABER, *supra* note 61, at 58; Gershenson, *supra* note 64, at 163. *But see* Graney, *supra* note 59, at 303 (noting there is a technical problem with grandparent and grandchild studies because they are generally retrospective, and not prospective).

68. *See* KORNHABER, *supra* note 61, at 8. One grandmother was quoted as saying that grandparenthood is "what my life is all about." *Id.*

69. *Id.*

70. *Id.*

71. *See* Gershenson, *supra* note 64, at 156.

72. *Id.* at 165-66.

73. *Id.* at 167.

74. *Id.*

75. *See id.* at 163-64.

76. ANDREW J. CHERLIN & FRANK F. FURSTENBERG, JR., THE NEW AMERICAN GRANDPARENT 194 (1985).

77. Judith Treas, *Aging and the Family, in* AGING: SCIENTIFIC PERSPECTIVES AND SOCIAL ISSUES

seems unfair to deny benefits to such a sizable and rapidly increasing group.[78] The traditionally dominant style of interaction between grandparents and grandchildren has changed for the most part, but many grandparents believe this is good.[79] Grandchildren are beginning to play a substantial role in their grandparents' lives as grandparents are living longer,[80] are more affluent,[81] have more leisure time,[82] and less grandchildren.[83] As a result, the grandparent-grandchild relationship counts even more than in the past. One study suggests grandparents and grandchildren are starting to be closer, because the relationship is now less about assuming a parental role[84] and more about being a companion.[85] The relationship between grandparents and grandchildren still includes family rituals,[86] as well as a fairly high intergenerational transmission of values.[87] Therefore, not only do grandchildren believe their grandparents are important, grandparents take pride in fostering their beliefs to their grandchildren.[88]

V. THE BENEFITS TO THE GRANDCHILD OF AN INTERGENERATIONAL RELATIONSHIP

Statutes authorizing grandparent visitation are based on the assumption that contact between grandparents and grandchildren is in the child's best interest.[89] The benefits of a healthy grandparent-grandchild relationship were recognized and eloquently described by the New Jersey Supreme Court in a case which has often been cited by legal authority, including the Ohio Supreme Court:

> A very special relationship often arises and continues between grandparents and grandchildren. The tensions and conflicts which commonly mar relations between

---

98 (Diana S. Woodruff & James E. Birren eds., 1983). Treas identifies five styles of grandparents: formal, fun-seeker, distant figure, substitute parent, and reservoir of family wisdom.

78. Vern L. Bengtson & David Haber, *Sociological Perspectives on Aging*, in AGING: SCIENTIFIC PERSPECTIVES AND SOCIAL ISSUES, *supra* note 77, at 90.

79. *See* CHERLIN & FURSTENBERG, *supra* note 76, at 8.

80. *See id.* at 27-28.

81. *See id.* at 32.

82. *See id.* at 31.

83. *See id.* at 35.

84. *See In re* Whitaker, 522 N.E.2d 563, 567 (Ohio 1988) (noting that where grandparents do not play a primary role in dispensing discipline, they are able to form relationships with their grandchildren which are free of the tensions and pressures which commonly mar parent-child relationships).

85. *See* CHERLIN & FURSTENBERG, *supra* note 76, at 55-58, 64. In the late 1800s, the average birthrate was greater than four children, thus grandchildren and children often overlapped in age ranges. Today, there is a lower birth rate, so grandparenthood is more of a separate stage of life without all of the child care obligations.

86. *See id.* at 114.

87. *See id.* at 172.

88. *See id.* at 169.

89. *See* Peter A. Zablotsky, *To Grandmother's House We Go: Grandparent Visitation after Stepparent Adoption*, 32 WAYNE L. REV. 1, 45 (1985). *See also In re* Griffiths, 353 N.E.2d 884, 885 (Ohio 1975). By the express language of section 3109.11 of the Ohio Revised Code, visitation may only be granted when in the best interests of the child. *Id.* The companionship and visitation rights of the grandparents are subservient to the best interests of the child. *Id.*

> parents and children are often absent between those very same parents and their grandchildren. Visits with a grandparent are often a precious part of a child's experience and there are benefits which devolve upon the grandchild from the relationship with his grandparents which he cannot derive from any other relationship. Neither the Legislature nor this Court is blind to human truths from which grandparents and grandchildren have always known.[90]

Grandparents offer themselves as a positive role model to their grandchildren because the child does not feel the overwhelming need to be different from them in the same way that they do with their parents. The intense need for a child to distinguish herself or himself from the authority of their parents is not part of the grandparent-grandchild relationship. Grandparents can provide an emotional sanctuary for their grandchildren, particularly during the adolescent stage of life. Moreover, youth have shown a decline in negative attitudes toward senior citizens as well as sympathizing with the plights of the elderly.[91] Not only do grandparents provide an outlet for their grandchildren, but more and more youth are understanding the new and challenging circumstances that arise as their grandparents age.[92] Positive opinions about old age are being disseminated and are taking hold.[93] According to one author, the grandparent provides an entire spectrum of roles for their grandchildren: (1) living ancestor and historian, (2) role model, (3) teacher, (4) mentor, (5) student, (6) nurturer, (7) genie, (8) crony, (9) wizard, and (10) hero.[94]

While grandparents are not necessarily the most prominent or visible actors in our family system, they are important backstage figures. Grandparents are called upon to act when problems arise. Grandparents plainly take an active role in families that are experiencing problems. Disrupted families are more likely to mention their grandparents than those with intact households.[95] This aspect of the relationship lends to the argument that it is all the more important for grandparents to maintain rights of visitation in order to continue providing support to the family network.[96]

---

90. Mimkon v. Ford, 332 A.2d 199, 204-05 (N.J. 1975).

91. ACHENBAUM, *supra* note 9, at 121.

92. *Id.*

93. *Id.*

94. *See* KORNHABER, *supra* note 57, at 59-89. *See also* Jackson, *supra* note 4, at 568. This article found that grandparents play four roles which encompass the aforementioned ten:

> First, they maintain the identity of the family, mitigate disturbing events of the outside world for children, and provide a stabilizing influence for children; second, grandparents can serve as "family watchdogs" for abuse or neglect; third, grandparents may play arbitrators between parents and children; and finally, grandparents allow children to build connections with their family history which can lead to a firmer self-identity.

Id.

95. *See* CHERLIN & FURSTENBERG, *supra* note 72, at 183.

96. The breaking down of family life has had a devastating effect on American society. Kenneth L. Woodward with Phyllis Malamud, *The Parent Gap*, NEWSWEEK, Sept. 22, 1975, at 48, 48-56. The *Newsweek* article also remarked that:

> Few contemporary American families include grandparents, aunts, uncles and cousins—all of whom used to be around like the front porch, to widen the family circle . . . .

VI. COMBINING SOCIOLOGICAL STUDIES AND INFORMATION WITH THE BEST INTERESTS TEST IN ORDER TO DETERMINE GRANDPARENT VISITATION

When petitioning for visitation rights, courts examine each family situation on a case-by-case basis.[97] The courts then determine what is in the best interest of the child. The Ohio Supreme Court has held the same factors used to determine the best interests of the child in custody cases may also be applied to visitation cases.[98] According to the Ohio Revised Code,[99] the factors a trial court may consider in determining the child's best interest are: (1) the prior interaction and relationships of the child with her or his family, relatives, and other parties, as well as the party petitioning for visitation rights; (2) the geographical location of the parents' residences to each other, as well as to the party requesting visitation rights; (3) the child's and parent's available time; (4) the age of the child; (5) the child's adjustment to her or his home, school, and community; (6) the wishes and concerns of the child following an interview conducted with the child in chambers; (7) the health and safety of the child; (8) the amount of time that will be available for the child to spend with her or his siblings; (9) the mental and physical well-being of all parties involved; (10) the willingness of parents and outside interested parties to reschedule missed visitation; (11) whether either parent has been convicted of, or suspected of, acting in a manner resulting in a child being an abused child or a neglected child; (12) whether the outside interested party has ever been convicted of abusing or neglecting a child; (13) whether the residential parent, or one of the parents subject to a shared parenting decree, has continuously and willfully denied the other parent his or her right to visitation in accordance with the court; (14) whether either parent is planning on moving out of state; and (15) any other additional factor in the best interest of the child. This list is certainly not exhaustive of all the factors that U.S. courts have considered.[100] Moreover, while courts will consider the totality of the

---

> . . . .
>
> If current trends and parental problems suggest anything at all, however, it is that the stripped-down nuclear family needs support in the rearing of kids . . . . In turn, the pressure on today's American family argues strongly for greater reliance upon relatives and friends.

Id. at 53, 56.

97. In *In re* Hartley, No. 1399, 1988 Ohio App. LEXIS 4071 (Ohio Ct. App. Oct. 13, 1988), the Athens County Fourth District Court of Appeals painted a very realistic portrait of the American family that supports why judicial discretion is necessary in such a diverse society:

> Ohio law recognizes that in a society as culturally diverse as ours is, some families are nuclear while others are extended. In some families, each household cares for itself without the assistance or intervention of relatives. In other families, ties are much closer and members feel a moral obligation not only to their own household but to grandchildren, grandparents, uncles, aunts, nieces, nephews and cousins.

Id. at *8.

98. *See In re* Whitaker, 522 N.E.2d 563, 567-68 (Ohio 1988).

99. OHIO REV. CODE ANN. § 3109.051(D) (Anderson 1996).

100. *See generally* Phyllis C. Borzi, *Statutory Visitation Rights of Grandparents: One Step Closer to the Best Interests of the Child*, 26 CATH. U. L. REV. 387 (1977) (noting preferential factors to

circumstances, the best interest test is not precisely defined. The unfettered exercise of judicial discretion can lead to inconsistent results.

The best interest of the child in a family situation is certainly ideal. The grandparent-grandchild relationship benefits the grandparent in so many ways that it seems unfortunate not to place some emphasis on the value visitation will have for the grandparent. The relationship works both ways, and for many elderly people, while the relationship has positive aspects for the grandchild, the grandparent-grandchild relationship may be more beneficial for the grandparent. Sociologists have established that interaction between grandparents and grandchildren mitigates ageism.[101] Nonetheless, the indeterminacy of the best interests standard leaves the door open to consider the positive influence the relationship will have on the grandparent. Moreover, it does not seem unfair to consider the impact a grandparent-grandchild relationship, or lack thereof, will have on the elderly person in a country that is to be heavily populated by senior citizens in the near future.

The grandparent-grandchild relationship is precisely that, an association between those two parties alone. If the grandparent and grandchild would each be affected in a positive manner by the relationship, then it seems irrelevant for the parent's wishes to be placed above that of the other two parties in awarding a grandparent rights of companionship. Arguably the power of *parens patriae* covers such a situation.[102] Further, the notion of the child as an individual with separately defined rights has emerged over the past several decades.[103] Therefore, if the child wishes to further the relationship with their grandparents, or they are at least ambivalent as to the decision, it is in the best interest of society to allow grandparents to have visitation rights. The mental and physical well-being of such a growing segment in our society should be a priority. However, until that time, an effective elder law attorney must couch the wishes of the grandparent in language favorable to the grandchild in order to be granted visitation rights.

VII. THE FUTURE OF GRANDPARENT VISITATION RIGHTS

As one commentator noted, "recognizing third-party rights to visitation is a move toward recognizing children's rights to have important relationships protected, and toward the emancipation of children from the idea that they are merely the chattels

---

consider in granting visitation rights).

101. *See* Zablotsky, *supra* note 85, at 46.

102. *Parens patriae* is "the principle that the state must care for those who cannot take care of themselves, such as minors who lack proper care and custody from their parents." BLACK'S LAW DICTIONARY 1114 (6th ed. 1990).

103. Early American law adopted the eighteenth-century English common law view that children were to be regarded as chattels of the family and wards of the state. JAMES KENT, COMMENTARIES ON AMERICAN LAW (Oliver Wendell Holmes ed., 12th ed. Boston, Little Brown (1873)). Only during the past fifty years have the courts begun to note that the constitution allows recognition of the rights of children. Tinker v. Des Moines Sch. Dist., 393 U.S. 503 (1969) (protecting the right of children to wear a black armband to protest Vietnam War); *In re* Gault, 387 U.S. 1 (1967) (adult procedural protections in criminal trial extended to delinquency proceedings); Brown v. Board of Educ., 349 U.S. 294 (1955) (recognizing that all children have the right to an equal education); Haley v. Ohio, 332 U.S. 596 (1948) (protecting against a coerced confession extended a fifteen-year-old boy in a state criminal trial).

of their parents."[104] The best means of furthering the interests of children is to continue to expand upon grandparent visitation rights. While children are our future, the elderly are as well, particularly with the aging baby boomers. In furthering grandparent visitation rights, the child's interest is not played down, but rather, the grandparent's rights are elevated to a more acceptable level. More equality in the family is desirable to prevent a disintegration of the family and concede to a better coexistence. This is likely to happen whether as a result of powerful senior citizen lobbying groups,[105] or simply as the legislature and judiciary age.[106]

Clearly, there needs to be a consistent framework[107] for determining grandparents' rights because litigation is plainly not in the best interests of the child nor the grandparent. As an elder law attorney, one might want to consider that the time, effort, and expense of litigating grandparent visitation rights would be better spent by families working through their own problems and facilitating their own negotiating and communicating. The answer for increasing grandparents' visitation rights may not be legislation, the answer may be simply the communication of grandparents with their own families.

---

104. *See* Harpring, *supra* note 13, at 1692.

105. It is very likely that lobbying groups may exert more pressure on the legislature in the future as the demand for grandchildren increases (based on increasing numbers of elderly and elderly that are living longer), but the supply decreases (based on reduced fertility rates).

106. Additionally, as minority representation in both the legislature and judiciary increases, this may have a positive influence on grandparent visitation rights because minority groups in the United States have a higher percentage of extended families. *See* MULLEN, *supra* note 1, at 1.

107. For a proposed Model Grandparent Visitation Statute, see Jackson, *supra* note 4, at 593-96.

Acknowledgments

Klicka, Christopher J. and Douglas W. Phillips, "Why Parental Rights Laws are Necessary," *Educational Leadership* Vol. 55, Nov. 1997, pp. 80–83. Reprinted with the permission of Association for Supervision and Curriculum Development.

Woodhouse, Barbara Bennett, "Child Abuse, The Constitution, and the Legacy of *Pierce v. Society of Sisters,*" 78 *University of Detroit Mercy Law Review* 479–489 (2001). Reprinted with the permission of *University of Detroit Mercy Law Review.*

Holmes, Gilbert A."The Tie that Binds: The Constitutional Right of Children to Maintain Relationships with Parent-Like Individuals", Vol. 53 *Maryland Law Review* 358–411 (1994). Reprinted with the permission of the University of Maryland School of Law.

Boccaccini, Marcus T. and Willemsen, Eleanor, "Contested Adoption and the Liberty Interest of the Child," Vol. 10 *Saint Thomas Law Review* 211–227 (1998). Reprinted with the permission of St. Thomas University, School of Law.

Haury, Cassandra S., Note, "The Changing American Family: A Reevaluation of the Rights of Foster Parents When Biological Rights Have Been Terminated," Vol. 35 *Georgia Law Review* 313–344 (2000). Reprinted with the permission of the *Georgia Law Review.*

Palmore v. Sidoti, 466 U.S. 429–434 (1984).

Santosky v. Kramer, 455 U.S. 745–791 (1982).

O'Brien, Raymond C., "An Analysis of Realistic Due Process Rights of Children Versus Parents," Vol. 26 *Connecticut Law Review* 1209–1260 (1994). Reprinted with the permission of *Connecticut Law Review.*

Bitensky, Susan H., "The Child's Right to Humane Discipline under the U.N. Convention on the Rights of the Child: The Mandate Against All Corporal Punishment of Children," Vol. 4 *Loyola Poverty Law Journal* 47–53 (1998). Reprinted with the permission of Loyola University, School of Law.

Orentlicher, David, "Spanking and Other Corporal Punishment of Children by Parents: Overvaluing Pain, Undervaluing Children," Vol.

35 *Houston Law Review* 147–185 (1998). Reprinted with the permission of the University of Houston Law Center.

Wadlington, Walter, "Medical Decision Making for and by Children: Tensions Between Parent, State, and Child", 1994 *University of Illinois Law Review* 311–336 (1994). Reprinted with the permission of the *University of Illinois Law Review.*

Dwyer, James G., "Spiritual Treatment Exemptions to Child Medical Neglect Laws: What We Outsiders Should Think", Vol. 76 *Notre Dame Law Review* 147–177 (2000). Reprinted with permission. Copyright 2000 by the *Notre Dame Law Review*, University of Notre Dame. The publisher bears responsibility for any errors.

Armacost, Barbara E., Affrimative Duties, Systemic Harms, and the Due Process Clause," Vol. 94 *Michigan Law Review* 982–1040 (1996). Reprinted with the permission of the Michigan Law Review Association.

Woodhouse, Barbara Bennett, "Protecting Children's Relationships with Extended Family: The Impact of *Troxel v. Granville*," Vol. 19, No. 5 *ABA Child Law Practice* 65, 70–71 (July 2000). Reprinted with the permission of the American Bar Association.

Weiss, Elizabeth, Comment, "Nonparent Visitation Rights v. Family Autonomy: An Abridgement of Parents' Constitutional Rights?," Vol. 10 *Seton Hall Constitutional Law Journal* 1085–1131 (2000). Reprinted with the permission of the *Seton Hall Constitutional Law Journal.*

Strawman, Erica L., "Grandparent Visitation: The Best Interests of the Grandparent, Child, and Society," Vol. 30 *University of Toledo Law Review* 31–47 (1998). Reprinted by permission of *The University of Toledo Law Review.*